Mr. Ambassador

Edward J. Perkins at his desk in Cape Town, South Africa, 1989.

MR. AMBASSADOR

Warrior for Peace

EDWARD J. PERKINS

with Connie Cronley

Foreword by George P. Shultz
Preface by David L. Boren

UNIVERSITY OF OKLAHOMA PRESS : NORMAN

The opinions and characterizations in this book are those of
the author and do not necessarily represent official positions
of the United States Government.

Library of Congress Cataloging-in-Publication Data
Perkins, Edward J. (Edward Joseph), 1928–
   Mr. Ambassador : warrior for peace / by Edward J. Perkins with
Connie Cronley.
      p. cm.
   Includes bibliographical references and index.
   ISBN 0-8061-3767-3 (alk. paper)
1. Perkins, Edward J. (Edward Joseph), 1928– 2. African American
diplomats—Biography. 3. Diplomats—United States—Biography.
4. Ambassadors—United States—Biography. 5. United States—For-
eign Service—Biography. 6. United States—Foreign relations—
1945–1989. 7. United States—Foreign relations—1989– I. Cronley,
Connie. II. Title.
   E840.8.P4255A3 2006
   327.730092—dc22

                                    2005053882

The paper in this book meets the guidelines for permanence and dura-
bility of the Committee on Production Guidelines for Book Longevity
of the Council on Library Resources, Inc. ∞

1 2 3 4 5 6 7 8 9 10

To
Lucy Liu Perkins,
my partner in all things

Happy is the man that findeth wisdom, and
the man that getteth understanding.
For the merchandise of it is better than the
merchandise of silver, and the gain thereof than fine gold.

—*Proverbs 3:13–14*

CONTENTS

Illustrations xi

Foreword, by George P. Shultz xiii

Preface, by David L. Boren xv

Introduction: Fire with Fire 3

Jesus Christ and Huey Long 13

High School in the Big City 37

Portland—Portal to the World 51

Young Warrior 73

Japan, Land of the Rising Sun 83

The Few. The Proud. 105

Taiwan, the Beautiful Island 123

Education and Eisenhower's Little War 137

The Foreign Service of the United States 147

Ghana in a Time of Turbulence 169

Liberia in Revolution 195

The Office of West African Affairs 217

Mr. Ambassador 235

A Black Ambassador to South Africa? 247

Let Them Know I Am Here 273

Making Policy in South Africa 289

The White Tribe 331

Reporting In 351

Tightening the Screws 365

Angola-Namibia: The Long Struggle for Peace 405

Postscript: South Africa 421

Director General: Changing the Foreign Service 435

The United Nations 461

Australia: Down Under and Beyond 497

Note and Sources 533

Acknowledgments 543

Index 547

Illustrations

Edward J. Perkins, ambassador to South Africa *frontispiece*
Bust of Martin Luther King Jr. at the U.S. Embassy, Pretoria 2
Emerline Stovall 17
The Noble family in Louisiana 21
Tiny Grant at her home in Portland 66
High school portrait in Portland 71
In uniform in Korea 79
Tomiko Kyoya 90
In Japan with sailor Thomas J. Rittenhouse 120
Lucy Cheng-mei Liu 127
Lucy's family when she was a child 131
The wedding 133
In an airport in Bangkok 142
The Perkins family in Ghana 175
Ambassador Robert Smith and Perkins calling on a tribal chief 179
Ambassador Smith and Perkins with Peace Corps volunteers 181
With James Washington at the burial place of W. E. B. DuBois 186
J. J. Rawlings and Perkins 193
Perkins with President Doe of Liberia 201
The staff of the Office of West African Affairs 219
The new ambassador to Liberia and his wife 234
Perkins's official portrait as ambassador to South Africa 246
Secretary of State George Shultz and Perkins 249
With Vernon Jordan Jr. 263
The Perkins family with Sen. Nancy Kassebaum 267
Perkins and family with President Reagan 269
Kappa Alpha Psi fraternity brothers and Perkins 271
Reporting in to President Ronald Reagan 276
Presentation of credentials in South Africa 286
Albertina Sisulu during her visit the United States 311
With Chief Mangosuthu Gatsha Buthelezi 326

Alan Paton at his home in South Africa 341
Giving a report on South Africa in the White House 353
Toasting the bicentennial of the Constitution 398
Perkins with Nelson and Winnie Mandela 425
With Rep. Constance Morella of Maryland 437
With James Baker as U.S. ambassador to the United Nations 460
The Perkins family meets with President George H. W. Bush 467
At the American Mission to the United Nations 469
At the General Assembly of the United Nations 482
With Colin Powell 484
President Clinton, Warren Christopher, and Perkins 499
Secretary of the Navy John H. Dalton and Perkins in Australia 509
Former President Bush, David Boren, and Perkins 528
Perkins and family in an informal moment 529
James Michener and Perkins 532

(All photos from archives of Edward J. Perkins)

FOREWORD

Ed Perkins leaves a lasting impression on all who meet him. He has made a tremendous impact as a professional diplomat and is doing so again in the academic world. His memoir is bound to be—and is—instructive, even moving.

I welcome this autobiography because Ed Perkins was one of those special Foreign Service officers who made a real difference. Foreign Service is a demanding occupation; the entry bar is high, the competition is strong, and the rewards are great in terms of the satisfaction derived from making a difference. I vividly remember the process of sending Ed to South Africa as our ambassador. The fact that he is black was intended to send a message. The fact that he is extraordinarily capable reinforces the message that talent knows no racial boundaries.

Ed's performance in his post was truly exemplary. His professionalism won respect on all sides and helped lay the groundwork for the end of apartheid. He played an important role in the extraordinary diplomatic process that brought about the independence of Namibia. As our ambassador to South Africa, he could see that independence meant the end of apartheid in that country and that South Africa, by withdrawing its forces, was acknowledging that a beginning had taken place.

Ed now serves as a professor at the University of Oklahoma, where he is doing an outstanding job directing the International Programs Center. He is plowing new ground, pulling together people with different viewpoints, and using dialogue to advance the understanding of many issues. He is adding life to the campus by his very presence and by the people, ideas, and events that come to the university because he is there.

Anyone who knows Ed Perkins will look forward to reading this book.

GEORGE P. SHULTZ
Former Secretary of State of the United States

PREFACE

If I were asked to describe the core values that have made the United States a great nation, I would illustrate them by citing the life and career of Edward J. Perkins. His guiding principles and personal integrity represent the best of American values. His career, which has required personal sacrifice and moral courage, helps us better understand the real meaning of public service. The opportunities that society has given to him remind us that equality of opportunity must be the hallmark of our country if it is to remain great in the future. Every child must have a chance to become all that she or he has the potential to be.

Edward Perkins grew up as an African American on a Louisiana cotton farm when America was still a segregated society. He was raised by grandparents who could not read or write. He served with distinction in both the United States Army and the United States Marine Corps. He worked hard to obtain the best possible education, receiving his bachelor's degree from the University of Maryland and his master's degree and doctorate in public administration from the University of Southern California. He married an extraordinary woman, Lucy Cheng-mei Liu, who is his effective partner in life and in diplomatic service. Edward Perkins is a black man who successfully navigated the mainly white and, at that time, elitist Foreign Service of the United States to become its director general. He served as ambassador to Liberia, South Africa, the United Nations, and Australia. Among the many honors he has earned are the Presidential Distinguished and Meritorious Service Awards, the Department of State's Distinguished Honor and Superior Honor Awards, and the Director General's Cup for the Foreign Service.

It was during his ambassadorship to South Africa that I first came to know him. As a U.S. senator and chairman of the Senate Select Committee on Intelligence, I had the chance to go to South Africa and, under his leadership and tutoring, meet with leaders of all segments of South African society. I observed his incredible self-restraint and personal dignity in the face of racial insults hurled at him in a private meeting with then President P. W. Botha. I was privileged to carry messages from Ambassador Perkins to President-elect George H. W. Bush, which helped to modify American policy toward South Africa and hastened the release of Nelson Mandela and others from prison. In my opinion, no person who was not a South African citizen played a greater role in the dismantling of apartheid and the transition to full democracy than Edward Perkins. He achieved it all while confronting a system in that nation that placed substantial burdens upon him because of his race.

As a scholar, student of Asian philosophy, warrior, and diplomat, he has been a gentle revolutionary and agent for change in some of the world's political hot spots. While he teaches students at the University of Oklahoma and leads the university's International Programs Center, he also brings together opinion leaders all around the world. From the Middle East, to Africa and Asia, he continues his quiet work to bring people together to devise peaceful solutions to conflicts that lead to violence if left unattended.

Edward Perkins is a worthy role model for young professionals who seek to serve our country as diplomats. His integrity and strength are exemplary. His life story gives us all a candid insight into the sometimes inscrutable worlds of the State Department and the American foreign policy. Above all, his life teaches us what it should mean to be an American.

DAVID L. BOREN
Former United States Senator and
President of the University of Oklahoma

MR. AMBASSADOR

As ambassador to South Africa, a document I found invaluable was *Letter from Birmingham Jail* by Martin Luther King Jr. I commissioned this bust of Dr. King to stand for perpetuity at the United States Embassy in Pretoria, South Africa.

FIRE WITH FIRE

Apartheid South Africa was on fire around me.

Just after dawn one December day in 1986, I was riding in the back-seat of a United States Embassy limousine on a quiet mission that would shake up the South African government. I knew that the black townships were burning with riots, bombings, gunfire, looting, and vandalism.

As the black resistance to white rule intensified, the South African government clamped down on the majority black population and declared a state of emergency. Curfews were imposed. Media coverage was limited. State police raided townships and arrested people by the hundreds. Some 20,000 political prisoners were jailed. Thousands of children, some as young as nine years, were arrested and detained, their whereabouts unknown. More than 200,000 other black children protested against the government by boycotting Afrikaner schools; they roamed the streets undisciplined and unsupervised. Public meetings, especially those held by political organizations, and even funerals were banned. And still the revolutionaries continued their protests against apartheid with boycotts, stay-aways, marches, revolts, and uprisings. "The struggle," as it was called, was growing in ferocity. The entire country was on the verge of exploding.

I had arrived in November as the United States ambassador, America's first black ambassador to South Africa. My appointment had made headlines, but I was far from being a popular choice. Most Americans had never heard of me. Many of those who had, black and white, thought me an unfortunate choice for the job. "They'll eat him alive," a colleague told the press. Some black leaders in America scorned me for accepting the appointment and murmured that I had sold out. The black South African revolutionaries disdained the United

States as unsympathetic to their cause and considered me President Ronald Reagan's "house nigger." The white South African government claimed the president of the United States as its friend and ally, so officials were confused and insulted by my appointment.

What nobody in South Africa yet knew was that I had been sent to change America's policy in South Africa. I was a career Foreign Service officer with a singular charge. On direct orders from President Reagan, my assignment was to dismantle apartheid without violence. To accomplish this, I was given the rare leeway of making policy on the ground.

It is understandable that few people thought me exceptionally qualified for the job. South Africa was only my second ambassadorial appointment. I was such an unknown quantity that when President Reagan announced his intention to appoint me to South Africa and the press scrambled to find out who I was, they could not locate a photograph of me in their files.

I refused to let any of this criticism distract me. I had the backing of the president and Secretary of State George Shultz, as well as the confirmation of the Senate. I had a big job to do and a short time frame in which to accomplish it. I embarked on a crash course, learning as much as I could about South African history and politics. I already knew something about segregation. I grew up in the segregated South, raised on a cotton farm in Louisiana by grandparents who could neither read nor write but who believed that education would be my road to a better life. I lived through an ugly time in American history, when familiar sights were signs such as "No Coloreds or Dogs Allowed." As a young man I took the only jobs available to blacks, working as a redcap at a bus station, as a janitor, and as a waiter. I was refused service at soda fountains, and I rode in the back of segregated buses. I never, ever, let any of that slow me down.

I was trained as a soldier in the U.S. Army, spent four years in the U.S. Marine Corps, then joined the Foreign Service when it was considered a traditionally white elite organization. Along the way I acquired a Ph.D.

Here I was in South Africa, a country where segregation was the law of the land and sanctioned by religion. In the one month since my arrival, I had conferred extensively with the staff of the U.S. Embassy, being briefed by the people on the ground. I had given no interviews to the press and made no public speeches. Now the time had come to stand and declare myself and the new policy of the United States. I wanted to capture the attention of not only South

Africa but the world. This was a seminal moment. I chose the time and place for that declaration with great care.

An hour's drive from Pretoria, in the little farming town of Delmas, a trial was dragging into its second year. Despite its remote location, the Delmas Treason Trial was the most important political trial since that of Nelson Mandela two decades earlier. The defendants in Delmas were black political activists. Many of them were members of the United Democratic Front (UDF), a strong umbrella organization of South African anti-apartheid groups. Their crime was advocating alternative structures of government, which meant they had agitated for equal representation under the law. To the apartheid government, this was tantamount to waging war against the nation. The State charged the young activists with high treason and conspiracy to overthrow the government by treason, murder, terrorism, and subversion. The South African government put the revolutionaries on trial for their lives.

Originally twenty-two men were charged, but some were discharged and others were allowed out on bail. By the time the case came to trial in Delmas, six defendants were in court and denied bail for the duration of a trial that would drag on for almost four years. The public focus fell on the three most prominent defendants—Moss M. Chikane, Mosiuoa Gerard Patrick Lekota, and Popo Simon Molefe. This trial had become a focal point in the struggle between blacks and whites in South Africa.

The government had chosen the out-of-the way location of Delmas in the hopes of diffusing public outrage and discouraging any demonstrations in support of the defendants. It did not work. People flooded to Delmas as if on pilgrimage—poor black South Africans, wealthy white foreign visitors, religious organizations, clergy, journalists, scholars, and some American politicians. They filled the courtroom day after day, sitting in respectful witness to the historic trial.

Delmas, I decided, was where I would make my first public appearance in South Africa, signaling the new direction of U.S. policy in that country. It was not a rash decision. I had consulted extensively with key staff members of the U.S. Embassy in Pretoria. One morning, without announcing my visit, I instructed the embassy driver to take me to Delmas. I was accompanied by two political counselors from the embassy, Karl Beck and Robert Frasure. This morning my work in South Africa was beginning.

The Delmas courthouse was small and built in the English design, an influence from South Africa's English-speaking colonials. As usual, the courtroom was full of observers, and security was tight. A legion of armed police was stationed both outside and inside the court. Some carried machine guns. I got out of the embassy limousine, walked past the armed guards without looking at them, and climbed the stairs into the courtroom. The dark wood paneling cast an atmosphere of doom over the place. Just inside the door, I paused for a few minutes, standing silent and still. I did not want fanfare, but I had not come to South Africa to slide through the country as quietly as a mouse through meadow grass. I wanted them to know that I was there. I could feel an awareness of my presence spreading through the courtroom like a hum. I am a big man, 6 feet 2 inches and 240 pounds, so it would have been difficult to miss me standing in the doorway. Another thing that set me apart was my attire. In a sad commentary on the economic condition of the black citizenry of South Africa at the time, I was the only black man in the courtroom wearing a suit and tie. Most of the Africans in the gallery were poor workers dressed in humble work clothes.

I stood there surveying the legal drama being played out before me. I saw the judge, Justice Kees van Dijkhorst, in his scarlet robe seated behind a massive throne of a bench. The long trial was beginning to wear on him, and he looked tired. There was no jury because the South African government had outlawed jury trials. The white judge rarely looked at the black defendants because in the culture and laws of South Africa, they were not his equals. Despite the crush of supporters in the gallery pulling for the defendants, the courtroom did not suggest a seat of justice.

I saw the prosecution, white men in black legal gowns, led by elderly P. B. Jacobs and his younger colleague, P. Fick. Occasionally they spoke in English, but usually they spoke in Afrikaans, the official language of Afrikaners.

In contrast to the white prosecutors, I saw in the defense barristers and advocates a team of men and women whose ethnicity was black, white, and Indian. Notable among them were the tall and impassioned Arthur Chaskalson and senior counsel George Bizos, a short man who had immigrated to South Africa from Greece as a boy fleeing the Nazi persecution of his homeland. The Delmas defendants nicknamed Bizos *Mathlathlo*, or "the power of an elephant," for his crushing cross-examinations. In the coming years I would come to know

Bizos well, but I already knew him by reputation. He was a stalwart anti-apartheid advocate. In the 1950s he had defended Albert Luthuli and Nelson Mandela in the first ANC treason trial. In the 1960s he had defended Mandela, Walter Sisulu, and Govan Mbeki in the Rivonia trial.

Most important, I saw the defendants. Two of them sat on a hard wooden bench while one stood in the dock testifying. The defendant in the dock was Patrick Lekota, nicknamed "Terror" for his fame and prowess on the soccer field. He spoke fluent Afrikaans, but he was reading his testimony in English. When I stepped into the courtroom, he glanced up from his notes to see me, blinked incredulously, and then went back to his testimony. Without looking up again he continued reading, but suddenly he thrust his fist into the air. The unspoken signal was unmistakable: "Power to the People. Black Power. The American ambassador and justice have arrived." It was a powerful gesture.

When he raised his fist, the emotion in the courtroom was palpable. I sensed incredulity in the air, too. The image that flashed in my mind was the scene during the Olympic games in Mexico City when two black American athletes raised their fists in a Black Power salute. Terror Lekota told me later that he meant his spontaneous gesture as a welcome to me, as a symbol of black solidarity, and as a signal to the authorities that the defendants and the black South Africans would overcome the oppression. His silent gesture was a shout of triumph. That single black fist in the air was so mighty that if I had been the presiding judge, I would have been uneasy. If I had been a South African reporter covering the trial, I would have researched the genesis of the gesture, but the significance was not understood, so the gesture went unnoticed.

Teatime came at 10 A.M. and I walked down to the bar, where the defendants crowded around me. Terror was their spokesperson. "Thank you for coming," he said. "We don't have any reading material. We don't have any foreign newspapers. Could you make sure that somebody from the embassy comes here once in a while to keep these people honest?" I promised him that someone from the embassy would be at that trial every day, and we kept that promise. We also supplied the defendants with newspapers and magazines.

I was very moved by their reaction to my presence in the courtroom. My being there as a representative of the United States was a strong infusion of energy and hope to them. Although the trial crawled on for two more years, they were inspired after that. They wore red, yellow, and black UDF pins and buttons with the slogan "UDF unites, apartheid divides." They and their legal representatives used UDF slogans such as "power to the people." The Delmas case was the longest trial in South African legal history: 450 days in court, an indictment of 386 pages, more than 14,000 exhibits, 459 volumes of final records, and a 1,521-page verdict.

That December day in Delmas was the first time an American ambassador to South Africa had ever set foot in a courtroom to attend a political trial. The very fact that I had traveled to this remote area was a message to the South African government and everybody else that, unlike my predecessors, I was going to be an activist. Delmas was my first platform for showing the governmental officials what my administration was going to be. I was in South Africa to deal with the governmental policy of apartheid and to communicate to black South Africa that the United States identified with their plight. Later I would make many appearances and speeches in South Africa, but none were ever as forceful as that day at the Delmas Treason Trial.

My appearance at Delmas had an impact on the South African government. It moved the trial back to Pretoria. That first visit to the trial transformed me, too. I saw that whether or not I liked it, I would have to be an instrument of change. Once I had taken that first step, there was absolutely nothing I could do to reverse this course or even to slow it. If I was to stay in South Africa, my only path was to carry on this effort.

I would attend the trial several times during the next couple of years. In the summer of 1988, I took my daughters, Katherine and Sarah, to the trial. When U.S. senators David Boren and Sam Nunn visited South Africa in December 1988, I asked them to go to the trial, and they did. I made the Delmas Treason Trial the U.S. wedge into the apartheid system. The United States was slow to the battle, many argued, but at Delmas we declared ourselves. The South African apartheid policy was like a hollow oak tree, strong and impenetrable on the outside but rotten at the core. When the United States struck its first blow, the oak started to teeter. The resistance had been building for decades, and I will always believe that the entrenched system of apartheid began falling that December morning in Delmas.

I was in the Pretoria courtroom November 19, 1988, when the verdict was read. Terror Lekota was among those found guilty, and he was sentenced to twelve years, a harsh punishment. After the sentencing, the defendants wrote me a letter that began, "Mr. Ambassador, we would be remiss if, as we go to prison, we did not write to you and tell you how much you have meant to us. Your embassy kept the window to the world open to us." From inside prison, Terror wrote to his teenage daughter a much more remarkable letter, asking her to not hate his captors. That letter became not only famous but prophetic for the future of South Africa.

"My darling Tjhabi," Terror wrote, "I am in prison for the sake of peace for our country and the world. I am in prison so that our generation may leave to your and later generations a country and a world that has the greatest potential for progress. I shall be happy if you forgive but not forget all the ugly things the Afrikaners have done to us. You must remember them so that you do not commit the same acts of barbarism on other human beings, particularly the Afrikaners themselves. Let us build our future on the love and mutual respect of all our country's people."

In my career I have been stationed around the world in places where I have seen unspeakable atrocities and evil. It was a great lesson in humanity for me to witness, after their bitter history of oppression, the magnitude of spirit exhibited by black South Africans. Lekota, who spent so many years of his life behind bars in the quest for freedom and justice, was a teacher for me. I saw the principles of forgiveness and reconciliation embodied in him. He had learned them, he said, while imprisoned in the 1970s on Robben Island for his participation in student demonstrations. In prison he learned from South African elders Mandela, Sisulu, and others.

South Africa was a difficult and a dangerous place to be. White men and women hissed at me when I walked down the streets of Pretoria. Black and Indian revolutionaries refused to meet with me when I first arrived. Coloured citizens accused me and the United States of stirring up trouble in their country. White government officials controlled their rage at my appointment with varying degrees of success. The possibility of assassination was very real. I knew that my own life might be in danger, and I accepted that in the line of duty, but I wondered sometimes how I could have placed my family in such a precarious life. On our posts abroad, my wife and daughters had lived through revolutions, uprisings, and difficult conditions, but South Africa posed a special risk to them. In this white-supremacist nation, I wondered how my Chinese wife and our two mixed-race daughters would be treated.

South Africa was a dangerous place politically, too, because I was operating in uncharted foreign-policy waters. I doubt that any American ambassador has ever been given as much leeway as the president and secretary of state gave me. That freedom was risky. I knew very well that with bad judgment or even bad luck, my career could be ruined on this continent, and my lifelong dream of serving in the Foreign Service would end in failure. I was so far from the safe political shores of Washington, D.C., that I might have been an Arctic explorer, trying to chart new territory with no guarantee that I would succeed and no assurance that the State Department would support me if I failed.

Finally, South Africa was a dangerous place spiritually. To me this nation often seemed soulless, and in the years ahead I would struggle to hold fast to my religious faith.

I would be tested, exhausted, and stressed to the point of illness, but I was never afraid. I had come to South Africa armed with an unusual quiver of tools—a long study of Asian philosophy (especially Sun Tzu's *The Art of War* and Miyamoto Musashi's *The Book of Five Rings*), a reverence for the Constitution of the United States of America, a copy of *Letter from Birmingham Jail* by Martin Luther King Jr., a commitment to the oath of office I had taken as an officer of the Foreign Service, and the discipline of a marine. I know the importance of comprehending both the battlefield and the opponent. I understand the art of diplomacy. And yet, South Africa was a different kind of warfare. I was creating policy day by day with no guidebook or reference source. As black resistance grew and state control tightened, South Africa was a powder keg. Still, I was wedded to the concept of conflict resolution. I saw all of the violent activity around me, but I believed it could be settled peacefully. In a highly unusual assignment, I was a warrior of peace on a strange shore.

I would use these eclectic tools, plus my military training and diplomatic credentials, to try to understand the Afrikaners, the minority white tribe that ruled South Africa. I wanted to see them not as an enemy to be crushed, but as a unique sociological-political-religious force that could be diffused. By understanding them, I reasoned, I could find an opening to slip inside, and from that place, I could begin a discussion. From there I hoped to dismantle apartheid. Understanding the Afrikaners was key—which nobody in the United States government had ever said before.

As much as I revere my own nation's Constitution, I admire the African National Congress's Freedom Charter, which states, "South Africa belongs to all who live in it, black and white, and no government can justly claim authority unless it is based on the will of the people." My work in South Africa would strain to the limit my skills in patience, communication, and diplomacy. I knew that we could not and ought not try to impose American ideals on another sovereign nation. I knew that we could not force change on South Africa from the top down. What I had to do was work from the ground up, marshaling a grassroots effort, but first I had to capture attention. In fiery South Africa, I had to start a fire of my own. That was the purpose of my visit to the Delmas Treason Trial. I was fighting fire with fire.

How I had arrived in this dangerous country with this strange mission is the story of my life, my career, and this book. To write it, I consulted voluminous official documents from the Department of State, the diaries and journals that I have kept throughout my career, personal and official correspondence, and even newspaper and periodical clippings from my files. My notes opened scenes of recall, and I remembered details of conversations and meetings. I double-checked my recollections with colleagues, friends, and relatives who were present on my journey.

This memoir of my career in the Foreign Service might be termed a study in conflict management. I have spent my life trying to bring about change. Some of my work as director general of the Foreign Service entailed wrestling with hidebound policy and, as the U.S. permanent representative to the United Nations, working deep inside international diplomacy. On many of my postings—Ghana, Liberia, and South Africa—I was operating in whitewater. In those posts, stationed in hot sociopolitical situations prone to violence, I saw my wife and daughters held at rifle point by rogue soldiers and wondered what the hell kind of life was I making for my family. Both in America and on foreign shores, I was so embroiled in the action of the moment that I spent little time looking back. Now that I see the arc of my long, exciting career in the Foreign Service, I see how much I have learned from those experiences. I recognize the people who taught me along the way, and I realize how far I have traveled from where I began—as a boy on a farm in the American South.

JESUS CHRIST
AND HUEY LONG

I grew up during the Depression on a cotton farm in Louisiana, where the house of almost every black family had pictures of two people hanging on the wall: Jesus Christ and Huey Long. I have felt the influence of both of these figures all my life. They were my introduction to the forces of religion and government, subjects that have been my life's work and my lifelong study. Geography was another primary force I discovered early. In the global travel that is the life of a career diplomat, I have witnessed the influence of geography on peoples around the world. The cultural history that gripped me from birth and was a looming force in my life and in the generations of my family before me went by the name segregation. "If you were black you caught hell wherever you were," a friend from Arkansas said, "but some states were worse than others." Louisiana was among the worst.

I was born Edward Joseph Perkins Jr. on June 8, 1928, in Sterlington, Louisiana. An astrologist would tell me sixty years later that the scattered planets of my birth chart indicated that I would be a person of multiple facets, a private person but one who would follow his destiny, although many of my successes would be delayed until later in life. I found that astrological reading to be eerily accurate.

Sterlington is a country village on the banks of the Ouachita River. The nearest town is Monroe, named for the steamboat *James Monroe*, which chugged up the river in 1819 when waterways were the principal paths of transportation. This was the setting of my family's history. My extended family was a blend of the area's colorful societies. Monroe is the dividing place between two Louisiana cultures influenced by their geography: timbered hills with small farms lie north and west of the city; and the lowlands stretching south and east to the Gulf of Mexico are the lands of bayous, marshes, and cotton country. The

13

arrival of the *James Monroe* launched the prosperous cotton era for the area, and King Cotton reigned, mighty and unjust, until gas fields were discovered in 1916 and an industrial era began, just twelve years before I was born.

In the 1800s, the era of my great-grandparents, cotton and sugarcane plantations flourished on the backs of slave labor. Louisiana was one of the states that seceded from the Union during the Civil War, and for a few weeks before joining the Confederacy, it declared itself an independent republic under its own flag. The end of the Civil War brought new rights and freedoms for southern blacks, but racial equality would be a long time coming to Louisiana. After the Civil War, Republicans and southern Democrats signed a compact to stop the move toward Reconstruction, and blacks were disenfranchised economically, politically, and socially. A specially called state convention in 1898 had modified the state constitution to stop the tide of black votes. Under the revised constitution, only adult males who could read, write, tell time, and remember dates and places or who owned property valued at three hundred dollars or more were permitted to vote. This precluded many black men, including my grandfather, from voting. The Ku Klux Klan enforced the system into the 1930s, when I was a child. When the Supreme Court ruled that public facilities and schools could be separate if they were of equal quality, neither my family nor other blacks could enter a building using the same door as whites, use the same toilets, sit in the same seats in streetcars, or go to the same schools. This was not changed until the 1954 Supreme Court ruling of *Brown v. Board of Education*. The institutionalized system of segregation existed until the 1960s, too late to help me. I knew only a childhood of segregation.

When I was born, more than one-third of the state's population was black. Louisiana ranked third among the states in black population. Race was such a paramount obsession that an entire vocabulary was developed to define the type and degree of interracial heritage: Sacatro (Negro and Griffe) 87.5 percent, Griffe (Negro and Mulatto) 75 percent, Marabon (Mulatto and Griffe) 62.5 percent, Mulatto (Negro and white) 50 percent, Os Rouge (Negro and Indian) 50 percent, Tierceron (Mulatto and Quadroon) 37.5 percent, Quadroon (white and Mulatto) 25 percent, and Octaroon (white and Quadroon) 12.5 percent. My maternal grandfather was identified as Mulatto on the official census of the time. Blacks were not the only group to be victimized by discrimination; Jews had been prohibited from settling in the area until after the Louisiana Purchase of 1803.

Southern Louisiana projects a romantic image: the wafting influence of New Orleans, Spanish moss, jazz, and the lilting French patois spoken by the Creoles and Cajuns. Monroe was proud of its southern traditions, including barbecues, hospitality, chivalrous attitudes toward women, and segregation of blacks. When I was born, about 40 percent of Monroe's population was black, and most lived in a district separate from the whites. I grew up in a parish of small farms near this city, and I felt its cultural influence.

My boyhood stomping ground, northern Louisiana, was rough-hewn and synonymous with Protestantism, fieldworkers, and hardscrabble farmers. Huey Long was a native of northern Louisiana, and he fondly called the area "my little pea patch." Some towns posted signs warning blacks not to remain in city limits after sunset, yet many of the northern Louisiana parishes were heavily or predominantly populated by blacks. My childhood home, in Claiborne Parish, close to the Arkansas border, was located in such a community. Our family farm was near the village of Pleasant Grove, where black farmers lived side by side with white neighbors.

My earliest memories are of that farm, where I lived with my grandparents and their two grown daughters, Savannah and Tiny Estelle. For generations, my grandparents and great-grandparents had owned property and lived on a cluster of farms in these rugged hills. My grandparents' farm was the center of my youthful world. One of my favorite places was the pond with catfish and perch. Although my eating habits have since changed, two foods from my boyhood— fried catfish and barbecue—are still delicacies to me.

Pleasant Grove, so small it does not appear on the map, consisted of a school and a Baptist church serving a scattering of twenty-five or thirty families. The school was for the black children; white children were bused to Haynesville, about eight miles away. Whenever we rode by horse and wagon to Haynesville, I looked in awe at the homes of the white farmers with their neat yards and painted houses, so different from the black community I knew. I wondered if I would ever be affluent enough to have a painted house.

The central figure of my young life was my grandfather, Nathan Noble, a big man who stood six feet tall. He was handsome with a light complexion, reflecting a racial mixture of half black and Irish/American Indian, perhaps of the Seminole tribe. He was a great father figure to me, kindly and stern, and the person I wanted to emulate—a good businessman, a deacon of the church, and a fine singer. My grandfather was a quiet and introspective man, even around the family, and he never engaged in small talk. Perhaps it was from him that I inherited my subdued nature. One journalist described me as "a quiet giant of a man," and that is how I saw my grandfather. He was the most mysterious member of the family. I never heard him talk about himself, and I know little about him or his family. Records indicate that he was born in Georgia in 1860. Some say he was born a free man, but others believe that he was born into slavery. His African ancestors were from West Africa. His mother was of mixed blood, part African and part Caucasian. His grandmother reportedly was part Osceola Indian. Nathan Noble arrived in Louisiana, met my grandmother at church, and asked for her hand in marriage.

My grandmother, Sarah Elizabeth Stovall (known as Sally when she was young), was born a slave, but her parents, Emerline and Benjamin Franklin Stovall, became affluent and exhibited an aristocratic quality. The founding patriarch of the Louisiana Stovall family may have emigrated from Jamaica. My great-grandfather, Benjamin Stovall, was a rural schoolteacher. My great-grandmother, Emerline, a strict matriarch, had high cheekbones indicative of her half-Indian heritage. By the time my grandparents met, the Stovall family was part of an established family of farmers with a tenacious reverence for their land. In their own lifetime they had made the miraculous transformation from slave to landowner, and they were determined to pass this legacy to their children. It was difficult to impress this proud family, but they considered Nathan Noble a man of good substance, so Benjamin Stovall devised a plan to help the young couple to a future of freedom and independence. "I'll sell you five hundred acres," my great-grandfather told my grandfather, "and that way you will be anchored to the land." For a while, my grandfather made the farm flourish. He became a pillar of the community; his name is enshrined in a little local church in Pleasant Grove, and a road was named after him. My grandparents considered their family a class above most families in the community—the Noble family was "highfalutin and uppity," a cousin told me. Both Great-grandmother Emerline and Grandmother Sarah established two rules for their children: (1) always maintain self-discipline and (2) remember that you are wellborn. My grandmother admonished us all, "Don't be pushed. Stand your ground. Sometimes it might hurt, but you cannot live unless your head is held high."

My grandparents had ten children. One died in infancy, but the other nine

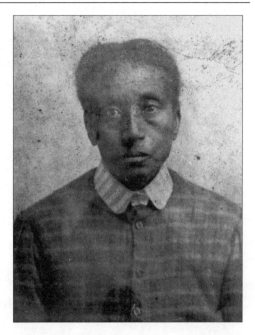

My great-great-grandmother, Emerline Stovall. Her husband was a rural schoolteacher. They made the miraculous progression from slaves to landowners in Louisiana. They were a proud family, as my grandmother Sarah reminded us.

grew to adulthood. This extended family and a hired hand made up the population of the farm, which was the small, secure universe of my boyhood. Although my grandparents could neither read nor write, all of their children attended college. For additional cultural education, Grandfather made his children study music, and the big farmhouse was furnished with an organ and a Victrola. Saturday evenings the family would gather for dinner and somebody would sing or play an instrument. As the Noble family grew up, married, moved away, and made lives for themselves elsewhere, I became the child my grandfather hoped would keep the farm in the family. I spent more time there than any of the other grandchildren did, and the colorful Noble family fascinated me.

Anna, the oldest of the Noble siblings, married a successful farmer named Moses Thomas, who liked to ride a horse and wear a top hat, riding boots, vest, and a pocket watch with a big gold chain. This high-stepping style did not go over well with the whites of the community, who considered it impertinent, and one night Moses was assaulted and beaten. This did not stop him, though. He had a great singing voice and loved to take a nip once in a while.

Jo Willie, much lighter than her sisters, was a good-looking woman, a successful teacher, and married to Robert White. The Whites were considered city people because they lived about fifteen miles away in Homer, the county seat. My cousins in Homer were reluctant to make the trip to visit us on the farm because, according to them, we lived "way out in the country."

Mattie Oney married Thomas Salter, a no-nonsense person and a prosperous farmer in the community, but my grandparents did not approve of him because he had been married before. Like Uncle Moses, he stood up for himself among the white population almost to the point of folly. He once took a rifle to a confrontational meeting with white businessmen.

Savannah, the aunt who had the most influence in my life, was a spinster who chose to stay on the farm rather than marry. She was in her forties when I was a boy on the farm. Savannah was plain and deeply religious. She read the Bible often. The center of our family's social life was the Baptist Church, and Savannah was there every time the doors were open. She went to Sunday School every Sunday, even if nobody else in the family did, and when Savannah went to Sunday School, so did I. We walked together, and when I wanted to wander away, she called me back to her, saying, "A gentleman does not leave a lady unattended." Savannah had a well-defined set of rules for young boys, and any lesson that she felt I needed to know she found in the Bible. The Ten Commandments were the law, directed principally to the youth of the community and to me in particular. In rural Louisiana, the Baptist Bible hung over us like a mighty scythe. The verses Savannah quoted to me most fervently were those about carelessly spreading one's seed. Every time I said hello to a young woman at church, immediately I could see Savannah thinking, "Sin! Boy, you're going to go to Hell for sure." She was determined that I grow up with a thorough understanding of the moral rules of behavior. According to her strict religion, those rules meant no dancing, no drinking spirits, no card-playing, no gambling, and definitely no casual seed-spreading.

Minnie Pearl married a man named Jameson from Smackover, Arkansas, where they lived with their four children. Because of the distance and difficulty of travel in those days, I knew her and her family least of all the siblings and their families.

Elmer, always known as Bud, was the oldest son and a veteran of World War I. He was more like my grandfather than his brothers, and perhaps this similarity in temperament is the reason he and my grandfather did not get along well.

Bud's wife became mentally ill and was admitted to an institution, where she remained for the rest of her life. Uncle Bud and his five children came to live with us, and he helped with running the farm.

Ellis was a high stepper who liked to keep moving, so he was on and off the farm throughout my childhood. I would not say that he was unkind, but he was given to acts of unkindness and provoked people. One Monday, the county sheriff appeared at our farm with a citizen's complaint that had been lodged against my uncle. The charge was that a talkative neighbor had pontificated in church until Ellis said loudly, "Why don't you shut up and sit down."

Nobody knows how many times Ellis was married, but one day he caused quite a stir in the community when he showed up with a new bride and her two children. This was Katye Bell, a mysterious, statuesque Cajun who practiced voodoo. My Aunt Katye Bell cast spells and curses, told fortunes, and made voodoo dolls of people who angered her. She scared the daylights out of me. Once, when I raised her wrath, she pierced me with a ferocious look and hissed, "I will not forget you." From then on I was careful to cut a wide swath around her. After we both left Pleasant Grove, I did not see her for almost forty years, and then I called her, where she was living in Kansas City.

"Katye," I said, "this is Edward Perkins."

After a pause she said, "Eddie Joe?"

"Yes."

"Boy, you talk like a white man."

Virgil, the youngest son, married Matilda, a fascinating woman in the community who did something unusual for the time: she conducted adult classes for women who wanted to learn to read and write. One summer about 1935, Virgil, not yet forty years old, caught viral pneumonia and died. Matilda, a member of the Pentecostal Sanctified Church, arranged the funeral. She brought in a minister from Homer who arrived with an entourage playing tambourines and guitars. This strange funeral ceremony, so alien to the conservative Baptist church I knew, was a version of religion I had never seen before. The Holy Rollers were happy, singing, dancing in ecstasy, and speaking in unknown tongues of praise. The minister ascended the pulpit shouting, "Brother Noble is not dead. He is just asleep, and he is coming again, so we don't want any tears." I sat dumbfounded and frightened at the commotion. When I stole a look at my grandmother, I saw that she was stoic and immobile in the pew beside me.

Tiny Estelle, the youngest daughter, was a kindred spirit with the exotic Katye Bell and Matilda. These three intriguing women, so different from everyone else in the community, seemed bonded by that difference. Tiny had a good education, had lived away from the farm for a few years, and was more sophisticated than my rural grandparents and Savannah. She was as tall as I am, 6 feet 2 inches, carried herself well, had a beautiful face, liked nice clothes, and was a lovely singer. She was the belle of that community and attracted men like a magnet, but country men held no interest for Tiny. The most glamorous of the entire family, she was a caged bird on that farm. When I was about six, my grandmother took me aside and told me that Tiny was not my aunt; she was my mother.

Tiny had been away at school, either Grambling College or the Louisiana State Normal School in Natchitoches, studying to get her teaching certificate, when she met my dashing father. Edward Perkins, from Monroe, had been a soldier in World War I and was an evangelistic minister of the gospel, traveling from church to church to lead revivals. He was also, my mother told me years later, "a no-account rascal," but she laughed when she said it. My traditionalist grandmother did not approve of this young man, whom she did not know, or of his family, who were "not our kind of people." She was scornful of migrant ministers, who seemed more interested in the flock's revenue and attractive women than in their eternal souls, and she opposed a hasty match. She expected a young couple to go through the ritual of courtship and spend time getting acquainted. Despite the family's opposition, my parents wed anyway in 1927. My father was twenty-nine and my mother was twenty-four. I was born the following year.

My parents divorced when I was three. "We were not compatible," is all that my mother ever said about it. "He was not ready to settle down," an aunt told me later. I do not remember much about my father except that he was a fancy dresser. I saw him only twice in church, when I was about seven. He wore a nice suit, shiny shoes, a hat, and a pocket watch with a long chain. He seemed to have money, because once he gave me a dollar and another time he bought me ice cream. He had not come to see me, though, and I never saw him again. I wrote to him occasionally at the prompting of my mother, and sometimes he would respond with a money order of ten or fifteen dollars. There are no photographs of him. When I asked his sister, my Aunt Viola, what he looked like, she said, "Look in the mirror."

The Noble family in Louisiana.
(*front row, left to right*) My grandfather Nathan, grandmother Sarah (Stovall),
with their children Elmer and Ellis. (*back row, left to right*) Mattie,
Tiny Estelle, Virgil, and Savannah.

After the divorce my father moved to Natchitoches, on the west side of Louisiana, where he married two more times. My mother left the Monroe area, taking me with her, and went back to her parents' farm. The arrival of a divorced woman was unsettling to that little community. Some saw her as a failure; others viewed her as a loose woman and a threat to their marriages. I remember a great argument and a woman shouting at Tiny, "I saw my man looking at you out of the corner of his eye."

Tiny was restless on the farm; she saw a future for herself over a dazzling horizon. When I was about ten, a traveling minister, the Reverend Henry Titus Grant, came to Pleasant Grove to conduct a week-long revival. He noticed Tiny immediately because she was the prettiest woman in the congregation. She returned the attention and, against the objections of my grandmother and

Savannah, invited him to Sunday dinner. I could feel the tension in the air, as taut as a wire. My grandfather was unperturbed by the visit, but my grand-mother, a moralist and a strict disciplinarian, was rigid with disapproval. She considered traveling evangelists little more than vagrant seducers of women. Savannah was distressed by her younger sister's risky behavior. The Reverend Grant was from Arkansas and Oklahoma, an older man who had been married before and had three or four children, some the age of my mother. The age dif-ference further distressed my grandmother. In southern black families, an older man who courts younger women is considered a lecher preying on inno-cent women.

Savannah believed that Tiny's association with this man would bring ruin to her and dishonor to the family. All the following week, I saw the three women in intense discussions. "What does he do for a living?" my grandmother asked in exasperation. "You'll be throwing away your life." Nothing she or Savannah said could dissuade Tiny. In that dreary routine of farm life, Reverend Grant was a door flung open to the world. To her, he was an exciting figure. He had a car, he dressed well, he was flamboyant, he was persuasive, and he liked her. The following Sunday, when Reverend Grant came back, he and Tiny went into the front parlor to talk, locking the door behind them. I was disappointed that they preferred to be alone and did not welcome my company. Midweek, he came again, this time to take her away. Grandmother stood in silent anger, Savannah clutched a meat cleaver, and I watched quietly as Tiny and Reverend Grant left together. "She ran away with a man," Savannah cried. They were not married when they left, and although I was too young to understand why, I knew that scandal shrouded the farm in despair.

Slowly the gloom lifted when we learned that Tiny and Reverend Grant had married and were living in Pine Bluff, Arkansas, where he was a minister, although still a traveling evangelist. My mother always worked outside the home. At various times she taught school, had a job at an arsenal, trained as a nurse, and cared for home patients. Despite their respectability in Pine Bluff, my grandmother never forgave the vagabond preacher. Reverend Grant was never once invited back into my grandmother's house.

I stayed behind on the farm, living with my grandparents and Savannah and going to school. I did not feel abandoned or deserted by my mother. To me this arrangement seemed the most natural thing in the world. Even when she was there, my mother had been more like a friend than a parent. For most of my life my mother was a stranger to me, and it was a long time before I looked upon her as my mother. I always called her Tiny.

I called my grandmother Mama. She was strong willed and hefty, with lots of hair piled high on her head. She was not a sour person, but she was serious. I rarely remember her laughing. She had a commanding demeanor, influenced by her own mother, and she was clearly a matriarchal figure, with a penchant for discipline. "You can be a man," my grandmother said to me, "only when you learn to accept discipline from others and from yourself." She was quick to dispense the discipline. If I transgressed in any way, she would send me to get a switch off a peach tree. Peach tree switches are strong and willowy, and they hurt. I quailed to hear the dreaded words, "Bring me a switch." When she judged a switch too small, she used it until it broke and then sent me to get another. Her strong arm marked her determination to bring me up right so that I would "be somebody." Then I got to the age of rebellion. She came toward me for a beating and although I was afraid of her, I did an unheard-of thing—I ran. She chased me, but she could not catch me. I was at large in the countryside for half a day. Eventually I had to go home, and she got her revenge, but that was the last time she whipped me. I will not say that I did not commit some acts that were unacceptable. Once, when I broke a post hole digger, I hid it for days, afraid to say that I had broken it. My grandfather finally discovered it. He knew I had done it, but all he said was, "Oh, this thing was about to break, and it looks like it has broken." So he fashioned another handle, bolted it on, and it was as good as new.

Savannah assumed for herself the role of surrogate mother to me. Her guide for child rearing was the Bible, with its dictates about being truthful, upright, studious, chaste, and hard working. Idle hands and idle minds, Savannah told me, were fodder for the devil's workshop. She kept me so busy working in her magnificent flowerbeds that I did not have a spare minute for the devil.

Almost daily my grandmother lectured me about proper relations between the sexes and the wickedness of crossing the line. She was adamant about my steering clear of girls. "You're too young to know what you're doing, so don't do it," she said, implying that there would be a high price to pay if she caught me. "Time enough for you, my boy!" The moral atmosphere that I grew up in has stayed with me. My grandmother thought my mother had married badly, twice, and she said so. "Make your grandfather the model for your life," she admonished me. She always referred to her husband as Mr. Noble. When she sent me to ask my grandfather to come to eat, she said, "Call Mr. Noble for dinner." I called him Pa.

My aunt preached, my grandmother disciplined, but my grandfather demonstrated. Much of what I learned about living an upright and honorable life came by watching him. My grandfather was a stickler for fair play. The unwritten rule of farm life is to not let livestock wander and damage other people's crops. I remember an incident when a neighbor's cows kept getting out of their fenced pasture and finding their way into our fields. My grandfather would round them up and take them back, and Mr. West would say, "Thanks very much." It happened again and again until my grandfather said, "This has got to stop." So the next time the cows came into our property, my grandfather put them in his own pens and kept them there. Eventually Mr. West came looking for the cows. "Thanks for keeping them," he said. "I'll take them now."

"No, you won't," my grandfather said. The cows had caused a specified amount of damage, "And we'll milk them until it's paid for." I was concerned that there would be bad blood between the two of them, but there were no lingering bad feelings. He never humiliated Mr. West, and the next Sunday at church they were talking and shaking hands. The lesson to me was that if you do not get justice one way, you can get it another.

The Noble family farm was diverse, with timber as well as crops. Two kinds of syrup were produced there: ribbon cane syrup, which we sold because it brought a better price, and sorghum syrup, which we ate although it did not taste as good. Sorghum is used to make beer, but none was made on our teetotaler farm. No liquor of any kind was poured in my grandparents' home. Grandfather raised swine, cattle, chickens, ducks, and guinea fowl. It was my grandfather's dream that I continue that family-farming enterprise. "Stay attached to the farm," he told me, "and you will always have enough to eat." Part of this dream was driven by family pride, but another part was practicality. It was the Depression, and people across the country were unemployed and hungry. My grandmother, however, had other plans for me.

A great crop of the South, then and now, is cotton. Growing cotton—chopping it, cultivating it, and harvesting it—is deservedly one of the most hated of jobs. It is hard and brutal work. Cotton is planted in late spring, as soon as frost clears. Picking cotton begins in summer and lasts into fall. When I was a boy, school was delayed so we children could help in the fields. Everybody on the farm participated, and all of us despised the entire process: hoeing weeds, eliminating wild cotton plants to get one healthy stalk, making sure it gets enough moisture, and keeping the space between the rows clean. In the heat of late summer, our work from dawn to dusk was picking the cotton, bending over all day, pulling a sack along, and stuffing in the damn stuff, constantly weighing it to get enough to make a bale, which requires a lot of cotton. After it was picked, it was taken to the cotton gin. That was a different kind of pain. I will never forget how hard my grandfather had to fight to get an honest deal from the broker and from the dealer. Being a black man, he had to fight to be treated as well as white farmers. Seeing how rejected and beaten he looked coming out of those sessions affected me a great deal, because I looked up to him as a hero. I thought he could do anything—and then he came up against that cruel and impenetrable wall.

One year I rode along with my grandfather in the wagon full of cotton to Haynesville to see the banker. My grandfather was asking for a loan to purchase equipment and expand the farm. The banker was a white man in a seersucker suit who shook his head and said, "I ain't gonna do it." "I have collateral," my grandfather repeated, but the banker only shook his head: "I ain't gonna do it." My grandfather was crushed at the refusal, but he was also angry that I had to see it. Years later I understood that the banker's denial of a loan was calculated to wrest the farm away from my grandfather.

The part of existence in the community that we detested most was negotiations with the whites, negotiations on every front. I know now how humbled and broken they left my grandfather. He had the knowledge, the pride, and the skills to be a prosperous businessman/farmer, as well as the desire to succeed, but he had no opportunity. I do not know how I avoided growing bitter at the racism I witnessed at that young age because, as Martin Luther King Jr. wrote so eloquently in his *Letter from Birmingham Jail*, little minds are formed when they see the different treatment for blacks and whites.

An asset to growing up on a farm was the experience I gained from being part of nature. I learned to acquire food by fishing and by hunting squirrels and partridges. In the spring I picked berries for canning. I can remember how pleasant it was to see the spring come because it is a rebirth: birds come back from migration, flowers begin to bud, and it is time to go fishing. I grew up observing the cycle of nature and learning that all of life is a cycle.

As a child I spent a lot of time roaming the woods alone. The rural setting was a constant adventure for me. In that solitude, I developed a keen imagination.

Once I saw a lone airplane overhead and wondered what it would be like to be in that plane, flying away. I was also an insatiable reader, and I could not get enough books. Savannah subscribed to the weekly newspaper, and I waited impatiently for its arrival—my glimpse into a world beyond the farm. In retrospect, the enduring lessons from my childhood were the power of imagination and the gift of curiosity.

When I was about twelve and the nation was mobilizing for World War II, the U.S. Army trained soldiers in the area. One day I looked up to see troops on a training march crossing our farm. I was so transfixed by these men with such strange gear that I did not know if they were friend or foe. They took a rest break in front of our farmhouse, picked vegetables from my grandmother's garden, and paid her for them. This was one of my first glimpses of people from outside my small, confined community.

The other side of bucolic farm life is the constant demand of work, especially work for a young person—gathering eggs and cleaning out hen houses and stables. My grandmother's big garden produced beans, cabbage, turnips, mustard greens, sweet corn, muskmelons, lettuce, and other vegetables. My grandmother raised and gathered our food, prepared three meals a day, then canned and preserved the surplus for us to eat through the winter months. She had Mason jars of green beans, tomatoes, and preserves. From my grandmother I learned how to milk cows, churn butter, make cheese, and pasteurize milk. She believed that everyone, boys included, needed to learn how to feed themselves, so she taught all of us grandchildren to garden and to dress and cook chickens, pigs, rabbits, and small game. Our house was lit by kerosene, and my jobs included filling the lantern with coal oil or kerosene and cleaning and trimming the wicks. My grandfather and I cut timber for firewood, and it was my responsibility to keep the containers by the fireplace or heaters filled with firewood. After I started grade school at the age of seven, I was considered big enough to use a plow pulled by a workhorse or mule, and I learned to cultivate that red earth and to prepare it for planting. The ability to plow straight was the mark of an accomplished farmer, so I knew it was a compliment when I heard my grandfather say, "Junior can plow a straight furrow." I worked with my grandfather mending fences; clearing the land; and planting, cultivating, and harvesting corn, beans, alfalfa, peanuts, sweet peas, black-eyed peas, cotton, sorghum, sugarcane, and soybeans. My grandfather also experimented with growing tobacco. Rewards came in simple pleasures. "I think those sweet potatoes are about ready for harvesting," my grandfather would say. "Dig up five or six, and we'll roast them tonight."

I came to know the nuances of the seasons. I learned how to read the almanac and how to know the best times for planting and pruning. I learned the best time to castrate hogs and, consequently, to appreciate what we called mountain oysters. I learned how to butcher and bleed animals, and how to use all parts of an animal for food and to cure it. We made sausages, chitterlings, and hog maws. We pickled pigs' feet and pig ears. Every part of the animal was used. Nothing was thrown away.

Most of our corn was taken to the miller to be ground into meal, but we bought flour. That was a luxury. Lard and sugar were other luxuries. When the Depression made spending money scarce, my grandmother cut down on things that had to be purchased in town, such as candy or a toy. I was not aware of suffering in the Depression, but there were things I could not get. At the beginning of the school year usually I was given new trousers, a new shirt, and a new pair of shoes. I had one set of Sunday-go-to-meeting clothes and another set for school, but as the Depression closed in, instead of getting two pairs of trousers for school, I had only one pair and an admonition to take care of them.

In warm weather, after the day's work was done and evening settled in with birdsong and locusts' rasp, my grandparents, Savannah, and I sat on the porch. Sometimes we sang, mostly hymns led by Savannah, and I listened to my grandparents talk about events of the community. Many stories came out of those get-togethers. I was never invited to participate in the conversation, but occasionally I asked questions, especially when they were talking about someone's behavior. Throughout my career I have been told that I'm a good listener. Perhaps I learned that trait as a little boy listening to my grandparents talk on the porch on long summer evenings. In the winter we gathered inside the big house, around the stove. A family ritual was having a hot drink, sassafras tea or apple cider.

There was no such thing as a vacation. If it wasn't the growing season, we took a break by sleeping an hour later, but we filled the workday with mending harnesses, greasing buggy wheels, or other chores. Sunday was a day of worship and self-denial. In Pleasant Grove, everyone went to church at least once a month to exchange the news of the community. Saturday, however, was for fishing or the ultimate adventure for me, a trip to Haynesville. Pleasant Grove had no stores. The nearby village of Dykesville consisted of a cotton gin and a gasoline service station. But Haynesville had it all. Besides a cotton gin, Haynesville had two drugstores, a couple of cafés, a bank, and three or four saloons. The saloons were for whites; blacks drank from bottles out back.

Christmas was a festive holiday in the country. We cut a holly tree from the woods, decorated it with cranberries and popcorn—nothing was ever bought for that tree—and everyone had presents. The presents for the younger people were always practical items: a cap, a pair of gloves, toothpaste and toothbrush, a bar of soap. The big Christmas dinner was traditional with two kinds of meat, a turkey or guinea hen and pork roast, and lots of pies. The women worked for days making fruitcake and pies: mincemeat, apple, and peach. Although nobody would admit it, the fruitcake was laced with rum—I found the bottle once, in the back of a big cupboard. Decoration Day, in late spring, was another big holiday. The entire family went to the cemeteries to clean the grounds and put flowers on the graves. A picnic followed, with watermelon, cantaloupes, sweet corn, English peas, and pork, cured beef, or fowl from the farm. That family gathering at the cemetery was one of the rare occasions I saw my grandparents be merry.

The big farmhouse had lots of rooms and a kitchen separate from the house. I did not see a separate kitchen like that again until I went to Thailand and Africa. I shared a bedroom with Savannah, with a little divider separating us. The biggest room in the house was my grandparents' bedroom, large enough to have a stove, a fireplace, and a few chairs. When some kind of natural disaster threatened, whatever relatives were living in the little house came to the big house to wait out the storm. Afterwards we had a snack—roasted sweet potatoes, popcorn, or peanuts. It gave everybody solace.

I grew up not knowing much about the opposite sex. When we were adolescents, my friend Henry Scott and I decided to go to a neighboring church one Sunday because we had heard about twin sisters in a black family that lived not far away. Those girls were the prettiest things I had ever seen. We talked to them at length that day and caught a ride home with them in their father's buggy. For the first time I realized there could be mental pleasure from being around the opposite sex.

As an adult, I became (and remain) a Roman Catholic, but the religion of my youth was hymn-singing, scripture-based, baptism-by-immersion, hellfire-if-you-sin Baptist. In the rigid religious stricture of our community, drinking spirits was strictly forbidden, and only twice did I see a man drinking whiskey.

One was a hired hand from a neighboring farm. My cousin and I met him walking along a country road, and we saw that he was drinking something from a
fruit jar.

"What are you drinking?" we asked him.

"Whiskey," he said. "Want some?" We drew back in shock and said no. "Well,
I wouldn't give it to you anyway," he said. "It's not good for you." He might
indulge, but he enforced upon us the morals of the community.

The other occasion was more colorful. A touring group of male singers
came to our church, and before their performance I walked around to the back
of the church to get a look at them. I saw them having a surreptitious drink to
fortify themselves for the audience.

In 1936, when I was eight years old, just at the advent of autumn, my grandfather caught pneumonia. Savannah and my grandmother nursed him with
herbs, especially Mullen tea, but he got worse and was taken to the doctor in
Haynesville. The doctor treated him with the all-purpose medicine Black
Draught and prescribed bedrest, the standard treatment for pneumonia, but he
did not improve. The nearby family was summoned—Mattie, Jo Willie, and
Bud. Virgil had died a year earlier, and the others were too far away. Every person who arrived added to the growing sense of urgency. Then, with the family
gathered anxiously in the farmhouse, sitting quietly or talking softly, my grandfather died. The women began to keen, making a sound of grief that cut
through the walls. My grandmother wept, not much, but it was unusual to see
her weep at all, this strong woman who never expressed any emotion. The
women sat in a circle in the parlor; the men congregated on the porch, all
grieving; and I went outside to be alone among a grove of pecan trees on the
farm. The farm seemed to die with him. Even the wind in the trees fell silent.
My grandfather's death devastated me. He was the foundation of my life and of
the family. I did not know what to do. I did not know how to live without him.
While my relatives were occupied making funeral arrangements and settling
his accounts, I kept myself busy gathering pecans. I did not understand my own
emotions. Years later, in Ghana, when I was getting ready to go to Mass with my
younger daughter Sarah one Sunday morning, I suddenly felt ill, strangely
light-headed. The embassy nurse told me to lie down until she arrived, and a
friend took Sarah out of the room. As they left I saw the stark terror in my
daughter's eyes, and I knew then what it was I had felt as an eight-year-old boy
when I saw my grandmother grieving over my grandfather: stark terror.

The whole community came to his funeral. He was buried and the family was broken, but life went on. My grandfather died disappointed that his sons did not preserve the big farm. He had tried to keep it going with hired help, but it became too much for him. Merchants would not provide long-term credit for a planting season, and the only loan available was from Mattie's husband, who was impatient and wanted immediate repayment. Finally, to pay accumulating tax debt, my grandfather sold part of the farm. The new owners were white. After he died, Bud stayed on to manage the farm, and Savannah remained, but it was never the same. Today, farms in that area are catfish farms or hunting retreats; none are working farms. Years after all of us had left, oil was discovered on my grandparents' farm. It was a lucrative place at last, but too late for the Noble family.

My grandmother was adamant that I get an education. This woman, illiterate all her life, had a granite faith in the power of education. She had me read to her anything that had print on it, everything we could lay our hands on—the local newspaper or books around the house left by her children who had gone off to college. We never passed by a piece of paper on the ground if there was printing on it; she made me pick it up and read it to her. She dictated letters that I wrote to her relatives in Louisiana, Arkansas, Illinois, California, and Texas. At Sunday School or any outing, I was presented as a little scholar. She never once let me believe that I was meant for anything but the top. Once I finished grade school, she vowed to do everything she could to get me out of Louisiana. She succeeded, but it was a struggle.

When I started school, I walked down a dirt road to the two-teacher, two-room wooden school building in Pleasant Grove while the white children rode a school bus to a school made of bricks. I knew that was not fair, and my grandmother did not accept it, either. She told my cousins and me that education would be our way off this dirt road, that we could "push the bottom out." The heroes of my little community were the two teachers and the minister.

Young people were taught to be respectful of all adults, especially accomplished community leaders and founts of knowledge. I once referred to the woman who lived over the hill as "Suz," and my grandparents said, "Who are you talking about? That is 'Mrs. West' to you." I was twenty-one years old before I could bring myself to call older persons by their first name.

A cousin once told a reporter that I was "a skinny, polite boy who did well in school and sang loudly in church." I was not as outgoing as my cousins were, and although not exactly a "goody two-shoes," I was too correct for the few playmates that I had. The training of my grandmother and aunt had taken hold, and I thought the worst thing in the world was telling a lie. In our little schoolhouse, I once got a cousin punished when I volunteered information to the principal about his playing hooky. "I know you don't want to tell a lie," another cousin said, "but you didn't have to say anything because the principal didn't ask you directly." That did not make sense to me, but I knew enough not to get on the wrong side of my cousins, so in the future I remained silent. It was another learning experience.

I was a quiet boy, with limited opportunity to engage in idle conversation and nobody to talk to except my grandparents and aunt, who did not encourage chatting. In my professional life I have been described as unemotional and criticized for my reluctance to talk about my personal life. These characteristics have their roots on that Louisiana farm. Reserve is a trait I learned from my grandfather; personal control is a characteristic I developed through my studies of Asian philosophy. I believe that we should not be intrusive or impose ourselves on other people, that a sense of privacy gives one the power to deal with personal environment, and that personal environment is something that must be controlled.

When I finished elementary school in Pleasant Grove, I faced a crisis. What would I do next? I liked to read and enjoyed science, but with no academic challenges for me, I found myself losing interest. In that rural community there were no opportunities for further schooling. The high schools for blacks were in Homer and Haynesville, but neither was an option in my grandmother's opinion. She wanted me to leave the state. "There is nobody here to teach you," she said. "You won't learn anything here."

I was caught in a dilemma that lay over that abject state like a pall. In the 1930s, Louisiana rated next to last in literacy among the forty-eight states. About 16 percent of the state's population, black and white, was illiterate; four out of ten farm men had not finished the fourth grade. This was a time when the majority of the state's population, 60 percent, was rural. One of the reasons educational opportunities were almost nonexistent was the state's poverty level. The average gross income was about thirteen hundred dollars, which ranked the state thirty-ninth in the nation. Compared to the other forty-seven states—in property value, income, conveniences such as running water and electricity, and social services, from transportation to health care—Louisiana was considered so backward that it was described as primitive. The state was not classified as urban until 1950. In our small community the infant mortality rate was so high that burying babies was routine. Now I know that they died as a result of dehydration caused by unclean drinking water, and that simple oral rehydration salts could have saved their lives.

In this bleak economic climate, Huey Long was a hero of the common people. My interest in the career of fiery Huey and his brother, Earl, both of whom were governors of the state and then elected to Congress, began as a child when the Long dynasty reigned. Huey Long was a different kind of politician, a radical populist who burst onto the scene with the blaze of a meteor. He campaigned for equal economic justice for everybody. "I come from the common people, and I am a friend of labor," he said. His slogan was "Every man a king, but no one wears a crown."

In the South, racism was an established way of life, as common as the sultry air we breathed. He had empathy not only for blacks, but for all downtrodden people, including the farmers with no adequate roadways to get their produce to market. When he became governor, only three hundred miles of roads were paved in the state. When rain made dirt roads impassable, farmers could not get their goods to market to feed their families—nor could they get to the polling place to vote. Governor Long developed a road-works program and built highways from one end of the state to the other. He built free bridges and improved state hospitals and institutions.

He wanted to make Louisiana progressive and educated. He introduced the concept of the state providing free textbooks for the schools in Louisiana, and that was a hard-fought battle. He started a school-lunch program so every child would have at least one genuine meal a day. "A student whose belly is empty can't learn," he said. The state contracted food preparation to local women, and I remember having delicious school food—stew, soup, lots of rice, some chicken occasionally. My grandmother made sure I had balanced meals because she was bound and determined that I not get rickets or some other ailment. She fed me milk, cornbread, meat, and lots of vegetables and sent me to school with huge lunch boxes. But I am sure that for many children, the school lunch was the best food they had. "Our kids deserve one balanced meal a day," the governor said, and he made it possible for that to happen. He also made it possible for rural children to study at the university. Until Long was elected governor, Louisiana State University was a little backwater school ranked near the bottom of state universities. He claimed that he moved it to number four in the nation. He was exaggerating, but it did improve mightily.

Studying Governor Long's career taught me that he was a political behaviorist genius. To fund much of the state work he passed laws requiring oil companies to leave some of their profits in the community where they made their money. Years later in South Africa, I would use Long's model for bringing business and government together. Whereas Long forced it, though, I used persuasion.

Huey "Kingfish" Long was cock-of-the-walk and king of the state from 1928, the year I was born, to 1935. He became a virtual dictator and in doing so created a lot of enemies, but he was revered by the people, especially by the black people. No one had spoken up for us before or included us as part of the citizenry; no one had championed us. We could not identify with the elected gentlemen in white jackets and goatees, but here was an ordinary man of the land who honored the working man. I was only seven when he was shot, but I remember how black people grieved. We had lost the man who seemed to be our only advocate. He was assassinated in the corridors of the Louisiana State Capitol at Baton Rouge and buried in front of the new Art Deco capitol he had built. His last words were reported to be "God don't let me die; I have so much to do."

If I stayed in Louisiana, my grandmother saw my future as clearly as if it were a plowed furrow stretching before me. She thought that I had intellect and education would be my escape, so she pushed me off that poor land. How this humble former slave came to believe so fervently in education I do not know, but she was right. I owe her the professional life I have been able to have.

Going away to school was the principal reason she wanted me to leave, but she was also afraid I was too involved with my white playmates, who lived on the next farm. My friendship with the Worley daughter especially disturbed my family. Blacks and whites did not mix in that time and place, not without problems and sorrow. "White girls and colored boys don't play together," my grandmother said. "This is trouble just waiting in the wind." She was determined to get me out of there. But where could I go? No one would accept me, not even my own mother. Reverend Grant refused to have me live with them in Arkansas. He did not want to be encumbered or responsible for the upbringing of a young person entering his teens.

Savannah orchestrated the plan for my departure. She had me write a letter to Jo Willie in Homer asking if I could stay with her while I was going to high school, but my aunt also said no. Then we appealed to Pearl in Arkansas, but she had a family of her own and she, too, said no. So Savannah wrote my mother and laid it on the line. "Look," she said, "he has to continue his schooling. He has a chance to go to high school, and the only avenue left is for him to go and live with you and your husband."

It was a crossroad in my life. I was at a vulnerable age, that critical time when young people need help from others to grow up and get the tools of life that make it possible to exist in society. Such support cannot be taken for granted. We have only to look out on the streets and see in society's rejects the people who did not get the necessary assistance. The Noble family values were already so ingrained in me that I doubt I would have done anything to embarrass my family, but none of us makes it through life alone and unaided.

It took some time before my mother could convince her husband to agree, but finally, exhibiting hidden steel, she said, "This is what I want." And that is how I came to enter high school in Pine Bluff, Arkansas.

Before my mother died, I wrote her a ten-page letter for Mother's Day telling her what she had been to me. "You offered me that step from a precarious world of nothing except the circumscribed life of a farm hand," I said, "and gave me a chance to go to high school and to move on to a white world which was so different from anything I had ever envisioned. And in that white world, the first thing I learned is how limited I was in my preparation, even for high school. I had not the slightest concept of the correct use of the English language for speaking or writing. The eight parts of speech were foreign to me. I did not have a good reading program and all of a sudden, I was introduced to William Saroyan and Greek history. Greek fables suddenly became a living thing for me." I said to my mother in that letter, "You are the instrument that made this happen." She gave the letter to her pastor, and he had it read out in church to the congregation.

Savannah stayed on the farm. Late in her life, surprising all of us, she married. A widower named Abner Gibson, who lived on an adjoining farm, paid court to her and asked for her hand, and my grandmother agreed. My grandmother lived to be 103 years old. I was in Japan after my army service when she died. My cousins told me that my grandmother always talked about me, wanted to know how I was, and wondered if I would ever come back. About a year after my grandmother's death, in 1960, my mother wrote to tell me that my father had died. He was such a shadowy figure to me that I felt nothing at the news. My grandmother, however, represented a seminal chapter in my life. She pushed me out the door and set me on the road of life, and I have been traveling around the world ever since.

When I was ambassador to Australia, I gave the keynote address for a conference and afterwards met a woman who was attending from Baton Rouge. When I told her that I had been born in Louisiana, she would not believe it. "I didn't stay there," I told her. "If I had, I would not be here today." She and I talked about Louisiana and how that state's development has been a lesson to other nations. Louisiana is a state that picked up its shoes and shawl and marched forward, but not without controversy and hindrances.

HIGH SCHOOL
IN THE BIG CITY

I left the farm when I was fourteen and moved to Arkansas to attend high
school. This journey of fewer than 150 miles was tantamount to entering
another galaxy. My grandmother and Savannah drove me in the wagon to
Haynesville, where I took my first train trip, north through the Cotton Belt to
Pine Bluff. It was early autumn, and some of the fields were still white with
cotton. When I caught a glimpse of a plantation, I saw roof railings on the big
houses, architectural remnants of the time the overseer stood on the roof to
survey the work of his slaves in the fields. Those empty roofs told a silent story
of the nation's history that affected my own life. They were mute reminders of
entitlement for one segment of society and the beginning of a new kind of life
for the black people. It was because those plantation roofs were empty that I
could make this journey for education.

During the Civil War, Arkansas allied itself with the Confederacy. After the
war, Confederate states, including Arkansas, were placed under military rule
until they adopted new constitutions and ratified the Fourteenth Amendment,
which granted suffrage to blacks. Before then, blacks were not legal citizens,
did not have the rights and privileges of citizenship, and were prohibited by law
from learning to read. After the Civil War, freed blacks worked in the fields as
sharecroppers instead of slaves. They could now be employed in trade, including businesses that required literacy, and segregated public education was made
available for black youth. Schools were built for black children, and a state college for blacks was established in Pine Bluff. Almost everything in the state—
education, economics, social structure—was changed by the Civil War.

When I arrived in 1942, Pine Bluff was a small agricultural community on
the banks of the Arkansas River, but to me it was a metropolitan city, with two
railroads, stockyards, lumber mills, cotton mills, department stores, movie

theaters, and skyscrapers eleven or twelve stories high. When I lived on the farm in Louisiana, going to Haynesville, with its dirt main street had been a festive occasion. Wearing our best clothes, we climbed out of the wagon and looked in wonder at the array of merchandise for sale in the stores and buildings. Those awestruck memories shrank to Lilliputian dimensions in Pine Bluff, where the population of about twenty-one thousand was almost ten times the size of Haynesville. I had stepped from a world that moved at the pace of a plodding horse to a modern city with streetcars and automobiles. In Louisiana, it had taken us an hour in a buggy to get to town, but here all I had to do was walk around the corner to find a store. Towering over the heart of the city was the Jefferson County Courthouse, an antebellum building with a great gilded clock that I could see from almost anywhere downtown. Nearby was the historic Jefferson Hotel, where riverboat gamblers, plantation owners, cotton buyers, and pontificating politicians had once gathered, and which still operated in glory. In its cotton heyday, Pine Bluff had been the state's leading cotton port. Now, as the nation geared up for World War II, the town was flourishing with the booming wartime economy. Jobs were plentiful, and I was not the only new arrival—people were flocking in from the East and the South, many to work in the new arsenal, where they would manufacture guns and ammunition to fight the war with Japan and Germany.

For all its cosmopolitan flair, Pine Bluff had an agricultural heart. On Saturdays, the farming community came to town. Women wore freshly ironed dresses; men put on their cleanest overalls and—winter or summer—wool hats and went to town to trade and socialize. The farmers' market was a rustic bazaar: chickens, hogs, pigs, cotton, potatoes, collards, cabbages, radishes, onions of all kinds—red, white, Vidalia—and freshly baked cakes, pies, and breads.

To a raw boy just off the farm, Pine Bluff was Xanadu. All I saw were the good things, but in reality it was a city sharply segregated, where the boundaries were clear. My mother worked for a while at the new defense plant, which manufactured ammunition in multiple shifts. Blacks and whites were employed there, but like other U.S. government workplaces of the time, facilities such as the lunchroom and toilets were segregated to separate the races. Forty years later I would battle the South African government to eliminate segregated work facilities like this.

The white population of Pine Bluff was incomprehensible to me, but the cosmopolitan black community was a glorious revelation. The city's black population was about six thousand at the time, and most lived northwest of the downtown area in a self-contained community of black stores, churches, schools, and a cemetery. I had never before seen so many black people congregated. Most blacks were employed in the sawmills, railroad repair shops, warehouses, and cottonseed mills and as domestic workers, but Pine Bluff also had a professional class of black people: dentists, doctors, chefs, and lawyers. To my amazement, in a drug store on Main Street I saw a black pharmacist who seemed to have equal status with the white pharmacist. There were no black motormen, however, and no blacks were allowed to drive the streetcars or buses. Blacks sat in the back half of the bus and whites in the front half. If the bus was crowded and whites overflowed into their half, the driver asked the blacks to move farther back. Restaurants were segregated, sometimes in a way that seems laughable today. A coffee shop I frequented was designed with two counters and a serving area in the center. Whites sat at one counter, chatting with us blacks at the counter across the way, but we came and went through separate doors so that we would not touch one another.

Whites and blacks tolerated one another in Pine Bluff, but an uneasy relationship existed under the façade of co-existence. One day a single event shocked us out of this faux tranquility. A black man boarded a city bus and, instead of moving to the back, took a seat in the front. It was the first black sit-in on a bus, more than a decade before Rosa Parks's heroic bus ride in Montgomery, Alabama. The incident hit Pine Bluff like a lightning bolt out of a blue sky. A short but spontaneous demonstration unfolded. It did not last more than an hour or so, but it was a clarion signal of the discord that lay just beneath the serene surface of day-to-day life. The next day, I read the editorial in the *Pine Bluff Commercial* newspaper, which said, "As long as Anglo-Saxon blood runs in our veins, we will never agree to the mixing of the races."

Pine Bluff marked a lot of firsts for me: the first time I saw a bathroom with a commode in it, the first time I saw stained-glass windows in a church, and the first time I owned a suit of clothes. My first suit was blue serge, and with it I got a white shirt and black shoes. The suit was second-hand, but I did not care. With that blue serge suit, I thought the world had come to me.

Tiny, Reverend Grant, and I lived in a one-room apartment that had a little addition for me. Our apartment was on the outskirts of a lower-middle-class area that was primarily, but not exclusively, black. The area had been built for the newcomers flooding into Pine Bluff and was grievously overcrowded. Although not as commercialized as the larger black community, our neighborhood had a few small stores, a Baptist church, a Methodist church, and several honky-tonks. By today's standards it would be considered a ghetto. Our black community was tight-knit. We made do with what we had, shared resources, and sometimes delighted in outwitting the whites. All black adults seemed to assume responsibility for us young people. "Who's your father?" one would ask. "Where do you live?" The parental grapevine was always humming. If a young person was seen where he should not be or was caught telling a lie, an alert adult would call his parents. Civil rights activist, former Atlanta mayor, and ambassador to the United Nations Andrew Young has said that integration has brought some unintended consequences, and loss of community solidarity is one of them.

I attended Merrill High School, the only black high school in town, which had an exceptional black principal and cadre of black teachers. The high school was in the segregated northeast section of town, quite a distance from my home in the southeast, and to get there I rode the streetcar if I had the fare or walked. Eventually I saved enough money from my jobs to buy a second-hand bicycle.

All of the teachers, from the youngest to the most experienced, were committed to the students, constantly urging us to greater heights. If a student was not in school, they called the parents to find out why. Not only were they dedicated to excellence in education, they were active members of the churches. Inside the classroom or out, school days or weekends, they were still teachers, and I lived in veneration of them. The Latin teacher ended class with the phrase *finis est non tamen*: "the task is not yet complete." Mr. Cheney, the principal, concentrated on scholarship, deportment, and appearance. He was tall and imposing, a serious man who never laughed. When he walked through the halls surveying his kingdom, we students barely breathed. Mr. Cheney ensured that the teachers stayed on top of us, and if we did not master the subject—and did not have a valid excuse—they smacked our hands with a ruler. The school's discipline was rigorous. In the words of Miss Jones, who taught physics and mathematics, "No student here is allowed to be a slacker." She was the meanest person I had ever come across. When segregation ended and the teachers were integrated into other schools, Miss Jones became a truant officer, a calling that fit her personality.

The first time I addressed a teacher as "Ma'am," she bit off my head. "Don't you use that term with me. You call me Miss Jones." In Louisiana, I had been brought up to never address people by "Auntie, Uncle, Boy or Girl"—handles ascribed to blacks by our white neighbors—but at Merrill High, the teachers were rebelling against any antebellum subservience, which extended to the titles "Ma'am" and "Sir." High school in Pine Bluff was not a pleasurable experience for me, but the education was good. Merrill High School taught me the gratification of pursuing excellence, and I have strived toward it ever since.

Our school assemblies featured visitors such as an Egyptian wearing a fez, a parade of black Americans held up to us as role models, and local white dignitaries whose condescending speeches were meant to be inspiring: "You can be a credit to your race." When successful graduates returned for a visit, Mr. Cheney presented them at school assemblies. "Observe," the principal said. "See how he sits." We saw that the visitor on the school stage sat properly with heels together, wearing a coat and tie, and looking serious. When he rose to speak, he spoke in a well-modulated voice. "He is representative of what we are trying to produce here," Mr. Cheney said, "educated young men and women." I saw, almost within my grasp, a new image for myself. My grandmother had planted the seed that grew into my lifelong respect for education, but it was in this high school that it took root. I felt as if I had discovered a secret passageway to a life I could barely imagine, a life of broad vistas that offered dignity, respect, and reward. It gave me a hunger for something just beyond my reach.

Latin was a staple at that high school. I saw my first Shakespeare production there when the drama department presented *The Merchant of Venice*. We studied black heroes—W. E. B. DuBois and Booker T. Washington—and read black literature—Richard Wright, Countee Cullen, and Langston Hughes. Our assignments were heavy with book reports and oral presentations. The teachers promoted reading above all other extracurricular activities. We were sent to the Carnegie Library, which was as segregated as other city facilities, and although we had to stay in the black section, we could request books from the white section.

We called our history teacher "Bulldog." A Civil War expert, she had us memorize the Gettysburg Address and dissect it to understand its meaning. We studied the Constitution of the United States and learned that the Fourteenth Amendment to the Constitution was the best protection black people had. Thus I began my study of the Constitution, with its opening phrase of beautiful simplicity—"We the people . . ." The document would become the touchstone of my life's work in the Foreign Service. That high school teacher instilled in me a reverence for the Constitution as the landmark document of liberty and justice.

It was in history class that I developed an interest in government, and where I first glimpsed something of my destiny. The teacher insisted that her students scrape together enough money to subscribe to the weekly publication *Current Events*, which was a compilation of significant world news of the week. One issue contained an article about South Africa and the plight of South African blacks under the reign of Prime Minister Jan Christian Smuts, head of the United Party of South Africa. This party was perpetuating a racist system, our teacher explained. "We have to help the black people of South Africa," she said. "Every black person everywhere needs to contribute to the African National Congress because they are fighting for justice. Their fight is your hope." We were black teenagers in the middle of Arkansas, young people discriminated against ourselves, black boys and girls who could barely find South Africa on a map, but we contributed our pennies and nickels for this noble fight. Beyond this, we did not study South Africa in school. It might as well have been in another galaxy. I was aware, however, that two U.S. senators from Mississippi commented on what they considered to be the liberal and uncommon worry about the blacks in South Africa. Theodore Bilbo, the senior senator, and James Eastland, the junior senator, said that as far as they were concerned, the Afrikaners had it right. Many years later, when I was being nominated to be ambassador to South Africa, the first thing that popped into my mind was this episode in that Arkansas high school history class.

The teachers themselves were role models. They dressed well, exhibited high moral standards, and earned the respect of the community. Any student who did not treat them with propriety was thrashed or expelled, and then the rest of the community got involved.

"Why aren't you in school, boy?"

"Got expelled."

"Expelled! What for?"

"Sassing the teacher."

"You talked back to your teacher? Which one?"

"Miss Stevens."

"Miss Stevens who's in church every Sunday? You talked back to her? Shame on you."

Not every aspect of high school was a watershed experience for me. School sports were not emphasized as much then as they are now. We had no football team, but we did have baseball, basketball, and track. I played some basketball, but I was not very good at it.

The high school had a cooperative relationship with the college, which was then Arkansas Agricultural, Mechanical, and Normal College. Twice a week we went to the college for classes in manual arts and shop training. The shop teacher taught us practical skills such as hanging wallpaper, machine tool work, welding, and carpentry. We learned the mathematics of the trade, used compasses and squares, and acquired practical experience restoring some college-owned houses. Years later, in my first house in Washington, D.C., I tried resurrecting this skill on a home-renovation project and almost cut off my finger with a power saw.

Usually we walked to and from the college, and sometimes we stopped for a few minutes at a snack shop with a dance floor. No alcohol was served there, but we could get a candy bar and a Coke, if we had any money. For anyone with an extra nickel the jukebox had popular black music: "Sweet Slumber" by Lucky Millinder, "Don't Get Around Much Anymore" by Duke Ellington's orchestra, sung by Al Hibler, and "Tippin' In" by Coleman Hawkins. Big-band music was at its pinnacle, so we saw advertisements for the regional and nationally known musicians coming through Pine Bluff: Louis Armstrong, Cab Calloway, and Duke Ellington. Everybody talked about how to get money to go to these dances. I was shocked to learn that a couple of my female classmates, perfectly respectable girls from the neighborhood, had gone to the dances. Even if I had the money, I could not dream of going to a dance, not living under Reverend Grant's rules. The four places he allowed me to go were school, church, work, or the library. This was years before the coining of the terms "nerd" or "square," but that was the stereotype of someone who did not jitter-bug, who was quiet, studious, and popular with the teachers but socially awkward with peers. That painful description applied to me. I tried to get out of that box, but it was a snug fit.

I had little social life, but I did make two close friends in high school: Leo Clinton and Cornelius Jackson. Cornelius was a sharp dresser and almost effeminate, but he was such a fierce fighter nobody called him a sissy more than once. He was bigger than I and became my protector. It was Cornelius who urged me to walk Ola Mae Cotton home from church one evening.

"I can't," I said. "She's going to walk with someone else."

"Don't you let him cut you out," Cornelius said. "You go take her hand."

My heart was pounding as I went over to her. To my shock, she said, "Let's go," and we walked off holding hands. From that moment, Ola Mae became my first love. The first time I had invited a girl out, she laughed at me and said, "Oh, you country boys!"

It was an innocent era, when high school boys and girls exchanged notes of undying love under the watchful eyes of teachers. One day in class the boy sitting next to me whispered, "Touch her here," indicating his side. I did and was surprised that it was so soft. The next thing I knew, I was seeing stars. Ola May had slapped the daylights out of me and then gone back to her studies. Mrs. Atkins, the Latin teacher, saw it all and smiled. After class she said, "Eddie, some things you don't do without permission."

The snappy attire of the day was a jacket, hat, and watch chain (not everybody had a watch at the end of the chain). Shoes were two-toned, whitened or alligator. The far-out dressers wore trousers called drapes, tapered to small cuffs, and balloon trousers. Pressed razor sharp, drapes looked great. Sundays, young men going to church wore a hat, white shirt, coat, trousers, and a chain. Being "on the block" meant being seen, on display, and whistling at the ladies as they went by. I dressed appropriately, but I could not afford a finger coat or a pair of drapes, the attire of my dreams. I never wore the clothes boys my age so admired, which was a zoot suit with wide shoulders and a wide-brimmed hat. My clothes were all suitable for work and church—a practical jacket and a raincoat. I have always dressed conservatively, which was certainly the correct attire when I entered the Foreign Service in 1970. At that time, it was rare to see a Foreign Service officer wearing something as flamboyant as a red tie. I love tailored shirts with French cuffs, and I love shoes. In the Marine Corps I learned to appreciate a razor-pressed uniform and well-shined shoes. No marine worth his salt would be seen without spit-shined shoes. I believe the way we dress not only reflects our respect for our work, it affects the way we perform and how people respond to us. I expected Foreign Service officers to dress professionally as befitting officers of the United States government. When I was ambassador to Liberia, a young officer said to me, "Some of us are thinking about not wearing a tie to the embassy." "Not on my watch," I replied. I gave them the option of dressing appropriately or asking for a transfer.

My family had implanted in me a strong work ethic. I scrambled to find part-time jobs after school and in the summer. I was industrious, energetic, and I liked to work; it gave me a sense of self-worth and maturity. My mother and stepfather were struggling economically, so I contributed my earnings to the family coffers and paid for my school expenses. One summer I worked in a lumber mill as a laborer, getting my hands full of splinters. After school, I worked the night shift as a redcap at the bus station, where my job was handling luggage and cleaning. For a wide-eyed, innocent young man, this was a high-risk work experience. I was confronted with the vices and lax discipline of the inner city, such as prostitution and drug handling. My eyes popped when I saw two men walking down the street holding hands. I had never heard of homosexuality, but I saw that there was no discrimination against them in the black community. Three or four of my classmates were children of clandestine liaisons between blacks and whites, so I became dimly aware that interracial sexual relations, however taboo, were a reality. Once, a white female ticket clerk at the bus station made friendly overtures to me and just for a moment, I was tempted, but I knew that was a sure path to disaster. Not only did my grandmother's warnings buzz in my ears, I was under the watchful eye of the older black redcaps, all church members or officers. Only one young ticket agent was white. While there was camaraderie between him and me, it was clear that we were not of equal status. Ticket agents were my first professional role models because they wore blue ties, white shirts, and dark trousers. The bus drivers, too, seemed dashing in their uniforms, but driving was an occupation closed to blacks; only white men could drive buses.

Since I was invisible in most of my jobs, as an unobtrusive cleaning person at the Great Masonic Temple and at private parties, I could observe the chasm of social differences between the races. Sometimes I got a memorable lesson in human behavior. I worked as elevator operator and janitor in the Old National Bank building, where white doctors and lawyers had offices. I thought the chiropractor was seeing patients after hours until I realized that he was entertaining girlfriends. I was shocked to discover that one girlfriend was a black woman. The doctor had not minded my knowing about the white women, but once I learned about the black girlfriend, he became hostile. Having a relationship with a black woman seemed to reveal something about him that he did not like my knowing. Years later, my study of ancient history helped me understand this. When Sextus Pompey was stabbed by the Egyptians, he saw his own blood and realized he was going to die. "I am a Roman nobleman," he said. "They must not see my face as I die; they must not see that part of me which makes me a man," and he covered his face and his manhood with his toga. That is what motivated the anger of the white doctor in Pine Bluff; he was uncomfortable with my knowing that he was just a man.

I was learning how to navigate the complicated social structure of blacks and whites. My stepfather had acquaintances of both colors, and I met whites through him, but my first direct contact with whites in a semiprofessional way came when I worked as a copy boy at the *Pine Bluff Commercial*. I liked the newspaper job, but it was short-lived. When I showed up wearing a clean shirt and slacks, I was considered too grandiose—I was forgetting my place. I was fired for being "too familiar" with the whites, which meant not speaking subserviently and—my worst offense—sitting down in the presence of whites. That was absolutely forbidden for a young black person. I had come up against prejudice in its worst form and that, too, was a good lesson.

Meanwhile, my home life was traumatic. I was having a difficult time adjusting to my new environment, especially to my stepfather, who was not enthusiastic about my being there. He and I were never close, and in a contentious struggle for control our relationship grew tense. He wanted me to call him Father or Dad, but I never did. I always addressed him as Reverend Grant. My stepfather was handsome, well-educated, community-minded, and a thirty-third-degree Mason. Most important, he was a certified minister of the Gospel, which was an esteemed occupation in the black community, and although he did not have a church of his own, he was a visiting pastor for several churches. He was knowledgeable about theology and the Bible, and he was a preacher so passionate about hellfire and damnation that he made people feel guilt-ridden and uncomfortable. In the tradition of black ministers, Reverend Grant was a flashy dresser. Black ministers of that era were elaborate, even ostentatious, in their clothing; they were an example to us young, aspiring black men to be fastidious about the way we dressed.

Although Reverend Grant was not particularly kind to me, in retrospect, I was both stupid and blatantly ungrateful to a man who had agreed to give me shelter. After that first year in Pine Bluff, I found his authority so rankling that

I left and went back to Louisiana. It took only one summer on the farm for me to realize I had made a mistake. "You can't see beyond the tip of your nose," my grandmother said. She told me I had to return to Pine Bluff and school, however difficult the situation with my stepfather. I wrote to my mother and told her that I wanted to go back. She had fled the farm herself as soon as she could and rarely went back, so she understood my feelings of wanting to escape. Before Reverend Grant would agree to my return, he laid down some rules. To his credit, he insisted that I get into class immediately, study hard, and make good grades. I agreed and returned to a home life of fragile peace in Pine Bluff. "If it weren't for you and your mother, I could live sumptuously," Reverend Grant told me, "but I love your mother and she wants you here." One of his rules was that I was to have a job. Another was to allow him or my mother to handle the money I made. For a while I did turn over my pay him, but one day I saw him leaving the office building where I worked. "Eddie, your stepfather was here," the building manager told me later, "and he asked me how much money you make. I told him he would have to ask you. What goes on between you and your stepfather is none of my business." I was outraged by Reverend Grant's inquiry, which questioned my integrity, and I was humiliated to be supervised as if I were a child. That event ruptured our relationship. I flashed with rebellion. From then on, I told my stepfather, I would give him some, but not all, of my salary.

About a year later, when I was fifteen, my mother and stepfather moved west and left me in Pine Bluff. They left in January, and since I had very little money, for the first time in my life I began to figure out how to exist on my own. I went to school, attended church every Sunday, and worked a full shift, four to ten o'clock, at the bus station after school. I lived in a rooming house and paid rent out of my earnings. Occasionally my mother sent me a money order, which allowed me to buy luxuries such as a winter coat. I have been asked if I felt abandoned by my mother when she left me behind not once but twice. Pride was a stronger feeling; I was proud of my self-reliance. I was still a young teenager and everybody knew I was alone, so that tight-knit black community kept an eye on me. The woman who owned the rooming house took it upon herself to see that I was comfortable and that I was not going to the dogs. The other four lodgers treated me as a younger brother, and the black community as a whole assumed an unofficial guardianship of me, *in loco parentis*. Someone always asked what I was doing and how I was faring. Usually I cooked for myself—hamburger, bacon and eggs—but occasionally a coworker would take pity on me and invite me to supper.

When my mother left, I had a degree of false freedom. I was living on my own, and suddenly, a whole world of innocent pleasures opened to me. I had a newfound sense of independence. For the first time, I could go to a movie without fear of being caught. My family had considered movies wicked and a waste of time. The first movie I saw was a Frank Sinatra film in which he sang "The music stopped, but we kept on dancing." That lyric struck me as the height of sophistication.

The second thing I could do was court a girl, an old-fashioned term for a formal social procedure. I had lived a sequestered life, barely able to have a conversation with the opposite sex. The object of my attention was an older woman—in her twenties. Her name was Parthenia, and she lived in the same boarding house. I was attracted to her, and I made shy, awkward advances at her. I went to my first movie with her. My idea of romance was not to take her flowers, but to give her a book. She could have made a fool out of me at any moment, this green young man barely out of short pants, but she was peaceful, patient, and understanding.

One of my closest friends in those days was Johnny Shaw, a senior cook at the bus station and my neighbor at the rooming house. He was the worldliest person I had met. One evening he took me to a honky-tonk, practically dragging me in because I was so paralyzed by my strict religious upbringing. Inside, I saw an element of society that I thought of as the underworld. I stood gaping at the people drinking spirits and dancing to loud music, thinking, "My God. What is all of this?" It was my introduction to jazz.

I could have spent my life in Pine Bluff, working in service jobs, earning what I would have considered quite a bit of money and eventually marrying and having children, but by the time I was sixteen, I could see the limitations. Excellence and achievement were closed to me. My life there would always be second-class life. I remembered my grandmother's fear, that if I stayed in Louisiana and Arkansas, my desire to experience other worlds would wither. I knew I had to get out. I still had to finish high school, but dreams of a distant horizon were stirring in me. My teacher had introduced me to a faraway place called South Africa. I had friends who traveled regularly to Chicago and described the city as sophisticated beyond my imagination. I longed to go to a place where I could achieve by my own ability and efforts. I was impatient for the day when I would be old enough to join the army and get into the ongoing war with Japan.

When school was out that spring, I still had not heard from my mother. They had gone first to California and then to Oregon. My mother and I had talked about my joining them in the West when they were settled, but to this day I do not know if Reverend Grant left Pine Bluff with that expectation. At last, a letter came from my mother inviting me to come live with her and my stepfather in Oregon, and once again my life changed. *Finis est non tamen.*

In August 1945, just after turning seventeen, I bought a ticket with my earnings and rode a bus alone from Pine Bluff to Portland, Oregon. We crossed the grandeur of the Great Plains and stopped in cities such as Salt Lake City, where there was no segregation at all. That was a dizzying experience. We drove through Nevada, Wyoming, and Idaho and finally arrived in Oregon. It was not winter, but the air seemed crisp. I saw the immense expanse of this nation out the bus window as I crossed a country as new and free to me as the lands described by the authors I had recently discovered—Willa Cather, Sinclair Lewis, and Alexis de Tocqueville. I could hardly believe I was a citizen of this grand place. I met new people on the trip and struck up conversations with strangers. On the last leg of the trip, I noticed a man and a woman, glamorous figures to me, having a great time in each other's company. They were effervescent with their enjoyment of life and being together. I had never seen anything like this before. I wanted to have a life like that. It was an exhilarating adventure. The journey took three days, and I sat at the front of the bus all the way.

PORTLAND—
PORTAL TO THE WORLD

That bus trip was my first great trek. I was on a quest, headed for Portland, where Lewis and Clark's fabled expedition to the Pacific had culminated in 1805. After their historic 4,000-mile journey, the explorers were acclaimed as heroes who had pierced the wilderness, crossed wild rivers, and cut a path through a vast unknown territory. I felt just as adventurous on my solitary journey. To a young man who had never been outside a small circumference in Arkansas and Louisiana, Portland was the other side of the world. Like those who had ventured before me—the fur trappers, explorers, farmers, and gold miners—I saw myself heading to a lush land of opportunity.

I had not heard of Portland until the letter from my mother arrived. I then threw myself into learning everything I could about the place of my destiny. Before leaving Arkansas, I went to the library to research the city methodically. As I studied, Portland began to shimmer with mystery in my imagination. I read about Oregon's history of bloody Indian wars, the imported Asian labor who constructed the transcontinental railroad, the empires of lumber barons and cattlemen, and the solitary work of homesteaders and gold prospectors. I read of the Northwest's geographic wonders—mountain peaks towering into the sky and cascading rivers fueling some of the first hydroelectric power plants in America. I learned that Portland was one of the nation's great freshwater ports and the largest city in Oregon. From the relatively land-locked South, I was going to a state on the edge of the Pacific Ocean, ringed by mountain ranges, meadows of alpine flowers, wheatlands, salmon rivers, and evergreen forests. I was leaving the South, where the heat hangs over the countryside like an orange blanket, for the rain-kissed Pacific Northwest. Instead of barefoot summers on dusty roads, I would grow up carrying a raincoat or an umbrella. I would live where the climate was so mild and the soil so fertile that the grass was green even in winter, where roses and rhododendrons flourished in head-high mounds of red, pink, purple, and fuchsia.

I was entering a different economy, going from a rural farmland anchored in cotton to a state teeming with industries: lumbering, fishing, wheat, cattle, food processing, and the mighty World War II war enterprises. My mother and stepfather were part of the gargantuan workforce streaming into the city. Most were headed for the plants and factories of the round-the-clock war industries that fueled the economy of the region. Factories cranked out automotive equipment products for the war effort; an aircraft industry sprang up, and electrochemical and metallurgical plants churned. Even the state's farmers were enjoying a new prosperity, driven by the Allies' demand for food. Ship-building, the greatest of the war industries, employed more workers than any other sector. In five years, Portland's six shipyards launched more than twelve hundred Liberty and Victory cargo ships, oil tankers, aircraft carriers, minesweepers, and other war and supply vessels. Three shifts of workers kept the shipyards grinding twenty-four hours a day. Black workers, historically shut out of many occupations, seized the opportunity to join this burgeoning work force and migrated to Oregon in droves.

An estimated 160,000 immigrants had poured into the city in a matter of months, increasing the population by one-third. Half of the state's 1.2 million residents lived in the Portland area. When I arrived in 1945, Portland was one of the most exciting cities in America.

I would find in Portland the largest black community I had yet known in my young life. Before the war, Oregon's black population was about 2,000. Now with a desperate labor shortage, in less than three years 20,000 blacks had flooded into Portland to work in the shipyards. Most black employees were recruited from Arkansas, Louisiana, Oklahoma, and Texas and came on specially chartered trains.

Emergency urban projects were built to accommodate the population explosion. My home was in Vanport, the largest and most progressive of these housing developments. This monumental project was a wonder of wartime ingenuity built on vacant land north of Portland, between the city and the Columbia River. Almost overnight, Vanport became the second largest city in Oregon with 40,000 residents living in almost 10,000 units. The temporary, hurry-up city was a model of planned housing and a pioneer in integration, but it was also plagued by rats, mosquitoes, and cockroaches.

I believed that Portland was a place free of racism. To me, this port city was ripe with promise and burnished with dreams. I expected to excel here. My first sight of Portland lived up to my expectations. It was just as I had imagined it—a big, beautiful city, nestled between the Willamette and Columbia Rivers and lively with river traffic. The brawny waterfront captivated me, and I spent hours at the wharves watching the fishing boats, the ship traffic, the freight moving up the river, and the ships arriving and departing. A friend's grandmother had sailed sometimes with her sea-captain husband on a merchant freighter, and she told me tales of voyages to the Orient, transporting Oregon pine lumber to China and returning with cargoes of silk. Ports have held a fascination for me ever since my arrival in Portland; they are the hub of a country's economy, alive with the movement of its people.

Elysian Fields, unfortunately, are the stuff of mythology. Most places, even the citadels of young men's dreams, ultimately are dulled by reality. I would discover that Portland was almost as segregated as the South I had left. Racism was more insidious in Portland than the overt discrimination called Jim Crowism I had experienced in Arkansas and Louisiana. Yet even this grave blemish did not tarnish the city in my eyes. Sequestered in my heart, Portland will always be as I first saw it: a great door open before me, pocked with imperfections but shining with opportunities to learn and discover. Portland became my home, physically and spiritually. The people I met there changed my life, and the friendships I formed there were lasting.

As a black family we were excited about the possibilities open to us for employment and education. My stepfather was minister at an African Methodist Episcopal Church, and my mother was working as an in-home caretaker of elderly people. I intended to find a job, too, but my first order of business was to finish high school.

I would begin high school that fall as a sophomore, and to make sure I was prepared scholastically for Oregon's public-education standards, I enrolled in summer school. It was the beginning of a fantastic academic journey. I met teachers who took a personal interest in me and encouraged me. I know that teachers can shape young lives because in Portland, they shaped mine. They told me, "Eddie, you have a good mind, and you should develop it," and "You have great potential." They advised me, tutored me after hours, invited me into their homes, outlined courses of study, and monitored my progress.

Two summer school teachers, C. S. (Cecile) Oliver and Ruth Arbuckle, were of paramount importance. They immediately recognized my weakness in grammar and set about improving my skills by prescribing regimens of remedial work. I soaked up their attention like a thirsty plant.

That first summer session, I met Miss Oliver from Franklin High School. She was an intelligent, intense English teacher who resembled Bette Davis. "Eddie," she said to me on only the second day of summer school, "you do not know enough about English." When Miss Oliver set out to improve my language skills, she took over my life. "Do you know where the public library is?" she asked me. Then she took me to the library to get a library card and designed a reading program for me. "When you are not working, I want you in the library reading." Every day of summer school she asked me about my library work. Under her guidance I read shelves of books and began a lifelong love affair with literature. In the Portland library, for the first time in my life, I did not have to worry about touching the books; here I began to really read. The first book I checked out was by William Saroyan.

The Multnomah Public Library is a majestic building of Italian Renaissance design that covers an entire city block. Three stories and a basement brimmed with books, periodicals, slides, research facilities, and knowledgeable librarians. It was considered one of the finest libraries in the Northwest. Here I could be alone, read, and dream. Searching the open stacks was a hushed adventure. Years later, when I visited San Joaquin Valley, the setting of *East of Eden*, I pointed out landmarks to my host. "How can you recognize it when you've never been here?" my guide asked. "Because I read John Steinbeck's novel," I answered. Next door to the library were several theaters, including a classics theater. Quite by accident I learned that foreign movies were shown there, so I discovered the cultural world of cinema. I saw my first John Gielgud movie there.

Miss Oliver put me on a regimen of subscribing to literary magazines and periodicals of book reviews that continues to this day. At the time, I had only enough money for one magazine, so she decided it should be a subscription to the *Saturday Review of Books*.

That summer, Miss Oliver seemed to adopt me as a son. She invited me to her home to talk about books, literary ideas, writing style, and authors ranging from Winston Churchill to Carl Sandburg. Sometimes our conversation went beyond literature, and we talked about the social situation in the United States. "The most segregated hour in America is Sunday morning," Miss Oliver said, "when everyone goes to their separate churches." She talked to me about prejudice, not bitterly but hopeful that post-war America would eradicate segregation.

I never had her as a teacher again, but Miss Oliver continued her guidance long after summer school had ended. Although she taught at a different school, she occasionally called me at home. "Eddie," Miss Oliver would say, "what are you reading?" Then she would recommend a book. Long after I had graduated from high school and left Portland, Miss Oliver wrote to me. Her letters often included gentle corrections of my grammar. When I told a friend about Miss Oliver's mentorship, she was shocked. This was not the image the teacher manifested to her students at Franklin High School. "I had no idea she was that kind of person," my friend said. I do not know what prompted Miss Oliver to extend herself to me as she did. My mother was astonished at the attention Miss Oliver gave me, but with the egocentricity of youth, I accepted the tutelage without question. She seemed to see something in a young boy that she could develop, and she stretched her teacher's creed to help me bring it forth.

The second summer at Milwaukee High School, I met Ruth Arbuckle. In those days, Milwaukee was a separate town, and I rode a Trailways bus to get there. Miss Arbuckle was stern, overweight, and all business. This formidable, mirthless woman who never smiled was a stickler for the correct use of language, and she focused on improving my composition and writing skills. Miss Arbuckle had survived a dismal childhood during the Depression, and as an adult she lived on the financial edge, supplementing her teacher's salary by working part-time as cashier and cloakroom attendant at McElroy's Ballroom. She became a legend as a teacher and counselor for thirty-four years at Lincoln High School. Despite her meager circumstances, she was known as a generous person, deeply dedicated to her students and family. Miss Arbuckle did not subsume my life in the all-encompassing way of Miss Oliver, but she gave me extra time and attention, which shocked even me, as this was such a contrast to her autocratic demeanor. Miss Oliver and Miss Arbuckle became so important to me that I visited them whenever I returned to Portland throughout the years, inviting them to my ambassadorial swearing-in ceremonies in Washington, D.C., and keeping in touch with them until their deaths.

In the autumn of 1945 I enrolled full-time in Jefferson High School, where I was considered studious and quiet to the point of shyness. My friends saw me as a very serious person. The education system was of a higher caliber than I had known in Arkansas, and I thrived on it. I met outstanding educators there who encouraged and inspired me: Carly Gilstrap was a history teacher who challenged us and made us think; and Ralph Bassett was a returning veteran who taught English, Latin, French, and Spanish. Bassett was a small man, about 5 feet 7 inches tall, with glasses, a receding hairline, and a distinctive speaking style. It was rare to have a male teacher at all, and because Bassett was recognized as an intellectual, I was doubly honored that he took an interest in my educational progress. When I had problems with an assignment, Bassett invited me to stop by his classroom so he could help me. He talked with me about my plans for the future and told me that he wanted me to matter in the world. His wife, Mildred, was a teacher at Lincoln High School, and she also counseled me. It would be inaccurate to call these mentoring teachers "friends." They were friendly professionals who extended themselves beyond the call of duty.

Marian Meacham, a supervisor at the Vanport recreation center, was another white woman who came into my life during my high school years and introduced me to a different culture. She was one of the most beautiful women I have ever met, a brunette with piercing blue eyes and a fascinating personality that was an alchemic mix of poetry, intellect, and political liberalism. She believed in another kind of America, one that lived up to its promise of equality. Marian became my guiding light. Her husband, Merle, a bomber pilot in the war, was a psychology major at Reed College. Occasionally they invited me to dances given by veterans' organizations or to social functions of college students and faculty. I felt awkward and inadequate among these learned people, but I was intrigued by this glimpse into their world of higher education. Reed College was considered the Pacific Northwest equivalent of the University of Chicago. At a cocktail party I saw the professors laughing and playing a word game that involved quoting lines from classics, then guessing the source. It was like a scene from a Noel Coward play. I was speechless at this erudite entertainment that they played so effortlessly. "My God," I thought. "Is this how well-educated people behave?"

One Friday evening at a gathering of Reed College people, I met Monte Griffin, a professor of ancient history and the classics. Griffin, too, was a returning veteran, a stocky man who looked like a bearded Karl Malden. Although he did not have a Ph.D., he was arguably the most respected professor at Reed. When he invited me to visit him Sunday at the college, it seemed an honor beyond measure, tantamount to entering an inner sanctum. Despite his brilliance, Griffin never reached his professional potential. His personal tragedy was alcohol, but I was unaware of that at the time and for many years to come. For now, the war was over, the economy was booming and it was a euphoric time of new beginnings for us both.

"Let's go for a ride on the streetcar," Mr. Griffin said when I arrived at the college that Sunday. We climbed aboard, riding from one end of the line to the other. First, he asked me about my life, and I told him everything—about my grandfather, Louisiana, my mother, and my stepfather. He listened intently. Then he began talking. It was the start of a private tutorial by rail. We spent several Sunday afternoons riding the electric streetcars while Griffin talked. Sometimes the public parks were our classrooms. He talked to me about my future, about going after what I did not have and believing that I could get it. "You have to be selfish with yourself before you can be helpful to others," he said. He was the first person to tell me that education is more than learning facts and figures. "You have to be able to relate what you learn to life," he said. "Be curious. Ask questions. Look at everything around you. And read. That is how you learn." He talked about books, the classics, and history. He passed on to me an enduring passion for learning and classical literature. He taught me about the world of the Greeks, the history of the English-speaking people, the United States, the Constitution, and injustice. It distressed Griffin to see blacks who had fought for the cause of democracy in Europe and Japan, only to come home to find the segregated social order unchanged in the United States. Discrimination against nonwhite people was just as it had been before the war. Portland exhibited a belligerence against people who had been abroad and found equality in France and England, as if to say, "Do not try to impose those ideas on this society." Griffin was terribly upset by this.

In my memory I see the two of us in that postwar American scene of tender poignancy—a quiet young black man thirsty for knowledge and a white war veteran battling his private demons. The student listened, and the professor talked. He talked, perhaps, to keep from drinking. Sunday after Sunday we rode the streetcar together, back and forth across Portland, discussing ancient history, contemporary inequality, and the way to a brighter future.

I have always learned by watching people and observing their behavior. Listening to Griffin and seeing my older friends from Reed College play word games, I saw not only what it was like to live in the world of educated people, but also the procedure they had undergone to arrive at that place. With this epiphany, I said to myself: "These people were not always this accomplished; they did not start life this way. It was a *process* and I can do this, too." And in that moment, I thought triumphantly, "The world is mine."

These Portland educators—Carly Gilstrap, Cecile Oliver, Ruth Arbuckle, Mildred and Ralph Bassett, Marion and Merle Meacham, and Monte Griffin— were enlightened, if somewhat eccentric, mentors to me. I do not know how they became progressive thinkers or what quickened the flame of racial equality within them. I know only that they stepped quietly, even bravely, into the tide of popular culture. They were as singular in their mission as Arctic explorers, a small band venturing into the frozen white world of segregation to plant a flag and name a new territory. It was my great, good fortune to be there and be discovered by them.

These few, however, were among the exceptions. Although the level of instruction in Portland high schools was excellent, most of the teachers were as prejudiced as the rest of the populace. Many were blatant racists, and some were so cruel that sixty years later, when black alumni meet, we can recite, not with rancor but with an awful clarity, bigoted behavior too painful to be softened by even the rolling decades.

Today, Jefferson High School is multicultural. When I visited the school in 1999, 62 percent of the students were minorities (African-American, Hawaiian, and Latino), and the principal and many of the faculty were blacks. But when I was a student there from 1945 to 1947, all of my teachers were white. In my graduating class of 360, only 8 of us were black.

One of the required classes at Jefferson was dancing. Probably because it was classified as physical exercise, it was taught by basketball coach George Hibbard, an All-American from Oregon. Hibbard was assiduous in keeping the races separate. He wanted no interaction between black and white students, and most especially he did not want a black boy to touch a white girl. When he taught ballroom and folk dancing, Hibbard went to great lengths to make sure that black boys danced only with black girls. Once I was paired with a white girl, but before we could begin dancing, Hibbard rushed over to separate us. "There's a mistake here," he said, switching us with other partners.

For today's black youth, sports are often seen as a career track out of a disadvantaged society. That was not true of the 1940s. College and professional sports were segregated, and high school athletics were not emphasized as they are today. Jefferson High School offered competitive sports, and though I participated—football, basketball, and track—it was without enthusiasm.

Although I was considered a good football player, I took the field only once or twice. What kept me benched was not lack of talent, but my race. I was the only black on the football team, and the experience ended badly. Eric Waldorf, one of the best coaches in the Portland school systems, was an aloof and strict disciplinarian who ran football practice much like Alabama's Bear Bryant, emphasizing tactics and physical exercise. One evening as we finished scrimmage and headed back to the locker room in a run, Hibbard, the assistant football coach, wanted us to pick up the pace. "Okay let's go!" he yelled. "Last one in is a nigger baby." I stopped in my tracks. The rest of the team ran, but I walked to the lockers. I continued to play football, but I lost all interest in it after that.

Hibbard did not encourage me in sports, but other people did. A businessman watched me at one track meet, and after watching my shot-putting, he came over to me.

"You've got good form," he told me, "but you've got to make your body hold that shot put. What do you do after school?"

"I work," I told him.

"What do you do when you're not working?"

"I go home."

"Spend all your time on track," he said. "You could be a track star."

If I had cultivated that ability, perhaps I could have done well, but sports were not my primary interest.

Most of the faculty and administrators at Jefferson High School treated us black students as if we were invisible. Sometimes their behavior was subtle or unspoken, but however they communicated it, we got the message. The black girls had an especially hard time. The teachers discouraged them from trying to join social clubs and sororities that were exclusively white, or from competing for honors such as Rose Festival Princess. When careers were discussed, only menial jobs were mentioned to them. Minority students never heard about the available scholarships. Discrimination was such a routine part of life that most students were oblivious to it. They did not see the "Whites Only" signs in the restaurant windows. Joy Brock Pruitt was one of the eight blacks in my graduating class. At a high school reunion years later, Joy was surprised to learn that her white colleagues remembered her as being popular. "How can you be popular," Joy said, "when you are not allowed to dance at school dances? When you are not allowed to join the clubs? When there are skating parties but you are not permitted to go into the skating rink? When you are not allowed to go to swimming parties because you are not permitted to swim at Jantzen Beach? When everyone else is eating hamburgers at Jonna Jones, but you can't enter the place?"

Her colleague was shocked. "I wasn't aware of that," she said.

"I know you weren't," Joy said.

Years later in Bangkok, I met Jacqueline Swint, a colleague in the Foreign Service who had grown up in Portland at the time I did. She had gone to a different high school, so we did not meet as teenagers. "I never saw a black person until I was eleven years old," she said, "and that was on a trip to Washington, D.C." The city of Portland is divided by the Willamette River, and in the 1940s, people stayed on their side of the river. "We did not have Negroes on the west side of the river when I was in high school," Jackie said. "A restaurant on the other side of the river was called Coon Chicken Inn and the entrance was a door shaped like the mouth of a black face. I never thought about it except as some kind of decoration. I am happy to report that it no longer exists."

Miss Arbuckle was Jackie's high school debate coach when the debate topic was whether or not the races could live together well. "Two persons on our debate team argued no," Jackie said. "One was a Japanese boy who had been interned during the war, and the other was Jewish. Only two of us, white girls, argued yes, which shows how ignorant and innocent I was of the race issue. I did not know about the problems of people of color because I had not encountered them. That was 1946, my senior year. Oregon was hard on black people. It was a closed society, but I was not aware of it." She speculated that I not only survived it with help from people such as Miss Arbuckle, but also grew into a stronger and more determined person because of it. She may be correct. Other young blacks were not so lucky. One friend who graduated from Reed College with a degree in psychology could never find adequate housing or employment in that segregated city. Over the years, as she was consistently beaten down, I saw the spirit bleed out of her.

After the war, fissures of unease began to appear in the unfolding years of peace and prosperity. Patriotism still ran high and pure, but the war had wounded and scarred ordinary people. The low rumble of the civil rights movement was beginning to be felt across America. In high school we said the Pledge of Allegiance every morning, but a classmate standing beside me refused to recite it. He was a returning veteran, an older student completing his education. His silence was unsettling and slightly frightening to me. I asked him why he did not say it.

"I can't do it," he said, "because this country is so hypocritical about liberty and justice. I can't do it, and I won't do it." He looked at me as if to say, "How the hell can you do it? They are going to treat you worse than me, and you are one of the reasons why I can't do it." Perhaps the idealism of youth kept me from empathizing more with this embittered veteran, but I could not share his anti-American sentiments. I chose another path.

In school and in the community, we felt the steady pressure of segregation. Not all discrimination was spelled out. We understood without seeing a sign that blacks were not welcome in Alberta Park. Signs or not, blacks were not allowed to enter hotels, except as employees. Joy Brock was a young girl when she went downtown with her mother and sisters to watch a parade and got caught in a sudden downpour. They stepped inside the Benson Hotel lobby to get out of the rain, and a staff member rushed over. "You can't stay here," the hotelkeeper said. "Niggers can't stay here." Her mother said, "We're not stay-ing. We're just standing here until it stops raining because I don't want my chil-dren wet." The mother did not move. She just stood there with her four daughters, not disrespectful but firm.

Most people were less vocal than the hotelier, but all of us remember inci-dents like that. We sat at counters without being served, or we avoided those places that were off limits to us, but still we were sometimes caught off guard. I worked after school as a busboy and waiter at the elegant Hotel Portland. One day after work another busboy suggested we go across the street and get a soda. He was white, so the waitress asked him what he wanted, but she ignored me. When my friend realized she would not serve me, we both got up and left. All minorities, especially blacks and American Indians, suffered from racism, but those of us who were not defeated by it chose not to be bitter. I was deter-mined to not let it get in my way. I did not have the time. I learned to ease the frustrations by reading, by talking to my mentors, and later by traveling the state sightseeing, where the beauty offset some of the negative factors. I under-stood to my bones William Cullen Bryant's poem "Thanatopsis":

> Or lose thyself in the continuous woods
> Where rolls the Oregon, and hears no sound
> Save its own dashings.

The Jefferson High School administrator most notoriously hostile to blacks was Dorothy Flegel, vice principal and dean. Her discouragement was blatant. When Joy was invited to join an all-white club, Miss Flegel called her into the office and said, "I suggest that you not accept the invitation; the parents would be upset." Miss Flegel continued her anti-black crusade well into the current era, but memory is malleable and vulnerable to revisionist history, and at the end of her life Miss Flegel remembered her racism differently. She spoke proudly of the black students who became successful professionals, claiming a role in their achievements. "I tried to fight and make a difference," she said. Joy confronted her. "Miss Flegel, how can you possibly say that?" she asked. "You know that is untrue."

I knew Miss Flegel and her sentiments well, but I prefer to remember Port-land people who set a different example. One Sunday evening on my shift at the Hotel Portland, I served a dinner party of ten, being especially careful because I anticipated a good tip from a group of this size. Suddenly, one of the young ladies at the table moved unexpectedly, and I spilled something on her. I apologized, and she apologized, too, but the man at the table exploded. He began yelling and cursing at me. The young woman apologized again. "No, no," she said, "I raised my . . . ," but the man would not hear it. He kept swearing at me. "If I had you back in Kentucky," he said, "I'd put you in your place." He went on and on with a string of epithets. In his culture, I was a defenseless black man who could do nothing but stand there and silently bear the whip of his fury. Finally, he finished and I went back to the kitchen. By that time the maître d'hôtel had called the hotel manager, an Austrian immigrant named Hermann. He and I had exchanged no more than ten words the entire time I had worked there, so he barely knew me. Hermann went to the customer and spoke to him calmly. "Sir, you are registered in this hotel, but you have needlessly abused one of my employees. I would be much obliged if you would finish your meal and check out of the hotel. We do not need your patronage." I was stunned, but the man from Kentucky was flabbergasted. Neither the maître d' nor the manager ever mentioned the incident to me.

The Hotel Portland, where I worked, was an elegant European-style service hotel designed by New York architect Stanford White and built in the 1880s. It covered an entire downtown block between Sixth and Broadway. At the hotel I met Jesse Owens, the great star of the 1936 Olympics. When Marian Anderson gave a concert at Symphony Hall, I went backstage to get her autograph. This gracious lady behaved as if I was the only person in the room, and I felt as if I were in the presence of a goddess. In that era, Marian Anderson, Paul Robeson, and other black entertainers might sing for audiences of Portland, but they could not rent hotel rooms, not even at the fashionable Hotel Portland.

My adopted home state had a paradoxical history leading to segregation. Markus Lopius was a black member of Captain Robert Gray's maritime expedition to Oregon in 1788; a black slave named York was among the expedition led by the Meriwether Lewis and William Clark Expedition of 1804–6; and black fur traders penetrated the Oregon frontier of the early 1800s. However, by the time the wagon trains rolled over the Oregon Trail in the 1840s, the predominantly white populace was resisting integration and passing black-exclusion laws. When I arrived in Portland, segregation had been legal for more than one hundred years. Under the state constitution of 1859, blacks and mulattos were excluded from using the judicial system or making legally binding contracts. They were banned from legitimate sources of employment and from owning real estate. The state constitution denied the vote to blacks, mulattos, and Chinese, disenfranchising in a stroke an ethnic population that included Portland's Chinatown, the second largest in the Northwest. American Indians fared no better. When white settlers had clashed with native tribes in 1855, the Portland *Oregonian* called for the extermination of Indians. "The idea of humanity to the Indians is preposterous," the editors declared, "if not criminal." State legislation of the Civil War era subjected blacks to a special poll tax, excluded them from jury duty, and prohibited the intermarriage of whites with other races. Blacks could not rent hotel rooms or be guaranteed service in restaurants. When they went to a movie, they had to sit in the balcony. Legalized discrimination existed until the 1950s.

For a while I worked part-time for the Urban League stuffing envelopes and distributing literature. Formed in 1945, the Urban League focused on housing and employment discrimination, civil-rights legislation, and informational programs in the 1940s and 1950s. I joined the Urban League's Youth Forum, a mixed ethnic and racial group of eight or ten young people who met periodically to discuss social, political, and interracial issues. Dick Bogle, who became a Portland city commissioner, was a member of that group. "There were more restaurants we could not eat in than we could eat in," Bogle remembered, and that was the sort of thing that drew us together.

During this time I witnessed the entrance of blacks into state politics and saw the first black person run for the state senate. In 1953, a historic civil-rights bill co-sponsored by Rep. Mark O. Hatfield declared it illegal for restaurants, hotels, and other public establishments to discriminate on the basis of race, religion, color, or national origin. In 1957, with Hatfield as secretary of state, Oregon passed the State Fair Housing Act, which opened housing to blacks in all parts of Portland.

Although the war industry wrought employment breakthroughs, work opportunities for blacks were limited. I saw firsthand that the jobs open to blacks were confined to domestic work, railroad redcaps (baggage handlers), or Pullman porters. The railroad was the backbone of the black economy. Even black college graduates, few though they were, worked for the railroad. Discrimination at the workplace was common. Black shipyard workers were paid less than their white counterparts. When black skilled workers were allowed to join unions, their identity cards were stamped "Temporary." During the war, the Boiler Makers Union, which dominated the shipyards, did not accept blacks for full membership, but enrolled them in an auxiliary unit without regular union benefits. There were virtually no black professionals—one physician that I remember, and a couple of black lawyers. Joy's husband, Clarence Pruitt, was the first black to graduate from the University of Oregon Dental School. Such professional breakthroughs were oddities.

In our small black community, professional role models were scarce. Beyond the churches, socialization opportunities were limited for black young adults. Most of us relied on strong family support for guidance, but this was of little help to me. My home life was so quiet that it bordered on solitary. As an only child I learned to be self-reliant. My mother and I had spent too many years apart; we were strangers to one another. Most of the conversation at home was between her and her husband. Relations between Reverend Grant and me were not as volatile as they had been in Pine Bluff, but we were never close. As a minister, he was an idol within the black community and he held high positions in Masonry, but his strict dictates about hard work and high morals extended more to young people than to himself. He began every meal at our house with long prayers. He preached hellfire and damnation with sulfur thrown in, and to many people he epitomized the teachings of Jesus Christ, but I did not see him in that exalted light. Some of his friends were notorious racketeers in Seattle. My cousin Estella knew Reverend Grant well and denounced him as a scoundrel. Other relatives considered him a womanizer who had several affairs during his marriage, and they detested him for the thoughtless way he treated my mother. In retrospect, those who knew him well believed that his most grievous flaw was a lack of self-discipline. On the surface he was a man of the Bible, but the true tenets of Christianity seemed not to be in him.

Neighbors in Louisiana who knew my father hoped that I would follow in his footsteps, and parishioners in Portland wanted me to become a preacher like him, too, but religion as I knew it held no career interest for me. The faith of my youth was too stern, too straight, and too unyielding. Doctor and teacher were suggested vaguely as professions, but these did not appeal to me either. I knew which careers I did not want to pursue, but as yet I had not found the right profession for me.

I discovered early on that when families are broken, separated, or less than ideal, we can be inventive about creating new paradigms for family. I had been on my own in Pine Bluff; I was virtually alone in Portland, building a life for myself while I was sixteen and seventeen years old. Although my mother was interested in my education, academic subjects were not something I could discuss with either her or Reverend Grant. That is not to say that my mother was disinterested in my life. She had strict guidelines about acceptable rules of behavior. She wanted to associate only with churchgoing people who could be invited to her house for Sunday dinner, and she set out those guidelines for me in a protective way. One subject my mother had especially strong ideas about was the kind of woman I should marry. She was even more adamant about the women I should not associate with and at the top of that list was Inez Freeman. When I met her, Inez was a student at Reed College and was dating a friend of mine, a waiter from the Hotel Portland. Their relationship did not last, but my friendship with Inez continued, and occasionally I visited her on campus in Anna Mann House, the progressive, even permissive, student center. One day when I came home from school, my mother and her husband were waiting for me in the parlor.

"Reverend Grant would like to talk to you," my mother said.

"Oh, not me," he said. "Your mother wants to talk to you about Inez."

Tiny at her home in Portland, Oregon—3138 North Albina Ave.

So my mother carried the conversational charge. "We don't think Inez is the proper woman for you." I considered Inez a respectable hat-and-gloves lady, but to my mother, she was a woman with a past and she listed Inez's faults: she had worked as a wardrobe lady to Billie Holiday, she was the divorced mother of a son, and she was seven or eight years older than me. "She is too old," my mother said. "When you get married, you will want someone your own age, someone who has never been married, someone from a good family. You will want a churchgoing person who is not yet involved with boys."

"Inez is not my girlfriend," I said.

"She calls to talk to you," my mother said, "and I can tell she is interested in you." Mothers must have strong intuition, because later Inez and I did become close, but the relationship was short-lived. I went away, and the next time I saw Inez, she was married to a social worker at Walla Walla State Prison.

I kept myself so busy with work and study that I had little time to socialize. Tall and thin in high school, I was too shy to date. When the senior prom came, I did not know any girl I could ask. My closest female friend was white—a blonde who wore her hair over one eye like Veronica Lake—and in those days it was impossible for me to invite her or for her to accept, so friends arranged for me to escort Betty Mann to the prom. She was a nice young woman from another high school, a girl who would have won the approval of my mother.

My two close friends in high school were both born in Portland, good students and ambitious. Glenn Pattee was white, had a summer job with the Forest Service, and shared with me such an enthusiasm for physics that we worked together and did the experiments early. He became neither a physicist nor a forester, but an insurance broker. George Hill was energetic, ambitious, and unusual in several aspects. He was the only black student I knew who was a member of the National Guard and who had a car. He worked after school at a mortuary with a goal to become a mortician, which he accomplished.

The Vanport Recreational Center was the hub of my emotional and social life. Because of the segregation limitations of high school, this facility was invaluable to me. It was visionary in organizing activities for teenagers and developing us into well-rounded, responsible adults. We did not realize it at the time, but the goal was to shepherd us into wholesome, educational activities and keep us occupied in our spare time. A staff of college-educated supervisors brooded over us in the best sense of that biblical verb. They took us on field trips, from ski lodges to courtrooms, and they organized activities, from badminton games to choral music. We went to symphonic concerts, and we took classes in what today would be called personal development: goal-setting, family relations, health, and hygiene. We studied art appreciation and the legal system. Two counselors there, Marian Meacham and Carmen Parrish Walker, seemed closer to me in some ways than my mother.

Carmen was a young and idealistic college graduate from Mississippi who found the job of her dreams at Vanport. "I was young," she said later. "I was motivated, and this was truly a godsend for me. All my life I had felt that this was the way we were supposed to live—helping everyone who needs help, learning to get along."

The only black member of the staff, she passed on to me her boundless ideals. "I don't believe in boundaries," Carmen said. "If you set your mind to it, you can do it. Don't let doors be closed to you." She never let me forget that as a black person, I had to excel, not only then, but all of my life. She introduced me to black history, determined that we few black students in Portland's public schools should not be deprived of our heritage or remain ignorant of achievements of black Americans. Some black youth were like runners at the blocks waiting for the gun. "You only said the word and they were ready to go," she said. I was one of those, in Carmen's opinion, and she became my steadfast booster. She saw me as a quiet diplomatic leader at the recreation center and a young man with aspirations to make the world a better place. Almost forty years later, when Secretary of State George Shultz called Carmen to ask about my nomination for ambassador to South Africa and my ability to make a change in the entrenched apartheid system, she did not hesitate with her answer. "I have no doubt that he could be the person to take that leadership," she said. "If anyone can do it, Ed can do it."

I worked and went to school, and all the while graduation day loomed as a finite date. I was moving inexorably toward a precipice. On the other side lay my future—unknown and undiscovered—but I did not know how to reach that place, because I saw no bridge between my present and my future. I was willing to work and study hard to accomplish whatever it took to close that gap, yet I could not get a firm grasp on anything to pull me across. I knew vaguely what I wanted my life to be, but I had no precise career goals. I realized that I needed a college education, but I did not know how to finance it. All I saw was a chasm of uncertainty separating me from the rest of my life. I did not feel despair, only a deep frustration coupled with the impatience of youth. I was hounded by the questions: What? When? How? And then, almost by accident, the way opened before me. It was just as Goethe said: "The moment one commits oneself, all sorts of things occur to help one that would never otherwise have occurred. Whatever you can do, or dream you can, begin it. Boldness has genius, power and magic in it."

One of the most romantic aspects of my job as a waiter was meeting visiting diplomats from around the world who were posted in the Northwest. This was my first encounter with foreigners, and it was heady. I met the Soviet consul general—the first time I had seen a Russian—and the man and his culture seemed daring and exotic. About the same time, Carly Gilstrap, our history teacher, began organizing noontime lectures by outside speakers. One day we gathered with our sandwiches in the school library and heard two Foreign Service officers from the State Department in Washington, D.C., speak about their profession. I did not understand everything they talked about, but their life seemed alluring. It dovetailed with my own aspirations—traveling, learning languages, and representing the United States in foreign countries. Joy and I were the only minorities in that class, and we realized they were not talking to us as prospective Foreign Service employees, but I was riveted by what they said. From that moment, I was hooked on the Foreign Service.

I became acquainted with the president of the Junior League, which sponsored dances at the hotel for servicemen. She took an interest in me and my future and took me to meet a businessman to advise me about a career after high school.

"What do you want to do in life?" he asked me.

That question was much on my mind. In a flight of fancy, I wrote for the high school yearbook that my career goal was psychiatry, but this was less a professional choice than an esoteric interest in the subject of human behavior. The mystery of human behavior is what drew me to become both a reader of ancient history and a devotee of Sherlock Holmes. I told the businessman about another alluring interest that was capturing my attention: diplomatic service.

"Do you see that as a profession for a black man?" he asked, thunderstruck. Obviously he thought that was a nice aspiration, admirable even, but unrealistic. "The most important thing for you to do," he said, recovering, "is get an education. You could get a job here," he said, gesturing at his insurance company, "run errands and learn about the business, but if you are going to have a career, you have to have a college education." It was a refrain I heard with increased frequency.

Among the guest speakers at the Vanport Community Center's International Relations Club were consuls general from Australia, Great Britain, Canada, Mexico, and South American countries. When they talked about promoting commerce between their countries and the United States, it sounded esoteric and interesting. I knew almost nothing about the reality of the Foreign Service, and in my innocence, I romanticized the work. I had read in a history text the phrase "relations among nations," which captivated me. I joined the high school's International Relations Club, sponsored by the prim Spanish teacher Kay Dilio, which invited foreign diplomats stationed in the area to speak to us. Suddenly, I was immersed in the subject of foreign affairs. George Hill and I became members of the club's speaking group, and we spoke on the subject of the United Nations to area high schools. The highlight of our speaking career was an invitation to a luncheon at a big downtown hotel to hear Secretary of Commerce Henry Wallace, former vice president of the United States. He talked about the United States and the Soviet Union in the United Nations, urging cooperation and communication. I met him after his speech and told him that I planned to be an American ambassador. I do not know what Secretary Wallace thought in 1947 of a black teenager's chances of getting into the Foreign Service. I did not ask him; I just told him I intended to do it. I had hitched my dream to the Foreign Service, and I never let go. Portland would be my portal to the world of faraway places where I could achieve, accomplish things on my own, and make a difference.

When the war ended, Vanport's residents began to drift away, but the housing addition's end came dramatically. In May 1948 a heavy snowmelt swelled the Columbia River. The dikes broke late in the afternoon of Memorial Day, releasing a ten-foot wall of water. In minutes, Vanport disappeared, gone as surely as the lost city of Atlantis. The community was never intended to be permanent; it was poorly built, and it had existed only five and a half years, barely a flicker in the long reach of history, but it had an abiding impact on me.

My mother and stepfather had moved away from Vanport to another part of Portland before the flood. Marian and Merle had gone, too, first to the University of Washington and then to the wilds of Washington, where they cleared land and built a cabin in an idyllic setting. While I was in Japan, Marian wrote to me about their cabin, the paintings on the wall, and the bears that ate cherries off the trees. Carmen Parrish Walker went on to have a successful career in education as a teacher and counselor, one of the first blacks in the Portland school district. She was always a role model; in the 1950s she sat quietly in protest at counters where she was not served, and in the 1960s she bought a home despite the protest of white neighbors. After a brilliant college record, Joy Brock Pruitt persevered through employment discrimination to become a notable teacher and administrator in Portland's school system. I was gone, too, graduated from high school and out into the world, but Carmen, Marian, and Joy remain lifelong friends.

I have always considered Portland to be my hometown. It was not the city of my birth or of my childhood, but it was much more to me than the place where

My high school portrait in Portland.

I attended high school. It was here that I shaped a boy's dreams into career goals, here that I formed enduring friendships, and here that I was launched into the world of adulthood. Throughout my career I have returned to Portland, visiting my mother until her death and reconnecting and consulting with the people who became some of my closest friends. Over the years, this handful of intimates, speaking to reporters and writers, has expressed surprise that I sustained communication with them from my posts around the world, but I see it differently. I keep in touch not out of courtesy, but because their friendship and counsel are important to me. Before going to South Africa as ambassador, I sought information and guidance from the nation's experts and advisors, but I also wanted to hear the opinions of people across the country, because I believe that foreign policy is a responsibility not just of professionals, but of all citizens. I made a special effort to meet with my friends in Portland. I rely on them to speak candidly and knowledgeably. It is easy to get caught up in the trappings of international diplomacy. I have seen many diplomats stumble on pride of office. In the formal world of my profession, others may call me Mr. Ambassador and open car doors for me, but my colleagues in Portland keep me grounded. They have been my true north, the place I return for replenishment. I believe there is such a thing as a spiritual hometown, and Portland is mine.

On the last day of school, just before I graduated, Bassett asked me to go for a walk, and as we walked up the street, he did something that shocked me. He lit a cigarette. I had never seen such behavior from a teacher before; I thought they were perfect people. "Teachers smoke, too," he said, when he saw the surprise on my face. "They just don't do it in the presence of students." We walked for a couple of blocks, and he said, "Well, Eddie, what are you gong to do? Going to college?"

"I'm thinking about joining the army," I said.

"Why?" he asked. I told him that I had applied for some scholarships and had received a couple, but not enough to cover tuition and expenses. The military intrigued me, and when my tour of duty had ended, the GI Bill of Rights would pay for college.

"Do what you really want to do," he said, "but let's face it, you are a black man, and you have to have a college education. Even if you go into the army now, never give up the idea of going to college. You are going to need a degree. You won't be able to advance without it." He invited me to his home that evening for dinner. His wife, Mildred, picked up the conversation where he had left off, and she was even more insistent than he had been.

"Here is what you need to do when you leave," she said. "Get yourself a reading program. Then I want you to write me and tell me what you are doing. And don't ever forget that you have to come back and go to college because life for you is not going to be any good without that." I wrote to her regularly, and she continually asked about my plans for further education. Once when I was visiting Portland, she introduced another plan.

"What you need to do," she said, "is meet a nice girl." A nice girl to her meant a nice, educated black girl who would pull me back to Portland, where I would finish my college education and become an active member of the community. Mildred was disappointed that I never made Portland my permanent home.

By graduation I had seen the future I wanted and had charted my course. I graduated from high school with a list of cities I wanted to visit by the time I was twenty-one: London, Paris, and Tokyo. I had a career mission—to become a diplomat. I would need a college education and the means to finance it. The vehicle for these dreams would be the U.S. Army, so I volunteered for military duty. Next stop, back to the South and Fort Knox, Kentucky.

YOUNG WARRIOR

In June 1947, I graduated from high school, turned nineteen, and joined the army. I had the world on a ribbon.

I did not tell my mother about my enlistment until I passed the recruiting-office examination and was scheduled to be sworn in. She was distraught that I was leaving home and that I might be involved in battle. My stepfather generally thought the army would be a good experience for me. In truth, getting away from him was one of the reasons I had joined. At nineteen, I bristled under the restrictive home atmosphere he imposed. With the hindsight of maturity, I realize I had other choices, but I have always told myself, "Never look back." And I did not.

I boarded a Trailways bus for Fort Lewis, Washington. It was the second momentous journey of my life. My first trek had brought me to Portland; now I was leaving not only Oregon, but my boyhood as well. The military would take me into manhood. It would be a journey fraught with adventure and new experiences, but even in the military, I encountered the familiar twin dragons Racism and Segregation.

The seven of us who had enlisted at the same time were given a battery of tests and sent from by train Fort Lewis to Fort Knox, Kentucky, which would be my home for the next ten weeks. We left July 3 for the two-day rail trip. The train seemed to stop at every station in Washington, Idaho, Montana, the Dakotas, Minnesota, Wisconsin, Illinois, Indiana, and finally Kentucky. I felt a swelling appreciation for the nation's birthday as a panorama of small town patriotism unfurled before me: flags, firecrackers, balloons, bunting, grand speeches, and slogans challenging all to "Love America or Go Back Where You Came From." At one stop, a delegation from the Ladies' Auxiliary came aboard and handed out cookies and lemonade to us boys going off to serve our nation in defense of freedom. Perhaps the holiday flurry was an effort to erase the fresh memories of World War II and savor the affirmation that God and the angels are on the side of democratic America. I had been in the army three days, it was the eve of Independence Day, and I was enjoying a new independence myself. I settled into the rhythmic sway of the train and simply enjoyed the expanse of summer skies, the spectacle of holiday celebrations, and the pride of postwar national unity. Before me was a sprawling, happy nation, and I was glad to be an integral part of it.

That contentment lasted until we reached the Indianapolis train station and were separated by race. All six of my colleagues went into the "Whites Only" rail cars. I was the only black in the group. A few moments earlier I had been among fellow soldiers in a car noisy with camaraderie. Now I rode alone in the "Blacks Only" car for the silent, final leg of the journey. It was the Fourth of July.

This was my introduction to the army's segregation. I was surprised at the rigidity of the military policy and said to myself, "It's the same old stuff." This segregation was a manifestation of American society at the time, especially in Kentucky, where we were trained. Fort Knox is outside Louisville and just south of the Mason-Dixon Line, which separated the slaveholding states of the South from the free states of the North before the Civil War.

The army was establishing a new postwar racial policy, wrestling with the idea of maintaining a quota on the number of black troops and trying to upgrade the quality of black troops by admitting men who scored higher on the intelligence tests. The military was caught between two forces, pressed on one side by the predominant segregation of American society and buffeted on the other side by civil-rights organizations, especially the National Association for the Advancement of Colored People (NAACP), headed by Walter White. The army did not see itself as an instrument of social reform. After the war, many black officers who had been given commissions during the fighting found themselves either mustered out of the army or reverted to enlisted status. In 1947, when I entered the service, a quota prohibited black troops from exceeding 10 percent of the army personnel. Black troops were also limited in their assignments and duties. According to the policy in effect, they could be sent to Japan or Germany, but not to China, Iceland, or the Panama Canal Zone. They could not be used in infantry units, in the constabulary, or in supervision of white civilians; they could not be buried among white soldiers in national cemeteries. We were segregated unto death.

Reform was in the air, however, and moving inexorably across the land, even to the southern states. For all its policies of separateness, the army was one of the nation's leading employers of blacks. The army's senior black officer, Brigadier General Benjamin O. Davis, declared it "the dawn of a new day for the colored soldier." The armed forces were pulled screaming across the line of change, but once they changed, they became institutions that America could be proud of. President Harry S Truman signed Executive Order 9981 in 1948, which decreed the end of segregation in the U.S. military. No great nation, he said, could afford such a contradictory policy. The forces were to be integrated gradually with the goal of total integration by 1950. Some units were already integrated, but the policy had not yet reached Kentucky. At Fort Knox, black soldiers and white soldiers lived in separate barracks, ate in separate dining areas, and relaxed in separate recreation facilities. The only areas not segregated were the retail facilities such as the post exchange and snack bars, although I do not remember ever seeing a white soldier in the snack bar located in the black troop area.

I trained with a company in an armored division, an all-black unit with an entire cadre of black officers: a captain and four or five lieutenants. The commanding officer, Captain Samuel S. Brown, and the lieutenants were the crisp essence of military bearing. I saw a white officer only when the regimental commander or the battalion commander came around. It was the first time I had seen black people in command, and I liked what I saw. This meant there was a chance for me. My future looked brighter.

Fort Knox had a regimen of academic and physical training that began with a 5 A.M. roll call and a few miles' run before breakfast. We learned the academics of being a fighting person, elements of personal grooming, care of military clothing, respect for fellow soldiers, and how to make beds. There was never enough sleep. No liberty was granted for the first four weeks, and in that time I learned the palliative value of music. One Sunday at mandatory chapel, the black troops were entertained by an open-air concert of a black choral group named "Wings Over Jordan." It was a mesmerizing performance—the power of the male baritones and tenors combined with crystal-bell clarity of the female singers. The women sang like celestial beings, and after our weeks of restriction to male company, they were visions of earthly beauty. The sight of these lovely young ladies made me acutely aware of my own shortcomings—awkwardness and shyness—which I silently vowed to correct posthaste.

When we were finally allowed off base, I joined a group of soldiers going to Cincinnati, Ohio, just across the river. One of my colleagues arranged for me to accompany his female cousin to church, and I knew then that God had chosen me for a special blessing, because she was the loveliest thing I had ever seen. I was learning that feminine charm surpassed even music's power to comfort and soothe. Other forays took me to Elizabethtown, Cincinnati again, Louisville, and to the Service Club on base, which was run by a woman of indeterminate beauty whom everyone called by her first name, Gwen.

While at Fort Knox, I caught a glimpse of America's experiment with Universal Military Training (UMT). At that time, a great debate was rumbling in Congress and among the people about compulsory national service for all of America's youth. UMT was an alternative national service for those who conscientiously objected to military service. A contingent of UMT trainees wearing special uniforms arrived at Fort Knox about the same time I did, but I saw little of them on base. We know from history that the American nation chose not to institute compulsory military training, and in my opinion, that is unfortunate. I believe that when young people are brought together in organized training to serve their country, the learning they derive is invaluable.

In that black unit at Fort Knox I saw, for the first time, the range of diversity possible among people of the same color. We were all black, but we represented a rainbow of skin tones, backgrounds, demographics, and religions. I met Black Muslims and Catholics from across the country, as well as hard-shell Baptists from Alabama, Mississippi, and Louisiana. A gang member from Chicago's south side baited me until the two of us clashed like young mountain rams. He was a small, street-smart tough, familiar with knife fights. I was big, quiet, and fond of reading poetry, far too much of a goody-goody in his opinion. It was the only barracks fight I ever had. We fought with no holds barred while the rest of the troops gathered around, enjoying the entertainment, until a noncommissioned officer broke it up. Even that experience did not diminish the esprit de corps that developed in the unit. When graduation day came and we donned full dress uniforms, I felt like strutting. We personified military pride and prestige. It was our day in the sun, and we were bound for glory.

My unit had trained in infantry tactics; then we were given a choice of service overseas or further training in the continental United States. I chose overseas duty. My Fort Knox training was completed in September, just as the Kentucky countryside was bejeweled with autumn color. My orders sent me home to Portland for thirty days of leave, then to Camp Stoneman, California, and from there to Korea, a country known as "The Land of the Morning

Calm." I was off for adventure in East Asia, where I would explore a new culture, discover a new philosophy, and begin to plumb depths within myself that I had not known existed.

Korea: The Land of the Morning Calm

Camp Stoneman was a transfer point for military personnel embarking and returning from duty in Japan and Korea. Crossing the Pacific Ocean by ship, I discovered two things: seasickness, which lasted only a couple of days, and poker, a game that has fascinated me ever since. It was December when we docked at Inchon Harbor on the Yellow Sea. We had arrived in the teeth of Korea's winter. The land appeared to be a cold, forbidding place of bare hills, nothing at all like its romantic name.

We unloaded in full field pack for transport by truck to the Replacement Depot in Seoul. A friendly group of returnees awaiting transportation back to the United States offered to exchange their military scrip for our U.S. dollars, which could not be used in Korea. We had been warned of this scam before boarding the ship. In an effort to control the black market, the military occasionally changed the scrip without notice. The scrip these accommodating servicemen were offering to us green soldiers was outdated and worthless.

Christmas at the Replacement Depot was a lonely time for young soldiers away from friends and family for the first time. The Christmas dinner was bountiful, but the underlying mood was as desolate as the landscape. Except for Antarctica, Korea was the coldest place I have ever been. In January, the average temperature is about 27 degrees Fahrenheit, but the water surrounding the peninsula and the winds from the mountains drive the wind-chill factor much lower. Our government-issued cold-weather gear included parkas, snow boots, and leather boots with cold-weather inserts. None of it was effective. When I was outside, I was always cold.

The Replacement Depot was a former Japanese military base that had been taken over by the United States at the end of the war in the Pacific. We were housed in an old Japanese barracks, which had been built for convenience rather than comfort. It barely protected us from the elements. The diesel oil space heaters produced more stench than warmth. Chain-operated windows near the high ceilings were kept open to release carbon monoxide. Fireguards posted throughout the night were to insure against accidental fires from the space heaters. Our sleeping bags, fortunately padded like comforters, were effective against the piercing Korean cold. The only time I was warm was when I was sleeping.

I was assigned to a black unit at the Quartermaster Depot just outside of Inchon. The commanding officer of this black unit was a white captain, a fine man, with a staff of two black lieutenants and a couple of white lieutenants. The captain, named Kunkle, walked into the officers' club to find a sign from his colleagues that read, "Kunkle got the niggers!"

My unit was the 175th Military Police Patrol platoon, a small and elite group that provided security for base and ancillary activities. The Russians were occupying northern Korea, and the American military had an assistance program for the struggling South Korean government. My military-police unit helped to provide training for a newly established Korean constabulary, which was the nucleus of what would become the South Korean, or Republic of Korea, Army.

I was stationed in Korea in 1947–48, before the country erupted in what became known as the Korean War. That war was the culmination of a troubled history for the peninsular nation. Korea was a land that had wrapped itself in its misty antiquity and so preferred self-sufficient isolation that it became known as the "Hermit Kingdom." Although the country respected China, it scorned the Japanese "dwarfs," as Koreans called them, and forcefully resisted western aggression from both the British and the Americans, whom Koreans considered barbarians. Korea wanted neither cultural intercourse nor trade with outside nations, yet peaceful seclusion was not to be the country's destiny. For centuries it endured waves of foreign invasions by Mongols, Manchus, and Japanese. At the end of the Sino-Japanese War in 1895, Japan triumphed over both China and Russia, colonized Taiwan, and set its sights on Korea. When this happened, clouds of disaster began to form.

Russia insinuated itself into Korea, and in 1904 the Japanese responded with an attack, emerging victorious as the United States and Britain looked on indifferently. Only World War II would release Korea from the long occupation that ensued. When the Japanese surrendered unconditionally, the Allies divided Korea arbitrarily at the 38th parallel. The Soviets, who had been fighting the Japanese in the north, were assigned protection of northern Korea, and the United States, which had been battling Japanese in the south, assumed responsibility there. Rivalry and mistrust between the two great powers began to take root as the seedlings of the cold war. Ultimately, the United Nations supervised

In the army I was stationed in Korea and was assigned to the 175th Military Police Patrol Platoon, a small and elite group that provided security for base and ancillary activities.

elections that resulted in the 1948 creation of two republics, North Korea and South Korea. Until then, Soviet and American troops were on the ground as occupational forces, and that is how I had come to be assigned to southern Korea.

Shortly after I arrived, the United States made a major decision to develop South Korea into a self-sustaining nation. President Truman saw a significant part of the world becoming communist and thought that if it were not stopped, communism would overwhelm us all. Dwight Eisenhower, following Truman as president, said that our job in Korea was to reestablish the original borders; once that was accomplished, we should leave. Some of America's most outspoken politicians and generals declared that we ought to march into Russia and "finish the job." Although I was sure that saner heads would prevail, a trace of uncertainty lingered in the air, and many a night patrol was edged with anxiety.

One midnight, the fellow who relieved me on patrol said gravely, "We're going to war with the Russians." I was gullible and wide-eyed at the news, a fact he never let me forget.

During the year I was in Korea, we saw a constant struggle between the North and the South. The Americans and Russians sparred verbally. Under Japanese occupation, northern Korea had been the industrial area, while southern Korea remained a farm country. Consequently, the South had no power plants and relied on power sources in the North to provide electric power. As a form of psychological war games, either the Russians or the North Koreans frequently interrupted power. The electricity went off repeatedly and at the most inconvenient times. This single irritating fact probably accounts for South Korea's speedy creation of an independent industrial state. The U.S. military command gradually established power plants to reduce reliance on North Korea.

The United States and the Soviet Union had agreed that the two Koreas were to be united, which did not happen, but for a while the Russians were given permission to leave grim North Korea and come to Seoul for rest and relaxation. I had my first look at buxom Russian female soldiers walking along the streets in huge fur parkas that seemed far more appropriate for the Korean winter than my own gear.

Just when I thought winter had settled in permanently, spring brought South Korea to life. The clear skies of robin-egg blue, the mountains painted with wildflowers, the countryside farms roused from winter, and the elegant dress of the women transformed a strange place into a land of beauty. Even so, it was a bleak country. The Korean people had just come out from under the yoke of Japan and had few luxuries. Neither Seoul nor Inchon had the financial means to be attractive cities.

Most places of leisure were off limits to military personnel, but the U.S. forces maintained a recreational lodge in Sang-Do. This gave me an opportunity to travel, explore the countryside, get acquainted with local families, fish in nearby rivers, and develop a taste for local cuisine. There were few uniformed people assigned to Korea, so those of us who did travel got to know not just girlfriends, but local butchers, schoolteachers, and other citizens. One colleague and I agreed to coach a basketball team at a women's college. We were not very good at it, but we tried valiantly.

At that time in Korea, human sewage was collected from the commode system and deposited in great vats below ground. From here it was used as rich fertilizer. We were warned repeatedly not to eat fresh greens unless we washed them in a sodium concentrate solution, never to eat salads in restaurants, and to wash and peel fruit before eating it. Human waste is arguably the richest manure in the world, but the odor from those sewage pools was god-awful. The smell is still with me. One night as a friend returned to camp, he took a shortcut across the fields and fell into one of the vats. What a commotion. It was one of the worst things anyone could have gone through. He was hosed down thoroughly and his clothes were burned before he was allowed to enter the barracks.

I had been in Korea about six months when my commanding officer asked me to apply for a public-relations job for the outfit. After the interviews, the job was between me and another black solder. My competitor liked to write poetry, and I was trying to write short stories, so we joined forces and bought a typewriter, which was unheard of in those days. He kept it for a few days, and then I took possession for a few days. It was on that typewriter that I taught myself to type in a five-finger style, which I use today. I got the public-relations job, and I also put out a little outfit newspaper called *The Scandal Sheet*, which I typed on the jointly owned typewriter. The soldier who did not get the public relations job was Alvin Aubert. He later became an English professor at Wayne State University in Detroit and was an award-winning poet, playwright, editor, and literary critic.

In 1950, after I had left, North Korean forces invaded South Korea in an effort to unify the nation by force under communist rule. This action ignited the Korean War. Chinese forces swarmed into North Korea to battle defending United Nations forces led by the United States. Finally, in 1953, a truce was reached with an armistice that did not involve signing a peace treaty. There is no peace treaty to this day, but the UN forces and South Korea continue to meet in a small house that straddles the demarcation line between North Korea and South Korea. Miniature flags representing each nation adorn the table where the meetings are held. Like chess players, the representatives compete silently with a flag race, a contest initiated by North Korea. Each nation periodically replaces its flag with one just an inch or two taller than the other flag. I am told the flag race continues yet.

JAPAN

LAND OF THE RISING SUN

When the United States reduced its presence in South Korea in 1948, I was transferred for the next two years to Japan to join the U.S. Eighth Army. I was stationed there when Japanese general Hideki Tojo, the minister of war who ordered the attack on Pearl Harbor, was convicted as a war criminal. He was hanged at Sugamo prison two days before Christmas in 1948. The hangman offered me a piece of the rope as a souvenir, but I would not take it.

In Japan, I saw the floods of war recede to the calm of rebuilding a society in a defeated nation. At the end of World War II, the Pottsdam Declaration called for the occupation of Japan by the Allied Forces, led by the United States. Commanded by General Robert Eichelberger, the Eighth Army was the occupation force with the massive and unprecedented duty of governing Japan under the directives of General Douglas MacArthur, the supreme commander of the Allied Powers. MacArthur was making history, and I was witnessing it. From that time, I became a student of both the general's career and Japanese culture.

Some biographers describe MacArthur as imperious and born to lead; MacArthur appeared to consider himself born to rule. He lived at the American Embassy in Tokyo, where he formally received the emperor, and established his general headquarters in the Dai Ichi Insurance Building, located in front of the Imperial Palace. *Dai* means "big" and *ichi* means "one," so this was the Big Building or the No. 1 Building. On a dare, another young soldier and I ginned up our courage and set out to meet MacArthur. We went to the Dai Ichi building, where the military policeman on duty agreed to introduce us when MacArthur departed for the day. Morning and evening, hundreds of Japanese citizens stood silently, ten-deep outside the Dai Ichi to get a glimpse of the general they so revered. About twenty minutes after we arrived, the general appeared, met us, shook our hands, took the corncob pipe out of his mouth, and made small talk: "Where are you from? Glad to see you here." Then General MacArthur put the pipe back into his mouth, paused just a moment for the cameras, got into the car waiting for him, and drove away. Some forty years later, when I was appointed the United States permanent representative to the United Nations and was in residence at the Waldorf-Astoria in New York, I called on his widow, Jean Marie Faircloth MacArthur, who also lived there. I told her about the day that we young soldiers met MacArthur, and she beamed. "How wonderful," she said. "How my General would have loved that story."

It was in the Dai Ichi building that MacArthur wrote the current constitution of Japan. The constitution's famous Article IX forswears war, emancipates women, legalizes labor unions, disestablishes business conglomerates, and empowers peasant farmers to own land, a policy that revolutionized the rural agricultural system. Another paramount element of the constitution involved the emperor. The divinity of the imperial family was rooted in legend. For centuries the Japanese people had believed that they were favored with a heaven-born sovereign and that their ruler on the Chrysanthemum Throne was a descendant of the Sun Goddess. With the stroke of pen, the constitution reduced the emperor from a god to a mortal man like his subjects.

MacArthur knew that the Japanese mindset needed a remnant of that supernatural belief, so in the new constitution the emperor was retained as a figurehead. MacArthur understood completely the Asian philosophies, peoples, and sense of balance, so he prevailed in urging that the emperor not be tried as a war criminal. By that act alone, the Japanese were able to develop relations with westerners, and especially with Americans. General MacArthur built the bridge into the future by allowing the emperor and his people to retain a shred of dignity.

When I arrived in Japan, the trial of General Yamashita Tomoyuki was still in the news. Some of the people I worked with in the military-police battalion had been in the Philippines when MacArthur ordered that Yamashita be brought to trial under the terms of the Pottsdam Agreement as MacArthur interpreted it. MacArthur took that action with no authority beyond his own, because Yamashita had treated the Philippines so badly as the governor general during the Japanese occupation. I heard it rumored that as psychological warfare, Yamashita violated the room in the hotel where MacArthur's late mother had lived, a room MacArthur retained almost as a shrine to her. The two generals never met but found themselves as adversaries; when MacArthur returned to the Philippines, he ensured that Yamashita was tried and convicted of war crimes of a heinous nature and subsequently executed.

The occupation of Japan thrust the United States, for the first time, into a position of imperial power. Uniformed personnel and civilians who worked for the U.S. government were virtually imperial agents. This gave all of us, me included, enormous psychological power. Perhaps more by luck than wisdom at my young age, I was able to keep my feet on the ground and not succumb to delusions of grandeur.

I was assigned to the 212th Military Police Company, an all-black company in a white battalion, the 519th Military Police Battalion. The job of the 212th, "The Lighting Company," was to maintain law and order in Yokohama and its environs by working in cooperation with the local Japanese police. Military police patrols consisted of one black serviceman, one white soldier, and one Japanese counterpart. Americans had the authority to arrest Japanese citizens, but no Japanese could arrest or discipline Americans. Consequently, Americans had an unusual degree of authority. The violation of this authority by individual Americans troubled me. I never saw any brutality, but I saw rudeness and excessive brusqueness when a military policeman thought a Japanese citizen did not move out of his way fast enough. The terms "gook" and "slant eyes" were commonplace among the uniformed people. These terms of disrespect meant the same thing to me as "nigger." One night I almost got into a fistfight protesting the use of these words. What bothered me most was that black troops also used the derogatory terms. I saw that the habits of the dominant group could sometimes permeate subgroups as acceptable behavior.

I did not do any patrol work. Somebody had decided that I was a personnel specialist and assigned me to the administrative unit. Every day, two of us from the black 212th company traveled by jeep to work on "The Hill," the popular name for the white 519th administrative unit. There we all used the mess, service, club, and library facilities of our parent unit, but in the bizarre segregation system of the day, we could not sleep among our white colleagues, so at night we drove back to the 212th.

All of the officers of the 212th Military Police Company were white and severe; they went out of their way to punish the black soldiers under their command. Army captain Robert G. Remley, the commanding officer, was a vindictive man and a zealous disciplinarian who destroyed the careers of several promising black soldiers. He and his lieutenants seemed to feel insulted to be assigned to a black unit, embittering them. They court-martialed many people who did not deserve it. On two occasions, high-ranking black noncommissioned officers were court-martialed, reduced in rank, and given prison sentences. The commanding general's review party, however, threw out the judgments as unwarranted and unsubstantiated. Clearly the judgments were motivated by racism.

During my days as a member of the Eighth Army, I saw the remnants of segregation in the occupation force displayed by those around MacArthur, such as General Courtney Whitney, who functioned as MacArthur's real chief of staff. On numerous occasions, black troops were less favored than white troops. My disappointment was that MacArthur—who was adulated and acclaimed as a wise conqueror who had been given what some considered divine inspiration to govern this conquered nation—so easily could have said, "We want to make sure that we manifest, in all of our actions, what we believe in as a nation. That includes the elimination of any vestige of segregation which is so at variance with what our forefathers intended in an enlightened Constitution." Sadly, he did not say it, either in word or in deed.

Prejudice was not limited to military compounds and authorized recreational facilities. It was also present when we were off duty. Some white military personnel bridled at the notion that black military personnel could openly pay courtship to Japanese women. I encountered this myself one Sunday afternoon while escorting a Japanese date to a seaside resort just beyond Kamakura. Half a dozen white soldiers confronted us, and one of them with eyes as sharp as a knife told me, "Boy, I wish I had you back in Texas."

Whipping the furies of prejudice, white troops spread the rumor that black men had tails and warned of dire consequences awaiting any Japanese woman who dated a black man. Hostilities simmered and sometimes boiled over into near-race riots. After a white unit clashed with a black unit, General Eichelberger called a meeting of all soldiers in the Yokohama area. Gathering them in the Octagon Theatre, he said, "I am used to talking to armies about tactics and winning, not to a group of soldiers who have exercised an evil side of man— racial prejudice." He said that this doctrine had no place in the United States, a country based on principles of democracy, and that he did not expect such incidents to happen again. General Eichelberger lived the American dream the way that it should be. He was intent on making sure that we had a fighting force of men, and some women in those days, not handicapped by racial prejudice. Clashes between black servicemen and white soldiers did recur, but less seriously. The last year of a segregated U.S. defense force was 1950. When the Korean War started in June of that year, white troops were transferred into black units and black servicemen into white units.

An official no-fraternization policy was in effect primarily to govern relations between Japanese women and American men in uniform. This policy existed until September 8, 1951, with the signing of the San Francisco Peace Treaty and the U.S.-Japan Security Treaty. Usually, wherever troops were concentrated, the recreational activities included sanctioned nightclubs where American servicemen could dine, dance, and arrange dates. Japanese authorities urged MacArthur to enact this policy in Japan because they were fearful of a full-scale assault on Japanese women. The Japanese authorized specific nightclubs and canteens that were little more than highly regulated brothels. Both black soldiers and white frequented these recreational spots but never together. The Kanko, one of the biggest nightclubs in Yokohama, reserved some floors for white soldiers, some for black GIs, and left one floor undefined.

As I remember, the military authorities did not generally permit overnight liberty. Weekend passes began on Saturday at noon and ended on Sunday at midnight, but ingenious American servicemen found other ways to establish informal living arrangements with their Japanese *koibitos*, sweethearts. Some liaisons were temporary, but other colleagues married Japanese women who became their lifelong mates. Meanwhile, chaplains and others preached the consequences of hell and damnation for those who engaged in illicit sexual encounters. The effect of the sermons and moral lectures lasted no longer than the time it took to get out the chapel door.

American-born wives tried valiantly to limit contact with the Japanese women, but with little effect. American soldiers were fascinated with Japanese women, not because we had never seen them, but because we had never seen so many of them going about their lives as Japanese citizens. Almost immediately, conflicts arose. Soldiers—mainly officers—and their wives began to divorce over liaisons with Japanese women. When General Walton H. Walker assumed command of the Eighth Army, his wife became a force to be reckoned with. In her personal campaign that the soldiers not go astray, she became a walking moralist on the subject of fraternization with Japanese women. Mrs.

Walker was known to stop servicemen early in the morning and quiz them about where they had spent the night. If she found their explanation unconvincing, the errant men were referred to their commanding officer. She was also a strict disciplinarian regarding the role of the military wife. She not only advocated but commanded that they attend tea parties and help at Red Cross functions. None of this behavior won her many friends. After the Korean War began, General Walker led the reconstituted Eighth Army into South Korea, leaving Mrs. Walker in Japan. He was killed in that conflict, and a sad footnote to their story is that Mrs. Walker became a lonely person.

The Japanese were no strangers to racial prejudice. Before World War II, racial superiority was a part of the *Kokutai no hongi*, the national policy. Japan considered itself the purest of the Asian nations and far superior to the white race. The *Ainu*, white aborigines of northern Japan, were viewed as barbarians by the rest of their countrymen and were isolated in a separate region. It remains that way today. Still, some Japanese noted the hypocrisy in the U.S. Constitution and in the American national anthem, which trumpeted "the land of the free and the home of the brave." They saw segregation as evidence of American duplicity. Those Japanese who were familiar with U.S. propaganda of democratic equality found it strange to witness separate military units and recreational activities. They saw the contradiction of our trying to restore Japan to sovereignty and change that nation from a dictatorship to a democracy, while at the same time bringing the ills of racism from the United States. Ironically, we transferred not only racism, but also the institution of racism with our segregated military club system.

Life in uniform was leisurely as a member of MacArthur's Occupational Forces. For recreation, there were mountain retreats and golf clubs available to officers and enlisted. I became a member of the Hakone Recreational Club and the Yokohama Golf Country Club, although I never played well enough to warrant the status. Traditional Japanese recreation facilities had been set aside for the American uniformed personnel to play golf or tennis, spend time on the beach, or row boats. When military integration began in Japan, it started with these recreation clubs. A couple of years later, all the clubs were integrated.

Every Japanese person I encountered was a model of politeness. It was some time before I realized that their courtesy was a façade masking their intolerance towards the inferior Americans. Sometimes their courtesy was insincere, but at other times it developed into genuine respect. The best example of this was the obeisance of the Japanese to General MacArthur. They might have viewed him as little more than a war marshal, but by seeing him as someone sent by the gods, they could accept him as a conquering hero. The first time I saw the quiet crowds of Japanese standing at the entrance of the Dai Ichi building waiting to catch a glimpse of him, it struck me as so strange that I felt pinpricks over my body. They stood in silent respect of the gentleman general. All during my time in Japan, an aura of omnipotence surrounded MacArthur. To my knowledge he did not travel much, if any, in Japan. He did make one trip to Yokohama, where I was stationed, and inspected the troops. That was the first time I ever saw him. Mrs. MacArthur, however, did travel, and much later the American biographers would say that he used her as his eyes and ears.

The citizens of Japan were digging themselves out of the debris of war and trying to rebuild their lives, but a national mantle of shame and guilt weighted some down. Many Japanese believed that their defeat in war was the result of some error in their collective behavior. With their strong feeling of national superiority, they thought the Japanese race must have done something inexcusable, and as punishment the clouds had rained down the unworthy race of Americans to govern them. Tomiko Kyoya, a woman as ethereal as a nightingale, illustrated this belief of dishonor. She came from a classical Japanese family, but she was a lost woman emotionally and philosophically. In the traditional Japanese custom, Kyoya had been betrothed to a young Japanese man and a lavish ceremonial wedding was scheduled, but the young man became enamored of a nightclub hostess of a lesser rank and broke off the match. Both families were devastated, and Kyoya was crushed. A mutual friend contrived for us to have dinner together. When I suggested to this proper Japanese lady that we might become friends, she was horrified. She said, "I don't believe that you understand how impossible it is for me to be a friend of an American. I could not possibly have a friendship with an American, a citizen of a country that has demonstrated its barbarity in such stark terms as the bombing of Hiroshima and Nagasaki." She went on and on. I retaliated by saying that a nation that engaged in the rape of Nanking, the forced march of Bataan, and the slave-labor camps in Thailand was also barbaric. My insult of Japan so enraged her that I believe she really would have killed me had she been less restrained. However, she did not appear to mind working for the Americans, and I asked myself why. I suspected that beneath her icy exterior burned a hot hatred for Americans and that she found a vicious self-punishment in being close to the cultural and

Tomiko Kyoya was a classical Japanese lady but tormented by her nation's defeat in World War II. Ofuna, Japan.

political enemy. The next time I saw her, she had retreated behind politeness and was as courteous and professional as ever, sometimes consenting to have coffee or tea with me during the workday. Never once did she mention the encounter.

In her personal romantic tragedy and in her nation's downfall, Kyoya represented the Japanese concept of culpability and atonement, which includes the belief that ill fortune befalls us because of some flaw within ourselves, and that we must atone for these personal or collective failures. Years later, Kyoya married an American from Hell's Kitchen, seemingly the most objectionable choice of partner for a classical Japanese woman of her upbringing. This appeared to be such a harmful thing for her to do to herself that I believe she married him as atonement.

The 212th Military Police Company was stationed near Idogaya, a suburb of Yokohama where the servicemen and the community forged a cordial relationship. Any soldier from that unit who went astray for a few hours was sheltered in the village until he was ready to make it back to base. For our part, the company supported schools, orphanages, and other community activities. Despite Japanese authorities' hope that any cultural effect would be fleeting, Idogaya seemed a microcosm of the influence that uniformed Americans had on larger Japan—notably baseball and jazz. American jazz records, introduced by black soldiers, were played in coffee shops in Tokyo, Yokohama, and Yokosuka, where the music became popular among the younger Japanese. One of the first Japanese jazz musicians was Hideiko "Sleepy" Matsumoto, who had worked for an all-black Yokohama Port unit. Matsumoto was a male household servant, an employee called a houseboy in the terminology of the era. The black band members of the unit taught him music. Matsumoto became famous as a jazz saxophonist. I first heard him at one of the military-sanctioned nightclubs, playing with a Japanese band made up principally of black soldiers. Now some of the world's greatest jazz impresarios come from Japan. These include several women, notably Keiko Matsui.

American GIs, in turn, were avid consumers of Japanese classical arts. *Kabuki* and *Noh* were staple fare for many of us. Asian culture and philosophy became a central part of my life. I had been studying the Japanese language since my arrival and this helped unlock the culture for me. I studied Japanese painstakingly, making many mistakes, but that taught me tolerance. By studying the language, I developed the ability to listen intently. Usually we hear people talk, but instead of listening fully, we are preparing our response. I learned to listen to people and to try to respond thoughtfully to what I heard and saw. I also became acquainted with Japanese woodblock prints and masks.

Almost imperceptibly, avenues of learning opened before me, and teachers appeared in my life. Some were Americans; others were Japanese. I worked for Staff Sergeant James Howell Roland, a superb personnel specialist who became my mentor. He taught me the rudiments of public personnel management, accepted me as a colleague, and became an enduring friend. He also introduced me to Futaba Meike, an extraordinary woman from a traditional Japanese family. She was about thirty, well educated, serious, slender, tall for a Japanese woman—about 5 feet 9 inches—and rather theatrical. She had been married to a soldier of the Japanese Imperial Forces who was killed in the Pacific war, leaving her widowed with a young son named Kiyoshi. Futaba lived with her mother and younger sister, Noriko. The sisters worked in a large downtown Yokohama department store, which had been taken over by the

Eighth Army as an Army Exchange Store (a large PX). It was Futaba who first took me to the traditional Japanese theater. On Sundays, I would take an *obento*, lunch box, to *Kabuki* and stay for the all-day performances with intermissions for lunch and tea.

I studied the paintings of the Shinto religion and went with her into the temple to offer prayers and light incense on her ancestors' day. Japanese festivals took on a drama that I never would have seen were it not for Futaba. The first time I was at a Japanese tea ceremony, I thought it was like playing house; it was years before I saw that the depths of one's being are exhibited both candidly and subtly in the tea ceremony. Slowly I realized that partaking of tea mixed by my host is an honor, and the shape of the leaves, the rocks placed carefully in the tea garden and the message on the cup are all part of the service. The concept of beauty, too, was a revelation to me. I had been wearing blinders, but through the Japanese people I began to see beauty in everything: every birdsong and flutter of a balloon, and especially the beauty of the *bonsai*, dwarf trees. I learned that the beauty in flower arrangements is the beauty of the arranger. When a woman arranges flowers in a classic way, she presents a portrait of her heart and soul.

With Futaba as guide, I discovered the real Japan—totally different from what we uniformed people saw each day. I traveled extensively by train and bus to parts of Japan unknown to most Americans. I saw beyond the cosmopolitan glitter of Yokohama and Tokyo and into the countryside and the little villages. Every stop of the train or bus was a rest stop that included tea, buns filled with bean paste, and eggs boiled in hot mineral springs, all served with courtesy and small amenities, such as a warm towel from the mineral springs to wipe away the dust from hands and face. I began to understand the subtleties of the country, including Japan's intolerance of non-Japanese. Their historical experience with white people was largely limited to priests, missionaries, and sailors on merchant ships; it was a new experience to meet black people, and especially to have large numbers of black Americans constantly stationed in Japan. Since their sense of superiority extended to other Asians, all whites, and all blacks, they were intolerant of liaisons between black Americans and Japanese women. Futaba was a rarity. Like many other Japanese women, she did not see color. She saw me as a person, not as a black person, and considered me a valuable friend. I felt her respect for me, and for the first time in my life, I was acutely aware of the power of another person's perception. I was a young country bumpkin in a strange land, learning strange customs, both astounded and thrilled at the unfolding path of this adventure. Futaba was the first woman I knew closely, and she was an important part of my new life experience. I did not realize until years later how much she gave me, or how gently and how generously she guided me through Japanese culture and toward maturity.

This extraordinary woman taught me the concept of "face," which means that no one should take away any part of another person's dignity or worthiness. I learned from her that when we enhance a person and increase his "face," we then enhance ourselves. She said, "You cannot live if you take something away from me. I will be half naked." I heard that term often from her and from others as I began to understand the sense of balance in everyday life. I learned that every morning when I awaken to take on a new day and a new world, I see that day as the beginning of the rest of my life. I have an opportunity to do something for myself, but I can never do it for myself alone. I must add others—a sweetheart, a colleague at work, or even someone long departed, by burning incense at the shrine. This took me a long time to grasp.

In June 1950, troops from North Korea, a satellite of the Soviet Union at the time, crossed the Imjin River intent on conquering South Korea. President Truman asked the United Nations Security Council to intervene under chapter seven of the United Nations Charter, which meant using armed activity to stop the aggression and to return the aggressors to the status quo ante. Ordinarily the Soviet Union would have vetoed the resolution and the UN would have taken no action, but the Soviet Union was boycotting the Security Council, so its representative was not present to cast the veto. The Security Council quickly approved the resolution, and a UN force has been in Korea ever since. It is the largest UN force assembled since the inception of the United Nations in 1945.

When the Korean War began, I had about a month left to serve in the army. I was discharged on the eve of the deployment of my outfit to Korea. The 212th and the 25th Infantry Divisions were among the last deployment of all-black units. My unit, the 212th, would have a rough time in the war before the North Koreans were sliced up and pushed back across the Yalu River. General MacArthur wanted to go across the river and immobilize the armed capability of China, which was supplying armaments to North Korea, but President Truman saw the futility of a land war with China and forbade the action. General MacArthur skirted the order from his commander in chief, continued to call on the commanders of the Chinese armies to meet with him, and urged Congress to force Truman to authorize armed action against what MacArthur called "a godless nation." Ultimately, Truman was forced to fire MacArthur, so ending the career of a brilliant officer, a great tactician, and one of the youngest generals ever made. As supreme commander of Allied Powers Japan, MacArthur had nursed that country back to civility and stability, orchestrated a constitution that is still in place in Japan, and accomplished many good things, but he came to an end because he forgot that he was a servant of the government.

The radio bulletin of MacArthur's recall on April 11, 1951, hit Japan like the a lightning bolt. The news was broadcast over and over to the stunned nation, every radio account beginning, "MacArthur *Gensei,*" which means "Supreme Commander MacArthur." He left Japan on April 16, 1951, amid a hero's departure. Before he left, the emperor of Japan called on him at the embassy, a last gesture of supreme respect. He made the courtesy call because MacArthur had saved the institution of the emperor. Later I read that this was the eleventh call the emperor had made, but this time only, MacArthur did something he had never done before—he escorted the emperor to his car as a symbol of humanness. Here were two giants stepping down from their thrones to meet as men. I remember the newspaper picture of MacArthur walking across the tarmac at Haneda Airport to his official plane for this final trip. When he learned that President Truman had fired him, he called his wife and said, "Well, Jean, we're going home at last." I was only twenty-one and witnessing the end of a legend.

After I was mustered out of the army, I chose to remain in Japan and work as a civilian. I asked the military to delay my repatriation back to the United States and to permit separation in Japan, where I worked for a component of the Eighth Army. I was employed by the Maintenance and Supply Division of the Japan Central Exchange, an organization that operated post exchanges on military bases. My title was storekeeper, a glorified warehouseman, but it was another step toward the career that involved a life of travel and foreign ports in the service of my country.

The early 1950s were grand years for young black Americans to be in Japan. I enjoyed being immersed in a new culture, and I reveled in the freedom that I had not experienced in my own country. Once in Yokohama, a friend and I went into a bar frequented by U.S. military soldiers, and the madam refused to serve us because we were black. She feared that she would lose her white customers or that a fight would erupt between the white soldiers and us. I fetched a Japanese policeman and explained, in Japanese, that the woman wouldn't serve us. "What!" he said. "You cannot do that," he told her, and he closed the bar. She pleaded with him, and we compromised, asking the policeman not to shut the bar if she would agree to serve us. "May I have a beer?" I asked, and she practically stumbled over herself getting it for me. I have never been anywhere in the world where I have not come across racism in some form, but institutionalized racism was not the Japanese way, as reflected by the policeman's shocked reaction.

During the next three years in Japan, I continued to study the language and explore the subject of Asian philosophy. A colleague and I became acquainted with a small group of literary artists who enjoyed practicing their English with us. They were pleasant and personable, yet they exuded a profound sense of loss. Among the group was a young Japanese poet who dressed elegantly in the double-breasted suits of prewar fashion. He had sensitive eyes, thick black hair, and a suffering face I can see yet. His face bore the torment of all the world's grief, much of it wrought by the defeat of Japan by the United States and its allies, but I also saw something else in his expression. Occasionally, his grief seemed to lighten, and then his face would shine with the glimmer of hope. Everyone in Japan in 1950–52 was looking for a place to fit, because the world they had known was turned upside down. For centuries they had been members of a great fraternity headed by the emperor, safe in the security of their superiority. Now that national identity was gone, and they were asked to be individuals, leaving them emotionally adrift and far from shore. The poet was one who wore the loss physically, almost as visibly as if he had been seared by hot metal and come away with a white wound burned into his flesh. I came to see the Japanese—merchant, poet, girlfriend, or Shinto priest—as a people of solemnity. By looking inward, they could maintain individuality without leaving the clan. Their stoicism shrouded their tears and was a palliative for their souls. The lyrics of a Japanese song express this emotional conflict:

> Man was made to cry
> like raindrops from the sky.
> I cannot cry,
> but I cannot forget, either.[1]

Some students of contemporary Japan proclaim that a new Japan is emerging, combining individuality akin to that of robust American achievers with the ancient culture. I see a Japan that has been able to put a new culture under the wings of an old culture, but when the new does not enrich the national identity, it is expunged. I believe that Japan has emulated the West monetarily, socially, and politically when necessary to exist with the West, but that the nation's art is slowly reverting to prewar styles, shown by some modern Japanese jazz that features flutes, summoning the imagery of a soft night and bamboo swaying beside a lake.

One school of thought in foreign policy is that the U.S.-Japan relationship is as close as it will ever be. Although some believe Japan and the United States are blood allies, a stronger argument can be made that, in actuality, we are convenient allies.

The friends and artists I met showed me the literary world, the countryside, and the essence of Japan. They took me to Kamakura, an ancient classic city, where I became acquainted with the Great Buddha and its history. Tourists find Kamakura a colorful city, exquisite in spring under a canopy of cherry blossoms. Westerners rarely see the side of Kamakura where the history of Japan still breathes: Samurai ghosts stride in splendor, honored sacraments are stored, and one prays to be worthy of the ancestors. Kamakura is a place where a man, young or old, can enjoy an almost giddy pleasure from strolling along the streets with his girlfriend on Sunday, stopping in a *sakiya* to drink *sake* or share a meal. In Kamakura I stayed in little houses designed for weary travelers, not more than three or four rooms with a restaurant and a hot bath.

One weekend in Kamakura a Samurai's armor and sword were stolen from a little hotel where they had been on display. The news of the theft shook the city. Consternation rippled through the streets and jangled the citizenry. To compound the offense, someone had seen a uniformed American soldier taking the armor. I am sure he took it on a lark, much like a fraternity boy's prank. He did not understand the magnitude of the violation, which disrupted hundreds of years of harmony in Kamakura. After a frantic search of several hours, the sword and armor were found. With the return of the sacred items, all order was restored. This demonstrated to me that one lives in a set of order and behavior, and when that rhythm is disturbed, one's own life is disturbed.

I learned to appreciate the written Japanese language, which had adopted the classic Chinese language, then initiated two others, *Hiragana* and *Katakana*.

One is an enabling language of a classical nature and the other is a language for writing non-Japanese words, such as "baseball" and "beefsteak." Those weekends in Kamakura were geographical seminars to a young man from Portland, Oregon.

South of Kamakura lies an idyllic seaside and the city of Zushi. This was the home of Miura Teiko, of such a fragile beauty that she looked like a gardenia. She was a small woman in her early twenties, about 5 feet 2 inches tall, with a square face and oval eyes. Sometimes she wore a kimono, other times Western clothing. She loved walking on the beach in all kinds of weather. I called her the "Lass of the Water" because of how deeply she loved the water, the inlet, and the island. Although I did not know her long, she was the woman whose hand in marriage I came closest to asking for. That alliance was impossible because she was the most classical Japanese woman I knew and completely wedded to her traditional family. Of all my acquaintances in Japan, she was the least likely to ever marry a foreigner, but we were young, and there was something in the wind that I called love.

I met Teiko in Ofuna, the Hollywood of Japan at the time, where the movie studios were located. I was there on business, and with the brashness of my age, I asked her to dinner. As unlikely as it seemed, she agreed. Going out to dinner in that part of Japan was a pleasure of simplicity, which usually meant being the only guest at a small country inn and receiving lavish attention. After only a few meetings, I was convinced that I wanted to marry her. We spoke about it, she talked with her parents, and they said flatly, "Do not see him again." With that dictate, she attempted to disappear from my life, but I knew where she lived. I persuaded my friend Matthew Brown, a black American and a great Japanese linguist, to go with me to talk to her parents. "I think this is futile," he said. "You don't know Japan the way I know it. You are up against a typical Japanese family who want their daughter to have nothing to do with Americans, especially black Americans." I persisted, however, and we called on her mother and father. Teiko sat by silently, never saying a word. The mother spoke. "Do not bother our daughter again," she said. "You have violated her by leading her astray." The terrible meeting continued in this vein until we left. My friend said, "Forget it, Ed. There is no way she will disobey her parents." He was right. That was the end of our relationship. We corresponded for a while, but her letters were polite and distant, making no reference to our relationship. She wrote about Japan, flowers, her garden, her parents' health, her work, and the beauty of the sea. She neither offered nor invited any hope of resurrecting our relationship. When I met Teiko, I thought nothing and nobody could stand between me and a desired goal, but I had come up against a code that had been operational for five hundred years. I thought I could circumvent that code, but that was impossible. It was a lesson about limitations; it was a young man's lesson.

The Way of the Warrior

In Japan, I began to study Asian philosophy as an intellectual exercise, and it was as comfortable to me as fitting a key into a lock. I felt as if I had come home. I have continued the study to this day, and my understanding continues to unfold. Initially, I thought this was a uniquely Japanese philosophy, but I learned that it had come from India thousands of years ago and was adopted first by China and then by Japan in the ninth to twelfth centuries. The wisdom of Asian philosophy has been of benefit to me both personally and professionally. At first, I did not realize the full ramifications of what I was undertaking, but I was intrigued by the ancient warrior philosophy. As I began to learn more about the age-old Asian concepts of leadership, war, and peace, I discovered that this philosophy is more holistic than any others I have investigated. It embraces mind, body, and spirit. I came to know the "way of the warrior" as a way of personal discipline. The Samurai's task was to follow the eight dictates of the warrior's code: right belief, right thought, right speech, right conduct, right occupation, right effort, right mind control, and right meditation. This was the source of the early leadership that helped fashion modern Japan. The practitioner/warrior forgets the eight dictates at his peril. When I have forgotten these, I have suffered the consequences rather than learning from living.

Three principal books have guided me in the study: *The Art of War* by Sun Tzu (Master Sun), *The Book of Five Rings* by Miyamoto Musashi, and *Bushido: A Modern Adaptation of the Ancient Code of the Samurai* by Mark Edward Cody.

Sun Tzu wrote his classic work of combat theory more than two thousand years ago in China, incorporating precepts of economics, politics, and psychology. This book of martial strategy, arguably the first of its kind, became the fountainhead of Oriental military philosophy.

Musashi was the greatest Samurai, a writer, poet, painter, contemplative, and master swordsman who fought his first duel at age thirteen. When he felt he had mastered the art of killing, he became a hermit, isolating himself in a forest cave in 1645 at the age of sixty and writing his book of strategy. *The Book of Five Rings*, or *Go Rin No Sho*, is as relevant today as it was then.

While I was studying the Japanese language, especially the ideographic writing, a young woman gave me an English translation of a book about *Bushido*. *Bushi* means "warrior," and *do* means "way," so the word *Bushido* translates to "the way of the warrior." This was a valuable gift to a young American in a foreign country, a young man slouching through life. It shocked me into standing upright, and from that time on, I became a student of *Bushido*. This 400-year-old code of Samurai ethics emphasizes such principles as honor, courage, and loyalty. Originally written for feudal warriors, *Bushido* has wielded such a forceful influence throughout contemporary Japanese culture that it is characterized as the heart of the nation.

These three books, never far from my side, are weatherworn and filled with my marginal notations. I reread them every year because I believe the way of a person is always in the making.

My initial encounter with Asian philosophy began as a flirtation with *kendo*, sword fighting now done with lances. I considered this a romantic sport and became a superficial admirer and naïve student at one of Japan's many *dojos*, or *kendo* fencing schools. Although I studied it for a short while, I never mastered the art, but it introduced me to martial arts as the concept of spirituality of the whole being. In Asian philosophy, the intent of martial arts is not just to knock down the opponent, but also to comprehend life's circular nature. A warrior is an artisan, a poet, a farmer, a merchant, and a warrior—a circle of life.

In the *kendo* studios I was privileged to see old masters, men who seemed to be ninety years old, easily hitting the young swordsmen on the head and punching them in the stomach. It was as if the old men had the vision of several eyes. I realized that physical strength is but a small portion of one's true strength, which comes from within. When physical strength is combined with self-reliance and self-discipline, the spiritual self is activated. This is the true self, which the old masters call "the mighty strength" and which no adversary can overcome. If we can triumph over one person, Musashi has written, then we can triumph over ten thousand people, but the first opponent is oneself. One Sunday morning in Tokyo in 1954, a young Japanese houseboy presented me with a short-bladed *katana*. This Samurai sword, wrapped in silk, was a family heirloom a couple thousand years old. I then learned that the blade of a Samurai's sword is made of several layers of steel, polished and honed to such a sharp

edge that even the lightest touch cuts the skin. In the code of the Samurai, the
sword is never drawn until it is intended to kill. The sword is the soul of the
Samurai and the path toward moral teachings, which includes an awareness of
mortality and a sense of intent. I learned that the "way of the sword" is to never
be foolish, but rather to be purposeful in everything we do. A companion philosophy is the concept of "the pen and the sword." They go together. Like a
sword, a pen is a way to defend oneself, defend ideas, and defend the nation.
My craft is diplomacy, and it is my soul that allows me to believe in the work
that I am doing and to attempt to do that work with knowledge, wisdom,
mindfulness, and compassion.

It was years before I understood the value of the houseboy's gift. A sword is
a living thing and crafted with such care that a sword made a thousand years
ago looks as if it were made yesterday. Each blade has a life of its own and a history that is inserted into the handle. The handle of my ancient sword was empty
when I received it, and that was symbolic to me. It pointed to the void in my
knowledge, and I saw there was much I did not know. In that moment, I began
to understand there was another side to the sword. Much later, I realized that
before I could learn, I had to feel the need to learn, that I had to feel the need
for philosophy before I could study philosophy. I have studied it ever since. The
warrior code has been my career. I never saw the young man again, but I have
taken the *katana* to my posts around the world, and I keep it close to me. It represents a spirit of generations gone by, the best of the warriors, and the high
moral code by which they lived.

The book I have had longest is Musashi's *Book of Five Rings*. The "Fire Book"
section instructs the warrior to be careful, to be watchful and, when necessary,
to be fierce. Several quick sword cuts disable the body. In my work I apply that
to the value of learning different techniques of strategy. For a diplomat, that
means negotiation. The "Wind Book" is a collection of traditions with the message to study well and not forget the old as we try to see the new. The "Ground
Book" is about strategy; the "Water Book" is a discourse of the spirit, which,
like water, can fill any vessel; and the "Book of the Void" refers to a cycle without beginning or end and beyond human understanding. I try to live by the precepts in Musashi's five books of strategy, to control and understand myself. As
I began to incorporate this study into my life, I saw personal flaws that I might
never have seen before: how I treat people and how I evaluate them. In my
approach to challenges I saw fault lines that had prevented success. With every

disappointment, I learned to look at myself and realize, however reluctantly, what I must do to correct it. I began to understand the warrior's quest: "Today is victory over yourself of yesterday. Tomorrow is victory over lesser men." To achieve mastery over myself I must study continually, avoid slackening my efforts, and strive to keep fit my skills, my body, and my spirit. To me, practicing self discipline is a method of honoring the sacred gift of life.

I learned from reading Musashi that change is inevitable, and therefore we must be flexible and prepared to change as necessary. An old Japanese man told me, "Walk with meditation, and see all about you." That is wisdom.

From Musashi I learned to develop inherent mystical abilities and pay attention to what appears to be insignificant. Everything is important. Unless we know the smallest things, we will never know the biggest things. The shallowest can be the deepest. In diplomacy, this has been helpful to me in overcoming difficult objections to a course of action that might enhance the national interest. The purpose of these concepts is to win, to be successful, to achieve the highest of which one is capable. My copy of Musashi's book is now falling apart, and when I look back at the notes I have written in the margins, I see the slow progress of a young man's understanding. Over the years, I have written:

> Never be out-hustled by the dimwitted.
> Always see the approach of surprise and be prepared for it.
> Never let your enemies know what they have inflicted on you.
> Win over all else. Do not draw out the fight. Move quickly. Win quickly.

Humility is incorporated into the philosophy of the warrior's way. Sun Tzu combines the art of war with the art of peace, and these two concepts embrace a true appreciation of peace and humility. I have learned to be humble and to feel a sense of humility as I use myself in whatever I am doing. It is an ongoing practice, illustrating Musashi's observation, "Step by step, begin the thousand-mile road."

Patience is a lesson in Asian philosophy. "You cannot rush the bloom on the rose" is an adage that teaches us to be mindful of time and its proper flow.

Industriousness is another aspect of the warrior code, which may contribute to the perception that the Japanese are more industrious and work harder than other nationalities. In the context of *Bushido*, industriousness means more than busyness; it means teaching, learning, and not wasting time.

Bushido is the way of life for the Japanese from birth to death, enfolding one's spirit, corporeal body, and philosophy. It directs the way to learn, to approach art, to accept filial piety, to understand marriage, to be a member of community, to fight, to be loyal to the nation, and to embrace death. Acceptance of death is an essential part of the warrior code. The more we expect death as resolute, the more we see that our body is a temporary vessel for our spirit or soul and must go back to the earth. When we accept that, we are free of the things that hold us down. *Bushido* says that when we end the day, it is not necessary to have completed everything we set out to do, but we must be satisfied with everything we have done. Did I do anything foolish? Did I waste time? Did I hurt someone needlessly? If I can answer those in a positive way at the end of the day, then I should not fear death if it comes before I can start again the next day. When death comes, I hope to feel that I have completed my life. Until then, the important thing is to go to bed satisfied that I did the best I could for the day that is now ending.

The seminal teaching from Sun Tzu is that the essence of war is to win without fighting. That opened more lessons for me than I can recount. I learned the importance of vision and obedience. Moral, emotional, and intellectual qualities are essential. When I learned that the first step is knowing one's own weaknesses and strengths, I understood that a warrior fighting for a nation must understand the nation. To save a nation, we must first understand the nation. Mao Tse-tung proclaimed himself a student of Sun Tzu and referred to this principle when he advised his soldiers approaching a village, "Be a fish in the river when you are among the people. Swim among them, but do not harm them."

Sun Tzu, Musashi, and *Bushido* have been profound teachers for me. Every time I reread the books, I add notes that are important guidelines. *Bushido* teaches:

> Never being late for work is the way of the warrior.
> Be useful to your master or boss.
> Be respectful to your parents.
> Get beyond love and grief and use the best of charisma.
> One's strength lies in teaching and receiving.

And I wrote my definition of the way: "Here is meant living, learning, teaching, and experiencing. All front line. Each day. With full knowledge that the end is death, but fulfilled."

Every day I try to be alone with myself for a while and think about these lessons. In the morning, I normally wake up at 4 A.M. and have a half-hour before

I go to the gym. This is the time for meditation and to review my life or the previous day in the context of this philosophy. At the gym, exercise is a time for meditation. By exercising among people but not with people, I use my time for remembering and for strengthening my spirit. Spirit and body together are more powerful than my physical strength alone. This was especially true in South Africa. I needed every bit of my time there to review these principles because it was these principles that made it possible for me to do what I did in South Africa. I close the day with a review of what I did in light of these theories. I evaluate whether I am satisfied with my work that day. I cannot say that at the end of every day I feel I did the best I could, but I can say that I am better because of this discipline than I would have been without it.

The longer I stayed in Japan, the more seductive the lifestyle became. I was learning Japanese, I liked the culture, and I enjoyed the comfort; but I recognized the superficiality of my life in Japan. I had been promoted to a respectable position, but my job did not require me to work hard, so I saw my initiative begin to erode. I recognized, too, that without a college degree, advancement was limited in both the military and in the private sector. Several people were encouraging me to think about my future and continue my education. One was Frank Kopp, the company's comptroller, a friendly, no-nonsense man who spoke to me in a straightforward style.

"What do you want to do with your life?" he asked.

"I want to be in a position to make a difference." I answered. "I would like to be head of this outfit or something like it. And I'd like to be ambassador to Japan."

"If you stay here, you'll never make it," he said. "What are your plans?"

"I'm giving it some thought," I said. "Originally I thought I would stay here for a couple of years and then go back to a university in the States."

"Go back," he said. "This looks like a nice life, but it is all artificial. Go back and go to school." He told me what I had heard before: "You are a black person, so you have that strike against you. If you want to do anything with your life, then you have to complete your education and get a degree. You won't be able to succeed without higher education." Once again, I had heard the whisper of divine guidance from the mouth of a mortal. I took his advice, got on a

ship, went home to Portland, enrolled in college, and embarked on another
chapter of my life.

When I returned to the United States, I lost contact with Futaba, the woman
who had so much impact on my life in Japan. She never remarried; it was not
in the stars. Japanese widows of her era usually did not remarry. Many contemporary Japanese women are trying to achieve a more balanced sense of
equality, but in Futaba's day—from the end of the war until about 1952—
Japan was remaking itself socially, politically, and economically. Japanese citizens like Futaba and her sister were caught up in the occupation activities. After
that, Japan found itself a new nation with old habits, and the people had to find
a new way of existing. Years later on a consultation trip to Okinawa, I phoned
Futaba. She did not come to Tokyo to meet me, but as an honor in the Japanese
tradition, she sent her son to greet me in the name of the family. He was now
a young man out of college. "I have come to represent my mother," he said.
"Her heart is too full to come herself. My mother sends her respects and her
regards and told me to stay with you as long as you need me." I was almost
reduced to tears when he said that. He and I had dinner at an elegant hotel in
Tokyo, and when he took his leave, I sent my greetings to his mother. I have not
heard from either of them since.

THE FEW. THE PROUD.

And so I sailed home and enrolled in college in Portland. I disagree with Thomas Wolfe about not being able to go home again. If we can't go home, where can we go?

My 1953 application to Lewis and Clark College included a list of books I had read recently: *An American Tragedy* by Theodore Dreiser, *The Fountainhead* by Ayn Rand, *A Generation of Vipers* by Philip Wylie, *The Prophet* by Kahlil Gibran. It further stated that my career goal was "international affairs," because I had some murky notion of a career in the Foreign Service. Lewis and Clark accepted the college credits for courses I had taken at the University of California campus in Japan, so I did not feel like a raw freshman. Since World War II, returning GIs had been a familiar sight on college campuses, and I was part of that tradition.

I began studying political science and economics under the tutelage of Dr. U. G. Dubach, a brusque, aristocratic Missourian who was head of the political science department. He challenged me intellectually and pushed me to achieve. When I had trouble mastering economic theory, he pushed me even harder. He had no sympathy for anyone not working up to his or her ability. "You've got the means to go all the way," he told me, "so do it. You have to prepare yourself to do something for your people."

I was not convinced, and one day I confided my uncertainty to the president of Lewis and Clark College. "I'm not sure that I'm studying the right thing," I told him. He replied with wisdom I have never forgotten: "I graduated thirty years ago," he said, "and I'm still not sure I made the right decision. What I'm telling you is this: You will never know with certainty. If you ever do get to the place where you are confident that you made the right decision, you will not continue to search and seek out other avenues that might have been, and that search is what makes life worth living."

I had high-flying academic ambitions, but they exceeded my grasp at that age. I lasted only a year at Lewis and Clark.

Now Portland seemed smaller than I remembered it. I went to college during the day, worked in the evenings, traveled about the state on weekends, joined the Urban League, and did community work, but I was dissatisfied with this life. I could not see a rewarding future. Exacerbating the situation was my living arrangement. I had returned to the home of my mother and stepfather, and this felt stifling to a young man who had tasted the freedom of foreign shores. Like most mothers, especially black mothers, mine worried about my plans for marriage. When I again began dating Inez, divorced and with a young son, my mother's protectiveness transformed her into Hera, the ferocious mother-goddess of Greek mythology. "You cannot start your life with this heavy burden," my mother admonished, and she conspired with well-meaning matrons to introduce me to eligible young women. She was chagrined at my rebellious lack of cooperation.

In my eyes, Portland had become provincial, but in truth, I was obsessed with a different kind of life and this fueled my restlessness. I talked with friends and fellow students about my frustration. One confidant was John Arten, an American Indian who believed that the Christian religion had been used to subjugate the Indians. He castigated the Bible with slicing sarcasm. "Bibles are for sale," he said. "Salvation is guaranteed." John died of alcoholism, but some said he grieved to death over the injustice to his people. My closest friends were Joan and Don Palmer. He was a former marine who had fought against the Chinese in the Battle of Chosin Reservoir during the Korean War. Fighting under cruel winter conditions, those troops became known as the "Frozen Chosin." Palmer had lost three toes to frostbite at Inchon Landing, which forced him to take a medical retirement from the Marine Corps. He was tough, lean, intellectual, and he was first and foremost a marine. I heard pride and reverence in his voice when he spoke of the Marine Corps and its high standard of discipline.

I left college determined to break free of my hometown and to find a life of adventure. With cocksure boldness and a flash of derring-do, I announced my plan: I would join the French Foreign Legion. I had read *Beau Geste* and was caught up by that romantic notion of male adventure. The French Foreign Legion proclaimed itself to be the best fighting force in the world. Legionnaires trained hard, lived hard, and fought hard. The promotional pamphlets emphasized loyalty, duty, and honor to fellow legionnaires. I longed to be part of such a highly disciplined outfit that would bring me to task and imbue me with steely self-discipline.

Luckily, the gods who watch over young fools were vigilant. The oath of allegiance for the French Foreign Legion had to be taken on French soil, and the French consul told us that the nearest port was Le Havre, France. Although I completed the paperwork, I could not afford the fare to France. If I'd had the money, I would have found myself in the French Foreign Legion fighting the Vietnamese.

As my misty dreams of service in the French Foreign Legion evaporated into the ether, I remembered Don Palmer's tales of the Marines. Providence guided me to join the United States Marine Corps, and at last my life began falling into place.

After passing the examination, I was sent to San Diego for ten weeks of training at the Marine Corps Recruit Depot, and there I entered a world I never knew existed. Nothing—neither anything Don Palmer told me nor my own experiences in the army—prepared me for the Marine Corps.

I was the only black among about twenty recruits from the West Coast who arrived at San Diego. I expected that we would be told to eat, wash, get a good night's sleep, and be prepared to start training first thing in the morning. I could not have been more wrong. Hazing began as soon as we entered the depot reception center. We were issued shaving gear and soap, and then we were taken to the mess hall where we tried to eat amid a cacophony of planned pandemonium. The drill instructors shouted that the Marine Corps was on its last leg if people like *us* tried to join. If the corps had to take *us*, they yelled, it was in dire straits. From the outset, they told us straightforwardly that the goal was to strip a recruit of any semblance of his past life and to create a new person. We were lowly recruits, they reiterated, and only if we survived these ten weeks of boot camp would we be entitled to call ourselves marines. We were given the work uniforms of recruits and ordered to keep the top button of our blouse buttoned at all times. Furthermore, we had not yet earned the right to wear our trousers bloused at boot top in classic marine style. Those were privileges to be earned by only the few who successfully graduated.

That first night, far into the early morning hours, we learned how to make beds the marine way; we were put through drills with mental games; and we were stripped of extraneous materials we had brought with us. I had a book of poems by Edna St. Vincent Millay. The drill instructor picked up this book and held it as scornfully as if he'd discovered a lace handkerchief among the gear. "Who does this belong to?" he asked.

I raised my hand and he called me over.

"Do you read this?" he asked.

"Yes, I do."

"Yes, I do, *what?*" he shouted.

"Yes, I do, *Sir.*"

His eyes raked me with repulsion, and then he dropped the book into the trash barrel. It was part of the psychological warfare being played that night, and he would have reacted the same to any book.

It was a rigorous night. About 2:00 or 3:00 A.M. we were told to hit the racks, but we were up again at 5:00 A.M. reveille. "What have I gotten myself into?" I asked myself. I realized I had two options. I could quit, or I could make it. If I quit, I knew that I would be lost. I was determined to succeed and vowed that nothing they could do would overcome me.

After a night of harassment and mental games, we were a ragtag bunch when we marched to the mess hall for breakfast.

Marching alongside us in crisp uniforms the DIs shouted, "Why are you here? You should quit."

Probably because I was the tallest recruit, one of the DIs stomped on my foot. "Does that hurt?" he shouted. I didn't answer, so he asked again, "Does that hurt, boy?"

I think I answered in the negative. "No, what?" he shouted. "The word is 'sir.' You are lying, boy. Does that hurt?"

I said, "Yes, Sir," and he said, "You think you are a marine and *that* hurt!"

We were given ten minutes for breakfast—not enough time, and not enough food. There was never enough food during boot camp. I was never so hungry in my life as during my weeks of instruction. That was part of the training.

The next ten weeks were a blur of mental and physical exercise, but I soaked it up. We spent half of the time in school; through the other half we engaged in rigorous physical activities. Boot camp was a trial of fire, flame, and inferno. For all recruits, the persistent message pounding through every day's training was: You are not good enough to be a marine.

It is, indeed, hard to measure up to the historic ideal that is a marine. A grizzled master sergeant told us an old Marine Corps joke. When this elite band

was formed at Tuns Tavern in Philadelphia in 1775, the first marine recruited
was told to wait until others arrived. Finally a second man appeared, took the
oath and sat beside the first recruit.

"Who are you?" asked the first.

"I'm a marine," the second replied.

"Ah," the first one sneered, "you should have seen the *old* Marine Corps."

The Marine Corps believes that intellectual soldiers make the best soldiers,
so training was both intellectual and physical. I had not expected the intellectual challenges to be so intense. The sign over the training room office
reminded us that all training was for combat. In class, we learned about the history of the Marine Corps and the history of the United States. The Marine
Corps was extraordinarily concerned with citizenship and the role of the citizen in a democracy. We studied the U.S. Constitution and the role of the military in a just society. For the first time, I began to see the Constitution as a
living document, crafted by and for the people of the nation. Outside the classroom, I heard another marine talk about what it means to be a marine defending that Constitution and the Republic for which it stands. Then I realized that
all the security afforded me as a citizen and as a black American rests on the
strong shoulders of that Constitution. Until then, the "Star-Spangled Banner"
and the "Marine Corps Hymn" had been songs. Now when I heard them, they
unfolded over me like a protective canopy.

I read about great warriors, generals, and military strategists: Clausewitz,
Marshall, Montgomery, Patton, and Sitting Bull. I heard my first discussion of
Karl Marx's major work, *Das Kapital,* in those training sessions. In between
classes, we learned how to kill people.

The drill instructors were merciless, but they were not racists. Never once did
I come across anything indicating racism. The black DIs were even tougher than
the others. The first day of training, the DIs gave a race-relations lecture. A
marine from Oklahoma told us that the Marine Corps abhorred racists and that
anyone discovered persecuting another because of skin color, religion, or ethnic
origin would be kicked out. "The Marine Corps does not tolerate that," he said.
I was shocked, because until 1945 the Marine Corps had accepted very few
blacks. When I entered the corps, only half a dozen officers were black, and none
were generals. It would be thirty years before the first black was made general.

During my training, the Supreme Court handed down the *Brown v. the Board
of Education* decision. Except for one other man, my platoon consisted of white

Texans. When the decision was announced, one of the Texans shook his head and said, "It will never be accepted."

"It's the law of the land," I said.

"I don't care," he said. "It will be the Civil War all over again." Even this landmark case was but a momentary diversion for us; we were too busy learning to be marines and trying to survive training.

Early in boot camp we were marched off to a swimming pool and separated into those who could swim and those who could not. The swimmers were taken to the shallow end of the pool for additional instruction. We non-swimmers were taken to the deep end.

"I can't swim," I said to the senior swimming instructor, a black marine as big and as tall as I.

"It's a known fact that anybody can float," he said, "and if you can float, you can swim. Don't be afraid. I want to see whether or not you can float. There are some things that militate against your being able to float. One is fear. The other is a failure to obey the rules. These are the rules: I want you to jump into the pool. Remember that if you sink, you will come back to the surface. When you come up, keep your eyes open. If you keep your eyes open, I will pull you out with this bamboo pole, but if your eyes are closed, I will push you back in."

For a second, I refused to jump. "If you don't jump," he said, "we'll throw you in." I had never been in a swimming pool in my life, but I jumped. As I expected, I sank. When I came gasping to the surface, my eyes were closed. I opened them and, mercifully, the bamboo pole was right above me. I reached for it, but he yanked it away. I went down again and when I surfaced he shouted, "I told you to keep your eyes open!" I went down a third time and when I came up, my eyes were still closed. "Keep your eyes open!" he ordered as he pulled the pole away again. A fourth time I went down, and this time when I came up, I did not look for the pole; I instinctively began paddling. When I reached the side of the pool, he was standing there laughing. "I told you that you could swim," he said.

I was determined to succeed despite my fears. As a marine recruit and throughout my career, the hunger for knowledge drove me to take chances, perhaps even to recklessness. It also buoyed me from the bottom of the pool to the surface. Learning to swim in the Marine Corps was a turning point in my life. I sank four times, but in the end, I swam.

I managed to get through the San Diego training and was graduated with my training platoon, except for the three or four who washed out. After ten weeks, I was in top shape, mentally and physically. At 6 feet 2 inches and 215 pounds, I felt better and had more confidence than I ever had in my life. My body had changed, my face had changed, and I walked with a spring in my step. The Marine Corps brought out attributes, physical and mental, that I did not know I had in me. The morning of graduation, when the instructor said, "Unbutton your collars," our pride radiated over us like heat waves above the sand. We were physically and psychologically exultant when the senior drill instructor walked down the line saying to each of us, "Congratulations, Marine." We had succeeded, we had proved ourselves, and we were now part of the best.

The lessons I learned in the Marine Corps have stayed with me from that day. I have applied these skills in everything I have done: continuing my education, pursuing a diplomatic career, and joining an institution of higher education. Those attributes, cemented within my character as solidly as bricks mortared into a wall, include:

* PRIDE. I learned the difference between false pride, which is founded on shaky ground, and pride in being a marine, which was the belief that we could overcome any obstacle that came our way. This translates into authentic pride in self.

* SELF-DISCIPLINE COUPLED WITH COOPERATION. Marines who are loners get killed. Marines who can cooperate with fellow marines live to fight another day. Self-discipline begins with getting up on time rather than sleep, because the day stretches before us laden with opportunity to do, to learn, and to accomplish.

* GOOD GROOMING. Marines pride themselves on dressing well, either for combat or for a stroll in the park. Good grooming includes personal hygiene, pressed clothes, shined shoes, and appropriate dress for each occasion. When one looks good, one feels invincible.

* CONTINUED EDUCATION. All learning is for combat. A well-educated marine makes a good marine. We were encouraged to read and to take classes and correspondence courses. The Marine Corps taught me to consider education a necessity for developing and maintaining a strategic advantage in everything I do. To not continue one's education shows no respect for self.

* PREPARATION. I learned the value of preparing for a task, whether it

was training for a mock battle or planning for a business meeting, in minute detail. Machiavelli wrote in *The Prince* that the most critical undertaking for a head of state was preparation for battle. The Marine Corps feels the same way.

★ RESPECT. I learned true courtesy. The Marine Corps puts a premium on respect for others—respect for fellow marines, citizens, and other nationalities. If one does not have respect for others, one cannot respect oneself. Without respect for others, one cannot know others. If one does not know them, how can one beat them in battle or influence them in a boardroom? It is a practical philosophy for first-class warriors.

★ PHYSICAL AND MENTAL FITNESS. A good marine must be in optimum condition, physically and mentally. The purpose of the Marine Corps is to fight. Every marine—cook, typist, or rifle carrier—has to be ready to fight and ready to die. Life is heightened when fighting and dying are the bookends of a personal philosophy.

I came out of the Marine Corps at age thirty with a sense of adventure embedded in my soul. Every day of my life since then I have awakened with a sense of anticipation that something exciting was going to happen that day. I hope to feel that way all of my life.

Historically, the Marine Corps was the most hard-core segregationist of the armed forces. It assumed that nonwhites, and especially blacks, could not measure up to its high standards. Neither was it willing to challenge the conventional customs of society, such as segregation in small towns where military units were located. In 1946–47, when black marines were proposed for assignment to a base near Weatherford, Oklahoma, the commander of that base made an impassioned plea to the commandant not to send black marines. Civilians visiting the base would object so strenuously to being questioned or searched by a black marine standing guard, he said, that a racial incident would ensue. The commander prevailed, and no black marines were sent to Oklahoma at that time. A base near San Francisco was then considered, and that base commander also wrote the commandant relaying the protests of the chic, upscale community. The presence of black marines on leave, the citizens argued, would threaten the high-class tourism of the community. Black marines were not sent to California, either. Next, a Massachusetts base rejected the proposal. Finally, a Pennsylvania base accepted black marines. So did one small base outside New York City, with the provision that buses transport them to places where they could socialize with black females. Some of the strongest opposition to black marines came from well-educated generals and colonels. An old black sergeant told me of standing in formation at Camp LeJeune, North Carolina, where the commandant looked at the smattering of black marines and said, "I know that we are in a war when I see you people in my Marine Corps."

When I joined the Marine Corps in 1954, this rigidity was slowly disappearing; still I rarely saw a black officer. Black marines were not encouraged to try for the academy or for Officer Candidate School. After I had been in the Marine Corps about three years, I set a goal for myself of attending the U.S. Naval Academy and took the tests and passed them. However, according to the rules of the time, I would have been too old to be commissioned when I finished the necessary training at the prep school in Bainbridge, Maryland, so I was taken out of consideration for the academy. The one hurdle I was unable to overcome in the Marine Corps was the age limit of being admitted into the academy.

Korea, Again

From San Diego, I went to Camp Pendleton, California, for Fleet Marine Training, which means advanced infantry training for "duty beyond the seas." In those days, that was the official nautical term for going to Korea to fight in the Korean War. In 1954, I was sent to South Korea to join the well-decorated First Marine Division and I was assigned as a rifleman to George Company, Third Battalion of the Fifth Marines, a famous outfit with a distinguished record of heavily fought battles.

I returned eagerly to Korea, anxious to test myself in battle, but I never saw combat. A cease-fire had been announced, and there were no more skirmishes, only an uneasy peace. I went on only one patrol to the Demilitarized Zone, but the North Korean force did not appear. During the year I was stationed in Korea, I did not fire a shot in anger. Years later when I went to the 38th parallel as U.S. Ambassador to the United Nations and viewed the demarcation between the two Koreas, I looked through binoculars across No Man's Land

and saw North Korean soldiers patrolling the demarcation line and looking at me through binoculars, just as I had seen them some thirty years earlier when I was there as a marine.

For the first few months in Korea I managed a small club for the company, which entailed keeping plenty of beer in stock for the troops. Bob Hope, often in Korea entertaining the troops, was a welcome face from home for us military personnel who were unable to see family or friends on holidays.

When I was transferred to an investigation unit, I embarked on one of the most fascinating assignments I have ever had. This unit dealt with the seamier side of life in a war zone where people were under great stress, and the ordinary rules of civilized behavior were in abeyance. The valuable life lesson that I learned from this experience is the reality of life that lies beyond the policy book and the manual. My responsibilities included investigating line-crossings of people infiltrating from North Korea, tracking AWOL marines (which was the closest I came to having my brains blown out by a .45 pistol), investigating rape cases involving uniformed personnel, and serving as amateur marriage counselor for marines and sailors having domestic problems with their Japanese wives and in-laws.

My assignments were wide-ranging. Early one morning I was sent to investigate the site of a fatal accident where a bus, full to overflowing with Korean passengers, had overturned, killing many of them. I had not expected to be so affected by the death of people.

Another case involved the contraband section in our outfit, which seized illegal narcotics, liquor, watches, and other goods. Once we found a cache of Sapporo, a brand of Japanese beer, and we drank it with relish.

One of my strangest assignments was helping to supervise the health of female camp followers. The commanding general took the realistic viewpoint that because women were going to be present around the troops, he wanted to ensure that they were healthy so the men did not contract venereal disease. The unofficial policy was that all women in the First Marine Division area had to report every two weeks for a medical examination by the division doctor and carry a health card. I have never seen anything to parallel this pragmatic but unorthodox policy, which was tantamount to sanctioning prostitution. When the head of our detachment succumbed to the charms of one of the women, he exempted her from the medical requirement. When he contracted a venereal disease he was stupefied until he had his girlfriend followed and discovered that she had another boyfriend, a Korean major. The woman was expelled from the area and lost her means of livelihood.

In my job of investigating criminal activities, I dealt with a case of narcotics trafficking within the First Marine Division. I had just joined the outfit when the commanding general's chief steward, a black master sergeant, reported that he suspected drug trafficking within the general's mess groups—the cooks and stewards, most of whom were black. Because I was new and unknown, I was assigned to the mess. Only two people knew I was there undercover, the commanding general and the chief steward. Only later did I realize what a risky assignment I had undertaken. After I had infiltrated the group for two months, I was removed and it was raided. It was a Korea-wide drug ring run by a technical sergeant in the U.S. Marine Corps who almost got away with the crime. He had been transferred back to the United States and was on the ship ready to depart. We knew that he was transporting a large shipment of heroin, but we could not find it and the ship had raised anchor. Then the agent assigned remembered that the sergeant always had two cameras with him. A shipboard search revealed that the cameras were hollow and filled with heroin. The sergeant was arrested at sea, turned over to federal authorities in San Francisco, convicted, and sentenced to a lengthy term.

Another investigation was a murder case involving two friends, marines from Baltimore. One of them apparently committed suicide on Christmas Eve, but just as the case was about to be closed, another agent expressed doubt. Further investigation disclosed that the dead marine had married his buddy's girlfriend. Under interrogation, the surviving marine confessed. "Goddamn it, he took my girl and it didn't mean anything to him. He always got whoever he wanted." They were drinking when the old animosity erupted. The jilted marine shot his friend with an M1 rifle, and almost succeeded in making it appear to be suicide.

In my work with the Korean National Police Force and the Korean Military Forces I learned dozens of ways to get people to talk during interrogations. I never dreamed that a human could conceive of such inhumane ways of extracting information. Nor had I comprehended how much punishment a human could take. I saw how some humans acting as agents of a country could carry out their mission not in accord with goodness of human character. It was a sobering look at man's capacity for brutality.

In 1955, the cease-fire was signed, the draw-down of the First Marine Division began, and I was sent directly to Hawaii, where my life would take yet another unexpected turn.

HAWAII

I was assigned in garrison to the Naval Ammunition Depot at Lua Lua Lei, an arsenal near Honolulu. This ammunition depot and nuclear-weapons storage facility was under the executive control of the U.S. Navy and under the security control of the U.S. Marine Corps. I was required to stand watch only about once a week. The rest of the time I trained and enjoyed almost unlimited privileges. This undemanding tour of duty on the tropical island of Oahu left me uneasy. I have always been uncomfortable with inactivity.

To counter the temptation of idleness, I set myself on a rigorous reading regime. I arranged with the base librarian to regularly order interlibrary loan books from the Library of Hawaii. Every week, a new shipment of books arrived for my use: *The Fall and Decline of the Roman Empire*, the Greek philosophers (Plato, Cato, Epictetus), and similar works. I spent the next fourteen months reading the classics. The more I read, the more interesting life became.

The rest of the time, I immersed myself in the history of Hawaii and discovered the spiritual culture of the island of Oahu. I became acquainted with the old Hawaiian men who played checkers in Kapiolani Park in midtown Honolulu. They talked to me about their history and the ancestors who had come across the waves, paddling canoes by moonlight and navigating by the stars. They told me about their gods and the *Menehunes*, the mythical "little people" of Hawaii. According to legend, the fairy race of *Menehunes* was the first to inhabit the islands, and it was they who planted the lush fauna and flora. It is believed that these shy folk ride on the backs of seagulls, protect ordinary mortals, and come out only at night to do good deeds.

In Hawaii's mountains, daylight disappears as quickly as if a great velvet curtain were pulled across the sun. Then, in the abrupt cloak of darkness, magic seems released from the night. One of the posts at Lua Lua Lei was halfway up Koli Koli Mountain. Japanese planes had flown over the mountain near Koli Koli Pass on their way to bomb Pearl Harbor in 1941. One Sunday morning as I was standing guard at this isolated post, a woman drove up. She was a *haole* woman, a white woman, and she said, "I grew up here and part of my spiritual life is here." She began to tell me the story of Koli Koli Pass, where the ancient gods reside, and of Sacrifice Rock. This huge platform of stone is a legendary landmark where Hawaiian warriors supposedly sacrificed young maidens to appease the gods. In the 1930s, the U.S. Army engineers building the pass utilized a bulldozer to shove this enormous rock down into the valley. According to legend, the next day they returned to find Sacrifice Rock in its original position. Again they pushed it down the mountain, and again it made its way back up. The engineers did not touch the rock again. "This is a sacred place," the *haole* woman said. "The gods are here and they watch over us. The ghosts of these maidens walk this valley all the time. The legends of Hawaii are wise, and I believe them."

Standing sentry duty one evening as twilight closed on this mystical place, I felt a presence join me in the guard booth. I thought I saw the *Menehunes* inside the booth, not threatening me but cavorting to music. I must have been in a trance-like stupor. Then they vanished as quickly as they had appeared. Reason told me it was my imagination, until I shared this experience with some of the old Hawaiians I had come to know.

"Was my mind playing tricks on me?" I asked.

"Boy," one old man said, nodding sagely, "the *Menehunes* were protecting you. I know you think that is not possible, but how do you know? Reason goes a long way, but it reaches its limit. They were there," the old-timers nodded sagely. "The *Menehunes* were there to take care of you."

Another marine had a similar experience, but without the benevolence I felt from the spirits. I was sergeant of the watch that evening when the marine called from a post deep in the jungle area, a booth on stilts.

"Sergeant," he said, "somebody is out there." He could not see them, he said, but he could hear them. I told him to call back if he sensed it again. Five minutes later, my phone rang again.

"They are here," he said, his voice wobbling with panic. "Somebody is here. I think they're coming to get me."

"Get hold of yourself," I said. "Look, you are armed and you are in a tower. Nobody can get at you." But he was so frightened, he would not stay. He ran all the way back, some two miles. We could never get him to return to that post.

Life in Hawaii was not all light duty, self-study, and skirmishes with the little folk. For entertainment, my colleagues and I went deep-sea fishing, hunted for boar with bow and arrow, toured the erupting volcano on the Big Island, retraced the trek from Southby Island to the Pacific Islands, enjoyed recreational excursions to Doris Duke's palatial estate, explored the islands with James Michener's historic novel as my guidebook, and engaged in hard training. With Robert Ward from Oklahoma, I became an accomplished party crasher along Waikiki Boulevard in Honolulu. With complete aplomb, we were one white marine and one black marine in aloha shirts, sampling free food and drink and mingling easily with the invited guests.

On duty, I gained the reputation of being a polite marine, which brought me to the attention of the commanding officer. Standing guard at the front gate, I was extraordinarily nice to the officers' wives visiting the area. I commented on how nice they looked, remembered them from previous visits, and made small talk about the weather. I paid attention to them and soon found myself being cited by the commanding officer for extraordinary courtesy. I then was promoted. It taught me these lessons: people want to be noticed; it does not cost anything to say nice things; people will reciprocate. Just as my tour was about to end, this commanding officer recommended me for extended duty and transfer to Japan, which is what I wanted, but I could not have achieved it without his assistance.

I learned that the U.S. presence in Hawaii was one of conflicted history. During World War II, the racial values of the white mainland occasionally clashed with the nonwhite status of Hawaiian men. A cause célèbre was the murder of a young Hawaiian singer who fell in love with the wife of a white naval officer. When they were discovered, she claimed rape, and the naval officer killed the young man. The establishment was bent on hushing up the incident rather than meting out punishment to the officer. It almost caused a race riot in Honolulu before he was court-martialed and sentenced. In the culture of that era, the Navy corps of officers was outraged that the Navy would court-martial one of its own for the murder of a *kanaka*, a non-white person.

Some remnants of that racism still existed when I was stationed there. I first heard the word *kanaka* uttered in contempt by a white sergeant; the word is akin to "nigger." Several marines were Hawaiians, and one of these was arguably the best marine I ever met. All marines are well dressed, but he took it an extra mile. Despite his professionalism, he lived on a personal precipice of rage. He and the white sergeant who had uttered the pejorative word *kanaka* collided in a mental battle royal. The sergeant had his own simmering anger which alcohol unleashed. If they had not been separated, one surely would have killed the other.

When Hawaii became the fiftieth state in 1959, a young Hawaiian man told a mainlander white man, "Now we are the same as you. We are white, too." His comment encapsulated years of pent-up frustration at being considered second-class citizens and the overwhelming domination of the American defense establishment in Hawaii—the island of Oahu, Pearl Harbor, Waikiki Recreation Center, Schofield Barracks, and the continuous presence of uniformed people. I filed away in my memory what Hawaii taught me about native peoples under the rule of a minority race. It was a lesson I would need in the Foreign Service.

Despite the Marine Corps' reluctance to accept blacks and women into its ranks, my service as a marine was one of the most enriching experiences I have ever had. Inside the Marine Corps, the rules of the game were 95 percent performance. Anyone who could perform was considered a marine first and a black second. I applaud the Marine Corps for maintaining a tough, disciplined, and living esprit de corps based upon a sense of comradeship that is essential in a fighting unit. It is one of the best things I ever did with my life. In my experience, every marine, black or white, will stand up and say the same thing, which is a monumental accomplishment for a regimented outfit to instill in a group of men and women. Years later, after my retirement from the Foreign Service, I mentioned my service in the Marine Corps while giving a speech in Florida. Afterward, one man approached me and said, "I just want to shake your hand, Mr. Ambassador. *Semper fi.*" Then he turned and walked away. That is the comradeship that prevails among marines.

Marines strive to carry proudly the banner of the legends—the fighting servicemen of Mexico, Italy, North Africa, Korea, and Vietnam. That mantle weighs heavy on the shoulders of every marine, and the longer one stays in the corps, the heavier becomes the burden of proving that one is worthy of being a

marine. I found my fascination with the legacy growing into near obsession.
The four years I spent in the Marine Corps were intense, with extraordinary
physical and mental challenges. My life was forever influenced with self-discipline and the will to achieve against all odds. An old master sergeant who had
been with the horse marines in China taught tactics when I was training at
Camp Pendleton. "When you finish your training," he told us, "you will be so

In Japan as a marine, I was
assigned to an investigative
unit, one of the most fascinating
assignments I have ever had.
My official photographer was
sailor Thomas J. Rittenhouse
from Litutz, Pennsylvania.

well trained that someone can give you an order to 'Take that hill!' You may know that you will die as soon as you get up there, but even as you are thinking this, you will already be up there." There is no evaluation for what being in uniform meant to me, both in the U.S. Army and in the Marine Corps. I credit those two experiences as crucial to the making of the man I am. They are priceless. I came out of the Marine Corps thinking those four years were the best educational experience I ever had. I still feel that way.

In 1956 I was transferred to the Marine Corps Barracks at Yokosuka Naval Base in Yokosuka, Japan. I spent the next eighteen months there and in Yokohama, Zushi, and Kamakura, assigned to an investigative unit in the barracks, investigating the misdemeanors of marines, sailors, and other U.S. Forces personnel. I traveled extensively, continued my study of Japanese language and culture, and felt myself being pulled inexorably back into the spiritual world of Japan. The marines in the barracks dubbed me "Professor" because I always carried a briefcase full of books and papers. I took my discharge in Yokosuka in 1958. Once again I chose to become a civilian employee on foreign shores—in Taiwan. What awaited me there was a double rendezvous with destiny. One was the Foreign Service. The other was Lucy Cheng-mei Liu.

TAIWAN

THE BEAUTIFUL ISLAND

When I arrived in Taipei in 1958, the city was as rowdy as San Francisco in the 1800s. People poured into the city by the thousands, most from Mainland China. Taipei lies tranquil in a valley overlooked by misty peaks, but the poetic geography was deceptive. Up close, the capital city was alive around the clock with a gaudy nightlife of clubs, brothels, gambling, and Chinese theater. Day and night, the streets were choked with merchants on foot and in drawn carts. I became a devotee of the food carts—noodles from one cart, shrimp from another, and fried fish from a third. The aroma of the foods, the clatter of the carts, and the hawking calls from the peddlers jangled the air.

Like a beautiful woman hiding her grief under excessive makeup, the city's festivity covered a more serious mien. Like most foreigners, I first knew the island as Formosa, from the Dutch name *Ilha Formosa*, "beautiful island." The Taiwan I met was indeed beautiful, but troubled. It was a country still rocked by a decade of tumultuous political tension and bloodshed. Although it had prospered as a Japanese colony, the country longed for independence.

I was posted to Taiwan when Dwight Eisenhower was president and U.S. foreign policy in Southeast Asia was changing. After its defeat in World War II, Japan lost its colonial territories, and Taiwan reverted to Chinese control under Chiang Kai-shek. The U.S. foreign policy was that colonial peoples were entitled to self-determination and a chance to express what political status they wanted, but that policy was not applied to Taiwan. Nobody wanted to cross Chiang or "China Inc.," which meant Madame Chiang and her wealthy siblings and associates.

In the eyes of the outside world, Chiang had emerged over the previous decade as the most promising leader of China, overshadowing Mao Tse-tung, who was the more popular leader among the people of Mainland China. Chiang was the darling of some of the American press, Republican political leaders, and a powerful U.S. organization known as the Committee of One Million. In truth, he was a controversial figure and little more than a warlord. Still, American political leadership saw Chiang as a God-fearing man and the most Westernized leader to emerge after the fall of the Tang dynasty. The Generalissimo and Mme Chiang were so popular in the United States that they were featured on the 1937 cover of *Time* magazine as "Man and Wife of the Year."

When I was in Taiwan, Mme Mai-Ling Soong Chiang was already a legend. She was an exquisite beauty who represented the moneyed class, a graduate of Wellesley College who spoke English flawlessly and who often interpreted for her husband. I heard stories of her fabulous dinner parties. She invited westerners as guests, and after the generalissimo had retired for the night, she sat up until the early hours drinking scotch whiskey with those who could keep up with her. She dressed in the most fashionable *chi'pao*, the traditional Chinese dress of silk sheath slit up the side with a high neckline. She ordered a specially made rice face powder, and she often wore gloves because she was averse to having her hands touched. Most Taiwanese considered her autocratic, condescending, and a grand lady albeit misguided. Mme Chiang was as brilliant and manipulative as she was lovely, and she wielded considerable influence in the United States. It was she who persuaded President Franklin D. Roosevelt to send military aid directly to Chiang instead of through the more customary route to the U.S. Mission in China and Ambassador Patrick Hurley.

A decade before I arrived on the scene, Chiang and his armies had taken refuge in Taiwan after Mao defeated him in the Chinese civil war. The Taiwanese resisted Chiang's intrusion and the subsequent corrupt, often cruel, administration, but Chiang burrowed in, established a nationalistic government, and became a virtual dictator, all the while harboring his dream of "retaking the mainland." Thus began four decades of martial law on Taiwan.

At least one million Chinese went with him, and they were amazed at the richness of Taiwan, which was a far superior geopolitical entity than the poor nation they had left behind. The immigrants, especially the soldiers, grabbed with both hands, behaving like a conquering army. Chiang initiated a land-reform program, seizing property from wealthy Taiwanese landowners and dividing it among the peasants. The natives of Taiwan became an oppressed people, treated by the Nationalists as if they had been collaborators with the Japanese.

After Chiang holed up on Taiwan, the Committee of One Million pressured the U.S. government to support him and Nationalist China instead of Communist China. American diplomats protested, but the cold war was beginning, and the fear of communism clutched American throats. In 1947, the House Un-American Activities Committee and a subsequent Senate committee that included the vocal Joseph McCarthy launched highly publicized investigations of the motion-picture industry, branded many American citizens as communist sympathizers, and accused President Truman and the Democrats of "losing China." The committee's investigation fueled a national "Red Scare" and ruined the career of several brilliant Foreign Service officers who disagreed with the U.S.-China policy. These career diplomats had dared to say, "We do not quite understand what is happening in China, but it is not being steam-rollered by a mob of Communist brigands. Mao's leadership is acting the way the people want them to act." Their temerity in questioning the popular support of Chiang cost them their careers.

This was the troubled history of Taiwan in the decade immediately preceding my arrival in 1958. Martial law was still in effect, and over the island lay an uneasy truce between the mainlanders and the Taiwan natives. Chiang was obsessed with maintaining physical and mental control of the people. He employed the tactics used by the Communist Party in the Soviet Union: enforcing strict censorship, limiting or forbidding travel abroad, and utilizing covert government intelligence networks among the people. I saw Chiang's secret police everywhere. Cell organizations similar to those within the USSR permeated every aspect of life, including the organization that employed me. I was recently separated from the U.S. Marine Corps and had begun a new job with the Army and Air Force Exchange Services.

The U.S. foreign policy in Southeast Asia was then based on the "domino theory," the belief that if one nation fell to communism in Southeast Asia, all nations were likely to fall. Staunch anti-communist Secretary of State John Foster Dulles coined the term "brinksmanship," which advocated the use of nuclear weaponry, if necessary, to contain the Soviet Union in Southeast Asia. In this shifting light of international affairs, Taiwan began to assume greater importance to the United States. A huge U.S. military presence—army, air force, and navy—was established on the island to help Taiwan develop its military capability, to defend Taiwan against China, and to deter Soviet designs on Southeast and North Asia. The defense was taken on by the Taiwan Defense Command as part of the

7th Fleet under the U.S. commander in chief, Pacific; and the 13th Air Task Force was there as a fighter arm of the U.S. Air Force. The U.S. Military Assistance Advisory group provided military aid, advice, guidance, and training. It was within this organization that I entered, joining the Taiwan Central Exchange, which operated post exchanges, commissaries, and snack bars for U.S. civilians and military personnel. In this job, I was learning to look at the profit line of an enterprise and to deal with an organization I considered the epitome of disorganization. This alone would make the assignment a seminal learning experience for me. Furthermore, I was in the midst of an ideological struggle between the mainlanders and the Taiwanese. I began my job not fully aware of these boiling political passions and prejudices but soon discovered that if I were to survive this political cauldron, I would have to learn fast.

My first assignment was in personnel management; later, security was added to my duties. I was constantly caught in the seething antagonism between the Chinese and the Taiwanese. If I hired a mainlander for a supervisory position, the native Taiwanese judged me to be insensitive to the downtrodden and favoring people who had no right to be there. Mainlanders, meanwhile, were determined to hold on to every remnant of authority and position. My every decision of hiring, firing, training, and placing personnel involved a balancing act of national sensitivities.

A greater problem was the climate of raw avarice in Taipei at the time. It was a wildcat city, with fast fortunes to be made and people clawing to make them. Many of the American civilians in Taipei were expatriates, soldiers-of-fortune, and people of malleable virtue. I could almost smell the intrigue and temptation in the air. Desire was everywhere, from the Chinese women desperate to secure American husbands to the people of all nationalities hungry to advance themselves. The lures of whiskey, opium, women, and monetary bribes were dangled before us daily. Every pleasure of the flesh seemed within grasp. In that unrestrained atmosphere, I witnessed far too many Americans in high-level positions succumbing to addiction and lechery. When one senior employee was reported missing, I suspected he had been killed, but we found him drunk and living in a house of prostitution.

Since my job put me in a position of some responsibility with contracts and jobs, I was faced with enticements and bribes of all kinds. It was a perilous path to traverse. I was young, just thirty years old, I had not yet completed a formal education, and I was not yet in the Foreign Service with its training behind me.

Once again, I encountered people who echoed what I had heard before: complete your college education. I listened to them, and this helped save me.

My experience in Taiwan would stand me in good stead in future postings. I was torn between two views. I saw that because mainland China had been under siege by the Japanese since the 1930s, the mainlanders were an economically deprived people, unprepared mentally, educationally, or philosophically to assume control of Taiwan. I saw how harshly the Nationalists had treated the natives. I saw what oppression can do to a people. I would see it again in South Africa, in Liberia, in Australia, and (from the vantage point of the United Nations) among the native peoples of the United States and Canada. All of this became a part of the professional repertoire I could draw on, and it began in Taiwan.

Then my personal life took a dramatic turn: Lucy Cheng-mei Liu. I was working in Taipei as a personnel officer with the Army and Air Force Exchange Services in 1960 when I became aware of a seemingly quiet, strikingly beautiful colleague with black hair that reached to her waist. This was Lucy. Sometimes she dressed in Western clothes and other times she wore the *chi'pao*. Eventually

My personal life took a
dramatic turn when I met
Lucy Cheng-mei Liu.

I summoned enough nerve to ask her to dinner, and she accepted. We dined at one of the best restaurants in the world, located in the Grand Hotel, Taipei's biggest hotel, which was owned by Mme Chiang. Later I found out that accepting my invitation was a daring thing for Lucy to do because she came from a high-born, protective Chinese family who managed the lives of the young women in the family until they were married. To the Chinese, it was understood that marriage meant a union with another Chinese, but at the time, I did not understand the rigidity of the Taiwanese family unit and rituals of engagement. Perhaps it is a good thing that young Americans do not know all the strictures when they deal in things like love and courtship. That dinner at the Grand Hotel's Mandarin restaurant was the only time we went out together in public. We dated surreptitiously, taking drives, having dinner at my home, or dining in places where we would be unlikely to meet someone she knew. She had to be home early in the evening to meet the family's strict curfew. We never went to a movie. I never walked her to her door, but let her out of the car a couple of blocks away from their family residence in Taipei. Until this time I had not seriously considered marriage, but with Lucy I had a change of mind. After paying court for almost two years, I proposed.

"My parents would never agree," she said. She was thirty years old, an educated and independent woman with a job, but this was not the United States, where young women followed their hearts and made their own decisions.

"I will adhere to the ancient custom," I said, "and send an emissary to your parents."

Lucy's family home was in the village of Miao-Li, in the center of the island of Taiwan. She was one of ten siblings in a wealthy Hakka family. The Hakkas are considered the "Jews of China," because historically they were wanderers, clannish, and devoted to academic excellence, commerce, and successful work in government at the highest levels. Her father was the third generation of a family that had emigrated to Taiwan from southern China. Usually he wore Western suits, but occasionally he dressed in Mandarin robes. He was a member of the local senate, had a patrician's long fingernails, which symbolized idleness and wealth, and was one of the landowners whose property had been confiscated by Chiang Kai-shek. Unlike some other upper-class Chinese, Lucy's father had only one wife, although his mother had urged him to take another. He refused, saying he had seen too many unhappy families of multiple wives.

Beyond race, religion was another potential obstacle to our union. Lucy's mother was Christian, but her father insisted that the children be raised Buddhist. "When I was old enough to make up my own mind," Lucy said, "I became a Catholic." The phrase "to make up my own mind" is a significant insight into Lucy's personality. She has always been independent with her time, her money, and her decisions. As an energetic and athletic child, she slipped outside to swim or play when the rest of the family lay down for an afternoon nap. She was so stealthy, she was found out only because she tanned darkly in the afternoon sun. As a schoolgirl, she spent her allowance as she chose, often treating other students to snacks.

According to Taiwanese custom, her father had attempted to arrange betrothals for her, but she resisted. She rejected two prospects outright and finally agreed to be engaged to an engineering student. Then she had second thoughts, and without consulting her family, she called the young man to break off the engagement. He was shocked at her breach of protocol.

"What will I tell my family?" he asked.

"I'll take care of it," Lucy said, and she delivered the news to them. Only then did she tell her father of the broken engagement. He was furious.

One thing she and I shared was a love of learning and reading. She had received a classical education, and when the schools were closed during the war, Lucy continued her own education in her grandfather's library, reading extensively—from Chinese classics to Russian and English novels.

She was a young lady in her twenties when she went to Taipei to visit her brother. Out of boredom, she decided to get a job. Once again, it was an action she took without her father's permission. She told him only after she had secured a job, but assured him that it was a temporary diversion. She was still working two years later when she met me.

As Lucy tells the story, every time she walked by my office, I had my head down and was writing. She considered me serious and studious, characteristics she admired. One day she looked in at me at my desk—and this is her account of that day: "My heart jumped," Lucy says. "Just once. One jump. 'What's the matter with my heart?' I asked myself. And I realized it meant I was in love with him."

Her friends advised her to find somebody more docile, somebody she could control. "Why would I want that?" she asked. "I want someone I can respect. To me, respect is love. And Ed is choosy, too."

So we came to the point of wanting to marry, and I faced the dragons of religion and family tradition. I spoke first with the priest in the Miao-Li parish of Lucy's family. His response was predictable; he warned me of the high likelihood of the marriage's failing because not only was I an American, I was a black American. I heard him out and then said, "Thank you, Father, you have done your duty. Now what do I do next in order to marry her?" When he saw my determination, he warmed to the idea of my sending an emissary.

One weekend when Lucy went home for a weekend visit, I sent a colleague, Calix Chu, to call on her father. It was a risk, I realized, to send someone not from the Hakka tribe, but Calix was a learned man and from a family her father could respect. Lucy did not concur.

"My parents will never agree," she repeated. "If you want to get married, let's just do it and take the consequences."

"No," I said, "I can't do that to your parents. I have to try." So, following Chinese custom, I sent Calix to make the proposal to the family leaders. After her parents sat to receive him, Lucy said, "Mr. Chu has come to discuss something important." Calix came back to Taipei and over dinner reported to me that Lucy's father was impressed that I respected Chinese custom, that he asked a number of questions about me, and that he ended the interview by saying, "You tell Mr. Perkins that I will think about it. I will give him my answer."

"I think things are okay," Calix told me. "It's in the bag."

Lucy has another version. "Mr. Chu heard my father's words, but I saw my father's eyes and I knew the answer was no."

Lucy was correct. What she saw in his eyes was steely resolve. The next day I received a message from Lucy's cousin saying that not only had her father refused the proposal, Lucy was forbidden to return to Taipei and was a virtual prisoner at the family home. Her younger brother and the family's servants were assigned to watch her. Lucy sent another message to me by a friend: "Get word to Mr. Perkins that if he wants to contact me, do it through you and not through my cousin, whose first loyalty is to the family." We communicated through the friend, my asking if she still wanted to get married, and her saying that it was hopeless.

"Leave everything to me" was my reply. I knew we had to act quickly. As an employee of the U.S. government, in order to marry a Taiwanese citizen I had to request permission from the State Department and then arrange for a representative from the U.S. Consulate in Taipei to be present at the ceremony to ensure the marriage was legal in the eyes of the Chinese. After that, I arranged

Lucy's family when she was a child.
Lucy is the little dark-haired girl standing beside her father.

for a municipal court judge, a church, the license, and the certificate of marriage; I set the time for early in the morning. Finally, I sent her word of the
wedding date—September 9, 1962. Her birthday. Now I had to get Lucy out of
her family home and back to Taipei.

Under martial law, Lucy could not be married without her identity papers.
Either by luck or premonition, she had left her papers with a friend, so once

she escaped from her father's house, she would have access to her identity papers. I arranged for a driver to go to Miao-Li, where he would meet Lucy and her friend at midnight. The hour came and went without any sign of the friend with the ID papers. Afraid that Lucy's father would wake and discover her missing, the driver took Lucy to Taipei then turned around and repeated the two-hour drive to Miao-Li. This time the friend appeared, the driver received the papers and got them to Taipei just minutes before our scheduled civil wedding at the municipal court. Lucy retrieved a blue dress she had left behind at a Taipei cleaners, and this became her wedding dress.

Late that afternoon we were married again in a Catholic ceremony. Father Edward Murphy, a Jesuit priest at the Beda-Tsang Chapel at the University of Taiwan, had agreed to marry us if I would go through the church's instructions after the wedding. Only three Chinese guests attended; the wife of Lucy's boss, Calix Chu, and another friend. None of Lucy's family attended either wedding ceremony. That evening, we went to the home of her boss for a reception, drank champagne toasts, and cut the cake her boss's wife had made for us. Then we retired to my house, anxious to learn of her family's reaction to our elopement. It did not take us long to find out.

About nine o'clock that night, Lucy's older brother appeared at our home in a highly agitated state. He would not come inside, so we stood outside in the courtyard while he derided us. Speaking Chinese, he said to Lucy, "What have you done? What has happened?"

"I am married," she replied.

"You have dishonored the family," he shouted. "Our mother and father deserve better than this. You are Chinese. You should have more discipline."

Then he turned to me. "You have violated all civilized precepts," he ranted. "You have taken my sister into her doom." I tried to explain about sending an emissary.

"What did you expect!" He was incredulous. "Did you expect my father to say yes?" On and on he went, berating us for about an hour. All the time he had his hand in his pocket and I wondered if he had a gun. Because he was so angry and our breach of custom was so severe, I thought anything was possible.

Finally he left, and about eleven o'clock another of Lucy's brothers appeared. He was calmer and told us what had transpired within the family. As soon as they noticed her missing, they set out in search. They suspected she might have fled to Taipei to be married, so the first place they went was the

Our wedding.

courthouse. Their suspicions were confirmed; we had been married at nine o'clock in the morning. "It is done," her father said sadly, and ended the search.

That night, her brother repeated the proclamation. "It is done. Now you must make the most of it." It was a hell of a way to start a marriage.

Her parents were enraged. About six months later, her father came to bring us traditional wedding gifts—very expensive scrolls—as a way of saying, "Peace be with you." It was eight years before Lucy's mother would see her.

My own mother received the news of our marriage with apprehension. She was concerned about my marrying someone from another culture, especially since she and her friends had devoted the past ten years searching for what they considered a suitable partner for me in Portland. Now I was halfway around the world with a wife my mother would not meet for three years. For her, this seemed to deepen and finalize the chasm between us.

I applied for a transfer out of Taiwan and sought application for Lucy to seek

American citizenship, and we were sent back to the United States. When I saw how slowly Lucy walked toward the plane with her head lowered, I realized the magnitude of her decision to make her life with me. She had never been off the island of Taiwan, and now she was leaving her home, her family, her country, and the life she had known for an uncertain future with a virtual stranger.

Today, Lucy speaks philosophically about the rupture in her family. "I wasn't worried. I knew my family. I knew they would speak to me eventually. They had to save face."

I am in awe of Lucy for defying everything that she grew up believing in. Although I occasionally worried about how Lucy would be received with me, I was not mature enough at the time to be fully aware of the hidden currents of possible conflict in an interracial marriage. Without the normal courtship pattern, we had not gotten to know one another, so some might say it is miraculous that our marriage prospered. We relied on faith and determination. Allying yourself with a person of another culture is not easy. It will not be red roses all the time. It takes work on both sides, and we have both worked because we value one another. Out of this marriage have come unexpected growth and a lot of flowers. For me, to not marry Lucy and witness the birth of our two daughters would have been a personal tragedy.

Married to me, Lucy learned to live outside a cloistered environment. She laughs when she tells the saga of becoming a wife: "My mother sent me to sewing classes, but I did not know how to cook or clean house. My family always had servants to do that. After I married, I decided to do all the cleaning myself. It took so much time! I thought I had to clean the oven every time I used it. I could not understand how the neighbors could leave their homes at 7:30 or 8:00 in the morning when I was still cleaning. Then I found out they just made the bed and left. I thought I had to clean the entire house before leaving it. And people expected me to know how to make Chinese food! When I had to host a dinner, I got a Chinese recipe book and gave it to the cook." Eventually, Lucy's family came around. The thaw began with the birth of our daughters, but I had to take the first step. In the Chinese tradition, the grandfather is invited to name the first child. I invited my father-in-law to name both children. We were stationed in Okinawa, Japan, when our first daughter was born June 2, 1965. He gave her the Chinese name Shih-tzu, meaning "Pearl of the Orient." She was born during typhoon Karla, so her anglicized name is Katherine Karla.

Our second daughter was born November 9, 1969, in Bangkok, Thailand. She was a premature baby of only three pounds and was in an incubator for a month. Since she was born early, we had not chosen a name and the hospital named her Marie. We changed her American name to Sarah Elizabeth, for my grandmother. Lucy's father gave her the Chinese name Shih-yin, "Pearl of the World." It was then that Lucy's parents accepted our invitation to visit us, and the break in her family began to mend. Before they left, my mother-in-law was praising Lucy's child-rearing skills and giving her advice on how best to care for a fine husband like me.

I wanted to shield Katherine and Sarah, the children of a mixed marriage, from racism, but I realized that was the worst thing I could have done. They needed to experience the dregs of society as well as all of its plusses. They have lived and traveled all over the world. They have both learned Chinese. They tell me they feel fortunate to have this mixed lineage and that they have the best of all possible worlds—half black American and half Chinese. I tell them, "You represent what our country thinks it stands for—that we are a diverse society, made up of people from all nations. Be proud of your heritage and be proud of your citizenship. You are true Americans. Stand up proudly. Hold your head high. And if people give you a tough time, push them out of the way. Keep going. You do not have time for people like that." I am convinced that the best way to help our children is to teach them to accept that they are the masters of their destiny.

EDUCATION
AND EISENHOWER'S
LITTLE WAR

S uddenly, I was in a hurry to complete my education. Since high school, people had counseled me about the importance of obtaining a college degree. I was ready to act on their advice. I was a married man, my military experience was behind me, and I had acquired some professional skills during several enjoyable years abroad. Now was the time to focus on my dream of joining the Foreign Service and finish my formal education. I wanted to make up for lost time.

I enrolled in the University of Maryland in Taipei, majoring in public administration and political science. I took every personnel course I could find, including seminars in manpower planning, wage and salary exercises, and workforce planning. Before long I had developed an expertise. While working in Okinawa, I satisfied requirements for a bachelor's degree.

In 1967 I was accepted as an intern in the U.S. Agency for International Development (USAID), an independent agency within the State Department, and was sent to Washington, D.C., for six months of intensive training. The program included courses and instruction at the Justice Department, General Services Administration, State Department, Capitol, National Archives, and on-the-job training in other U.S. government offices. On my own I began studying the administrative law pertaining to USAID. I read it all, volume after volume. Because of that self-study, when I was assigned to my first post, I happened to be the only person in the mission who knew most of the administrative law governing USAID.

All twenty of us in that USAID internship cohort were destined for Southeast Asia, which was a new area of foreign policy for the United States. I had been intrigued by Thailand after seeing the movie *Anna and the King of Siam* (1946) and had read a great deal about the country, which had never been colonized. I asked to be sent to Bangkok and was detached there for a tour of duty with the U.S. Operations Mission (USOM) to Thailand, a part of the U.S. Embassy. USOM was responsible for the management of United States–financed economic development programs in Thailand. The Soviet Union was funding what it termed "wars of liberation" in Latin America, Southern Africa, and Southeast Asia, specifically Cambodia, Laos, Vietnam, northeast Thailand, and peripherally in Burma. In Thailand, the United States was making a stand to prevent the domino effect, using the tools of economic assistance for social and community change and battling insurgencies supported by communist states.

The job of the USOM was to assist Thailand in economic and social development and to help Thailand fight the insurrection. Thai guerrillas, trained by or funded by the Soviets, were making a concerted effort to communize Thailand, first in the rural north and then moving south toward the capital of Bangkok.

This was the setting for my USOM posting, where I was assigned to the Office of Assistant Director for Management. Lucy was with me every step of the way, and by now we had Kathy. In Washington, during my long orientation, we had rented an apartment in Foggy Bottom, 2401 H Street N.W. When my orientation was completed and I was posted to Bangkok, we lived in rented housing. Lucy was an active member of the mission wives' club, and Kathy started school at the International School.

Among my other duties at the Bangkok mission, I was in charge of transportation, including the scheduling of two airplanes used almost exclusively by the ambassador, the director, and an enormous public-safety contingent, which had an overwhelming role in Southeast Asia, especially in Laos and Thailand. The public-safety contingent was funded in large part by the CIA. I spent considerable time in the air with Howard Parsons, a senior Foreign Service officer and head of the mission, and other mission members. We traveled into the north to supply the local Thai fighting force, and occasionally we ventured into Laos, where the United States actively managed a war that came to be known informally as "The CIA's Secret War in Laos." There were no uniformed military in Laos, but plenty in civilian clothes. I watched Ambassador MacMurtrie Godley direct the war in Laos from his office. In this assignment he was virtually a proconsul ambassador, managing a fighting force of civilian soldiers, working with a cadre of Laotians, and making policy from day to day. President John Kennedy completely supported him.

Ambassadors Godley in Laos, Leonard Unger in Thailand, and John Gunther Dean in Cambodia were among the last of the proconsul Foreign Service officers and they exercised extraordinary powers and authorities. They interpreted their oaths of office as the president's representative to mean that no other officer, even the vice president, could impose interpretations unless the proconsuls wanted it. They took their orders solely from the president. Although I would come to have almost that much authority in South Africa, these men were the last of an era.

In Southeast Asia we were learning about a different kind of war. We were keenly interested in Vietnam because we believed that a similar war would erupt on Thai soil, where it would be even hotter and more destructive. My superiors wanted me to be up to date on the procedures of helping to fight such a war, so I found myself in meetings to develop foreign policy for the Thai insurgency and the war in Vietnam. It was a heady experience for a junior officer. I was taking official notes for spies as they discussed how to develop Vietnam and Thailand into flourishing economies with stable socialization programs, as well as how to kill people. It was my first taste of foreign policy in real time.

My assignment to Southeast Asia placed me in one of the most exciting locales in the world. During the 1960s and 1970s, Southeast Asia was a stage of great drama and tragedy created by a cast of larger-than-life characters determined to write their name in history. Ho Chi Minh, the leader of North Vietnam, and Ngo Dinh Diem, president of South Vietnam, were a contrast in personalities. Preparing for his leadership, Ho Chi Minh had been a world traveler, working as a stevedore and an able-bodied seaman and visiting New York's Harlem and the black communities of New Orleans. He lived in France, where he was one of the founders of the Chinese and French Communist Parties, and he went to Russia to study Marxism and Leninism. He was a genius who looked like a peasant. He wore a peasant's simple clothing, including rubber sandals cut from old tires, and he worked in the fields with the peasants, helping them harvest. All the while he was gathering around him a strong cadre of committed communists and nationalists, who were one and the same. Ho Chi Minh's great strength was that he remained true to his people.

Ngo Dinh Diem in South Vietnam dressed in white suits, the uniform of the colonialists. He was the aristocratic son of a Mandarin, educated in the best French schools, unmarried, and Roman Catholic in a predominantly Buddhist country. If he had not been a statesman, he likely would have been a priest, but he was corrupted by the love of money. He was a strict disciplinarian but without an expressed purpose accepted by the people. His regime became known as unscrupulous, repressive, and nepotistic. His brother was his chief aide-de-camp, and his sister-in-law was the quintessential Dragon Lady, a beautiful woman who could slowly carve out your heart without wrinkling her delicate brow. When Buddhist priests were immolating themselves in flames, she said coolly, "If they want to barbecue themselves, let them go ahead." Ho Chi Minh and Ngo Dinh Diem both vied for U.S. support. The United States had indicated that it might support the Geneva Accords, leading to the reconciliation of the two Vietnams, but Ngo Dinh Diem could not create a unified Vietnam. Ho Chi Minh, on the other hand, could win the elections, but Vietnam would become a communist state. That possibility was too much for America to accept. We were afraid of communism, plain and simple. Consequently, the United States reneged on an implied promise and supported South Vietnam, which was tantamount to supporting the division of Vietnam at the 17th parallel.

This policy required that the United States position substantial resources in Thailand, Vietnam, and Laos. For the first time, we faced a land war different from anything we had experienced as a nation. Ho Chi Minh was a Communist, but he was also a Vietnamese patriot who had vowed to expel all colonials and unite Vietnam. In at least one part of the country, the majority of the people would risk everything for the cause of liberty. Perhaps more than any other person except Nelson Mandela, Ho Chi Minh was able to successfully mobilize people in the fight against colonialism. We did not understand this ideology, nor did we recognize how much more powerful it was than communist ideology. Much of that knowledge is hindsight. What was clear to me at the time was that we were being involved in guerrilla fighting, and our fighters could not see the enemy.

In Taiwan a few years earlier I had watched the arrival of U.S. military planes filled with fresh-faced, young troops. The soldiers marched into buildings wearing military uniforms and came out the other side dressed in civilian clothes, headed for Vietnam as advisors. That was the beginning of U.S. involvement in

Vietnam. First came the civilian advisors, then the uniformed advisors, then the military combat units, and now I was participating in Vietnam policy conferences in Bangkok and Singapore determining how to deploy economic, social, and military assistance in Vietnam. We still believed we could win the war.

Congressman Otto Passman from Monroe, Louisiana, the most influential person in Congress in allocating economic assistance, was an important participant at one high-level conference in Bangkok.

"Well, Mr. Congressman," I said when I picked him up at the airport, "the war will soon be escalating."

"Yes," he said, "that little war that Eisenhower started down there in Vietnam. Now look where we are." That was the phrase he used—the "little war that Eisenhower started."

One school of thought said, "They are all the enemy, including the civilians. Kill them." Another school said, "My God, what are we becoming? Why are we killing all these people? What is it going to get us?" I was among the latter.

The war did escalate. We sent more troops into Vietnam, and then bombs began to drop. "Operation Rolling Thunder," under President Richard Nixon and Secretary of State Henry Kissinger, was an around-the-clock bombing of Hanoi, all to no avail. This led to a reevaluation of the U.S. role in Vietnam. The question asked in the national interest was: "What do we have to do to win?" and the answer was: "Obliterate Vietnam." And thus began the excruciating effort to extricate ourselves from Vietnam.

The officers serving in Vietnam were on an unaccompanied tour, and Thailand was a safe haven for their dependents. Part of my job was supervising the Bangkok support for the safe-haven families, a number of whom were black. In Thailand, black Americans were a curiosity. I was standing alone on a street corner when a couple of young Thai women began talking about me in their native language. "Look at this big black man," one of them said to the other. "I wonder if he is hairy like some of the whites." I answered in Thai, "No, I am not." They screamed and ran away.

Other incidents were less innocuous. Unfortunately, Americans arrived on the scene shadowed by racism and some native people absorbed the prejudice. I encountered landlords who did not want to rent to black families and white

In an airport in Bangkok. My career in the Foreign Service has meant a life of travel for me and my family.

military families who did not want black families to use the swimming pools at apartment complexes. When a group of black USAID and military wives came to the mission hurt and angry, I was given the assignment of talking to them. It was a heartbreaking experience. They were halfway around the world and subjected to racism similar to what they had experienced on occasion back home. They said they were treated unequally in shops and in housing assignments. They felt isolated in this foreign land, not a part of the larger American community, and they believed that their white fellow Americans conveyed the message to the Thai people that black women were second-class citizens.

My immediate boss was not sympathetic. "We cannot change the hearts and minds of people," he said.

"I am not suggesting that we try to change the way the Thai think," I said, "if indeed they do think that. I am suggesting that we live what we think we are as a nation. I do not intend to let people hide behind the U.S. flag to exercise their prejudices."

"What do you think we ought to do over here?" the ambassador asked me. (Because I am black, I was expected to have the answers to race problems.) I suggested that the ambassador invite them for coffee occasionally and continue the conversations.

"Ask them how they are getting along," I suggested. "Don't try to come up with answers, just listen. Listening is the hardest thing you can do." Slowly things began to get better for the black families, but the undercurrent of racism continued. When Martin Luther King was shot, I was in Bangkok on my way to a function at the home of a Foreign Service officer. The news destroyed me. My host said only, "He probably brought it on himself."

Bangkok is the Venice of Southeast Asia, a city of canals in a land of sunshine, beautiful people, flowers—especially orchids—and snakes. In Buddhist Thailand, temples are a part of everyday life. Buddhism influenced me to become more considerate of myself and of others and to understand that we can be considerate of others only if we are considerate of ourselves. I came to have a new respect for non-Christian religions and to appreciate the quiet, meditative nature of Buddhism that seems to embrace everything around it. I did not need to go to church to feel virtuous. In Thailand I continued to meditate, and I found increased compatibility with the concept of looking for an inner peace. I found solace in being alone and learned how to be alone in the middle of crowds. In theory, every Thai man serves some time as a monk. I will never forget the former general who was prime minister when I arrived. A palace coup forced him out of office, and the next day I saw him wearing a monk's robe begging for food with a wooden bowl. There was no shame in his actions; it was merely another facet of his spiritual journey.

I fell in love with the Thai language. Languages are fascinating puzzles to me: once I find the key, a new culture springs open. Some people think I have an affinity for languages, but I have to study hard to learn them. What has helped me is the ability to quickly mimic the accents. My accepted Foreign Service languages were Japanese, French, and Thai. I had become fluent in Japanese while in Okinawa. To satisfy the Foreign Service requirement that every officer be fluent in a world language, I chose French, a grand language. Things can be said in French that cannot be said in English, especially when paying court to a woman.

In Bangkok, I began to study Thai. Mrs. John J. Peurifoy, the wife of the first American ambassador to Thailand, introduced me to Pali, the ancient Thai language. The Indians who built Angkor Wat thousands of years ago probably brought this language. Today, only monks speak Pali, and they must give permission for others to study it. Pali has the same status as Latin in western languages. Studying Thai was hard work because it is an esoteric and tonal language, yet the more I learned about the language, the more I learned about the Thai people. If every officer were required to learn the language of the country in which he served, he would be able to do a much better job.

In Thailand I also set upon another course of study that would serve me well. It began with a traumatic experience. I was called upon to be a master of ceremonies for a function with a visiting dignitary. Although I had studied public speaking both in high school and in college, I was in a fright. The evening was interminable agony for me. I did not feel in control of myself. When the experience was finally—and mercifully—over, I vowed to solve the problem and joined a Toastmaster Club. There I received some of the most important training I have ever had. It taught me to be confident when communicating with mass audiences, to make eye contact, to emphasize key words, to understand the audience, and to empathize with the listeners silently and psychologically. I was chosen to represent the Bangkok Toastmasters Club in a yearly speech contest, and I pulled off a win. I can still feel the exhilaration of winning that cup. People comment on my measured speaking style and the deliberate way I choose my words. "As precise as a cat on a ledge," someone said. The training garnered from the Toastmasters Club in Bangkok taught me self-control and self-confidence at the podium.

Then I took another leap of learning. I requested educational leave, equivalent to a sabbatical with pay, and began graduate school at the University of Southern California. The professors were impressed by my sense of urgency and made accommodations to help me with a heavy class load. I wanted to earn a master's degree in record time, and I accomplished the task in about a year and a half. I did not spend much time with my poor family. I went on for a Ph.D. in public administration at usc, which had a campus in Washington, and I was among the first usc doctoral candidates to be registered with the Washington Center. Of the thirty-two people who began the program, fewer than ten of us completed the degree. My doctoral dissertation was a case study of Henry Kissinger's method of managing the State Department through the allocation of resources for the greater consideration of foreign policy. I finished it in one year. When it came time for the comprehensive exams, I decided to ignore most of the conventional wisdom about behavioral science and the theory of public administration and take a new approach. I coined the phrase "Mao Man" and used it to refer to Mao Tse-tung's revolutionary public administration in China, the most populous state, as well as in Vietnam. For two days I typed eight hours a day in one of the most intensive projects I have ever done. Then I sent off my exam and awaited the results. When a thick letter from the university arrived, I drove to a nearby Irish tavern, ordered a large glass of Guinness stout, and opened the envelope. The letter from my advisor began: "Dear Ed—Your readers were impressed with your treatment of the questions, which were certainly original and unorthodox, but which made sense. They are pleased to recommend you highly for the defense of the dissertation."

My approach to the questions had been so unorthodox that before the exam began one of my colleagues said, "You are crazy to introduce something new. Get away from me. I don't want to hear it. You'll muddle my thinking." I recognized that it was a daring approach, but I have always liked living on the edge. I would not have it any other way.

In Bangkok, mission director Howard Parsons took me under his wing and began to counsel me about the direction of my career. "You are having a great time here as an USAID officer," he said, "but you have the potential to make a difference in the shaping of foreign policy. You will not be able to do it, however, unless you become a commissioned Foreign Service officer."

I knew that he was correct. With my formal education well in hand, I set my sights on another career mountain peak. In the 1970s, the Foreign Service was known as a closed, elite organization of white, Ivy League men. For a black man, a female, or a member of any other minority to aspire to a career in the Foreign Service was more than life on the edge. It was over the top. In the face of that challenge, I first had to pass the notoriously rigorous Foreign Service oral examination.

THE FOREIGN SERVICE
OF THE UNITED STATES

I intended to enter the diplomatic service under the Foreign Service Act of
1946, which allowed officers serving in other branches of the U.S. government to be considered for lateral entry after passing the oral examination.
Although I had taken the Foreign Service examination a couple of times and
had not been called, I was not deterred. While in Bangkok with USAID, a secretary in the mission played a brief but pivotal role in my career.

At a party one evening, a lovely Australian named Fay Thorne introduced me
to her husband. Nicholas G. W. Thorne was a Polish count who had immigrated
to the United States, served seventeen years in the U.S. Marine Corps before
being medically retired early, and then joined the diplomatic service. He was a
tall, handsome man with a handlebar moustache. As a senior Foreign Service
officer in the Bangkok post, Nick was the mission coordinator, organizing the
core mission elements, political, economic, consular, military attaché, CIA,
USAID, FBI, and others, on behalf of the ambassador. His job was to insure that
in this large mission all elements worked in accord with mission policy, on
which the ambassador had the final say. Nick's mandate also included coordinating the U.S. assistance program through USAID and other elements in the
mission special to Thailand as it strove to both fight an insurgency in the north
and to accelerate its economic development. He asked why I was not on the
diplomatic side instead of being a Foreign Service reserve officer in the USAID,
and I told him my story: that I had longed to join the Foreign Service since high
school, that I had been trying for several years, and that I was preparing to try
again.

"Let's see if we can't speed things up," he said. He critiqued my application
papers and contacted a friend on the Board of Examiners. Within a week, I
received a letter inviting me to take the oral examination the next time I was

in Washington. "Now we have to get you back to Washington," Nick said. Upon the advice of friends, I had spent four months studying world affairs by reading back issues of *Time*, *Newsweek*, and the prestigious journal *Foreign Policy* and by researching artists and authors. I felt ready for the notoriously rigorous examination.

Nick saw to it that the oral examination was scheduled, and he arranged my transportation with VIP status on a U.S. Air Force aircraft headed back to the United States. I was the only non-air force passenger aboard the C-130 Hercules, a colossal aircraft known as "The Mighty Herk." In a climate time warp, we flew from balmy U-Tapao Air Base, Thailand, to Kadena Air Base, Okinawa, and from there to Minot Air Force Base in North Dakota, where March snowbanks towered higher than the cars. From Warner Robbins Air Force Base, Georgia, I caught a small plane to Washington, D.C., and began final preparations for the examination. Friends spent five days quizzing me on everything from art to quantitative analysis and world states.

The oral examination was scheduled for one o'clock on a Monday afternoon in March 1971. It would last for only one hour, but it was one hour of hell. The examination was designed to be as intense as possible. Many people passed the written examination, which was academically difficult, only to wash out in the oral examination. Sometimes they wore a tie of the wrong color, the wrong suit, or made the wrong use of English. Sometimes it was some other nonquantifiable thing such as reading habits, knowledge of current events, or interaction with the interviewing panel. I wore a very conservative suit and tie, but I was superstitious enough to wear jade cufflinks and a certain scent of men's cologne that I considered lucky.

When I arrived, the secretary gave me ten minutes to read a short biography of each of the three members of the examining board. I entered the examination room, sat in a chair facing the three examiners, and they began asking questions. As I saw it, their job was to flunk me, and my job was to refuse to be failed.

I had formulated my own approach to the examination. I knew they could keep me for only an hour, so, playing for time, sometimes I restated the question for clarity or asked them to repeat it. When I answered, I took my time and answered thoroughly and at some length. Relying on the biographies I had just read, I personalized my answers. I addressed the examiners by name and referred to their Foreign Service experience: "I think Mr. So-and-So, who served in Such-and-Such post, would agree with this approach. . . ."They asked me practical questions and "what if" situations, such as how to deal with mobs. They asked ideological questions—the concept of communism, why it was controversial, and if it had ever been tried in the United States. "Yes," I answered, "in Ohio." When they asked me to discuss art, I talked about Picasso and Cézanne. When they asked me about literature, I discussed Willa Cather and Ayn Rand. They followed up by asking me to explain Rand's view of collectivism in *The Fountainhead*.

At last the ordeal was over, and I waited outside while they tabulated the results. After about forty-five minutes, they came out and said, "We are pleased to tell you that you did quite well." That is all they told me. I returned to Thailand. Several months later, I was transferred back to Washington to take the oath of office. In 1972 at age forty-four, I became a commissioned officer in the Foreign Service of the United States. I was by all accounts a late entrant, but I did not intend to be a placid one. I was resolute about being a proactive professional.

Years later, I ran into one of the examiners. "After you finished the exam," he told me, "we took a bet about how long it would take you to become an ambassador." At the time I was about to become ambassador to Liberia. It was an appointment against long odds. Approximately 5 percent of Foreign Service officers become ambassadors, and the average length of time in the Foreign Service before receiving an ambassadorial post is 20 to 28 years. I managed to make it in twelve. This accomplishment was not achieved alone. Every success that I have enjoyed I owe to the generous help of others. For every peak I attain, I stand on the shoulders of others.

Nick Thorne and Howard Parsons were mentors with invaluable guidance. "First, learn every bloody thing you can about the Service, its traditions and its history," Nick said. "Know more than anybody else about it. The more you know, the better you can understand where the traps lie that will affect your progression. Second, learn languages. Third, take the jobs that nobody else wants—jobs in developing countries or hardship assignments. You take them. Show that they can be done exceptionally well. You will find yourself being noticed as someone who can do a job. Stay away from Europe—do not ask for that assignment. Everybody wants to go there. The places to be in the Foreign Service these days are Africa and Asia. That is where the work is. That is where the United States has to make its mark. We are now fighting a war in Asia, so we need people who understand Asia. We need people who understand Africa. That is where you need to go."

He also advised me to reassess my career every January and ask myself hard questions: How am I doing in the service? Does my last efficiency report reflect my own assessment? Will this report contribute to promotion? Do I need extra training? His advice was so sound that I practice this professional inventory to this day.

I had, at last, scaled the Matterhorn of my youthful dreams and was a commissioned officer in the Foreign Service. Now, I asked myself: "What have I done? What is this mysterious organization I have managed to join?"

I discovered that I had worked hard to become a member of a profession popularly considered to consist of posh men in striped pants who gave tea parties and ate small sandwiches. To the general public, diplomats are often seen as little more than caricatures of highbrow affectation. Yet others consider the Foreign Service to be "the overseas arm of the government," the "first line of defense," "soldiers of the front line," and "the eyes and ears of the president and the secretary of state." More plainly, the term "Foreign Service officers" generally refers to those men and women who carry out diplomatic assignments abroad—the entire body of people who run embassies, consulates, and legations.

After almost thirty-five years of service, I still appreciate the grand mystery of the service. It is difficult for even a career officer to fully comprehend the complexity and subtlety of the organization. I came to understand the necessity of maintaining a professional Foreign Service as America's first line of defense, which means achieving advantages through the diplomacy of negotiation rather than the extreme diplomacy of war. When I joined the service, there were 195 overseas posts and a force of about 7,000 officers and specialists working abroad. Today, there are about 12,500 Foreign Service officers and specialists in 250 posts abroad. These diplomats and professionals are essential for preserving the peace, promoting U.S. interests and values, reporting on political and economic developments, providing services to American citizens abroad, and interpreting U.S. policy to foreign governments.

Foreign relations is a governmental activity that predates the government itself. A decade before the Declaration of Independence of 1776, Benjamin Franklin and others represented the colonies abroad. Before the Revolutionary War, these representatives were referred to as secret agents. The early Americans who followed Franklin in foreign affairs include stellar names from history books: Thomas Jefferson, John Adams, James Monroe, and John Quincy Adams. It is humbling to step into this long, proud line of American diplomats. Years later, in a more contemporary setting, I would say the same about many of the people I followed as ambassador to the United Nations.

While considering entry into the Foreign Service, I read as much as I could about it, including a 1946 series of articles published in *Fortune* magazine that presented the Foreign Service as a paradox of images. On one hand, except for a few noble individuals,* the Foreign Service had suffered during World War II when the president and the War Department took the lead roles, and the Foreign Service trailed behind doing grunt work. Although the Foreign Service had been formalized in 1915 and 1925 and rejuvenated with the milestone Foreign Service Act of 1946, the institutional elitism that had been fostered since the late 1800s still stuck. As a diplomat, I wondered if I would be expected to mingle with high society, chatting about art and culture.

I was comfortable with the fundamental requirements of the job. I understood that 60 percent or more of my service would be overseas and that glamorous locations were unlikely. I knew that assignments were typically three years, so transfers would be frequent. I was more uncertain about the risky "up or out" system. Patterned after the U.S. Navy officer personnel system, Foreign Service officers are either promoted up or selected out. I knew a Foreign Service officer who committed suicide when he was not promoted and faced expulsion from the Service. Nick Thorne had warned me of the dangers of being selected out and of the subtle ways that I could be targeted for extinction. "Because you are a black officer," he said, "you will be expected to jump higher than anyone else. You have to be better than anyone else." What I was least prepared for was the impenetrable maze of the organization. At that time, only a couple of us utilized lateral entry to join the Foreign Service, where we found ourselves babes in a polite but bare-fisted world. As director general, I later would champion special programs to redress the balance of ethnicity, and by then I knew full well the extra challenges presented by lateral entry. Maneuvering one's way through the Byzantine layered system was difficult enough while coming up through the ranks, and to try to do it after jumping into the deep end by lateral entry was well-nigh impossible. I was determined to not only survive this system but master it.

---

*Robert Murphy, Llewellen Thompson, Foy Kohler, "Chip" Bohlen, and Joseph Grew.

I was posted in Washington for six months of training in the "A-100" basic officers' training course and in my initial assignment. I was thrilled to be there. As
a young man, I had privately thought of the nation's capital as the City of
Power. That first cold morning as I walked up 19th Street toward the State
Department building to report for work, the massive structure was formidable. Architecturally, the building, with its mammoth columns, symbolizes a
government that is solid and enduring. The dreamer in me saw the building as
a vision of the Parthenon. Ferocious gargoyles peer down from the building's
corners, and a marble balustrade encloses a minipark built to hold a statue of
Benjamin Franklin, the father of American diplomacy. I seemed to float rather
than walk through the diplomatic entrance, which is flanked by the national
ensign flying on my left and the flag of the secretary of state on my right.
Behind me was the Lincoln Memorial. I climbed the stairs, stepped into the
hushed hall of ochre-colored marble, and stood in silent awe of the mystique of
the place. My first thought was not about forging a diplomatic career of accomplishments and satisfaction. It was, "How can I keep from being swallowed up
by this building?"

The building seemed to personify the old Foreign Service—white men of
moneyed, well-established, New England families who were educated at private schools and Ivy League universities. I represented none of that. My first
day of work in the State Department building, I was welcomed correctly but
not cordially. I could have felt like an interloper in that setting, a black man
who had not yet completed an advanced degree. But for some reason I never
once doubted that I would rise to the highest levels of the Foreign Service and
have challenging assignments around the world. I was focused solely on my
ability to achieve by doing a superlative job. What absolute nerve.

To my wry sense of humor, the State Department building reminded me
occasionally of the steep road ahead of me. The eighth floor holds art treas-
ures—paintings and furniture that constitute a history of the nation—and is the
location of the ornate Benjamin Franklin Room, the site of high ceremonies. It
is here that ambassadors are sworn in and where diplomats from around the
world gather for formal lunches and dinners. And in this room on such an occasion I heard, for the first time in my life, diplomats discussing how to eat soup.
This was not a discussion topic for most black communities of that era.

I had not been in Washington long when I attended a diplomatic reception in the Ben Franklin room. I stood chatting with John Burroughs and John Gravely, the only other blacks in the room, when two elderly women approached us. One of them said to me, "Sonny, would you get me a Coke?" My colleagues stifled their laughter and walked away. The women were perplexed and could not understand what was happening. I indicated the direction and said as politely as I could, "The bar is there, ma'am." With only a handful of blacks in the service, it would not be the last time I was mistaken for an attendant.

From the beginning, I knew that the life of a diplomat was more rigorous than sipping tea and giving parties. The discipline of the U.S. Marine Corps stood me in good stead. A typical day was to awaken by 4:30 A.M., run five miles, and help get the girls ready for school, arriving at work at 8:30 A.M., a half-hour early. While I was writing my dissertation, I wrote from 3:00 to 5:00 A.M. When I was studying foreign languages for the Foreign Service requirement, I either attended French classes beginning at 7:30 A.M. or had a Thai tutor after work. It was a most hectic period for me.

Much of my time those first weeks was spent in the Foreign Service Institute learning the niceties of diplomacy and studying USAID economic assistance, which was the foreign policy of special interest to me at that point in my career. A memorable lecturer was Bishop John Walker, who rose from a childhood of poverty in Detroit to become the first black senior official of the Episcopal Church. He spoke to us about the role of community organizations in diplomacy, a subject that would serve me well in South Africa. "Here I am lecturing to you in the State Department," he said, "and yet down the road in Virginia I was stopped a few days ago by a policeman because the parishioner in my car happened to be a white woman. For a moment, I feared that something violent would happen. You have two burdens to carry. First, the burden of a powerful nation. Second, the fact that this nation still condones racism. You must overcome that." In contrast, Henry Cabot Lodge Jr., another noteworthy lecturer, seemed oblivious to social relations among peoples. He spoke about applying the country's economic power to diplomacy.

I was assigned to the Office of the Director General of the Foreign Service and detailed temporarily to the Office of Equal Employment Opportunity. Almost immediately I came face-to-face with the problems facing minorities and women in the Foreign Service. Two black female Civil Service employees officed in the basement told me about working in the State Department when the main cafeteria was segregated and therefore closed to them. Blacks with university degrees had spent their entire career in the mailroom. It was shameful. I vowed then to do what I could to change the Foreign Service and make it both equitable and better.

Another Civil Service employee, a black Washingtonian with a master's degree from Howard University, had begun as a messenger, the only job he could get in the State Department. Ten years later, he was still a messenger. It was a privilege, he assured me, for blacks to work in the State Department, even if only in menial jobs because then, as now, State was considered the most prestigious department in Washington. The Constitution gives the president the authority to manage foreign relations of the United States and appoint ambassadors, ministers, and envoys "by and with the advice and consent of the Senate." Consequently, ambassadors are direct representatives of the president. In practice, though, the State Department manages the foreign relations, embassies, and activities abroad, except for military forces in the field. The State Department is prestigious because it is the first department of the federal government.

The messenger spent hours sharing with me his in-depth knowledge of the city, Washington society, and the State Department. What he taught me was priceless. Most people, even presidents, dreaded working with the State Department because it was like dealing with a great vat of Jell-O—they could not get their hands around it. From these invisible civil servants—chauffeurs, secretaries, and mail clerks—I learned that the department consisted of both a formal and an informal organization and that the latter drove the former. Here was the theory of organizational behavior in operation. By understanding what made the informal organization tick—by knowing the people in the bowels of the building who got the work done—I could feel the pulse of the organization. The secret of accomplishing the impossible was in knowing the people who did the work. It was a piece of information I held close to the vest. Like a sleight-of-hand trick, the power was in secrecy.

It was in the Office of Equal Employment Opportunity (EEO) that I first met

John Gravely, another black Foreign Service officer who shared my passion for
making the Foreign Service more representative of the face of America. John
had grown up in Virginia, where his schoolteacher father was an activist
involved with the NAACP. In the late 1930s, John's father and a colleague had
been wrongly accused of burning down a shabby black school in protest of
black education and were run out of town. In 1956, John participated in a test
case of *Brown v. the Board of Education* and was one of four black students to integrate a white high school in West Virginia.

John and I were both junior Foreign Service officers, both working on our
Ph.D. degrees, and both avid students of public administration, organizational
behavior, and organizational theory. In 1973, with seven or eight other black
officers from USAID, USIA, and State, we helped established the Thursday Luncheon Group, dedicated to advancing the cause of blacks in the Foreign Service. I became the executive secretary. Not only were black Foreign Service
officers scarce—numbering only about twenty-five—but traditionally blacks
did not fare well in promotions or assignments. European assignments were
rare; black officers were typically assigned to Africa. The Thursday Luncheon
Group would lead the charge to make a dramatic change for blacks. We wanted
to open the Foreign Service to accepting and promoting more minorities. How
brash we were, two junior officers working for a purpose at variance with the
traditional beliefs of the department. Our plan of attack was to send a senior
delegation to Secretary of State Henry Kissinger and petition him to elevate
the status of the EEO office. John and I spent several months preparing our
strategy.

We began by researching Kissinger himself. On our own time, we read his
books and his papers to understand how he thought as a strategist and what
methods he used, albeit on a global scale. We referred to our research as "Sher-
locking" because we were both aficionados of Arthur Conan Doyle's work and
Sherlock Holmes's deductive reasoning. We tried to anticipate all possible situations, oppositions, and contingencies that might arise in the meeting with
Kissinger. We were keenly aware that we were dealing with the ultimate diplomat. Because we were too junior in rank to attend the meeting ourselves, we
had to first convince the delegation to carry out our strategy. This, itself, was
an exercise in diplomacy. Some wanted to go in aggressively with figurative
fists raised; others wanted to beg the issue or argue the cause of right. These
tactics would have been absolutely wrong with Kissinger. The Foreign Service

Act of 1946 dictated that the Foreign Service must look like America, but the key argument for Kissinger, we believed, was efficiency of resources. John and I were careful to write in the memorandum to Kissinger that our only desire was that the Foreign Service represent America. Still, some of our delegation wanted to make a moral argument.

"Oh, come on, Ed," one of my colleagues said. "The man must have a heart."

"Henry Kissinger's passion is statecraft," I said. "He lives it. He is the foremost authority in the world. You have to appeal to his desire to run a good foreign policy and persuade him that bringing in more blacks and minorities will help him better manage foreign policy."

Meanwhile, a number of officers wrote a letter protesting what we were doing. I was shocked to see that one of them was a black officer until I realized that he, too, was part of the elite mafia from a certain geographic section of the country and with a certain kind of education. He, therefore, empathized with those convinced that the Foreign Service constituted an elite corps of people. To them, our work was threatening a way of life.

The meeting was an unprecedented success. Kissinger approved our request on the spot without its going through channels. It was one of the most remarkable things I have ever done. That meeting resulted in monumental changes in the State Department. Until then, EEO had been a quiet little Civil Service office. Kissinger elevated the rank of EEO (now known as the Civil Rights Office) to an office headed by a deputy assistant secretary (which gave it clout), and installed a Foreign Service officer to direct it (which was unheard of at the time) and career Foreign Service people to staff it (which helped close the divide between Foreign Service and Civil Service). The Foreign Service began to recruit more blacks and expand their career opportunities, assignments, and promotions. Later this would include other minorities and women. In retrospect, John and I are astonished at our audacity. "To think we could read some books about Henry Kissinger," John said, "and devise a plan to make a difference takes a certain kind of thinking. We had to have confidence in ourselves. To be able to think that way in the early 1970s took a lot of gumption."

One of the few people of that era, and perhaps the only white person, who sought to make a difference for minorities in the Foreign Service was William "Mac" McElroy, deputy director of EEO and a Civil Service employee of some thirty years. He brought a significant number of minorities into the Foreign Service through special programs and assignments. His work was so prescient

that the Thursday Luncheon Group cited him as worthy of being called a
"brother."

Ultimately, some time after that heart-pounding walk up 19th Street to
enter the hallowed diplomats' door, I came to see the State Department building as a receptacle of all that is good in government. It was a place where I felt
I could accomplish something meaningful. I awoke each morning eager to get
to work. Despite the discrimination, the atmosphere in State crackled with
excitement and a sense of public service. With Secretary of State Henry
Kissinger and his executive assistant, Lawrence Eagleburger, at the helm, the
windows of the building had been flung open for fresh air and change rode the
breezes.

In 1975, the 119th Foreign Service officer class was sworn in, and I was
invited to attend the ceremonies. Kissinger, who won the Nobel Prize for
Peace that year for negotiating America's withdrawal from Vietnam, was the
scheduled speaker, and I wanted to hear what he had to say. His statements, so
direct and profound, rocked the building. For the first time since 1946, the
State Department faced an upheaval. State learned that day that Kissinger took
no prisoners. Foreign policy is important to our nation, he told the new officers; it must be developed and pursued in an orderly manner. "And you, ladies
and gentlemen, are the means by which this is carried out." He told them that
he intended to appoint young ambassadors as well as older ones. For the first
time, a low-grade Foreign Service officer, FSO-4, had been named ambassador
to Rwanda. "Even an FSO-4 can find the ambassadorial baton in his knapsack,"
Kissinger said, "and there will be more appointments like this." Then he
announced the establishment of the revolutionary Priorities Policy Group
(PPG) to be chaired by the deputy under secretary for management. "We must
have a better way of allocating resources for the broader consideration of foreign policy," he said. The mission of the PPG would be to review all policies, lay
them beside the budget, and then allocate the resources to fit the policies.

With that "little secretariat," Kissinger centralized the budget process of the
State Department, taking it out of the basement and the province of people
wearing green eyeshades. He now controlled the money, the resources, and the
people. It had never been done before. The PPG gave Kissinger the power, at a
moment's notice, to take funds from one bureau and give to another. I never
doubted that it was the right thing. The only period in my career when the Foreign Service and the State Department were successful in convincing Congress

to make the appropriations necessary for adequate resources for the departments was during the tenure of Kissinger as secretary of state and Eagleburger
as deputy under secretary for management. They understood absolutely the
concepts of management and strategic planning, and they presented the material so clearly that Congress could easily understand the logic of the request.

PPG, in essence, controlled the entire foreign-policy apparatus in the State
Department and overseas in the name of the secretary of state. Six regional
bureaus exist now, but at that time there were five—European Affairs, African
Affairs, Inter-American Affairs (South America), Near East and South Asian
Affairs, and East Asia and the Pacific.[†] Under the stringent new procedure,
every assistant secretary came before the PPG and presented the policies for his
or her bureau. Each had to justify the requests for budget and personnel and
answer the question: "What policies will this advance?" Policy and money were
bound together. The assistant secretaries who were responsible for the geographic bureaus were mightily displeased. The Bureau for Europe, the premier
bureau, was considered first among equals, and when some of its resources
were allocated to another bureau, the European bureau was incensed. The
indignant assistant secretary appealed to Kissinger and Eagleburger, but their
answer was abrupt and final: "This is the way we are going to manage the
department on foreign policy." They were standing the State Department on
its startled head.

In 1975, as I was completing my doctorate in public administration, I cast
about for a subject for my dissertation. The more I studied Kissinger's theory
and operational style, comparing them with popular views of public administration, the more I appreciated their profundity. With Kissinger's approval, I
wrote my dissertation as a case study of the PPG. I created a mathematical
model and sent a questionnaire to Foreign Service officers and Civil Service
officers all over the world.

Computers and software were new, so when I persuaded a friendly person
in Central Computer Services in the Personnel Bureau to run the data and help
interpret it, we helped start a new trend of using computers in the Foreign Service. People were eager to participate in my study because I was writing about
Kissinger and his work. The dissertation, "The Priorities Policy Group: A Case

---

[†] In 1993 the Near East and South Asia bureau was split into two bureaus. The bureau of South Asian Affairs includes
India, Pakistan, Nepal, and Sri Lanka.

Study of the Institutionalization of a Policy Linkage and Resource Allocation Mechanism in the Department of State" (June 1978), became an unofficial handbook for that management office. I understand it is still being used to brief new officers.

Kissinger's many attributes and faults are legendary. He was an erudite, egotistical, and Machiavellian tactician who created an aura about himself. By holding the limelight as secretary of state, he made it impossible for diplomacy to revert to being a bilateral exercise. Since he was foreign-born and therefore ineligible to be elected president, being secretary of state was the highest position he could achieve at the federal level. For a time, he jointly held the title secretary of state and national security advisor, spending mornings at the White House dealing with issues before the National Security Council, and then, for the remainder of the day, moving over to the State Department. With his insatiable appetite for work, it was not unusual for him to arrive at the White House at 5:00 A.M. and not leave the State Department until 11:00 P.M. He had several aides and two sets of secretaries who worked in shifts. Few people challenged him in his quest to harness the State Department because few people were smarter than he was. To enhance his success, he surrounded himself with bright people, none surpassing Larry Eagleburger from Wisconsin. They were a dazzling team. The PPG was Kissinger's little think-tank. He created it; Eagleburger operated it. Both were skillful with the press and with Congress. Foreign Service officers sometimes erroneously believe that politics stop at the water's edge, but Congress holds the purse strings and Eagleburger never forgot that. He knew congresspersons, informed them, cultivated them, and played the system like a jazzman on the vibes. Working with the PPG changed forever my modus operandi for managing foreign policy.

Although I do not admire everything that he did, Kissinger was the right person at the right time for the State Department. He gave the department a sense of renewal, and he brought together all of the foreign-affairs activities under the secretary of state, coordinating the programs of Defense, USAID, USIA, Commerce, Labor, Agriculture, and the CIA. In my judgment, the management of foreign policy has never been as efficient as it was under Kissinger's direction. He instituted a wrenching policy of regularly transferring every Foreign Service officer to different bureaus to insure that the officers had a global perspective of foreign policy; it became known as "GLOP." Heretofore, some ambassadors homesteaded in one country or region for their entire career. Now, officers were routinely reassigned and would say, "I've been glopped." He invented "shuttle diplomacy," traveling to Egypt to Syria to Lebanon and back again. When he engineered the beginning of the reestablishment of U.S.-China relations, he inscribed his name in history. He shaped groundbreaking policy with the Middle East, he put Africa on the foreign policy radar, and he expressed an interest in the United Nations. I came to view him as the foremost foreign-policy theoretician and practitioner in the world. The man has had an immeasurable effect on the world, for good or bad. Kissinger and President Nixon wanted to run the world, and to a great extent, they did.

My first permanent assignment in the Foreign Service was to the Policy Office in the Bureau of Personnel. For two years, 1972 to 1974, I worked with personnel policy and served as liaison with the General Accounting Office, watchdog over the rest of the government. Among other things, this office has the responsibility of interpreting Title V of the United States Code, which governs personnel in the federal government. Title V is the basic law upon which all other personnel laws and regulations are based. As liaison in the director general's office, I found myself researching complex issues of personnel law from all reaches of the personnel bureau. Three cases I encountered were especially educational.

The concept of overtime was one of those complex issues. Traditionally, commissioned officers in the Foreign Service were not paid for overtime because rank is in the person, not in the position. After the Foreign Service Act of 1946, the assumption was that officers were on duty twenty-four hours a day. This policy was challenged by Allison Palmer, and the case wound its way through the State Department mechanisms for resolving grievances. The ruling was that Foreign Service officers, like employees of the Civil Service, should get paid for overtime until they reach a senior grade and receive a reduced allowance.

Alcoholism was another tangled issue assigned to me for research. In the 1970s, the question was whether alcoholism was a disease or just bad conduct. Until this time, it had been the practice to consider officers who were addicted to alcohol as undisciplined and unprofessional. If alcoholism was a treatable disease, however, these officers might be rehabilitated and continue productive careers. My researched report on the issue supported the medical division's recommendation that the director general and the secretary of state consider alcoholism a disease. While attending seminars and investigating treatment centers then available in the United States I learned, among other things, that gin is so potent that it is absorbed into the blood stream through the tongue. I quit drinking martinis immediately.

The third substantive issue dealt with sexism. Until about 1970, female officers had been forced to resign from the Foreign Service when they married. When that policy was changed, those who wanted to return to the Service were invited back. I had the job of welcoming them aboard.

Lucy not only had the lion's share of raising our daughters, she also had enrolled full-time at the University of the District of Columbia to complete her bachelor's degree in accounting. We bought a home in the Chevy Chase area of the District of Columbia for what seemed at the time an exorbitant price—$42,000. I took the bus to work at the State Department every morning while Lucy carpooled the girls to Blessed Sacrament, a Catholic school. Occasionally, as is life's wont, this pat routine was upset. One day, the school nurse called me to say that Sarah had a piece of chalk stuck in her nose. Lucy was in class, so I went to the school, took Sarah home, and we dislodged the chalk. Since five or six hours were left in the workday, we took a taxi to the State Department, where I bought her ice cream in the cafeteria. No babysitting services were available at the workplace in those days, but a friendly nurse in the dispensary came to my rescue and looked after my daughter for the rest of the day.

When I came into the service, one part of an officer's evaluation was secret, and this portion included an evaluation of his spouse. Questions included: How well does the officer interact with people in the embassy? Does he socialize? Does he play bridge? What does his wife do? Is she part of the community? Does she help the officer in his work? Is she available when the ambassador's wife calls for assistance with a social function? After the Foreign Service officer's suicide, the American Foreign Service Association and the Association of American Foreign Service Wives (now American Foreign Service Women) worked to eliminate secret evaluations. Changes in the service were forming as clouds in the distance and were moving toward us in a gentle storm. An old-line Foreign Service officer admonished some of us for writing letters to the president in support of the raise being advocated by the American Federation of Government Employees, the Civil Service union. "It is not done," he said. "A Foreign Service officer does not lobby for such a mundane thing as a raise in salary." Until then, the American Foreign Service Association had been a gentleman's club, but it was taken over by a group of young Turks who changed its culture completely. I would not say I was one of them, but I worked with them. The Foreign Service has turned around 180 degrees since 1925, and the profile of the elite, old-guard Foreign Service officer has slowly disappeared.

At the same time, the Association of American Foreign Service Wives lobbied to be excluded from the husbands' evaluations. With Leslie Dorman as president, the association also changed its name to the American Foreign Service Women, acknowledging the fact that all women—wives, secretaries, female officers—had a rough time in the service. This was the beginning of a solution, but by no means was it the end of the problem. During my entire career, the issue of minorities and women never left my desk.

When it was time in my career to move from personnel to a geographic bureau, Mac McElroy, a mentor from the EEO, engineered my first assignment of substance in the State Department. Through his efforts, I was assigned in 1974 to the Bureau of Near East and South Asian Affairs, where I cut my teeth on managing foreign policy issues in Washington for posts abroad. As a post-management officer, I covered India, Iran, Lebanon, Sri Lanka, and Nepal. My job was to backstop the posts in Washington and get the ambassadors whatever they needed—personnel, housing, supplies, vehicles, and diatomaceous earth—and to manage relationships with other agencies such as the CIA, Treasury, Agriculture, Labor, Atomic Energy Commission, Library of Congress, and State Department. Iran was a hot spot because it was a major source of oil for the United States and unrest was stirring in the country as the Shah attempted to transform his nation's economy rapidly. The Gulf States had just come into their own, and the United States was scrambling to establish embassies in all of them: Bahrain, Qatar, the United Arab Emirates, and Kuwait. This bureau assignment put me in contact with almost every person on the Hill who dealt with foreign affairs, and it sent me traveling to far-flung places. India seemed to be another world. I was struck by the castes, the poverty, the intensive labor market, and the practice by parents of crippling children so they could beg in the streets. The Taj Mahal, seen by both day and night, enthralled me. I flew into Katmandu so close to the majestic Himalayas I thought I could touch the snowy peaks, and I was in Tehran when the first shots were fired at a U.S. Defense attaché in front of my hotel near the American Embassy.

The executive director of the bureau was Leamon Ray Hunt, a senior Foreign Service officer from Oklahoma. He believed in giving his officers latitude, so we had the authority to go as high as needed to get things done. I encountered only one person, a deputy assistant secretary of state, who resented being addressed by a junior officer and complained to my superior. Ray was later chosen to be head of the Sinai Multinational Force and Observer Group, the first peacekeeping mission in the Sinai Desert, headquartered in Rome. On his way to the Rome office the morning of February 15, 1984, he was shot through the back window of his sedan by a terrorist and killed.

In 1975, I had an intriguing phone call from a friend in the Office of the Under Secretary for Management, who was working for Eagleburger, who was now deputy under secretary of state for management. In his slim book, *American Foreign Policy, Three Essays*, written while he was on the Harvard faculty, Kissinger espoused the theory that in order to control the making of foreign policy, one must control the resources. Kissinger instituted the concept into the PPG, which consisted of the deputy under secretary for management as chair, the director of the policy planning staff, the director general of the Foreign Service, the inspector general, the counselor of the State Department, the assistant secretary for Administration, and the director of Management Operations. The group reviewed the entire budget and policy. Kissinger's operative phrase was "the allocation of resources for the greater consideration of foreign policy," which meant micromanagement from a macro vantage point. This model, Kissinger's personal management style, worked because Eagleburger had total access to Kissinger, and Kissinger had complete trust in Eagleburger. They were a symbiotic team that virtually directed the entire State Department and the rest of the foreign-policy community.

The phone call was to ask if I wanted to be a part of this group. "But," my friend cautioned, "it is not a permanent mainstream position. It could hurt your career."They were assembling a small staff of Foreign Service officers capable of exercising intense control of management and policies, but they wanted only officers who were willing to take calculated risks. These officers could not be anxious about making the right move to advance their careers. They wanted a group of daring people. I did not hesitate. "I want to be a part of it," I answered. Thus I joined the PPG staff of five Foreign Service officers. Working for Kissinger's management tool, the PPG, opened doors quicker than *alakazam*. We operated with a great deal of autonomy; senior officers found themselves justifying budgets and policies to us. This was perhaps the most powerful job I had in the Foreign Service, doubly remarkable for my age and rank. From 1975 to 1978, I was in the Office of Management Operations, where my responsibility was to follow policy on Africa, the Middle East, human rights, humanitarian affairs, and the law of the sea.

Our blue-ribbon staff was housed on the prestigious seventh floor, the command center of the State Department. Gaining access to the seventh floor was a heady experience. A special pass permitted me to enter restricted areas, to receive special intelligence briefings, and to be in the vicinity of luminaries such as Kissinger and his successor, Cyrus Vance. The seventh floor was resplendent with the ghosts of former secretaries of state and heroic figures of diplomacy: George Marshall, Dean Rusk, Dean Acheson, Edward Stettinius. This is where the action took place and the air was charged with power. Overnight, my status changed in the eyes of my associates. Eagleburger detected this as well, and soon after our arrival he talked to the staff about it. "You are in the center of power," he said, "but remember, you will not always be here. So, make your decisions with the realization that one day you will be where those people are—at posts overseas and occupying jobs in the geographical and functional bureaus of the department. Be fair and useful. Never use your power for the sole purpose of exercising power. Make it work for what Kissinger wants, and that is the greater consideration of foreign policy." It was a valuable piece of advice. Immediately, I changed my attitude from being a staffer impressed with the glow of the job to realizing that it was one of the greatest learning opportunities that might ever come my way.

Eagleburger is a blunt bulldog of a man who played classical music in his office. We could detect his mood by the volume of the music and the composer—if it was Bach, watch out. He smoked incessantly, with a cigarette in one hand and a nose spray nearby. "You are killing yourself," I once told him. "Who asked you?" he replied. When smoking was prohibited in federal buildings, Eagleburger's office was an exception. He had a sign made touting the fact. It read: Smoking Area.

Eagleburger is an intellectual who can be rough and testy and is intolerant of small talk, scathing of mediocre thinking, and curt with foreign secretaries and ambassadors. He knows behavioral science and foreign policy down to the ground. Unusually early in his career, he became known for being precise and decisive. He never backed away from making decisions, popular or unpopular, but nor did he fail to listen. One issue I was assigned to research was the movement of Jews from the Soviet Union to Israel with American aid. Legislation called for the Jews to transition through London or elsewhere before going to Israel. Occasionally, refugees wanted to go directly to the United States. A colleague urged me to permit their bypassing the law, but I would not do it. We went before Eagleburger with our opposing views. Mine was based on reading the sense of Congress when it passed the legislation. My colleague's view was based on expediency. I made my case, my colleague made his. Eagleburger sat for about five seconds, then rendered his decision. "Ed is right, you're wrong. Goodbye." Precise and decisive.

Not every issue was a victory. On another occasion, the Foreign Service came to a crossroad of change and backed away. American business had been complaining that American embassies were not responsive to helping American business abroad. As the criticism grew, chambers of commerce and business organizations wondered aloud if the Commerce Department might do a better job promoting business than the Foreign Service was doing. The Commerce Department leapt aboard this moving train and made a pitch to absorb the Foreign Commercial Service, taking it away from the State Department. No Foreign Service officer believed that would happen. The Office of Management and Budget got into the skirmish to examine the situation, and I was the staffer assigned to backstop the issue. Senator Daniel Inouye (Democrat–Hawaii) asked that a hearing be held inside the State Department so Foreign Service officers could voice their opinions. I attended the session and was astonished to hear an economic commercial officer from the State Department say, "I did not come into the Foreign Service to work in Commerce." The prevailing attitude was that Foreign Service officers tolerated commercial activities, but did not want to dirty their hands with them. The moderator replied, "I am quite sure that Commerce won't mind if you do not." That signaled to me that Senator Inouye was leaning toward sponsoring legislation to give this commercial activity to Commerce.

I went to Eagleburger and asked if the secretary of state would make a fight to keep it.

"No," Eagleburger said, "the secretary will not."

"Why not?"

"Because I am not going to recommend it. The bunch of pantywaists that made those dumb statements about commercial affairs do not know that the world has changed and that we have to have people to do this work. If Commerce can do it better than we can, let them have it. American businessmen have already made the decision."

It was the right move at the time. As Senator Inouye asked the protesting Foreign Service officer, "What do you think keeps this country going?" The objective was to sell more cars, more electricity, more technology—more American products and services—because the nation realized that we cannot consume everything that we produce. If we were to remain a first-rate country, and that was the argument we made in those days, we could not rest at that level of production. We had to keep moving forward. It was a long time before Foreign Service officers realized that the Age of Commerce had arrived and that the day was fast coming when economic affairs would be the new boy on the block, followed by science and technology and then the environment. When Eagleburger became deputy secretary of state and I became director general, one of his first conversations with me began, "We have to change the Foreign Service. These bloody pencil pushers and political officers have to learn that their bread and butter is promoting American products, selling cars, or whatever else our country produces." Later, Eagleburger became secretary of state himself, to date the only career Foreign Service officer to hold that post. Throughout his twenty-seven-year career in the State Department he defined his work as "a servant of the people." That definition parallels my own philosophy. I have asked myself, "Why am I serving as a Foreign Service officer? What is the business of a diplomat?" The answer is because it is the rule of the people to have a number of people in government representing it. Foreign Service officers are no less representatives of the people than extension agents of the Department of Agriculture working in lower Alabama. When I saw Eagleburger at work, I always felt that not far from his mind was this question: "Is this beneficial for the American people?" It is a good and sound question for all of us in public service. I like to think that I have always kept in mind the interest of the people.

The staff of the Department of Management Operations rarely met directly with Kissinger. He met only with Eagleburger, although there was one exception. We had been trying to get a meeting with Kissinger for a week to get his decision on a major foreign-policy issue. One Sunday afternoon, my direct boss called me at home and said, "Can you come in? We're going to see The Man." Kissinger saw us, outlined what he had in mind, and we had our marching orders.

When we saw him at ceremonial functions at which he presided, he always acknowledged us. Always. We ran into him in the hall, and he made sure he spoke to us. He never ignored the staff or appeared to be too imperious to notice our existence. Once in a while, he sent back a piece of paper with a single comment: "Excellent. HAK." That is the most he would allow himself. I received one of those laudatory memos and wish I had it still. Today, it would be a collector's item.

These experiences and people during my first few years in the Foreign Service formed me professionally. I learned the characteristics required of good Foreign Service officers. To be successful, they must be daring, confident, curious, and love continuous education. They must be not only unafraid of change, but welcoming of it. As noted theologian Presiding Bishop John Hines once said, "You either seize change by the hand, or it will seize you by the throat." Good Foreign Service officers must love reading and writing. "You have to be reflective," Nick Thorne told me. "You have to think." A Foreign Service officer must also learn how to be alone, even in a sea of people. I learned to cultivate solitude in the midst of controversy or in a raging river of conflict in order to bring myself back to a sense of balance. That lesson served me well. The overriding requirements are a sense of mastery over self, the ability to communicate, a good sense of history, and the ability to figure out for oneself where the world is going and what role the United States has to play in that world. These are not things that can be taught in a foreign-policy course.

I had spent six years in Washington, completing my graduate education, learning the intricacies of the Foreign Service and the State Department, researching and tracking foreign policy abroad, and riding the whirlwind stirred by Kissinger and Eagleburger. No longer was I a fledgling Foreign Service officer. My wings had been strengthened on the domestic front, and I was ready to test myself in the field. It was 1978, and I wanted a foreign post.

GHANA IN A
TIME OF TURBULENCE

My first overseas assignment as a Foreign Service officer would be Ghana, the Black Star of Africa, but first my career took a detour. The customary route for a Foreign Service officer was to serve in a geographic bureau in order to study a region and to learn one of its languages before being posted abroad. After two years in my selected parent bureau, Near East and South Asian Affairs, I was headed for the Foreign Service Institute to study Arabic in preparation for going to the Middle East, but this plan was interrupted by my stint with Kissinger's PPG. After that, a position became available in Maputo, the capital of Mozambique, one of the new independent states in Africa. I applied for deputy chief of mission in that small post, but word came back that the ambassador there would not accept me. I had no experience as a political officer, he said, and he did not think I could write a Foreign Service dispatch.

I was shocked and angry, but strengthened in my determination. I would not let the rejection be a setback. Instead, I remembered what Singapore prime minister Lee Kwan Yew said when he learned that the Malaysia-Singapore Federation had been broken by his Malaysian counterpart: "Let us shed one tear, and then let us go to work."

I enrolled in a political reporting course at the Foreign Service Institute while I spent another year working in the Office of Management Operations. By then, the position of political counselor had become available in Accra, Ghana, a hardship post that the personnel bureau had a difficult time filling. I applied and was accepted as counselor for political affairs. And so I went to Ghana. I was fifty years old and headed for my first overseas job as a Foreign Service officer—and a baptism of fire.

The American Embassy in Accra (consisting of about twenty officers, most of whom were in the USAID mission) was minuscule compared to the Bangkok mission, where I had served previously. A mission is the name given to the U.S. government entity on foreign soil responsible for the conduct of relations between the host country and the United States. Comprising many sections, a mission is commanded by a chief of mission, also referred to as an ambassador, who is appointed by the president with the advice and consent of the Senate. The deputy chief of mission (DCM), never called deputy ambassador, is appointed in partnership between the ambassador at post and the director general of the Foreign Service. Mission sections are headed by counselors, an international term signaling functional rank. Depending on the size of the operation, a mission could have counselors for political affairs, economic affairs, administrative affairs, consular affairs, and agricultural affairs. The section heads of a mission constitute what is known as the "country team."

In some large missions, such as Tokyo or Paris, the DCM may have the title "minister," an international rank just below "ambassador," appended to his working title to give the officer more prestige. In a sizeable mission, a counselor of consular affairs, referred to as consul general, is an independent post that reports to the ambassador. Other mission employees include secretaries, support staff, officers, and specialists.

As a political officer, I would hold one of the most romanticized jobs. From the beginning of the Foreign Service, political officers were the core of a mission and responsible for political reporting and analyses. Political officers have always held themselves in high regard. By the time I became a political officer in 1978, much of the glamour had dimmed, and it had become a job of hard-edged demands of contemporary foreign affairs. It is the job of a political officer to develop a broad range of contacts from every walk of society (governmental leaders, educators, labor leaders, private sector, clergy, military officers, press, and others), to gather information, and to report and analyze political events. An effective political officer must have good interpersonal skills, effective communication abilities (oral and written), an aptitude for clear thinking and analysis, and the courage to report objectively and honestly. Political officers find that truthful reporting can be risky to a career when he or she reports information that disagrees with the opinion of the ambassador or Washington officials. More than one political officer caught in that predicament has been tempted to adopt Emily Dickinson's poetic advice—"tell the truth, but tell it slant."

When I was assigned to Ghana, President Jimmy Carter's administration was expressing interest in Africa. Ghana was important to the United States because it was the first African nation to win its independence and, therefore, was the pacesetter for our relationships with the continent and with other emerging nations. To illustrate the importance of our relationship with that country, the U.S. Embassy in Ghana was built in the image of a chief's palace. Constructed of Ghanaian wood and octagonal in shape, it sat on stilts and was open to the breezes in that equatorial climate. The graceful embassy building was one of the United States' few attempts to replicate native artistry. The open architecture, however, proved to be a security impossibility, so it is no longer used as an embassy.

The U.S.-Ghana relationship began in 1957 after Ghana acquired its independence from Great Britain. When I came on the scene twenty-one years later, the country was under military rule, beset by governmental corruption, financially bankrupt, and seething with frustration. In this political climate, the purpose of the U.S. Embassy was to maintain good relations with Ghana; to support the return to civilian rule; to foster the development of investment codes and other elements, which would result in economic stability and growth; and to promote peaceful relations amongst Ghana and her neighbors: Togo, Benin, Nigeria, Côte d'Ivoire, Kenya, Sierra Leone, and Haute-Volta (now Burkina Faso).

My family and I arrived in July in the midst of the rainy season. It was hot, muggy, and wet. We stepped off the plane to see a city surrounded by banana trees and climbing, trailing, towering vegetation. The climate was so lush and fertile that I could imagine Accra being swallowed in a gulp by the steaming jungle. Yet, when the heavy rains stopped, the tropical weather swung radically 180 degrees, and the country became dry and dusty. Malaria was ever-present.

The capital city of Accra was patterned after London, and the populace clung to Ghana's sunset glory as a British colony. Cars imported from England whirled around the many traffic circles, ladies met for afternoon tea, and men left their offices for a ritual of scotch and soda before dinner. Accra was accustomed to being a throbbing center of activity, but political upheaval and economic hardships had dealt harshly with the city. When we arrived, Accra was faded and weary.

The houses for U.S. Embassy employees were private residences scattered across the city. Our furnished house was located in a suburban area. That first day, with geckos climbing up the walls of our home, tropical birds screeching in the forests, and the air blanketed with wet heat, Lucy asked, "What have we done?"

What we had done was come to the Gold Coast, to a once-flourishing country that was an impoverished nation not only down on its luck, but almost down on its knees. Ghana had become rich from the trade of gold, ivory, diamonds, cocoa, and slaves. As one of the jewels of Britain's colonies, wealthy and well-educated Ghana seemed destined for a bright future. It is a hospitable land of gentle beaches, savannas, rain forests, and superior game reserves. By 1948, a movement for independence was being championed by the United Gold Coast Convention Party (UGCC), led by Ghanaian elites. Many had been knighted by the queen; most had been educated in England. The man the UGCC chose to carry the country forward into independence was Dr. Kwame Nkrumah, a teacher educated in Britain and the United States. Before I could understand Ghana, I had first to know about Nkrumah.

Nkrumah's dream for Ghana was that it would lead all of Africa in establishing a United States of Africa. He was a northerner, an important consideration in that country, a charismatic ebony man of average height but Romanesque hauteur who usually dressed in colorful robes. In the United States and London he became acquainted with black Americans and early civil-rights leaders such as W. E. B. DuBois and Marcus Garvey. Nkrumah left America to become secretary general of the UGCC, taking with him his dreams for Africa. He was a populist in the manner of William Jennings Bryan—advocating equal justice for everybody—but he was also a power-seeker and an ineffectual leader. His dreams were forever beyond his reach.

Nkrumah was independent Ghana's first prime minister, and when it became a republic in 1960, he became president. Along with independence, Britain left debt-free Ghana a treasury of $200 million. The country had a shipping line, an airline, and a huge infrastructure of state buildings, but the wealth began to melt away. Nkrumah envisioned Accra as the host country to organize African unity, and he built edifices to support huge conferences, built an industrial park outside of Accra, built up the port of Tema, and brought in so many advisors they were falling over one another: black Americans, left-of-center English authorities, and advisors from East Germany. Many of the advisors were sociologists and social theorists who saw Ghana as a laboratory for theoretical experimentation. An East German woman was brought to Ghana to establish, of all things, a glider corps.

The darling of the communist world, courted by the Soviet Union and China, Nkrumah instituted in his own country what a *New York Times* writer described as "idiotic African Socialism." He instituted a centralized economic model, patterned after the Soviet Union system, but it broke down. Nkrumah had great vision and energy, but because he had little knowledge of people or sense of practicality, he was unable to bring his vision to fruition. An onlooker told me of a visit by a delegation from a small African country. As they were leaving, one of them said to Nkrumah, "*Osagefo* [leader], what about the loan?"

"Oh, I almost forgot," Nkrumah said. He turned to one of his aides and said, "By the way, I promised them $2 million."

Nkrumah financed incipient movements in various parts of Africa. Consequently, Ghana was soon broke, and Nkrumah was overthrown by a cabal of military generals and exiled to die in Guinea. This was the first coup. The unstable country was jolted by military overthrows in 1966, 1969, and 1972. The last installed Lt. Colonel Ignatius Kutu Acheampong as head of state. Acheampong's government was known for its incompetence, greed, corruption, and immorality, and Ghana continued to deteriorate. In 1978, a palace coup displaced Acheampong and installed General Frederick W. K. Akuffo as head of state with a government made up of military generals, paramilitary generals, the police department, border guards, the air force, and the army. I arrived as political counselor at just about this time.

I welcomed my new professional challenges. Political reporting is like transcribing a theatrical performance and observing all of the actors. I looked at the players from the perspective of a behaviorialist. The most important element of my posting to Ghana was the learning experience. I would be an eyewitness to a country using its resources and political leadership to become a respected member of the larger world of nations. Before I went to Ghana, I had a conversation with Andrew Young, U.S. ambassador to the United Nations. He told me of standing at the border of Ghana and commenting on the abundant food production in neighboring Côte d'Ivoire.

"Yes," his Ghanaian host said, "but Ghana is a freer nation."

"The first duty of political leadership," Ambassador Young replied, "is to make sure the people are fed."

Ghana, a country once ruled by the great Ashanti Empire and then a strutting British colony, was now in shambles. The entire state-directed infrastructure—communications, sanitation, transportation—was collapsing. Electricity was sporadic, and water systems were failing. We do not understand deprivation until we cannot get water—to drink, to take a bath, to cook, to flush the toilets. The lack of products in the stores indicated the scarcity of foreign exchange. Basics such as rice and bread were scant and the people could not find enough food to eat. What food existed fell victim to a failing distribution system. Crops rotted on the ground because trucks were inoperable or roads impassable. A civil servant told me, "I get up in the morning knowing there is no food in the house. So I spend the next several hours searching for food for my family. By the time I get to work, I have a couple of hours before noon, when I need to start thinking about where I am going to get lunch. I'll search for a place where I can maybe buy food for lunch. Then, dinner, same thing. And then I am able to go to bed."

Although the common people were preoccupied by subsisting from day to day, a special black market existed for the privileged who could have cases of beer delivered to their homes. Liquor, chocolates, luxury items, watches, and briefcases were all sold at a duty-free state store. Yet the system did not apply to all of the elite. A law professor at the University of Ghana with a newborn baby could not find milk. He asked if there was any way that I could help him get a supply of milk that did not require refrigeration. I violated all the embassy regulations, bought milk from our commissary, took it to his villa, and gave it to him. I later overheard him relating this with incredulity, describing me as "the guy that exhibits the milk of human kindness."

The American Embassy ran its own commissary of basic staples and, because morale was so low, made shopping runs to Togo. For a few days, American personnel could escape the oppressive atmosphere in Ghana, stay in a comfortable hotel, and eat in nice restaurants. The embassy also brought in generators for employees' homes for when the electricity went off. Each house had a refrigerator and a food freezer to stock up on food purchased in Togo or shipped from the United States. American companies operating in Ghana—oil drilling, tuna canning, aluminum mining—built their own small, self-sufficient communities and flew in food and goods for their employees. This was a way of life,

Ghana, a country once ruled by the great Ashanti empire and then a strutting British colony, was in shambles. The entire state-directed infrastructure—communications, sanitation, transportation—was collapsing. Electricity was sporadic and water systems were failing. Even worse, a violent coup would soon follow. And this is where I had brought my family.
(*left to right*) Our cook Garuba, Sarah (*front*), Katherine, Lucy, Perkins, our dog Gabby, and two Embassy drivers.

but obviously the self-sufficiency affected our host country, and I worried about what effect it had on our relationship with the Ghanaians who worked for us at the embassy.

Our family settled in. Kathy, thirteen, and Sarah, nine, were enrolled in the International School. I served on the school board and sang in the British Choir, where I heard ladies talk about Ghana's golden years while they took afternoon tea at the King's Way Hotel. At first, Lucy was a member of the Foreign Wives Club, then she went to work as the accountant for the defense attaché. Lucy and I belonged to a club at the port of Tema, but it rarely had anything to sell, so we always took a portable cooler stocked with sandwiches and beer. One Sunday I offered a Ghanaian member a can of imported beer. "My God," he said, "I haven't seen a Heineken in years." I gave him the six-pack to take home. Thereafter whenever I saw him, I gave him four or five beers. His deep gratitude embarrassed me, because I realized that my small gesture took away part of his dignity.

Nobody could get a handle on running the country. By 1978, the country was bankrupt. Inflation had risen to 116.5 percent; agricultural productivity had declined, exacerbated by drought and bush fires; unemployment was high; exports, especially cocoa, were low; industrial productivity sank; the cost of living was skyrocketing; and rampant corruption became a way of life. The fault lay with the failures of government policy, mismanagement, and *kalebuleism* (from irresponsibility to profiteering in trade). Kickbacks were the normal way of doing business with the government. The cruelest element in the Ghanaian construct was the corruption of government officials and their neglect of the country.

I spoke with Ghanaians who remembered the last high official from the United States who visited the country: Vice President Richard Nixon. Most memorable about that visit was how quickly the United States set up a communications system at the Continental Hotel. "Why can't we have a system like that?" they asked. "In a country so rich with natural resources, why can we not feed ourselves?" The poignancy of that longing demonstrates how difficult it is to govern a country, to facilitate the best efforts in the interest of a country, to satisfy the needs of citizens, and to champion the intrinsic values of statehood and sovereignty. I learned in Ghana the value of taking pride in the ability to till a field, to work in a factory, to sweep a street clean, and to develop new products. It was heartbreaking to walk into a hospital and see the unmet needs of the halt and the lame, knowing that a system of triage was always in effect because of lack of medicine, lack of training, and lack of doctors.

Repeatedly I asked myself, "Why doesn't the United States do more?" But the answer was not in bringing in truckloads of goods to fill the stores of Accra. What happens when the products are gone? How could we keep the system going? I recognized that it is impossible for outsiders to institutionalize a system. The citizens themselves must do this work. I would feel this sense of inadequacy, face this temptation, and come to this understanding again and again in underdeveloped countries around the world.

How does a Foreign Service officer reach the point of wanting to do more?

The answer is that one must become a revolutionary oneself and develop a revolutionary mentality. How does one be an effective change agent as a Foreign Service officer? It seems to me, as it was proven to me in South Africa, that one must be a revolutionary at the bottom of one's heart before beginning to use the tendency toward revolution as a foreign-policy tool. Why did I challenge the status quo, ostensibly without fear or concern for my career, and why did I go to South Africa? Because I believed in what was being attempted by the different groups: to overthrow the regime in a revolutionary sense. So one must become a revolutionary at heart in order to make it work for the United States. I do not think the president of the United States would put that in the instructions to any ambassador going out, but if I had been writing my own instructions, I would have written, "Mr. Ambassador, for you to manage the conduct of relations between South Africa and the United States, you will have to change the system in South Africa, which means you will have to become a revolutionary."

Since my time in Thailand, I have worn a medallion with a likeness of a dragon, the Asian sign under which I was born. The dragon mirrors my zodiacal sign of Gemini. An element of both signs is being a revolutionary person, not being satisfied with the status quo. I do not take this frivolously, but instead I embrace it and act on it when necessary. I also wear a jade cross, which represents to me the Christian philosophy and the umbrella of Christ's teachings and blessings. The two, the dragon and Christ, meet halfway and form, in part, my personal philosophy.

Revolution is a great mystery. Mao Tse-tung was a dreamer who was in love with continuous revolution. I believe that such a thing as continuous revolution exists, and that it is working in our country. I have said in many speeches that America is a revolutionary society. I counted out our myriad revolutions to an audience of clergy, listing the Revolution of 1776, the Civil War, the revolution of labor and employee rights about 1912, the second phase of the feminist movement in 1925, the civil-rights revolution, which began in earnest in the 1940s, and more until the present day—women's rights, gay rights, and the rights of people with disabilities. With each revolution we said the world was coming to an end, but every revolution in this country has made us better as a people, more sensitive and more appreciative. America is an imperfect society. As long as we can remain a revolutionary society, we will continue to grow as a nation. The United States is a unique country, as I have learned in the past thirty-five years through representing it. I could not represent it well unless I knew it and believed in it. The aphorism is true: If you want to learn something, teach it.

Now I was in Ghana representing the United States, and because that job is a two-way communication, I had to learn about Ghana. Ghanaian culture is a mix of tribal affiliations (primarily Ashanti, Ga, Fanti, and Ewe) and colonial influences (Portuguese, French, and British). The British colonial system left behind a costly class system. Colonials had lived in grand houses and enjoyed food allowances and "home leave," in which they could visit their homeland or lavish vacation spots such as Kashmir in India or the Cameron Highlands in Malaysia. Ghanaian government officials were still trying to maintain colonial pretenses. Native Ghanaians, already at home, went on "home leave" at government expense to visit their villas in Switzerland or elsewhere. This was not only a drain on the treasury; it widened the class division, fostered elitism, and further separated the government's hierarchy from those who were being governed.

The Ghanaian elites I met clung to British colonial habits of tea mid-morning and mid-afternoon and a drink before a leisurely dinner, all to the detriment of work habits. The British educational system had provided Ghanaian students with a free education, free food, and free books. When the government could no longer support the university system and initiated a loan system to begin the process of students bearing the cost of their education, unhappy students protested. The great divide was between the colonial luxuries that Ghanaians wanted and the reality of what the country could afford.

While they treasured protocol, Ghanaians also could be remarkably informal. Social functions are a part of a diplomat's life, so I often hosted Saturday afternoon lunch. Ghanaians like picnics with stews, lots of rice, and beer. At one more formal, sit-down lunch for elites, the incoming minister of the interior arrived with seven or eight extra people in tow. "I knew you would want to meet these people," he said, "so I invited them to come along. They don't have to sit at the table. They can sit in the corner and have a plate." That is what happened, and we all had a great time.

It was my job to report on both the central government, whoever was in

The majority of Ghanaians lived outside Accra in rural villages. I got to know the tribes
of the four regions and learned that tribal and family connections are ironclad. Under a
thatched open-air pavilion, Ambassador Robert Smith (*in a white suit*) and I called on a
tribal chief, who sat under a fringed umbrella, which symbolized his status. We were
accompanied by a representative of the Ghanaian government.

control at the time, and the regional governments of traditional rulers in the
complex of tribes. I traveled all over the country, getting to know village leaders, regional chiefs, and the emerging political elite. For the first time in my
life I was in a totally developing country in Africa whose problems were different from those I had encountered in Thailand or Vietnam.

The majority of Ghanaians lived outside Accra in villages. I got to know the
tribes of the four regions, and I learned that tribal and family connections are
ironclad. The most successful individual was expected to make sure that his
family benefited from his fortune. The Fantis, the first tribe in Ghana to relate
with the white world, considered themselves to be avant-garde, cosmopolitan,

and closest to the English. Other parts of the country considered the northerners to be backward people, mere hewers of wood. I discovered the low regard for northerners when President Hilla Limann's name was mentioned at a party I hosted.* Limann, like Nkrumah, was a northerner. A guest muttered something derisive in Fanti.

"What did you say?" I asked.

"She said exactly what you think she said," the woman's escort laughed.

"They have always been the people to carry the water," the woman said, "and to clean the ditches. They have always been servants."

The Ga tribe consisted of commercial traders who saw themselves as the center of power because of their proximity to the capital. The Ewe tribe (pronounced EV-ee), were traders and farmers and most akin to their Togo neighbors. The royal Ashanti, the most powerful tribe, considered themselves the leader of the elites. Ashanti are big people, tall and haughty. "If you had been fortunate enough to have been born in Ghana," my colleague George Owusu-Afriye told me, "you would have been an Ashanti." In his eyes, this was the greatest compliment he could pay me.

I began by trying to get to know the government and the political parties seeking to be re-enfranchised. My predecessors had limited acquaintances, but I wanted to understand the force fields and have unlimited contacts. I hoped to report from every corner of Ghana about the actual situation. I tried to ferret out people who could make a difference. I went to villages of thatched huts and met the elders. They did not know much about the United States in those days, and they were curious. We drank tea, coffee, or sorghum beer and talked about the ills of the people. The elders believed in discipline, but the central government had never learned to work with them to make things happen in the villages.

Wherever I went, I saw Ghana's rich agricultural potential being unrealized. The central government was inept, so the country was poor. My dispatches included all of this—accounts of people starving and babies dying of dysentery because of lack of an appropriate saline solution. The Peace Corps was growing disillusioned after seeing its efforts appropriated by a corrupt authority for personal gain. The Catholic Church, especially the archbishop and some of the

---

* In 1979 Hilla Limann was elected president under the People's National Party (PNP), a reincarnation of Nkrumah's old socialist UGCC party.

senior priests in Accra, appeared to make no effort to effect change. Some of the priests, including one or two from America, had gone to seed. I do not know that any priest was killed in the ensuing coup, but they were not loved.

Part of our work with the Limann government was to help develop the economy, a protracted struggle. The Ghanaians were reluctant to approach the International Monetary Fund (IMF) for a loan because of the stringent controls

The Peace Corps was one of the most settling influences in both Ghana and Liberia. Ambassador Robert Smith (*front row, in sunglasses*) and I (*back row*) gave the Peace Corps volunteers in Ghana our fullest support, but I saw them grow disillusioned when their work was appropriated by corrupt Ghanaian governmental officials.

attached. Failure to meet these requirements had toppled the previous govern-
ment of Kofi Busia. "We do not intend to make that mistake," said Owusu-
Afriye, Limann's chief of staff. "You have a choice," I replied. "You can take an
IMF loan, or you can muddle along. No government, including mine, will give
you the kind of loan necessary to establish economic stability in the country."
Eventually they took an IMF loan.

When Limann was elected president, out of the woodwork came people
reincarnating the old CPP and all its socialist ideology. Some had been educated
behind the Iron Curtain, and some in the United Kingdom and in the United
States. They believed that the first rule of government was to do the bidding of
those who wanted largess. One man had several Cadillacs, but no fuel.

The first political rally I attended was a closed meeting. I was the only foreigner there and I stood at the back, never dreaming they would let me stay.
One of the key party leaders gestured toward me and spoke quietly to the president. "Leave him alone," the president told him. "He is always among us."
Slowly and suspiciously, the Ghanaians began to talk to me and help me understand Nkrumah and his grand dreams.

I operated differently from some other reporting officers because I wanted
to get to know every element of Ghanaian society; I found it fascinating. I
served as the embassy's labor reporting officer and reported on the Labor
Congress, an important element in Ghana, where my contact with the AFL-CIO
was Pat O'Farrell, an Irishman from Philadelphia. I went to labor congresses
and conventions, visiting and drinking coffee with labor leaders in the office
and interacting with them in ways I never envisioned a political officer doing.
Until then, I had not understood the importance of labor in a constructive
society.

I developed a large network of contacts stretching into every nook and
cranny across the country. Nothing was off limits to me. I went to homes and I
met people in cafes and taverns. I drank with young comrades, firebrands in the
villages, and students at the University of Ghana, and I listened to their criticism of the United States, which they considered an imperialist nation with no
concern for little people. A huge bookstore on campus was stocked with books
and music from Eastern Europe and with propaganda critical of the West, especially of the United States. The young comrades would parrot this material and
challenge me to show them just cause for being friends with the United States.

Many of them had been educated in the USSR, and they considered the Nigerians, the British, and the Americans to be their enemies. They wondered why the United States did not help Ghana with technology, such as installing a telephone system that worked. They were scornful of what they considered America's opulence as depicted on television programs. The Carter administration had begun to talk about human rights, but "you don't practice what you preach," the comrades told me. I was often hard-pressed to explain the United States in terms they could understand, but patience won out and eventually I made a few friends among them. They accorded me the ultimate honor of inviting me to drink beer with them in the campus beer hall.

During the Carter presidency, Muhammad Ali was sent to Africa to talk about human rights. The government plane carrying Ali landed in central Africa, and the public-information officer accompanying Ali handed him a paper with talking points that included such platitudes as "America, the land of the free" and "protector of the downtrodden." Ali, who had refused to be drafted into service to go to Vietnam, had his own views of America. He began to read from the talking points, then he stopped in mid-sentence and said, "I don't believe this." That was the end of his trip. He got on the plane and went back home.

Eventually, it seemed that everywhere I went in Ghana, I was known. It was important, they told me later, to feel that somebody in the American Embassy empathized with them. I do not know what prompted me to take the risks I did or to go to such lengths to meet the people. It seemed natural. A reporting officer can do his job in two ways. He can read the newspapers, call somebody, and write a report, even fabricating generously. Or, he can do what Mao Tse-tung advised to his army: "Be as a fish in the sea. Swim among the people. Get to know them." That was also Sun Tzu's philosophy.

Since this was during the cold war, a central interest for our embassy was to scrutinize the East-West struggle of politics and ideology. We were to exercise peaceful activities to thwart the East from making inroads into Ghanaian society. I was expected to report on the diplomatic relationships between Ghana and other states, especially the Soviet Union and its satellites: East Germany, Hungary, and Libya. I met the task head on.

The Soviets were mounting a cultural assault on Accra with music, theater, books, and records subsidized and sold far under market price. They financed ASTAB,[†] a large bookstore in Accra run by a staunch ideological leftist. One of the first places I went was to that bookstore to beard the lion in his den. The proprietor was surprised to see me, but he was affable, and we became relatively good friends. When I could not get an answer from the Ghanaian government regarding, for example, Ghana's policy with respect to Eastern Europe (Hungary, Romania, and the Soviet Union), I went to the bookstore to ask the veranda boys. (Ghanaians often gathered on the veranda on Saturday afternoons to drink beer, eat barbecued goat, and debate political issues, hence the term "veranda boys.")

My first call to the Soviet Embassy surprised my counterpart. Nobody from our embassy had ever called at the Soviet Embassy. We had a morning meeting in a conference room, not his office, where he served me a hefty glass of vodka and excellent caviar. We chatted as I sought to assure him that I wanted nothing more than for us get to know one another. He eyed me skeptically.

One evening I was invited to a cultural event at the Soviet Embassy and was given a seat down front. I was the only American present. On my right was the Hungarian ambassador, until then a great friend. An East German gave a major speech in English, lambasting the United States and President Carter. "He's pretty vitriolic, isn't he?" I said to the Hungarian, who stared straight ahead. "Well, Mr. Ambassador," I said, "I will not sit here and take this." I got up and left. The next morning, the news had spread that the American representative had walked out on a speech given by the honorable representative of the East German Republic. Totally doctrinaire. I would become more comfortable with the Russians, but I was always uneasy with their satellites—the Yugoslavs, Hungarians, Romanians, and especially the East Germans. In retrospect, that is nonsense. I should have learned more about the force field in play in Ghana before I got there.

It was in the national interest of the United States to keep track of the other superpower wherever it had an embassy or wherever the Soviet Union or its satellites attempted to make inroads. Both China and the Soviet Union ogled

---

[†] Named for the bookstore's owner, Kofi Batsa, spelled backwards. Kofi means Friday and, in that tradition, a boy's name includes a day of the week.

Ghana as a succulent plum ready for the picking. Naturally the CIA was active in Ghana's subtle struggle between East and West. The CIA's main objective was to serve as an advisor to the chief of mission, just as I did in my role as political counselor. The role of intelligence is often exaggerated. Laymen tend to view the CIA as super sleuths wielding powerful influence. On the other extreme, a secretary of state once criticized an officer for obtaining information through intelligence. "Gentlemen don't read one another's mail," he said, with remarkable naïveté.

After I had been in Ghana for a couple of years, I joined with another black officer, James Washington, on a quest to find the grave of W. E. B. DuBois, educator, author, activist, expatriate, pioneering sociologist, and father of the civil-rights movement in America. DuBois was the first black man to earn a Ph.D. from Harvard and was the founder of the National Association for the Advancement of Colored People (NAACP). "The spell of Africa is upon me," DuBois had written, and at age ninety-two he left the United States and went with Dr. Kwame Nkrumah to take up residence in Ghana. There he began writing *Encyclopedia Africanus*. When DuBois died in 1963, a Ghanaian told me that he lay in state at his home for days while people streamed in to view the body. The last to come was Nkrumah, who closed the coffin. Now, fifteen years later, nobody remembered where DuBois was buried. We interviewed people, especially old Ghanaian men who remembered the great American. Finally one old man told us to search in the walls surrounding the Christiansborg Castle, the fort that held the seat of government in Accra. We walked all around the stone wall, much of it overgrown, and in one place we pulled away weeds to find a brass plaque with the simple words: "Crypt of W. E. B. DuBois." We cut away the weeds, and I went to my friend Owusu-Afriye on the president's staff, saying, "Come with me." He could not believe what we had found and sent a cadre of workmen to clean the site. Jim and I sent a photograph of the plaque to the NAACP publication, where it was featured in the issue commemorating the magazine's one-hundredth anniversary.

In Ghana, James Washington and I set out on a quest to find
the lost burial place of W. E. B. DuBois. And we found it.
Our discovery was featured in an article in a NAACP publication.

With all the distress and unhappiness stewing in Ghana, we knew a revolution
was coming. The country had been a pressure cooker for years and it was going
to blow. Early on May 14, 1979, a young flight lieutenant in the Ghanaian Air
Force, angry that he could not get parts for his MG sports car, tried unsuccess-
fully to overthrow the government. During the public trial that followed,
Flight Lieutenant Jerry John (J. J.) Rawlings became a folk hero. He admitted
what he had done, testifying: "I tried to overthrow the government because it
is sucking the people's blood dry. I want justice. I want the criminals brought
to book." His eloquent testimony was what the populace was saying. The trial
progressed into June with more and more people crowding into the courtroom every day to watch it and to hear him.

Before dawn on June 5, I was jogging in the neighborhood when I became
aware that a strange silence had settled over Accra. Everything was hushed, and

the streets were empty. A lone fighter plane circled overhead, flying dangerously low over the city. Something was very wrong, and it scared the bejesus
out of me. I hurried home to find the radio silent. Nothing was being broadcast. Then the radio's hum was replaced by martial music, signaling that a coup
had begun. I left Lucy and the girls at home and went to the embassy, where we
began to piece together what had happened and notified Washington of the
unfolding drama.

The evening before, a group of young officers and enlisted men broke Rawlings out of jail, asking him, "Sir, will you lead us in the revolution?" "Yes," he
replied. I learned later from intelligence sources that if his answer had been no,
they would have killed him and made him a martyr. But he answered "yes" and
led a cadre of military personnel known as the Armed Forces Revolutionary
Council (AFRC) in overthrowing the Akuffo government.

Akuffo tried to mount a counter-coup, and we heard gunfire in the streets.
Mid-afternoon, I was relieved at the embassy and sent home. On the car radio,
I heard a woman's voice come over the American radio network saying, "Two
soldiers have just come into my house." It was Lucy speaking. The driver and I
turned into the little street leading to our house to see Katherine, my four-
teen-year-old daughter, and two neighbors standing with their hands in the air,
a soldier pointing a rifle at them. We stopped the car, and the driver asked,
"What should I do?" "Nothing," I said. "Don't move. Just wait." About that time
another soldier marched Lucy out of the house at the end of a rifle. Sarah, our
younger daughter, was nowhere to be seen.

The two renegade soldiers in camouflage uniforms, both of whom had been
drinking and smoking hemp, had burst into our house to loot it. Lucy gave
them what cash she had, and they took an official radio and a short-wave radio.
After herding my family outside, the soldiers stood with raised rifles for several
long, frozen minutes. Then they got into a white Peugeot and slowly drove past
us, never taking their eyes off us, as if daring us to make a move. I am convinced
if we had moved, they would have blown us out of the street. Sarah, it turned
out, had slipped behind the sofa to hide. Lucy handled the incident calmly. She
told me our two daughters asked, "Where's Daddy? Why isn't he here taking
care of us?" That was a good question. It stuck with me.

It was the first time I had been involved in a complete breakdown of law and
order. Nobody was in charge, and anything could have happened. I realized just

how vulnerable one can be and how vulnerable one's family can be in a hostile situation when nobody knows who the enemy is.

The bloody coup raged unabated for four days. In the heat of the battle, some of the Akuffo government sought sanctuary in the Holy Spirit Cathedral, but the archbishop convinced them to turn themselves in. They went to the police headquarters, where the head of the border guards, head of the army, head of the air force and Akuffo, the head of state, were holed up. I was two blocks away when Rawlings pulled up a tank outside and ordered them out before he blew the place apart. They came out. Akuffo was jailed and the coup was over, but order was not established immediately. For about a week, the university students assumed a role of self-imagined importance and were especially vocal in their support of Rawlings and the AFRC.

Eventually, things settled somewhat across Accra, but a sense of unease hung in the air. The day was clouded by discernible feelings of hostility, revenge, and instability.

Meanwhile at the embassy, we did not know what kind of government was coming to power or what to expect next. Rawlings, of the Ewe tribe, was half-Ghanaian and half-Scottish, light-skinned, tall, and intense, with piercing eyes. He was a young man with a military background who seemed determined to right a society that had gone wrong, and who was willing to take rough action en route. But, he announced, in four months he would turn over the country to an elected government. Several times in June he assured the citizenry with radio broadcasts that "Our resolve is not to entrench ourselves in office; we are professional soldiers and we want to return to the barracks. We are in for a housecleaning." The action of June 4, he said, was "a revolt against injustice, against economic hardship, and against the cancer of corruption that had eaten deep into the fabric of our society." He vowed to punish the corrupt and the guilty. Here at last, Ghanaians believed, was a man who truly understood the little people.

The soldiers under Rawlings' command characterized the coup as a moral revolution rather than a political revolution. It was a *jihad*, a moral crusade, Rawlings told a Muslim audience. The AFRC disciplined with a rod of vengeance and fear. Some of their methods were brutal and barbaric, such as the public caning of nude women, but the most grievous action was the trial of six former government officials in a people's court that operated behind closed doors. Even the six men on trial could not see their accusers or jurors. Three of those on trial were former heads of state, including Akuffo, and one was the minister of foreign affairs, whose primary interest had been getting visas for his girlfriends to go to the United States.

The Americans, British, and Nigerians urged the new government to observe due process of law and human rights. This outraged the students from the University of Ghana. To protest the interference of these three governments in the affairs of Ghana, the students announced plans to march on the three embassies. First, they marched on the British Embassy, but the British Embassy was on the third floor of a downtown building with steel doors. The students stood on the street and railed for a while, then they marched on the Nigerian Embassy. Finally they headed toward the U.S. Embassy, where our handsome open architecture was defenseless. As they approached, my boss said to me, "Ed, we just had a little meeting and decided that if they want to talk to somebody, if you don't mind, we'll ask you to go out and talk to them." I was still a young officer and said, "Okay. I'll do it." Around the world, U.S. embassies are guarded by the Marine Corps, so the head of security said he would send marines out with me. "No," I said, "you won't. That would be the worst thing you could do. If you have marines there, I won't go."

The compromise was that he could go with me since he was wearing civilian clothes. A demonstration arrived; thousands of students singing revolutionary songs surrounded the embassy. Their chants were so loud, the building began to shake. They pulled down the American flag and tore it apart. I thought we would have to restrain the defense attaché when he saw that. After they had damned the United States, the leader and some of the hostile crowd started up the steps to the door and shouted, "We have a message for President Carter if anyone will come out here and take it." I asked the marine standing post at the front entrance to open the gate, and I went out with my escort. Recently that marine, Stephen T. Lyons, wrote me of his recollection of that event. "Once the large front doors were unlocked," he wrote, "you raised your hand and the crowd went silent. You spoke to the leader of the demonstrators with great poise and confidence. I don't know what you said, but it calmed them down. I have never seen a man, then or now, command such instant respect. They instantly stopped to listen to what you had to say." Stephen thanked me in his letter for my courage and wisdom, but perhaps the demonstrators were shocked into silence. They had not expected a black man to step out of the U.S. Embassy. We stood there quietly looking at one another, and then I reached out my hand for the letter. The student leader looked at me, turned to the assembled group, threw his arms in the air and said, "Let's hear it for our American brother!" They cheered, I took the letter, we shook hands, and they left. The marine told me that he reclaimed the torn U.S. flag, and he has it packed carefully away in his home.

The trials continued, but I was not permitted to attend because the proceedings were secret. All six men were convicted of crimes against the state. Every day I called the Ghanaian chief of protocol or a contact in the military to find out what was happening. When I heard that soldiers were installing stakes in the parade field at an army encampment, I got a driver and went out to investigate. What I saw told me they meant business. Six stakes were driven into the ground, each tall enough to hold a tied man. Bales of hay were stacked behind each stake to stop bullets. One morning not long after that, I awoke with a dark feeling, more of dread than fear. The air was strange. I knew that something had happened, so I immediately phoned the chief of protocol and asked him about the six convicted people. "Mr. Perkins," he said, adopting a formality he had never used before, "I am authorized by the Armed Forces Revolutionary Council to inform you, and through you, your government, that at six o'clock this morning, those convicted of crimes against the state were executed on orders from the People's Court." They had been tied to the stakes and shot.

This was a turning point for Ghana, and it changed the nature of the people. Something had been unleashed, and it had to run its course. Outside of invasion, there was no way to stop the execution because it was a popular act among the younger people. Some time after that, several Supreme Court justices who had ruled against the government on a human-rights case were found assassinated on their front doorsteps. Before, it was unthinkable that such things could happen. The Ghanaians were a tolerant people; they loved life. Now excesses had brought them to the point of executing people. The AFRC had waited to see if a great outpouring of outrage would arise from the people during the trial, after they were sentenced, when the stakes were installed, and before the execution. It was a way of asking, "This is what is going to happen. What do you think of it?" No opposition was heard, so the executions were carried out. We observed all of this with growing concern because we did not think it would stop there. Most Americans, me included, suspected that the AFRC had taken a page from the communist Soviet Union and would replicate the Stalin purges.

Gradually, normality returned to the city, like the dawn of a clear day after a night of violent storms. Rawlings and the AFRC seemed intent on keeping to the four-month timetable. Two months later, however, three members of the AFRC visited me and my counterpart in the British embassy. "Rawlings is having second thoughts about handing over power," they told us. "We feel he needs to keep to the schedule to maintain a sense of honor." They asked us to help. We were impressed by the sensibility of these military men. We told them that Rawlings was the head of state and we were but minor players on this stage of political events, so we had to consult our respective governments.

"Don't get involved in things like that," my boss told me.

"Maybe we can change the course of history by helping them," I said. "This could affect the way civilian government returns to this country."

"We don't get involved," he repeated.

"But they came to us," I said.

"Why can't they go through channels?" he asked.

"There are no channels. The channels have broken down." I kept talking until he gave in as much as he could.

"If you are crazy enough to do something like this, don't tell me about it. And if you do it and get caught, expect the consequences. Remember, you are alone."

"Thank you for that endorsement," I said, and I did not involve him further.

My British colleague, John Brown, and I agreed to help. We were the only diplomatic officers in Ghana who knew the members of the new government. We had known them before they shot their way to power; we had drunk beer with them in the villages and at the University of Ghana. When we met at John's home, the young military men came dressed in battle fatigues and, to the dismay of John's wife, carried AK-47s, which they laid on the kitchen floor while we talked. They asked us one simple question: "What can we do to convince Rawlings to keep his promise?" We advised them to resurrect the speech that Rawlings had given on the day of the coup in which he said he had come to power to rout out the corruption and that civilian rule would be returned in four months. We suggested they go to Rawlings with that speech, remind him that they had come to power because of the "call of the people" to turn Ghana around, so it could reach its potential as an "honorable nation." I kept saying, "You've got to talk about honor because the people have given you a big trust and a part of that is believing that they can trust you." I knew that Rawlings was an honorable man. I had sat on the front row of the rallies and heard him deliver soul-stirring speeches about the responsibility of government to the people and the responsibility of people to themselves. I further recommended that they take with them Elizabeth Ohene, a newspaper editor, an Ewe tribeswoman, and the self-appointed conscience of Rawlings. She did, indeed, accompany them; she was a brave woman.

A couple of days later, Rawlings delivered a speech in which he announced that government would not only return to civilian rule, it would do so one month earlier than promised. I was present at Parliament House when he symbolically stepped off the dais and handed the mace of power to Limann. Rawlings' parting speech was prophetic. "We came to power to right the wrongs of a lot of people and to bring a better life to the Ghanaian citizens. We think justice has been obtained and we are now on the road to a good system." Then he looked at President Limann on the dais and said, "You guys had better behave, or we'll be back."

John Brown and I had set out some good strategy, and it turned out all right.

When it was all over, John's wife, Christine, said to him, "We're going home. I don't ever want to serve in a country like this again."

In 1981, my assignment in Ghana ended, and I was posted elsewhere. A year later, in December 1982, the ineffective Limann government was overthrown. Again, the coup was led by Rawlings. This time Rawlings did not say when he would return the country to civilian rule.

No Hollywood scriptwriter could have written a more dramatic assignment for a beginning political reporter. In Ghana, I wrote my first political dispatch. I learned how to observe what is important and how to report it. I learned what a policy-maker needs to know. I tried to write reports that would convince my government that Ghana could be a substantial ally, even though it was a country that might seek relations with cold-war opponents.

What went wrong with Ghana and Nkrumah's dream? Nkrumah had the monumental task of creating an institution of governance by native Ghanaians, in the wake of a white colonial government. I think he failed to understand how the country had to be governed, disregarded fiscal prudence, and did not understand the importance of a flourishing private sector. He failed to create a political ideology that was suitable for the country; the idea of socialism was a total disaster.

When I first met J. J. Rawlings in 1979, he was a folk hero in a military uniform who had led a successful overthrow of the government. After he was elected president, he dressed in African robes. In Ghana, his stature is akin to George Washington in the United States.

My biggest disappointment in Ghana was its inability to develop itself into a society in which all the people could participate and contribute to the greater good. The execution of those six people in 1979 released a dark vengeance, one that Ghana is still paying for. Yet the nation did turn itself around in developing the private sector and encouraging individualism and excellence in achievement. Rawlings seemingly has been an honest head of state and a model Ghanaian citizen with an influence akin to that of George Washington.

Ghana has not been the hope and promise of Africa as Nkrumah envisioned; far from it. It has not been the Black Star of Africa. Neither has Nigeria, which was the next hope. The star is hovering above South Africa now; perhaps South Africa is the hope of Africa.

The role of Ghana, Liberia, and Ethiopia in America's civil-rights revolution is often forgotten. The United States was eager to establish relationships with the newly enfranchised African countries, but we were naïve in how we would behave as a host nation for those diplomats accredited to the United Nations. They appeared in New York in native finery and established embassies in Washington, but they soon confronted a segregated society. Where could they eat, travel, get a haircut, stay in a hotel? Diplomats told me that when they wore their African robes, they had no problem being served, but the situation was different when they wore Western clothes. Their dilemma embarrassed the United States and, in so doing, inched the race issue toward resolution. Africans in native costume helped push open the doors of American segregation.

The last time I called on Rawlings was in 1997 when I took a group of university professors to Ghana. He was serving his final term as president, and he had a sadness about him that was unlike the resolute young leader I met in 1979. Then he wore military uniforms; now, as elected president, he dressed in African robes. He was still concerned about corruption; he wondered aloud what might have happened if different concepts had been institutionalized, and he worried that students studying abroad would not return. "We need our people back," he said. "That is our only assurance of progress." We talked about the old days, and he told me that he appreciated my stepping out of the traditional role of a diplomat. "You did a lot of things that no one expected you to do."

As I took my leave, Rawlings said, "By the way, Mr. Ambassador. We have moved the remains of Dr. DuBois to a place of honor. I hope you have a chance to go by and see it. We have put him where he belongs." Until that moment, I had no idea he knew about my finding the crypt. I did visit the memorial, a beautiful structure, and thought how appropriate that DuBois, this man who had such a profound impact on the social development of the United States, is buried in Ghana.

LIBERIA IN REVOLUTION

I went from Ghana, a country whose future held special interest for the United States, to Liberia, where I discovered a web of personal conflicts and love/hate diplomatic challenges.

Liberia was my first management assignment in the Foreign Service. I was deputy chief of mission, second in command at the U.S. Embassy. It was a most unusual situation. William Swing, who had been named ambassador to Liberia, was in Washington undergoing confirmation procedures, and as soon as I reported, the DCM I replaced left for another posting. I found myself in charge of the embassy at a time when Liberia had just undergone the overthrow of the elected government by a group of enlisted military men.

I knew that Liberia's history was strangely tangled with that of the United States. In preparing for my new assignment, I studied the background of Liberia and discovered a spellbinding story. None of my extensive reading prepared me for the clash of ancient and current history. In 1822, amid a cloud of murky motives, the American Colonization Society, aided by other white groups in America, began resettling freed or escaped slaves in Liberia. Some praised it as a missionary movement to spread civilization and Christianity in Africa, but others denounced it as an easy answer for the race issue. Far from being benevolent, abolitionists said it was merely a way "to get clear of the coloreds." Resettlement on the West Coast of Africa was a panacea for the awkward problem of the offspring of slave mothers and white slave masters. These mixed-blood people had no place in the majority white American society of the 1800s, and they were troubling to the Christian conscience of the time. The society's aim was to remove all blacks from America. The emancipated slaves were set ashore to create a new nation, which became known as modern Liberia, a name that means "freedom."

Liberia is a tropical country boxed by the Atlantic Ocean, Côte d'Ivoire, Guinea, and Sierra Leone. Here the freed slave emigrants built a community that resembled America's antebellum South, renamed the capital city Monrovia in honor of then-U.S. president James Monroe, established a government patterned after that of the United States, and recreated a strict class society similar to the one they had known in the slave states. They considered themselves akin to the landed aristocracy of southern plantations and modeled their new lives after that system. Even the flag of modern Liberia resembles the U.S. Stars and Stripes, with alternating stripes of red and white and one star in a field of blue in the upper left corner. They took as their motto: "The love of liberty brought us here." Their sense of liberty, however, was totally different from that of the majority people, who were indigenous to Liberia. The emigrants called themselves Americo-Liberians, to distinguish them from African-born Liberians. These former slaves and their descendants set up a class structure designed to advance their personal social and economic welfare. The African-Liberians got the scraps from the table.

Americo-Liberians believed fervently that they had a special relationship with America, historically, culturally, and emotionally. Eventually, indigenous Liberians also came to believe that Liberia was the favorite son of America. Unfortunately, I never found this feeling reciprocated in the United States. The two nations were as two ships passing in the night, neither seeing the lights of the other. It is the same today.

I found it grievous but factual that some of the descendants of slaves came to behave as slave masters themselves. Not only did the Americo-Liberians oppress the indigenous Liberian populace, they trafficked in slavery. They captured boys and young men, "like stray animals being hunted by animal control to be taken to the pound" and exported them to labor camps and cocoa plantations. Most were sent as indentured labor to Fernando Po to work on plantations. Clearly, the African-Liberians were considered less human in the eyes of the Americo-Liberian establishment. As late as the 1930s, a scandal revealed the sale of native people to Spanish territories that involved some Liberian government officials.

I saw in Liberia's history a story I would see repeated around the world: the tragic tale of native people being controlled by aggressors. I saw it in the experience of Native Americans and white settlers, and with the Aboriginals in Australia. The only difference in Liberia was that both the oppressed and the oppressors were black. At first, the African-Liberians fought the intrusion of the unwanted settlers and battled to force them off the land. All of their struggles failed, however, and the Americo-Liberians clung tightly to their new land

and to their power. From 1944 to 1980, Liberia was ruled by the Americo-Liberian administrations of Tubman and Tolbert. William V. S. Tubman had been a benevolent leader who served as president for twenty-seven years, until his death in 1971. In the hot African sun, Tubman personified the landed gentry from another time and era. He set men's fashion, dressing in a top hat and swallowtail coat. On more casual occasions, he wore a straw boater and smoked a big cigar. "Blacks were in the big house," *Life* magazine reported, but black labor received little share of the wealth. Tubman was succeeded by his kinsman, William R. Tolbert, who was nothing short of a psychopath. Tolbert was a Baptist minister who traced his roots to Kentucky. He had been elected vice president of the national Baptist convention in the United States and had a penchant for young girls. When he became president, he had a law passed that lowered the age of consent to twelve, and he was known to have chosen many young girls as consorts. Tolbert was a tall, sloppy man with a cruel face. He required his wife to walk two paces behind him in deference to his status as head of state. When I met her, she was recovering from the effects of a beating he had given her.

In the first minutes of the revolution that began April 12, 1980, Tolbert was killed by Harrison Pennue, a vicious man with a hard grudge against the president. Pennue was a country person whose applications to go abroad to school had been repeatedly turned down by the government. "You wouldn't let me go to school," Pennue told Tolbert, bayoneting and disemboweling the president. Pennue, short, stocky, and brutal, was a sadistic killer who became the new government's "tax collector," a term that gave him the authority to raise or extort funds by any means possible. I was astonished the first time I walked into Pennue's office and saw sacks of money piled on the floor.

By 1980, 5 percent (or less) of the elite Americo-Liberian class controlled the majority population of 95 percent indigenous people. This ruling class was educated in the United States at institutions such as Harvard or historically black universities such as Howard University or Lincoln University. Occasionally, a country person was allowed to go abroad to study. He or she often returned with the extremism of the newly converted, becoming holier than the pope, more "Americo" than the Americo-Liberians.

The rift between the Americo-Liberians and indigenous people never healed. Racial rivalry, bitterness, and struggle seethed for more than 150 years until it exploded in a revolutionary coup in 1980 led by army Master Sergeant

Samuel K. Doe. He was the first non-Americo-Liberian to come to power. Managing the fallout of that violent revolution would constitute most of my work in Liberia and that of my embassy colleagues.

Even before my posting to Liberia, I had witnessed the ethnic-racial chasm that ticked like a time bomb within the country. In June 1979, I went to Monrovia as a representative of Kissinger's Priorities Policy Group. That visit was a chilling experience, like being transported back to the United States of the early 1880s.

On that visit, my traveling colleague and I were invited for Sunday lunch at the mansion of Charles C. Dennis, an Americo-Liberian who was Speaker of the House of Representatives and father of the foreign minister, Cecil Dennis. The Speaker was a tall and imposing man, very light complexioned, and obviously of mixed blood. The wife of the foreign minister was an American born in St. Louis. She was vehement in her analysis of U.S.-Liberia relations. "The United States is not giving Liberia its just due," she told me angrily. "After all, we are your best ally in Africa." This was my first taste of many dialectical discussions I would have with Americo-Liberians regarding this issue.

Liberians call the big midday meal a "country chop," and it reminded me of a leisurely Sunday lunch in Alabama, Missouri, or Louisiana. The table and sideboard were laden with various Southern greens (collards, turnips, mustard) and meats (turkey, chicken, ham, ham hocks). The black people serving us clearly were considered a lower class. They looked different and acted different. I learned later they were tribals whom the Americo-Liberians referred to as "country people." After lunch, when we retired to the library for local wine and conversation, I asked my host about the servants. From my experience in Okinawa I knew that servants can harbor a bitter dislike for their employers, much the same hatred a slave feels for a master. I had seen this hostility in the eyes of the people serving our meal.

"Oh, they're just country people," Dennis said, dismissing the subject.

"One day," I warned, "you may find them on the outside throwing bricks at you."

"You damned Americans!" he exploded. "Always making trouble all over the world. Don't bring your ideas here. We are kind to these people. We're bringing Christianity to them." He was mouthing the clichés of the American Colonization Society, using religion as a cloak for other motives.

"I'm sorry, Mr. Dennis," I apologized. "I was merely speaking from my own experience." Two years later, when the country people came to power, the people pulled Dennis from his home, tied a rope around him, and dragged him through the streets of Monrovia until he was dead.

I was sent into this maelstrom in June 1981. My daughter Kathy was in boarding school at Emma Willard in upstate New York, so only Lucy, Sarah, and I boarded the plane for the forty-minute flight from Ghana to Monrovia, Liberia. Once again, we entered a tropical country during the rainy season. That December, I brought Kathy home for Christmas, the season of the *harmattan*, the gargantuan dust storm from the Sahara Desert that turns the country brown. Visibility is so limited in the heavy dust that planes rarely can land, but these pilots managed it and the entire plane full of people stood and applauded.

It was an anxious time to be in that country. Liberia had recently survived a bloodstained coup patterned after that in Ghana, but Ghana was righting itself and returning to civilian rule. Liberia, by contrast, was not yet out of its descent. If Ghana had been corrupt, the Liberia I met in 1981 was Sodom and Gomorrah, with the military revolutionaries still in power.

Monrovia looked like a Southern riverboat town. Small stores and little chop shops (cafés) lined the streets. One big hotel topped the hill, and the city buzzed with activity—artists carving ivory and bone, Lebanese merchants at work in their retail stores, and pedestrians up and down the sidewalks. As DCM I often would walk along these streets, getting to know the place, and every journey was like stepping back in history. Portions of Monrovia reminded me of the Louisiana towns of my childhood, Haynesville and Homer. All that was missing was a cotton gin.

Until Ambassador Swing could take command in August 1981, I was chargé d'affaires ad interim with a snarl of issues needing immediate attention— almost all revolving around the new head of state, Samuel K. Doe, who had shot and butchered his way to power.

My first morning at work I began endless briefings from the country team about the political and economic situation. After the country team, I met with the only other black officer at the mission, William Stevens, a young air force lieutenant and one of our military attachés. "Now you'll get a real briefing," he said. The picture spread before me was horrifying.

My second day at work, I went to the executive mansion to meet Doe. The minute I met him, I knew I was in for a long ride. A massive, curved desk reaching from wall to wall almost filled the room. Behind it sat a young man, about twenty-eight years old, dressed in camouflage fatigues with sleeves rolled up. The uniforms of the Liberian army were identical to those of the U.S. Army. On the desk was a sign with his full name and title: Master Sergeant Samuel Kanyon Doe, Head of State and Commander-in-Chief of the Armed Forces of Liberia. From our perfunctory conversation, it was clear to me that he was uneducated. At most, he had a diploma from Marcus Garvey High School in Monrovia. He was a member of the Krahn tribe, a minor tribe known for its warlike characteristics and which traditionally hired itself out as mercenaries. In retrospect, Doe reminded me of boxer Mike Tyson, both physically and mentally. His colossal desk was piled with papers, but Doe was illiterate and could read none of them. He spoke to me in memorized phrases and quotations, yet he seemed to feel an affinity to me, presumably because I, too, was a black man. He assumed that I would understand him and his work. Doe had been trained by the U.S. Special Forces in Liberia, where he developed a passion for military might and a craving to be recognized as a military man. His regalia for public occasions was army fatigues, a .357 Magnum on his hip, a ceremonial sword in a sheath of elaborate tribal beadwork, and sunglasses dangling from a jacket pocket. It had been less than a year since he and his cadre of young noncommissioned officers and privates had seized control of the government.

After I had called on Doe, my second official call was to Vice Head of State Lieutenant General Thomas Weh-Syen, until recently Private Weh-Syen. I was ushered into his office where he, too, sat behind a desk and wore military fatigues and a field cap. It struck me as a scene from a play, with the desk as scenery. He seemed to be sitting properly in the office for the express purpose of receiving me. I stood before the desk and said, "Mr. Vice Head of State, I am here to pay my respects. I have just called on the head of state. I am here to help Liberia and to keep the good relationship going that has existed for a long time between our two countries." I waited for a reaction. There was none. An eternally long period of time passed as he sat staring at me. Nobody spoke. Then he jumped up, rushed around the desk, grabbed my hand and said, "Welcome, my brother!" and returned to his chair. That was all he ever said to me. He did not live long enough for us to have another conversation. I would not wish to portray him as mentally deficient, but he was an uneducated private who had been promoted to lieutenant general—a position far beyond his capabilities.

I present my credentials to Samuel K. Doe, Head of State of Liberia, on August 28, 1985.
Note the curved desk with his full name and title.

Doe's revolution was the second attempt to overthrow the government. The
first insurrection had been put down when Guinea sent in troops. Tolbert
sought help from the United States, but none was forthcoming. Then the
Movement for Justice in Africa (MOJA), consisting largely of a group of well-
educated young Liberians, convinced Doe to take control of the government.
MOJA was a left-wing political organization that advocated socialism. In the
cold-war skirmish, the Soviet Union and Libya had increased their presence in
Liberia with the intention of edging out the United States. MOJA was known to
be funded by the Soviet Union and Libya. It intended to manipulate the soldiers
into being the muscle of the revolution, wait for Doe's group to fail, and then
step in heroically to take the reins of government. I heard from both sides that
Doe asked the young men of MOJA to establish a new government, but they
refused, biding their time. Doe's junta did prove to be inept and incompetent,
but to the horror of MOJA, once in power Doe clung to control as tightly as an

eagle with prey in its talons. Speaking patois, Doe told me, "They think we crazy. They think we make a mistake and then they take over. We fool them." I heard the same thing from Foreign Minister Baccus Matthews, a young revolutionary Americo-Liberian. "All of us thought that these soldiers would botch things up and we would pick up the pieces and run the country the way we thought it should be run. Doe was a lot smarter and more clever than any of us gave him credit for."

Violence and bloodlust were excessive in Liberia's revolt. This was a part of the world where individual human life was not highly valued, so human-rights violations were rampant. Soldiers, armed and undisciplined, roamed the streets of Monrovia as a law unto themselves. They confiscated cars, ransacked homes, and looted property. They raped countless women and girls. Hundreds of defenseless civilians were reported missing or killed. Scores of government officials were jailed. Less than a week into the revolt, thirteen leading members of the Tolbert government were publicly executed on the beach in Monrovia. They were stripped to the waist, tied to electric poles, and shot by a firing squad. The corpses were loaded onto a truck, taken to the middle of the city, and dumped into a common grave dug by a bulldozer at a crossroads. Their bodies lie there yet, to be trampled eternally by the traffic of vehicles and pedestrians. Among those executed were the brother of President Tolbert and Foreign Minister Cecil Dennis, whose father had hosted me for country chop Sunday lunch.

A year later, on the anniversary of the revolution and Tolbert's murder, Doe declared April 12 a holiday: National Redemption Day. Although Tolbert's ministers had been executed for corruption, misuse of public funds, and high treason, Doe put Liberia's leading soccer team on the government payroll and promised to triple the soldiers' salaries.

It was a dangerous time to be a diplomat, and all of the cars of the chiefs of mission were armored. Until Ambassador Swing arrived, I rode in his Lincoln, which was as heavy as a tank. Even a tank, however, is no guarantee of protection. Guns were everywhere. Every day I rode through streets full of revolutionary soldiers, all armed. In this milieu, our family settled in to live as normally as possible. Sarah enrolled in school and Lucy became an award-winning bridge player. I set about my work, learning the lay of the land and implementing U.S. policy as best I could.

The foremost interest of the United States was to insure the safety of the numerous Americans in Liberia: businesspeople, missionaries, and a huge contingency of Peace Corps volunteers. The U.S. Embassy was one of the largest in the world, the military mission was big, the CIA ran a facility, and the Voice of America station had its own large compound. Liberia was a sizeable post because the United States had invested a great deal of money there during World War II.

Doe's junta was a ferocious debacle, and Liberian society was shattered. It was the embassy's job to help restore the country to order and to rebuild the infrastructure. Competent human resources were limited, however, because a mass exodus of Americo-Liberians had depleted the country of its best-educated and most competent citizenry. The Americo-Liberian leadership had called on the United States to put down the civil war and restore their group to power. The United States responded by offering amnesty to almost any Liberian who sought it. Ninety-nine percent of those seeking asylum were Americo-Liberians.

Luckily, the U.S. Peace Corps stayed, and this had a settling effect. In the villages where even small-scale health-delivery systems were rare, the Peace Corps was invaluable in teaching the people about health, education, clean water, and livestock development. I often visited the Peace Corps volunteers in remote locations where they were living and working on the front line. In the deepest poverty and deprivation, where infant mortality rates were high and education was low, the Peace Corps worked to educate the villagers about nutrition and good health. They dug wells and taught young mothers how to boil water and mix it with dried milk to feed the babies. They not only provided these services, they institutionalized them so the systems would continue after they returned to the United States. Of all the American presence overseas, Liberia included, the Peace Corps is the closest to the people.

I visited one village in which a solitary Peace Corps volunteer had dug a well and made a pump out of spare parts. He had taught the villagers how to dig wells that would not be contaminated, how to boil water, and how to keep water in a central distribution place—all to lessen the spread of disease. The village elders were in charge of water distribution. Then the volunteer introduced new crops so the village would have fresh vegetables to eat year round and he taught them crop rotation to replenish the soil. He also taught barefoot doctors how to administer vaccinations in small health stations. All of this by one volunteer.

In another village a female Peace Corps volunteer was so inventive that the headman relied on her as his assistant. She established a school where she taught English and mathematics, working in cooperation with another school and native teachers who were teaching her their dialect. She was practicing a wise lesson. In order to maintain honor and respect, there must be consideration for what one gets and for what one gives. Some kind of exchange is important.

The entire foreign business community stayed, becoming an endless source of frustration for me and the rest of the mission. The businesspeople were often at the embassy doors, asking us to intercede with Doe on their behalf. The foreign corporations had money, provisions, hotels, liquor, and private planes—all the shiny things Doe's regime wanted. The junta, circling the flush foreign business community like a pack of ravenous wolves, demanded, threatened, bullied, and sometimes went armed to the business or corporation, but they never carried out their threats of violence.

The United States did not want a runaway geopolitical entity that could fall prey to Libya or the Soviet Union, so I worked hard to establish a professionally friendly relationship with Doe and his junta. One of my initial tasks was persuading Doe to permit Tolbert's widow and son to leave Liberia for the United States. Doe, meanwhile, was securing his position by removing anyone he suspected of insurrection. One Saturday afternoon when I was relaxing at home, a big Mercedes belonging to Doe pulled up in the driveway and a couple of bodyguards came to the door. "The Chief wants to see you," they told me. I started to call my driver, but they said, "No, we'll take you." Instead of going to the executive mansion, they drove to an apartment hideaway in the suburbs. Soldiers were everywhere; all of them armed and waving weapons unsteadily, most of them sprawled in various stages of drunkenness. Many had been drinking palm wine, a powerful hard liquor that ferments two hours after being harvested from a tree. Some of them were nearly comatose.

"He has come to see the Chief," one of the soldiers said, and staggered forward to frisk me.

"You can't frisk him," another soldier told him. "He's the ambassador."

"Oh," the first soldier stopped and considered the dilemma. "Have you got a gun?"

"No," I answered, and he gestured me inside.

Doe was watching television. He offered me a soft drink, asked me to sit, and after about fifteen minutes said, "I asked you to come, Mr. Perkins, because

I got word that some members of my council are going to attempt to over-throw me in the next day or so."

"Oh?" I said. "Who are they?"

"They will be led by my vice head of state, General Weh-Syen. Have you heard anything about this?"

When I told him that I had not, he asked me to check with the intelligence personnel at the embassy and to see him again at 10 P.M. "You haven't heard anything, but I have," Doe said. "My sources are different from yours."

Ambassador Swing had arrived by this time, and I reported the meeting to him. Immediately, he called a country-team meeting. We had eyes and ears everywhere, and none of us had heard anything about a threat against Doe. We concluded that this was the beginning of his plan to eliminate competitors.

That night, I told Doe straightforwardly that we had heard nothing of plots against him. "Thank you very much, sir," he said. "Have a good evening. But remember," he reiterated, "my sources are different from yours." The next day, Sunday, Weh-Syen and another of Doe's council were arrested coming back from a soccer match and charged with plotting to overthrow the head of state. They were scheduled to be put on trial Monday, the same day Ambassador Swing was to present his credentials to Doe. I called for an appointment to plead for the men's lives. Doe said he would receive us at 10 P.M. that same day.

On Monday, Ambassador Swing presented his credentials in the morning, and that evening he and I and the senior military attaché went to see Doe at the Executive Mansion. He was watching CNN as usual. In the name of human rights we made the plea that Wey-Syen and the other persons arrested with him receive a fair trial and that they be spared the death sentence. Doe listened almost sullenly. "I cannot interfere with the court system," he said. Then he received a telephone call, spoke briefly, and brightened visibly. His attitude toward us changed 180 degrees. "Thank you for coming," he told us. "Hope you had a pleasant day, Mr. Ambassador," he told Swing. "Come see me any time."

Once outside the ambassador asked me, "What do you make of that?"

"These people have just been executed," I said. It was true. The phone call was to tell Doe the deed was done.

I followed the routine that I had established successfully in Ghana: traveling across the country to get the feel of Liberia. From the port city of Buchanan to

Doe's village of Tuzon, I saw Liberia as a poor nation that had been exploited by two factors, the foreign business community and the Americo-Liberians.

The economy had teetered precariously for decades, bloated by foreign investment and dependence on foreign money. Americo-Liberians and True Whig party leaders grew fat and prosperous from their relations with the foreign companies, but the African-Liberians were the hungry have-nots left on the outside. Thus the distance grew between the two groups. The spark that ignited the 1980 coup was a demonstration a year earlier protesting the rise in the price of rice, the staple diet, from twenty-two dollars per one hundred pounds to thirty dollars. For the want of a bowl of rice, a government was lost.

Restoring Liberia's political stability was the first concern of the United States; establishing economic stability was next. The country was still in turmoil, and clearly economic stability could not be achieved until political soundness was accomplished. To accomplish this end, Liberia's political leaders had to adhere to the strictures of the World Bank and the International Monetary Fund. Persuading them to do this was an uphill battle. Confidence in the country's economic stability had evaporated, so we concentrated on stabilizing Liberia's two essential products: rubber and iron ore.

Rubber had been the country's first major export, beginning with the first British rubber plantation in Liberia in 1904. Firestone Plantations acquired this operation in 1926, and rubber production accelerated as the American company cleared African jungles and built plantations to produce raw rubber for its factories. The Liberian government had been more than generous with concessions to foreign companies. By leasing millions of acres—4 percent of the entire nation—to Firestone, Liberia came to be known as "the Firestone Republic." Firestone became the main entrepreneur in Liberia and a reasonably good employer with fair wages, good working conditions, and medical services for the employees and their dependents. The Firestone manager was almost as powerful as the American ambassador.

I worked to get the iron-ore industry on its feet. Liberia's ore deposits were first discovered in 1941 when U.S. military pilots flying over the country noticed their planes' instruments spinning awry. These deposits, located in the Bomi Hills north of Monrovia and surrounded by dense jungles, would prove to be among the highest quality in the world. Mining iron ore is labor intensive and hampered by a tropical climate where rainfall exceeds 150 inches during the rainy season. Still, the market is intensely competitive, and producers attempt to extract and refine it at the lowest cost possible. The Swedish conglomerate LAMCO was the primary extractor in Liberia; the German firm Bong Mining Company was also quite active.

Firestone, LAMCO, and the Bong Mining Company were the three largest commercial enterprises in Liberia. Each had its own self-contained compound with stores and a hospital for its employees and their families, as well as a hotel for guests. I toured all three operations for overnight visits in their facilities. The accommodations were lavish in comparison with most in the country.

Citibank, Chase Manhattan, the Stanley Corporation (an Iowa farming group), and MESURADO, a large fishing operation co-directed by an American businessman and Tolbert's son, were other important American businesses operating in Liberia. All of us were frustrated by the foreign businessmen—Americans, Europeans, and some Asians—who were trying to continue work as usual and make money in this ill-managed country. When Doe blundered by issuing Liberian currency not backed by the U.S. dollar, big industries found the conditions almost intolerable. Eventually, all the large banks except Citibank pulled out of Liberia. Doe could not understand why they left. He never understood that the coup upset confidence, which is one of the most essential qualities of the economy. "We are a friendly country," he said—all the while looting the country instead of building it up. He did not understand that the treasury was limited, not a bottomless source of funds for his personal use.

Liberia's other revenue-generating activity was the registry of ships. Years earlier Liberia had set itself up as a nation willing to let its flag fly over ships of other nations or ships of companies located in nations that might tax them excessively, withhold access to a deep-water port, or impose other hindrances. For a fee, Liberia would register a ship to sail the seven seas. Only two or three countries in the world offer such a "flag of convenience."

I devoted considerable effort to understanding the Americo-Liberians. The three pillars of the Americo-Liberian culture were the True Whig party, the Masonic Order, and the church (Baptist and Methodist). Until the revolution, this iron triangle ran the country and dictated societal terms.

The True Whig party had been in power so long that it was synonymous with Liberia. For 133 years, from independence in 1847 to the coup d'état in 1980, Liberia prided itself on being a peaceful, one-party country. In fact, the True

Whig party was dominated by privileged Americo-Liberians who favored class structure and repressed the African-Liberians. The party was rife with nepotism, and party leaders chose the candidates for office. The party withheld suffrage from the indigenous or rural people. (Until 1963, 97 percent of the population was denied the vote.) Furthermore, it flaunted its power and was notorious for election fraud. According to an oft-repeated tale, President Tubman once dressed a monkey in a frock coat and took it to the polls to cast a vote.

The True Whig party created by Americo-Liberians was influenced by the nineteenth-century Whig party in the United States, with historic roots in class-conscious England. The political party in Liberia established an elite social class, which was kept small and exclusive through intermarriage. Repeating a pattern established by some European lines of royalty, the Americo-Liberians set themselves beyond the normal bounds of propriety. Within their closed class structure, promiscuity and wife-swapping became acceptable, partying was ongoing, taboos eroded, and satisfactory social behavior dissipated.

To ensure their class privilege and to keep the indigenous population subservient, Americo-Liberians followed the paradigm of slavery in the United States: they kept the African-Liberians ignorant, they limited ethnic Liberians' communication with the outside world, they installed a system of employment and economic control, and they exhibited a sense of superiority by virtue of birth. The disintegration of morality, the greed of True Whig party leaders, and the exploitation of the indigenous Liberians planted the seeds for the coup that would overthrow the government.

The Masonic Order, the second pillar of the ruling class in Liberia, was a secret society of men who considered themselves respectable members of the community, gentlemen who believed in God and were dedicated to uplifting society through charitable events and the Masonic community. In Liberia, the Masonic Order was exclusively an organization of Americo-Liberians. When I visited Monrovia in 1974, the Masonic temple was a commanding edifice, situated at the end of a street for effect and illuminated in splendor. Now it stood empty and in disuse. The revolutionaries had stripped it of its glory, and the Americo-Liberians who remained in the country were no longer influential members of society.

The church was the third hallmark of Liberian upper-class society. On that earlier trip, I had seen a large Methodist church in full bloom resembling nothing so much as a prominent Southern church in its heyday. The choir was extensive, and the congregation was dressed in its best finery. Now the churches were still active but not as prominent. Some of their activity was political. One Sunday I attended a songfest at a Baptist church crowded with about three hundred people. When a singer began a revolutionary song directed against the regime in power, the United States, and me, the effect on the congregation was electric. The singer did not look at me steadily, but her gaze kept returning to me. As her song grew to crescendo and the rhythm increased, I felt as if all three hundred pairs of eyes were on me. Americo-Liberians still hoped that the United States would come to their rescue and restore them to the position they held before the coup.

Right away, the Americo-Liberians let me know they were accustomed to their extraterritorial relationship with the United States. A visitor called on me about a project he wanted to undertake. "Before we do anything," he said, "I was told to come and see 'the Man on the Hill.'"

"Who is that?" I asked.

"You."

At that moment, I understood firsthand the meaning of the word "proconsul." It means a representative of a government outside the host country, but it implies the power of a governor general. Americo-Liberians felt they were duty-bound to see the U.S. ambassador. This is the way they had been brought up.

They saw me as a conduit for their views to the U.S. government and exercised an exhaustive campaign to ally me to them. When that did not happen, when neither the United States nor I could be the special friend they wanted, they were angry and disappointed. To this day, I am unpopular among many Americo-Liberians.

We were never able to communicate effectively to the Americo-Liberians how the United States saw our relationship with their country. Repeatedly, my conversations were fraught with emotion. Liberians considered their nation to be important to the United States, yet here were Americans in the U.S. Embassy presenting a different picture of U.S.-Liberia relations. They wanted their world back the way it was before the revolution, and they wanted the U.S. to make that happen. Some argued bitterly for U.S. intervention, and were totally crushed when we said it would not happen. Even more poignant for them was that the message often came from me, a black man whom they felt would be sympathetic to their plight. "But these people don't know how to run a government," an Americo-Liberian aristocrat argued.

"They are citizens of Liberia," I said, "and America makes no distinction between Americo-Liberians and tribal Liberians." When I said that, the expression on his face was utter dismay. I was speaking the language of modern America during the Carter administration, which had adopted human rights as part of its enduring foreign-policy plank. All they saw was a black man sitting in the embassy saying what they would expect to hear from a white person. It was one of many similar painful experiences for me. It was a terrible time to be in Liberia, but it prepared me for what was to come in South Africa.

A recent ambassador to Liberia, Bismarck Myrick, phoned me in total frustration to say, "I can't stand it any more. They have not changed a bit since you were here." General Stevens, the young air force lieutenant who gave me the grim briefing, also called. "Ambassador, they still say the same thing. They have not yet understood that their conception of the relationship between the United States and Liberia is different from reality."

The United States recognizes countries, not regimes. The United States will take extraordinary efforts to distance itself from a rogue government, but our position in Liberia was that the upheaval was a civil war in which the United States would not intervene. The American Embassy worked closely with Doe to guide him quietly, but the United States never harbored the opinion that Doe was a good leader and worthy of support. This was a stakes game, and Doe and his colleagues were the cards we had to play in the best interest of the United States. We had to sell this philosophy even within our own mission. I spent a lot of time talking to young officers in the embassy who saw Doe only as a man who shot his way to the top. Our goal, I reminded them repeatedly, was the stability of the country and the return to representative government.

The people of Liberia had mixed feelings about Doe. Most of the African-Liberians liked him because he was one of them. They referred to him as the "Abraham Lincoln of Liberia," who emancipated the tribals from the yoke of Americo-Liberian control. MOJA seethed behind the scenes and underground, agitating constantly to oust Doe and his government, and turned increasingly to Libya and the USSR for assistance in their goals. Americo-Liberians opposed the revolution and despised Doe as a pretender to a position he did not deserve. They believed that the United States was committing an unpardonable sin by working with him. Eventually, however, some Americo-Liberians began to work in the Doe administration, some because they felt they were serving their country, others because they liked the power and money.

Doe and his palace guard, all country people from eastern Liberia, were now on top, and they wanted all the accouterments of prestige and privilege that they had seen the Americo-Liberians enjoy. The country people wanted the means to acquire big houses, automobiles, and beautiful women. The United States, on the other hand, wanted a stable government with economic and political order; it wanted to restore the people to health. Even before the revolution, the USAID program in Liberia had been less than successful. I do not know why. When President Tolbert visited the United States, President Kennedy asked, "What can I do for you?" and Tolbert answered, "We need a hospital." So the USAID program built the John F. Kennedy Memorial Hospital, a large training facility in Monrovia. But it did not succeed. When I arrived, the hospital was barely keeping its doors open; unable to maintain an adequate staff of doctors and nurses, it was on the brink of financial ruin. And the hospital was only one of the U.S. failures in Liberia. After the revolution, much of the annual $90 million USAID program in Liberia was spent on military activities such as barracks and training activities for defense. The military could be used for such purposes as building roads, but the new Liberian government was not interested in rebuilding the infrastructure. Doe wanted flash—airplanes, tanks, guns, helicopters, and new military uniforms. Doe wanted a first-class army with shining boots, a sharp-looking honor guard, a great military band, troops on parade; he wanted the symbols of sovereignty. He was less interested in the essential minutiae such as creating postage stamps and becoming a member of the International Postal Union, which was necessary for getting the mail out of the country. Our frustration was in trying to persuade him to think in broader terms and to understand that Liberia must adhere to international principles. The Liberian economy was a dominating issue for the United States; I got a battlefield tutorial in the importance of economics in foreign relations.

The American Embassy had a role in determining how funding from the United States was to be spent, and we advocated paying down Liberia's national debt instead of initiating new programs. Liberia had incurred enormous external debt after the revolution, and in order for it to be accepted back into the world community of nations, it had to be creditworthy. It was in the interest of the United States that Liberia pay its debts, especially to the World Bank and the International Monetary Fund. Convincing Doe of this was a nerve-wracking adventure, much like driving a sputtering jalopy in the Indy 500. If Liberia defaulted on its debts, it could never borrow money again. Part of U.S. policy was to reduce the debt, using a law at the time that provided for Economic Support Funds. In an effort to influence economic stability, this law permitted loans with no collateral. If Liberia did not contribute to servicing the debt, however, another law would kick in that prevented us from giving them these funds. The Liberian government always made its payments at the last possible minute, constantly tottering on the edge of financial ruin.

The United States wanted to protect its private investment in Liberia. We wanted to preserve Roberts Field, the international airport, which had been built by the U.S. Air Force during World War II to bring men, materials, and guns to North Africa. We wanted to keep the port open and operating. Furthermore, we were deeply concerned about the efforts of the Soviets and the Libyans to make inroads in Liberia. The Soviets worked to become a dominant force on Liberian soil. This would have been a particular triumph in a nation where the United States had such a large presence. When I was posted to Liberia, I understood that one of the most important U.S. goals was to keep Libya, the USSR, and their Eastern Bloc allies out of Liberia by using all means necessary—intelligence, machinations, and money. Consequently, the U.S. civilian and military aid programs were accelerated.

The ambassador and I realized it was our job to keep Doe stable and to ensure he provided no surprises. The two of us spent considerable time with him. Liberia was probably the only country in the world where the U.S. ambassador was likely to receive a call from the head of state every day. Day and night, much of our time and attention was given to talking to Doe, talking about Doe, or thinking about Doe. It was difficult to present issues to him because he had a short attention span and was unable to grasp a bundle of facts. An issue as complex as balance of payments is difficult for almost anyone to understand, but Doe would simply say, "Oh well, the United States has a lot of money," referring to Liberia's perceived special relationship with the United States, which would surely bankroll its favorite African country.

The more I worked with him, the more clearly I saw several distinct facets of his personality. He was a young man who had no prior contact with the world beyond the borders of Liberia, his tribal background, and his military experience. His army career was his most important accomplishment. The army had given him a purpose in life. He considered being a senior master sergeant as the pinnacle of success, and he saw the military as the only stable activity in the world.

He was forming his vision of what a head of state should be and wrestling with the concepts of efficiency, authority, and power. In the United States, I told him, we see the head of state as the first among equals with responsibility for administering the government effectively. When we discussed the possibility of Liberia's eventually implementing three branches of government as in the United States, he replied, "Africa is different. African people are different." "Chief," I said, "people are the same."

We steadily urged Doe to turn the country back to civilian rule, but first we had to explain the theory of elections to him. He came from a society of tribal chiefs. The chief is the wisest person and tells the people what they should know. By extension, the head of state is the biggest chief. We tried to talk to him about the concept of international acceptance, which necessitates a stable economic, political, and social society. We were trying to persuade him that a head of state demonstrates fiscal prudence and discipline. We wanted him to have a lean civil service and a disciplined military, but he wanted a first-class military. "Your borders are permanent," I told him. "You don't need a large military because nobody is going to try to take territory away from you, and therefore you are not going to fight anybody." We agreed to build barracks and to provide a limited amount of ammunition so he could conduct training for border-guard capability, but we would not fund huge armaments of tanks and armored vehicles. We urged him to take the guns from the soldiers on the street and to stop the rampaging. We tried to persuade him not to be so friendly with the Soviet Union and Libya if he wanted to be friends with the United States.

In Doe's vision, a head of state must have the trappings of position. He wanted a fleet of cars, a big mansion, and lots of walking-around money. Mostly, he wanted a plane. A number of people were eager to sell him one. We tried repeatedly to explain the excessive expense of the fuel, the maintenance, the crew, the ground fees, and the per diems and expenses of an entourage of people to travel with him. When we finally had to say flatly that the United States would not pay for it, he was hurt and could not understand. His sycophants whispered in his ear: "Americans are stingy. They are not helping us. Don't listen to them. You are the head of state; you are the chief."

Doe also had a dark side. He was a nefarious man and clever in disguising the savagery of his dictatorship. At the drop of a pin, Doe could order an arrest or the disappearance of a person, but he was careful to see that the most blatant human-rights violations were exercised through other people. He was a dictator who knew the ever-present danger of being toppled from power, and he secured his position with a cruelty some might call self-preservation.

Finally, he was an uneducated man who wanted to learn. A major part of my job involved the education of Doe himself. He wanted to become what he called a "book person"; he wanted to become literate. He enrolled in home-study courses at the University of Liberia. A tutor went to the mansion to help him with lessons. As head of state, he was often too proud to ask any of his colleagues for help, so occasionally he would ask Ambassador Swing or me for an explanation. As he navigated his way toward education, we realized he needed a special kind of nurturing, and we arranged for him to receive CNN, which was new. We wanted him to know something about the world, and we thought exposure to CNN would be the best way. Liberians could not receive it because they did not have the appropriate technology, but we installed it in the executive mansion. Every time I called on Doe, he had his television tuned to CNN.

In August 1982, Doe decided that he wanted to make a state visit to the United States. Presidents rarely make state visits because of the associated pomp, so we asked President Reagan to invite him instead on an official visit, which involved less ceremony. This trip was another aspect of our care and treatment of Doe, to guide him along the right path, to avoid totalitarianism, and to protect American assets in Liberia. The icing on the cake would be a visit to the White House. President Reagan agreed and issued the invitation.

The preparations to get him ready for the trip were extensive. When we discussed dress protocol, Doe declared that he would wear a military uniform. "It won't work," I said. At the time, Doe was wearing his hair in an Afro, a big bush, and the image that popped into my mind was the "Beetle Bailey" cartoon strip in which a black officer wore a garrison hat perched on his bush. I could see American cartoonists having a field day with the Liberian president. We told him that a head of state holds a higher status than a military man and persuaded him to wear tribal robes. We also briefed him and his assistants on the role of the press in a free society, which most emerging societies do not understand. They are baffled that the U.S. government does not control the press. We told Doe not to take the American press for granted. I accompanied Doe,

Ambassador Swing, and their assistants to the airport, saw them off, crossed my fingers, said a silent prayer, and wished them good luck. They needed it.

When President Reagan met Doe on the South Portico for photographs, he introduced him to the press as "President Moe." Although Reagan corrected himself later, the press picked it up. That was the first misadventure. Then, at the Liberian Embassy reception, Doe spotted a beautiful woman and asked about her. When told that she was the style editor of the *Washington Post*, he said, "I want to give her an interview." Ambassador Swing tried to persuade him otherwise, but Doe was determined. "No, no," he said. "Nice woman. I want to give her an interview." He did. He gave her an exclusive interview. And she crucified him. He made every mistake possible, and she reported every one. I talked with her years later. "It was a great interview," she laughed.

Doe was aghast when he read the story in the *Post*. "This woman! We had a great conversation!" The more he read it, the madder he got.

"What do we do now?" he asked.

"Nothing," the ambassador told him.

"We can't take that. She has insulted us."

"You gave her the interview freely. You have to take what she gives you." So Doe began sulking. The final leg of the trip was Los Angeles, where it had been arranged for him to meet with movie actors and executives interested in doing business in Liberia. Doe refused to come out of his suite.

"I ain't coming," he said in patois. That is all he would say. "I ain't coming."

Finally, Ambassador Swing talked him out of his deep funk, and he met the motion-picture people. I understood his reaction. He behaved much like a disappointed child who was hurt and had no inner resources to fall back on. He was in a strange country with strange habits and mores, and he did not recognize the inherent danger. He had been wounded, and he had nowhere to fall except down. All was well when he returned to Liberia with pictures of himself and President Reagan—evidence that he was playing with the big boys, proof that he was an authentic head of state. This was just another episode in our efforts to make a silk purse out of a sow's ear.

During the trip, he visited a big U.S. military base in South Carolina. When he stepped out of the plane, he saw acres of helicopters and his eyes glazed over. Back in Liberia, one of the first things he asked for was some helicopters. "I saw them," he said. "You have thousands of helicopters." He wanted helicopter gunships to transport him around the country quickly. Our job at the embassy was to say, "You don't need it," in a way he could accept. He simply could not understand that he could not have everything he wanted when America had it.

It was hard work keeping Doe on the straight and narrow path, and his relationship with Ambassador Swing was often rocky. One evening at a resort hotel, the ambassador encountered Nicholas Podier, vice head of state. Podier was loaded to the gills, belligerent, and began to verbally abuse the ambassador. Swing's only reply was to say, "I'm sorry you feel that way, General." The next day, Doe called the embassy furious with the version of the story he had been given, in which it was Swing who attacked Podier. We tried everything we knew to restore relations, but Doe was so angry he would not budge. Swing was crushed. The strained relations hung on like bad weather. About that time, Anwar Sadat was assassinated in Egypt, and Doe went to the funeral, taking an entourage with him. As a last-ditch effort to mend fences, we asked for help from U.S. representatives attending the funeral. "Relations between the ambassador and head of state are at an all-time low," we said. "Would you pay some attention to Doe?" Former secretary of state Alexander Haig took Doe by the arm and introduced him to former U.S. presidents Carter, Ford, and Nixon. Doe was elated. He returned to tell Swing, "All is forgiven, Mr. Ambassador. Just a misunderstanding."

I intended to serve a full three-year term in Liberia, but I was unexpectedly posted again to Washington in 1983. When I left, Doe had agreed to elections and the return of Liberia to civilian rule. But he quickly added, "Maybe I'll run for president. Who would run against me?"

When Lucy, Sarah, and I looked out the departing plane's windows to see Liberia growing smaller below us, I never dreamed that my destiny would bring me back to this troubled country for another tour of duty. That future was beyond my line of vision. For now, I was headed for the Office of West Africa Affairs, more responsibility to master, and new worlds to explore.

In hindsight, the cold-war mentality and the U.S. anxiety about Soviet and Libyan influence led us to spend more money in Liberia than we should have. Today, the result of that money is not apparent anywhere in the country.

THE OFFICE OF
WEST AFRICAN AFFAIRS

My career was on the ascendant. I had intended to serve a customary three-year appointment in Liberia, but after two years I was offered a position in the Bureau of African Affairs at the Department of State. I had my choice of three jobs. The one I chose was director of West African Affairs, also known by the title of country director. This job was to manage from Washington the conduct of relations between the United States and sixteen countries in West Africa. I realized immediately that the job was much more than I expected. What astonished me—almost frightened me— was the enormity of the position without underlying solidity. We were always flying by the seat of our pants, getting things done by any means possible. As director I gained a new respect for ambassadors, and at the same time I was surprised at how vital a country director is to an ambassador in the field.

I was about to learn that a country director is one of the most important jobs in the State Department, because it is the office in the U.S. government that is expected to know everything about a country or a region. One phone call has gone down in legend. A desk officer picked up the phone to find President Kennedy on the line. "Do you handle country X?" the president asked. "Tell me about it. Why do we have representation there? What are the issues of interest to us? What would happen if we closed our embassy?" In a system rooted in the chain of command, the desk officer was nearly apoplectic.

A bureau serves as a big switchboard, moving information constantly among the countries. Dividing the West African region into Francophone and Anglophone countries, two deputy directors assisted me. Every day, missions and embassies report by cable (now by e-mail), to the bureau's desk officers, although all cables are addressed to the secretary of state. A cable either requests action or reports action; each is read and directed to the appropriate country

217

director. Then, action is coordinated either within the bureau or outside, in another part of the State Department. Our job at the directorate was to support the countries in Washington and to ensure that the ambassadors convey to the governments abroad what the U.S. government wants said to them.

This required me to stay in communication with every Washington agency involved in overseas operations, including but not limited to Defense, CIA, Justice, USAID, Commerce, Agriculture, Treasury, Labor, and Energy. We also dealt with other State Department activities, such as the Foreign Buildings Office, a congressionally mandated office to build and manage properties of the U.S. government abroad. I was responsible for maintaining a continuous liaison with the intelligence activities in Washington, including the Bureau of Intelligence and Research (INR) in the State Department, an intelligence-gathering agency that works with the CIA. As the Washington eyes and ears of overseas posts, we were responsible for collecting and interpreting information. The desk officers were in regular communication with INR about anything dealing with post-analysis of conduct of relations, including background information on heads of state. They could provide me with anything I needed to know when traveling in those countries—what did the heads of state like or hate, or how did they feel about the United States?

The directorate of West African Affairs was a dynamic office due to the number of countries in our area and their range of issues. I remembered the lessons learned as a desk officer, and I gave my staff the same freedom of operation that I had been given, instructing the staff to do its job without regard to rank. Granting junior officers this freedom is unusual in government. I also told them, "Never let there come into this office a problem that cannot be solved. If the post sends it in, we have to solve it." The third rule was "Never let me or the deputies be surprised by something. Keep us informed."

The country director has a responsibility for public relations with the public at large, so I traveled extensively in the United States making speeches. Narcotics was a subject of increasing interest, and a number of my speeches were on that subject. During the Carter administration the Bureau of Narcotics had been created, and the United States made narcotics a diplomatic initiative. When we began having embassies report on drug trafficking in their countries, we discovered that in Nigeria such trafficking was extensive, elaborate, and lucrative. Nigeria was often a transfer point between Southeast Asia and Sydney or Melbourne, then on to the United States. Nigerians were some of the

THE STAFF OF THE OFFICE OF WEST AFRICAN AFFAIRS.
I am in the back row. Our job was to manage from Washington the conduct
of relations between the United States and sixteen countries in West Africa.
The enormity of my responsibilities as country director was astonishing.

most clever narcotics smugglers in the world. We worked with the U.S. Bureau
of Narcotics and Dangerous Drugs, and the FBI increased the number of agents
overseas. In this way, the United States spread its tentacles overseas through the
country directorates. Our role was to try to stop drug trafficking in Nigeria
and elsewhere. This did not make us very popular.

An effective Foreign Service officer is knowledgeable about the countries of his
or her responsibility, knows the issues between the United States and that
country, and is familiar with the issues that affect regional solidarity. In West
Africa, we also had to understand each country's potential for development.

These criteria applied no less to me than to the ambassadors accredited to countries in my region, so my immediate task was to learn as much as possible, as quickly as possible, about the sixteen countries in my directorate. The Office of West African Affairs has since been divided into two directorates, but when I was there, it was the largest directorate in the State Department. Consequently, I logged thousands of miles by almost every mode of transportation touring the countries of my responsibility: Ghana, Liberia, Niger, Senegal, Côte d'Ivoire, Sierra Leone, Nigeria, Mauritania, Gambia, Guinea-Bissau, Cape Verde, Guinea, Togo, Mali, Chad, Benin, and Western Sahara.

The political hot spots were Liberia, Ghana, and Nigeria. After my last two posts, I was well versed with the issues in Liberia and Ghana, where people still were being killed. I was less knowledgeable about Nigeria, so I set out on an orientation tour to get to know it and the neighboring countries of West Africa.

Nigeria had been the hope of West Africa after colonialism. The country had a dynamic population with an achievement-oriented mentality, so it was expected to lead the way in development. The population was teeming; every fourth African is said to be a Nigerian. The country was rich with resources, and by the time I took the directorate, Nigeria had discovered oil. Oil would be both a bane and a blessing. It was a blessing because it is a marketable resource, but it was a bane because it pulled enormous numbers of people away from agriculture and into the cities and small-scale jobs. Regrettably, the cities were not equipped to handle the influx of people, and agriculture languished. Nigeria's oil economy created millionaires in both the private sector and in government. The money attracted a military-officer corps into government, and once ensconced there, the military wanted more power and more control. This led to multiple coups and military dictatorships. Only once did the military return the country to civilian rule.

While in Nigeria, I visited the working farm of Olusegun Obasanjo, a former general who was elected president in 2001. When I first met him he was operating a huge farm activity and market. A non-traditional product at the farmers' market was palm wine, made from the sap of a specific palm tree that must be tapped before noon. In the morning the juice is sweet, but it ferments quickly and by afternoon, it is a potent alcohol. Obasanjo bottled and sold the palm wine for a tidy profit, and he built a pub for his farm hands to drink it in a safe environment.

When I assumed office, debt and inflation were high, and Nigeria's relations with the United States were tenuous. But overall, the country seemed to be peaceful and tranquil. Within months, though, a coup had taken place. I was awakened one morning about two o'clock to be told, "Mr. Perkins, this is the operations center at the State Department. We regret to inform you that a coup is underway in one of your countries—Nigeria." So I dressed quickly, went down to the department, and took over the task force. Within a very short period, a new set of army officers had taken over Nigeria's government. Nigeria became a political and economic basket case, having squandered its opportunities through poor administration and bad political judgments. Working with Harvard University, we set up management-training series for young middle-managers. That was going quite well until the price of oil dropped and Nigeria's economy stumbled, never to regain its balance. Now, corruption is so rampant that it is difficult to get from the airport into downtown Lagos without having to resort to bribes. Lagos Murtala Mohammed International Airport has been branded by the Federal Aviation Administration as the most unsafe airport in the world.

A major concern when I was director was the relentless drought in the Sahel countries, some of which were within the West African directorate—Mali, Niger, Mauritania, and part of Senegal. We worked with USAID and Treasury to provide relief missions and keep people from starving. Economic development was a prevailing issue, and it was ongoing work to arrange loans from the African Development Bank in Abidjan, Côte d'Ivoire, and the International Monetary Fund. Part of our job was justifying such loans based on a country's potential. The countries in French West Africa—Côte d'Ivoire, Senegal, Mali, and Niger—were very likely to grow, and we pushed the World Bank to be generous in granting concessions to them. Chad, by contrast, was at that time a cattle country with no natural resources and seemed the least likely to be developed. Recently, however, oil was discovered in Chad, giving the country a new lease on life. It remains to be seen if success is in the cards.

Human-rights issues were continual problems, in Liberia particularly but also in Guinea. One of the great African revolutionaries, Ahmed Sékou Touré, died in Guinea while I was head of the office. He was the first black to become president of independent Guinea, which had been a colony of France. When Charles de Gaulle granted independence to the French colonies, he asked them to join the French Financial Union so that the African-French franc would be backed by the Central Bank of France. Sékou Touré adamantly opposed any further relations with France. De Gaulle, in turn, ordered everything French removed from the country, including the telephones. Guinea never recovered economically.

When I heard that Sékou Touré was seriously ill, he was already in a famous hospital in Cleveland, Ohio, and he died there soon after. Because Guinea is Muslim, friends supplied a plane, belonging to the king of Saudi Arabia, for the body's transport home. Sékou Touré had such a stranglehold on Guinea that no recognizable successor was in the wings. The country was thrown into total chaos. I was concerned about the upheaval in the country and anxious to make sure the transport of the body went smoothly, so I sent Nancy Morgan, the desk officer for Guinea, to Cleveland. There she found some of Sékou Touré's closest advisors frozen into inactivity. She called me and said, "They don't know what to do." She discovered that no arrangements had been made for an airport ceremony to receive the body. I told her, "Get on the plane and go with them." She accompanied the body back to Guinea on the king's plane and made the arrangements herself. For a couple of days, this Foreign Service officer virtually ran the country. Upon returning, she shook her head and said, "After what I did, I will never be satisfied with desk officer work again." In my judgment, this was a natural duty she was called upon to do, and she did it well.

Up the coast, another nation I inherited in the directorate was the Western Sahara, a little piece of land between Morocco and Mauritania. It is rich in phosphates, and it could have a lucrative fishing industry. Once a Spanish territory, Spain ceded control to Mauritania, Algeria, and Morocco. When a revolutionary movement arose in Western Sahara, Mauritania quickly abdicated responsibility and wanted nothing to do with it, but Morocco hung on, angling for hegemony over the entire area. The issue has never been settled.

Mauritania, the only Arab country under my directorship, is a poor country with enormous problems. When I was director, Mauritania still practiced slavery. It is a sandy country—most all the trees have been cut down for firewood—and the sands are always shifting. I saw the capital being overtaken by sand. A sandstorm came up when I was there, and I quickly learned how to wear the burnoose to protect myself from the relentless sand.

East of Mauritania is Mali, which has the great, open-air market in the capital city of Bamako. This 4,000-year-old bazaar swirls with colors, smells, and activi-ties. Everything is for sale here—incense, myrrh, amber, silver, fresh fruits, and produce. During my visit, the ambassador, a former Peace Corps volunteer who shared my passion for the historic richness of the market, spent a lot of time exploring it with me. We then went to Mali's other capital—Timbuktu, which has a huge sandcastle university resembling a set from *Beau Geste*. Timbuktu was an ancient seat of learning, where the sons of black Africa and Arabia went to be educated. Historically, Timbuktu has been divided into three sections: Arab, black, and Tuareg, a Muslim, Berber-speaking people. Each has its own culture intact—food, clothing, music, literature, and architecture. The Tuaregs are a mystery; nobody knows where they came from. The name means "mixture," so the likely explanation is that they were nomadic people descended from the ancient Garamante people of Libya with strains of Negro blood. Tuareg women are known for using indigo as a beauty preparation on their fingernails and lips. Some have an indigo figure painted on their palm. The ambassador and I walked into the wee hours of the morning, strolling through the three sections of Tim-buktu. It was one of the most exciting orientations I have ever had. The city was alive all night with poetry readings, musicians on stage, and people cooking food in narrow alleyways. Even more fascinating was the knowledge that peo-ple had been doing the same thing on this spot for thousands of years.

Niger, an agricultural market economy, was a French-speaking country under the rule of a general who had come to power through a coup. The U.S. Embassy there is very small. I had previously been to Niger and there had my first expe-rience with problems wrought by a unique American phenomenon—a political appointee as ambassador. This is a practice that has passed along through the years, but the United States remains practically the only country in the world that assigns political appointees to overseas posts. Other countries have non-career ambassadors, but it is a rare occurrence. The ambassador in question was a non-career appointee from the Reagan administration. The inspection team reported that morale at the embassy was rock bottom and asked me to visit it on my way to Washington to take over the directorship of West African Affairs. The inspectors attributed the problem to two things: (1) the ambassador and (2) his wife. I spent two days there trying to sort out the trouble.

The first problem was that the ambassador did not speak French, although he thought he did. I have studied French for ten years and still do not presume that

I can speak it fluently. He should not have presumed that after three months of study he could carry on a diplomatic conversation in French, but he refused to take his DCM with him on calls to the Nigerian head of state. Finally, after one bumbling day, the foreign minister said, "Please bring your deputy with you next time, Mr. Ambassador." It was very embarrassing for the ambassador.

I talked with the troops to see what I could do to improve morale. As soon as I hit the ground, I realized that I was dealing with an individual who had low self-confidence and a big ego, a deadly combination. When I met the DCM, I asked, "What in God's name is going on here?"

"The ambassador suffers from a lack of confidence and a suspicion that all of the career people are out to do him in," the DCM told me. "Consequently, he tries to do everything himself and he doesn't know what to do. And his wife feeds his suspicions." I met with the entire mission and heard the same thing repeatedly.

The next day I met with the ambassador's wife, who told me that nobody appreciated what they were trying to do, which was to have a happy, well-run embassy.

"Your husband can make a success of this or he can bollix it up," I said, "in which case he will create a reputation that will be with him for the rest of his life. You have a deputy chief of mission . . . ," I began.

"But we don't know if we can trust him or not," she said.

I explained to her, as well as to the ambassador later, that it was not in the interest of the Foreign Service or the State Department to have an ambassador fail. One of the major functions of the DCM was to help an ambassador operate a successful mission. "Call on the DCM," I said. "Do not consider him a threat."

The final evening of my visit I scheduled a meeting with the ambassador, an encounter I did not relish. An ambassadorship is unlike any other appointment in the government. He is a direct representative of the president, and no one can dismiss him except the president. It is a powerful position, even for a small, insignificant post like Niamey, Niger. Obviously the ambassador was appointed there because he had made a contribution to the Reagan campaign, although it was such a small post I do not think it could have been a significant contribution.

"Mr. Ambassador, you are missing a golden opportunity to have a great functioning post," I told him.

"What am I doing wrong?" he asked. We were drinking wine, a hell of a mistake on my part, because I told him what he was doing wrong, chapter and verse. About two in the morning he said, "I checked on you before you came, and the one thing everybody said about you is that you don't pull any punches. What you say is what you mean. I see they were correct. So, what shall I do?"

"It's up to you," I said. "You and your wife. You have a staff of people willing and able. It is up to you to lead them. Trust them. Use your DCM as your alter ego. Travel around the country. Get to know it. That way the government will have more confidence that you care."

He tried to change and to do what I suggested. About a year after I became director of West African Affairs, his tour ended and he was advised by letter to prepare to vacate his post. He asked permission to come in on consultation and the first person he had to see was the country director—me. He came in with the cable in his hand.

"I am not ready to accept this as the final authority," he said. "I was appointed by the White House and I am going to the White House. Who do I see over there?"

"The director of the Office of White House Personnel," I said, and I offered to call and make an appointment for him. He refused my help, saying he would handle the matter himself. About an hour later, he was back looking sheepish. Clearly, the meeting had been decisive. Now he had a new plan.

"What can I do to get appointed as ambassador in Geneva?"

"You go back to the office you just left," I told him. "All of the ambassadorial appointments are made in the White House."

"Would you give me a recommendation?" he asked. It must have galled him to ask this favor of a midlevel officer. I explained that it was the secretary of state, not the country director, who should make such a recommendation and suggested he go to talk with the secretary of state. That was the last I saw of him. One Saturday morning some time after that, a package arrived for me. He had sent me a camel saddle as a gift. To this day I do not know why he sent it. Camel saddles are notable for two things: (1) they are precious artifacts, and (2) they are cured by an unusual process—the repeated application of camel urine. I do not know what silent message he was sending me with a camel saddle, but I phoned him to thank him for the gift.

The smaller countries in West Africa include Cape Verde, Togo, Benin, Guinea-Bissau, and Gambia.

Cape Verde was a Portuguese colony of seafaring people. At one time, more Cape Verdeans lived in the shipbuilding town of New Bedford, Massachusetts, than in all of Cape Verde. The country was stable when I was director, and it had the distinction of being one of only two countries in Africa that would allow South African planes to land (Côte d'Ivoire was the other country to grant South Africa landing rights). While under the apartheid government, flights from South Africa to Europe took an inordinate amount of time because planes were not allowed to fly over land until they reached North Africa, but they could refuel at Cape Verde.

Guinea-Bissau, another former Portuguese colony, rumbled with unrest but suffered no blood baths.

Benin is French-speaking and is the third point from which slaves were shipped, especially to Brazil. When I went to Benin, former general Mathieu Kérékou was president. Benin was a socialist country that flirted with extreme socialism until France indicated its disfavor; then the Beninois practiced socialism more discreetly because they did not want to lose French support. When I crossed the border I saw likenesses of Lenin and Stalin next to a sign that said, "The Democratic Republic of Benin Welcomes You." When I expressed surprise at this paradox, the ambassador escorting me explained, "They don't let socialism get in the way of capitalistic tendencies." Benin was a country that practiced socialism in the wings and capitalism in the markets. Our foreign policies included trying to move Benin to democracy. Problems were few with Benin, but one issue I encountered involved the embassy of Benin in Washington, D.C. It asked permission from the city of Washington, under the leadership of Mayor Marion Barry, to construct a tower to communicate with its home country. We were inclined to urge the city to grant permission until one of the Washington neighbors complained. The neighbor was Helen Thomas, the doyenne of the Washington press corps. She would not have it, so permission was refused.

Togo is a very small former French colony between Benin and Ghana. This beautiful seashore country was a popular holiday location for European travelers, who found it much like vacationing on the Riviera. Sergeant Gnassingbé Eyadéma had wrested control of the country years earlier in a coup and was, at the time of his death in 2005, Africa's longest-serving head of state.

Senegal, on the West Coast, is one of my favorite countries. It is known for its art and music. Senegalese women are some of the most beautiful in the world, and they carry themselves with a regal bearing. Leopold Senghor, the first Senegalese president, was a world-class poet who sent numbers of young men to Paris to get a classical education. His successor, Abdou Diouf, wondered aloud, "What does a classical education do for Senegal? We need agriculturists who can get their hands dirty." Perhaps the country needs fewer poets, librarians, and literature professors and more mining engineers and topographic experts. Senegal exploited its rain forests and then discovered that once the ecosystem is disturbed, it cannot be restored. So Diouf began sending government-sponsored students to the United States for education in more practical fields.

Senegal is the location of Gorée Island, a slave shipping port. On a tour of the island I met the son of renowned historian John Hope Franklin, who, with a Senegalese curator, was working to restore Gorée to a tourist attraction. Gorée had not changed much in the past two hundred years. One day, the full story will be told of the time when slavery was a business and humans were a commodity, and it will include the complicity of Africans and Arabs in enabling the slave trade to flourish. On Gorée Island, I came to a full stop when I saw the ports that were built into the side of the building, through which the slaves who died were pushed out to sea, without burial.

Côte d'Ivoire, the other big Francophone country, was also stable and never had a revolution until longtime president Félix Houphouet-Boigny died and a struggle for power ensued. Houphouet-Boigny, the head of state when I was director, was French down to the ground and he loved Côte d'Ivoire. Houphouet-Boigny was an entrepreneur—a dreamer, grower, and builder who promoted agriculture and created markets in Europe for produce grown in Côte d'Ivoire. Even today, cabbages, carrots, and greens are loaded on a plane in the capital of Abidjan and are offloaded in France a few hours later, destined for the markets. He promoted the innovative production of the country's pineapple crop into a delicious, effervescent non-alcoholic drink called pineapple champagne. In Abidjan, he built one of the world's largest Catholic cathedrals, the Basilica of Our Lady of Peace, modeled on St. Peter's in Rome and constructed at an estimated cost of $150 million (in U.S. dollars). He built paved roads across this poor bush country, installed some ten thousand streetlights, built colleges, presidential and parliamentary palaces, an airstrip to accommodate jets, and a five-star hotel. He also tended to build monuments to himself, including a palatial home surrounded by a moat stocked with crocodiles, held sacred by his Baoulé tribe. Côte d'Ivoire is one of the world's largest suppliers of cocoa, produced in part by child labor, one of the scourges of the West Africa region. Another blight of the area is female genital mutilation, an age-old practice of some tribes that will be eradicated only by the slow practice of education.

The fact that I was the highest-ranking American official to visit Mauritania in several years indicates that the country was not a priority in United States relations. The ambassador pulled out the stops to welcome me, and my visit concluded with a *mish-oui*, a lavish feast hosted by one of the ministers. Mauritania is an Arab country, so we sat on cushions on the floor. The centerpiece of the banquet was a whole roasted sheep. Since I was the guest of honor, I sat on the minister's right and he presented me with a great delicacy—the eyes of the sheep. No alcohol is served in Arab countries, but we drank cup after cup of strong, sweet tea. My Arab hosts were attired in robes and sandals, and throughout the feast, my host picked his toenails. The *mish-oui* was a grand occasion, and I enjoyed it thoroughly.

Gambia is a curious geopolitical entity, which by logic should have been part of Senegal. One of the smallest countries in the world, it is about twice the size of the state of Delaware. I was familiar with Gambia as the country popularized by Alex Haley's book *Roots* and the site of his maternal ancestor's kidnapping and enslavement. Later, Senegal and Gambia would combine their two small countries and refer to the resulting nation as Senegambia, but it would not be a success.

Sierra Leone was established as a haven for freed slaves from British possessions in the Caribbean, and for some time the inhabitants considered themselves more British than African. Their descendants constituted the elite class, similar to the Americo-Liberians, and when Sierra Leone became an independent country, they constituted the ruling class. Sierra Leone had been a free country since the end of colonialism in West Africa, and for a while it enjoyed a placid life seemingly bereft of tension. Later that would all change. In a repetition of a familiar story, the indigenous people became restless, and a series of struggles for political power has almost destroyed the country. Warlords compete for the only resource that makes sense to them—diamonds. In a shameful continuing saga, some American entrepreneurs try to take advantage of the warlords' greed by financing the illegal extraction of diamonds. A temporary government was cobbled together hastily, and today an uneasy peace hovers over Sierra Leone, as a United Nations peacekeeping contingency monitors, in theory, the cease-fire between contingencies vying for political power.

Burkina Faso, a land-locked French colony on the Volta River, was earlier known as Haute-Volta. Ouagadougou, the capital city, is a microcosm of a small, sleepy rural French town; the only difference is the color of the inhabitants. The economy of Burkina Faso is based on cattle driven through the country to market or to pastures. Established as a convenience colony for the French, it was not developed to be a freed country with a thriving mercantile. Consequently, since 1960 the country has had a difficult time finding a balance in its new incarnation as an independent nation. It is, however, a country known for its hospitality and for its arts and crafts, especially rugs, robes, sheeting, and more recently, its film industry. A coup occurred in Burkina Faso while I was country director and a government was established that was less friendly to the United States.

There would be more trips to West Africa, but for now I returned to Washington to begin my stint as director. I had seen the economic plight of these poor countries, so I dealt extensively with the International Monetary Fund and the World Bank trying to arrange loans. I worked with the private sector as well, trying to persuade companies to invest in these countries, to create jobs and market opportunities, and to help the countries produce what they did best and sell it. Long before it became popular, we were thinking about a regional organization to facilitate trade among these countries.

I had not been in Washington long when I encountered a situation that went against my management style. The former director, Bob Bruce, was a good friend of mine. He was an obsessive worker recovering from a heart attack and working at quarter-time. He reported to a deputy assistant secretary (DAS), a fine Foreign Service officer and a perfectionist. Every day at five o'clock, Bob reported and recapped everything that had transpired in the directorate that day while the DAS analyzed and approved or disapproved each action. I realized that Bob was spending most of the day preparing for this anxiety-ridden briefing. My first day on the job, I, too, went upstairs and reported everything that had taken place.

"That is very good," I was told.

"I'm glad you liked it," I said, "because it won't happen again. I don't intend to do this again." I told him that two deputies and I were paid a significant amount of money to manage the directorate and to alert him and his superior to matters of importance to them, but that we were all too busy for me to report every detail every day at five o'clock.

He heard me out and then said, "Well, okay." That was the end of that.

I also told him that I realized we would not always see eye-to-eye, but when that happened I would find a way to see him before I left for the day and get it off my chest. Life is too short for me to go home worrying, I said. I had already told him that instead of waiting for the traditional annual job evaluation, I would prefer to meet with him every three months for an informal review. "Tell me how I'm doing. Give me some suggestions about how I could do better. Don't wait until the end of the year and a rushed evaluation." I have practiced this with every supervisor I have had, and I practice it with subordinates. It is a procedure that works.

When the DAS gave me my official evaluation, he wrote in part: "This is a fine officer. Doesn't waste my time and doesn't waste his. When he talks to me he has notes, a clear issue, and a recommended course of action. I can say either yes or no or change it. Then we get on with business."

The walls of the directorate are hung with the portraits of the sixteen ambassadors and their predecessors. One afternoon Shirley Temple Black came to see me, and as she left she said, "I'll bet you don't have my picture." I said, "I bet we do." And I led her to the collection of ambassadors to Ghana. There was her portrait from when she had served in the 1970s. "My, what a beautiful woman," she said with a twinkle.

The directorate operates with a great deal of autonomy—until it gets into trouble. I made a lot of decisions that were beyond my level for decision-making, but only one backfired. Based on the precedent of a former action, I sent instructions on an issue to an ambassador. The decision was of such importance that normally it would have come from the secretary of state, the deputy secretary, or the under secretary for political affairs, who was Larry Eagleburger. On this occasion, I made the decision myself, an action that reverberated through the department. I decided to ride it out and say nothing. One morning, a staff assistant to Eagleburger came to see me. She said, "Mr. Eagleburger asked me to come and tell you that you don't run the State Department."

"That's all?" I asked.

"That's all." Eagleburger never minces words, and he knows when to make a reprimand official and when to send a warning. He never mentioned the incident to me.

Throughout this time, the relationship between the United States and the Soviet Union simmered silently. The Soviet Embassy in Washington assigned an officer to be my contact, which meant to watch me. Occasionally he would come to see me and we would spend most of a morning talking about human rights, arms transfers, and trade agreements, but I never returned the calls to his embassy.

As director, I also managed official visits from the heads of states of countries under my responsibility when they came to the United States to meet the president. These could be either official visits, or the more formal state visit, with a panoply of bells ringing, sirens blaring, black-tie dinners at the White House, and twenty-one-gun salutes. Most recent presidents prefer official visits because they entail less hoopla. I oversaw visits from President Eyadéma of Togo, President Houphouet-Boigny of Côte d'Ivoire, and President Diouf of Senegal. They came to be recognized as being worthy of a call on the president of the United States, but everybody comes wanting something such as a new trade agreement or an aid program. Preparations are thorough. The chief of protocol of the United States, a presidential appointment in the Department of State, plans all protocolary elements of the visit using the Geneva Convention as the basic document of reference. This includes who precedes whom, who sits where, and the like. In welcoming the visiting dignitary, the president might slip into a formal speech a nugget of substantive information. For example, "Country X has been a friend of the United States for a hundred years. We have thus today decided to grant Nation X 'most favored nation' treatment for the next year." In an exchange of formal dinner parties, the president does not usually attend the dinner at the head of state's embassy, but everybody else in Washington does. It is all part of an ancient ritual supposedly begun in China, when heads of state paid tribute to the emperor and empress. On the surface, the ceremonies seem unimportant, but in reality they give heads of state an opportunity to exhibit their prowess, to say personally what they would like the United States to do for them, and why it is in our best interest to do so. In return, it permits the United States to accord the visiting head of state some degree of status that we consider to be in the national interest. It gives us a platform on which to say forcefully what we would like the country to do for us. In my experience the British and Germans have been most effective in these ceremonial visits. Nelson Mandela was very good, President Salvadore Allende of Chile exhibited the real promise of a nation on the move, and, in the developing world, President Diouf of Senegal was quite capable.

When I review my tenure as director of West African Affairs, what I learned was an intimate knowledge of Washington bureaucracy that I never could have gained from serving at posts. I learned my way around the Atomic Energy Commission (now the Department of Energy), the Treasury Department, the Attorney General's office, the FBI, the Agriculture Department, and the White House Public Information Office, which gave me practical experience in dealing with the press. My policy has always been to be as open as possible with the press and to recognize that the press can be, and often is, a useful tool in carrying out conduct of relations. I have always made myself available to the press. If journalists asked a question that I did not want to answer, I would say so. The press can be a help or a hindrance. It is fickle, just like a person, but if treated with respect, most of the time it will work to the advantage of the office, bureau, or post.

Most heads of state outside of Western Europe and Canada do not understand the press in the United States. Some of the newer countries, especially African nations, think the press can be controlled by the government. When they learn it cannot, they think the press is irrelevant. Because they have no appreciation for the institution of the press, they frequently make mistakes. Even the Afrikaners, as astute as they were, erred with the press, which increased their enmity for it. Sometimes they jailed journalists. The more unfavorably the U.S. and British press wrote about the Afrikaner government, the more the government tried to control the press's access to news sources. And the more it failed. Afrikaners could not understand why I was so adamant about treating the press fairly. "Why do you waste so much time fighting for them?" they asked me. "Actually I am fighting for myself," I replied. "It is another element of freedom."

Within the United States, I dealt with cities that had extensive commercial and cultural relations abroad, especially Los Angeles, San Francisco, Atlanta,

Chicago, Dallas, and New York. The Pearson Amendment, initiated in part by President Truman, authorizes the State Department to assign Foreign Service officers for a tour of duty to inter alia state and local governments and to non-governmental institutions within the United States. Part of the officers' job is to learn about the operation of these offices, and part is to promote the Foreign Service. I made it my business to travel around the country to check on the Pearson Fellows and see how they were doing. I encouraged them all, white and black, to go into the minority communities. When we are abroad we never talk about the social problems of the United States, but our colleagues abroad are not stupid; they know we have social problems. I wanted the officers to be informed about these issues and able to talk about them knowledgeably. I also had the job of finding Pearson Fellows assignments in committees on the Hill. For the first time, I was in direct contact with Congress and I learned about the workings of the committees. This range of duties gave me invaluable training that I could not have received anywhere else in the world. The directorate is considered one of the best jobs in the State Department for an aspiring mid-level officer because it is usually the springboard for a senior assignment. It was that way for me.

One morning in 1984, my secretary, Beverly Alexander, came into my office rather wide-eyed. "The White House just called and said we are to expect a call from the president." A few minutes later, the call came through for me. "Mr. Perkins," I heard the distinctive voice say, "this is Ronald Reagan. I was wondering if you would be willing to represent me as ambassador to Liberia."

Lucy and I returned to war-torn Liberia for my
first tour of duty as an ambassador.

MR. AMBASSADOR

An ambassadorship. Here was my dream on a platter. Not only was this a chance to become an ambassador, it was achieving the appointment in record time because I had been in the Foreign Service for only twelve years. I told the president that I would be honored if he nominated me.

But I did think it over. Liberia would not have been my first choice as a place to go as ambassador. I had left that war-torn country less than two years earlier, so I was keenly aware of the impossibility of helping to establish a formidable government that was economically viable and socially strong. How could I return my family to a country where law and order were tenuous at best? Additionally, how could I ask them to live in a society devoid of peace, tranquility, and orderliness?

I talked with Lucy and our daughters about what this appointment would mean to our lives. Sarah was our first consideration. Kathy was almost twenty and in college at Mount Holyoke in Massachusetts, but Sarah was only fifteen, and we would not ask her to go back to Liberia. The country was too unstable, and the school system was inferior. If Lucy and I returned to Liberia, we decided that Sarah should attend boarding school in the United States and receive a first-class education. Once the nomination was a certainty, Sarah and I set out to visit schools, although it was March and late in the season to be accepted. She chose Phillips Academy in Andover, Massachusetts, making the difficult decision to repeat a grade so that she would be at the school for two years and benefit from a full Andover education. A month later, she was happily ensconced there, and Lucy and I began preparations to move to Liberia.

Once again, my regular tour of duty had been cut short. My nomination for ambassador ended my assignment as country director of West African Affairs one year before the customary three-year term ended. I discovered there was a reason for the haste. The ambassador to Liberia who I was replacing was Bill Swing, who had hit a patch of rough road with Samuel Doe and the Liberian foreign minister, Ernest Eastman. Bill had spent three years in a nightmarish assignment, constantly taking guff from Doe and his administration and trying to run the country without appearing to act as a proconsul. Bill was justifiably wrung out. Furthermore, his relationship with Doe seemed beyond repair. As DCM, I had managed to maintain cordial relations with Doe, so now I was being sent back as ambassador to bail water and try to keep the U.S.-Liberia relationship afloat. At the time of my appointment I was recovering from knee surgery and was walking with a cane, a detail that would have political ramifications later on.

I had left Liberia as Edward Perkins; I was arriving as Mr. Ambassador. Most of the embassy staff were those with whom I had worked earlier, so this made for a seamless transition. The American Embassy is on a hill called Mamba Point, so named because of the profusion of deadly mamba snakes. We paid five dollars for every mamba snake caught until we discovered that one man was submitting the same snake. This could be a metaphor for my experience in Liberia—elusive surface solutions in a dangerous and deadly society. Lucy and I arrived in August 1985 to find the country in turmoil and an election approaching. The Americo-Liberians were sidelined in anger and pain at seeing their hopes disappear with the coup. They were bitterly disappointed that the United States had not come to their rescue and reestablished the *status quo*. They were incensed that the United States considered the country people to be their equals as Liberian citizens.

Influenced largely by the Americo-Liberians, some members of Congress were unhappy with our support of Samuel Doe. A leading voice of opposition was Howard Wolpe, the representative from Michigan, an African expert, and the chairman of the House Subcommittee on Africa. Wolpe considered Doe a right-wing dictator, a humanitarian violator, and an unstable leader. "We need to be tough on heads of state who shoot their way to power," Wolpe said, "and on the apartheid government in South Africa."

Wolpe was at odds with Assistant Secretary of State for African Affairs Chester Crocker, who was the author of the constructive-engagement policy on South Africa. The best way to change South Africa, according to Crocker, was to work with the Afrikaners rather than make enemies of them. Through benevolent diplomacy, the basis of constructive engagement, black South Africans would slowly inherit their share of political power and participate in governing the country. The Carter administration had tried to use a big stick with South Africa, but it did not work, so the Reagan administration was intrigued with this new approach. Largely because of his diplomatic theory, Chet Crocker, a respected academic, an African specialist, and a descendant of President Chester A. Arthur, was named assistant secretary, beginning a new chapter in United States–South Africa relations.

Right away, Crocker and Wolpe clashed over Liberia. Wolpe decided to hold subcommittee hearings on African policy, and he wanted either Crocker or me to appear informally. Crocker was not about to do it, so I flew to Washington. The long flight did not help the healing of my leg. The night before I was to testify, I had a call that began, "Mr. Ambassador, a coup attempt is ongoing in your country." Thomas Quiwonkpa, Doe's former army chief, had led a group of soldiers across the border from Côte d'Ivoire and was attempting to seize power in Liberia. Americo-Liberian Ellen Johnson-Sirleaf reportedly had encouraged Quiwonkpa to believe that America would support him in the coup. I canceled my appearance before the subcommittee and left. Wolpe was livid, but the State Department supported me, saying, "Get back to your country."

I got as far as Sierra Leone, but Doe had closed the borders and I could go no further. While the revolt stormed, Lucy was holed up in the residence with the servants and only one guard. A crazed Liberian jumped the fence and tried to break his way into the residence. Both this incident and the coup attempt were short-lived.

Quiwonkpa was one of the most tragic figures I have ever come across. He had a childlike innocence about him, and he was genuinely liked by the Americans who met him. An embassy staff member reported to me almost sadly, "He doesn't have a clue what an army commander should be doing." Doe and his regime overpowered Quiwonkpa. They killed him, dismembering and cannibalizing him. The press did not report this last grisly detail. Some tribes believe that to eat a part of a vanquished warrior is to capture his soul and absorb his power. One of Doe's tribal kinsmen, the minister for state affairs, told me about the assassination. A soldier came to him and said, "Sir, we saved a finger for you." "Get away from me," the minister replied. "Get that thing out of my face."

A few days later, when Doe reopened the border, I flew to Monrovia and took command of the embassy, this time in a radically changed country. We had worked for years to persuade Doe to return the country to civilian rule, but the coup attempt threatened to undermine all of that. Doe wanted to cancel the elections, and I had to persuade him not to do it. He finally agreed that the elections would go forward.

In this tense atmosphere, it was obvious that we needed to establish election observance to ensure that the elections were free and fair. We installed monitors in unannounced locations, we watched the ballots being counted at the polling place, and we saw them taken under lock and key to Monrovia in the custody of the electoral commissioner. When the counting was complete, the entire diplomatic corps was invited to the Hotel Africa to be present for the announcement of the results. The electoral commissioner read out the results county by county and when it became clear, to nobody's surprise, that Doe had won, everybody stood to applaud—everybody except me. My leg was still weak and standing was very difficult. The press noticed that I did not stand and the *Washington Post* wrote that apparently the United States did not like the results because the American ambassador remained seated when Doe was announced the winner. Doe and his staff were offended, and an emissary was sent to ask me tersely about my breach of courtesy. I reminded him of my bad leg, and immediately the tenseness in the air broke. "Oh, I knew that," he said. "Why didn't I think of it?" Obviously relieved, he went off to report the reason to his chief. Once again, we had maneuvered a perilous path around Doe. All was well, and now we prepared for the inauguration to take place in January 1986.

Our dilemma was finding a suitable representative of the U.S. government to attend the inauguration. Doe's people knew that a representative of low-level stature would indicate a vote of no confidence from the United States. I sent an urgent cable to Washington: "Please select a super representative to represent the president at the inauguration of Samuel K. Doe and Harry F. Moniba [his running mate]." The representative chosen was Bill Harrop, inspector general of the Foreign Service and a distinguished senior Foreign Service officer. Doe was pleased.

The lavish inauguration begged description. Doe wore a dark suit with a big presidential sash across his chest. He was not only sworn in by the chief justice, but he kissed the Bible and was blessed by three bishops: Catholic, Methodist, and Baptist. He and Moniba and their wives were in the limelight for almost five hours. Harrop, Lucy, and I were there for every event of the entire day and part of the next day. We stood the course to make sure that Doe knew, by our presence, the support of the United States was steadfast. The legality of his victory has been questioned ever since, and many believe that Doe bullied or cheated his way to power. Nonetheless, Doe was the victorious candidate,

elected to a presidential term of four years, and therefore the United States
recognized him as the head of state.

Doe began his administration by shedding his five-star military uniform and
adopting mufti clothing. He always had ample self-confidence, and now he
adopted the more serious mien befitting a president. He declared amnesty for
all political prisoners. He promised to return the country to material economic improvement and to improve relations with other African states. He was
particularly interested in a letter he had received from President Reagan, urging him to be generous in observing humanitarian laws and enforcing economic discipline.

Almost immediately, fissures appeared across newly calmed Liberia. The
defeated candidates and their supporters were distressed. Jackson Doe, a failed
presidential candidate and no relation to Samuel Doe, came to see me with a
stash of burned ballots he had discovered. I suggested that he call on the electoral commissioner and request an investigation. "He will do nothing. Only the
United States can make a difference," Jackson Doe said. The Americo-Liberians still expected the United States to behave as a special friend, and again their
hopes were dashed. An early missionary described an American Indian tribe "as
stubborn as the devil's pig, which would be neither driven nor led." That
description reminds me of the Americo-Liberians who hold fast to their belief
in a special friendship with the United States. Little by little, some Americo-
Liberians returned to serve in the Doe government. Although there were some
exceptions, they were honorable people intent on rebuilding the country. But
it was an impossible task.

Not long after that, Ellen Johnson-Sirleaf, the woman who had encouraged
revolutionary Quiwonkpa in his effort to overthrow the Doe regime, was again
jailed as a political prisoner. I almost lost count of the number of times I asked
Samuel Doe to release her. Johnson-Sirleaf, a prominent Americo-Liberian
with world-renowned financial expertise, is a woman fearsome in her beliefs.
When I was sworn in as ambassador, she was in jail because of a Philadelphia
speech that she made criticizing the Doe government. As soon as she returned
to Liberia, Doe had slapped her in jail. At the request of Deputy Secretary of
State John Whitehead, one of my first duties was to try to get her freed. I had
to use a lot of muscle to persuade Doe, and when he did release her, the
younger officers at the embassy were jubilant. "You did it!" they exclaimed.
"Don't say that to anybody," I told them. "The head of state, in his wisdom,

decided to release her. The Americans had nothing to do with it. That is our story."

Johnson-Sirleaf came to thank me for my work and quickly segued into lecturing me on what she thought the U.S. policy should be. Within a month, she was back in jail. The State Department, under pressure from Howard Wolpe, Citibank (which had interests in Liberia), and Senator John Kerry (Democrat–Massachusetts), cabled me to get her out again. The question was how to do it. I had used up my persuasive powers with Doe. "Why do you worry about these people like Ellen Johnson-Sirleaf?" Doe asked me. "She wants to be president of Liberia. Have you ever heard of a woman president in Africa? She can't be president."

I had been to the well too often on Johnson-Sirleaf's behalf, but after Quiwonkpa's death I decided to do something that diplomats never do. I would try to manipulate the head of state with people inside his own government. First, I consulted Minister for Presidential Affairs Peter Naigow, a well-educated man who was also from Doe's tribe. We both knew that Doe believed in ancestor worship, relied on paganism, and appealed to the gods of his tribe for instruction.

"I am willing to concede that there is some value in that," I said. "How can I influence those who influence the president?"

Peter considered the question and then said, "I will do it in the name of Liberia." We would appeal to Doe's religious beliefs through an emissary whom Peter would find. One Sunday morning not long after that, Peter called me to meet an imam, a Muslim leader, from Togo. With some trepidation, not knowing the price that would be extracted from me in return, I laid my request before him. I wanted to manipulate the president, I said, but for his own good. I asked the imam for his help, in his role as special advisor to the president, influencing Doe to do the right thing and accede to my requests. I wanted Doe to observe human rights, the rule of law, and the court procedure. Most immediately, I wanted Doe to release a number of political prisoners, including Johnson-Sirleaf.

To my surprise, the imam agreed—with a proviso. He would do it if I could show him how my requests related to Islamic truth. "You must frame your request in language from the Koran," he told me. That was the price he asked of me—to recognize the importance of Islam in Liberia. The political hot potato was back in my lap.

He gave me a battered copy of the Koran, and I began to study it. Then I sought Peter's help in phrasing my requests to Doe within Islamic teachings. Nobody in the embassy ever knew; nobody in Washington ever knew. They thought I was working miracles. It was Peter and me, one Liberian and one American, working together in a circuitous route to accomplish the desired results. This was, of course, totally outside the realm of acceptable diplomatic activity.

After the presidential election, Johnson-Sirleaf left the country and eventually made her way to the United States. The next time I saw her was at a function in Washington, where she pointedly snubbed me in disgust.[1]

Not all of my exchanges with Doe ended as happily. One serious run-in involved Jean-Claude "Baby Doc" Duvalier, who was forced to leave the presidency of Haiti and was searching for a country to accept him. Haiti was a former French colony with a French culture, so Baby Doc and his wife sought asylum in France, but France did not want them. They were given permission to stay in the United States a few days while American officials tried to persuade France to accept them. While this negotiation was underway, a reporter spotted Liberia's foreign minister changing planes in Rome and asked him if Liberia might grant Baby Doc asylum. The minister should have said that he had no authorized answer, but as many people are wont to do when talking with the press, the minister stepped into the spotlight. Liberia's name means freedom, he expounded, and we have always offered freedom to the oppressed, so, yes, we would seriously consider it. As soon as the interview appeared on CNN, I was directed to check out the story with Doe. It was a Sunday afternoon and I phoned Doe. "Maybe we decide tomorrow," Doe told me. That was a clue that something was wrong, but I did not heed it. The next morning I phoned for an appointment, but Doe was not available. By now I realized that I had affronted Doe by phoning him instead of calling in person. When I finally got to see him, he ranted and raved for a while and I apologized profusely.

"Mr. Head of State, I am grieved about this. It is clearly a breach of protocol on my part," I said.

"You come and see me," he said. "We are brothers. You don't have to worry about protocol." Then we got down to business. He asked my opinion about Baby Doc, and I told him that the State Department supported the idea and would consider it a favor if Liberia would solve the placement problem and take Baby Doc. I told him that I had argued against it, saying that Liberia had enough problems without imposing Baby Doc on the country, but that I had been overruled. Doe thought it over for a few moments and then reached his decision. "I don't think we want him," he said. "Too much of a problem." I was very happy to hear this and reported it to Washington. When the news reached Under Secretary Mike Armacost, he was angry and called me to ask if I would go back to see Doe and ask him to reconsider. "Mike," I said, "the answer is no. It would not be useful." Eventually Baby Doc and his wife landed in a little city outside of Paris, where they celebrated with a champagne party that lasted twelve days. They are still there.

This was the closest I came to a rift with Doe. It was my mistake. He was a moody person, and one should always talk to moody people face-to-face in order to observe their facial expression, their eyes, their hands, and their body language. I never again spoke to Doe on the phone.

Since my arrival in Liberia, I had been juggling several fragile issues—trying to keep the country going, trying to free political prisoners, and trying to keep Doe on the path toward elections. To complicate matters, a couple of officers in the embassy openly disagreed with the U.S. policy toward Doe. One was a political officer, the other was the public-information officer. While it was acceptable to express diverse opinions within the embassy while we were forming policy, once that policy was established, I expected unified teamwork. We might argue like cats and dogs inside the embassy, but when the decision was made we had to present a united front outside the door. These two officers were not insubordinate, but neither were they circumspect in their outspoken opinions in public. The political counselor told me plainly that she was not comfortable with a policy that supported Doe. "Either support our policy, or ask for a transfer," I told her. Then Doe got wind of some of the comments she made in a speech, and he was outraged. He called me to his office and demanded that I get her out of the country. Although I did not countenance her behavior, I could not accept his dictate. "Chief," I said, "international law does not permit you to do this unless you are willing to risk some rupture in relations between the United States and Liberia. You are attempting to interfere in the affairs of the United States. The embassy is the sovereign ground of the United States." He capitulated. "Okay, you handle it," he said in patois. "But she no good. She is no good to you, too."

My next talk with the political counselor was solemn. "You have made it tough for me to conduct business here," I told her. "I do not like doing this because you have dug this hole yourself, but I am going to support you because you represent a principle. However, I think you ought to go." She wanted to extend her stay in Liberia, but I refused her request and when her tour ended three months later, she left. She remained in the Foreign Service, but she never recovered professionally from the damage done by her lapse of judgment.

The incident with the public-information officer was more serious. When I discovered his public missteps, I used my full power as the ambassador. In a face-to-face meeting I told him, "I no longer have confidence in you, so I am declaring you persona non grata, and I am asking your agency to recall you immediately." He was flabbergasted. "I know you will call Washington," I said, "and you have my permission to do so, but this is an irreversible decision. The only person who can change my mind is the president of the United States. I suggest that you start packing." His career was finished.

I had served as ambassador to Liberia for only one year when I was called to another appointment. When I left, the country still was not stable, but we had done our best. Our job was to hold the country together, and we did it. We had guided Liberia to elections and to the return of civilian rule. We had subordinated the relevant ministries, except the foreign minister, to oversight by outsiders. The only thing we had no direct control over was law and order, and we effected that through our military mission, bringing in police trainers to work with the Liberian police. We invested a lot of money in these training activities, and we worked hard to get guns out of the hands of the renegade soldiers and off the streets.

The role played by the Agency for International Development (USAID) was important in Liberia. USAID is the arm of the U.S. government responsible for economic recovery activities throughout the world. Its predecessor organization was the International Cooperation Administration, a product of World War II. When President Kennedy was inaugurated in 1961, he and his colleagues were determined to make better use of the economic development program. He changed the name of the agency to the Agency for International Development, which is more in line with its legislated purpose of international development. It was a watershed. The agency has kept that name ever since and remains active. USAID was invaluable to me as ambassador to Liberia, and it was critical to my work later in South Africa.

Liberia was a regional center of the Voice of America, the official broadcast-ing service of the United States government, and supported broadcast facilities for the entire region, stretching from the southern tip of Africa to northern Africa. The station was located in Liberia because of our relationship with that country, as well as the fact that we were able to get a huge tract of land on which to build these facilities plus housing for the hundred or so technicians working there. The compound itself was similar to a country club, with an eighteen-hole golf course; most of the embassy personnel were members. It was a place where we could entertain Liberians, enjoy a meal, and escape the atmosphere of Monrovia. The Voice of America has been a significant force in influencing the way people think all over the world, winning adherents to American jazz, to American literature, and to the history of the United States. It introduced people to our Constitution as a unique instrument created by Americans, who are a unique brand of people. The Voice has remained remark-ably uninfluenced by our politicians, with regard to what they think the serv-ice should say in selling America; it tells its vast audience about America as America is—including the good and the bad—and that has been one of its sin-gular merits.

Still, despite our accomplishments in Liberia, we made a lot of mistakes. The first wrong turn was assuming that we could keep the country afloat by look-ing over the shoulders of the new political aides and recommending a course of action. A second mistake was not having sociologists among our policymakers to help us understand the nature of human behavior in these circumstances. We should have known more about their likely reactions. When the Tennessee Val-ley Authority was proposed in the 1930s, the U.S. government planners took sociologists to help the farmers about to be displaced and to talk with them about the likelihood of unhappiness that lay ahead. In Liberia, we should have learned from that history. A third mistake, among many, was that we did not act soon enough to insist that the government have competent players at the min-isterial level and that they understand the economy. We waited too long. They did not know where the money came from. In their minds, since they were ministers, funds would magically appear and could be used for their own per-sonal gain. It was impossible to pull them back from that fantasy. Corruption in government is insidious and hard to eradicate. It was clear to me that we were holding the country together by force of will. That could not go on forever. I asked myself repeatedly: When is this place going to blow up? In what form will it come?

I had my answer three years later. On Christmas Eve 1989, Charles Taylor, an Americo-Liberian educated in the United States, crossed the border from the Côte d'Ivoire leading a band of rebels bent on overthrowing Doe. They allegedly had been trained in Libya, the constant nemesis of the United States, under the leadership of Muammar Qaddafi. Libya funded terrorist activities and incited revolutions in order to destabilize the United States in the region. Once the Taylor-led revolution began, Liberian tribal dissidents leapt to arms and the country erupted. The battle for Monrovia was long and bloody. Doe tried negotiating with a warlord, "Prince" Yeloue Yormie Johnson, but at the meeting he and his bodyguards were overthrown. Doe was slowly tortured to death. A homemade film recorded the grisly episode, and Johnson was quoted as saying, "I cut off his ears and made him eat them." Doe died September 9, 1990, ten years after he had seized power. His butchered body was paraded through the streets. Doe's death did not end the fighting of warlord factions. The civil war and ethnic cleansing raged for seven years. An army of child soldiers, barely in their teens, revolted the world with their atrocities. Before the violence ended, an estimated 700,000 people were killed and as many as 1.2 million fled the country. The United States did not intercede. When the blood stopped flowing, Liberia lay in ruins.

I was spared the sight of Liberia's most deadly saga. I had been pulled from the country in 1986 and sent on the greatest challenge of my career—to South Africa. My mission, a seemingly impossible charge that came directly from the president of the United States, was to dismantle apartheid without violence. "Without violence" was the crucial phrase. I did not know if it could be done. I did not know if I could do it. Still, that was my assignment.

My official portrait as the U.S. ambassador to South Africa.
"Who is this guy?" the press wanted to know.

A Black Ambassador
to South Africa?

A chance to go to South Africa as ambassador came to me as if out of the blue. When I got the call, in the summer of 1986, my first thought was: "In a stroke, I am both in luck and out of luck." I was in luck because the opportunity brought to a close my chapter in tumultuous Liberia. I was out of luck because it was South Africa—one of the most heatedly discussed U.S. foreign-policy relationships in the world.

I knew the geopolitical forces on both continents that had brought U.S.-South Africa relations to this point. Recently the African National Congress (ANC) had been very successful in mobilizing public opinion outside of South Africa against apartheid. The year before, in 1985, the churning anti-apartheid movement in the United States almost brought the Reagan administration's congressional-policy relationship to a standstill. Prominent people protested and demonstrated in front of the South African Embassy; many were arrested, and Congress jumped into the fray by drafting a bill calling for across-the-board sanctions against South Africa.

The Carter administration had been the first to take proactive notice of the apartheid issue and talk about "one-man, one-vote," a concept that the Afrikaners and their government hated passionately, because it implied black political equality. After a significant speech by Carter's vice president, Walter Mondale, the South African government branded the Carter administration its enemy. The administration began to dismantle cooperative business and military agreements with South Africa. It emphasized, for the first time, the importance of the U.S. Information Services library in Soweto, a black township in South Africa, as part of the change-agent process. The Afrikaner government was incensed at the assimilation of propaganda into U.S. foreign policy.

The Reagan administration followed, with Chet Crocker's criticism of the

Carter policy and a new policy of constructive engagement with the South African government. In the meantime, the ANC stepped up its efforts world-wide to cast the Afrikaner government as a pariah. Outside of South Africa, the Free South Africa movement and the Free Mandela movement were loud drumbeats announcing and supporting the war against apartheid. Randall Robinson of TransAfrica, an organization that spearheaded the movement to influence U.S. policies toward international black leadership; the Reverend Walter Fauntroy; and countless others protested the apartheid policy and the imprisonment of Mandela and others. It became a badge of honor to be arrested and jailed for demonstrating in front of the South African Embassy.

Crocker and the Reagan administration felt they should not give in to pressure tactics, and they stuck loyally to the constructive-engagement policy. Consequently, in its first four years, the Reagan administration was seen as advocating a policy of appeasement toward the South African government. The administration had not reckoned with the influence of special-interest groups outside the U.S. government or the vehemence of the American people against South African apartheid. The administration missed this because it was not in tune with the minority population of the United States.

Then Secretary of State Alexander Haig, who was far from innovative in the job, was replaced by George Shultz. I liked Shultz immediately because, among other things, he was a former marine. Still, Shultz took his time making rec-ommendations about South Africa to President Reagan. While Shultz delayed, the Free South Africa movement pushed and pushed for the administration to enact economic sanctions against South Africa. Still, the administration did not move. Crocker, the chief Africa policymaker, was determined not to bow to the Congress. He was a highly intelligent academic, but, as I told him, his fault line was not understanding Congress and co-opting it to his position.

President Reagan issued an executive order imposing sanctions on some but not all items, a measured action that infuriated the anti-apartheid movement. "He is trying to appease us," the protesters railed. Shultz, Crocker, and the White House political gendarmerie had been working on a presidential speech for almost a year. They wanted a speech that would put the president and the administration solidly in favor of doing the right thing: vigorously opposing the apartheid system, making proactive efforts to dismantle that system, working to ensure a non-racial government, unbanning political activity, and freeing Nelson Mandela, the most famous political prisoner in the world. They urged

It was Secretary of State George Shultz who recommended me to President Reagan as the ambassador to South Africa. I liked Shultz immediately when I met him because, among other things, he was a former marine.

the president to let it be known publicly that the South African government had to deal with black South Africans. Shultz and Crocker failed to influence the president. The extreme conservative right of the administration prevailed, and on July 22, 1986, the president delivered a conciliatory speech that might have been acceptable three years earlier, but now was seen as too little, too late.

I now know that the president was swayed in part by White House staffer Pat Buchanan and others who wrote a significant portion of the speech. What's more, the director of the Central Intelligence Agency, William Casey, seemed to be running his own foreign policy with the South African government.

In the wake of the president's disappointing speech, Congress created a bill establishing economic sanctions as law, including a prohibition against South African aircraft landing in New York or any other port in the United States. Significantly, the Senate discussion was led by Richard Lugar, a moderate Republican from Indiana and a member of the president's political party, and on August 15, 1986, the bill was passed by the Congress. Reagan vetoed it. Although Shultz and Crocker worked around the clock to prevent an override, on October 2, 1986, the Senate overrode the president's veto by a vote of 78-21. In the midst of this turmoil, I entered the scene.

By July 1986, relations between the United States and South Africa were so hot as to be at combustion point. To take the heat off the administration, some of President Reagan's close circle of advisors suggested sending a black ambassador to South Africa. The idea created a sensation because nobody had ever considered posting a black ambassador to apartheid South Africa. Initially, the administration considered a black political appointee, not a black career ambassador. The first candidate's name to surface was that of Robert J. Brown, a long-time Republican and a black businessman from High Point, North Carolina, who had been a special assistant in the Nixon administration. Brown's business activities in Nigeria appeared to be a conflict of interest, however, and he withdrew his name.

Secretary of State Shultz stepped in and said, in essence, "Mr. President, it may indeed be time to send a black ambassador to South Africa, but if we do, we need to accomplish change in South Africa. I would like you to let me find a career officer to fit that bill." Shultz had an unusual confidence in the ability of a career Foreign Service officer to perform both in deed and in rhetoric. His principal advisors were Foreign Service officer Charlie Hill and Deputy Secretary of State John Whitehead. I do not think either Shultz or the president has been given the credit they deserve for the decision to turn around the apartheid policy. Against the advice of his political advisors in the White House, the president said, "Go to it. Find one."

The list was short. The Foreign Service had only nine senior black officers on the rolls at that time. At the top of the list was Terrance Todman, then ambassador to Denmark and one of the most senior officers, black or white, in the Foreign Service. The press surmised that Todman was the likely candidate and asked him about it. He replied that the administration would have to change its policy before he went there. His remarks were reported as if he had been offered the job, but both Todman and President Reagan told me later that he had not. Then someone remembered me, tucked away in Liberia.

Since I was one of nine senior black officers, it was understandable that the press ferreted out my name as a prospect. In Monrovia, Lucy woke me up the night of July 22, 1986, to say that CNN had just reported the speculation that I would be sent to South Africa. "Forget it," I told her. "Nobody is going to ask me to go to South Africa." I was neither senior enough, nor did I have any experience on that part of the continent, I said, so I went back to sleep. Three days later, Crocker called to assure me that the speculation was without basis. The morning of July 29, 1986, Secretary Shultz called me on the secure phone line to ask my permission to submit my name to the president as the next ambassador to South Africa. "I can understand it if you would say no," he told me. "Nobody has the right to ask you or any other black person to go down there in that situation, but the president is going to send a black ambassador, and I told him we need to appoint a professional if we are going to bring about change. I don't know you, I have never met you, but I think you're the person to go." I told him that I would give him my answer in a couple of days. I was not allowed to discuss it with anyone but my wife.

Lucy and I talked most of that night. We agreed that the optimum phrase from the oath of office I had taken years ago was "to go where needed." We thought I might be able to do something in South Africa. I called Shultz on July 30 and told him that if the president and the secretary of state thought so, too, I was willing to go. "I have even more respect for you," he said graciously. "You will hear from me." Then we waited for the White House to decide whether or not I was to be the president's candidate.

I learned later that my dossier was put together and forwarded immediately to the president. I was asked to return to Washington no later than August 10 to begin a round of interviews with White House principals. I was also instructed to enter the United States as quietly as possible in order to avoid media speculation. The international press was already beginning to sniff out this news story. I would not talk to them; I referred them to the press person in the State Department. Before leaving Liberia, I issued a set of talking points for everybody in the mission:

"Question: Is Ambassador Perkins being considered as the next ambassador to South Africa?

"Answer: No one in the American Embassy knows anything about Ambassador Perkins being suggested as the next ambassador to South Africa. For further information on this, you should call the press office in the Department of State." Period. I went to Washington. As I suspected, TV cameras were waiting at National Airport when I arrived, but they did not know me or what I looked like, so I walked past them. I heard someone call out, "Mr. Ambassador," but I kept walking. One man hurried after me, calling my name, and finally he said, "Mr. Ambassador, I'm from the State Department." It was the desk officer who had come to take me to an obscure hotel before I began a series of interviews from August 10 through August 16.

During that trip to Washington I spent much of the time in talks with Chet Crocker. Even before I left Monrovia, he had sent a South Africa specialist to Liberia to brief me. Ray Smith, the deputy director of the South Africa desk, had arrived with an enormous briefing book and spent two days with me. We talked well into the night about South Africa. Chet had sent the right person. When Ray left Liberia, I felt as if I had been drenched with buckets of cold water. No gauzy illusions remained. He had given me straight facts and nuances about the history of U.S. relations with South Africa and about our successes and failures, both overt and benign. By the time I arrived in Washington, I was prepared to talk substantively about South Africa.

In Washington, I met with Chet four or five times. His special assistant, Robert Cabelly, was also in the room with us. I told Chet up front that I wanted always to be of service to my country. I also wanted to establish some ground rules and ascertain the corporate administration's position, so I asked questions geared to see if Chet was supportive of (1) sending a black ambassador, (2) sending a Foreign Service officer, and (3) sending me.

"What do you expect will be accomplished with my appointment?" I asked him.

"The president wants to accommodate all voices," he replied, "and he wants to show that this administration is committed to making a difference in South Africa." Chet danced around the rest of the question. Understandably, since he had authored the constructive-engagement policy, he equivocated somewhat and seemed reluctant to move too far from the status quo. I later learned that Frank Carlucci, Reagan's national-security advisor and later secretary of defense, said bluntly, "I intend to make sure that this president does not leave office with the reputation of being anti-black."

When I had talked with Secretary Shultz by phone from Monrovia, I asked him, "There has been little movement in the South African government toward meeting us halfway in a genuine effort, what comes next?" That was a key question. Then I asked, "Will I be a participating member of this policy-making group? Can I expect to have my voice heard in the State Department and in the White House?" I now asked Chet the same things.

It is rare for potential ambassadors to ask such questions. Chet replied that an attempt would be made to ensure that no daylight existed between us. I asked if I could be assured of backing and that I would not be surprised in the field. I told him I wanted the best Foreign Service officers to be appointed to South Africa. I asked if I would be able to consult widely before leaving. "It is important that I have a good understanding of the depth of feeling both ways before I go." Then I asked a cards-on-the-table question: "What is our ultimate goal in the Southern Africa region?" Until that time, our goals had been obscure, at least to me.

The problems in southern Africa were legion, but the most significant were:

1. Zimbabwe, which had recently become independent, had a new president in Robert Mugabe. The prevailing question in this country was how whites, especially white farmers, and the new black government could get along. Mugabe leaned toward socialism and had floated the idea of breaking up the big white farms to give blacks a chance to buy farmland and obtain a stake in the economy. For the time being, he had retracted the proposal.

2. In the Cape of Good Hope region, the United States was redefining our strategic interests.

3. The United States and the South West African People's Organization (SWAPO) were working for the independence of Namibia, which South Africa opposed adamantly.

4. Angola and Mozambique were both locked in civil war. The key issue in Angola was getting the Cuban troops out of that country and at the same time convincing South Africa to grant independence to Namibia in accordance with UN Security Council Resolution 342.

5. In Liberia, the concern was how Doe would interpret my removal after only one year as ambassador. Would he think it signaled displeasure with him or his regime?

6. The most serious issue was South Africa itself, with looming problems
   of such complexity that they almost defied comprehension. I had reason later to ask myself if Chet understood the ambiance of the entire
   South African panoply —the history of the blacks, the Afrikaners, the
   English-speakers, the San people, the Coloureds, and the Indians.
   Which black leader was most acceptable to us? What was our view of
   the ANC? Do we consider the ANC to be a terrorist organization? Was
   it using hardware from the Soviets? How did we view Oliver Tambo,
   then president of the ANC, who was persona non grata in South Africa
   and based in London? What about Thabo Mbeki, the head of foreign
   relations in the ANC, who was asking repeatedly to meet with Shultz?
   Every question opened volumes of debate.

During a subsequent Washington visit, I spent considerable time with
Deputy Secretary of State Whitehead, who had the task of getting me success-
fully through a series of interviews, approval by the White House, and final
Senate confirmation.

"Where do I stand in this drama?" I asked him. "What is the mood of Congress?"

Whitehead, a former New York investment banker, personified the cool
financial professional. "There is some hysteria ongoing," he answered, but he
thought the key players in Congress would support my appointment.

"I can't go to South Africa and just be there," I told him. "It cannot be business as usual after I am on the scene. That would be disastrous. I want to maintain confidence and credibility." I could not be benign; I would have to be an
activist. I had to get out and be seen as working for political change. Non-action
would signal broken promises, I said, and it would destroy South Africa's faith
in the Reagan administration, which already was tenuous. South African president Pieter W. (P. W.) Botha, so belligerent that he was popularly known in his
country as the Great Crocodile, was mistrustful of the U.S. State Department,
so how could I be intellectually convincing in my dealings with the South
African government?

Whitehead agreed with the need for action and said he thought that eventually I could instill in South Africa's black community confidence regarding U.S.
antipathy to apartheid. He said that I should get out into the South African
neighborhoods and the townships, talk to people, and let them know that the

American Embassy was an activist embassy. To my knowledge, this was the first time that the American ambassador made continuous entry into black neighborhoods as part of the change-agent strategy. I had heard this suggestion first from my private brain trust, three black men who are not only fine professionals but personal friends: John Gravely, Herbert Harrington, and Harold Sye. I consulted them confidentially, and their advice was invaluable. Aside from Lucy and my daughters, these were the only people I talked with outside of official interviews. My three colleagues and I had personally experienced segregation in this country, and we knew the difficulty in getting people to change.

John, my collaborator in drafting the strategy to open opportunities for minorities and women in the Foreign Service when we had been junior officers, reminded me of the incipient resistance to change. "If you could get rid of that feeling of threat," he said, "you could erase most of the racial problems in that country." If whites could see that their fortunes and the blacks' were intertwined, their value judgments would change.

My three friends warned me of the dangers. "You will be hated by the white minority, especially the Afrikaners," they said, and they raised the possibility of my being killed. My activism in South Africa would exacerbate the risks to my family. "If you make too much of a wave," Herb said, "the South African government might have you assassinated." "What about your family?" they asked. "How are you going to protect them when we cannot even protect the presidents of the United States from assassination?"

The flood of information, questions, concerns, opinions, and ambiguity I was receiving reinforced my initial recognition that the job was bigger than I was. Obviously the tools I used would have to be bigger, too. It was then that I began to form an invaluable theory. Perhaps my association with Asian philosophers could provide a valuable tool to use in conflict resolution in South Africa. It was an epiphany. Sun Tzu's *The Art of War* and Miyamoto Musashi's *The Book of Five Rings* would be my big tools in South Africa. I would also make wide use of James Michener's book *The Covenant*, which included his seminal research on southern Africa.

My August 1986 White House interviews proceeded exactly as if I were being interviewed for a job. The first person I met was Robert Tuttle, the White

House personnel officer, whose father was a friend of Ronald Reagan. The purpose of this unprecedented interview was to determine my suitability for this sensitive appointment in terms of the administration's political values. "South Africa is not simple," I told him. "We must get used to incrementalism. The air is poisoned on all sides, and we must figure out a way to cool down the rhetoric and get everybody to talk to one another without restrictions." I used the term "without restrictions" because the South African government was dragging its heels in talking with the black citizenry until the black activists renounced violence.

I was next interviewed by the personnel officer's deputy, who was the only person who asked my political affiliation. "Is the answer to that question necessary?" I asked her. I said that I had never been asked that question before. Clearly she did not expect that response from me. I did answer her question, however, and told her that I was registered as an Independent.

I met with National Security Advisor John Poindexter, a penultimate military intellectual, and finally with the president's chief of staff, Donald Regan, an unfriendly man who was the most contentious of the interviewers. I asked Regan about the sanctions bill.

"We will veto it," Regan said without hesitation.

"The Congress expects a veto," I said, "so why not compromise?"

"Never."

The only remaining interview was with the president himself. While I waited for that meeting to be arranged, I stayed with my daughter Kathy, who was a student at George Washington University's School of International Relations in Washington. I had dinner with her and her friends and tried not to behave as if the most important decision of my career was hanging in the balance.

On Friday, August 18, I was told that President Reagan wanted to see me the next morning. At 9 A.M., I was driven to the White House, where I entered surreptitiously through a little-known entrance and was taken to the map room to wait for the president. About five minutes later—which seemed an eternity—the president breezed in dressed in western clothes. He was accompanied by Don Regan and John Poindexter.

"Excuse my dress, Mr. Ambassador," the president said cordially. "I'm on my way to Camp David. Have a seat here on the couch next to me. George Shultz wants me to send you to South Africa. I think I need to get to know you first."

He asked me about my family, where my wife was born, how many children we had, what they were doing, and how they might view an assignment to South Africa. He wanted to know about my hobbies and interests. He told me a couple of jokes. After about twenty minutes of preliminary discussion, he said, "If I send you to South Africa, what are you going to do down there?"

Answering such a direct question by the president of the United States was quite a challenge. "Mr. President," I answered, "the situation in South Africa is inimical and not at all in accord with what we believe in as a nation. A significant part of the world is against the system in South Africa and is watching us to see what we are going to do. We need to think of something that we can tolerate as a country and support it. Frankly, if you send me, I will try to change that system using the power of your office." Both Poindexter and Regan were in the room and although neither of them said anything, I could feel the disapproval emanating from Regan, who was not happy with my response. I think he wanted a political appointee instead of a career officer.

"That's interesting," the president said. "How are you going to do it?"

"I don't know all the answers to that, Mr. President. I'll have to discover them as I go along. Certainly I'll try to get to know everybody in the townships. I'll try to get to know all of the black actors. I'll also try to get to know all of the white actors, as well. And I'll try to convey the message, through our actions, that the United States stands for something, and that what we stand for is not what they have going on in South Africa. I don't believe our country is perfect, and I am not going to go down there and say that it is, but I will say that our country offers the opportunity of getting a little better than we were yesterday. I hope that through some innovative activities we might be able to convince the Afrikaner government that their time is up and that they need to change. I hope we can do it without violence."

"Do you know any black leaders in this country?" he asked me.

"A couple."

"I suggest you get to know a lot more of them.[1] You will need their help if you are sent to South Africa. What do you think the blacks in this country will think of you for accepting such an important appointment from me?"

"I haven't given it any thought."

"Well I can tell you that they won't like it. If I send you, you need to get to know as many black leaders as you can and tell them what you'll do if you go down there."

We talked further about South Africa, the sanctions by executive order he had tried to impose, and the bill that was soon to be on his desk. He did not say that he would veto it. He did say, however, that he wanted "that business" out of the way before any announcement was made about my going to South Africa if he should decide to nominate me. "No need for you to be caught up in that and be compromised by political rhetoric before you start," he said.

As we concluded the interview, he said, "I would ask you to come out and see me off at the helicopter, but if the press sees you, they'll know something is up, and it is not yet time for them to know if you are my choice if I decide to send you. I'll make the announcement in my own time in my own way."

At the door, he turned back to me and said, "By the way, Mr. Ambassador, I would like you to go to South Africa."

I found President Reagan extremely likeable, and frankly, I was surprised that the president knew as much as he did about South Africa and the issues there, and that he recognized the need for a new policy. "Mr. Ambassador, if you go," he told me, "you'll have to establish your own policy. We don't know enough about what is happening there to make policy at this end. You come back every six months and tell us and the American people what is going on in South Africa and what you are doing."

The president asked me matter-of-factly if I would consider this assignment as a risk to my career. "I imagine it will be, Mr. President, but when I took the oath of office, I didn't take an oath to go where there were only risk-free assignments. That is the way we are taught in the Foreign Service." This was the second time I was being offered a high-risk job, and Lucy and I had talked about the possibility of this being the end of my career. There was no guarantee of success. Neither the president nor the secretary of state gave me any assurances that everything would be all right or that they would pull me out of the river if I slipped in.

"Everybody says you are a good professional," Secretary Shultz said later. "I am impressed with that." That is all he said on the subject, but I had a good feeling about the secretary. I felt that he would back me. It is one thing to have the backing of the president—that gives stature and clout—but it is another thing, and quite crucial, to have the backing of the secretary of state. I never doubted that Shultz was behind me, even when I did some outrageous things in South Africa.

Shultz is an economist, a graduate of Princeton University with a Ph.D. from the Massachusetts Institute of Technology. He is a successful businessman, an academic, an author, and a reflective intellectual. I found him to be approachable, deeply principled, and totally unflappable. Much earlier he had taken a stand against the president, who wanted to initiate lie-detector tests in some departments. At a cabinet meeting in which the president requested comments on the proposal, Shultz said, "People in the State Department will take a lie-detector test when I take one. I do not intend to take it." That killed the proposal.

Secretary Shultz has another quality that I admire tremendously: he never allows himself to be managed by the press—or anybody else. While being interviewed on "Face the Nation," his response to a question was: "That is none of your business." While testifying before a Senate committee, he took an inordinate amount of time, several minutes, before answering a question put to him by one of the senators. He said nothing, just sat in silence. Finally the senator said, "Well, Mr. Secretary?" Shultz replied, "Just a minute. I'm thinking." I used the same effective strategy myself once, and Senator Nancy Kassebaum told me, "I've never seen anyone else use that technique—except Secretary Shultz."

In our Saturday morning meeting, President Reagan was totally at ease with me, and I with him. It was one of the great interviews in my professional life. I was overwhelmed that here was a country boy sitting in the White House with the most powerful man in the world, discussing with him how best to deal with the issue of South Africa and apartheid. Nobody from the State Department was with us. At that moment, I was the only person in the administration who was given the privilege of making points with him. He did something that presidents do not do: he gave me carte blanche authority to make policy from the embassy in South Africa. That authorization would stand me in good stead much later—with the State Department, the White House, business, and other nongovernmental activities. I had to call often on my conversation with the president and say something that ambassadors do not often say or, if they do, say at their peril: "I am the president's representative. This is my view." I got away with it, and the reason was that the president let it be known at large that the United States was changing its policy toward South Africa and was sending one of its most trusted senior diplomats to turn the policy around.

Now came the preparation. I had to get another security clearance—and quickly. I was cleared in record time. Everybody moved heaven and earth to make sure it happened. The State Department sent a request called *agrément* to the South Africa government asking that I be accepted as the next U.S. ambassador. This request for *agrément* is an ancient procedure used by all nations in accordance with the Geneva Convention. I knew that being asked to receive a black ambassador would throw the South African government into turmoil. Later I was told by one of the officers in the South African Embassy in Washington that the president's request exploded like a rocket in Pretoria, South Africa. "Who is Edward Perkins?" the South African government wanted to know. "Dig up everything you can on him and let us have it immediately." They could find nothing except that I was a former marine. They searched newspaper archives, but my name did not turn up. Finally they went to the State Department to request background information on me. The appointment was so delicate that nobody in the South African government felt comfortable approving it so the decision went all the way to the top, to President P. W. Botha himself.

I received a telegram in Monrovia saying that the South African government had granted *agrément,* and authorizing me to notify President Doe that I would be leaving. Doe interpreted the news as a compliment to his country. "It says something about Liberia, doesn't it," he said, "that the American ambassador to Liberia has been picked to head this important post." He gave me a big farewell reception and conferred upon me the Order of Liberia, which is the country's highest decoration. Lucy and I packed our household effects and flew to Washington.

In October 1986, the president ordered the press secretary to post a little notice on the bulletin board in the pressroom—not to make an announcement, just to post the notice. The notice said in its entirety: "Today the president decided to send the name of Edward J. Perkins to the Senate in nomination to be the next United States Ambassador to the Republic of South Africa."

Somebody wandered over to read the notice and, I am told, all hell broke loose.

"Who is this guy?" the press wanted to know. "*Where* is he?"

It was big news that President Reagan was appointing a black ambassador to South Africa, but to some it was not good news.

None of the South African press was friendly. An editorial in *The Sowetan* newspaper was bluntly titled: "Dear Mr. Perkins, you are just not welcome."[2] I did not take it personally. What they resented was the Reagan administration that I would represent.

In the United States, both blacks and whites were skeptical. William (Bill) Gray III, a black congressman from Pennsylvania and the majority whip of the House, spoke for many blacks when he said, "We do not think that changing the messenger is going to make any difference unless the message is changed." I had never met Bill, but I called on him at his House office and told him what the president had told me. "You can expect to have my support," he told me. "We will wait and see if he backs you up."

I called on every member of the Congressional Black Caucus and told them what I intended to do in South Africa. Standing as a solid block, the Black Caucus was unequivocally committed to change in South Africa. They believed that the president and his administration had attempted to apologize for the Afrikaners, a stance they abhorred. In fairness, the Reagan administration had done little to dissuade them from that view.

Some black leaders I met with were supportive. Some were noncommittal, adopting Gray's "wait and see" philosophy. Others were negative:

"It will not work," they said flatly.

"This is just another trick of the administration."

"His is a token appointment."

"He will have no power."

"He will just do the bidding of the administration."

Some people openly doubted if I was the man for the job. "He is too controversial."

Jesse Jackson and Randall Robinson were among those who said, "He won't know when to talk back to the administration." When the press ferreted out a former professor of mine at USC and asked his opinion, he replied, "They will eat him alive." Despite such public doubts, it never dawned on me that I would not be successful. I approached South Africa as a problem that needed to be solved.

I held no press conference, and I made absolutely no comments to the press. This was not a deliberate strategy; I simply did not have anything to say at this point. By and large, the American press was supportive. One exception was *The Washington Post*. The *Post* asked for a special interview, which I was not inclined to give. Publisher Katharine Graham called Crocker and asked him to persuade me to reconsider. The *Post* had a poor relationship with the black community and was losing black advertising and subscribers. Mrs. Graham and her staff were looking for ways to redeem the newspaper. They proposed that Juan Williams, a black reporter, write a weekend magazine piece about me. My instincts told me to stay away from it, but Chet urged me to agree and I did. Juan wanted to go to Portland and follow me around the old neighborhood, then spend six months trailing along with me in South Africa, but I nixed both suggestions, so he interviewed me at the State Department. When his article, titled "Man in a Trap,"[3] came out, it was not entirely favorable, and the black community was incensed. Even today black people tell me they are still angry with Juan about his article.

Juan quoted former co-workers who described me as "one of those ex-marine, no-nonsense types who get recognition for keeping their mouths shut" and critics who derided me as unimaginative, unemotional, and aloof. He wrote that I likely would wait for policy to be formed in Washington and not be upset if that policy was slow in coming or flawed. He quoted Americo-Liberians critical of my work in Liberia and my seemingly favorable relationship with President Doe. Ellen Johnson-Sirleaf, my nemesis from Liberia, was quoted as saying, "I don't think he's going to assist in the process of change in South Africa. He's a good man to send to protect the status quo and U.S. economic and military interests there." Juan also wrote that Jesse Jackson had met with me twice, trying to convince me not to take the job. That statement was not only accurate, it summarized one of the more colorful aspects of my preparation.

Before going to South Africa, I made a point of meeting with as many black leaders as possible, especially the movers and shakers around Washington: attorney and civil rights leader Vernon Jordan; charismatic Philadelphia minister Leon Sullivan; The Council of 100, a black Republican political organization; and the long-time Jewish legal counsel to the NAACP, Jack Greenburg. I had lunch with Coretta Scott King, a strikingly beautiful and level-headed woman who was interested in establishing a Martin Luther King Center for Non-Violent Social Change in South Africa in honor of her late husband. She told me about her recent disastrous visit to South Africa. She attributed much of her poor reception there to a few prominent men in the civil-rights movement who had poisoned the well because they resented her marching alone, without their participation. She had committed several political blunders that further blemished her trip, such as scheduling a call on the president of South Africa before meeting with the revolutionary black leadership. This created such an uproar that she was forced to cancel her meeting with the president.

I met with people in Washington, New York, and London, but none of my meetings were more dramatic than those with Jesse Jackson, who was the most vocal opponent of my going to South Africa. Jesse first visited me in the State Department. He arrived one Friday with two aides. I began to tell Jesse about being approached to go to South Africa, but he interrupted me, saying, "Brother Perkins, I have come here today to ask you not to go." He asked if I thought it appropriate for a racist president like Ronald Reagan to nominate the first black ambassador to go to South Africa.

"Reverend Jackson," I said, "I am a career diplomat and not a politician, and as a Foreign Service officer, I agreed to go where needed when needed." Jesse

With Vernon Jordan Jr. at the reception celebrating my swearing in as U.S. ambassador to South Africa. Vernon, a Washington attorney from Atlanta, was the principal black leader I spoke to as I prepared for my South Africa post. He was a member of Secretary of State George Shultz's blue-ribbon South Africa Group and had studied South African policy.

is shrewd, calculating, and attractive, especially to women. He spoke in staccato bursts like a preacher—a powerful rhetorical technique—and I replied quietly, making my points in an understated way.

"I can understand why you say that, Reverend," I said. "It is the Christian thing to do. I will try my best to walk in the path of Jesus Christ while I am down there."

We had a good conversation. We will never be bosom buddies, because philosophically we are different people. I think he is an effective political activist, but that stance raised a question for me: When does theology cease to be theology and become political dogma?

After about an hour, our meeting ended, and I escorted him downstairs to make our farewells in the glass foyer. He seemed reluctant to leave, and I wondered why he lingered so long with me in the foyer. Then I saw cameras outside the building and understood. This would have been a fine photo opportunity—Jesse Jackson appealing to the potential ambassador not to go to South Africa. We were at an impasse. I would not go outside, and he would not leave. Finally I wished him well and returned to the seventh floor.

A few days later, I was a speaker at the Black Women's Political Caucus. My hosts were Malcolm X's widow, Betty Shabazz; Representative Shirley Chisholm of New York; and long-time New York political leader Gloria Toot. A messenger arrived during the meeting and said to me, "Reverend Jackson would like to speak to you in a room down the hall."

"Wait a minute," Gloria said. "I smell a rat. I'm going with you." Sure enough, as she suspected, a large gathering of press was assembled in the hallway with cameras at the ready. "You go on in, Mr. Ambassador," Gloria said, and as the press surged forward, she shut the door behind me and stood guard. Once again, a photo opportunity was lost for Reverend Jackson. He had to address me behind closed doors. "Brother Perkins," Jesse said again in what was likely intended to be a highly publicized plea. "I appeal to you one more time—do not go to South Africa. They might kill you down there." I told him again that I had promised the president that I would take the job. "Since you have promised the president," he replied, "maybe I can help you."

The State Department saw to it that my preparation for South Africa was thorough and in-depth. I had briefings from numerous sources and Washington agencies including Defense, the CIA, Treasury, Commerce, Agriculture, the U.S. Information Agency, and the Agency for International Development, which was responsible for administering a $45 million program unlike any other that Congress had ever authorized. The financial aid was not government-to-government; it was designed to further the revolution, to aid cottage industries among women in the townships, and to train lawyers and community activists under the guise of education and health workers.

An Africa expert whom I consulted, then and throughout my tenure in South Africa, was Helen Kitchen, of the Center for Strategic and International Studies, under the aegis of Georgetown University. She was a long-time observer of the African scene and one of the few U.S. experts on Africa's emergence after World War II.

According to formal procedure, once the president sends an ambassador's nomination forward to the Senate, the nominee is obliged to call on the chairman of the Senate Foreign Relations Committee and as many individual members as possible. With fifteen members on the committee, it was not possible for me to see them all, but it was important for me to see those on the Africa Subcommittee. I left Liberia on October 22, 1986, and as soon as I arrived in Washington, I began making my official visits. My first calls were to Senator Lugar, chairman of the committee, and Senator Nancy Kassebaum (Rep.– Kansas), subcommittee chair. The administration considered them turncoats because they not only had opposed the administration's South Africa policy, but also had led the sanctions bill through Congress. They then had supported the fight to overturn the president's veto. Furthermore, Senator Kassebaum was among those who criticized the current ambassador to South Africa, Herman Nickel, a political appointee, for not interacting with the black population or spending enough time in the townships. The battle was over, but not forgotten. Senator Lugar told me that there had been no subsequent communication between the administration and the Senate. He asked me to meet the press with him for photographs. "I thought it would be helpful to all of us if the world saw us getting ready to talk," he said. I was happy to oblige. I found him to be one of the finest individuals I have ever met.

"This is a turning point in America's fortunes," Senator Lugar told me when we met privately. "At last we can be seen as representing what we stand for as a country. I have been troubled by the view of the administration that we can work with the Afrikaner government. The impression of the majority of the population is that we are insensitive. Finally, we are getting away from that. There is not one person who can pull this off except you. You have both my prayers and my support." I felt quite humbled by his remarks.

Senator Kassebaum quickly scheduled the hearings and invited all committee members to attend. As I recall, six of the fifteen attended. Senators Orin Hatch and Jesse Helms, the two most conservative members of the committee, were not in attendance. The hearing was held in the Senate Foreign Relations Hearing Room, where the senators sat on an elevated dais facing me and I sat at a big polished table. A sunken floor separated us. I wore my green jade cufflinks for good luck. My wife sat behind me. The hearing room was packed with my family and friends, a delegation from the State Department, and an overwhelming number of press stationed in the no-man's land between me and the committee. Flashbulbs popped in my face during the entire hour-long hearing. To describe this photography and press activity as disconcerting is an understatement.

Senator Kassebaum asked the first question: "You've got your work cut out for you. Tell us a few things you will do when you get there." I told her I would get to know as many South Africans as possible—South Africans of all colors. Senator Thomas Eagleton of Missouri asked about sanctions, and I replied that I had taken an oath of office to uphold the law, the same as he had done, and that was what I intended to do. Senator John Kerry of Massachusetts asked about constructive engagement and how Congress's overturning the president's veto indicated a disapproval of this policy. I had anticipated this question. I did not concur with Chet Crocker on the policy, but my reply was to say only, "Constructive engagement means many things to many people, Senator. As for me, I do not intend to use those words in my administration of policy in South Africa." This was the beginning of the end of the policy of constructive engagement. It was never again mentioned as U.S policy, and it was not pursued thereafter.

After the questions were completed, I made a statement. I well remember what I said that day to the Africa Subcommittee of the Committee on Foreign Affairs in the Senate.

"I promise that if confirmed I can assure you I will do everything in my power to advance United States interests in the Republic of South Africa. There is no difference between the executive branch and Congress on what those objectives and interests are, notwithstanding recent disagreements of the most

My family with Senator Nancy Landon Kassebaum from Kansas. She was chair of the African Subcommittee in the Senate Foreign Relations Committee and had criticized the former ambassador to South Africa for not interacting enough with the black population of South Africa.

appropriate means by which to pursue them. As the president stated during Congress's debate on the Comprehensive Anti-Apartheid Act of 1986, and I quote him, 'It is clear that my administration's intentions and those of the Congress are identical.' That is the basis on which I appear before you now. The message I will carry to South Africa, if I am confirmed, is therefore that our relationship is united on the central questions confronted by South Africa today. I shall devote myself to communicating United States policy to all important groups in that troubled and divided land, and I will lend all of my energies and skills in pursuit of that policy.

"I hope I can play a role in helping South Africans to move their nation toward the president's vision of a new South Africa, a new nation where all that has been built up over the generations is not destroyed, a new society where participation in the social, cultural, and political life is open to all people and a new South Africa that comes home to the family of free nations where it belongs. To that end, I plan to listen carefully to the views of South Africans inside and outside the government. I believe it is essential that the United States work with every element of South African society. I will do my best to ensure that our own government has the best possible information and understanding of trends and events in South Africa so as to assist the president and his advisors as they consider how best to advance our goals.

"I am, of course, acutely aware of the special challenges that appointment as ambassador to South Africa must pose. But at the same time, I believe that my experience as a career officer in the Foreign Service and in previous postings abroad prepared me to serve in that position. I am honored by the president's confidence in my qualifications and in my capacity to make a contribution to our nation's interest in South Africa.

"Our nation is strong. That strength derives in no small measure from the vigor with which we Americans can pursue open debate and then compose our differences and work together for common national objectives. It comes from our diversity and our inherent tolerance of all people. But above all, I believe we are strong because of our respect for the dignity and worth of the individual, our encouragement of individual excellence, and our insistence that each person enjoy the right to achieve the highest of which he or she is capable. We are far yet short of perfection, but no one who knows us can doubt that we are committed to ceaseless striving for it.

"So I look on my appearance here today and the assignment I hope shortly to take up as a small example to South Africa of how a nation's strength may rest on its diversity. This and many other reasons make me especially proud to have the opportunity to serve our president, our government, and our people as ambassador to South Africa."

That little speech was the manifesto for my work in South Africa. I did everything in my power to follow it to the letter and uphold my pledge to the subcommittee, the Senate, the president, and the people of the United States.

If it is possible for senators to be supportive in a hearing atmosphere, then they were supportive that day. Finally Senator Kassebaum said, "I won't adjourn the hearing. I will recess it in case Senator Helms or Senator Hatch would like to enter questions directed for you. I would like to be the first to congratulate you, though." That was the end of the hearings. After waiting the minimum time of one day, the Senate voted. All one hundred senators voted yes. My family and I went to dinner floating on a cloud.

November 3, 1986: The swearing-in ceremony for career ambassadors, replete with drama, is held traditionally in the ornate Benjamin Franklin Room in the State Department. Here, under what is perhaps the world's largest chandelier, I sat at my first formal dinner as a young Foreign Service officer learning etiquette and conversational discourse techniques so important to diplomats. Now, the room was packed with about four hundred people, including the press, awaiting my arrival. The secretary of state commented that this was the largest audience in memory for a swearing-in ceremony. The dress for the occasion is coat and tie. I wore a blue suit and a red striped tie.

This official White House photograph of my family with President Reagan was taken in November 1986. Kathy is far left, Sarah is on the right. I was surprised at how much the president knew about South Africa and how much authority he gave me to make policy on the ground.

While guests assembled in the Ben Franklin Room, my family and I were in a holding area in the adjacent Monroe Room, along with the secretary of state and the chief of protocol. Lucy, my mother, and my two daughters accompanied me. At exactly twelve o'clock, we entered to a completely hushed audience. Then, the entire audience burst into applause. I had an extremely difficult time holding back tears. It was wrenchingly emotional.

This is the oath of office I took that day: "I, Edward Joseph Perkins, do solemnly swear that I will support and defend the Constitution of the United States against all enemies, foreign and domestic, that I will bear true faith and allegiance to the same, that I take this obligation freely and without any mental reservation or purpose of evasion, that I will well and faithfully discharge the duties of the office of which I am about to enter, so help me God." That oath is the same one that is taken by every official in the United States government, in all three branches of the government, as an officer of the government, including the president and vice president.

I had extended an invitation to Carmen Walker, my high school counselor from Portland, and she was in the audience. Neither of my former Portland English teachers, Ruth Arbuckle and Cecile Oliver, could make the trip, although both had been invited. Secretary of State George Shultz officiated at the swearing-in ceremony. He was eloquent and straightforward. He referred to Hemingway's definition of courage as "grace under pressure" and described me as "a truly courageous professional diplomat" for the challenges I had faced in Liberia and now would face in South Africa. This assignment, he said, would require both courage and moral strength. In the "noisy divisiveness in South Africa," Secretary Shultz said, "our diplomacy is conducted in a minefield. It will take a man of Ed Perkins's strength to keep U.S. diplomacy aimed resolutely at its goals when so many will be trying to twist our arm, warp our message, or manipulate our efforts." The critical question in all foreign policy arenas is not only what we want, the secretary said, but how practically we can get from here to there. Ultimately the South Africans would decide their country's future. "Our role is to help create conditions that will draw people of good will, the overwhelming majority of South Africans, together," he said.

In my response, I thanked everybody for coming. South African ambassador Herbert Beukes was present, probably feeling like a mouse in a room full of cats. I extended a special welcome to him. Later, in South Africa, he told me, "That was a hell of a day."

"Herbert," I said, "it was a hell of a day for me, too. I'm sure you were afraid I was going to damn the Afrikaners."

"A lot of us were relieved when you finished speaking," he said.

My remarks had been crafted with care and with the help of several people. I went through several drafts before arriving at the finished product. I wanted to send a message to several quarters. "I do not go to South Africa as a representative of any special group of people," I said. "I go as a representative of the American people and the administration, and I hope that I can have their backing. America's hopes for South Africa are based solidly on our national experience, which teaches us that the seemingly impossible may, in time, be achieved by men and women of good will." I cited our struggle against colonial rule and our many revolutions—the abolition of slavery, the establishment of the rights of labor, the extension of civil rights to all Americans, and the fight for women's rights. "That is why we dare to trust that peaceful change can come about in South Africa," I said.

I have been asked what this assignment meant to me as a black American. I told the audience, "I accepted the president's offer as an American, and as an

My brothers of the Kappa Alpha Psi fraternity (international) at the reception following my swearing in as the U.S. ambassador to South Africa. Some years later, nominated by the Alexandria-Fairfax alumni chapter, I was awarded the Laurel Wreath, the fraternity's highest award. This honor was one of the seminal experiences of my life.

American who believes that we should not stand as cheerleaders on the sidelines of the great issues of our time, but that we should have the courage to engage ourselves in them. I accepted this assignment as a Foreign Service officer who took an oath to go where needed, when needed. I believe President Reagan chose me for this challenging assignment on this basis: that I am a Foreign Service officer who by training and experience can help him pursue American objectives in South Africa, and that as a black American, as a member of a minority that was long oppressed, I might have a special empathy for both the minority and the majority in South Africa."

The ceremony closed with a receiving line, after which I hosted a little reception. The U.S. government does not fund cocktail parties when an ambassador is sworn in, so I paid for it. That evening, a group of black businessmen gave a spectacular party in my honor, the first of several celebrations. Our daughters went back to school, and Lucy and I went to New York, where I spent a couple of days making official calls before our departure to post. This entire episode—rumors of my nomination, community reactions, the Senate confirmation, and the swearing-in ceremony—was the most exciting time of my life. With pounding heart and surging adrenaline, I felt as if I were walking a tightwire across the Grand Canyon with no net or safety harness and winds blowing from all sides, while I tried to keep my balance in midair and my eyes on the goal.

Frankly, I was glad to get out of Washington and away from the hoopla. It was wearing, although I understood the reason for it. The administration was changing its policy. A hard-fought war was over and people were giddy with relief. The celebrations for me were fueled by powerful expectations. I felt the full weight of these expectations on my shoulders.

The following December at the U.S. Embassy in Pretoria, I received a holiday letter from Senator Kassebaum that included this quotation from war photographer Carl Mydans: "I cannot tell you where our history is leading us, or through what suffering, or into what era of war or peace. But wherever it is, I know men of good heart will be passing there."

That observation, she said, is a favorite of hers because it captures the essence of faith in the human spirit. "Faith in the human spirit"—I would hold that faith like a lamp before me as I strode deeper and deeper into the Republic of South Africa, a country where the government believed apartheid was a policy sent by God.

LET THEM KNOW
I AM HERE

Edison Mmusa, at the wheel of the limousine, rolled up the driveway of the ambassador's official residence to drive me to the U.S. Embassy in Pretoria. It was my first day as ambassador to South Africa. Edison was the embassy driver who would transport me all over the country during my tour of duty, but he was much more than a chauffeur. He is a tall, wise black man who speaks several languages. I would come to rely on him as one of my most influential advisors and as a guide into the black townships. He taught me to walk through the townships and hear the different languages being spoken. At first, I could not understand any of them, and to my ear they sounded like a musical cacophony. "Just listen," he said. "Eventually you will hear."

The embassy limousine was a gray armored Cadillac. The tinted windows were bulletproof, and the body was reinforced with steel. It was as heavy as a tank. Unfortunately, the engine was not beefed up to support the additional weight, and the car would sputter and die at inopportune times and places. When that happened, I sat in the back seat—sometimes decked out in top hat and morning coat if it was an official function—while Edison swore into the radio and called for help. In 1986, cell phones and pagers were communication devices of the future. When the limo stalled, we were stuck except for the short-wave radio in the car.

Those vehicular adventures lay ahead of us. This morning was a solemn occasion. I was the new and controversial ambassador of the United States, venturing for the first time into the turbid waters of apartheid. I felt as if both nations, the United States and South Africa, held their breath to see how I would fare.

"Put the flags on," I told Edison. A U.S. ambassador is entitled to fly two emblems on the official vehicle. One is the Stars and Stripes of the United States; the other is the president's flag, since an ambassador is the president's direct representative. Usually an ambassador's vehicle travels unadorned, reserving the banners for ceremonial functions. Today would be different. Edison affixed the flags, one to each front fender of the Cadillac. They fluttered in the soft breeze and bright sunlight of one of the most beautiful countries in the world.

"Roll down the windows," I told him. "I want everyone to see who is in this car."

We began the drive down the hill from the ambassadorial residence toward the city. The ambassador's residence in Pretoria is located in a region called Waterkloof, which means "water cliff," and which was one of the whitest areas of Pretoria. The neighborhood that day was strangely quiet. Lucy and I were acutely aware that no welcoming neighbors were present. Although I saw black servants coming and going to work, the white neighbors were not in evidence. The residence is a Cape Dutch style, landscaped with beautiful terraced gardens and a heated swimming pool. The head gardener was an Afrikaner woman who did not speak to me the entire time I lived there. From our residence on the hill we could view a sea of blue jacaranda trees. It was one of the most beautiful views in the world. How could a city hold both so much beauty, I wondered, and so much evil?

Edison and I drove slowly through the city streets toward the U.S. Embassy, and out the car windows I watched downtown Pretoria glide by. As the capital of the South African government and an administrative city, Pretoria is not unlike some areas of Washington, D.C., or the capitals of many eastern states in the United States. It is a modern city with solid, high-rise office buildings and busy, street-side shops and cafés. As in many state and national capital cities, its architecture conveys strength and stability rather than charm. Pretoria is a no-nonsense city of industry and administration laid out on a practical grid of streets. In October, some seventy thousand jacaranda trees bloom, but I arrived in November after the blue froth of blossoms had faded, leaving behind a solemn city. In the years to come I would often walk alone, foolishly perhaps, through Pretoria, and I could feel its unkindness. The city had a militant air. It had been the headquarters of General Andries Pretorius during the Boer War, and a dedicated band of followers still celebrate Adolf Hitler's birthday there every year.

The atmosphere I felt in Pretoria was like the threat of a cocked hammer. This was the seat of the official governmental policy of racial segregation and, for any who challenged the policy, swift punishment akin to Old Testament vengeance. Pretoria was the heart of Afrikanerdom, and in 1986 it was a hard heart. The residents were shocked to see me, a black man, walking down the city sidewalks as bold as brass. Women dressed in fashions of the 1950s and pushing baby prams hissed at me as they passed; men glared ominously.

South Africa is a large nation, five times the size of Britain and almost twice the size of Texas. Pretoria is not far from sprawling Johannesburg, known as "the gold city." Both earth and air near Johannesburg seem to glitter golden, and no wonder; South Africa's famed gold and diamond mines are nearby. When South Africa became a republic and the location of the capital was being debated, the Afrikaners and English-speakers compromised by dividing governmental activities among three cities. Cape Town on the Western Cape is the legislative seat of government where Parliament meets from February until about June. The judicial center is located in Bloemfontein in the Orange Free State in the center of the country. The United States maintains embassies in both Pretoria and Cape Town, and I would divide my time between the two cities, living six months in each. In December, the foreign embassies move operations to Cape Town and then, because this is the summer season in South Africa, take a few weeks of vacation. Twice a year Lucy and I packed up the residence and moved cross-country to our other home. It was in the administrative center, Pretoria, that I would present my credentials and begin my work.

As we drove through the city, one of the newsboys selling newspapers caught sight of me in the backseat of the limo. "He is here," the newsboy shouted. His call was picked up by the newsboys on the next streets. Their shouts preceded us like clanging bells all through the city center. I heard their calls sounding even as the car pulled up to the U.S. Embassy.

The embassy at that time had little majesty. It was located in a building shared by the South African National Police Department. Downstairs in the lobby was a gun shop. Inside the building I saw three elevator doors. They were no longer labeled, but clearly the doors had been built for separate entrances by white, Coloured, and black races. Here was my first confrontation with the tangible barriers of apartheid, from the Afrikaans word for "apartness." I did not hesitate but walked steadily on, entering the most convenient elevator door. "Let them know I am here," I thought. Even without labels, South African citizens knew which doors were for which races and habitually conformed. The American Embassy staff, of course, ignored the distinction. Later I learned that the *Christian Science Monitor* had run what it considered to be a humorous cartoon suggesting a route I could take.

My first day was spent meeting the large embassy staff and in briefings by the country team. One of the first people I spoke with was the personnel officer, Sandy Siverson. Our recruiting policy must reflect our revolutionary stance on change in South Africa, I said. "From this time forward," I told the senior staff, "everything we do must show that the embassy is one giant change agent for South Africa. Every move I make, every speech I give has to be from that view. My entire tour hereafter will be acting as the head of a change agent." This was a dramatic shift. Until then Americans assigned to South Africa

Reporting in to President Ronald Reagan in the Oval Office. He recognized the need for a new policy, and told me, "Mr. Ambassador, if you go you'll have to establish your own policy. We don't know enough about what is happening there to make policy at this end. You come back every six months and tell us and the American people what is going on in South Africa and what you are doing."

had found it a comfortable life—a wonderful climate, plenty of sunshine, good transportation, a good financial rate of exchange, great food, and good South African wine. Most of them could afford to have servants. It was a good place to be, if one could ignore the apartheid system. All of a sudden the United States had shifted its stance. "We are going to be a revolutionary embassy," I told the staff. Some of the employees were unhappy with this turnaround.

Let them know I am here was my silent slogan, to be demonstrated by my every action. And just where in the hell was "here"? What was it? What kind of people inhabited it? I felt sometimes as if I were observing myself at a distance; I saw Ed Perkins being buffeted about, a small vessel in a rough sea, trying to get a bearing.

I knew that South Africa was (1) a country of exquisite beauty and rich resources, (2) at the southern tip of the continent and isolated from the rest of the world, (3) populated by about 33 million people, and (4) an institutionalized system that allowed a 14 percent white minority to rule the other 86 percent of the population consisting of black, Coloured, and Indian races. All of these factors were tangled together in a socio-political knot tied by history. The result was a society distorted by the forces of religion and revenge. In 1985, a state of emergency was declared in South Africa in order to impose extra-legal precedents to derail human and civil rights. The country was in such a state of turmoil and violence that the South African government had suspended all political rights. Although scorned by the world for its racial policies of apartheid, South Africa seemed locked in an impasse it could not break. I could not move forward until I understood how the country had reached this point.

Before going to South Africa, I had immersed myself in a crash course of self-study about the country. I did a great deal of reading and listening. The history of South Africa reads like a magnificent novel of adventure, courage, passion, and blood. White settlement in South Africa began in the mid-1600s when a ship from the Dutch East India Company ran aground at the Cape of Good Hope. A colony was founded near Cape Town, where the white settlers met the San people, a nomadic tribe that had existed there for centuries. The San were so closely attuned to the land that they considered themselves one with the animals, grass, and water. The Dutch company Heere XVII, which financed the Dutch East India Company, granted permission for settlers—primarily Dutch and some

Germans and French—to set up a whaling station at Cape Town and then allowed *burghers*, or farmers, to settle in the region but set a limit on how far inland they could intrude. Before long, the San people became their servants.

Originally, only white males settled in the area, taking African or Malaysian women for mates. The children of these unions were called Coloureds, which would become one of the four official races in South Africa. When the settlement appeared to be permanent, white women from European orphanages were sent to South Africa to become wives and mothers. With missionary zeal, the Dutch farming families began to raise their families according to biblical teaching. They became known as *Boers*, which was synonymous with poor and lower class. The Boer women would become revered for the hardships they suffered and the dangers they faced while "bringing civilization to the heart of this black continent," and their rock-hard determination. White settlements slowly crept farther inland from the western coast. Meanwhile, whole native kingdoms were moving south, including the Zulus under the great leadership of kings Dingane and Shaka. Inevitably, the two groups clashed in a spectacular battle between Boers and Zulus, a conflagration that would have grave consequences for the future of South Africa.

Meanwhile, the British Empire began to expand into South Africa with the dream of dominating the African continent from the Cape to Cairo. The dream was laid out in frighteningly clear language by Cecil Rhodes, a diamond mine mogul. The British followed Rhodes's lead and declared possession of several colonies in South Africa. In 1793, the British raided the Cape Province and took control of the castle, which held the Dutch government. That began what the Afrikaners call the Century of Wrong. The Xhosa tribe was among those resisting the British intrusion, and a series of battles were fought. Early in the 1800s, the British issued a proclamation that would reverberate for almost two centuries. It required every member of the Xhosa tribe to have a registered residence and a certificate authorizing travel from one district to another. This was the birth of the hated "pass law."

The Boers had their own problems with the British, especially the British policy that abolished slavery. They resented British rule with a bitterness that drove a group of several thousand burghers to leave their homes on the Western Cape in 1837–38 and to trek north and east. This exodus earned them the name of *Voortrekkers*, pioneers. Fleeing British authority, they headed toward what would become the Transvaal and Natal to form independent republics, hauling their possessions in ox-drawn wagons. Along the way some died of disease, and Zulus massacred many others—40 men, 50 women, and 180 children in one campsite. This trek hardened the Boers' fierce resolve to throw off British rule and to dominate black African society.

Then came the decisive battle in South African history: the Battle of Blood River on December 16, 1838. To the Afrikaners, it is not only history; it is sacred history. Literature told me that some 550 Boer marksmen, led by Andries Pretorius, faced a tide of 15,000–18,000 Zulu warriors. Along the Ncome River, the trekkers formed themselves into a *laager*, a circle of sixty-four wagons with women and children inside, while the men manned the outside of the circle armed with pistols and rifles. Before the battle began, a church elder led the group in prayer, asking that God deliver them safely out of this confrontation. The prayer ended with a vow that became their covenant: if they emerged victorious, they would interpret it as a message from God. They pledged that they would forever commemorate this date as a day of remembrance and thanksgiving like the Sabbath.

The Afrikaner women, unlike any other women I have met, developed the same strength of determination as Afrikaner men. I am sure that before the great battle in 1838, they encouraged the men to circle the wagons and vowed to go down in death together with the men if that was God's will. I emphasize their belief: *If that is God's will*. In the building of South Africa, the Afrikaner woman never faltered or doubted she could overcome any obstacles. A memorial to the Afrikaner woman who died during the Boer War stands at Bloemfontein with the inscription: *To our heroines and beloved children. Thy will be done.* "No Englishman can understand South African history," an English reporter wrote, "until he has seen this shrine."

The Ncome River lies in a plain with low hills in the distance. The Zulu regiments attacked over these hills, wave after wave of *impis*, warriors, wielding their traditional weapons, assegais or long spears. Wave after wave of *impis* was cut down by rifle fire. When the slaughter ended six hours later; the Ncome River ran red with the blood of some three thousand fallen Zulus, hence the name, the Battle of Blood River. Only three Boers were injured, none fatally. It was a divining moment for both the Boers and the Zulus, who were surrogates for all blacks of South Africa. The Voortrekkers accepted this as a sign from God affirming white supremacy. They had read in the Bible of covenants that God made with his chosen people, and they believed they now had such a covenant. The vow they took that historic day is included as the "Te Deum" in the liturgy of the Afrikaners' civil religion. As author Allister Sparks wrote, "The Lord did indeed deliver the enemy into their hands. . . . Here was the ultimate revelation of God's special favor and so it is recorded in the sacred history." The Boer victory at Blood River may be considered the birth of the Afrikaner national identity. From this day on, the Afrikaners considered themselves to be God's chosen people surrounded by evil. They saw all non-Afrikaners, especially non-whites, as hewers of wood and carriers of water until it was determined by the Afrikaners that the non-whites merited entrance into the kingdom of heaven. When the Battle of Blood River was over, the Afrikaners were on a political, social, and economic march to dominance.

Shortly after I arrived in South Africa, I visited the battle site. I had read so much about it, and I wanted to see the river myself and to walk on that battlefield. I wanted to soak up the spirit that still permeates those hallowed grounds, where so many African warriors died in battle. I sensed their ghosts around me. My experience there was surreal. It was a sinister place. As I walked back and forth on the battlefield, I had the very real impression that the people I was now working with, especially the Afrikaners, were not human beings like others of us. I had the strong image of a cornered animal determined to fight to the death. I remembered a female raccoon that I had once seen cornered for capture. Her babies were with her, and when it became clear that they would all be captured, the mother's reaction was totally unexpected. To prevent her babies' capture, she ate her young. I felt this paralleled the Afrikaners' position when I was there—we were approaching a time when the Afrikaners could emulate that mother raccoon and say, "This is the end for us, and we will now destroy everything we have accomplished, *along with the blacks.*" I thought it quite likely that they were considering using small-scale nuclear weapons on some of the townships, even with the knowledge that they would also be destroyed in the process. Intelligence information provided to the embassy would later confirm my intuition. My visit to the Blood River battlefield was as much a defining moment for me as it had been for the Boers. The air was full of messages for me, but, as if they were behind a veil, I could not decipher them all. I knew clearly, however, that the situation in South Africa was reaching the breaking point and that I had to take action.

In the 1800s, the racial friction among Boers, British, and black Africans continued to grow. In mid-century two mighty discoveries exacerbated the problem. In 1867 diamonds were discovered, and eventually diamond mining was dominated by the British. Then, in the 1870s and 1880s, gold was discovered, and the Afrikaners began to dominate this industry. In both cases, black Africans were relegated to migrant-worker status. In the late 1800s, land-ownership laws and taxes limited the amount of land blacks could own. Slowly the black population was being disenfranchised.

Much like the Battle of Blood River, the Boer War (1899–1902) would cast a long shadow over South Africa. This war, known to some Afrikaners as the English War, was the flashpoint of resistance to British rule by the Boers and some black tribes. For the Boers it was devastating: one-sixth of the population was lost. British troops battled the Boers' wily guerrilla forces with an intensity that some say was designed to destroy Afrikaner nationalism. The British high commissioner for South Africa was quoted as saying that his intention was "to knock the bottom out of the great Afrikaner nation forever and ever. Amen." Afrikaners told me horror stories of the Boer War that had been passed down by their parents and grandparents who were taken prisoner. They spoke about it as if it were yesterday, relating how the British had treated them with unusual cruelty. Some 136,000 women and children were sent to concentration camps, the first such camps in the world. In those camps, the Afrikaners died of starvation or disease. About 20,000 children under the age of sixteen died. Some prisoners reported that they found ground glass in their food. More than 30,000 Boer men were taken as prisoners of war and exiled to India, Burma, Ceylon, and Bermuda. At home, their farms and crops were burned in a scorched-earth war, and their sheep and cattle were slaughtered. The cruelty the Afrikaners suffered at the hands of the British in turn shaped them into cruel rulers when they came into political power. They were defeated in battle but not conquered in spirit. The Boers emerged from the war with a deep hatred for the English and a strengthened sense of Afrikaner nationalism. They were determined to preserve themselves as a people.

The church was the glue that held the Boers together as a people as they shaped themselves into Afrikaners. The South African Dutch Reformed Church grew out of the Dutch Church, which had its origin in Calvinistic philosophy. Calvinism has always been a strict religion, so it is no surprise that the Dutch Reformed Church developed even stricter rules of behavior. The Bible was the anchor. Most Boers had a habit of reading aloud from the Bible every night to the family. We are too far removed to remember the hardships of settling a frontier or to know the comfort of familiar pieces of home in an untamed land, but that was the Boers' experience. One thing that many Boer families brought with them from Holland was a huge crock used for making a favorite sweet pudding. The other treasure they brought was a big Bible, which they used as a shield in a hostile land. The Bible would become their weapon in establishing their dominance over the native peoples. As the church developed, God was defined as chillingly strict and demanding obedience. It was this God that identified with the Boers' hardships in South Africa.

With a constructionist interpretation of the Bible, the church used two scriptural passages as a foundation for apartheid. The meaning of Acts 17:26 is rather ambiguous: "And hath made of one blood all nations of men for to dwell on all the face of the earth, and hath determined the times before appointed, and the bounds of their habitation." The early *dominees*, Dutch for "priest," egged on by political leaders, interpreted this passage to justify the separation of those who are not yet ready to enter into the kingdom of heaven. In their thinking, it was the blacks who were not yet ready. They emphasized the word "bounds" and stretched it to mean "boundaries."

The second scriptural interpretation was quite ingenious. Genesis 11:6–9 tells the story of the Tower of Babel:

> And the Lord said, "Behold, the people is one and they have all one language; and this they began to do: and now nothing will be restrained from them, which they have imagined to do. Go to, let us go down, and there confound their language, that they may not understand one another's speech." So the Lord scattered them abroad from thence upon the face of all the earth: and they left off to build the city. Therefore is the name of it called Babel; because the Lord did there confound the language of all the earth: and from thence did the Lord scatter them abroad upon the face of all the earth.

The church's interpretation was "Who has the right to bring together people that God has separated?" From these two scriptures the Afrikaners concocted a witches' brew of theology.

Religion, language, and a widening gulf of class distinction divided the Boers and the British. The British immigrants and their descendants in South Africa became known as English-speakers. They were English, Irish, and Scots, urbanites who by profession were engineers, businessmen, and lawyers, as well as unskilled workers. They considered themselves a higher class of people. The Boers were farmers, considered by the British to be a lower class of white people. By the early 1930s and 1940s, Afrikaners were among the poorest people on earth, with intolerable living conditions.

All of this history cumulated in the making of the modern South Africa that

I knew in 1986. After the Battle of Blood River and the Boer War, the Boers ceased to be Europeans. They became Afrikaners, bound up by a religious, political, and social fervor. They declared December 16 to be the Day of the Vow, a national holiday commemorating their escape from death at Blood River. Their faith lay with the *Volk*, a word that translates as "the people," but which had a much larger meaning that embraced nationhood, community, language, and power. From that time on, the Afrikaners vowed to seize power in the banking institutions, the educational system, and the civil service. They made their plan in 1902, and it fermented for thirty-six years. In 1918 they formed the *Broederbond*, a secret society of Afrikaner men whose goal was to promote the Afrikaner culture and to gain control of the South African government. They not only spoke Afrikaans, a language that evolved from Dutch, but they also treasured their national language and refused to speak English. In 1938, they took a bold step and symbolically reenacted the Great Trek of their ancestors.

As much as I had read about South African history, nothing prepared me for the story that author Alan Paton told me about the Great Trek. In 1938, to commemorate the one-hundredth anniversary of the Battle of Blood River, Afrikaner leader Henning Klopper called upon all able-bodied men to reenact the trek of independence. The journey from Cape Town to a hill outside Pretoria, a distance of about one thousand miles, would take five months. They built nine ox-carts, a powerful Afrikaner symbol of determination, and named them after nine Afrikaner heroes. Thousands joined in along the route, coming from all corners of South Africa. When they reached the mountains near Pretoria, the leader said, "Unhitch the oxen and use your own brawn to pull the carts to the top." The Afrikaner women said, "If the men cannot do it, we will." That is the steel of the Voortrekker women backing up their men. The men dismantled the ox-carts and carried them on their backs over the mountains. Lucy and I visited those steep mountains, and looking up at them I wondered how the Afrikaners did it—how they pulled ox-carts straight up toward the sky. Such is the strength of the Afrikaner character. The Voortrekker Monument that now sits atop the hill is a national shrine to Afrikaners and a patriotic shrine to Afrikanderom as "a nation of heroes."

Alan was on the trek and gave me an eyewitness account. He was an English-speaker, of British descent, but he had allied himself with the Afrikaners out of a sense of justice, he said. He empathized with what the Afrikaners had suffered at the hands of the British. Like many of the men on the trek, he grew a huge beard for the march. Once they reached the pinnacle of the Voortrekker Hill, Alan said, the leader delivered an impassioned sermon about preserving the Afrikaner Volk and being masters of their destiny. Alan said that the men were crying, shedding tears of thankfulness that Klopper had led them through the wilderness the way Moses had led his people out of Egypt. Alan shed tears, too, he said, but his were tears of frustration because in that sermon he heard a doctrine of hatred. "They were determined to build a nation based on hate," he said. They hated the British, and they hated nonwhites, and when they came to power they would discriminate against all nonwhites. "Then I turned around and walked back down that hill," Alan told me. "I went back to my home in Diepkloof and shaved off my beard and there I began to write *Cry the Beloved Country*." We were sitting in his backyard when he told me this story, and I was in tears, too. I was learning something totally new to me. I was in a milieu that I never knew existed.

In 1938, the Afrikaners began to take their destiny in hand. They established their own bank, the *Volkskas* or People's Bank, and urged all Afrikaners to deposit their money there, even if it was only shillings. The *Volkskas* grew into an important economic institution. They created Afrikaner businesses that catered to Afrikaners; Sanlaam, one of the world's most successful conglomerates, emerged. They infiltrated the civil service, starting at the lowest level, and the school system. Eventually they decreed that only Afrikaans would be taught in the schools. In protest, a significant number of young black students left school, an action that would have dire consequences because it created a generation of uneducated citizens. The Afrikaners' intent to gain control was based on their belief that they were God's chosen people. By 1948, their political party, *Herenigde* [Reunited] National Party, campaigned on a platform of complete racial separation and won the elections. It became known as the National Party. For the first time in the history of South Africa, every minister of state was an Afrikaner. One of the first actions they took was to oppose missionary schools in the black townships. Then they took the Coloured people off the voter rolls. (The blacks had never had the right to vote.) Mixed marriages were prohibited, and sexual relations between whites and non-whites were banned. Hendrik Frensch Verwoerd, who later became prime minister, developed a diabolical scheme of a multi-racial and segregated society with whites at the top of the pyramid, Asians (Indians) next, followed by Coloureds, and with blacks at the bottom. Verwoerd was the architect of complete apartheid, one of the most evil social experiments in the history of the world, and he did it with the Afrikaners' fervent belief that God favored them and their racial supremacy. Few things in this world are harder to combat than homeland patriotism and religious belief. In South Africa, the two were intertwined in Afrikanerdom. This is what I was up against.

Presenting Credentials

My first order of business was to present my credentials to the president of South Africa. Until this protocol was recognized, my activities were limited. It was rumored that President Botha would keep me waiting for two or three months before receiving my credentials, but someone talked him out of it. Within a day of my arrival, I was invited to take my credentials to the foreign minister, which is procedure. He also invited news reporters and television cameras to publicize his reception of the black ambassador. A week later, I was asked to present my credentials to the president. The ceremony was lavish and formal.

I wore a gray top hat, black morning coat with swallowtails, striped pants, a pearl vest, and a four-in-hand silver tie. Lucy looked smashing in a long dress with hat and gloves. We rode with a motorcycle escort from the residence to the Union Buildings, the administrative center of government. The Union Buildings, magnificent, towered, and built with local red sandstone, were designed by the celebrated British architect Sir Herbert Baker. I was accompanied by my deputy chief of mission and the next senior officer, who was the counselor for economic affairs. President Botha, similarly dressed in formal attire, was waiting outside on the stairs, flanked by an honor guard consisting of two military companies, one white and one black. As I stepped out of the car, the band played the South African anthem, "Die Stem," and then the United States national anthem. I had been thoroughly briefed by Allen Harvey, chief of protocol, and as instructed, I removed my top hat and handed it to an attendant on the first step. I was then to proceed up three steps to where Botha stood. With him were two governmental officials who, like South Africa itself, were radical contrasts. One was the director general of the Foreign Affairs Department, a true professional who was a pleasure to work with. The other was General Jannie Roux, minister for presidential affairs, a fiendish despot of black South African prisoners.

In formal attire for my presentation of credentials as U.S. ambassador to South Africa. An official photograph of me with officials of the Nationalist government. (*left to right*) Director General of the Ministry of Foreign Affairs P. R. Killen; me in swallow-tail coat; State President P. W. Botha, *die groot krokodil* (the big crocodile); and Jannie Roux, South African minister for presidential affairs, one of the cruelest men I have ever met.

President Botha was standing one step above me. I suspect that the ceremony was choreographed so that he would tower over me and I would look up at him, but he is a short man and we stood looking one another straight in the eye. I was determined not to avert my gaze until he did. Tradition called for me to deliver a short set speech as I handed him my credentials. As I did so, he had to look down to avoid dropping them. When he did, he lost the staring contest.

One of the formal photographs taken after the presentation appeared in *Time* magazine. A polite little ceremony of conversation followed in an antechamber. On this occasion, the politeness was all mine. The air was electric, and I could feel an immediate dislike emanating from the president. My officers were not allowed to accompany me, but General Roux and the director general joined us, sitting on either side of Botha.

I began the conversation. "Mr. President, I am delighted to be here. Our two countries have a lot in common . . ." He stopped me.

"What do you mean, 'a lot in common?' How can you say that? Your Congress just declared economic warfare on my country. But not your president. He's a good guy."

"Mr. President, Congress represents the people of the United States."

"No people could be represented by such a stupid group," Botha said.

"Nevertheless, Mr. President, they are the representatives of the people." I could see that my remark made him angry, the first flash of raw anger. I was not surprised. Despite the institution of apartheid, the Afrikaner leaders before him had been well-educated men. Botha was not, and he distrusted academics. He ascended to his position as a ward politician, wielding bicycle chains to make sure that the party people obeyed. He was a toughie who wanted to be respected as a leader.

"I am glad to be here," I continued. "I expect to travel a lot in South Africa. I want to get to know all of the people."

"I don't want you getting involved in our affairs," Botha said.

"I represent the people of the United States to the people of South Africa. Until I get to know them, I don't think I can adequately represent my country."

He stuck his finger in my face. "Didn't I tell you that I don't want you to get involved in our affairs?" His two aides were shaking because they realized he had gone beyond the norms. When he put his finger in my face, it was like putting his finger in Reagan's face. He ranted on before he finally caught himself and ended the meeting. "Well, Mr. Ambassador, welcome to South Africa. Thank you very much. That is all." That was my first encounter with him. As I left I said to myself, "This is going to be a very unpleasant tour of duty." I had come face to face with the Afrikaners, their government, and their determination to keep their system of apartheid.

I did not see Botha for another two months, until we were in Cape Town at a banquet for the opening of Parliament. Botha was in the formal receiving line, and when I reached him, he turned baleful eyes on me and said, "Hello, Ambassador. How are you finding our country?" I had begun to make good my word to make my presence known in all walks of life in South Africa, and he knew it.

"I am getting to know the people of South Africa, Mr. President," I replied. I said nothing else and took my seat.

After the presentation of credentials in Pretoria, my first outing was a walk around the neighborhood. I met no whites. I later learned that some of the neighbors had circulated a petition trying to prohibit black people from coming to the ambassadorial residence or from using the swimming pool, the tennis courts, or the barbecue pits. They were prepared to treat me as an honorary white—as long as I did not abuse the privilege. Despite arthroscopic surgery, my knees were in terrible condition and walking was difficult. Still, every day I increased my walks farther out of the neighborhood. I never met a white. Except for the Afrikaner head gardener, the entire staff at the residence was black—the butler from Malawi, the cook, and the two stewardesses. The white people had mysteriously disappeared from the neighborhood.

I had grown up in a country that had a hard time overcoming racism, so I was not unfamiliar with separateness, but this was new to Lucy. More than anything else, she was concerned for me. She knew that I was in the spotlight, and she expected harm to come to me. Although she was never fully at ease with my actions, she knew, perhaps better than anybody else, that I had to do it. Never once did she suggest an alternative course. She was always there supporting me.

MAKING POLICY
IN SOUTH AFRICA

After my presentation of credentials, only about a month remained before breaking camp and moving to Cape Town for the legislative session. I spent some of that time calling on the ministers of the South African government, but my priority was meeting extensively with my country team to formulate and formalize the embassy's policymaking and lay out the first phases of our change-agent strategy.

"We are in a proactive fight together," I told the country team. "We will write the script as we go along." I repeated what President Reagan had said to me about making policy in the embassy. "This puts a great burden on all of us," I said, "because we are on the firing line. One false move can mean the end of my career, but more important than that, it will affect the way the United States operates in this part of the world for a long time. So, we cannot fail." After that, I never worried about my career.

I explained that I was wedded to the concept of conflict resolution. Despite the spreading violence and the magnitude of activities that denied the rights of a large body of its citizens, I still believed that the situation in South Africa could be settled peacefully. Toward that end, I introduced the theories of Sun Tzu, Miyamoto Musashi, Martin Luther King Jr., and Mahatma Gandhi.

The country team was extraordinarily accomplished. The three who were especially valuable to me in forming policy were Robert Frasure, Karl Beck, and Tim Bork. I wanted to understand both black and white South Africans, so I asked the country team to talk with me about the system of apartheid. Although I had read about it, members of my staff—especially Frasure, Bork, and Beck—were the people on the ground. They had seen apartheid in action.

Bob Frasure, my gifted political counselor, was the key. He knew more about the Afrikaners than anyone at the embassy. From the foothills of West Virginia, Bob received a doctorate in history from Duke University and had been an Africa watcher at the London Embassy before going to South Africa. I was always surprised at his tolerant attitude toward both the Afrikaners and the blacks, but perhaps that came from his background of living among coal miners, who often had a hand-to-mouth existence. Bob was the shrewdest analyst on the country team and asked me forthrightly at that first policy meeting if Crocker, Shultz, and President Reagan would support me. "Secretary Shultz, yes," I said. "Crocker— I am not sure. As for the president, I intend to take him at his word."

Karl Beck, a fantastic counselor for black political affairs, thoroughly understood the workings of the United Democratic Front (UDF), which was the largest antigovernment group in South Africa. He was an indispensable link to both the UDF and the African National Congress (ANC). From Fort Myers, Florida, and of German extraction, Karl was one of the most successful directors in the history of the Peace Corps. In the late 1970s, his Peace Corps tours included Togo and southern Africa (Botswana and neighboring states). He knew the objectives of the Peace Corps program and the needs of the countries and societies of his beat, and he spoke the languages, including Zulu and Xhosa. He had an excellent background for our work in South Africa.

Tim Bork, the USAID director, was a white lawyer from Chicago who had worked in the American Civil Rights movement and was so liberal that Crocker considered him rather radical. Tim was passionately committed to eliminating the apartheid system and supporting activists. He was so energetic in his work that sometimes I had to rein him in. He had a tendency to be a loose cannon, and occasionally this landed him in a contentious relationship with the rest of the country team. On one trip back to the United States, he paid a courtesy call on the assistant secretary of state for African affairs. "I had a hell of a meeting with Crocker," he told me when he returned to South Africa, and he certainly had. Chet had already called to tell me about it. Sparks had flown between measured Crocker and this fervent Foreign Service officer who believed passionately in social, political, and economic equality for the downtrodden. In his ardent fight for racial equality, Tim did not always recognize the conservative mindset of the administration, and he found it hard to trust the promises made to me by President Reagan. He was dispirited after the meeting. I told him that every perceived obstacle is a plus if he could see Sun Tzu's brilliant philosophy: "to win without fighting." It had taken me years to learn this theory and here I was asking Tim to learn and practice it now. Nevertheless, he buckled down and proved equal to the task.

Elizabeth (Liz) Pryor, press attaché, became the spokesperson for the embassy. When I arrived, a lot of people were speaking for the embassy. I stopped that. "We will have one voice," I said, "and that voice will be the ambassador. Speaking for the ambassador will be the press attaché." I issued a classified memorandum to the staff reiterating this new policy. Immediately, one of the voices that had been rattling in public leaked the memo to the *Christian Science Monitor*, which reported it in an article headlined "Ambassador Perkins Suppresses Press Freedom?" My reaction was to immediately declassify the memorandum and have it distributed to the entire press corps, taking the air out of that balloon.

For the first six months, I did not hold press conferences, but I gave Liz the responsibility of preparing statements when I was required to speak without a prepared text. With my approval, those statements became our policy statements of record. When speaking to the public at large I wanted to make four points: that the United States stands for (1) individual rights, (2) political freedom, (3) observance of human rights, and (4) due process of law. Afrikaners were famous for saying, "It is the law." My reply was to differentiate between just laws and unjust laws, quoting Martin Luther King Jr. "When is a law unjust? When it does not square with the teachings of Jesus Christ." The Afrikaners interpreted scripture to support apartheid, so we had to go one step further and elucidate Christ's teachings.

Norma Jaegar, my dedicated secretary who had followed me from Liberia, was an American of German descent, stubborn, efficient, and committed to my objectives. Norma was castigated by the Afrikaners. "How can you work for a black man?" she was asked repeatedly, but she was stoic and stayed the course. She became a sister to me.

The country team also included Ray Snider, a superb white politics officer; Jerry Rose, administrative counselor; and Gene Friedmann, the public affairs counselor and a solid staff member, but who was not accustomed to innovative thinking about the huge problem facing us.

Richard Barkley, deputy chief of mission, was most unlike the others, and that was his strength on the team. He played the devil's advocate and voiced opinions that contrasted with mine, which is what I wanted. Dick was a highly intelligent Foreign Service officer, but his shortcoming was a quick temper.

For a while I had a special assistant, Steve McGann, a black Foreign Service officer who asked to go to South Africa with me. He served as secretary to the policymaking group, and his job was to record minutes of meetings and draft them into a policy memorandum for circulation to the country team. I would conclude that he was the wrong person for the job of special assistant, and he returned to the United States a year later. He was not the only one.

Security officers tend to be conservative. My first security officer in South Africa disagreed with my policy of change, which he believed would exacerbate violence in the country. When his tour was up, he was transferred to Tokyo. The next person to question the policy changes was the senior defense attaché, a colonel in the U.S. Army. He first indicated his feelings one morning in staff meeting by saying that the Afrikaners would never accept political change. I wondered how much of this statement referred to his personal feelings. Then he expressed his concerns outside the embassy, saying, "The ambassador is leaning too much toward the blacks, but don't worry about it. There are some of us who don't agree with him." That shortened the colonel's days of service with me. Some months later, when I was back in the United States to report in, I learned that the colonel had censured one of his officers for being too close to some of the black South Africans and had criticized and sabotaged my policy to the military chiefs. I knew that of all people, as a U.S. military officer, he should have understood the need for respecting orders and the chain of command, and for voicing objections in private. I picked up the phone and called the Pentagon, reported the problem, and said that I wanted the colonel moved in two weeks. Upon my return to South Africa, the colonel asked to see me to negotiate a later departure. I would not meet him, and I let him know that he had burned his bridges himself and the sooner he got out of the country the better. I never saw him again.

I inherited an embassy staff of some seven hundred employees. The majority were white, but I wanted the embassy to be a model employer with a multiracial staff doing all kinds of jobs in the U.S. mission. I did not want to employ blacks only as chauffeurs, so among those we hired was a black researcher. The first time the researcher went to the Pretoria public library on a job of research for the embassy, he was refused admission. I sent word to the library that not only was he a member of the U.S. Embassy, he was also a South African, which authorized him to use the public library. If the library had a problem with this, I told them, I would like to hear from them. After that, we never had any trouble with library use.

Housing for our multiracial staff was a problem. The Comprehensive Anti-Apartheid Act of 1986, which guided our activities in South Africa, authorized the American government to support the buying of homes in white areas by embassy employees, white and nonwhite alike. When the foreign minister of the South

African government heard through the grapevine that we intended to do this, he summoned me to his office. It would not work for black employees to buy homes in white neighborhoods, he told me, and he began to offer a compromise.

"No, Minister," I said, "this will not be acceptable to the Congress."

"These things take time," he said. "We cannot go too fast. Our people need time to become accustomed to the idea."

"It is the law of the land, Mr. Minister," I said. "I am bound by the oath I took to support any black South African employee of my embassy who normally would not be able to purchase property. The idea is to integrate the housing areas, plain and simple."

He protested that we were getting involved in internal affairs, and he was correct. We were deliberately getting involved in internal affairs, because the United States policy was to push for political change in South Africa.

I included everyone in the embassy, including the subordinate officers, in that policy. "Everybody has to act as a change agent," I told them. I made sure that every American employee had a chance to read the letters from the president and the secretary of state affirming that it was my job to make policy from the embassy. Then I assigned all of them to geographical segments of the country. One of the rules I established was that the embassy was to be seen as intolerant of segregated establishments, especially in Pretoria. "I will take it as an act of unfaithfulness if any American knowingly patronizes a place that will not serve blacks," I said. The word soon got around to the eating establishments, and many called to assure us that they served everybody.

We sent frequent round-up cables to Washington under the heading "How We See South Africa Today." These cables reported what I had done, what effect it had, and what our strategy would be. We reported to Washington, but we did not ask for concurrence, although that did not keep Washington from reacting to those cables.

I kept a low profile my first few months in South Africa, but with the counsel of the country team I decided to attend two church services in the Pretoria area. The first was a Catholic church. I made sure that nobody called ahead to notify the church that I was coming. When the priest later told me that he would liked to have announced my presence, I replied that was not the purpose of my visit. "I am a Catholic and I wanted to attend Mass," I said. "I probably need it now more than ever."

My second church appearance was entirely different. "I need to make an appearance at some event to convey the message that I expect to be in touch with every element of South African society," I told the country team.

"Why not go to an Afrikaner church?" suggested Gene Friedmann. This would be my first political act. We planned it carefully.

The Afrikaner church we chose was in the black township of Mamelodi, a church pastored by the Reverend Nico Smith, a remarkable dominee and a social activist. He was one of three high-ranking officials in the Dutch Reformed Church who had taken the controversial and courageous stand that apartheid was not in accord with the teachings of Jesus Christ. The other two were Beyers Naudé and Johan Heyns.

We decided that it was unfair not to warn the dominee that I was coming. I would take no entourage; it would be just Lucy, the driver, and me. I finally conceded that the embassy security officer could accompany me, although his presence would do little good if somebody were intent on doing me in. As a rule, Lucy and I visited, shopped, and traveled in South Africa without body-guards, unless it was known that we would be involving ourselves in a life-and-death situation.

We arrived at the service to discover that the dominee had invited a German television station, whose crew recorded my first important outing in South Africa. After the service, they told me they suspected their film would be con-fiscated and asked me to transport it for them. "No, I cannot do that," I told them. "I did not object to your being present, and I have given you some good statements, but you can't ask this of me. There are some things I will not vio-late and this is one of them. We must all take our chances." They understood. My appearance at a Dutch Reformed Church in a black township with a pastor who disavowed apartheid astonished the South African government. It signaled that I really did intend to meet all segments of South African society.

THE PROBLEMS AND THE PEOPLE

We began to shape our policy by first identifying the problems and the people we were dealing with in South Africa.

The problems were legion, but I did not want to scatter our political ammu-nition. I wanted every action to be directed toward a target. We decided to focus our attention initially on those issues that were particularly offensive:

* THE DISAPPEARANCE OF BLACK CHILDREN. One of the most odious police practices was the arrest of children under the age of eighteen. Children often were jailed for throwing rocks at the armored military vehicles, called mosquitoes. Officials then refused to tell their frantic families where they were being detained. Earlier that year, a government official admitted that more than 13,000 people were detained. Some estimates said the actual number was closer to 30,000. Whatever the factual number, a high proportion of those detainees were children.

* THE ASSASSINATION AND PROSECUTION OF REVOLUTIONARIES. Frustrated by the growing agitation, the repressive government was determined to wipe out revolutionary voices. In 1984, 922 blacks in the townships were killed by South African police, soldiers, and undercover agents. In 1985, the number of fatalities had risen to 1,352 and in 1986, it was almost 3,000. When I arrived, 5,500 people were in jail as political prisoners.

* THE INVASION OF BLACK TOWNSHIPS. The Afrikaner government was acting in a fury, like a swarm of maddened bees. In one swoop, it would forcibly remove an entire community from one area to another. Some black township homes were nothing but makeshift cane shacks, but that was everything the family had in the world. Whenever we learned of a forced removal, we sent an embassy officer to be present and to witness the action. The officer did not speak, just stood by silently, writing observations in a notebook. Often that presence alone was enough to stall the removal, but inevitably the authorities returned when nobody from the embassy was there.

Understanding South Africa's people was more complex than identifying the problems. I set out to meet representatives from the four separate races as legally defined in South African society: whites (Afrikaners and English-speakers), Indians, Coloureds, and blacks. The Population Registration Act carefully distinguished among the races, using a series of absurd tests when racial origin was questionable. The pencil test, for example, involved putting a pencil in a person's hair. If the pencil stayed in place because the hair was kinky, the person was classified as nonwhite. The person was declared white if the pencil fell out, because evidently the hair was straight. After the Population Registration Act of 1950, every South African citizen was identified ethnically.

The intent was to separate the races "from buses to bed." Prime Minister

Hendrik F. Verwoerd did not equivocate. "Let me be very clear about this," he said in 1961. "When I talk of the nation of South Africa, I talk of the white people of South Africa. I do not say that in disparagement of any other racial group in South Africa. I do not see us as one multiracial state descending from various groups." Verwoerd was such a fervent Afrikaner that he was described as a xenophobe. In the 1930s, years before he began separating the races in South Africa, he opposed Jewish immigration from Nazi Germany. Verwoerd was a native of the Netherlands who migrated to South Africa as a toddler in 1903 with his parents. He became a professor of psychology at Stellenbosch University, minister of native affairs in 1950, and prime minister from 1958 to 1966, when he was assassinated. Verwoerd's name is inscribed in history as the man who designed apartheid and then legislated it into the most iniquitous form of social engineering in the post–World War II world.

In 1976 the South African government revoked citizenship from the blacks and assigned them citizenship in Homelands. In 1984, a new constitution established three houses of parliament—one for whites (178 members), one for Coloureds (85 members), and one for Indians (45 members.) The blacks, the majority population, were excluded. The state president was given responsibility for the control and administration of black affairs. Even to this day, I cannot understand why the Afrikaner government did this and why they did not account in some way for the blacks in South Africa. They could not ignore the Indians because they had been brought to the country, albeit by the British. They could not ignore the Coloureds because they were a part of them. The blacks, however, were relegated to citizenship in the Homelands. The Afrikaners attempted to render them invisible.

This blatant exclusion was the torch that ignited South African blacks into revolution. It convinced the ANC that the Afrikaners intended to eliminate blacks as a force, politically and economically, in South Africa and that they had to take matters into their own hands. The Coloureds were aware that they were living on borrowed time; the Indian parliamentarians I met were cautious and did not say much; but black leaders saw that the future was closed to them. The Afrikaners had sealed their doom. That was when revolutionary violence increased.

Classifying the multihued populace by race was a nightmare. An early crude method used the terms "general appearance" and "repute." Families were divided, marriages were declared illegal, and siblings were classified into different races. In the mid 1960s, the government was trying to classify some 150,000 cases described as "borderline."

I knew that Coloureds were the issuance of three hundred years of liaisons between black tribes and white people (European colonists, Malay, and Indonesian slaves). Much as the U.S. blacks in the southern states had been classified by blood degree, South Africa's Coloured population was divided into seven categories: Cape Coloured, Cape Malay, Grigua, Indian, Chinese, "Other Asiatic," and "Other Coloured."

Under apartheid, Coloureds had a marginally better status than blacks and this allowed them to have slightly higher quality homes, jobs, and educations. The prevailing question was whether or not the Coloureds were comfortable with the prospect of living under a black government. Some Coloureds I had met in the Mitchell's Plain township near Cape Town said they would not like to live under a black government and that they were satisfied with the *status quo*. "That is because you are not on the bottom rung of society," I told them.

"Why are you people making all this trouble?" one Coloured man asked me.

"You are completely oblivious to the fact that 28 million blacks are at the bottom of this arrangement," I said. Despite the protestations I heard at Mitchell's Plain, many Coloureds were activists in the revolution and some, such as Allan Boesak, were heroes of the struggle.

The largest Indian community outside of India is in South Africa's Natal Province. Indians were considered the second in the racial tier, a step up from the Coloureds and one step below the whites, which was the top tier. Where did the Indians stand on apartheid? I knew the history of the Indian population in South Africa. In 1860, after the Chinese laborers in the sugarcane fields had rebelled and were sent back to China, workers had been brought from India to work as indentured laborers, scarcely more than slaves. In the next few decades, the exploited Indian immigrants found employment as free workers in mines, gardens, and railroads and as domestic servants, but they were segregated into selected areas and even expelled from the province of the Orange Free State. In the early 1890s, a young lawyer named Mahatma Gandhi arrived to practice law. Before he left in 1913, he helped build the Natal Indian Congress and the Transvaal British Indian Association and established the *Indian Opinion* newspaper. He also led two historic resistance movements, one of which galvanized sixty thousand Indian laborers into the first mass strike of Indian workers. I was coming full circle— working on the same soil where Gandhi had initiated passive resistance, a movement that inspired Martin Luther King Jr.'s philosophy of civil disobedience, and using King's writings as my inspiration.

✭

The white race in South Africa contains two classifications, Afrikaners and English-speakers. The Afrikaners were more numerous, but English-speakers played a prominent role, especially in the country's economy. I first saw the Afrikaners—the great white tribe of Africa—as an almost inscrutable mystery. Our opponent seemed to be Afrikanerdom, whose Dutch Reformed Church and Broederbond were, with the South African government, a tangled force. Yet the more I understood the country, the more I realized that English-speakers, a term for white South Africans of British ancestry, were equally culpable. The English-speakers were newcomers compared to native black Africans and Afrikaners, who both justifiably claimed ownership of the land. The behavior of the British in the Boer War had so embittered indigenous blacks and Afrikaners that this historic moment appeared to be the headwater of apartheid. Afrikaners had given up their European connection, but English-speakers were considered to have one foot on the continent of Europe and one foot in South Africa. Every English-speaker was thought to have two passports. I never heard Afrikaners use the word "British." They called them "English-speaker," which meant people who spoke English, did not bother to learn Afrikaans, and still clung to the European continent. Most Afrikaners I met were suspicious of English-speakers. Sampie Terreblanche, the head of the economics department at Stellenbosch University, explained it to me this way: "Ambassador, I trust a British person about as long as a sand castle lasts in an oncoming wave. What the British did to us we will never forget."

On the surface, most English-speakers supported change, but I believe the prospect dismayed them. When the United Party lost the election of 1948 and it became clear that the Afrikaners were going to govern, the English-speakers appeared to make a pact with the devil. They conceded political power to the Afrikaners while they held tightly to the economic, entrepreneurial, and managerial power of the country, keeping their large farms, fortunes, and easy life. Unspoken was this English-speakers' sentiment: Let the Afrikaners keep the blacks in their place and take the heat for it. Our hands will be clean.

And yet courageous individuals, both Afrikaners and English-speakers, were active in the struggle. The Black Sash, a white South African women's organization, was adamantly, even militantly, opposed to apartheid. Since 1955 this group had held demonstrations, night vigils outside of Parliament, and protest marches and had established advice centers. Many of their protests targeted the government legislation of pass laws and forced removal of black communities. In the days of the Public Order Law, which prohibited speech-making, the Sash discovered a potent way to make their presence felt. They stood quietly, shoulder to shoulder, outside a minister's office, wearing their black sashes across their chests as a symbol of shame, grief, and protest. It was more effective than carrying placards, and it was intimidating to the authorities because it attracted publicity.

Nelson Mandela called the Black Sash "the conscience of white South Africa." One of the founders of the Black Sash was English-speaker Jean Sinclair, who served as its president for fourteen years. I knew her daughter, Sheena Duncan, an indomitable fighter who succeeded her mother as president of the organization and then headed an advice center, becoming active in the Anglican Church's Challenge Group. Sheena supported international economic sanctions as a persuasive force more powerful than company divestment, and she criticized the South African business community for its long silence about apartheid. "Apartheid has been in the interests of profits all along," she said, but business began to feel the pressure of economic sanctions and the refusal of international banks to roll over South African loans. In 1987, Sheena said the women of the Black Sash planned to dig their own graves and say, "We will stand beside our graves because we are not moving from here. You can shoot us, and we will lie in our land forever." That quote became famous.

Mary Burton was president of the Black Sash when I was in South Africa. She was born in Buenos Aires, Argentina, married a South African, and in 1969 moved to South Africa, where she became a well-respected human-rights leader. "After a short while I just couldn't sit back any longer," she said. She began taking soup to the poorest black settlements and soon was involved in the Sash organization. She told me about another mission of the Sash: searching for the whereabouts of missing children whom the police had either picked up and jailed or killed. The women of the Sash were harassed and their families were threatened. They discovered that their phones were tapped and their mail tampered with, but they stood firm and began to gain international attention. The presence of these white women, standing in speechless protest, seemed to quell some of the police violence at black demonstrations.

Helen Suzman, a white Jewish South African, was for thirty-six years a courageous voice and the lone woman in Parliament. For thirteen years she was the sole representative of the Progressive Party, speaking in Parliament against racial injustice and the only voice demanding information about the missing children.

"How did you find the courage?" this tiny woman was asked. "I didn't need courage," she replied. "I needed stamina. I hate bullies." Recently, a cultivar rose was named for this woman, who was a thorn in the side of the apartheid government. The rose is not white, which would recall white oppression; nor is it red, which would suggest a different political affiliation; and certainly it is not yellow, the color of cowardice. The Helen Suzman Rose is creamy pink, described as hardy, almost invasive. She chose the variety herself.

The white society also included rebel dominees, thuggish governmental officials, and the indomitable Afrikaner women who appear, erroneously, almost translucently fragile. I astonished Chet Crocker when I told him that we needed to understand the Afrikaners in all of their manifestations. Nobody in the United States government had said that before. This philosophy is straight from Mao Tse-tung and Sun Tzu: it is necessary to understand the opposing force in order to find an opening for your troops. Toward this end, I studied Afrikaans, the Afrikaners' guttural language akin to Dutch and German. This surprised most everybody, but it is important to speak to people in their own language, if only to say, "Good morning."

I had received extensive briefings in Washington and in London from U.S. agencies, private organizations, and South Africans. "You will be considered the stooge of the Reagan administration," Deputy Secretary of State John White-head told me. "Very few will accord you any degree of trust," I was warned by activist Allan Boesak, a Coloured minister of the Dutch Reformed Church. Upon arrival I began consulting immediately with university professors, bureaucrats, sociologists, newspaper writers and editors, revolutionary leaders, religious leaders, and officials of the Afrikaner government. Yet nothing— neither the stacks of documents and books I read nor the hundreds of hours of briefings I received—nothing prepared me for the quagmire I walked into in South Africa.

First, I turned my attention to the black South Africans, the overwhelming majority of the population. It was immediately clear that we were dealing not with one black monolith but rather with a number of different kinds of people united by one common theme: the abhorrence of apartheid. There the similarity ended. The blacks of South Africa were of varied economic and social views. I met many black South Africans who extolled the virtues of socialism and criticized the capitalist philosophy of the United States. The black revolutionary groups were rife with splits and fissures. If they had been unified without political disagreements, I believe that by their sheer numbers they would have prevailed more easily. But the black organizations were far from a united voice.

One fissure was between the township elders and the younger blacks. The harsher the Afrikaners became, the more strident grew the voices of blacks in their teens and twenties. These young people said with gathering intensity that they had been betrayed by the older generations, who had not fought the South African government. Almost immediately after I landed in South Africa, I saw two examples of the violence that drove the black youths to their enraged stance. Both incidents involved an element of the South African Defense Force that was dedicated to discovering and destroying revolutionaries in South Africa and the Cordon Sanitaire—Mozambique, Angola, Zambia, Namibia, and the Caprivi Strip. "Take no prisoners" was the motto of the South African military in its determination to obliterate all opposition by the ANC and other revolutionary groups.

The first incident involved a black physician. According to South African law at the time, any doctor who treated a gunshot victim in a township was required to report the fact to the authorities. Gunshot wounds were an everyday occurrence in the townships as black youths fled from South African police and defense forces patrolling the areas. Despite repeated warnings, Dr. Fabian Defu Ribeiro in the Mamelodi township continued to treat gunshot victims without reporting them. One December afternoon, two white men in black face drove to the doctor's residence and rang the bell. When he opened the door, they killed him and his wife, Florence, with sawed-off shotguns. I attended the huge political funeral that was held for him. No one was ever brought to justice.

Across the border in Mozambique the following spring, Albie Sachs, a revolutionary and attorney forced into exile, was targeted by the "Kill Squad," the South African national security forces. In April 1988, he was working as an academic lawyer and holed up in a safe house when he became the victim of a car bomb. He lived, but he lost his right arm and the sight in one eye. Even then, he never abandoned his political ideals. After Afrikaners fell from power, Albie was appointed to the South African Constitutional Court of the new government.

South African state president Botha had made a promise to President Reagan: there would be no further raids across borders of the contiguous nations by the South African security forces seeking to eliminate members of the ANC operating in these nations. When Reagan learned that Botha had broken his word and continued the cross-border raids, he was so outraged that he called a secretary and dictated a letter to State President Botha right then. I was told over the phone that President Reagan was "pissed off." "I don't want this to go through the State Department," President Reagan said. "I want someone to hand-carry it to our ambassador, and I want him to take it to the state president. I don't want anyone else to see it." This was most unusual.

Ned McMann, a Foreign Service officer, brought it to me, flying in on a military plane. Ned had the letter in a briefcase locked onto his wrist. President Reagan did me the courtesy of sending me a copy in a separate envelope. The transmittal sheet to me from the assistant secretary was titled: "Subject—Hot Potato. The President directs you to hand-deliver the attached letter to President P. W. Botha as soon as you can get to see him." Ned's instructions were to return to Washington immediately, without waiting for a reply from the state president. This was a one-way communication. With much opposition and stalling from Minister of Foreign Affairs Pik Botha, I finally got an appointment with the state president, and Bob Frasure and I flew to Cape Town to make the personal delivery.

President Botha insisted on seeing me alone. In my presence, he opened the letter and read it. The letter from Reagan was short and direct: "We have learned that forces of South Africa crossed the border into a neighboring country recently and shot up a safe house, injuring a well-known activist. You promised me that this was never going to happen again. You have broken your promise. We cannot continue our relationship this way." Botha then unleashed a firestorm, rising from his desk chair and pointing his finger at me as he said, "I will answer this in my own way and in my own time, Mr. Ambassador. But you have been getting involved in our internal affairs. I told you when you first came here that I did not want you involved in our affairs, and yet I learn that you have been giving speeches against my government in the United States and in South Africa."

"Mr. President," I said, "have you got any reports of anything I said that was not the truth?"

At that, he erupted and literally lost control of himself. Once more jabbing a finger at me, he spat out the warning, "You are treading on dangerous ground, Mr. Ambassador. I do not want you involved in our affairs."

"Mr. President, I do not intend to do anything that breaches the bounds of diplomatic correctness."

He ranted and raved for about twenty minutes before he regained some semblance of composure, and then, still fuming, he dismissed me. I rose to leave, but at the door I turned to him.

"Mr. President?"

"What do you want?"

"Please have a nice day."

In the outer office, Botha's secretary, a navy captain, was trembling, and Bob was smiling. "Well," he said, "that's why you get to live in the big house and ride around in a Cadillac."

The former Deputy Chief of Mission Dick Barkley told me about one of his meetings with Botha. He and Herman Nickel, my predecessor, had been summoned to the state president's office in Pretoria. Both Americans are shorter men, and as they sat in the waiting room, their feet didn't touch the floor. Dick said they looked like schoolboys waiting to be scolded, and once inside the office, Botha was fierce with them. Whenever I met with Botha, I could see him wondering, "Why the hell can't I intimidate this guy?" One reason was that I was bigger than him, and that advantage gives a person a lot of confidence.

The young black revolutionaries of South Africa blamed the older generation for not protesting more forcefully. They would not make the same mistake, they declared. They would fight. These were the most militant teenagers I have ever seen anywhere. Many were practicing criminals. The most dangerous were the young comrades, street boys who had left school in protest when Afrikaans became the required language in education—they refused to speak the language of the oppressor. Across the country, they forced other students to drop out of school until thousands of youth ages thirteen and older were on the streets.

One of the Afrikaners' first governmental actions was to eliminate missionary schools in the townships. Education fell under the control of the South African government and Minister for Native Affairs Verwoerd. The Bantu Education Act of 1955 institutionalized an inferior school system for black students. In Verwoerd's cold and calculating world, black youth did not need education, because they would be limited to menial work for the white economy. He redesigned public education to keep them servile. "There is no place for the Bantu in the European community above the level of certain forms of labor." He instituted an educational system designed for the four races. Open universities were restricted to whites, and separate universities were created

for Indians, Coloureds, and blacks. In 1986, my staff showed me statistics that
painted a grim picture:

* White students were 100 times more likely to go to college than black
  students.
* 48 percent of white men finished high school, compared to 1.8 percent
  of black men.
* 200,000 whites were attending public schools, compared to 5,400
  blacks.
* 71 percent of the population was African and 15 percent white, yet 65
  percent of the education budget was being spent on white schools and
  only 16 percent on black.
* Teachers for the black institutions were inferior to those at white
  schools. Only 10 percent of the black teachers had completed high
  schools, and a mere 2.6 percent held a university degree. They were
  often less prepared than the students they were teaching.

The descriptions I heard of the black schools still in session were scenes of
terror. At a Soweto school, male students set aside one day for open sex in the
classroom. Teachers did nothing as couple after couple made use of the designated area. Parents did not want to know about it, the teachers said. From 1985
to 1987, violence in the classroom was acute. Students accosted, molested, and
raped teachers who found themselves helpless to protect themselves.

Ten years before I was on the scene, frustration and anger over black education set off township riots that shook the world. The riots began with a large
student march in Soweto in June 1976. Some 15,000 students gathered in
protest. State security ordered the crowds to disperse, then released police
dogs and tear gas. Students began throwing bottles and rocks, then the police
started firing. Soweto exploded. Coloured and Indian students joined forces
with their black peers. They set afire government buildings, buses, white-
owned vehicles, community centers, and municipal beer halls. The riots lasted
for three days and spread to Pretoria, Durban, and Cape Town. It was the
largest outbreak of violent revolt in South African history. Hundreds were
injured. The official number of dead was twenty-three, but some said fatalities
numbered two hundred. Like a mighty forest fire, the Soweto riot was never
fully extinguished. All through 1976, violence flared up in one area after
another. A decade later, I found the embers of that riot still combustible among
the new generation of protesters.

In every township I visited, I tried to meet community leaders, proactive groups, and the South African student organizations. I spent many futile hours with groups of angry young comrades in Soweto, Crossroads, Durban Umshlangu, Port Elizabeth, and the Western and Southern Capes. I tried to convince them to stay in school. "You will be the leaders of tomorrow," I told them. "You need education for that." Their stonewall response was, "Political freedom first, education second." The tragedy, as I predicted, came when it was time for them to lead the country. They were uneducated, untrained, and unprepared. They had not gone back to school, and their life on the street had grown into a way of life. When I visit South Africa now, almost two decades later, I see how this uneducated mass of citizens became a burden on the country. It continues to drain the treasury.

No wonder we made education, a foundation of society, one of our priorities in South Africa. We increased the number of scholarships for black South Africans to study abroad. Tim Bork was assigned the duty of managing the funding and awarding scholarships. "This government is going to disappear in five years," I told him. "Suppose you had to form a government. Who would be the ministers?" I suggested that he work with the black political organizations to develop a way of tracking the scholarship recipients for such an occasion. The United States provided the computer hardware and software for the record-keeping.

An unforeseen problem was the resistance to the scholarships abroad from some of the socialistic black youth. "Until we can all get the same kind of education, nobody should get one," said the young socialists. Those who went to the United States or Europe to study often came home to find themselves scorned by the uneducated revolutionaries. I told a group of young comrades, "Unless you are willing to subject yourself to the discipline of getting an education and respect what it will do for you, you won't win this revolution." Revolutionaries often look for deviants to be eliminated. They see the power in the masses, not in individualism. This is how the young comrades saw the education program. It was a hot subject, but we had to deal with it. I laid down the law: We have to get to know this important group of teenagers, and we have to encourage them to go back to school.

Meanwhile, I moved on to other black protest groups, trying to sort out the differences that separated the principal black organizations—the ANC, the Pan-Africanist Congress (PAC), the Azanian People's Organization (AZAPO), the Black

Consciousness Group, the influential South African Students Organization, the Congress of South African Trade Unions (COSATU), the South African Miner's Union, and the Free Mandela Movement, among others. All opposed apartheid, but they had differing philosophies, goals, and strategies. The only thing these black resistance groups seemed to have in common when I arrived was their animosity toward me as Reagan's appointee as ambassador to South Africa.

The PAC believed armed fighting was necessary in order to achieve a true revolution. The Black Consciousness Group, manifested by the martyr Steve Biko, believed in black power and a construct in which there was no place for whites in a future South African government. When I made a quiet visit to his grave near Fort Hare, I stood in the small cemetery thinking ruefully that Biko was one of many heroes I met only in posthumous tribute. His grave, so green and serene, was a sharp contrast to his furious life. I was told that his public speeches were mesmerizing.

I knew about Biko long before I went to South Africa. Even reading about him, I found myself almost in a trance. I was awed by his unbelievable leadership skills and fascinated by his weaknesses, which he made work for him. He had an overriding fascination with his own power, but he recognized that this would be disastrous unless he brought other strong people into his circle. In his short lifetime—he died in 1977 at age thirty, beaten to death while in the custody of the security police—Biko was a philosopher, revolutionary, and charismatic leader who contributed immeasurably to the success of the black-led revolutionary movement in South Africa. He was an inspiration to the young students in the townships.

The legacy of Steve Biko is that revolutions succeed through the deployment of successive waves of young people led by bold and imaginative leaders. What he gave the young blacks was a sense of pride and faith in themselves. "The black man has become a shadow of man," Biko said, "completely defeated, drowning in his own misery, a slave and ox bearing the yoke of oppression with sheepish timidity." He inspired the young blacks of South Africa to become a militant new generation fired by pride. Biko said that he found his own inspiration in the works of Frantz Fanon, Aime Cesaire, and Martin Luther King Jr. He was the first South African leader in my experience to acknowledge King's early teaching. The ANC was leery of Biko's visceral approach and avoided him, but Winnie Mandela was captivated by the angry young rebel. She was perhaps the only member of the ANC with the courage to see him. "He gave me spirit," she said. I believe that the South African government of the day feared Steve

Near King William's Town, I visited the grave of Steve Biko, martyr of the anti-apartheid movement.

Biko and Robert Sobukwe more than any other black leaders, and thus the government brutally eliminated both. Sobukwe, one of South Africa's great anti-apartheid leaders, was a university professor and the founding president of the Pan-Africanist Congress. After the Sharpeville Massacre of 1960, he was jailed for nine years and then banned (which meant being prohibited from attending gatherings, educational centers, or courts) for a total of ten years. South Africa official John Vorster said he intended to detain Sobukwe "until this side of eternity." Sobukwe died while still under house arrest. His philosophy was "There is only one race to which we all belong, and that is the human race."

The dominant group was the ANC, which had been formed when the British ruled South Africa. The ANC was led early on by Walter Inbusana, who founded the organization in 1909 and became its first president in 1912. Albert Luthuli, the first South African to win the Nobel Peace Prize, was later president. Oliver Tambo and Nelson Mandela also served as presidents. The ANC charter called for political enfranchisement of black South Africans, a government based upon universal suffrage, and a multiracial society. It also called for nationalization of South African resources and, by definition, equal distribution to all.

The ANC did not immediately unify a significant number of people or establish political power, but it progressed as if eventually it could influence South African political society. Its non-violent program of action included marches, strikes, boycotts, and other protests. Only God knows how the ANC stayed non-violent for so long. The lid blew off in 1960 in Sharpeville, where South African police fired on a peaceful protest crowd, killing 69 people and wounding 186. The Sharpeville Massacre received worldwide media coverage.

From that point, the ANC abandoned a campaign of only peaceful protests. The *Umkhonto we Sizwe* (MK), which translates as "Spear of the Nation," the militant branch of the ANC, was formed in 1961 to take up arms against the South African government. The MK was established by ANC leaders who had studied the theory of guerrilla warfare available at the time—the writings of Mao Tse-tung about the Chinese experience and the career of Che Guevara, with its lessons of the American experience. Both authors emphasized the importance of enlisting the support of the peasantry for a successful revolutionary war. I do not know if the founders of MK had read King's *Letter from Birmingham Jail*, but their philosophy mirrored King's words: "Freedom is never voluntarily given by the oppressor: it must be demanded by the oppressed." From there, their course of action diverged. Whereas King advocated non-violence, the MK was aggressive with the manifesto: "The time comes in the life of any nation when there remain only two choices: submit or fight." The mission of MK was to "hit back by all means within our power in defense of our people, our future, and our freedom." In eighteen months, MK carried out at least two hundred acts of sabotage.

The South African government retaliated. A national state of emergency was declared. The ANC, the PAC, and other organizations were banned, and ANC leaders such as Oliver Tambo and Lithuanian-born Joe Slovo went into exile. New laws were passed to punish terrorists and saboteurs. In 1963, the MK leadership was arrested and put on trial in the famous Rivonia Treason Trial that sentenced Mandela, Walter Sisulu, and Govan Mbeki to life imprisonment. Also sentenced were Raymond Mhlavi, Dennis Goldberg, Ahmed Katrada, Andrew Mlangeni, and Elias Motsualedi. Only Rusty Bernstein was acquitted.

In addition to these major revolutionary organizations, we identified a sizeable number of smaller groups—women's movements, black-township civic groups, church-based organizations, professional organizations, trade unions, and youth groups. A unifying umbrella for these movements was the United Democratic Front (UDF), organized in 1983 to represent people of all colors in the struggle. The UDF saw itself as a group of grassroots activists unified to champion the oppressed masses.

I persisted in trying to meet activists from all organizations, but it was essential to our work at the U.S. Embassy that we have direct contact with the ANC and the UDF so we could help these two revolutionary movements stay alive. Meeting these leaders became my focus.

Getting to know the blacks of South Africa was not as easy for me as one might have expected. Even before I left Washington, I received word that the black leaders of South Africa had decided not to meet with me. They considered Reagan to be anti-black and the Reagan administration's constructive engagement policy to be favorable to the Afrikaner government. President Reagan knew of this perception. "You have your work cut out for you," he told me.

One black leader in South Africa who was most determined to boycott me was Anglican Archbishop Desmond Tutu, Nobel Laureate and pastor of St. George's Cathedral in Cape Town. He refused my requests to call on him. So be it, I thought. I have too much work to do to let this slow me down.

I wanted to meet black people instrumental in the revolution, especially four key leaders who were in Soweto, the black township near Johannesburg: Aubrey Mokoena, Ntatho Motlana, Winnie Mandela, and Albertina Sisulu.

Aubrey Mokoena was head of the Free Mandela Committee in Soweto, a powerful political group. I found him to be unfriendly and not inclined to ally himself to me. I moved on.

Ntatho Motlana was Mandela's physician and chairman of the Soweto Committee of Ten and of the Soweto Citizens League, a highly charged political activist organization. Dr. Motlana told me about the organization's vow to not pay for municipal services until they improved. Although the South African government resorted to all kinds of trickery to get payment, it did not succeed. The Soweto Citizens League collected the money and put it into escrow.

His ex-wife, Sally Motlana, was a true freedom fighter who used the Anglican Church as a weapon in the revolution. She was instrumental in organizing the women of Soweto into self-sufficiency cottage industries.

Winnie Mandela, then wife of Nelson Mandela, was referred to as "Mother of the Nation." Trying to arrange a meeting with her was an ordeal. She enjoyed having me leap through hoops like a performing circus dog. After repeated phone calls and requests, I rebelled and put an end to the game. An interesting drama then occurred.

Most important was Albertina Sisulu, co-president of the UDF and wife of Walter Sisulu, who was imprisoned on Robben Island with Mandela and other revolutionaries. Whereas Winnie was flamboyant and pushed herself into the public eye, Albertina was the real leader of the Soweto community. Karl Beck, my black political officer, had begun to arrange my introduction to her even before I left Washington. That meeting was on my calendar when I arrived in Johannesburg. The South African government was stunned that I had broken protocol by arranging to meet her before I presented credentials. It was deliberate. Meeting Albertina demonstrated my intent to be active with the black revolutionary leadership. Setting off a cannon could not have sent a clearer message. The activist organizations took notice and the South African government began to consider me a serious annoyance.

Albertina is a short, unassuming woman, a nurse and midwife by training who visited her patients in the townships on foot, carrying her medical equipment in a case on her head. Her role in South African history belies her small stature and modest disposition—she was a towering figure in the black resistance. Although she stayed in the background, she galvanized the revolutionary movement in a quiet, iron-fisted way. While Walter devoted himself to organizing the ANC and was then imprisoned, Albertina supported their family, five children of their own and three adopted children. "All these years," she said, "I never had a comfortable life."

Beginning in 1958 she was jailed repeatedly by the South African government, banned for five years, and then under house arrest for ten years. "That was the worst," she said. Two of her children were also jailed and then exiled. While banned, she was confined to her home and restricted to limited contact with the outside world between the hours of 6 A.M. and 6 P.M., and no contact at all after 6 P.M. Despite the banning and house arrest, Albertina continued to hold resistance organization meetings at her home. Occasionally the government caught her, but usually she was too clever. Whenever anybody unknown approached her house in her village, the people in the meeting were alerted and melted away.

From prison, Mandela urged the black leadership to meet me, but Sisulu advised Albertina against it. Luckily for me, she ignored him and acted on her own. Within the first two weeks I was in South Africa, she came to the residence to dine. As she left that evening she said, "Mr. Ambassador, I guess you're wondering why I am here in view of the boycott of you by the black leaders. It is very simple. You are a black man. You can't be all bad." She never again mentioned the boycott and she invited me to call on her from time to time, which I did. The last time I saw the Sisulus was at their home in Johannesburg in 2002. Walter was frail, but mentally and politically astute as always. Before I left, he told me, "I was wrong to tell her not to meet you." Albertina was astounded. "He has never said that to me before now," she murmured.

From the time I set foot on South African soil, I petitioned the government to allow me to meet Mandela. I had a mandate from the Senate Foreign Relations Committee to see him and then to get him freed. My requests were always denied. "Keep trying," advised George Bizos, the lawyer for the Delmas Treason Trialists. "Contact anybody you can. Wide and deep are the contacts you must make." When I finally met with Winnie, one of the things she said was, "My husband urges you to keep trying to see him. Each time you make this request, it makes him a little more powerful in prison."

My interlocutor was Minister of Justice Kobie Coetsee. My repeated

When to her astonishment the South African government allowed Albertina Sisulu to visit the United States, then-Senator David Boren (*third from left, back row*) and his wife, Molly Shi Boren (*second from right, back row*), hosted a reception for her and her entourage at their home in Washington, D.C. Lucy is far right. Albertina is the woman in the black dress and pearls. I am standing right behind her.

requests to him for a visit to Mandela in prison always elicited the same reply:
"The time is not right, Mr. Ambassador." After several attempts, I told him that
Mandela was becoming very powerful in prison, and the time would come very
soon when the South African government would find it impossible to keep him
in jail. Coetsee scoffed at that statement. However, after Mandela's eventual
release, I saw the minister one more time before the elections in which Mandela was elected president. Coetsee said to me, "Mr. Ambassador, I want to
thank you for one thing. You have not said, 'I told you so.'"

MEETING WINNIE

I was trying just as relentlessly to arrange a meeting with Mandela's wife, Winnie, his window to the world. I could understand the difficulty in meeting
Mandela, because he was the government's prize prisoner. Winnie, however,
was living in Soweto, just miles away. She seemed to enjoy playing a cat-and-
mouse game with me. When I had enough of this runaround and stopped con-
tacting her, almost immediately she was ready for a meeting. After four months
of trying, I finally met Winnie in March 1987.

Just as the Voortrekker woman held the clan together, the black woman in
South Africa was the glue of the family, including the family of the political
organization. Although Winnie and Albertina were distinctly different personalities, each was a political activist par excellence. Albertina was strategically
careful and very good at both planning and executing activities. Winnie was a
reactionary with an innate understanding of the effect of words. Her speeches,
animated with expressive hand gestures, excited audiences and created a following for her, but she was an incautious speaker, and her incendiary statements got her into trouble. To say that Winnie was a contrast to Albertina is like
comparing firecrackers to firewood. Winnie was flash and fire; Albertina was
steady and warm.

Nelson was sent to jail soon after he and Winnie were married, and in the
eyes of many, Winnie was left carrying the torch. Slowly, the press made her
into an icon, but she was not prepared for that exalted position. Winnie is
beautiful, sensuous, intelligent, clever, strategic, diabolical, and cruel. Every
time I saw her, she was dressed in Fifth Avenue high fashion. Men flocked to her
like forbidden honey, and the press loved her. The media, one writer acknowledged, "baptized her in the font of publicity." About the time I got to know her,
Newsweek magazine described her this way: "'Mother of the Nation,' Joan of

Arc, the Black Madonna. Winnie thrived on the celebrity. She was and is deeply charismatic, feisty, proud, photogenic, everything that a fearless fighter of injustice should be."

Winnie was high on the list of South African black leaders that Washington recommended I see immediately. Other black leaders might not meet with me, I was told, but she would. "She knows you are coming," her emissary told me. "She knows you want to talk with her." After her repeated delays, our meeting was finally arranged with theatrical intrigue. A black businessman in Johannesburg approached me at the Carlton Hotel and said, "If you and your driver go past her house next Tuesday about ten o'clock, she may be out in her garden."

At the appointed time, Edison drove to her house in Orlando in Soweto, and there was Winnie standing in her garden, dressed as a fashion model and holding a trowel in her hand like a prop. I asked Edison to stop, got out of the car, and addressed the lady in the yard. "I do believe that you are Mrs. Mandela," I said. She replied in silky tones, "And I believe that you must be the new American ambassador. Welcome. It is so nice to have you here in our country." During our conversation of about thirty minutes, she said, "My husband wants me to convey to you his best wishes and to tell you that he is pleased with the work you are doing. . . . If you want to communicate anything to him," she told me, "let me know, and I will get the message to him."

The next time I saw Winnie was at a function in Johannesburg where she was accepting an honorary degree on behalf of Nelson. As usual, she was accompanied by bodyguards, which the press called her football team. They were young men dressed in the ANC colors of green, yellow, and black. She saw me in the audience and floated over to me—Winnie never hurried—to chat for a few minutes.

She gave a good speech that night. "I have been asked to receive this on behalf of my husband," she said, "but I can't do it. The men here who represent the leadership of the struggle are not yet ready for a woman to play a prominent role like this. Just ask them. For that reason, I have asked Cyril Ramaphosa to accept the honor on behalf of my husband." At that time, Cyril was president of the National Union of Mineworkers, a powerful trade union.

Winnie's talk in Johannesburg was quite a contrast to an infamous speech she gave previously in Soweto. I have a recording of that reckless speech. "All traitors will be dealt with," she said. "We will necklace them." A "necklace" was the punishment for those deemed to be traitors to the cause; a tire filled with gasoline was placed around the neck of the traitor and set afire. Several people in Soweto lost their lives through necklacing. The necklace speech haunted Winnie. It was the beginning of her non-acceptance by the leaders in the ANC and the UDF. Some black political activists urged Mandela to banish her, to divorce her, or to distance her from the organization, but he would not do it. "She stood by me," he said. "She comes to visit me. I am with her all the way."

The event that would fatally destroy Winnie's public reputation was the murder of teenager Stompie Moeketsi Seipei in the late 1980s. She met Stompie when she was banned in Bloemfontein in the Orange Free State. Although not much more than a child, he became a young freedom fighter and one of her loyal fans until he fell out of favor. About this time, rumors circulated that Winnie was involved in the murders of several people whom she had declared traitors to the cause. She stood as judge and jury of their guilt and their fate. Stompie was one of those she accused of betrayal. It was said that not only did she order his death, she took a knife and dealt the fatal blow herself. Supposedly, to shift the blame, she concocted a scenario that required the help of a Coloured doctor in Soweto. He refused to cooperate and reportedly lost his life because of it. Winnie was brought to trial for the death of Stompie and was convicted and fined, but not jailed. The question lingered: Why did a white judge dispense such a light sentence? I believe that the judge thought she would have become an even greater champion of the people if jailed, so he freed her to let the ANC and other black people render their own justice. Winnie's dream was to become president of South Africa, but her credibility there was damaged beyond repair. She traveled back and forth to the United States, where some black Americans adopted her as a heroine. I have never met anyone quite like Winnie. The only woman in history I might compare her to politically is Cleopatra.

When I was growing up on a Louisiana farm, I learned the difference between edible plants and those you could not touch. Two plants were particularly dangerous: poison ivy and poison oak. Poison ivy is easily recognizable, but poison oak is difficult to identify until you see the flowers or the fruit. The flowers are seductive, and the fruit is almost humanly sensuous—it begs to be touched. The more I got to know Winnie and her activities, the more she reminded me of the poison oak plant. She was beautiful and wielded a powerful effect on men, and I felt that I always had to be on guard not to get caught up in her web. In the dark of night, I would think about the worst mistake I could make in South Africa, the worst thing in the world I could do, and I always concluded that it would be to get involved with Winnie Mandela. Yet she was part of what South Africa was at that time.

I estimate that three-fourths of my career has been spent in people-on-people situations. I was meeting South African leaders as fast as Bork and Frasure could set up the appointments. When obstacles arose and someone refused to see me, we went on to the next available person. Some people welcomed me, some were wary, and others were hostile. Each situation called for an individualistic approach.

In January 1987, just before I left for Cape Town, I called on the officers of the most extreme political activist group, the Azanian People's Organization (AZAPO). The name is derived from *Azania*. The origin of this word is not clear. Some say it is from a Zulu word for South Africa, but the prevailing view is that *Azania* is derived from Arabic and refers to the East African coast of current Somalia, Kenya, and Tanzania. The policy of AZAPO was black power. To them, there was no place in South Africa for anybody except blacks. They were rough and raw revolutionaries and among the black leaders most critical of the United States. I visited them deliberately to give them a chance to see me, to meet me, to test me, and to challenge me. They opened the meeting by calling President Reagan a black hater, his administration a racist government, and insulting me in some of the roughest language I had heard in my diplomatic career. I asked my note takers to wait outside, and then I replied to the AZAPO leadership in street language. Translated for a family audience, what I told them was that if they thought I came ten thousand miles to sell out black people, we could end the encounter right now. I said that I did not come to South Africa because they were in trouble, but because injustice was being practiced here, and that was a threat to me and to the whole world. I outlined what I intended to do while I was in South Africa. "But what I don't have to do," I said, "is listen to you. If that is the way you feel, we can cut this short right now."

Then I waited. They were stunned. Ambassadors customarily do not resort to this kind of language, but I was talking straight as shock tactic. When they regained their composure, they said, "Welcome to South Africa, Mr. Ambassador. We are glad to see you here and hope that you will work with us." Before I left they gave me a book and invited me back. "We'll be glad to talk to you anytime, Ambassador," they said in parting. So AZAPO and I now understood one another, and we began working together.

Labor is a critical force in any society. White workers did not begrudge the Indian labor its work in the sugar cane fields. Labor trouble erupted when blacks and whites met in one geographical area and competed in one profession for work. Black workers came in droves and worked for cheaper wages in the gold and mining industries and, to some extent, in the railroads. The lower-class Boers reacted to the competition by forming the Broederbond in 1915 to solidify the Volk and to control the nation. Not long before I was on the scene, black labor organized itself into unions. Because political organizations of resistance were banned in South Africa, labor unions often shouldered their role, too. In addition to campaigning for workers' rights, labor unions were extremely important in the political struggle. I did not spend much time with the white labor unions, because they were less influential than they had been in the 1930s and 1940s. The black labor unions, however, were strong forces. Although they were not organized until the late 1970s, just one decade later they comprised nearly one-fifth of the labor market and were ready to take on the South African government. The trade unions were making major gains in wages and benefits, but they also agitated for political power, organizing hundreds of labor boycotts, wildcat strikes, and demonstrations in mass gatherings. In 1987, trade unions called out workers on 1,148 strikes. This growing protest activity threatened the already staggering economy, and the government was trying to contain them. Labor unions against the South African government—this was a battle of titans.

One of my assignments from Washington was to try to reestablish relations between South African labor and the AFL-CIO. Cyril Ramaphosa was general secretary of the black National Union of Mineworkers, which had a membership of 500,000. He steadfastly refused to have anything to do with the AFL-CIO, which considered itself to be the premier American union. Black labor in South Africa disdained the AFL-CIO, considering it an appeaser of the South African government. In 1987, Ramaphosa led his union in a strike that lasted three weeks. When I met Ramaphosa in February of that year, the first thing he wanted to know was what I would do to end apartheid. Our meeting stretched on for several hours, but in the end he and I worked out a modus operandi, and eventually he agreed to meet an emissary of the AFL-CIO. Little by little, relations were resumed between the two unions. They began cooperating on such projects as labor training and bursaries.

It was a different story with the strong Congress of South African Trade

Unions (COSATU) and its large membership of black workers. Despite numerous ethnic and ideological hurdles, nearly three dozen black unions had reached agreement and established this major labor federation. It had been in place for about a year before I got there. We wanted to mend relations between COSATU and the African American Labor Center (AALC) and the AFL-CIO under the direction of Patrick O'Farrell. The dilemma was that we at the embassy needed the resources of the AALC, which wanted to be a part of changing South Africa, but it was an organization used to calling the shots. COSATU, however, would not be beholden to anybody, no matter what the other group brought to the table. The AALC had taken a swat on the nose when it offered too much advice and imposed too many conditions on COSATU. Black or white, South Africans are notably independent. COSATU had a strong integrity and was not about to take a back seat. I do not know of any other organization in Africa willing to say, "We do not need your money if you are going to try to tell us how to use it." I believed that both groups were needed in the fight to end apartheid, and that both would be more effective if they worked together. This was my goal when I called on Jay Naidoo, COSATU's combative secretary general.

Naidoo is Indian, tall, imposing, and charismatic. Fiercely passionate about his work, he reminded me of a young Ralph Nader. With long, straight black hair, Naidoo was as handsome as a movie star, but he looked at me with black eyes as hard as marbles. As soon as I met him, I realized that I was up against a master. He is an astute political operative with the focus of a coiled cobra. "Why are you here?" he asked, opening a confrontational meeting. When I told him that I represented a government that wanted to see change in South Africa, he laughed mockingly. I could have cut the acrimony in the room with a knife. "I am not going to justify my being here," I said finally. "I just wanted to meet you. Wait and see what I do."

For some time, Naidoo was one of my most forceful adversaries. I assigned Bork, our country team radical, to work with Naidoo. The two of them were well suited, and in time COSATU cooperated with the AALC and the AFL-CIO. Initially, Naidoo's stand was unequivocal: total sanctions by the United States government against the Afrikaner government, and possibly a break in relations between the two countries. I did not rule out breaking off relations, I told him, and the United States was moving toward total sanctions and making a much more decisive stand against the apartheid regime. In the meantime, it was in the best interest of the United States and South Africa to retain relations and to keep talking. Eventually Naidoo and COSATU softened toward the U.S. At a public function some time later, he even embraced me. At our first meeting, this action would have been unthinkable to both of us.

In the embassy's file of black activists, we listed about three hundred movers and shakers in the revolution. I met as many as I could, including Dr. Mamphela Ramphele, Steve Biko's consort, although that term does not fully describe the depth of the relationship between the two. They were political companions, freedom fighters together in the pursuit of justice, and they were committed to one another in a long-term relationship. She was one of the first black leaders to recognize the need for Afrikaners to work in partnership with blacks in the new South Africa. She also recognized how difficult it would be for the Afrikaners to believe that blacks had enough of a reservoir of goodwill to accept them as partners. "How can we make them understand that we need them?" she asked me. I suggested that she persuade the dominees in the small towns and rural areas take up the cause of the new South Africa in their Sunday sermons.

Then there were those who were offshore, declared persona non grata by the South African government. These included Joe Slovo, a South African Jew who was head of the South African Communist Party and in exile in Zambia; Oliver Tambo, president of the ANC based in London; Thabo Mbeki, the current president of South Africa; and Albie Sachs, a Jewish attorney with the ANC.

When I first went to Ulundi, the capital of Zululand, I was met by an unprepossessing young man in a business suit: Goodwill Zwelithini, king of the Zulus. "How very unroyal," I thought. Later I learned that he forbade pretentiousness. His princess was warm and beautiful but, like the king, played down her royal status. King Zwelithini graciously received me and my entourage, which included my visiting mother, and entertained us with a Zulu dance and festival. The warriors performed their war dance, their ferocious dance before entering battle. It put fear in my heart to see these tall, imposing warriors in war gear with spears, shields, and war feathers, synchronized like soldiers in their dance to the sound of war drums. Then the teenaged maidens performed a ceremonial dance. Later my prim mother remarked, "They didn't have anything on their tops."

In the Indian community, I worked with a number of members of the Indian National Congress. In Durban, Fatima and Ismail Meer, husband and wife, were famed as tenacious fighters. Ismail was a prominent member of the Indian National Congress and a close friend of Mandela. Ismail was such a revolutionary influence that in the mid-1940s, the South African government had prohibited him from writing. Fatima is a social activist, an educator who developed perhaps the first private school for blacks in Durban and an author. She wrote a biography of Mandela and a book about Gandhi.

The Meers took me to visit Gandhi's house, a little shack that is now a shrine, and to Ladysmith in Natal. In the 1960s, Indian businesses were forced out of Ladysmith's central business district by the Group Areas acts. This was another example of the apartheid government's removing "black spots" whenever and wherever they deemed it appropriate. One evening, the Meers gathered top Indian and Coloured revolutionary leaders to meet with me at their home, where we discussed Gandhi in detail. I was accompanied by Lucy, Sarah, Karl Beck, and his son. This trip to the Natal Province was one of the occasions I had to have security along, so security officer Pat McGee was with us. The Meers told me about the Natal Indian Congress that was founded by Gandhi in 1894, almost two decades before the ANC was established in 1911. It was not until 1946, they said, that the two organizations agreed to work together. White South Africans, I discovered, considered their treatment of Gandhi a mistake. In retrospect, they thought they never should have let him into the country.

It took me a long time, almost a year, to get a good handle on black South Africa. It is an easy assumption to think that people of one color think alike; they do not. The political activists were not united. One of my suggestions to the activists was that they needed to speak more often with one voice.

Chet and I talked many times about consensus building. It was some time before he saw black South Africans as a force to be reckoned with, as opposed to a force to be manipulated by the Afrikaners. He saw that the Afrikaners had the army, the police, and nuclear weapons, none of which the blacks had. Chet represented a popular view: "Since the blacks have no power base, let's go ahead and fix things our way and when it's over, the blacks will have a piece of the political pie." This is a false view that rarely, if ever, works because it does not take into account the years after the revolution.

TARGETING ISSUES

In December 1986, I made my first public stance by appearing at the Delmas Treason Trial. Now it was time for me to make another attention-getting public statement.

The country team and I chose the poignant subject of missing children. By orders of the South African government, thousands of black children had disappeared or were under arrest in locations unknown to their parents. This was the subject on which I would make my stand.

One of the things I asked to see when I arrived was the infamous children's graveyard. It is a chilling sight, this large, barren cemetery, about a city block square, in the middle of nowhere on the *velt*, countryside. No trees shade the cemetery. The little graves, so much smaller than those of an adult cemetery, were decorated not with flowers but with toys. Simple, childlike memorials had been erected. Siblings crafted them, I thought, or young friends.

The majority of children buried there had died between the ages of ten and eighteen, but some were as young as six. Some were killed when they stepped on land mines. Others had been caught in the crossfire of battles in the townships. Some had died of natural causes. I walked among the small graves with a feeling of incredulity—all these young lives cut short, all the mothers' tears that had been shed over them, and all the toys trying to cheer a cemetery into a happy place. I spent a long time walking among the children's graves. As a father myself, I was reluctant to leave the children's bodies there on that empty land. When I met the minister of justice, I told him about my visit. "Your blood is there," I said. "Your white blood is there."

By April 1987, the South African government was intensifying its efforts to quash political protests and control the black population. At the time, some two thousand children were in detention. The American Embassy was one of several organizations that spent considerable time tracking down the children. I assigned one officer the full-time job of trying to find them. I regularly went in person to the minister for internal affairs, protesting the jailing and asking their whereabouts. "We have this list of kids," I would say, showing him the paper. "We want to know where they are."

Eventually the government tired of this exchange and passed a law making it illegal to either inquire about the status of jailed children or to protest their jailing. The next day we learned that the leaders of all religious sects except the Dutch Reformed Church were holding a protest service at St. George's Cathedral in Cape Town, an Anglican church. They were flagrantly disobeying the government by putting their protest in a theological context. After deliberating no more than five minutes, we decided that I should attend. We did not consult Washington or ask for permission.

This would be my first public protest as the American ambassador and my coming-out with the press. I told the driver to hoist the flags on the car and gathered my deputy and press attaché and off we went to the cathedral. The entire press corps was shocked when we drove up. The air hummed at the sight of the official car. Until now I had kept under the radar of the press, and now here I was, publicly disobeying a law passed by the government. Martha Teichner, a reporter for CBS, ventured over to ask for an interview later. When I consented, she was thunderstruck. It was the first time I had agreed to an interview since being in South Africa.

The media followed me into the cathedral. Television cameras were set up aimed at me, recording my singing along with the rest of the congregation. We sang in Zulu "Nkosi Sikelel' iAfrika," "God Bless Africa," which was the outlawed black national anthem. It was great news that day: the American ambassador sang a condemned song. I became even more popular with the people after that. After the service, Teichner hung back in the press corps, hesitant to approach me until I caught her eye. Then she rushed over.

"I thought you wanted an interview," I said.

"I never thought you would give it," she replied.

"Ask your questions."

She was speechless. Finally, she asked, "Why are you at this protest?"

"Do you remember Martin Luther King Jr.'s *Letter from Birmingham Jail?*" I asked her. She shook her head no. I often couched our change-agent activities in references to King's classic work of protest literature, and I did so now. "I am here to represent the United States because injustice is being done. Human rights are being violated. That is something we cannot countenance. So, isn't it natural that I be here? The South African government has just passed a law. It is an unjust law. It seems to proscribe the activities of people seeking to exercise their rights as citizens. The United States cannot be a party to that." That became the lead of her story.

After the interview I said to Liz Pryor and Dick Barkley, "I may be recalled tomorrow, but for now let's go someplace and have breakfast."

It did not take Washington long to send a cable asking what was going on. We replied by cable what I had done. There was no response. Then Secretary Shultz was heard to reply, "Boy! That's the way to go!" Suddenly, all of the people who were getting ready to cut my throat got busy doing other things.

National Security Advisor Frank Carlucci sent me a letter that said, "I just want you to know that President Reagan is so pleased with what you did in Cape Town." The president himself sent me a note of appreciation. When former Secretary of Defense Robert McNamara learned that I had not requested

permission to attend the protest, he said, with muted approval, "I thought not."
An ambassador has to accept responsibility and sometimes take risks.

After my appearance at St. George's Cathedral, an editorial in *The New York
Times* began, "Thank you, Ambassador Perkins." The editorial went on to say,
"We can't think of many things that the Reagan administration has done in for-
eign policy that merits our thanks. President Reagan's appointment of Ed
Perkins to be ambassador to South Africa ranks among those things that we
think are exceptional."

The following day, the South African government rescinded the law. Archbishop Tutu was reported to have said to his aide-de-camp, "If Ambassador
Perkins keeps doing the things he's doing, it looks like we're going to have to
meet with him."

After that, my meetings with the press became more regular. My first press
conference was a mental battle between the press and me, then the press
sorted itself out. Some South African newspapers were extremely conservative, such as *The Citizen*, which was the English-language mouthpiece of the
government, and the Afrikaner newspapers *Die Burger* and *Die Beeld*. Other
newspapers were more objective, such as the *Johannesburg Star* and the *Cape
Sun*. Often Liz and Bob jointly determined when it was time to schedule a
press conference, recognizing that it was good to have them fairly often. We
held press conferences for two purposes. One reason was to impart information. I said that our two countries had a lot in common, that the United States
was wedded to the concept of change in South Africa, but that did not mean we
thought there was no place for Afrikaners. We thought it was possible for
Afrikaners and blacks to work together towards a common objective.

The second reason was to give the press corps a chance to see me, because I
was a strange animal to them. Never before had they seen a black person speaking on such a public stage. No black person had ever done anything like that in
South Africa.

It was my policy to never duck questions, and the press asked tough questions, sometimes in hopes of embarrassing me. I was frequently asked about
sanctions and if I thought they were unfair. I replied that, given the gravity of
the apartheid system, Congress had decided that the United States could not
support business as usual.

The press invariably asked about social conditions in the United States. They
expected me to react angrily, but Liz coined a phrase from my many speeches
that I incorporated into my answer. "The United States is a revolutionary soci-

ety," I said. "Our country was born in revolution. It continues to be revolutionary in a positive sense. If we reach a point where we are no longer a revolutionary society, I predict that we will atrophy. My country is far from perfect, but it is more nearly perfect than it was ten years ago or even yesterday. It will never be perfect. Your country is different from mine, because the Constitution of the United States has a promise in it, and that promise is that the country will get better all the time. Your constitution does not have that promise in it for all citizens."

Reporters often asked me if I had encountered discrimination in my own country and if so, how I handled it. "Yes, I have," I told them. "And it will come again. Usually I push them aside and remind myself that I do not have time for this. I also fight it when I find it because it is an insidious poison in any society."

The press watched every step I took. We did not court the press, and we did not tell the press where we were going, but after a couple of months the reporters ferreted out this information on their own. *Time* magazine was the first of the print media to ask for a special interview. Liz and Bob thought it was time to change my policy of not granting one-on-one interviews, so I met Bruce Nelan, *Time* reporter, in Cape Town. "We thought you were sitting in the embassy all these weeks," he said, "but you were out in the townships meeting people and understanding what is happening in South Africa." He was astonished that I was cultivating black contacts. He wrote that in addition to attending the white diplomatic dinner parties, I also set out "to grimy offices in Soweto or a spartan church in Mamelodi, the dusty black township outside Pretoria, or a listing shanty in Crossroads, a squatter camp near Cape Town." No American ambassador in South Africa had ever ventured into these places. This was the first major magazine article about my work as ambassador to South Africa, titled "New Man in the Townships."

Black Townships

I had indeed been out into the black townships and in the Homelands. This is a priority, I told the country team. "I have to travel constantly, and when I travel I want every trip to have a purpose. When I go to a township, I want to know why I am going there, what we expect to achieve, who we want to see, and what role they play in their community and in the political process."

The Homelands were a legacy from the British and nineteenth-century segregation, when tribes were conquered and pushed onto reserves and the rest of their land was opened to white settlement. Tightening racial segregation and discrimination, the white government passed laws, notably the Native Land Act (1913), which prohibited African ownership of land outside the reserves. Usually the reserves were in remote locations, consisting of land so poor that by the early 1900s, Africans could not produce enough food to feed themselves. Some reserves were divided into several areas. For example, Bophuthatswana was separated into nineteen sections that were miles apart.

In the apartheid era, these reserves would become the Homelands for what was termed African "nations" to be administered by hereditary chiefs. *Bantustan* means "black homeland," from the Afrikaner word *bantu*, which refers to a black who belongs in the Homelands. *Bantu* is a Zulu and Xhosa word that means "the people." The other term Afrikaners used for blacks was the Arabic *kaffir*. This word is akin to the word "nigger."

When the National Party came into power in 1948, more blacks were forced onto the Homelands until, eventually, half of South Africa's 29 million black citizens lived in Homelands that constituted only about 13 percent of the country. Ten Homelands were established: Transkei, Venda, KwaZulu, Bophuthatswana, Ciskei, Gazankulu, KwaNdebele, Lebowa, Qwaqwa, and KaNgwane. By law, Africans were not permitted to live anywhere else in South Africa. They could work elsewhere, but as soon as their labor ended, they were required to return to the Homeland. The hated pass laws prohibited them from visiting urban areas without special documents for more than seventy-two hours. In 1975–76, more than 380,000 Africans were arrested because of violation of the pass laws.

The South African government accorded the Homelands the status of nations, with all of the trappings of government such as legislature, department of foreign affairs, and police departments. The intent was to have every black person in South Africa be a citizen of one of the Homelands. With the blacks thus contained, the Afrikaners could claim there were no blacks in South Africa. "Sometimes the blacks come into white South Africa to work temporarily," governmental officials would tell me. "What about the two million people in Soweto?" I would ask. "Temporary workers," the officials would reply.

The South African government feted the Homeland leaders. Whenever the government hosted a state dinner or other event involving the diplomatic corps, Homeland leaders were invited as if guests from another country. Invariably, I was seated between a Homeland leader and his wife to give this person political legitimacy. I talked with the leaders, but I never recognized the status accorded them by the Afrikaners because this would have taken the heat off the South African government. I treated the Homelands as another part of South African territory, which angered both the Homeland officials and the South African government. "The United States government does not recognize Homelands as independent nations. We recognize only the government of South Africa," I explained. "We see the Homelands as a contrivance of the South African government to deny black citizens bona fide citizenship of South Africa."

Beginning about a month after I arrived, I began traveling unofficially to the Homelands and, eventually I visited all of them. The first Homeland I saw was KaNgwane, led by Chief Minister Enos Mabuza. My second trip was to KwaZulu Natal, the largest Homeland, governed by Chief Mangosuthu Gatsha Buthelezi.

The United States relationship with Zululand was different. Zululand was a well-established nation before the Afrikaners came on the scene, so we recognized Zululand not as a Homeland, but as a part of South Africa, and we recognized Buthelezi as the king's subaltern. The Zulus are fierce, proud, and warlike. When I served in South Africa, they were the most organized tribal group and numbered about six million. Buthelezi, who can trace his ancestry back to the first king of the Zulus, and his wife, Princess Irene, were the most influential people of the tribe. When I met Buthelezi, he was fifty-eight years old and had just taken his third wife. He had been a member of the ANC with Mandela but, for personal and political reasons, approached the struggle in a different way. Because he was head of the Zulu nation, various U.S. groups courted him assiduously. Buthelezi was the black leader most compatible with the South African government, probably because he was opposed to sanctions. That does not mean he was a toady, far from it. He was not collaborating with the Afrikaner government, but he was using that government to get his own way. He is astute, cool, cunning, and well educated. He holds honorary degrees from a number of prestigious universities, including Harvard.

Buthelezi can speak for hours. He was the luminary when we shared a speaking platform, so he spoke last. And he spoke and spoke and spoke. Finally, I did the unthinkable. I called over a Buthelezi aide and said, "The Chief always has a lot of good things to say and I want to hear them all, but I need to go to the bathroom." The aide led me offstage and then back to the platform. Buthelezi was still going strong. He spoke for another thirty minutes.

Above all, I characterize him as a Zulu. Like others of his tribe, he believes that the Zulus are the superior race of any color. I once carried a message to

On a recent trip to South
Africa, Chief Mangosuthu
Gatsha Buthelezi, now
Home Affairs minister,
entertained my traveling
companions and me at a
dinner. The blessing was
said in Zulu. He and I did
not laugh together like this
when I served as ambassa-
dor to South Africa.

Buthelezi from Jay Naidoo, who was asking that they meet to develop a common strategy of dealing with the struggle. Buthelezi listened to the message
with cold dismissal. "They know where I am," he said. Clearly, he was offended
that Naidoo did not ask him in person.

In 1989, the final year of Mandela's imprisonment, when his release was
imminent, a tremendous fight for power erupted in KwaZulu between the ANC
and the Inkhata Freedom Party, which was Buthelezi's party. Many people
were killed. The questions hover still: Could Buthelezi have stopped the violence and created instead an atmosphere for negotiation among the people
involved in the final stages of the struggle? Was he a smooth killer and fomenter
of violence? I do not know the answers. I found him to be a calculating politician who was capable of using whatever means appropriate to gain his objectives. The South African government needed a powerful black ally and thought
that Buthelezi was the most acceptable choice. English-speakers thought the
same thing. Perhaps the white South Africans even thought him pliable. If so, it
was like making a pact with a tiger. He was not openly aggressive, but patiently
awaited his opportunity. He was a skillful Homeland Zulu leader and warlord,
with emphasis on "lord," who felt that power was due him. I know that he
believed he should have been the first black president of South Africa.

Poverty on the reserves and in neighboring countries drove black laborers by the hundreds of thousands into the urban areas to seek employment. By 1910, the government sought to separate the urban Africans from the white residents by creating black townships adjacent to the urban areas. Modern city housing for the white residents ranged from middle-class homes to opulent mansions. Black or Coloured townships, synonymous with slums, resembled large villages with dirt roads, mud or tin huts, and no electricity or sewage systems. Crime and disease were permanent residents.

The pass laws were finally repealed in 1986, the year of my appointment, but by then the townships had erupted into violence. Audiences around the world watched nightly televised news reports of the battles in the townships—police and military against unarmed blacks. Suddenly, the bloodshed of apartheid, which had been isolated at the tip of the continent, was being broadcast into private homes. This television coverage inflamed the world's sensibilities. The South African government responded by prohibiting news coverage of the township wars, but it was too late. The world had seen it.

I needed to see the townships myself, so I walked the streets of Mamelodi, Alexandria, Soweto, Soweto-by-the-Sea, and others. I saw congested, sprawling, makeshift clusters of poverty. I witnessed conditions that appalled me.

Soweto-by-the-Sea on the Eastern Cape had no semblance of running water in the entire township. I could smell the open sewage a block away. Women walked a mile to a water pipe, then carried water in buckets on their heads. Although they lived in degradation and squalor, they maintained a sense of self-respect. Every morning, mothers sent their young children off to school carrying lunch buckets. The students were clean and dressed in freshly starched blue-and-white school uniforms. It was a valiant demonstration of dignity in deplorable circumstances.

Alexandria exhibited a heart-rending lawlessness that was condoned by the white government. It was commonplace in Alexandria for young black thugs to select girls as young as thirteen or fourteen for gang rape. The girls would be openly taken from their homes and dragged into a van outfitted with a bed. I knew of one woman who pleaded that her two daughters be spared. "Give us your daughters," the toughs said, "or we will burn down your house." The woman had no recourse, no authorities to call, and no one to protect her. She watched helplessly as her girls were led away.

Violence was so commonplace in the townships that, although the press described me as "a quiet giant" or "football big," officials in Crossroads were astonished that I would walk through their township unafraid. They were wrong. I did feel trepidation, but I refused to show it. If people could live there, I reasoned, the least I could do was walk there.

Eventually I would visit most of South Africa's townships—Mdantsane outside East London; Umlanga, outside Durban; District Six, Langa, Gugulethu, Nyanga, and Khayelitsha, adjacent to Cape Town; Alexandra and Thokoza, near Johannesburg; KwaMashu, outside Durban; and Fort Beaufort, Crossroads, Mamelodi, and Meadowlands. The first township I saw, however, was the mother city of them all—Soweto, an acronym for South West Township. It is South Africa's biggest and best-known township. By the 1970s, Soweto's population was one million people; today it is estimated to be more than three million. In this massive, sixteen-square-mile township between Pretoria and Johannesburg, all of the sins and problems of other townships were tripled.

Two South Africans invited me for a private tour of Soweto. That experience was like Dante's descent into Hell. My guides were Trevor Tutu, the son of the archbishop, and Don McRoberts, a white lawyer who was head of the Get Ahead Foundation, which created entrepreneurships among blacks. They wanted to show me the real Soweto, the go-to-hell Soweto, the in-your-face Soweto. We went to bars, restaurants, neighborhoods, and a workers' hostel, where I had my first view of living accommodations for migrant workers from neighboring countries. The hostel had the worst living conditions I have ever seen—a long, barracks-like structure with double-rack beds. All of the black migrant mine workers were men, but a concomitant of female camp followers was present. In this barracks, copulation occurred in community fashion, babies were born, and AIDS proliferated. I could not imagine such a life, and I was appalled at the degradation that so violated human dignity. I deliberately walked slowly through the barracks, absorbing everything that I saw—the smells, the filth, and the realization that this little space was the sole domain of many individuals. The men had come to South Africa to make a living, leaving their families behind. This was where they lived their lives. I looked in the eyes of the men present that day. What I saw was despair and anger, but mostly resignation.

The hostel reminded me of a visit to Calcutta a few years earlier. There in a railroad shed on a bare floor, I saw a three-generation family living in a space about the size of an American closet. Only two reactions come from an experience like that—either ignore it and forget it as quickly as possible, or be affected by it and wonder about a humankind that permits one class to live comfortably while another exists in misery.

When I returned to the embassy from my tour of Soweto, I talked about the plight of the men working for the mining companies. I wanted to know what we could do to change how they lived. The answer was nothing. We could do nothing at the moment, unless we could take over the mines. That visit to the hostel had a lasting effect on me, and it propelled me to include accounts of such degradation in our reports to Washington. We wanted the State Department to see the human suffering that we saw in South Africa. We wanted to remind Washington that foreign policy is not an impersonal geopolitical subject, but rather the day-to-day lives of human beings.

Townships were not limited to black residents. I visited Coloured townships, notably Mitchell's Plain, a bare stretch of sand that was established as a township when the District Six township near Cape Town was declared to be a white area and the Coloureds were forcibly removed. A large number of Indians lived in what amounted to squatters' camps, notably near Durban. To my surprise, I discovered white townships populated by desperately poor Afrikaners. Conditions were not as bad as those in the black townships, but the attitude of the whites was remarkably different. In black townships, citizens were making an effort to make do—to try to keep their children clean and educated, for example. The attitude was entirely different in white townships. Afrikaners seemed to accept their poverty as their due and God's will. This was coupled with extreme anger at blacks, whom they held responsible for their plight.

To Cape Town

In January 1987, it was time to move to Cape Town for the opening of Parliament. Lucy and I traveled on the luxurious Blue Train with our visiting daughter Kathy. The train snaked through the Great Karoo desert, one of the most beautiful landscapes I have ever seen. As we passed through little towns, I saw the faces of the blacks outside when they spotted me on the train. I could tell from their amazed expression that this was the most unusual thing they had ever seen—a black man on the grand train.

The opening of Parliament was an eye-popping drama, a formal occasion requiring top hat and tails. The ministers marched in, dressed identically in short black coats, striped pants, and black ties and resembling a line of penguins. I was struck by how carefully they adhered to formality and protocol on such occasions. The decorum of Parliament was a glaring contrast to what was going on in the streets of South Africa. P. W. Botha opened Parliament with a lackluster speech, partly in Afrikaans, along the line of "We shall not lose."

His wife, Elise, was in attendance to hear her husband speak. She usually wore dresses adorned with oversized bows, and she had a passion for polka dots—huge black or yellow polka dots—and she wore hats. Throughout our tour in South Africa, she lamented repeatedly to Lucy that her husband had not received an invitation from President Reagan to visit the United States. He will never receive such an invitation, I told Lucy. When Chet and others tried to engineer an invitation for Botha to meet Reagan quietly in California, I nixed it. What's more, I promised that I would never support such an invitation, because it would give Botha the legitimacy and endorsement he so craved. My interference with Botha's scheme enraged the South African government.

On the way to Parliament House, my official car stalled again. We had to rent a car. En route, the flag fell off twice. The Cadillac's electrical system failed two or three more times, on one occasion leaving me alone on a lonely stretch of road between Pretoria and Johannesburg while Edison went for help. The security officer, responsible for my safety, was shaken to his boots when he learned of it. After that incident, I called Washington and told them to send somebody immediately for the car. "To fix it again?" they asked. "No," I said, "to drive the damned thing into the Indian Ocean because I won't have it."

In Cape Town I turned my attention to getting to know the Afrikaners, the iron-fisted whites who loved their land with a passion beyond love, and their Dutch Reformed Church. Only James Michener's book *The Covenant* had given me a glimmer of insight into this strange religion. I did not fully realize how this church had bastardized the scriptures and twisted Biblical text to serve the racist views of the Afrikaner elders. I could not perceive the depth of evil allowed to permeate the teachings of Jesus Christ and then used to manipulate the masses to believe they were the chosen people of South Africa. The only person in the embassy who understood this culture was Bob Frasure, and I marvel yet at the knowledge of this craggy West Virginian. Except for Bob, none of us knew what we were dealing with. I was about to find out.

THE WHITE TRIBE

The Afrikaners are a white tribe. I saw that they were bound together by their culture, religion, language, and love of South Africa, their homeland. Their greatest loyalty was not to the flag, however, but to the Volk, their cultural clan. Many saw themselves as a nation of heroes who brought civilization to a wild land. They considered their political policy of apartness a divine mission.

I was discovering that Afrikanerdom is as multifaceted as any other society. Many were conservative and strict nationalists, yet some were liberal minded and open to progressive change. They were divided in political thought, even among families. Some held fast to traditional politics. Others wanted to change but did not know how.

The more the rest of the world criticized, scrutinized, and interfered, the tighter the Afrikaners, with their tribal loyalty, closed their *kraal* in proud defiance. As a representative of the United States government and determined to be an agent of change, I was a threat. As an invader of the homeland they defended, I was in the most precarious position for a soldier. Although their repression of the revolution created a mushrooming violence, I did not see the Afrikaners as an enemy—I saw them as a force to be redirected. The national policy of apartheid was much like a mighty river that had overflowed its banks and was wreaking damage: it needed to be channeled. It was my job to change the course of this river. What is more, I was directed to do it without dynamite—I was to dismantle apartheid without violence. I was a black man, an American, and an appointee of Ronald Reagan, who had, up until that moment, been sympathetic to their cause. Consequently, I represented everything they hated. Could I gently harness a raging river? Could I tame a crocodile?

I knew that the South African government leadership was unhappy with the idea of my being there. I never wanted them to like me, but I did expect them

331

to respect the United States, what it stood for, and its determination to be proactive in bringing about change. So, with measured stride, I set out to meet the leaders of the three powerful pillars of the Afrikaners society: the church, the Broederbond, and the National Party.

I started in Pretoria, calling on the ministers of the South African government. I had to work with these men professionally—at that time all the ministers were men—but it was important for me to try to understand them, as well. I wanted to get into their psyche and understand Afrikaner thinking. What a wild ride it was.

Willie van Niekerk, minister for National Health and Population Development, was a key governmental official. As I had with others, I talked with him about equal education and eliminating the dozen or so education departments spawned by apartheid. Most importantly, I talked to him about AIDS. For twenty years, the South African government had maintained that there was no AIDS in that country. In reality, AIDS was rampant in the townships, especially in Soweto, where I had seen the epidemic myself.

Van Niekerk stood fast in his denial. "I don't think there is a problem," he told me. What he meant was that he did not think it affected whites, and only black people were infected with AIDS. I made the point that education was essential and urged the South African government to mount an accelerated educational program about AIDS. "You cannot be fooled by the demographics," I said. I could see that AIDS would spread from the itinerate black labor force from Malawi, Zimbabwe, Mozambique, Angola, Zambia, and camp followers to the white areas of South Africa.

To the minister, that meeting was a historic occasion. He looked at me, aghast, as I told him things he had never heard before. I was sure he was thinking, "That's crazy! What white person is going to sleep with a black person?" The South Africa government did not acknowledge that black and white liaisons existed all over South Africa. The Sun City resort in Bophuthatswana, for example, was a notorious meeting place for white men and black hostesses. If a woman had AIDS, the man could infect his partner back in South Africa.

I spoke to van Niekerk many times about the likelihood of an AIDS pandemic, and his reply was always the same: "We don't have a problem." South African governmental officials put their heads in the sand and would neither hear nor see. As long as I was in South Africa, the government did nothing to indicate it was aware of this menacing health crisis. What a façade. Some of the ministers insisted that the government was trying to move toward a constitution that would share political power, but they were doing no such thing. It was a sham. It took me only about a month to become convinced that despite the government's rhetoric, it never intended to have a majority government in South Africa. Some of the ministers felt otherwise, but certainly not the state president.

Nonetheless, I persevered, working my way through the ministers. I met with Stoffel Botha, the bland but intelligent Afrikaner minister of Home Affairs and Communications, and with Chris Heunis, minister of Constitutional Development Planning, who was quite a character. It was the job of Adriaan Vlok, minister of Law and Order, to jail people who disturbed the social order. I called on him many times to ask him to release political prisoners. His demeanor was completely incongruous with his official behavior. His actions were monstrous, but on the surface he seemed to be a nice gentleman. This was even more horrifying.

In contrast, Neil Barnard, director general of National Intelligence Services, was rough ideologically and professionally. He appeared to me to be a man of limited intellectual capacity, and he was bitterly anti-American. He told me that the United States would not last as a country because we had too much freedom. "You can't control Congress," he said. He got that right. I told him that we did not want to control Congress and tried to explain the balance of power among the three branches of government. He just shook his head. "It can't last like that," he said. I learned that he had been rejected years earlier as a graduate student by Georgetown University. Perhaps that was a source of his hatred of the United States.

Barnard headed a secret intelligence group, sanctioned by President Botha, that harassed members of my staff. On one occasion, a white male accosted Liz Pryor in a *hyperama*, a supermarket, knocked her down, and dumped her groceries on top of her. Another time, a different white male abused her verbally, saying that he had embarrassing information about her personal life. Liz and Bob Frasure both received threatening calls in South Africa and on visits to London and the United States. "We're watching you. We're going to get you," the anonymous callers would say. I grew so uncomfortable with the threats that sometimes I had my official visits to Durban and elsewhere classified, which meant that the embassy did not announce my travel plans. I did not want to give the secret intelligence people any help in planting a bomb on the plane.

One of the most challenging ministers was Defense Minister Magnus Malan, a no-frills former general and a contact of Bill Casey, director of the CIA. Malan radiated power, spoke bluntly, and maintained that South Africa had held back communism on behalf of the Americans. He accused the United States of being two-faced.

"You are advocating change for South Africa," he said when he came to lunch. "But you are forgetting that we have done your work out here for you. We made sure that you had open sea-lanes through the Cape of Good Hope. We acted as your eyes and ears. Now you're saying you don't need us any more."

"It was very generous of you to have done this," I said, "but I am not sure that it is accurate."

"Oh yes, it's accurate. You asked us to do it. You go back and check the records. We went across the border and fought the Marxists so that you would not suffer a Communist-dominated geographical area. We fought your battle in Mozambique and Angola and you know it. You owe us something."

Malan considered himself a reincarnation of the Roman dictator Pompey. He held the party line absolutely. We let Malan know that we had irrefutable evidence that the South African dirty tricks people were involved in the murder of a Swedish embassy member, a car bomb in Botswana, an explosion at an ANC house in Lusaka, and other deaths in Mozambique. He dismissed the information as an orchestrated propaganda campaign. Malan spoke publicly about what he considered the real nature of the ANC. This was a part of an anti-ANC public relations effort created by the African Defense Force.

"The ANC has been guilty of numerous murders and the deliberate maiming of innocent civilians," Malan said. "They are guilty of serious crimes against humanity as well as infringements of basic human freedoms. . . . Many terrorists have been arrested, tried and convicted by the highest courts in the country. . . . Neither I nor the Defense Force will apologize for acting against terrorists in the best interest of all our people, creating a stable environment for the constitutional growth processes. To develop and safeguard the protection of basic human freedoms is a duty which we take seriously."

Malan was one of the insiders who knew about the South African government's dirty tricks played against black revolutionaries. He knew everything that went on in the government. He always professed ignorance, but if there was so much as a parade across the border, he knew about it. Consequently, Malan was our barometer of how the South African government was moving. It was important that we track his decisions and actions. I became acquainted with an Afrikaner woman who was so close to Malan that some characterized her as his mistress. "I see these ministers often," she told me. "If there is something you need to know, ask me. I'll find out for you." With her help and that of our other sources, we kept a close watch on him, especially in the period of February–March 1987. That barometer told us that the South African government had not made a decision and did not intend to make a decision to figure out some way to accommodate black South Africans. They were not moving. They had drawn a line in the sand and said, "We go no further than this."

As I got deeper and deeper into the inner workings of the South African government, I learned that it was not Malan and the defense department who engineered the fight against the revolutionary people. This fell to the National Security Council under the direction of General Pieter van der Westhuizen, one of the men closest to President Botha. It was van der Westhuizen who gave the order to shoot up the safe house in Maputo where Albie Sachs was wounded. Malan was a killer, but not even in the same league as van der Westhuizen.

Roelof "Pik" Botha, minister of Foreign Affairs, was the most forthcoming of the ministers in understanding what the United States was trying to do in South Africa. He did not like it, but he understood it. Pik was highly intelligent, and when he was in charge of his faculties, he was articulate and a good global strategist. The nickname "Pik" is roughly translated into English as "penguin," a bird he vaguely resembled in appearance and walk. My contact, Joe Marks, told me the nickname alluded to Pik's always "pecking around like a chicken."

An editorial in the *Sunday Times* newspaper told me clearly that Pik represented the Afrikaner Volk. "Mr. Pik Botha can look fierce and intense," the editorial said, "but he frequently adopts this mannerism to portray the feelings he most correctly thinks South Africans share with him." To make doubly sure that I got the message, the editorial's headline read: "Make No Mistake, Mr. Perkins. This Time South Africa is Behind Pik All the Way."[1]

One of Pik's flaws was drinking. When he drank, he could be mean, and this made him an unstable contact. I never knew what to expect of him when he was imbibing. I saw him in this condition many times, and I was with him on one drinking binge that lasted until three o'clock in the morning. A close colleague in the embassy told me of a drinking drama that took place in Cape Verde. Pik had been drinking since noon and was seen that evening, drunk as can be, walking on the beach with a drink in his hand, two drinks stuffed into the pockets of his safari suit, and a South African Airways flight attendant on each arm. He had been foreign minister for thirteen years, one of the longest-serving foreign ministers anywhere in the world. He became, however, the wrong foreign minister at the wrong time. Pik's world was coming to an end.

The head of the National Party in the Transvaal, F. W. de Klerk, minister of

National Education, was the third guest I invited to dine at the residence. De Klerk came for lunch, and we met in the study to get acquainted. He immediately lit a cigarette—he smoked incessantly—and asked for a scotch and soda.

"Welcome to the residence, Mr. Minister," I said.

"I'm glad to be here, Mr. Ambassador, but if you're going to talk about one-man, one-vote, we can terminate this conversation now."

"I didn't particularly intend to talk about one-man, one-vote," I said. Bob Frasure, sitting to one side, laughed.

De Klerk told me that the National Party intended to change.

"Events are moving faster than you want to change," I told him.

"We can handle it," he said. "I just hope the Americans will understand our situation. We are moving toward change."

I asked him if blacks would have a voice in how they were governed, and he replied with a classical Afrikaner phrase: "In their own way, in their own affairs." He said that the party was committed to separate development through the Homelands.

"You and I both know that is a farce," I said. "The Homelands are there for the convenience of the government of the Afrikaners." It is not customary for ambassadors to speak so bluntly, but this was an unusual situation. I told him that I did not intend to stand in the streets and condemn the Afrikaners, and I recognized that the Afrikaners belonged in South Africa just as the blacks do. Still, the Reagan administration's policy was change in South Africa.

De Klerk and I became good contacts, if not good friends. He was cordial when we met and a good conversationalist. I often saw him and his wife at social occasions, particularly at the opera, for they were avid opera aficionados. De Klerk was a realist, although in no way a revolutionist. His wife was much more conservative than he and not at all comfortable living with nonwhites. His brother, Wimpie de Klerk, however, was a journalist who had said publicly that apartheid was wrong. The de Klerk family illustrated how divided Afrikaners were on the subject of apartheid.

As I studied South Africa, two of the most informational books were Allister Sparks's *The Mind of South Africa* and Ivor Wilkins's and Hans Strydom's *Broederbond: The Super Afrikaners*. These books helped me understand that the historical goal of institutionalized apartheid, unlike the segregation I had known in the United States, was complete separation for whites. Blacks and Coloureds were intended to live apart in separate nations, and Asians, or Indians, were to be deported. Ahmed Ebrahim Laher, who schooled me on the history of the Broederbond, said that *The Super Afrikaners* was the definitive study of this secret organization in print in the English language. The book clearly stated the Afrikaners' intent: "The primary consideration is whether Afrikanerdom will reach its ultimate destiny of domination in South Africa. Brothers, the key to South Africa's problems is not whether one part or another shall obtain the whip hand, but whether the Afrikaner Broederbond shall govern South Africa." I consulted the book frequently as I developed scenarios for the United States's change policy in South Africa. I knew I was up against a tightly knit, highly sophisticated organization.

Hendrik F. Verwoerd, leader of the National Party, had developed the concept of apartheid or apartness in 1965. When I landed in South Africa, the official term in use was "our own affairs," which justified separateness as the Afrikaners' taking care of their own affairs under the guidance of the leaders and the strict constructionists in the church. The Broederbond's first comprehensive draft of the apartheid ideology was heavily based on Germany's National Socialism Plan. The primary aims of that first comprehensive apartheid ideology included:

* A national home for the Afrikaner Volk and its posterity;
* Separate homes for blacks and Coloureds where they could develop their nationhood;
* Complete racial separation, not segregation but separation;
* Special tolerance and "spiritual guardianship" for the development of the black man, since Afrikaners knew him better than anyone else, historically;
* Protection of the white race from the biological degeneration that would result from mixing of the races, since whites were superior culturally and biologically;
* Division of the country into several racial divides, with the white one being the largest (including all the harbors for international trade). The Indians were to go back to India; and
* Recognition that whites would eventually have to work and exist without black labor in order to keep blacks out of the economic mainstream.

The Broeders were the true architects of apartheid, so very soon upon my arrival I bearded the lions in their den. The second person I invited to the residence was Broederbond president Pieter de Lange. By this time, the Broederbond had altered some of its views. Professor de Lange told me that the Bond would not give up the idea of power, but that some accommodation with the blacks had to come.

De Lange, a Rhodes scholar, was president of the Rand Afrikaans University in Pretoria, a strict constructionist university. He had read Greek and Latin at Oxford and was an educated person, but he had an overdose of Afrikaner racism composed of equal parts religion, politics, and social status. I told de Lange that I wanted to understand Afrikanerdom and the Broederbond, this strict society of Afrikaner men. He was very pleasant when he came to lunch with Frasure and me. We talked about the history of South Africa, and he asked what I thought.

"I think you're heading down a road that has no return," I said. "Time is running out."

He shocked me with his answer. "I know that," he said. "We do have to change. The question is how. A few of us understand that we are facing demise, but the president of the country is not one of them. We don't know how to change. I guess you have to help us."

De Lange came to lunch several times, and we formed a tacit understanding that we would work together. Even Frasure was surprised. "Ambassador, I don't know what you did," he said. "Just remember one thing. The Afrikaners are one people and they'll go far, but there will come a time when they think of Afrikaners first." I found this to be true. Afrikaners are a complicated people.

THE DUTCH REFORMED CHURCH

Until the 1980s, the doctrine of separateness was accepted and blessed by the Dutch Reformed Church (*Nieuwe Gereformede Kerch*, or the NGK), a handmaiden of the Broederbond. In 1986 and 1987, the church shifted its position slightly. Some church members began to reconsider apartheid. One group said that God's word did not square with racial separateness, and this split the church wide open. In October 1986, in what was considered the most important synod in the history of the powerful Dutch Reformed Church, newly elected moderator Johan Heyns led a fight in which the majority of the church agreed that the teachings of Jesus Christ did not support apartheid. "Apartheid cannot be justified scripturally in a mixed society," the synod declared. Heyns called for radical changes in church policy toward other races and other churches. This signaled new social activism by the church, notably reconciliation with the estranged Coloured Dutch Reformed Church and a challenge to the scriptural basis for apartheid.

Just about the time I arrived, some two thousand dissidents broke away from the liberal greater church and established a new Dutch Reformed Church for whites only, the Afrikaans Dutch Reformed Church (the *Afrikaans Gereformeerde Kerk*, or AGK). The infant church had no standing, but it was an irritant to the mother church. Despite the split, the drama was far from over. It would smolder for years.

Johan Heyns was following a path of change set by Christian Frederick Beyers Naudé and Nico Smith, two prominent dominees. Naudé, from the core of Afrikanerdom, was the first to try to pull the church away from government ideology. He had been a professor of religion at Stellenbosch University, the premier Afrikaner university, and his father was a founder of the Broederbond Society, but in the early 1970s Naudé declared the church's policy heresy. "I must obey God rather than men," he said. It was a brave and fantastic stand, shocking because he came from such an illustrious Afrikaner family. Naudé had come to this conclusion on his own. He was the first of the prominent dominees to speak out, and he suffered for it. They defrocked him, declaring him an enemy of the church and a traitor to the Afrikaner people. They said he had lost touch with his tribe. The Afrikaners were hardest on their turncoat members. and I found them to be merciless on nonconformists. Esther Lattigan, a professor at Stellenbosch University and a candidate for Parliament, told me that when she broke with the National Party, she was castigated. She regularly awoke to find garbage and dead black cats on her lawn—symbols of the Afrikaners' contempt for her renegade activities. They called her at night, harangued her, and told her she had forfeited her right to be called a member of the Volk.

Naudé was harassed, ostracized, legally banned by the government for eight years, and under house arrest for years. They thought that this would drive him out of South Africa, but he stayed and became an even stronger fighter against apartheid. He resigned his membership in the Broederbond in 1963 because of its support of the Immorality Act, the Race Classification Act, Group Areas Act, and the Bantu Laws Amendment Bill. When I arrived he was a revolutionary and the spiritual conscience of the South African Council of Churches, a group united in its fight against apartheid. He was unbending in his devotion to God's word, and he believed that God intended for all people to be treated the same way. He was one of the first white theologians in South Africa to attempt to bridge the gap between black clergy and white clergy. He and the black theologians formed a powerful cooperative theological battle force. The blacks began to push all churches—Catholic, Presbyterian, United Congregationalist, and the South African Council of Churches—to take stands against apartheid.

Naudé was one of the first people I called on. USAID director Tim Bork and I visited him at Khotso House in Johannesburg. Tim was along because we were funding some of the activities of the South African Council of Churches. Khotso House very well could have been named Revolutionary House because it also housed Sheena Duncan, an English-speaker, and her Black Sash Advice Center. The Advice Center was dedicated to the professional development of black people, providing guidance to anyone with a problem—education, human rights, employment, or anything else. Sheena was a large woman who carried herself with stately dignity and never allowed herself to be intimidated by the authorities.

The Afrikaners had stripped Naudé of everything, but he was indomitable. He would not be defeated. When I first met him, he greeted me saying, "We've been waiting for you." He had been waiting for someone who would manifest a change of heart in the American administration. "I am here," I replied.

Naudé was a tall man, impressive in appearance with a craggy, artistic face. I could tell by talking with him that he was a deep thinker and certainly the most liberal Afrikaner I had met to date. I confess that I felt inadequate in his presence. His considerable knowledge included a deep familiarity with the teachings of Martin Luther King Jr. Even so, I did not realize the enormity of this man when I first met him, because at that time I did not yet know much about the Dutch Reformed Church. I was just beginning my study.

Naudé welcomed me profusely, saying, "It's about time the United States woke up." He was anti-Reagan and anti-Crocker. "They put the United States on the side of injustice," he told me. Just as Vietnam is a case study of the United States' betrayal of its ideals, South Africa exemplified its failure to act on those ideals. We seemed to have forgotten the words of the Preamble, the Bill of Rights, and the 13th, 14th, and 15th Amendments to the Constitution. Naudé was among those who pulled off our dark glasses and made us see clearly.

The lesson I learned from this experience is that the American people are known to stand for something. This has been our strongest suit. We may not realize it, but people all over the world have watched our evolution as a nation and have read our Constitution. Naudé was one of those in South Africa who had read it and said, "That is what we want." One reason I came out of South Africa a different man was that I had met people like him. These were substantial people.

The last time I saw Alan Paton, he talked about the people who championed South Africa—Steve Biko and Robert Sobukwe. Alan identified with their quests for justice. "I can't give up on South Africa," he told me. "That would be like giving up on life."

"Who else would you say is a real South African?" I asked him.

"Jan Hofmeyr, of course," he answered. Paton had written a biography about Hofmeyr and considered him the perfect Afrikaner. "Johan Heyns is in that category."

As soon as I could get an appointment with him, I went to see Heyns, moderator of the Dutch Reformed Church. He was one of the most enlightened Afrikaners holding an official position. The first time I met Johan, I called on him at his home, which was a modest residence in the nice neighborhood of Waterkloof. His wife, Renee, served us Koeksisters (pronounced "Cook Sisters"), a sticky, sweet dessert the Afrikaners love. He and I sat in his study, where I saw books by Martin Luther King Jr. I was flabbergasted to learn that Dr. Heyns was a student of Dr. King and, like King, a believer in the power of theology to produce change.

Johan and I struck an agreement to meet every couple of months and review where South Africa was at that time. He told me that I could help bridge the

At his home in Durban, Alan Paton told me how he came to write *Cry, the Beloved Country*. He talked about the people who championed South Africa. Alan identified with their quest for justice. "I can't give up on South Africa," he told me. "That would be like giving up on life."

gap between the different groups in South Africa. "We don't know how to talk to each other," he said. I was impressed that he knew that. "God probably sent you here because we are incapable of doing this alone."

Since the revolutionary General Synod, the church had declared membership open to all races. From the embassy, we pushed the church to open itself even more to black people. This would give Afrikaner farmers a chance to meet their counterparts, black farmers, or at least sit in the same building with them on Sunday. If the dominees were honest, they would read scripture to indicate all were the same.

It was far more common in South Africa than in Europe or the United States for ministers, especially of the Dutch Reformed Church, to become political leaders. Andries Treurnicht was representative of that. He was head of the far-right Conservative Party that had split from the National Party, and he was so pro-apartheid that he later earned the nickname "Dr. No" for opposing every reconciliation the government proposed. When I called on him in Parliament House, he answered the door personally and made the tea himself. No servant was in residence. It was the first time I had seen this in South Africa.

Treurnicht, a former dominee in the Dutch Reformed Church, counseled patience in the church fray, but he told me he thought the church had made a wrong turn in declaring separatism to be inconsistent with scriptural teachings. "The Conservative Party teaches separatism," he told me. "Not racism, Mr. Ambassador, separatism. The development of people separately assures that there is no interference, that we don't step on each other's feet, and that we develop according to what we culturally believe in. We can preserve our separate cultural manifestation—language, art, music, education. We want a separate homeland in South Africa, and we will not accept black labor in this homeland. We'll do it ourselves." He was courteous, an Oxford scholar and well educated, but rigid in his belief in separatism.

In 1986 and 1987, the Dutch Reformed Church was at a crossroads. Led by Johan Heyns, it was an emerging force for change, but it was too late. Events had passed the church by and left it beached in misguided history.

OTHER RELIGIONS AND THEIR EFFORTS IN SOUTH AFRICA

South Africa was my crucible and a defining point in my own religious journey. I had always looked at Christianity not as an ecclesiastical element, but as an intellectual exercise that one needs to bring into one's everyday life. It is a tool of life. Before I went to South Africa, I had not considered my religious belief in a wider context of the world, certainly not in a political sense. In South Africa, I found that Christianity played a prominent role in the battle against apartheid. We do not often refer to the United States as a Christian nation in a political sense, but it is accepted that our nation was generally founded on what we call Christian principles. I would use these words to try to define what the United States stood for in relationship to South Africa. I did not think of Jesus Christ as a philosopher until I reread the speeches of Dr. King and especially his *Letter from Birmingham Jail*. In that work, King explained the meaning of Christianity—the laws of man on one hand and the laws of Christ on the other hand. Any man-made law that does not square with the teachings of Christ, he wrote, is an unjust law. I was using King's concepts of nonviolent revolution, influenced by Gandhi and Reinhold Niebhur, a European theologian. When I found myself carrying on this religious dialogue in a public domain, I had to ask myself, "What do you know about Christianity, Perkins?" Suddenly I found myself in deep water, having conversations with representatives of Christianity. It was totally unexpected. It should not have been, but it was. For the most part, my findings were disappointing.

I began with the Roman Catholic Church, which is my own church affiliation. At one of the first Masses I attended, the priest in the pulpit did not say what I wanted to hear. He did not talk about man's inhumanity to man, which we saw manifested every day in South Africa, although one of his fellow priests, Father Smangaliso Mkhatshwa, was in jail in Central Pretoria Prison at that very time for advocating alternative structures. Father Mkhatshwa is a formidable combination of priest and politician who has been jailed numerous times, tortured, and denied freedom of speech. I was not permitted to visit him while he was in jail, and after his release he was initially reluctant to meet me. He had made a decision not to deal with the American Embassy because he thought the Americans were sanctioning the white South African government. After about six months of watching my activities, he changed his mind and we met and our relationship grew ever more cordial. He became a valuable contact as we planned strategy to try and contribute to the elimination of apartheid. Father Mkhatshwa was especially helpful to me as I sought to unravel the ideology of the Dutch Reformed Church.

He also helped me to analyze my own feelings about being a Christian in a place like South Africa at that time. While in the Pretoria prison Father Mkhatshwa had honed his theology, deciding how the tenets of Christianity should be interpreted and operationalized in South Africa as opposed to the United Kingdom, for example. To paraphrase his essential question, when we encounter evil in a place such as South Africa, should we approach it in the name of Jesus Christ the same way we would approach evil elsewhere, in London or New York? The answer, in his judgment, is no. He believes that we should see evil in its unusual situation and figure out what can be done about it. He and I spent some time discussing this. I also talked with him about my own spiritual trial. "Since I have been in South Africa," I told him, "I have questioned myself on what I believe."

"You could not be here without doing that," he replied.

The South African government had decided to treat Father Mkhatshwa like a revolutionary and jail him. The more they imprisoned him, the more famous and the stronger he became. He is not a large man physically, but when he starts talking he is bigger than life.

In contrast, when I called on the Catholic bishop in Pretoria, I was saddened to leave that meeting feeling unsatisfied. There was no passion in his talk with me. The Catholic Church did not come on board in an ardent way until about a year after I had been there. Then church officials became outspoken, making efforts to ameliorate the actions of the unjust government.

Next I spoke with the Methodist bishop, a black South African and the most active church leader. Bishop Mmutlanyane Stanley Magoba was on the ideological and religious front lines and saw his role as the head of a large religious order as an opportunity to use it as a change agent. I regard him as one of the most effective church leaders in South Africa, along with Mkhatshwa, Tutu, and Boesak.

Anglican Archbishop Tutu was in a category by himself, and there was no question about his being a fighter against that government and using Christianity as a fighting tool. I disagreed with him about his view of the United States's representation in South Africa, but I never doubted his devotion to justice.

Allan Boesak in Cape Town was the leader of the Coloured Dutch Reformed Church. He was an erudite, well-educated Coloured who was brash, brave, passionate about change, and far ahead of the Dutch Reformed Church. He was one of the first senior black leaders to break ranks and accept me as the new American ambassador. Boesak's openness was an important chink in the armor of silence. John Burroughs, the black consul general in Cape Town, had arranged it. We had dinner at the deputy chief of mission's house, which was a face-saving plan that enabled Boesak to meet me without openly violating the boycott. We talked about the struggle, the revolution, and the United Democratic Front, which was a surrogate for the banned ANC. Boesak was a leader in the combined efforts of the UDF-ANC.

Boesak reads, speaks, and writes Afrikaans perhaps better than any other person in South Africa. It stuck in the craw of white Afrikaners to have a Coloured be more scholarly and fluent in their own language.

"You've got to understand the Afrikaners," he told me that evening. "They are like no other white people you've ever met. They are on a spiritual mission." He explained how they interpreted the Bible, how they understood their small band to be God's chosen people, and how embarrassed they were not to acknowledge the existence of Coloureds as offspring of the Afrikaners. Some Coloureds, Boesak told me, were more comfortable with Afrikaners than with blacks. "But the generic term 'black' is applied by the Afrikaner to everybody who is not white. That means that there is a second- or third-class category that exists for the greater good of the Afrikaner, and that is what we are fighting. We want equal political participation, equal economic integration, and socialization." From then on, Boesak and I met rather openly. "You are representing the most powerful country on earth," he said. "It doesn't make any sense not to talk with you."

I found Boesak to be a deep thinker who was enlightened but also practical. He was also egotistical and had an unbridled eye for the ladies. It was dangerous to indulge this fancy in a place like South Africa, where the government had eyes and ears in every nook and cranny of life. I knew that I was in a great fishbowl and that if I so much as danced too long with some lady at an official function, it would be in the newspapers. Boesak should have known better than I that our lives were under scrutiny, but he became involved with a beautiful Afrikaner woman. The hotel room where they met was bugged, of course, and their affair was soon made public. The fallout was heavy. Boesak's marriage ended in divorce, and he had to give up his pastorate and resign as head of the Coloured Dutch Reformed Church. It did not, however, diminish his passion for fighting for justice and freedom.

The Congregationalists, an evangelical black group, were led by a charismatic bishop who was loved by the Afrikaners because he opposed sanctions.

He advocated change and abhorred violence, but he was willing to compromise, so he was suspected of selling out to the Afrikaner government.

Except for a few heroic leaders, the Jewish community did not participate.
When other religious leaders met to take concerted action, the rabbis were not
present. Only one rabbi, a man from Brooklyn, was active in revolutionary
protest. The Jews in South Africa were divided in their ideas about how to react
to Afrikaner separatism. For some, apartheid was painfully similar to Nazi Germany's socialism. That history was too terrifying and too recent, so they
avoided the issue and hoped it would pass them by like an avenging angel, leaving their house untouched. Apartheid was so close to the bone, they could not
address the issue. They looked away. These differences came to light in Durban
where a key member of the Jewish community was an active member of the
Nationalist Party. He was attending an open meeting when someone challenged him saying, "We cannot see how any Jew can be a member of the
Nationalist Party." I couldn't understand it either.

In Johannesburg, the American rabbi from Brooklyn was a real fighter. Two
or three members of his congregation were beginning to challenge the status
quo of the Jewish community. After I had been in South Africa for six months,
Bob Frasure began putting together lunches with the Johannesburg Jewish
community, which allowed me to challenge their position of benign neglect.
Helen Suzman was an institution in her own right, tirelessly fighting for justice
on her own. I felt the Jewish community should have been right behind her, but
I did not get any sense of that happening.

On the streets of Pretoria, white people hissed at me, but Cape Town was different—I felt a freshness that I had not known elsewhere in South Africa. Some
of this was geography. Cape Town is located on the coast and benefits from its
international traffic. This was the first entry point of whites into South Africa.
It became a place peopled by Coloureds, but not many black Africans. The cosmopolitan air of the city masked the apartheid system, but it was still there.

One of my first acts in Cape Town was to celebrate Martin Luther King Jr.'s
birthday at the American Center in January 1987. My speech was based on
three elements of King's fight: fairness, justice, and legal redress. I saw this as
a way to signal what we would be talking about in our campaign for change in
South Africa.

About this time, I had my first run-in with Chet Crocker about personnel for South Africa. The tour was ending for the American consul general in Johannesburg, and I wanted a black woman to take the job. Aurelia Brazeal, a long-time Foreign Service officer, was perfect for the post. She wanted to come and I lobbied for her. Chet did not support it, and I interpreted this as a signal that he did not support me wholly. Both Chet and Chaz Freeman, his principal deputy, supported Jim Montgomery for the post. It was suggested to me that I get on board with the team's decision, but I did not. I continued to support Brazeal, and I lost. Montgomery was a brilliant officer, and I did not argue against his appointment, but I did point out that of the three consuls general in South Africa, all were men and two were white. I had wanted a minority and a woman. To appoint Brazeal to a senior post in the financial center of South Africa would have driven the Afrikaners nuts.

In addition to the colonel, the security officer who was an outspoken opponent of our policy, the only other person I had to send home from South Africa was the political officer in Cape Town. This chain of events began when a black revolutionary, who was also an avowed communist, told me that he had met a CIA agent in the American Embassy and told me his name—that of the political officer. "He has been passing himself off as a CIA agent all over Cape Town since he's been here."

"He's crazy then," I said, "because he is not a CIA agent." Back at the embassy I learned that my predecessor also had trouble with this officer, but neither he nor my second-in-command had taken action. I was livid. "This is unsatisfactory to me," I said. "I cannot believe what I am hearing. Send him in to see me." I told him that I was declaring him persona non grata and wanted him to clear out his desk that afternoon and to be out of the country in two weeks.

"What will I tell my wife?" he asked.

"That is your problem. Today is your last day in the building. I am instructing the security officer to lock your file cabinets and your office. I don't want you in the embassy ever again. I'll have your orders within two days." He was transferred back to Washington.

Instances like these with Crocker and the faux CIA agent, while I was confronting the greater Afrikaner battlefield, forced me to stop and deal with skirmishes in my own ranks both in Washington and in South Africa. It was frustrating, but part of the job of ambassador.

★

One of my first appointments on the Cape was with Anton Rupert, a sophisticated Afrikaner of high intellect who showed me such a different Afrikaner philosophy that it was like turning a kaleidoscope. Rupert is an Afrikaner
businessman with worldwide business interests and headquarters located in
Stellenbosch, where he has several vineyards and an impressively restored
ancient Cape home. He invited Frasure and me to a sumptuous lunch at his
mansion, Cap de Fleur, which has beautiful gardens and exquisite architecture.
Where else in the world could I see such splendor and comfort? I wondered.
And the companion thought was: Cheap labor had made it possible. Artificial
economics skewed toward one end of the human scale in South Africa, aided
and, in some cases, abetted by corporate moguls.

Most of the Afrikaners I had met were hard-shelled and resistant to change.
Rupert represented another side of the Afrikaner. He welcomed me graciously
to his elegant home, but his self-effacing manner would never be mistaken for
weakness. "The color of our skin gives us an identification we really don't
have," he said. "We are a tribe seeking to be safe and comfortable in an
extended family manner. The Afrikaners are now in control politically. Everything they have accomplished here in this part of the world is for our country,
the Volk. They are now being seen as pariahs. The question is, 'How do we do
it?' I am not afraid of this struggle. I think out of all of this turmoil there will
be some good."

Rupert believed that Afrikaners had no future unless blacks were a part of
that future. "It is inevitable," he told me, "that if we are to have any salvation, it
will be a black person who will help lead us to that. And you are a part of the
leadership. I hope you see us sympathetically and not as a group of people without refinement."

I found that Afrikaners, far more than Americans, dot their everyday language with biblical allusions. They refer to "a Damascus Road experience" or
something multiplying "like fishes and loaves." In like manner, many of the
Afrikaner leaders I met who were outside of government couched my presence
in scriptural terms. They considered me to be God's messenger. Moderator
Johan Heyns, Professor Pieter de Lange, Reverend Nico Smith, and the influential Piet Cilliers, head of the giant publishing conglomerate Nasionale
Pers—all told me they believed that God had sent me to South Africa. "God's

will is being done through messengers," Smith said. Heyns cited both Old and New Testament messengers sent to prevent a people from destroying themselves through folly. I could not see myself as a divine messenger, but I realized that these leaders, albeit late in coming to their activist role, were thinking about change. They had come to realize that without change, the future was a road to destruction. Their saving grace was a vision of a future with blacks and they believed that I was a messenger sent to point the way to that future.

No discussion of Afrikaners would be complete without special consideration of the Afrikaner women, because historically they have been a mainstay of the Volk. The Voortrekker monument to them in Bloemfontein, a bronze statue of an Afrikaner woman, symbolizes white civilization and represents determination and triumph despite the dangers of the wild continent. The official guidebook says, "The woman suffers but she does not look down. She looks straight ahead."

The prettier Afrikaner women, with their translucent skin, reminded me of a fragile eggshell—too pretty and too white. In reality, they are very strong people. They never accepted the fact that black women could be their equals. In a speech, I once used the phrase "black is beautiful," and some of the Afrikaner women were horrified. To them it was an oxymoron. "How could he make such a statement?" an older Afrikaner woman exclaimed. "How could he say 'black is beautiful?'" In another speech, I said that the Voortrekker woman bore some similarity to stalwart women such as Sojourner Truth and Harriet Tubman. The audience of women was not happy. The next day the newspaper quoted an Afrikaner woman who was outraged that I had compared them to two black women.

When Lucy, daughter Katherine, and I first visited the northern Cape, I asked the protocol officer to arrange for us to spend the night at a farm. She arranged for us to be the guests at the large farm of Elizabeth van der Merwe, her husband, and two teenage sons. Elizabeth took charge, and make no mistake about it, Afrikaner women are in charge of the household. She fixed the beds, and she prepared the breakfast. An Afrikaner breakfast is unlike anything else I have ever eaten—eggs, five or six kinds of meat, potatoes, porridge, lots of jams, three kinds of homemade bread, home-churned butter, coffee, tea, and pitchers of milk. She had a black servant, but Elizabeth did all of the cooking and serving.

Elizabeth also welcomed the opportunity to debate apartheid with me. She argued the rightness, the biblical basis (Genesis and Acts), and the practicality of the policy. "The blacks are different from us," she said. "The things that are valuable to them are not valuable to us and vice versa. They are backward and not educable. Sometime maybe in the future they might be, but not now. Ours is a benevolent stand."

I argued from a world position. "You cannot sustain it," I said. "There are more of them than there are of you, and they will overwhelm you one day. Isn't it better to reach an agreement now and grow together?" The idea was abhorrent to her. She was bound to the idea that the Afrikaners would prevail over the blacks with armed power.

If South Africa were a great chessboard spread before me, these would be the central players: the black revolutionaries in all their manifestations of organizations, individuals, and labor unions; the Afrikaners in government, church, Broederbond, and society; the English-speakers; the religious communities; the international press; and other factors I would come to address, such as our European allies, with their policies of self-interest. My first six months as ambassador had been an intensive tutorial in South African history, religion, geography, economy, labor, and politics. Our embassy operations in both Pretoria and Cape Town arduously gathered and analyzed information. Working like wheelwrights, we had spent hundreds of hours crafting strategy and hammering information and activities into smooth and seamless policy. I had made dramatic and emphatic statements of intent in my private meetings with ministers of the government, with revolutionary leaders, with my selective press interviews, and in my public appearances both at the Delmas Treason Trial and at the St. George's Cathedral demonstration. Now it was time to apply more widely the policy of the United States as a change agent in dismantling apartheid.

But first, I was ordered home for meetings in Washington, D.C., and to give a series of nationwide speeches. I was reporting to my boss—the people of the United States.

Reporting In

My assignment upon my return was clear. President Reagan and Secretary of State Shultz instructed me to travel across the country and let the people know what was happening in South Africa. "Get out of Washington," Secretary Shultz said. "Go into America, and tell the people what you are doing."

But first I reported in to the White House. One morning in May 1987, I climbed into Shultz's limousine, the biggest Cadillac I had ever seen, and we set off for my meeting with President Reagan in the Oval Office. The president had allotted me twenty minutes, which is a long time for a presidential meeting.

I was mindful of what Frank Carlucci had told me about being determined that the president finish his term without being branded a racist and an enemy of black people. "This is especially true with South Africa," Carlucci had said, "and you can help. Every time you see the president, make sure that you let him know that America's credibility is on the line. Tell the president what he needs to hear, not what he wants to hear."

That Saturday morning, President Reagan asked me about Buthelezi, whom the conservatives touted. I said that Buthelezi was a political leader with his own agenda and that he wanted to be president of South Africa. He asked about Desmond Tutu and told me, "I don't think too much of him." Evidently Tutu had lectured the president when they met, which President Reagan had not appreciated. And he asked me about the Afrikaners—if I thought all the white people in South Africa were evil.

"Absolutely not," I said. "There are some very good white people in South Africa who also want to see change come about, but they are not doing enough to help effect change. I think they have a role to play, and we need to coach them."

Secretary Shultz asked me to repeat something I had told him about Afrikaner women, that they were dangerously closed off from the black community and had no clue what was going on in the townships.

A photographer came into the room, startling me slightly, but the president laughed and said, "Don't worry, Mr. Ambassador. He's one of ours." The president had a great sense of humor. I met with President Reagan four times, not enough to say that I knew him, but I observed him closely. I had heard the rumors that sometimes he did not focus his thoughts or his attention wandered, but that is rubbish. I saw no lapse of attention in our meetings, and it was he who took control of the conversation, not the secretary of state or chief of staff. The president opened the meeting with directness, saying, "Mr. Ambassador, it is good to see you again. How are things going in South Africa?" He was very interested in my responses.

"We have to show what we stand for, Mr. President," I told him, "and we do not stand for oppression. These people in South Africa have to have a say in how their country is run, and the only way we can do that is open elections—universal suffrage. That's what we believe in." I reminded him that we had given the vote to blacks first and then to women. "We've come through all these revolutions," I said. "We know what revolution means."

"You are correct," President Reagan said.

Most ambassadors never get the chance to have an intimate conversation with the president, so I was floating on high cotton because I had more than my share of conversations with President Reagan about how to run the mission and develop policy in South Africa. The photograph of that Saturday morning meeting is on my office wall. A visitor asked me why I am the person sitting next to the president and the secretary of state is sitting elsewhere. The answer is that the Constitution identifies an ambassador as the president's personal representative, so protocol demands that the ambassador sit next to the president.

Secretary Shultz wanted a separate briefing on South Africa. He considered it an important meeting, so he called in the top hierarchy of the State Department: Deputy Secretary John Whitehead, Assistant Secretary of State for African Affairs Chet Crocker, Under Secretary for Political Affairs Michael Armacost, Assistant Secretary for International Organizational Affairs Alan Keyes, some staffers from the secretariat, and Charlie Hill, a Foreign Service officer who was aide to Shultz.

Secretary Shultz asked me to lead off the meeting, and I told the group that we needed to remain involved in South Africa and take every opportunity to talk with the Boers, who do not see any need to talk. "That suggests another need," I said. "We have to look at our way of doing business with them and slowly distance ourselves from them." I invited the secretary to visit the southern Africa region and to say something to help dismantle apartheid.

Seated on the sofa on the right (*left to right*),
Secretary of State George Shultz, Frank Carlucci, and Hank Cohen.

On the agenda was a discussion of South Africa policy based on a memorandum by Keyes, a black Foreign Service officer who was bombastic, conservative, and not comfortable with me or with what I was trying to do in South Africa. In turn, I considered his ideology to be strange. He found an ideologically kindred spirit when he worked for Jeane Kirkpatrick, the U.S. ambassador to the United Nations. His memorandum recommended shoring up domestic politics with respect to sanctions, "before it rises up and overtakes us." After the great sanctions debate in 1986 (which resulted in the sanctions bill being passed over the president's veto), Keyes said we needed to think about how to negate anti-apartheid assertions that our sanctions were inadequate and that we needed more. He wrote the memorandum to Shultz but did not send a copy to me. Crocker saw it for the first time the day of the meeting. I argued that domestic politics had spoken and was manifested by the way the

Congress voted. To lobby against sanctions, I said, would be swimming against the tide and not a popular action.

Shultz said that Keyes was talking about domestic politics while I was talking about South Africa, "and that is our interest here." The secretary suggested that Alan and I get together and discuss the matter. We never did. It was quite clear that Alan was being rebuffed. As he left, Keyes said, "Well, Mr. Ambassador, I don't envy you your job, but I do envy you your opportunity."

I had a special lunch May 18 with Crocker, a meeting that indicated the importance of South Africa to him. We agreed on a new approach to South Africa, the basis of which was my last speech—"Time is running out." I was to keep saying "South Africa has to change" and reiterate the three fundamentals of U.S. policy: (1) the release of Nelson Mandela, (2) the unbanning of all political parties, including the ANC and the Communist Party of South Africa, and (3) the enforcement of sanctions. Even that was not enough, I told Chet. We stopped short of calling for one-person, one-vote, which the Afrikaners dreaded.

In Washington I attended a weeklong chief of mission conference, where ambassadors from the region met with the secretary of state, the assistant secretary of state, and others in the State Department. National Security Advisor Carlucci spoke to the gathered ambassadors. Carlucci was a brilliant Foreign Service officer. When he was beginning his career as executive officer to Ambassador John W. Tuthill in Brazil, the ambassador asked if there was a better way to organize an embassy. When Carlucci told him there was, he was given the assignment. He reorganized the mission along functional lines, regardless of the agency involved. It was the first time this had ever been done in the Foreign Service. Many of the ideas he incorporated there are now taken for granted. At a time when it was fashionable to have martinis for lunch, Carlucci had a sandwich and then went to the YMCA to play handball. He was always reading and studying. He had come up through the ranks—a stint in personnel, a post in Zaire, working in the Office of Management and Budget, and serving as deputy secretary in the Treasury Department, ambassador to Portugal, and deputy national security advisor to Colin Powell.

At the conference, Carlucci spoke to us about the "cumbersome and unresponsive" bureaucracy of the State Department, something of which he knew firsthand. "We Foreign Service officers," he said, including himself in our group, "need to stop talking about the ratio of career officers versus non-career officers as ambassadors. Quit spending your time trying to figure out where you fit in the ratio. Just do your damned job and do it well, and maybe you'll be noticed. We have to argue merit in order to make a case. To all of you who represent our posts in Africa, I want to tell you that Africa is not on the front burner in the White House at all times, South Africa excepted. We pay a lot of attention to what Ed Perkins is doing in South Africa." He reminded us of the value of the president's time and that sometimes a domestic agenda is more important than the foreign-policy agenda. "I promise you that I look carefully at the issues," he said, "and I try to keep in front of the president those that are important and that he needs to see and act on. If you need some information or if you need an opinion that you don't get out of the State Department, call me. I'll give it to you." Listening to Carlucci I thought, "Here is the ideal Foreign Service officer: totally holistic in his nature, not beholden to any one track of a political officer or economic officer or consular officer. He had learned all of those things and he did them well. The only other person who has done that is Lawrence Eagleburger."

Another major speaker at the chief of mission conference was Chet's nemesis, Congressman Howard Wolpe, chairman of the House Subcommittee on Africa. He was not a friend of constructive engagement, and he told the assembled ambassadors that he thought the U.S. policy on South Africa needed to be more assertive. His view was that we could not talk the Afrikaners into making change.

That evening, Chet assembled a small group of ambassadors at his house. We talked for almost three hours about issues in South and southern Africa, as well as United Nations Security Council Resolution 435, which dealt with the independence of Namibia.

My conversations in Washington turned again and again to the subject of sanctions, especially the tough new sanctions bill coming before the Congress in October. I discussed sanctions with House majority whip Congressman William Gray and with Senator Lautenberg of New Jersey. "Sanctions work," I said repeatedly. "It is a wake-up call for the Afrikaners, but we can do more with sanctions. We can make them more creative in enhancing black economic empowerment." I said we should drag business and enterprise activities into the effort and that United States' businesses in South Africa should be persuaded to leave some of their profits, both in capital and in technology, in that country.

The two people in the sub-cabinet level whom I dealt with most frequently were Hank Cohen, the Africa person on the National Security Council, and

Allison Rosenberg, deputy assistant secretary in the Africa Bureau. I listened to Chet and these two policy-makers prophesying about what actions Afrikaners would take toward political change, and I thought, "They are full of bull. It won't happen that way."

I tried to bridle their optimism. "Don't expect much from the Afrikaners," I told them. "We must be realistic about South Africa." I said that the Afrikaners were not going to change unless they were forced to change. They were prisoners of themselves living a comfortable life within that prison. I pressed Cohen, who was in the White House, to get the president to take a stand on detainees and to encourage Shultz to visit southern Africa.

In Washington, I went hither and yon in the State Department for meetings, having a new official portrait made for the press and working on three speeches. My talks would focus on South Africa's economy, current and future political situations, and the jailing of children and of people who advocated alternative systems. I wanted to be able to deliver these speeches from notes, rather than reading line by line. I spent one day working with Sharon Peterson, a public-speaking expert who had been Shultz's advisor. "You can say thank you when you finish a speech," she said, "but remember that it is the audience that ought to be thanking you for addressing them. If you can believe that, the speeches will be infinitely better." I still thank audiences for a chance to address them.

Jesse Jackson called on me and repeated his message to the waiting press. "Before Edward Perkins went to South Africa," he told them, "I asked him not to go. I was wrong, and today I have told him so." "Reverend Jackson," I said to him, "today you stand ten feet tall in my opinion." He was pleased to hear that.

With F. Allen "Tex" Harris, deputy director of the Office of Southern African Affairs, I went to a conference on South Africa sponsored by the Ford Foundation at Pocantico Hills in upstate New York. A number of South Africans, both black and white, were in attendance, including English-speaker Alex Boraine and Afrikaner Frederick Van Zyl Slabbert. They had formed the Institute for a Democratic Alternative South Africa, which was making waves in white South Africa.

Still, I was discouraged to hear at the conference such a wide range of views expressed with practically no substance. One such suggestion was that the United States take the lead in completely shutting South Africa off from the rest of the world until apartheid was changed. They did not realize that the Afrikaners would likely welcome this because they preferred to be isolated.

In New York I gave a major speech at the Council on Foreign Relations, one of the most prestigious non-governmental foreign-policy organizations in the world. Based on conversations with the country team, I reviewed for the council the past six years of relations between the United States and South Africa. These ranged from the semi-aggressive policy of the Carter administration to the constructive engagement policy of the Reagan administration. Now, I said, we had come to a point where the United States was slowly turning its policy about face, moving away from a benign policy of hoping that the South African government was willing to reach an accommodation with the disadvantaged South Africans. Time was running out, I said. Although I acknowledged that South Africa had a role to play in its own future, I said loudly and clearly that the South African government was just one element in that process. The country team suggested that I stress trade and the economic development aspect of change, so we came up with the term "Aid Plus Trade Plus Government Partnership." This was a necessary element in the coming change. We wanted to hone in on technology as opposed to political theology.

In Philadelphia, Tex and I called on Judge Leon Higginbotham, a federal district court judge who had been to South Africa and was outspoken in his opinion that the United States was not being assertive enough. This was the kind of person I wanted to talk with. I asked him what I asked many people: "How would you do it?"

"Concentrate on the legal profession," Judge Higginbotham told me, "people who deal in judicial activities, such as judges. Get them to stand up, to speak out, to try and make law that is favorable to providing equality across the board." It was exciting to talk with him because he said, simply and without equivocation, "Here is one way that societies change."

From there we went to see Reverend Leon Sullivan, a giant of a person both physically and morally. I thought of him as a coat-and-tie Moses, such was the power of his personality and church. Reverend Sullivan graduated from West Virginia State University, a traditionally black university, and further educated at Columbia University. He was an internationally known social activist and, for thirty-eight years, the pastor of the Zion Baptist Church in Philadelphia, one of the largest churches in the United States. In 1977 he had authored the famous Sullivan Principles, an attempt to end discrimination against black workers in South Africa by establishing within the international business community a code of conduct for economic, social, and political justice.

General Motors had a huge plant in the Eastern Cape region and since Sullivan had been appointed in 1970, the heyday of the civil rights struggle, as the first black American member of the board, this was his main focus. He became an activist board member. If U.S. businesses were going to continue to operate in South Africa, Sullivan said, they need a set of principles, and he created them.

The Sullivan Principles were overtly and directly related to business in South Africa, but the document was such a revolutionary move that it caught the attention of South Africa, Europe, and the United States, where it had an impact on the president and the State Department. The Comprehensive Anti-Apartheid Act (CAAA) did not require American businesses by law to disinvest in South Africa; it merely urged them to do so. When the Sullivan Principles were adopted by all American businesses in South Africa, it made American business a change agent. In 1999, the principles were expanded and known as the Global Sullivan Principles, described as an international standard for equal opportunity and human rights. Originally, there were only six Sullivan Principles:

1. Nonsegregation of the races in all eating, comfort, locker rooms, and work spaces.
2. Equal and fair employment practices for all employees.
3. Equal pay for all employees doing equal or comparable work for the same period of time.
4. Initiation and development of training programs that will prepare Black, Coloureds, and Asians in substantial numbers for supervisory, administrative, clerical, and technical jobs.
5. Increasing the number of Blacks, Coloureds, and Asians in management and supervisory positions.
6. Improving the quality of employees' lives outside the work environment in such areas as housing, transportation, schooling, recreation, and health facilities.

By the time I became ambassador to South Africa, Reverend Sullivan had painted himself into a corner by declaring that he would leave the Sullivan Principles Foundation if South Africa had not made a dramatic move toward dismantling apartheid in six months. As I took my leave from him in Philadelphia, his wife Grace took me aside to say that she was worried about her husband. His health was not good, and he had been hurt terribly by criticism from black leaders in the United States. When General Motors did not immediately disinvest after the passage of the CAAA, and since Sullivan was not aligned with the process of some anti-apartheid movements in the United States, his personal commitment and the effectiveness of the principles came into question. Some black American leaders did not give him much support or credit. When some said that he appeased Afrikaners by not demanding more of them, Reverend Sullivan felt forced to make his intemperate statement declaring a six-month deadline. It was not well thought out, Grace said, and was a reaction to that criticism. My view was that he was sorry he had made that statement and sorry that he had to disassociate himself in order to keep his honor. The Sullivan Principles did make a difference, but that difference was probably negated somewhat by those who criticized it. I learned a lesson from the visit to Reverend Sullivan. It reminded me of the precariousness of my own position. At what point would I be looked upon as appeasing the Afrikaners instead of pushing them? It was a concern I carried all during my tour in South Africa.

In Chicago I spoke to the Chicago Council, and in Kansas City I gave a series of speeches and was reacquainted with relatives and friends from Louisiana. In Boston, I met with Harvard president Derek Bok, who was secretary of labor in the Johnson administration. Harvard was heavily involved in South Africa and had given an honorary degree to Desmond Tutu. At one time, Tutu threatened to give back all of his honorary degrees if the universities that had conferred them upon him did not get more involved in trying to make a change in South Africa. Bok and I discussed education in South Africa and Harvard's participation in a new scholarship program that I wanted to initiate.

I also spoke at Phillips Academy Andover, my daughter Sarah's high school. The entire student body was invited to hear me. The question-and-answer session that followed lasted for an hour and a half. I was pleased with the intensity and substance of the students' questions about South Africa. Sarah had more questions, so she and I sat up late into the night talking.

In early June, before leaving the East Coast, Sarah and I toured colleges and universities to find one that was right for her, visiting Brown, Wesleyan, Yale, Princeton, Georgetown, University of Virginia, and Johns Hopkins. Finally she chose the University of Pennsylvania in Philadelphia. They were pleased to have her, and it was a good choice; she excelled and was happy there.

On trips back to the United States, I made it my business to reconnect with family and friends. On the way back to South Africa, Lucy and I stopped in Honolulu to visit with friends and to talk with people about South Africa. I found that their views differed from those of the continental United States;

generally native-born Hawaiians were much more detached, as I sometimes think people in Hawaii are.

On this speaking tour across the United States, I talked with businessmen, state legislators, community leaders, religious leaders, and civil rights leaders. I solicited their views and support. I elicited comments about South Africa, and the people had a lot to say. The statements I heard again and again, repeated like a mantra, were: "Keep trying to see Mandela. Keep trying to get him released. We support sanctions." Although business in general does not like sanctions, the people I met said business had concluded that sanctions were one of very few ways left to get the attention of the South African government.

I did not want only to address audiences in formal settings, being exclusively with people who considered me Mr. Ambassador. I wanted a two-way communication with people. I wanted question-and-answer sessions, informal conversations, and feedback. I wanted to know if they were hearing accurately what I was trying to say. On one testy occasion, that was not the case.

In Portland, I spoke to my mother's church as well as to corporate executive officers under the auspices of the City Club. I was in Los Angeles when Tex Harris called to read me the front-page headline from the *Washington Post*: "America's First Black Ambassador Breaks with the Reagan Administration." During the question-and-answer period after the Portland speech, I was asked if sanctions have been effective. "They have been extraordinarily effective in this way," I answered. "They have opened doors for us in the black communities and other places that we wouldn't have had otherwise. They have been a wake-up call for those who watch what America does." I also used the term "unequivocally successful."

The Associated Press reporter interpreted my answer a different way and wrote the story as if I were saying the Reagan administration had been wrong all along, that constructive engagement was a mistake, and now we were embarked on a different course. This was the story the *Washington Post* had picked up. Chet Crocker wanted to talk with me, Tex said. I called him.

"Well, Ed, you have stirred up quite a dust storm back here," Chet said, and he told me that he would like to have a copy of my speech.

"You can't have it," I said. "I didn't say what the *Post* said I said. Here is what I said in answer to that question." I repeated my answer for him. "I'd appreciate it if you told the secretary that. But I am not sending you a copy of my speech. You take my word for it. If you can't take my word, then you have the wrong person."

When the secretary of state heard about it he said, "Defuse it." The next day, at a press briefing, the first question asked was, "Has Ambassador Perkins broken with the Reagan administration?" The spokesperson had been instructed to say, "Ambassador Perkins speaks for the American people and for this administration." Period. And that was the end of it.

Before leaving South Africa for this speaking tour, the country team and I had met to analyze the South African elections of the white parliament that had taken place in early May 1987. In theory, the Nationalist Party put its mandate on the line and said, "Here is our policy. Do you agree or disagree with it?" The vote was overwhelmingly for the Nats, and P. W. Botha was re-elected president. The message was simple: The Afrikaner government had dug in and would go no further.

They would not change, so we would tighten the screws on them. We began to re-do our policy. We determined that the Nationalist Party had lost all of its intellectual strength, especially with the departure of a group of Stellenbosch professors, and since there would be no younger elements joining the ranks, there would therefore be no new blood. There was a possibility that a new political alignment might emerge from the wreckage of the election—independents, professors, and other academics—but that lay in the future. For now, our view was that the voting electorate had made a decisive and unequivocal shift to the right. As I put it, "This means that United States government policy has been 'diddled' for six-plus years. The South African government of the Afrikaners cannot be talked into change." It was a disheartening recognition, and the entire country team felt deflated.

What I told the country team, and what I put into my report back to the secretary was this: "Constructive engagement, as we know it, was a flawed policy when looked at in the context of Afrikaner history. We must now reexamine and change." Crocker often wanted me to be more academic in writing cables, but sometimes ambassadors have to be blunt to get anyone's attention.

I had stopped in London en route to the United States, once again consulting with Fleur de Villiers, a tall and beautiful, modern-thinking Afrikaner writer whose family goes back to the early Boers in South Africa. She was working for the Institute for Strategic Studies in London, and she was the first Afrikaner woman I met who was a professional in her own right, and the first Afrikaner I heard described as having been "de-tribalized." Fleur was a valuable contact because of her knowledge of Afrikaner history and because she was accurate in predicting the political alignment to come in South Africa. I met with Charles Price, the United States ambassador to the United Kingdom, and told him that the elections seemed to announce, "No change." I also told him the substance of my speeches, which was the United States' requirement that South Africa lift the ban on political parties and release detained children and political prisoners. This was not the British view. The British recognized British business interests in South Africa, which was unlike the United States government's stance. The United States had come to the point of saying, "Business interests must either be contributing to change or not be in business." This is not the way the Reagan administration started, but sufficient time for change had elapsed, and it was where we were now.

After about six months of serving as ambassador to South Africa and after listening to the American constituency, I knew that the time had come for the United States government to make a declaration about South Africa. The U.S. Embassy, with me as spokesman, had to stand for something. We had to put our imprimatur on something that made sense. The statement I made in declaring our stance was this: "South Africa is a land twice promised."

"A land twice promised"—a powerful phrase coined by Bob Frasure. It had never been said before. The first time I used it was in a policy speech in Portland, Oregon, in April 1987. From then on, I used it often in my public speeches. It was accepted variously as an effrontery and a reality. The president of South Africa did not like it at all, and some people in our own administration thought it was too adventuresome, but there it was. This was the phrase the United States planted in the earth like a banner, a declaration that both black and white South Africans had a legitimate claim on that country. We were saying that the Afrikaners do not have exclusive ownership of the country, but rather that South Africa must be a nation of all its citizens.

Back in South Africa, the country team and I reviewed my visit to the United States, discussing the people I had spoken with and their recommendations, as we sought to find a way to fit this information into our unfolding policy. From this point on, we would be striding boldly in a new direction in South Africa.

We decided that we needed to talk more with business and push them toward trying to make a difference, instead of hiding behind the skirts of the South African government. "Politics for politicians, economics for the businessmen" is a phrase they liked to brandish about. It was a convenient way to duck responsibility. "There is no separating the two," I said. White South African businessmen winced when I said it. I chose to concentrate on the duties of the businessmen in the struggle, both Afrikaner and *uitlander*, which means "outlander" or Englishman. I suggested that every businessman had to take a stand. When they argued, "We do business and leave politics to the politicians," I always answered the same: "If you pay taxes, you can influence it. Look at the end objectives of those who are fighting for change. One day you will wake up and black political leaders will be in charge, and you won't know what they are or who they are. You won't know their names. Businessmen have to decide if they want to be a part of a new South Africa and then decide how they can contribute to the transitional process."

We decided to work closely with the English-speaking, American, and Afrikaner chambers of commerce. A year later we were also working with the black chamber of commerce.

The team and I began redrafting the policy document to go to Washington vis-à-vis the South African elections, deciding that I should give more speeches, and we began working on a new one to talk about our objectives henceforth in South Africa. We concluded that we should widen our network. We would get to places we had not been—small townships on the periphery of Afrikaner towns where we could meet farmhands and domestic servants. We would talk more in general about the need for change, and in black townships we would talk about peaceable change rather than change at the point of a gun. This is when we decided unequivocally to use, in part, Martin Luther King Jr.'s philosophy of nonviolent protest as enunciated in his celebrated *Letter from Birmingham Jail* to his fellow clerics. We wanted to tell the black citizens that they could make a difference in a nonviolent way, but that they had to keep at it.

We needed to get a much better handle on education among black people and to mount an assault on the 7:1 ratio of education spending—seven dollars for a white child compared to one dollar for a black child. That same sort of ratio existed for health care.

It was agreed that I should visit as many southern African countries as I could, talking to my fellow ambassadors and to the people so they would know what was happening in South Africa. It was important to have diplomatic relations with the front-line states: Zimbabwe, Tanzania, Angola, Zambia, Malawi, Mozambique, Swaziland, Zaire, Lesotho, and Botswana. We needed to get a good hold on South Africa by ensuring that all of the southern African countries saw the United States as attempting to make a bona fide effort to change South Africa.

I finally decided to go to an Afrikaner church and be seen in a restaurant with Afrikaners. I deliberated long and hard about this and how it would be perceived, but I concluded that it is instructive to finally realize that you never, ever see yourself as others see you. About this time, a well-known Afrikaner businessman told Bob Frasure and me, "Things are getting really bad. I went through the immigration facilities at Heathrow a day or so ago, and they looked at me like I was a worm or something. Are we really becoming a pariah state? I'm not like that. I'm a perfectly decent human being." "Yes, but you are South African," I said, "and you have to be responsible as a citizen for the activities of your government."

In our new policy, I would make more speeches. Every time I made a speech, I would say what positive actions we were taking to dislodge the apartheid system. And—of paramount importance—the country team and I would determine when and how I would publicly utter the all-important statement, "one-person, one-vote." I know the South African government winced, waiting for me to throw down this final gauntlet.

TIGHTENING THE SCREWS

They haven't felt the pain, yet." That was what Congressman Ron Dellums (Democrat–California) meant in 1986 when he introduced a bill, H.R. 4868, urging stricter U.S. sanctions against South Africa. Ron was a civil-rights activist and a guiding force behind the Comprehensive Anti-Apartheid Act of 1986. I used to jog with him in Washington, and I found him to be intense and highly intelligent.

He was among the growing numbers of Americans, black and white, who found the situation in South Africa intolerable. Driven by his conscience, he wanted the United States to hasten change by unleashing a full range of economic and political sanctions against South Africa. American businesses, especially those with interests in South Africa, were hit broadside by this, and they fought back with what they considered logic. People will suffer, they said. This was one of the few times I agreed with Archbishop Tutu, who replied, "Nobody worried about this until it began to hurt."

Chet argued that the implementation of the CAAA had no effect. Following this line of thought: Sanctions do not work, so let's try something else.[1]

Ron stood firm. "Let's turn the screws even tighter. Crank it up." The Dellums bill did not pass, but this was because things were beginning to change in South Africa.

The South African election of May 1987 was one with a difference, according to an editorial in the South African newspaper *The Citizen*. It was a turning point in South African history. The campaign "forced the white electorate to a choice and the voters chose unequivocally to declare the values they hold most dear. They voted first and foremost to define themselves by pigmentation. . . . Voters squashed all cultural, religious, and language barriers to enter the white laager and to shut out the rest. The only binding factor was race." The editorial included a damning statement: "You Americans have caused this."[2]

The Cape Times adopted a similar warlike tone: "Eighty percent of South Africans who voted . . . opted for regression, or at best, highly defensive gradualism toward the future they dared not think about. State President P. W. Botha received a mandate for *Gotterdamerung.* The only question was whether he would have the political guts not to use it."[3]

We had tried gentle persuasion and called it constructive engagement, but the Reagan administration saw that the Afrikaners would not cooperate. The only way to get them to change was to hit them on the head, and that is what the sanctions were about.

In the embassy and in Washington we were searching for a model for a new South Africa. President Reagan and I had discussed proposing a cantonal country. "Suppose South Africa was partitioned," the president said, "like the Swiss cantons. Suppose they had a government like Switzerland, with the Germans in one place and the French elsewhere."

Back in South Africa I layed the proposal before the country team—alternating the presidency among black, white, and Coloured officials. I quickly realized I was out of my mind to even consider it, and I went back and told President Reagan, "It won't work, sir."

"Why not?"

"Because it's not Switzerland, it's South Africa."

"It's that different?"

"Yes it is. Everybody in Switzerland is white. They just speak a different language. But everybody in South Africa is multicolored, of many religions, and they speak many different languages. The one thing all black South Africans are united on is that they don't want to be governed by a white minority unless they vote it in. We can't do anything that would seem to impose the system." I am sure the president's advisors had lobbied him privately on a canton system. They likely told him that putting a black in charge would drive the country into the ground, and the United States could not possibly be involved in imposing a system that ruined a functioning country. To his credit, President Reagan never betrayed any of that to me. He listened courteously, setting up one suggestion after another as I, with equal politeness, knocked them down.

Finally he said, "Well, you know best." And we never again discussed partitioning South Africa.

A model we did discuss seriously at the embassy was a multiparty corporation, with the ANC taking the lead. Primary objectives of this model included
the overt integration of the political and economic activity, accelerating a
wider participation by the nonwhite population, and dramatically advancing
education across racial divides, including increasing the numbers of technolog-
ically qualified people. In a couple of speeches we offered this model for consideration, and we were pilloried.

This model would acknowledge that black South Africans and Afrikaners
had more in common with each other than with others outside their domain.
The Afrikaners disliked it instinctively because of their biblical interpretation.
They could not believe that any black could be the political equivalent of an
Afrikaner such as Henning Klopper.

The blacks disliked it because they were so adamantly opposed to the tenets
of Afrikanerdom. Later, after the heat cooled, members of both groups told me
that my statement was accurate and they were in the same boat together.

As another model, I considered the example of Singapore, where Lee Kwan
Yu had come to power on a platform of economic equality and housing. The
Singapore government passed a law providing everybody with a house of three
bedrooms, a master bedroom and a bedroom for each of two children. The
government also encouraged families to limit themselves to two children. A
third child would require by law a third bedroom that would not be funded by
a government loan. We thought the South Africans might employ a similar system, but I was keenly aware that it was easier to deal with a smaller population
such as that of Singapore than it would be with South Africa's twenty-seven
million people, many of whom had been deprived for so long and were hungry
for material goods. So this model, too, was discarded.

We wrestled with the massive problem of education. How do you go about
educating everybody at once? The answer is that it cannot be done. We could
not omit people ages 30–50 and above. So many in this age bracket had inadequate education, yet scores of productive years ahead of them. They needed to
be useful citizens and participate in society.

We talked with communists, as well as marxists who called themselves "scientific socialists." They all had a different view of a new model, but they felt
that government had to take a commanding lead. I agreed, but government
must be enlightened and inventive in such a situation. To be successful, government cannot adopt a "hands off" stance, but nor can government be the sole

innovator of change. We were fast reaching the point where we needed to con-
solidate the political and economic references we were gathering.

In Johannesburg after my U.S. speaking tour, I began reading a biography of
Miyamoto Musashi and rereading the philosophy of this sixteenth-century
Japanese warrior. As I read, I saw the past and present in a great circle that
moved into the future like a spiral. I recognized that my decision-making in
South Africa was influenced by my study of Asian philosophy and my experiences in Japan. There I took chances and went places where I never saw Americans. I learned to enjoy Japanese food, drink, and culture. It changed me
forever from a provincial American boy to someone who could appreciate
another culture. Gradually, in many ways, I shifted to the Japanese style, which
is a style of indirection, symbolism, and universal respect. First it became purposeful; now it is automatic to me, and I know precisely when I am using that
style. I used it a lot in South Africa.

From my boyhood, I remembered the populism of Huey Long, which I saw
manifested on both the black side and the Afrikaner side. Long had said, "Pick
up your shovels and hoes. I'll join you." He used the term "rednecks" and said,
"Everybody thinks you're nothing but rednecks, but I'll make it possible for
you to get those goods to market." In South Africa, they used the word *rooinek*,
which means the same thing. In a vein similar to Long's championing the poor,
working people of Louisiana, Afrikaner leaders at Voortrekker Hill in 1938 said,
"We do not intend for any Afrikaner ever to go hungry again." Huey Long
asked his Louisiana audiences to dream. The Afrikaners asked their constituents
to do the same thing when they won the election in 1948.

Fast forward to the blacks in South Africa of the 1980s with a similar dream:
"This great country has its promise for us and we want to control our destiny."
They did not aspire to unbridled capitalism because they wanted everybody to
get a piece of what the land had to offer. That was the essence of the ANC charter, yet here I was in 1987 using the phrase "a land twice promised."

Although I had granted no personal press interviews on my trip across the
United States, some of the American press had detected an atmospheric change
in our policy. Starting with my speech in Portland, we had begun tightening the
screws.

"Quietly, the way Edward Perkins prefers to do things," the *Christian Science
Monitor* reported, "the new American ambassador to South Africa is overseeing

a shift in the United States' approach to the political conflict here. On the surface, little has changed in American policy . . . yet Perkins said that in conveying Americans' moral outrage, [sanctions] had been a success." The reporter noted a tougher tone in my Portland speech, as well as a subtext about the necessity of the United States' distancing itself from official South Africa policies. "We have to make abundantly clear," I had said, "in almost any way we can, our abhorrence of a system which has a minority of the population enjoying economic and political rights at the expense of the majority." The article was a bit unfair to President Reagan, but dead on about the new tone of our policy.[4]

I kept up the pressure when I delivered a speech to the Executive Women's Club in Johannesburg, "Time is running out," I told the group, as proven by the demographics of South Africa. "By our account, the white population of South Africa is about 15 percent of the total population. By the year 2000, whites will constitute less than 8 percent of the total population." I looked at this audience, a powerful group of women with only four or five black members who sat together at one table. "What does that tell you?" I asked.

One of the black women jumped to her feet, threw her fist into the air, and shouted, "Tell it like it is, Ambassador!" The only people who laughed were the black women at her table. The rest of the audience sat in stony-faced silence.

As I left that evening, I was met at the escalator by Mona DeBeers, the wife of the president of the English-speaking Progressive Freedom Party (PFP). "Ambassador," she said, indicating the elegant Carlton Hotel where we were standing, "do you want to see all of this torn down and destroyed?"

"Mona," I said, "are you suggesting to me that a brick, or several bricks, of this building is worth one life? If you are, I disagree. If the place is torn apart, so be it." She was very angry at my answer.

Often I asked myself how the separate elements of South Africa could be so blind. I realized that they saw limited perspectives. They could not see the whole field, whereas I saw all of the players—total South Africa and its division. The American Embassy understood what was happening in South Africa better than any other single activity anywhere in the world, better even than the Afrikaner government. This is why my discussions with George Shultz and Ronald Reagan centered primarily on how to get people to communicate with each other. It meant breaking down walls of fear and the Afrikaners' god-awful interpretation of the Bible.

As the *Christian Science Monitor* correctly noted, whereas the previous ambassador had been identified with the South African government, I was intent on encouraging dialogue of all people, official and opposition. This strategy of trying to get people to talk among themselves had not been used before. It was specifically designed for southern Africa and South Africa. It did not come about all that quickly. We formed it only after I had been there a few months, had surveyed the ground, and got to know some of the people. While I was gone, Bob Frasure, Liz Pryor, Frank Parker, Steve Rogers, Karl Beck, and the political officers fanned out across South Africa to talk about what the United States stood for and what we hoped would obtain in South Africa. Without being too dramatic about it, we wanted them to know that a new day had arrived.

After one strategic dinner at the residence with younger South African politicians, I saw a new perspective: These Afrikaners were scared. They were concerned that the blacks were unhappy and wanted change, and they were even more frightened to realize that the United States appeared to be taking sides with the blacks. We talked that evening about the Group Areas Act, which determined where blacks could live. "You have created an unnecessary enemy in the affluent black person," I said. I had met several black millionaires who could not buy a home in the environs of Johannesburg or Cape Town. "You may have had some allies along the way if you had been more inclusive. Perhaps income, not race, should have been the dividing line." The deputy minister of Foreign Affairs considered that comment, and then said they worried about black people moving in and living in overcrowded houses. "That means that you don't know anything about people who are upwardly mobile," I said. Upwardly mobile people take on the coloration of the society they are penetrating.

Within white discussion groups, I heard South Africans say, "This is my country," at the same time they asked themselves, "Or is it?" They were afraid the blacks would say, "You don't belong here." They were wrong. The majority of blacks were very forgiving and said, "The Afrikaners have as much right to be here as we do."

We talked about a new model constantly. On a trip to a township in Pietermaritzburg with Liz Pryor, a political officer, and other staff members, we found ourselves at six o'clock still about an hour away from Durban, our destination. It had been a long day and I suggested we stop at a pub.

"Thank God," someone said. "The ambassador has a heart." It was a typical

English pub and, since it was winter, a big fire burned in the fireplace. The Afrikaners in the pub were somewhat surprised to see our mixed group—a white woman, a Coloured person, and me as the only black in the place—but we were welcome. The atmosphere was cozy, and we relaxed over our drinks. "Look at this," I said, indicating the mix of customers. "Why can't the country get along like this? But everybody here at this moment is on a collision course and all of this will be destroyed. This is what we have to try to prevent. This is the essence of our objectives."

No one had addressed the issue of a black government until I started talking about it. Even in Washington, none of the policymakers had considered the possibility. It was too alien. The first indication of anybody's taking it seriously came with the secretary of state's Advisory Council, which was meeting when I was appointed ambassador. In 1987, the Advisory Council released the report of its year-long study, with the important two-part conclusion that it was not possible to see a future South Africa as it existed currently, and that the ANC and other parties would eventually form the government. "The first priority of American policy toward South Africa should be to help facilitate real negotiations between the South African government and representatives of the black majority," the panel of experts said.[5]

So, the initial part of my strategy in South Africa was to plant the idea of a black government among the mission's senior staff members; I had to get them thinking about it. Some of them were comfortable with the segregated status quo ante. A black government was inevitable, I told the staff. That does not mean that everything admirable in South Africa—the buildings, the parks, the economy—will be torn down. It does mean that the standard of living will change. Our job was to try to take South Africa through a transition to something politically and socially different without destroying idyllic South Africa at its best. I did not know whether or not it was possible, but I was dedicated to that goal.

Bob Frasure understood immediately. Every time we wrote a speech, he helped address our three audiences: the American and South African employees in the American embassy, the white audience in South Africa, and the nonwhite audience in South Africa. Even among these three audiences, black and white, the people were fragmented, tribally, politically, and economically.

✫

About this time, autumn 1987, Secretary Shultz helped identify our new policy in an important New York address titled "The Democratic Future of South Africa." He cited current realities, listing the very issues that we at the embassy had identified as priorities—increased repression of blacks, detention of children, escalating violence, the economic plight of nonwhites, terrorist attacks such as car bombings, and the lack of negotiations between the South African government and its opponents.

"I particularly feel the frustration of having only limited influence," Shultz said, "and for not being able to make things right down there. That, too, is a reality. It is not within the power of the United States, or any other country, to impose a solution to South Africa's problems. The solution must come from South Africans themselves. The United States will not walk away as South Africans struggle to decide their destiny, and we are united in our opposition to apartheid. It must be eliminated and it will be eliminated." This is what we had been saying all along from the mission in South Africa. These words came from our embassy.

Shortly after that, Crocker also gave a speech in which he seemed to agree prima facie with Shultz, but he was reluctant to come down hard on the Afrikaners. Black South African revolutionaries heard the caution beneath his words and never quite trusted his sincerity. Chet had not let go of his belief in constructive engagement, which he characterized in this speech as "the power of persuasion and the efficacy of diplomacy." He also took a verbal swipe at the anti-apartheid movement in the United States, referring to it as "those who champion the policy of punishment and isolation."

South Africa was a complex subject, the most contentious and compelling issue faced by the United States at that time. It was a tangle of colonial history, American commerce, and the international intrigues of the cold war. In fairness to Chet, who had been the chief spokesperson for the Reagan administration on Africa policy, South Africa had not been dealt with satisfactorily by any American administration, including President Carter's, which had been the most proactive administration in seeking a United States policy toward it. What's more, Chet was not alone in his thinking. Others in the Reagan administration shared his sympathies, including Bill Casey, head of the CIA, who was totally against any change in South Africa. Casey's position was understandable, since he was the

United States' chief intelligence officer. We had relied on South Africa to tell us what was happening in that part of the world and to keep an eye on the Soviets and their dirty tricks. At that time, too, we still considered the Cape of Africa to be essential to us for ship commerce.

Chet and I continued to disagree from time to time on what the United States should say to South Africans, but he did use some of my comments in his New York address. Talking about how apartheid kept people separated and unable to communicate in normal structures, he quoted something I had said in a recent talk in Johannesburg: "If I were to choose the most poignant thing I have witnessed since my arrival here," I said, "it would be the lack of knowledge and understanding of each other among South Africans. You live in two different political and economic worlds. You come from different social positions, and you are only now getting to know each other. All over this lovely country, blacks have asked me, 'What is it that whites are thinking?' And whites have questioned me, almost wistfully sometimes, about life in the townships."

At this juncture I did what the South Africans had been dreading; I publicly proposed the concept of one-person, one-vote. Bob Frasure, Liz Pryor, and I caucused. "You have been here almost a year now," Bob said. "I think it is time to say one of the things that will help bring about peaceful change is one-person, one-vote." Liz approached Hugh Murray, the publisher and editor of a highly respected South African magazine, and he agreed to publish it. Bob, Liz, and I collaborated on the article, making it pithy but short.

The article "In Your Hands" appeared in *Leadership* magazine (vol. 6, no. 5, 1987). I wrote:

> If I had no concern for the future of South Africa, I would not be here. . . . The sad fact is that the policy of apartheid has been all too successful. It ranks as one of this century's most disastrous feats of social engineering. And now, somehow, it must be disassembled. . . . Somewhere down the road, South Africa faces a major transformation of its political structure. Almost no one I have met believes that the present constitutional system is sufficient to carry the country into the next century. I sense a growing realization that a valid political system here must be one that correlates with the demographics of the country—not merely black participation, or black cooperation, but a government which truly represents the majority of South Africans (and the term "South Africa" includes everyone inside the wide, traditional, national boundaries).
>
> . . . Afrikaners are now the governors of the nation. This means that they bear a special responsibility to take steps to create reconciliation, unity, and the extension of full democratic rights to all South Africans.

This was my throwing down the gauntlet, and on this occasion, I cleared the article in advance with Washington. I do not think Chet liked it much, but it was time. When that magazine hit the stands, it raised hell. The Afrikaners erupted like a maddened bull. They had consistently told me they could not live with that policy. One of the newspapers called for me to be declared persona non grata. I rode it out.

Accelerating the pace, I launched into tours through the provinces of South Africa, meeting individuals, addressing organizations, and talking with the press. The subtext of my message was "Time is running out."

In the Orange Free State, Karl Beck and I met with local labor leaders, who were so confrontational that I cut the meeting short. "There is no sense talking to you," one said. "Good night, gentlemen," I replied, "we don't have much to say to each other." Most times I could persuade groups to hear my points, but occasionally, we were so at odds that we had to agree to disagree. Otherwise, we might exhibit anger and show extreme weakness, and that incurs disrespect. One thing I required of everyone at the embassy is that we demand respect. We stood for something honorable. Our policy was an honorable policy. We would not take our cue from anybody; we marched to our own beat.

With its climate and geography, Port Elizabeth, on the Indian Ocean, should be pleasant, but I felt it to be an ominous place, perhaps because I knew the city's history. It was from here that South African authorities took Steve Biko on his fatal ride to Johannesburg. Many South Africans would agree with me. They are not a superstitious people, but some believe that the unhappy souls of the persecuted roam the countryside still, sometimes slipping through into our reality.

While in the Eastern Cape, I met with a group of National Party members of Parliament (MP) who were Afrikaners of French ancestry, as well as with MPs who represented the opposition party, the Progressive Freedom Party (PFP). I talked with black leaders and toured townships, advice centers, and Ina Pearlman's Operation Hunger projects. When several black ministers took me in a minibus to visit a township, a policeman stopped us en route and asked where we were going.

"We are escorting the American ambassador around the township," one minister replied.

"The American ambassador?" asked the policeman. "Where is he?" He looked at the occupants of the bus, all black, and the ministers pointed to me. Neither speaking nor smiling, I just looked at him. "Excuse me," said the policeman. "I have to call headquarters and find out what to do next." When he returned, his hostile attitude had changed to courtesy.

"Welcome," he said, saluting. On our way once more, the black ministers smiled victoriously. "Ambassador, please come back," they said. "We've got to do this again."

One evening, MP Saki Louw hosted Karl, Liz, Lucy, and me to a *brai*, a barbecue. The women stayed in the kitchen, and the Afrikaner men, all members of government, were in the front rooms with huge glasses of whiskey and great chunks of roasted lamb. Lucy commuted back and forth from the kitchen, but Liz stayed with us men. She is a tall brunette, brilliant, and lovely. Her stance that evening suggested a slight challenge, reflecting her unwillingness to be one of the women in the kitchen preparing food. I am sure many references were made in Afrikaans that we could not understand about her working for me, a black man. As the evening progressed, the Afrikaner men got drunker and cruder, but Liz toughed it out. I made a little speech partly in Afrikaans, and we left. It was hard for all of us to be cordial to people whose behavior, personally and politically, was so abhorrent.

Touring the Eastern Cape was a powerful emotional experience because the beauty of the land contrasted so sharply with the degradation of behavior. I saw the neat little English-style towns—Grahamstown, King Williamstown, Queenstown, and Port Elizabeth—and then caught my breath at the bleak poverty of the neighboring black townships. I also saw an overriding characteristic of the blacks—the enormous amount of goodwill they had toward the whites. Except for the young comrades, even black revolutionaries exhibited goodwill toward their white oppressors. I was further amazed to see how well the blacks coped economically. Many people did not have enough food, but the community rallied around and took care of its own. The black groups always held to the belief that change was coming.

In the Western Cape Province, I visited the famous township of Crossroads, which the government had tried to hide behind large berms. Behind these earthen barriers, bright lights flooded the black township. "The lights are there so the authorities can see when they go in and shoot up people and keep order," Cape Town consul general John Burroughs told a visiting group of Americans.

We also met black leaders, visited the black and Coloured townships, discussed the Coloured schools, and talked about the economic deprivation of a large segment of the Coloured population, especially those who work in the extensive vineyards. The workers were paid a *dop*, which is wine. Theoretically they were supposed to sell it, but most drank it, became drunkards, and were perpetually poor.

I saw the scars at the foot of Table Mountain, the remnants of the Coloured township of District 6, which the government moved to the sands of Mitchell's Plain. The relocated Coloureds reacted so angrily that no whites ever built on the ashes of District 6. All that remained were three churches—Methodist, Catholic, and a mosque. In Mitchell's Plains, the Coloureds planted trees and grass and turned it into a successful township with good schools and profitable shopping malls.

We continued to push for changes in education, including more bursaries and educational grants from the United States for South Africans, especially for disadvantaged blacks. I wanted the USAID mission to do in South Africa what it had never done: use the money to enfranchise the people by giving them economic power, social power, and political power. Tim Bork, with his intense commitment and his ability to reach out to the disadvantaged, was just the person I needed to head that USAID mission. We authorized him to hire a secretary/special assistant, and he told me he had chosen John Lee, a black man.

"Why are you telling me?" I asked Tim.

"Because he has AIDS."

"Hire him," I replied. "We won't broadcast that he has AIDS. He's going to have a hard enough time being black and trying to work in this situation." When John arrived I told him that he was there to do a job and that it was not my place to talk about his illness. He was so grateful that we understood the situation. He and Tim worked well together.

Carlos Pasqual, a dedicated social activist and a program officer for the USAID mission, was unbelievably effective in the black community. I insisted that the policy of the AID program be managed by the entire country team. We put our shoulders to this work. We needed all of the resources and all of the strength directed toward the enemy.

I wanted more money, $25 million to $30 million in USAID funding, to enhance the policies. The administration asked the Congress for $25 million. We used the funds in townships, creating leadership, working with women's groups, and supporting incipient cottage industries. The embassy's self-help programs ranged from making ceramics to kindergartens. A group of Soweto housewives used the financial aid to begin a silk-making activity. The Soweto Women's League utilized self-help funds for a club for making clothing to sell, enhancing township education, church activities, and advice sources for female victims of domestic violence. South African men, black and white, are unreconstructed regarding equality between the sexes. Sometimes the self-help funds helped rebuild a house or a church that had been destroyed by the South African authorities. This was done quietly and without fanfare. USAID often installs a plaque or sign featuring two hands shaking and the USAID shield, but I would not let that be done in South Africa. I considered that to be altruism in its worse sense.

We were moving as fast as we could, in as many directions as possible.

The Marine Corps was reluctant to assign black marines to guard the chancellery in the hostile environment of white South Africa, but I met with the commandant, telling him that times were changing and we had to take the bull by the horns. These young men would be examples of the best that America produces, I said, and I hoped they would be seen as Americans, not as black Americans. At the next opportunity, a black marine was assigned to guard the chancellery and it went quite well.

When the senior officer position in Durban was again vacant, I asked bigger-than-life Tex Harris to be the consul general there. Tex is a huge, savvy lawyer from Texas. I knew that he could deal with Buthelezi on his home turf. Tex is a computer whiz and said that he could not come without his super computers and a program called "Tempest." Much to the chagrin of the administrative officer, we spent $2,000 to set up the program.

Gingerly, I began to create a relationship with the South African military. I discussed with my military advisors what we wanted to achieve, and I vetted our objectives with the U.S. Defense Department. It was a bit of a problem bringing the military advisors' advice and guidance in line with the political counselors' advice and guidance, but Frasure was the most knowledgeable regarding South Africa's political ground and I wanted everybody to take their lead from him. We increased the embassy's civilian activity and quit relying on the uniformed people, who were ineffective as reporters because they failed to see the political element.

Our military-to-military objectives were multiple. First, we wanted to disabuse the South Africans of the thought that it was business as usual with the American military establishment. Furthermore, I wanted to make sure they understood we believed that change had to come to South Africa. I wanted to convey my view that the military was in the best position to begin to change by taking into its ranks members of the disadvantaged groups in South Africa and to train them to take their place as useful members of society. I also wanted the South African military to realize that we knew of the existence of its expansive dirty-tricks unit whose job it was to kill people, to conduct flash raids across the borders, and to disrupt the revolutionary movement in any way possible. The tentacles of that special unit reached as far away as London and Paris.

VISITORS

The International Visitors Program is a U.S. government program to fund potential leaders of a country to visit American institutions for thirty days. When I arrived, it had long been the responsibility of public affairs. I changed that, making the entire country team involved in the International Visitors Program as another element of the embassy's role as a change agent. I exerted greater pressure on all sections of the embassy to get to know people and then nominate them for this program. This ruffled feathers in public affairs, but as Frasure explained, "If we want to make a difference in this country in the future, we have to pick people we think will be constructive in their society." We began a different kind of selection. We chose professionals—teachers, legislators, small-city mayors, advice givers, lawyers—but we also selected many blacks. We also insisted that blacks and whites travel together; we would not issue separate tickets. We discovered that this was the first time 95 percent of them had ever talked to either a black person or a white person in an equal situation. Sometimes it was a great experience for them; sometimes it was not.

I set an open-door policy for visitors to the embassy for South Africans and foreigners alike. The officers at the embassy were astounded, because it is unheard of for people to stop by and ask to see the ambassador. When at all possible, I had them shown in, because I wanted the embassy to be known as an open place.

I welcomed visits from congressional delegations. Those who visited the American Embassy included Senators David Boren (Oklahoma), Sam Nunn (Georgia), Frank Lautenberg (New Jersey), Charles Robb (Virginia), Nancy Kassebaum (Kansas), and John McCain (Arizona). I considered congressional delegation visits an opportunity for the mission to interact with the other branch of our government, to tell them what we were doing at post, and to enlist their aid. We gave them unvarnished briefings, holding nothing back and made sure they went places they would not go as ordinary tourists. I always looked upon visits by members of Congress, in all of their manifestations and appendages, as a positive thing. Conversely, Chet sometimes seemed to consider Congress an enemy to be shielded from what we were doing.

American visitors included a group of congressional staffers on a fact-finding mission led by a woman who was the long-time chief of staff of the Committee on Foreign Relations, Oklahoma businessman Jake Simmons, Washington attorney Arnold Levy, and two state representatives from Oklahoma. The latter two were being squired by a Coloured member of the South African Bureau of Information. I told them they should see everything inside the country, not just white South Africa.

One of the most far-reaching visits was by Boren, who was chair of the Senate Select Committee on Intelligence, and Nunn, who headed the Senate Armed Services Committee. Both committees were important. They were permitted to visit because the Afrikaner government considered them to be conservatives and tending toward being a friend in court, possibly even allies—a misguided conception.

My staff and I put together a program that showed them as much of South Africa as we could squeeze into their visit. Boren, Nunn, and I met with State President Botha in a private conference room at Tuyn Huis in Cape Town. It was a signal meeting. Botha welcomed them, talked about what his government was trying to do, and said that troublemakers were trying to revolutionize South Africa. As I had asked them to do, Boren and Nunn protested the jailing of several people, including Father Mkhatshwa and journalist Zwelakhe Sisulu, son of Albertina and Walter.

"They are in jail because they violated the law," Botha said.

"It is an unjust law, Mr. President," Nunn said.

"Who said so?" Botha demanded.

"I say so," Nunn replied, "and the whole world says so."

Botha began to boil and to rant. Suddenly Boren said, "Wait!" He stuck his finger in Botha's face and said, "You listen. You've been doing all the talking. I came here to learn. Let me talk some."

Botha was so shocked that he sat back and did not say a word as Boren, who is very intelligent and articulate, made all of his points in fantastic oratory. He reacted spontaneously, and it worked. Botha was completely disarmed. Later Senator Boren told me, "I can't believe I did that."

I persuaded the Afrikaner officials to let the two senators visit jailed Father Mkhatshwa, whom I had not been permitted to see. Otherwise, I told the Afrikaners, they will go back to the United States and talk about being denied, and that would do more harm. They also met Albertina Sisulu, who gave them a tour of her *crèche* (kindergarten) and home in Soweto. On my suggestion, in 1989 Senator Boren persuaded President George H. W. Bush to invite Albertina to Washington. She was one of the first revolutionaries to be received in the Oval Office. President Bush sent me the invitation to deliver to her.

This woman, who had never been out of South Africa, was deeply honored. "It will never happen," she told me. "The government will never let me travel outside of this country. "You leave that to me, Mrs. Sisulu," I said.

I called on the foreign minister, and as she predicted, he said, "She ain't goin' nowhere."

"Mr. Minister," I said, "are you and your government afraid of this little old lady who is eighty years old? Are you so afraid that you won't let her travel to the United States and meet the president of the United States? Imagine how that is going to look in the press."

"Damn it, Ed," he said. "What are you trying to say?"

"I'm just saying that it's going to get out if you don't give her a passport and an exit permit and let her go." He looked at me without saying anything. He had a terrible temper, but he knew it did not work on me. The next day his aide called to tell me that she had been issued a passport.

Albertina went to Washington, and I presented her to several people. Senator and Molly Shi Boren had a big reception for her in his home in Alexandria. Lucy and I attended and saw the number of powerful Washington folks who came to pay homage to her that evening. When she met the president, he invited her to brief him and advise him on the situation in South Africa. It was the first time any president ever said that to a black South African revolutionary. Albertina had brought several people with her, mostly men, and she said,

"Mr. President, I would rather let them tell you about our revolution." Like a traditional black South African woman, she took a back seat and let the black South African men talk.

Because of Senator Boren's visit to South Africa and his involvement with a revolutionary such as Mrs. Sisulu, he was one of the first senators invited by Mandela to appear with him on television in New York during Mandela's first visit to the United States. Because Mandela was not yet president of South Africa, the Afrikaner government did not give a damn if he was killed or not. The senator rarely mentions it, but he arranged special security for Mandela during that U.S. visit. He used his position as chair of the Senate Intelligence Committee to have Mandela protected.

The embassy reported all of our activities in a weekly policy paper for Washington. We provided more information than they wanted, but I never wanted Washington to be in the dark about the mission's activities.

I established a policy of replying within twenty-four hours to any inquiry from a congressperson, even if our reply was to acknowledge the inquiry and say that we would have an answer as soon as possible. When we slipped up once and did not reply for two weeks to a call from a senior aide to Senator Ted Kennedy, the political officer wanted to manufacture an excuse. "No, you won't," I said, and I called the aide to say that it was our fault, that I had the answer for him, and I would apologize to Senator Kennedy personally.

My Fellow Ambassadors

It is protocol for a newly arrived ambassador to call on fellow ambassadors, which I had been doing, assessing the position of the embassies in South Africa and trying to enlist them all to our position. What I wanted was a series of statements that we could all agree on. I called on all of the European representatives, told them what we were doing, and asked that they join us. I was welcomed with varying degrees of success.

I was supposed to work closely with our allies, especially the British, Germans, and French, in that order.[6] The British never stepped out front because they had too many business interests in the country. Neither did France, Taiwan, or Portugal. The French ambassador never joined me in any of my causes—the French did not always seem to care. We knew that some of their businesspeople were making deals with the white business leaders in South Africa, and we finally let them know it.

The Swiss did not join us because of their South Africa business interests. When I asked the Swiss ambassador if he was trying to make a difference in South Africa, he said he was too busy with Swiss business to be out front making change or giving speeches.

The countries that did join forces with us included Germany (after a change in ambassadors), Australia, Italy, Sweden, Norway, Finland, and the Low Countries—Belgium and the Netherlands. The Low Countries began to invest considerable money for social and political change. Austria also joined us, led by the perceptive Austrian ambassador, Alexander Christiani.

The German ambassador, Immo Stabreit, was one of that country's most effective diplomats. Immo is tall, ascetic looking, and wears great ties. His predecessor had been sidetracked by his deputy, who had a personal friendship with Winnie Mandela, but when Immo arrived, he brought a new deputy and a new, more balanced policy from Germany. Before, the Germans had limited contact with the white South Africans, but Immo was determined to be all-inclusive and to do what I was doing, which was to see everybody. On occasion, the British ambassador, Stabreit, and I met to review the political situation and to compare policies.

The Soviets were not represented in South Africa. The Israeli ambassador consulted with me often, and I asked him once why we heard little from him about apartheid. Israel was very quiet about its interests in South Africa. Not much was known about the business relations between the two countries, but I did know that Israel provided technical assistance in different areas, including atomic energy. By purchasing technology and hiring technical experts from many places, South Africa had put together atomic nuclear activities. Some were trained on Soweto and Crossroads with the possible intent of putting down insurrections in these two townships. It became incumbent upon us to urge South Africa to adhere to the Nuclear Non-Proliferation Treaty and ensure that it put in place IAEA safeguards.

At that time, South Africa did not have relations with mainland China, the People's Republic of China, but maintained relations with the Republic of China (Taiwan). The ambassador of the Republic of China (Taiwan) was a venerable gentleman and something of an apologist for the Afrikaner government.

One of Lucy's cousins was an officer in his embassy. It was important for the Nationalist government in Taiwan to have a relationship with the dwindling number of countries accredited to Taiwan, so the ambassador was in South Africa to maintain relations and not to make waves. He and I agreed silently not to criticize each other.

THE BRITISH

The British never once forgot the economic side of the picture and did nothing that might harm British interests in the country. The uniformity of the Margaret Thatcher government dictated that British interests not be disturbed. A British Foreign Office memorandum in 1987 made the British position clear: "The government's policy toward South Africa is to further the considerable British interests in that country." The British did want apartheid eliminated, repression ended, the state of emergency lifted, and Mandela and other political prisoners released, but they preferred a policy of what they called "positive measures," which is akin to constructive engagement. Prime Minister Thatcher gave the impression that anybody who did not agree with her could go straight to hell.

The British wanted change, but Thatcher did not want to force businesses out of the country. She never imposed sanctions because, she said, sanctions would hurt the blacks. British interests in South Africa included such financial pillars as Barclay's Bank, one of the biggest investors, and Cadbury Chocolates. Whenever I met with British businessmen and government officials, they inevitably asked if their investments were safe. I could not give them any reassurances but told them that change, which was coming, would make investments safer than no change.

Margaret Thatcher's reign was so friendly that it suggested an in-bed policy with the Afrikaner government. State President Botha saw Thatcher as a kindred soul. About the time of summer 1986, the two of them met in the presence of South African ambassador Denis Worrall, who told me about the meeting. Thatcher was not forthcoming in condemning the South African government. When the meeting was over, Botha said, "We have our work cut out for us. She wants us to hold the line." Intentionally or unintentionally, Thatcher had conveyed the message that she did not want the South African government making any concessions to the black political leaders. I believe that was one of a number of reasons President Botha was so intransigent. The people of South Africa accepted the relationship between London and the Afrikaner government, and did not expect much help from Britain. Their expectations of America were different. Black South Africans expected the United States to take the lead in pushing for change, and they reacted with visceral disappointment when we did not push as hard or as fast as they thought we should.

In London in 1986, U.S. State Department officers met with key South African and British businessmen, U.S. ambassador Charles Price, and senior officials of the British foreign office, including Thatcher's private secretary, Charles Powell. I met with the same people about six months later, and my assessment matched the report of that earlier meeting. State President Botha was committed to ending the socioeconomic aspects of apartheid, but was not open to sharing political power with blacks. Pretoria's leadership, including Afrikaner military and security, had a profound distrust of Western intentions, which they saw as focusing on black majority rule. President Botha was increasingly reconciled to Western sanctions and was preparing, politically and militarily, to go it alone. In fact, he might welcome being relieved of Western interference. In summary, the South Africans repeated the mantra: Business takes care of business, and government takes care of politics.

When I arrived, the British ambassador was Sir Patrick Moberly. He was replaced by Robin Renwick, later knighted by the queen to become Sir Robin. Robin was not in tune with the activist policy we Americans were practicing. He wanted to pursue British interests, but he also wanted to be aboard this moving train headed for a destination not favorable to the British, so he tried to straddle the fence. Britain was considered our closest ally, but in South Africa we were sometimes at odds.

Britain did not trade arms with South Africa or export oil or sensitive equipment to the armed forces, maintained no military cooperation, withdrew their military attaché from Pretoria, announced a ban on new government loans to the South African government, and had taken other actions. Still, we understood that the British would only go so far and no further, but they were willing to take a lot of credit for change when it came. Prime Minister Thatcher opposed Mandela's ever achieving the respectability of being received at the highest levels of government. When Mandela finally appeared in the House of Commons, Thatcher was present, beaming like everybody else. A year earlier she had damned him for refusing to renounce violence. Now she embraced him like a long-lost son.

The British have a strange history with South Africa. After the Boer War, the British realized they could not control South Africa politically, because the Afrikaners outnumbered the English-speakers, so they began to focus on the economy and controlling the Afrikaners economically. That history helped form the policy in apartheid South Africa. The British were among the most oppressive colonial masters, and it was they who started the apartheid system. The French, I observed, assumed that it was possible for a colonial to rise to the level of a Frenchman through education and marriage. The British did not; they adopted a superior attitude and were not liberal with their colonials.

President Reagan's dramatic policy turnaround caught London unawares. Britain's foreign office talked to me repeatedly, trying to figure out what we Americans were doing. The more we talked, the more confused they became. It did not make sense to them that I was in South Africa to make policy, because that had never been done before. The British skillfully tagged along, neither condoning apartheid nor doing much to indicate disapproval of it. Unhappy playing second fiddle to the Americans in a place that had once been a former British colony, they never joined our team or acknowledged that the Americans were leading the cause. We tried to keep them informed every step of the way. In South Africa, the bottom line for the British was money. Perhaps only the Americans could afford to be humanitarians in this case.

AMERICAN BUSINESS INTERESTS

The United States policy did not require American businesses to leave South Africa, and we never urged any American firms to withdraw. We did say, though, that although the CAAA of 1986 did not require withdrawal from South Africa, it did encourage it. We saw some advantage in a decision by some of the signatories of the Sullivan Principles to remain.

My view, which I expressed in public speeches, was that American corporations ought to stay in South Africa if they were engaged in bringing about political change, but if they were not, they ought to leave.

The involvement of American business interests in South Africa ran the gamut, ranging from self-serving isolation to dynamic change agents. Historically, American companies had not always been the good guys, I learned from Johannesburg city councilor Molly Kopel. Early on in South Africa, American companies helped segregate employees and were as complicit in fostering apartheid as the South African companies.

A 1987 listing of the top U.S. employers in South Africa with more than 50 percent U.S. ownership included some big hitters: Mobil, RJR Nabisco, Goodyear Tire & Rubber, USG Corporation, Cal-Tex Oil, Johnson & Johnson, M. Hart Corporation, United Technologies Corporation, American Brands Incorporated, Joy Manufacturing Company, Minnesota Mining and Manufacturing, Xerox, Baker International, Colgate Palmolive, H. H. Robertson Company, Crown Cork and Seal Company, Unisys Corporation, American Cyanamid Corporation, PepsiCo, Dressler Industries, and Union Carbide. Beginning in 1986, some corporations began divesting, including Kodak and Bell and Howell.

IBM, too, left because stockholders insisted. Despite the efforts to eliminate racism, stockholders said, staying in South Africa with IBM's world-recognized name gave credibility to the South African government. Staying did more to advance apartheid than to hinder it. So IBM left.

Coca-Cola was one of the more successful corporations working in South Africa. Early on, largely due to Ernest J. Mcunu, a trade and community development manager, Coca-Cola realized that to be successful, the corporation had to work with the communities, not just sell the product. Coca-Cola was involved with schools and community development activities.[7]

In 1985 PepsiCo left, and in August 1987, Coca-Cola began to divest at the insistence of its shareholders. The Coca-Cola management was unhappy about leaving, so they sold the infrastructure to the black employees. It was just a paper transfer, but it enabled the black employees to receive a part of the profits. The bottling operations were moved to neighboring countries, including Swaziland.

Some of the U.S. firms that stayed became effective allies in change, either by corporate policy or by the work of individual executives. A few American businessmen were heroic in their efforts. Ford Motor Company operated a functioning plant near Pretoria, and when Ford executives asked me to assess the current political situation, I told them it was tenuous at best. "And State President Botha's mood?" they asked. "Combative," I said. He was combative without understanding what he was up against, much like a wild man flailing about in the bush who hears something but does not know what it is. Ford pulled out of South Africa in 1987, but Wayne Fredericks, a key Ford operative, continued his devoted involvement in change activities.

Wally Life, a South African and the manager of the Goodyear plant for the Goodyear Tire Company, turned that company into a change agent. Once black and white workers stepped inside that plant, they were treated exactly the same.

Representatives from Eli Lilly wanted to be assured that we could effect a policy of change without a civil war, but I could not give them that assurance. We did not know how the Afrikaners would react. "You ought to participate in this change," I told the Eli Lilly people. "You ought to help us create this."

Mobil Oil Company was one of the companies that did not divest, because shareholders voted against it in May 1987, but Mobil was an activist and a member of the Sullivan signatories. Georges P. Racine, chairman of the board of Mobile Southern Africa, often consulted with my colleagues and me. He and his assistant, Bob Angel, were helpful in rationalizing, to us and to their stockholders, why it was important for Mobil to stay. Angel was good at conflict resolution, and Mobil was involved, so they stayed.

Johnson & Johnson was another company heavily involved. It did not disinvest, but stayed. The manager of the South African project in the Princeton corporate office was Al Cooper, who was enormously talented in conflict resolution.

The American Chamber of Commerce performed well in South Africa, making known its antipathy to the government in many ways and working to create a new class of blacks. In Soweto it supported Pace College, an institution for black students and one of the best private high schools in the world. When young comrades trashed the school, the Chamber rebuilt it and picked a new no-nonsense person to be headmaster. He stood on the steps of the new facility, faced a group of young toughs, and said, "If it happens again, you'll be dealing with me. Every one of you."

"Weren't you scared?" I asked him later.

"No," he said, "I have gone beyond fear. What they saw in my eyes was my determination. They saw that I meant it." The young comrades never again bothered the school.

The majority of the Chamber was comprised of South Africans working for American companies. One of the most effective was Roger D. Crawford, an

executive of Johnson & Johnson at HalfWay House, which is halfway between
Johannesburg and Pretoria. He was one of the guiding lights behind the Sulli-
van Signatories' Association in South Africa. He was an Afrikaner born in the
Orange Free State, and in my judgment it was a miracle that he evolved into
the democratic, fair-minded person that he is. His wife Gillian and daughter
Bronwyn are also courageous South Africans and activists.

Not all Americans doing business in South Africa had operations located
there. A United Nations embargo prohibited entertainers from going into South
Africa. The UN could not enforce that ban, but it had a psychological impact,
and the number of American entertainers dwindled to a trickle. Very few were
willing to face the opprobrium of the industry or of other countries. Some, such
as Frank Sinatra and Eartha Kitt, were too powerful to worry about it. They performed in a world-class casino in a homeland called Bophuthatswana and in contiguous countries, so they could claim they were not literally working in South
Africa.

As I now look at the sanctions policy papers dating back to 1986, I am struck by
how they were written to convince Congress not to pass the sanctions bill. The
Department of Commerce assessed the impact on South Africa of a withdrawal
of U.S. investment under three scenarios: the continued withdrawal of U.S.
firms acting independently and voluntarily, a politically induced voluntary
rapid mass exit, and a congressionally mandated withdrawal within a specified
short period of time.

According to this Commerce report, termination of U.S. investment in
South Africa was projected to cause no drop in South Africa's gross domestic
product. Without additional productive capacity, however, the South African
economy and the country's GDP could not grow as rapidly. If U.S. disinvest-
ment occurred, 63,000 new jobs would not be created. Black South African
unemployment would soar. In a worst-case scenario, termination of U.S.
investment in South Africa would result in a loss to the United States of at
least $120 million annually in foreign exchange from repatriated profits and
$400 million in forgone export sales. Another $600 million in associated
exports would be in jeopardy; 14,000 jobs involved in the manufacture and
shipment of those exports and another 21,000 jobs would be at risk if associated sales were lost as well. Under the worst of cases, to this would be added

the loss of about $7.2 billion in proceeds of sale of U.S. corporate assets in South Africa. U.S. firms would not be able to collect the amounts still outstanding on the intercontinental loan economy, and new foreign exchange rules would be imposed by South Africa. I believe these statements were issued in good faith, but they were generated with the idea of making a worst-case scenario to the public.[8]

United States investment in South Africa was very important in 1986, and American banks played a big role in that investment. The U.S. bank claims on South African residents were considerable, about $300 million. This included claims on public borrowers, claims on banks, and claims on other private borrowers. As the Reagan administration sought ways to argue against sanctions in 1985, it considered their economic and commercial impact. The administration raised the possibility that South Africans would refuse to pay outstanding debts at the bank, which could affect the full extent of the U.S. bank claims, which amounted to $3.25 billion out of the residents of South Africa. Furthermore, sanction opponents were concerned about adjustments for guarantees; U.S. bank claims would be about $24 billion. The bulk of bank lending in South Africa, however, was from non-U.S. banks, and South African banks were accustomed to "rollovers," which means the debt is continued without the lender calling it in. We knew that South Africa had sold many bonds as government bonds. What we did not know was the value of those bonds held in the United States. We also knew that the value of American-owned shares in South African companies was considerable.

The South African economy was much like a pressure cooker about to explode. Foreign business interests were either pulling out of the country or staying on with trepidation. Some South African whites were tightening their hold on the status quo, fearful that a black revolution would destroy economic stability. Some black South Africans, forced into substandard living conditions for so long, were impatient to grab some of the luxuries of life, while blacks with socialist leanings wanted to do away with the capitalist society. Part of my job was to try to steer all of these diverse parties along a similar course and keep a lid on the economy. In so doing, I began to espouse a theory I called "community capitalism."

Whenever I consider methodologies for carrying out foreign policy, I concentrate on the role of the community, a concept that I formed in South Africa. Grasping for whatever methodology we could find to change things there, we began to articulate the role of the community and promote individualism in a land where individualism had lost its meaning among blacks. I remembered Huey Long's model for bringing together business and government in a cooperative venture, leaving some profit to benefit the community. Then, we brought in Robert Woodson, a black community activist from Washington, D.C., to conduct community seminars. He espoused the concept of promoting achievement as the ultimate goal of an individual. He also promoted community involvement in enterprises that foster employment while helping the community to have, among other things, cleaner streets, health-delivery systems, and *crèches*. From him I got the idea that we could work with a concept of enterprise, or capitalism, to turn the young comrades' negative feelings toward capitalism to one of support. If they could see it as an integral part of their lives, they might support it.

I discussed the idea with the venerable Govan Mbeki when he was released from Pollsmoor Prison in November 1987, where he had been confined with Mandela and Sisulu for twenty-five years. After being in prison for so long, the three had developed themselves into a force so powerful that the South African government could not deal with it. The first thing Mbeki said upon his release was "I'm still the same person I was when I went in." He knew the South African government was expecting him to say something quite different. Mbeki was the only avowed member of the South African Communist Party who was jailed with the Rivonia Ten. To see him, I had to get permission from his community, especially from the young comrades, who were reluctant to grant me access to their leader. When I called on him at his home in the township of Welcome, near Port Elizabeth, I found him to be gentle, very quiet, and a master politician. He was small, about 5 feet 2 inches, wizened, and reminded me of a superior swordsman, able to wield the blade with ease.

"Why should we be talking to you?" he asked softly. "You are an appointee of a racist president." Finally, over another cup of tea, we got down to business—the possibility of a socialist future for South Africa. When the ANC comes to power, Mbeki said, they would nationalize everything.

"If you do that," I told him, "I think you'll lose." I cited the negatives to him—that the black part of South Africa did not have the technology, the money, or means to exploit the country's natural resources or compete in the market place.

"We cannot come to power without doing something for the people who have been waiting too long to participate in the resources and the riches of our country," he said.

I began to talk about the idea of community cooperating with capitalism. I explained it much as Woodson had done, but I talked about big business that operated in South Africa—Ford, IBM, Coca-Cola, PepsiCo. Every business has a duty to make a profit, I said, and these corporations make their money in the South African communities, with help from community members who are workers. It seems to me, I said, that the corporations have a further responsibility to leave some of that profit in the community to build up the community—roads, sewer systems, health systems, educational activities, and the arts. A community would place a member on the board of this enterprise to help decide how to use the profits to benefit the community. "Individual development would result from some of the profits," I said. We talked about this concept for about an hour. Mbeki did not believe the U.S. government would support it.

About a year later, the United States confirmed that it would. At a meeting in Cape Town, Mbeki was the spokesperson for the black political groupings, and Secretary of State James A. Baker III was speaking for the U.S. government about the new South Africa. The well-known Baker Initiative for Economic Reform was summarized in this question: "Do proposed policy changes create the incentives and opportunities to acquire private property for all parts of the population of the country evaluated?" The true foundations of growth, therefore, were economic efficiency, competitiveness, and productivity. When I called on Mbeki, he had asked me about U.S. policies regarding the use of the natural resources. He wanted to know my views on private investment. People in the struggle considered a market economy to be capitalism, which the ANC saw as the enemy of the people. I had briefed Baker that he would be quizzed about the market-economy concept. One of the first questions was from Mbeki. "What do you mean by a market economy?"

"I can't explain it in a few words," Baker said, "but the closest thing to that is something I call 'community capitalism.'"

Mbeki was immensely pleased. "I don't know how you got him to say that," he told me. Baker did say it, and community capitalism became a policy that the United States would support. Since then, the concept of community has taken on a connotation of the unit of any group of people that can promote individualism and at the same time promote the well-being of a group or groups of people. It is a good policy.

The Black Economy

Many people were working to make a difference in South Africa. Some were black businesses, ranging from small township operations to very wealthy enterprises. Some white South African companies quietly integrated blacks into the upper reaches of the work force, a public-relations director for a beer company, for example, and a personnel manager for a small white company. Others were individuals striving to improve business possibilities for young blacks.

I met Gary Player, the champion South African golfer known as the Black Knight (because of his clothing style and skill of playing, not his race), and learned about the golf school being operated by him and his son to introduce golf to young black South Africans. It had never been done before.

Gordon Sibiya, South Africa's only black nuclear scientist, spent his weekends tutoring young black students in mathematics. One evening at a high-level dinner party at the residence with a guest list of people from industry and education, Gordon had a fascinating discussion with some of the Afrikaners and English-speakers. As one of the whites left, he said to me, "I didn't know there were black people like this in South Africa." "There are a lot of them," I replied. "A lot of black scientists, mathematicians, playwrights, actors, and businesspeople. In fact, you have the beginnings of a parallel society within the black community, one that will serve you well if you make use of it."

When I met with the South African minister of finance, I told him that we would push to empower black business people. "This is a way to eliminate the possibility of violence," I told him. "You have to bring more and more black people into the economic stream and close the gap between the haves and the have-nots." One way we tried to do this was by involving black businesses in "matchmaker affairs" funded in part by the Department of Commerce through its foreign commercial service under the embassy. In this program, we brought major U.S. and South African businesses together with struggling and incipient black businesses so they would have a chance to market their wares in an even-handed way.

I met with leaders from the black business community, including a group of Johannesburg companies trying to establish a black bank. I encouraged this, remembering how important it had been for the Afrikaners to have their own bank, and I persuaded USAID to send an advisor from the United States to help develop the bank. My black business contacts were individuals who had become financially successful despite all odds.[9] They ranged from Richard Maponya, the wealthiest black man in South Africa, to Lucky Michaels, the *she-been* (pub or tavern) king of Soweto. Lucky was a no-nonsense, no-romance realist whom I called on to give tours to visitors who wanted to see the real Soweto.

In a little Coloured township near Cape Town named Retreat, I met Joe Marks, a Coloured, and his wife Maggie, a Zulu. Joe is a big man, illiterate, and worked as a fishmonger. An ANC activist, he is one of the most effective community leaders I have met anywhere in the world. We arranged for him to receive some entrepreneurial grants, which he spread around the community with great success. In Gugulethu, a black township near Crossroads, I met with black leaders, including three doctors and several Catholic priests. The leader of the group was an eminently successful builder named Lester Patina who had taken nothing and built it into great wealth by the sweat of his brow. He had been to Washington, D.C., and could not understand how so many blacks there lived in inaction and poverty when they had so much opportunity. It is a good question, I told him: "Why does one person succeed and another not?"

Lucy and I spent a night at the home of Enos Mabuza and his wife, Esther, in KwaNdebele Homeland, which is in the northwest part of the Transvaal. There, in the heart of Afrikanerland, Enos was one of the most effective black leaders, and he walked a cool path. He brought in industry and agriculture that changed the economy into a Homeland of prosperity, but since he was head of a Homeland, he worked for the South African government. He opposed the government, but he was interested in justice and made sure that Homeland profits were plowed back into the Homeland and worked to the benefit of the citizens. One KwaNdebele industry was litchi nuts, which were harvested and sold to Asia and to the South African Winery Consortium. The first time I tasted delicious litchi wine was in South Africa.

In Pretoria I visited several businesses run by blacks that few whites knew about. One was a fashion shop run by a black milliner. In Durban, I met a firm of black lawyers. In Mamelodi, I encountered successful cottage industries, including a dressmaking school. In Winterveld on the prairie veldt in the Bophuthatswana Homeland, I had lunch at the home of the president of the Black Chamber of Commerce, Sam Motsuenyane, and his wife, Jocelyn. It was the home of a person of means. Sam was a black entrepreneur who made an accommodation with the white world to exist economically, if not socially. The more time I spent with people like the Motsuenyanes, the less concern I had for South Africa's future, because they were as capable of running the country as any white person.

Yet not everything was moving forward. In Johannesburg, I met a couple of black architects who represented the younger professional group of blacks with no place to use their skills. The apartheid system limited them. That same day, I visited MEDUNSA of the University of South Africa's medical school, the only place that provided medical training for blacks. Until this program was begun, only one black veterinarian and very few black medical doctors practiced in the whole of South Africa.

Some of South Africa's black leaders were corrupt, and some outside corporations were more interested in raping the country than in helping develop it. As the United States sought to make order of our policy in southern Africa, we found ourselves with some strange bedfellows. One of them was Lonrho Africa, a corporate empire run by tycoon Tiny Rowland. A British corporate executive who operated like a soldier of fortune, he had transformed a small Zimbabwe mining firm into a multi-billion-dollar conglomerate. By the 1970s, Lonrho Africa was so controversial that former British prime minister Sir Edward Heath described Rowland as "the unpleasant and unacceptable face of capitalism."

When Bob Frasure briefed me on Rowland, it was like hearing something that Somerset Maugham might have written about colonials who squeezed the riches out of a land for their own self-interest. Rowland and his company looked for special concessions dealing with the country's resources—diamonds, minerals, and some agricultural products such as timber. He was a world-class entrepreneur who was not interested in folding some of the profit back into the community that produced it—he kept it. That is not to excuse the leadership of Africa, but when the story is finally told about all of these activities, we will see some of the causes for the continent's degradation.

We were already concerned about the education and productivity of the vast number of black citizens who were undereducated, both by the Afrikaner educational system and by their own boycott of schools. Then, one evening at a restaurant, an Indian woman introduced me to another segment of black South African society—a former member of *Umkhonto we Sizwe*, the ANC army. She had warned me that he was different, and when I looked into his eyes, they were as flat as slate. He was a man of about thirty who had been trained since childhood to be a killer. He told me that he had gone into the army while barely a teenager. So for more than half of his life, he had developed himself into someone who would kill at the drop of a hat, never feeling remorse. He was pleasant enough to me and even asked about the possibility of his visiting the United States. When he left, my hostess said, "Our challenge is finding a place for people like that." Where do young, cold killers fit in a society?

A Heavy Personal Toll

I could sense that, like a great ship slowly coming about, South Africa was slowly changing course. I could almost hear the mighty creaks and groans, as if the land itself were heaving to, the earth's continental plates grinding on one another, as South Africa righted itself. Almost everybody suffered from the stress of this long struggle.

The mental health of many Afrikaners was precarious. They were caught between the oppressive Dutch Reformed Church and political pressure. I was not surprised when the foreign minister told me that every minister in government had a black mistress. Pik had been drinking when he told me this, and he was speaking unguardedly. Still, it may be more accurate to say that many Afrikaners had relationships with nonwhite women. They rarely had white mistresses because Afrikaners seldom mingled with English-speaking women, and the strict upbringing of Afrikaner women prohibited such behavior. It was easier for Afrikaner men to have a black mistress in a neighboring country, a Homeland, or a country such as Lesotho, Malawi, or Swaziland.

English-speakers, too, felt the stress. In a sense, they were the original creators of apartheid and the Afrikaner mentality of segregation. To have an anaconda for a pet is dangerous because eventually the snake gets too big to handle—that is what happened in the relationship between the English-speakers and the Afrikaners. John Wiley was the only English-speaking cabinet member in the South African government. He must have believed deeply in the government's mission and, like many converts to religion, he was more Afrikaner than the Afrikaners. Wiley was one of the last ministers to whom I paid a courtesy call. He lived at the foot of Table Mountain on the Hout Bay side in a big house adjoining an estate he had inherited from his family. The visit was surreal, because the house and the acreage were unreal. Wiley was minister of environmental affairs, yet I noticed that his estate was one of the few places in South Africa with plants not indigenous to the country. They were choking out the native flora.

"Your aide can stay in the waiting room," he told me. "Just you and me, Ambassador." As we sat down for coffee and tea, I sized him up. He was in his mid-fifties, tall and wiry with a craggy face and tense eyes. He seemed to be uncomfortable and under intense pressure.

"Why is America advocating change?" he wanted to know. "Do you know anything about the Afrikaners? I'll bet you don't even speak any of the language." I threw him off course when I told him I took Afrikaans lessons every morning.

"Not many Americans do that," he admitted.

"Not many Americans have to," I said. "Where else is Afrikaans spoken outside of South Africa?" He did not like that. I had completely disoriented him. We had the damnedest conversation, with my saying the land was twice promised and the blacks had as much right to be there as the whites, and his justifying the Afrikaner stance with growing intensity. "You have to understand," he said. "The Afrikaners are a different kind of people."

I was troubled by my meeting with him. I did not understand him—his demeanor, his movements, the way he used his hands, the slightly wild-eyed look, and the firm set of his jaw as if his teeth were clenched. He seemed guilt-ridden. One Sunday morning about a month later, his wife reported that he walked to the mailbox at the edge of his property to get the newspaper, walked back to the house, went into his bedroom, lay on his bed, and shot himself. No note was left. Our embassy investigation turned up two significant details. Some Afrikaners wanted to be like the Nazis, fervent in their sense of nationalism. Wiley was that intense about Afrikanerdom; he immersed himself in the culture and spoke Afrikaans, but he felt inadequate around Afrikaners. We also discovered that he was probably homosexual, which, in that society, was a dangerous thing to be. Wiley was a casualty of the strange juxtaposition of South Africa's rigid religion, social custom, and politics. He was a misfit in the society he coveted, and he became its victim.

My staff, too, felt the stress of South Africa. It was an intense assignment for everybody in the mission. My policy was to get everybody out of South Africa at least once every six months, crossing into one of the other countries for a little vacation and R&R. It was important to take a break from the storm. I also worried about the staff's becoming so involved that they began to identify with either the South African government or the revolutionaries. Tim Bork, for example, was so passionate about achieving equality that he was always in danger of over-identification with the leaders of the struggle. We all felt a constant sadness, and the magnitude of the work we had to do was a heavy weight. It was easy to become consumed by our work, including me and my family. When our daughter Katherine came to visit us, she took courses at the University of Cape Town, and our younger daughter Sarah volunteered as a candy striper at Groote Schuur hospital.

On top of our workload, we utilized American holidays and anniversaries to tell the story of the United States. The Fourth of July is an occasion for the ambassadors abroad to entertain, pulling out the stops displaying a typical American celebration. We hosted a Fourth of July celebration in every post in South Africa, and I attended as many as I could. We spent months in the planning, as I charged every section head to compile a list of South African guests. I prefaced the meetings by saying, "Here is another chance to demonstrate our policy of complete integration. We are going to invite people who need to meet other kinds of people." We invited some of the highest-ranking people in government, as well as people in the black communities. At the parties, we showed the colors, had a picnic of traditional American food—hot dogs and hamburgers—and featured American-style musical entertainment.

The 200th anniversary of the U.S. Constitution, September 17, 1987, was a special occasion in American embassies around the world. Retired Chief Justice of the Supreme Court Warren Burger was chairman of the Committee to Observe the Anniversary of the Constitution. Every ambassador was an honorary member of the committee. In South Africa, we observed the occasion with several black-tie dinners. At one dinner for thirty-five, the South Africans who were invited—white, black, Indian, and Coloured—all had a reverence for the U.S. Constitution, the oldest constitution and the most powerful document in the world. Alan Paton sat beside me, on my right.

"Your Constitution has made you better as a people than you would have been without it," he said. "It is a remarkable document—sparse and full of power."

"It also makes us aware that we can be better and more just than we are today," I replied. Ten years earlier, he reminded me, I would not have been able to walk freely around South Africa without being insulted. "Your presence has been instructive for all of South Africa."

I took pains to make a toast that evening that reflected my deep and abiding belief in the Constitution as the manifestation of the sure possibility that people can find ways to live together, remain dynamic, grow, learn, perpetuate themselves, and improve their societies, all without enslaving or killing one another. We must learn to live as brothers and sisters in the world, I said, talking about labor versus management, women's right to vote, sexual equality, civil rights, and abortion, among other things—revolutionary approaches that engage us as citizens and make us better people. Hosting a dinner in honor of the birthday of the Constitution was one of the highlights of my stay in South Africa.

Some of the stresses of the work were related to the embassy buildings and the official residence for the ambassador, since we divided our time between

In the Cape Town residence, I hosted a dinner to celebrate the two hundredth anniversary of the U.S. Constitution. I crafted my toast with care to honor this precious document.

Cape Town and Pretoria. Managing two large operations in two locations is a monumental task. In my absence, the embassies did not operate as smoothly or efficiently as I wanted, so I began visiting both embassies more frequently. At one point, the real-estate manager in the State Department wanted to buy another house in Pretoria for the ambassador. I could not see why we needed another house. True, we could have used another bedroom, but the Pretoria residence was beautiful. I told Chet I wanted him to know that I did not approve of getting another house and I considered it a waste of money. We did not get a new residence.

The embassy in Pretoria, however, was another matter. When I first arrived, the embassy occupied space adjacent to the headquarters of the national police force, and we knew they had penetrated our embassy. I wanted a new embassy building, and I wanted it right away—not just for security and symbolism, but for safety. I was sure that as things heated up, a revolutionary group would bomb the building. The police would be their target, but we would go up with them, too. At first, nobody listened. I had to go all the way to the secretary of state, explaining how cohabitation with the national police was seen by the black people as being in bed with the South African government. Finally, ground was broken for the new embassy in 1988, and it was opened in 1991. In the meantime, I had to go to Congress to try to get a temporary building. I failed. I called the chairman of the committee and said, "I have concerns for the safety of all employees of the embassy and especially that of the Americans. If I don't fight [for a separate space] the way I'm fighting, I would not be doing justice to the folks at home."

"All right," he said, "You've made your point. I get paid to carry out the people's business and to make sure that their money is spent wisely. I think you need a new embassy, but you don't need to build a temporary one before you go to the new one."

"In your role as manager of the people's money," I said, "that's probably a good decision. But in my role as manager and protector of the lives of people out here in South Africa, I don't like that decision. However, if that's your last word, there is nothing I or anybody else can do."

"That's my last word, Ambassador. You made a good fight. Thank you very much."

So, we did not move out of the shared space. As far as money was concerned, it was a good move. As far as safety was concerned, it was very risky.

None of us had a chance to relax. Every time I thought about tomorrow, it was about something that had to be done or a point that had to be made. The assignment was much like playing football and running a race at the same time. An ambassador's tour is about three years, a time that seemed too short for all I wanted to accomplish. Sometimes when I headed to the embassy in the morning, after only five minutes I felt as tired as if I had worked all day. Sometimes I would be so physically and mentally exhausted at the end of a day that I could not sleep. Often a person in a situation like that mixes a drink to help relax, but I never did. I read books instead; that was my escape. I also began to see a physiotherapist occasionally for massage to help me relax. When the fatigue would not go away, I consulted a South African doctor who diagnosed either a virus or debilitating stress. He insisted that I take a few days away from work and stay home. Lucy was surprised to learn how I felt and that I had consulted a doctor. She attributes what she considers my silent stoicism to being an only child and quietly independent. Obviously I was reacting to the magnitude of the task unfolding before me, but there was no way I could have prepared for this before going to South Africa. We never do that much in-depth orientation in the Foreign Service. All the briefings I got in Washington were just one narrow window into the multi-windowed world of South Africa. On the doctor's advice I spent a couple of days around the swimming pool reading and listening to music. The cooks were very solicitous and prepared comfort food that I liked.

The stress experienced by black South Africans was a special kind of hell, which they responded to in myriad ways. They fought, they endured, they suffered, and some tried to escape. One day while I was in residence in Pretoria, I was advised that three political prisoners had escaped from their Afrikaner guard at Diepkloof Prison and were holed up in the American consul general's office in Johannesburg, seeking asylum. Two of the prisoners were black and one was an Indian.

This called for some battlefield decisions. I assembled an emergency action committee at the embassy while Consul General Peter Chaveas told the prisoners that the United States could not offer them political asylum but could give them temporary refuge. I dispatched the security officer to Johannesburg to keep an eye on things, alerted Washington, and made the decision to give the prisoners asylum inside the mission. I extended the embassy to include the consul general.

South Africa revolutionary groups hastily formed a support group including Allan Boesak, Desmond Tutu, Albertina Sisulu, Frank Chikane, and others. The revolutionaries welcomed this public platform and prepared to milk it to the extreme. If the prisoners spoke to the press, it would dramatize their plight in South Africa. I knew the press was looking for me, so I met the support group and its lawyer, Chris Ngue, at the home of Commercial Officer Ben Brown.

We struck the agreement that two people would be allowed to visit the refugees each day to take them food. Family members could visit, and non-family members would be permitted to visit on a case-by-case basis. No press was allowed to meet with them. The refugees signed the agreement.

That evening Foreign Minister Pik Botha phoned me. "Get them out of the country," he said.

"I can't do that," I said. "As long as they are in the mission, they're on American territory, but the moment they step outside of the mission, you can arrest them."

"I give you my word," he said.

"I don't want your word. I'm not going to do it. It's not our job to spirit them out of the country. They're your citizens. If you want them out of the country, you pass word to them saying, 'You can leave South Africa and we'll escort you to the border.'"

Pik challenged the legality of declaring the consulate as sovereign territory. It was a legitimate challenge. Could I support my declaration? I took the position that I could.

"Mr. Minister, I'm saying that as a representative of my government personally appointed by my president, the consul general in Johannesburg is a part of the embassy of the United States and that makes the consulate sovereign territory. Constitutionally and in accordance with international law, if I want to say the consulate is a part of my mission, then it's a part of my mission."

In feverish phone-call exchanges between the embassy and the South African government, I spoke with Neil Van Heerden, director general of the South African Ministry of Foreign Affairs, and was summoned to the foreign minister's office for a meeting. Within the hour, Pik told me, he would release a statement declaring that the prisoners were free to go and would not be rearrested. By deflating the issue the South African government gained the upper hand. The support committee of revolutionaries was thunderstruck that the government had quietly stolen their public platform.

I did not meet with the refugees, but I did speak with them by phone. Through their attorney, I told them of their release. They told me that they did not want to leave the country, and since they had neither heard of the release officially nor had it in writing, they refused to leave the safe refuge of the consul general. We were at a standstill.

Although the press did not find me and could not speak directly to the prisoners, news of the event had reached the media. The prisoners became known as the Johannesburg Three and gained a brief notoriety. During the siege, I began to receive calls from many people, including one from Archbishop Tutu inquiring about the prisoners' well being and hoping that I would not turn them out into the street. A number of calls came from the United States. Two of the Americans who called were of national prominence. Senator Ted Kennedy called and asked about coming to South Africa. "Can I be helpful?" he asked. "I don't think there's anything you can do, Senator," I told him, and he accepted this.

The Reverend Jesse Jackson called with the same question: "What if I come down there?" I told him the same thing I had told the senator, and Jesse did not come to South Africa, either.

All of this transpired in a frantic thirty-six hours, but eventually the Johannesburg Three ventured out of the consulate to freedom, the South African government kept its word about not arresting them again, and the incident faded into history.

In the midst of this drama, Chet called to congratulate me on my promotion to career minister. "You're one of five people on the [promotion] list," he said. "You're in pretty illustrious company." Career minister is the highest rank in the Foreign Service. In the Senior Service, the first rank is counselor, the second highest is minister-counselor, and the highest operational rank is career minister. The final rank, which is honorary, is career ambassador. These require the president's approval of the promotion board's recommendation and the Senate's confirmation. I was so busy in South Africa that I had not noticed that time had arrived for the annual promotion board recommendations or considered that I would be on that list.

★

One of the most poignant victims of South African stress was the eminent journalist Percy Qoboza, one of the first people I met there. He was the editor of
the *City Press* newspaper, which was owned, ironically, by a pro-government,
white chain. I expected him to be as hostile as *The Sowetan*, but I could not have
been more wrong. He was a brave, outspoken critic of apartheid who had been
persecuted, harassed, interrogated, and imprisoned for his vehement press
attacks on the government, which had shut down two newspapers he edited.
When the government began to crack down on black journalists, he remembered coming to work to find that nine reporters had disappeared, as if wiped
off the face of the earth. He never saw some of them again. Under his editor-
ship, the *City Press* became the country's widest-read black-edited publication,
with a circulation of more than 200,000. His courageous voice rang out in his
column, "Percy's Pitch."

Percy was charismatic and brilliant, a Roman Catholic who had considered
entering the priesthood, a Nieman Fellow at Harvard, and a fighter. I called on
him in his office, as cluttered with paper as any editor's office, and I could see
that he was churning inside. The way he spoke, the agonized expressions in his
eyes, and the tense way he held his hands told me that apartheid was destroying him. He embodied the pain of a black man of dignity who had suffered so
much under the Afrikaner government. He died on his fiftieth birthday, January 17, 1988. He had suffered a heart attack, and I learned that he was suffering
from cirrhosis of the liver. I believe apartheid killed him: it ate out his heart.

A national monument had fallen. He was one of the heroes of the revolution, and his funeral reflected that. Government authorities tried to restrict
attendance at Soweto's Regina Mundi Catholic church to two hundred people,
prohibited political speeches, and limited clergy to one presiding priest.
Everybody expected trouble at the funeral. Aubrey Mokoena, chairman of the
Free Mandela Committee in Soweto and an outstanding orator, managed the
funeral. I was invited to attend and although my mother and Lucy demurred, I
took with me our daughter Kathy, who was visiting from school. The government had black agents among the congregation, but no uniformed police were
visible. A European ambassador, the Canadian ambassador, and four or five
other diplomats attended, and we were seated on the front row. Our presence
probably kept the authorities at bay. What took place at that funeral is almost
indescribable.

Winnie arrived late, making an appearance. She was dressed in royal green and flanked by her football team of eleven young men. She made a statement and left, marching out in regal style. Several tributes were made, flowers arrived, and the church overflowed with hundreds of people, perhaps thousands, as the local press reported. Then Mokoena took over. He was electrifying as he delivered the funeral oratory solely with biblical phrases and references, but it was the most political statement I have ever heard. With the powerful eloquence of Martin Luther King Jr., his voice rang to the rafters and back, and every line of scripture was a statement against the apartheid regime. The biblical quotes were molded into a mailed weapon of political attack. At one point, he reached a defiant crescendo, and I had to hold onto the pew to keep from standing in solidarity. Katherine was similarly moved. I learned that day that the Bible can be one hell of a political weapon.

The oration was punctuated by shouts from the congregation of "*Amandla Ayethu*," which means "power to the people." Percy's widow, Anne, and their four children sat through the four-hour service. When Mokoena asked mourners to rise and sing the freedom song "What Have We Done?" the Qoboza children stood with their hands raised in the clenched-fist salute. Mokoena thrust his fist in the air, too, and it was all I could do to keep mine down at my side. Plainclothes police filmed the mourners and coffin leaving the church and police in vehicles followed the procession to the cemetery.[10]

The next day a photo of Kathy and me appeared in *The New York Times* with the cutline "Ambassador Perkins in Township at Percy Qoboza's Funeral."

It took me a long time to get South Africa out of my system. I still feel the stress, and I dream about South Africa yet. But I could not stop to dream in 1988, because I was plunged into yet another monumental diplomatic test—trying to win the independence of neighboring Namibia.

ANGOLA-NAMIBIA
THE LONG STRUGGLE FOR PEACE

Dealing with the issues inside South Africa might have seemed to be a full plate for me, but I soon discovered that my assignment as ambassador was more than that. My mission was to promote peaceful change in southern Africa, and that meant my work extended beyond the borders of South Africa. It also involved a tangled situation in Namibia and Angola, which included, behind the scenes, Zimbabwe, Mozambique, Cuba, and the Soviet Union. This was unfinished business, which had started as an initiative of Secretary of State Henry Kissinger in 1976.

I traced the roots of the problem in Angola and Namibia back to World War I. The groundwork was laid by Germany's colonization of Namibia in 1884. At that time, the country was called South West Africa. After Germany's defeat in World War I, the League of Nations mandated Namibia to South Africa to be developed and prepared for independence. South Africa did not let go, however, and held on to Namibia as part of its own Cordon Sanitaire. Because Namibia is on the Atlantic coast, during World War II the Germans considered it a strategic area and used it as a submarine staging area. A fifth-column force of pro-Nazi Afrikaners attempted to arrange safe passage for German submarines in Namibian waters.

In 1966, the United Nations General Assembly revoked South Africa's mandate. In 1971, the International Court of Justice upheld the UN authority, determining that the South African presence in Namibia was illegal and that South Africa was obliged to withdraw from Namibia immediately. South Africa ignored the ruling, and guerrilla groups revolted with armed combat. Chief among these guerrilla groups was the South West Africa People's Organization (SWAPO), a Marxist guerrilla group with Angola as its ally, and the People's Liberation Army of Namibia (PLAN). SWAPO leaders told the UN that armed liberation struggle was the only language South Africa understood.

In 1976, Kissinger's first efforts in Sub-Saharan Africa signaled the end of his benign neglect of the continent. He concentrated on the most volatile target of the Afrikaner government in South Africa. He also determined that South Africa was determined to continue its hegemony over South West Africa/Namibia. Kissinger was not alone. On January 30, 1976, the UN Security Council adopted Resolution 385. This resolution implied that sanctions against South Africa were in store unless South Africa indicated it was moving to comply with the essential terms of 385: that Namibians be permitted to hold free and fair elections to determine how they wished to be governed. Because an election would mean the beginning of the end of South Africa's governance of Namibia, the Nationalist government stalled.

In 1977, the five western members of the UN Security Council known as the Contact Group (Canada, France, Federal Republic of Germany, the United Kingdom, and the United States) launched a joint diplomatic effort to bring a peaceful, internationally accepted transition to Namibian independence.

South Africa tried to thwart the loss of control over Namibia through the Turnhalle Constitutional Conference. Through this mechanism, South Africa would insure that white ethnic groups governed Namibia following its independence. The African Frontline States (principally Tanzania, Angola, Mozambique, and Zambia) opposed this plan. Kissinger tried to get all of the parties together in a conference to work out an agreement, but he did not succeed in this venture. This was a defeat for the United States.

Exacerbating the situation, neighboring Angola had been enmeshed in a great civil war since 1975, when it extracted itself from four hundred years of rule by Portugal. The resulting coalition Angolan government collapsed, leaving the Popular Movement for the Liberation of Angola (MPLA), a popular movement fighting for the liberation of Angola, in control. This delivered a one-two punch to the United States, because (1) the MPLA government was Marxist, and (2) the Soviets, Angolans, and Cubans conspired to dispatch Cuban armed forces to Angola to fend off enemies, primarily South Africa.

Where did Cuba fit into this maelstrom? In 1975 Cuba and the Soviet Union had intervened on the side of the MPLA. We were fairly certain that Cuba and the Soviet Union were calling the shots. MPLA was competing for power with another group, the Union for Total Independence of Angola (UNITA). After Angola became independent, SWAPO established bases in Angola. Still caught up in the cold war, the United States decried the involvement of the Soviets and

Cuba, but the Cuban force continued to strengthen. At the time of Angola's independence, Cuban troops numbered about 10,000. The following year they had increased by another 5,000. By the end of 1988, Cuba had a force of 50,000 troops stationed in Angola

The civil war in Angola, which spilled over into Namibia, was one of the most destructive smaller wars ever fought, and it was a battle between surrogates for the two superpowers. The Soviet Union backed the pro-Angolan government (MPLA), and the United States backed the opposition forces of Jonas Savimbi (UNITA) against what were considered "the godless forces of Communism." The U.S. support was managed by the CIA from Zaire, where an agent acted like a pro-consul. We in the foreign service did not always know what he was doing.

This was the situation in 1987 when I was thrust into the scene. Resolution 435 had been passed by the United Nations on September 29, 1978, almost ten years earlier. It reiterated the terms of resolution 385, which had been passed in 1976, set up a transition assistance group (Untag) to help ensure Namibia's early independence, and called on South Africa to stop impeding the electoral process. So far resolution 435 had been just a piece of paper that the South Africans ignored. For four years the principal issue had been South Africa's position that it would not agree to Namibia's independence until Cuban troops had withdrawn from neighboring Angola. SWAPO ran raids inside the Namibian border, attacking white farms and disturbing public activities. (The United States lost two officers in Namibia, a military officer and a Foreign Service officer, when their vehicle was bombed as they stopped at a gas station.) And South Africa had launched a major offensive against SWAPO guerrillas operating north of the Namibian border from Angola, intensifying hostilities.

Efforts were geared up again to remove the Cuban troops and bring about the independence of Namibia. Assistant Secretary Chet Crocker was wielding the baton. The Contact Group was still operative; the Frontline States were less so by this time. The Soviet Union played a silent role, and the Namibians were on the sidelines. Key players were South Africa, Angola, Cuba, and the United States. The UN's under secretary general, Perez de Cuellar, waited in the wings to declare victory and witness the lowering of the South African flag over Namibia, an action made possible, of course, by the United States. The expectation was that I would help persuade the South African government to comply with 385 and 435 and thus insure Namibia's having free and fair elections. It was a heavy expectation.

In this arena, the United States had no relations with two of the players—
Angola and Cuba—and a wobbly relationship with South Africa. With Cuba,
the United States was learning how to negotiate with a third-world country.
Much of the time, I felt as if I were juggling water.

This was a unique time in history. On the surface, our goal in the Angola-
Namibia peace talks was to influence the implementation of resolutions 385
and 435. In reality, much more was involved internationally. The peace negotiations were an unusual situation because of the players involved and the hidden
forces operating beneath the surface. South Africa and Angola were doing the
dance; Cuba and the United States were the orchestra; and the Soviet Union
was trying to call the tune. We were dealing with Afrikaners, Angolans,
Cubans, and Soviets. Oddly enough, we never talked to the Namibians themselves. This was a rare case in which the main players were excluded from the
process of independence.

The situation posed an interesting question of national interest: the chance
to make a difference, have friendly governments emerge in southern Africa,
and obtain clear passage by air or sea without circuitous routing. All we had to
do was provide arms and some cash. Were the results enough to warrant the
risks and the disparagement of what we stand for? I do not know. The national
interest is an elusive and dangerous concept.

THE STAKES

Everybody at the table had a monumental vested interest in the outcome.
South Africa had occupied and administered Namibia for seventy-three years.
It was hard for South Africa to give up the country, but bigger issues were at
stake. Unofficially, South Africa was at war with Namibia. Contingents of the
South African Defense Forces were stationed in Namibia to fight the insurgent
SWAPO troops and sometimes engaged them in battle. The white racist Afrikaners certainly did not want an independent Namibia next door, because that
likely meant a black government, which was exactly what the Afrikaners were
fighting to avoid in their own country. Crocker hoped that a mixed-race government would emerge in Namibia after independence, and that by getting the

Cuban forces out of Angola, we would win the cooperation of the South African government on a quid pro quo basis. Consequently, the negotiations were a great polite, diplomatic tug of war.

The stakes grew higher when we considered the very real possibility that we would be unable to bring South Africa into line with us on the Angola-Namibia issue. If that happened, the South African government would continue to flex its muscles in its homeland, and we would have to rethink our position there. I had pushed for peaceful change for two years, but any progress we had made could be gone in the blink of an eye if we failed to persuade the Cuban troops to withdraw from Angola. Then what? Could we tolerate indefinitely a South Africa where whites ruled blacks cruelly and with indifference to human rights? If the answer was yes, we would have to reduce our presence drastically, cut what contact we had with the Afrikaners, and do anything possible to show the illegitimacy of the South African government. The alternative to that was unthinkable.

In the Cuba-Angola alliance, Cuban troops had the job of protecting Angola from military invasion by South Africa. Cuba was not pleased to be known as the protector and wanted to be recognized as being legitimately in that country at Angola's request. Cuba and the United States had no formal relationship between them. This was the first time Cuba had worked openly with the United States, and this was the closest the United States had been to Cuba since Fidel Castro came to power. It was a heady experience for Cuba—collaborating with a great power (the United States), a friendly power (the USSR), and a belligerent power (South Africa). More than anything, Cuba wanted a recognized relationship with the United States.

This was the mix of agendas, and we could not move forward until each country's message was understood. We had to know institutionally what we stood for, who the players were, and how we had to play with them. It was a big task for the United States. We came to the table with superior strength, but it was a strength we held in abeyance. I did not understand all of this at the beginning, but from the first day of the negotiations I knew that we were in a situation we had never been in before.

The U.S. role was mediation, and this was part of my job, but Namibia was so important to Chet, who had such a tendency to hold everything close to the vest, that I had to force myself into the negotiations. I insisted that if I was going to bring the Afrikaners around to accepting this new construct, I would have to be involved every step of the way. This was part of the noose-tightening strategy to help convince the Afrikaners that they should be seeking the path to a new day. I did not want anything to happen that I was not aware of. I also insisted that if I could not be present at a meeting, somebody else from the embassy had to be present.

The embassy personnel I included in the process were Bob Frasure and Robin Raphel (Bob's replacement), Liz Pryor, and Larry Silverman, a Namibian expert. Chet resisted, because he was wary of people he did not know personally. He wanted total control, but I was adamant about being at the table. I was trying to move Chet toward institution-building, a philosophy that did not come to him naturally .

The Namibian government was under the executive power of Louis Pienaar, an administrator-general appointed by the South African government. When negotiations began, Pienaar welcomed me to Namibia with a dinner at his official residence and the declaration that "435 is dead, Mr. Ambassador. We will never agree to it." I told him that the United States was solidly behind 435, and moreover, we would hold it to be the basis for negotiations and eventually the independence of Namibia. I did promise that we would try to bring everybody to the negotiating table.

The U.S. objective in this exercise was to get the Cubans out of Angola. The South Africans wanted the same. Namibia's independence hinged on our achieving this goal.

I was instructed to go to the British, the French, and the Germans and ask them to make parallel *démarches* to the South African government. "Don't backslide on independence for Namibia," I said. The French notified us that they would not play the game. The Canadian ambassador said he thought he should and would ask his government for permission to do so. The British and the Germans supported us.

Not everybody backed us in our intention or expected us to succeed. The Belgian ambassador to South Africa was one of those. "Why does Chet Crocker want to go to the well on Angola?" he asked. The South Africans were "masters of deception," he said, and would prolong the chaos in Angola. He was speaking as a colonialist-minded European who deplored the passing of the torch from the sometimes-benevolent colonial countries to governance by citizens of the country, with all the turbulence that brings. It was exactly the same fear expressed by white South Africans at the prospect of the Nationalist Party losing power.

THE PLAYERS

THE UNITED NATIONS: Under Secretary General Martti Ahtisaari was the senior representative for the UN. I worked closely with him until he left to campaign for and win the presidency of Finland. His title was special representative of the secretary general of the United Nations. His team included Hisham Obayed and Merrick I. Goulding, both UN civil servants.

NAMIBIA: SWAPO, the revolutionary group that had launched a war of independence for Namibia in 1966, was led by Sam Nujoma, a medical doctor who would become the first president of independent Namibia. The South Africans considered him a joke, but the Namibians called him "Nujoma the Messiah" because he was delivering them from the yoke of South African colonialism. Even countries sympathetic to SWAPO dreaded dealing with Nujoma because he changed his mind faster than a swallow on the wing. He was so cautious that he often traveled in a bulletproof Mercedes, flanked by a phalanx of bodyguards.

ANGOLA: Two groups vied for power in Namibia from their base of operations in Angola. Jonas Savimbi, head of UNITA, was the darling of the right wing in the United States and was supported by U.S. funding. Savimbi was Chet's contact. The MPLA, the ruling party of Angola, was funded by the USSR and considered the Soviets' puppet. The Angola representatives in the negotiations included Manuela Pacivera, who was the Angolan ambassador to the United Nations, and Minister of Foreign Affairs Afonso Van Dunem.[1]

CUBA: In negotiations, I spoke primarily with Ricardo Alarcón, the key delegate. He later became the Cuban ambassador to the UN and then president of the legislative assembly in Cuba. At the time, we did not know he was so powerful. The no. 2 man in the Cuban delegation was José Arbescu Fraga. Cuban foreign minister Isidoro Malmierca Peoli was involved at the UN when the agreement among the United States, the Soviet Union, South Africa, Cuba, and Angola was signed in December 1988.[2]

SOUTH AFRICA: Neil Van Heerden, director general of the department of Foreign Affairs, led the South African delegation. Pik Botha was involved, along with General Jannie Geldenhuys and Minister of Defense Magnus Malan. They were joined by General Neels Van Tonder, a Namibia expert and former commander of the South African military force in Namibia. "Look at his eyes," Frasure told me before I met him, "and then look at his hands." Van Tonder had eyes as cold as ball bearings and the biggest hands I have ever seen. They were hands for strangling people.[3]

The South Africans were unhappy throughout most of the negotiations. They maintained that Namibia was part of South Africa's Cordon Sanitaire, and they considered this yet another battlefield between them and the United States. In their minds, Namibia's independence would reflect another U.S. victory, and they would be left empty-handed. Still, they wanted the Cubans out of their backyard. The longer the Cubans stayed, the more likely it was they would become civilians with access to Soviet and Cuban weapons.

The South Africans must have known they had to give up Namibia at some point. They had two options: they could give it up with honor, or they could give it up with some force. My preference was the former. I dealt extensively with Neil, whom I considered the most honorable senior official in South Africa's Ministry of Foreign Affairs.

THE UNITED STATES: Namibia was Chet's baby, and he led the U.S. delegation.[4] When Chet became assistant secretary of state in the new Reagan administration in 1981, he came prepared to resume the stalled talks about Namibian independence. He had studied South Africa, South West Africa, and Angola in some detail, and he took office ready to roll, visiting Angola in 1981 to discuss Cuban troop withdrawal, and in 1984 meeting in Lusaka with Angolans and South Africans.

In 1987, after six years of Crocker's constructive-engagement policy, the Cubans were still in Angola, South Africa still controlled Namibia, and South Africa was in turmoil. An alternative approach was called for. Chet's efforts were already *en train* when I joined the process in early 1987, attending a London negotiation session among Angola, South Africa, Cuba, and the United States. This was the start of one of the most excruciating diplomatic ventures of my career.

In Geneva in March 1987, we began to play hardball with the South African government. Chet laid down some strict rules to Foreign Minister Botha. He said the United States was attempting to be an honest broker, but if South Africa did not recognize that and wanted to go it alone, Botha could "Be my guest." He said that he was through with standing up for the South Africans in the face of worldwide opprobrium with no help from them. Nobody had heard Chet talk that tough to the Afrikaners before.

The task ahead seemed insurmountable. We were trying to persuade the South Africans to recognize the inevitability of independence for both Angola and Namibia, which they were loath to do. We wanted the South Africans to continue talking to the Angolans and the Cubans and trying to arrive at a solution to the Angolan problem. Sometime later at a meeting in New York, when I was in my next post, Secretary of State Cyrus Vance told me, "The United States should have recognized Angola long ago. It was a mistake not to have done so from the start. I should have just told President Carter to recognize Angola and take the flak from the right." That flak would have been intense, because Angola was considered to have a left-wing government under the MPLA.

With the Angola-Namibia negotiations, we were now fighting the Afrikaners on two fronts. They were losing the fight for independence of Namibia, as well as the fight for maintaining an apartheid system. Some of the more intelligent members of the South African government, Pik in particular, knew the time was up. They knew that they were going to have to take a political back seat and that the blacks were going to take over the government. Still, they fought on. A new day was dawning, but they were not acknowledging the sunrise.

THE LONG ORDEAL

On April 18, 1988, I arrived in Namibia to begin the process of negotiations. I was fascinated by the unique geography of this enormous desert country. Namibia is the thirty-first-largest country in the world, more than half the size of Alaska. The Namib Desert, the oldest desert in the world, extends along the west coast, and the Kalahari Desert stretches along the southeast inland border.

When I visited the town of Swakopmund, I saw a German town from another era: the streets, the taverns, the little coffee shops serving black walnut cake. It was like stepping back in time. I saw the German influence in the names of the principal cities—Windhoek, Keetmanshoop, and Grootfontein—and I saw the old German Lutheran influence in the dress of the tribal women.

Almost 90 percent of the Namibian population was black. The largest black tribe, the Ovambo, constituted about 52 percent of Namibia's population. When Namibia was a German colony, the Lutheran Church was imported. Ovamban women still dressed in the pre–World War I German fashion of blouses with long sleeves, long skirts with seventeen petticoats, and distinctive bonnets. Namibian Coloureds were divided into two groups, one of which is called *Basters*, meaning bastard liaisons between white South Africans and black women. They were proud of their name and mixed race. The *Basters* wanted group rights for protection, but they did not want to be governed by a black government. Whites were the minority population; 60 percent of the white population spoke Afrikaans, about 30 percent spoke German, and 10 percent spoke English.

I was met upon arrival by Harry Smuts, the great-grandson of Afrikaner hero Jan Christian Smuts. Harry, a human-rights lawyer, told me, "The South African Defense Force has gone completely awry in Namibia. The soldiers are beating the population at random, raping women, and killing villagers. The army is completely out of control." This was the first time a notable witness had said that. The next morning, Ken Abrams, a Coloured former member of SWAPO, confirmed that the South African army was running amok and doing everything to co-opt the Namibian people into voting for a party that was a surrogate for the Afrikaner National Party.

From April to December 1988, nine long months, we met in London, Cairo, Geneva, and New York for official talks, but we met most often in Congo Brazzaville at the invitation of President Denis Sassou Nguesso. Brazzaville is an exotic river-port city on the Zaire River. Kinshasa, the capital of Zaire (now the Republic of the Congo), is on the other side of the river. The travel alone was wearing, but the stress of the finicky negotiations had us all on edge. Institution-building is delicate work, particularly in the uncharted territory of these talks. Diplomats are not used to this sort of thing. I had done my graduate work in public-administration behavioral science, so it made sense to me, but this was not an academic exercise. We were playing for keeps, making history, and the pressure was exhausting. Often I was dog-tired. For relaxation, I began rereading *The Hero With a Thousand Faces*, Joseph Campbell's study of mythology. On top of all of this, upon returning home to South Africa, I learned about the three political prisoners holed up in the consul general's office seeking asylum. This gave me another issue about which to wrestle with the South Africans, yet another struggle for diplomatic prowess. The sky was raining problems and stress.

One Sunday, on the way across the Zaire River from Brazzaville to Kinshasa, Jeff Davidow, principal deputy to Crocker, was horsing around on the boat, and the seat broke. There was nothing but daylight between us and the river, which is notoriously full of crocodiles. Two years earlier, the German ambassador to Kinshasa had fallen overboard and was never seen again. This close call scared the breath out of me. "Jeff, I'm going to the other end of the boat," I said. "You stay here, and don't come near me again." He sat quietly for the rest of the trip.

I went back and forth from South Africa to Namibia as we held unilateral, bilateral, and plenary sessions and endless conferences, caucuses, and strategy meetings. We met for breakfast, lunch, dinner, and cocktail parties in the evening. Every time I thought the road was smoothed, the South Africans bombshelled us. Once, Pik, unreliable as always, took it upon himself to announce to the press that a timetable agreement had been reached, an announcement that was premature and not true. Occasionally, we wondered if the Cubans were forthright about the numbers of their troops in the country, or if a substantial uncounted number were stationed in Angola and planning on staying behind.

We felt our way among the minefields of international egos, always monitoring the South African mood. "It is like a dance of giraffes," I told the Angolans. Pik often reminded me that it was impossible for the Afrikaner government to appear to be the loser in the Angolan-Namibian situation. For this reason, most of the talks took place on the African continent. Twice in the midst of negotiations, the South Africans packed up and went home. They were called back, I presumed, by the elders for consultation. "When there's enough fire in their breasts," I assured the others, "the South African government will be ready to talk."

As the talks began in earnest, I spoke first with the Angolans and then with the Cubans. I asked the Cubans for their strength and urged them to say what

they had to say and then get on with the business at hand because we were trying our best to calm the South Africans and avoid drama. Both the Cubans and
the Angolans complied with my request. They were easier to deal with than the
U.S. assistant secretary for Inter-American Affairs, then a hard-line right-
winger. Until then, I thought he and I were friends, but he took a stand that
branded Cuba as a country not worthy of relations with the United States.

Occasionally Chet briefed Angola's Savimbi in Zaire. Sometimes Savimbi
showed up for these meetings; sometimes he did not. Savimbi distrusted Americans, and he got the jitters about meeting us. Once, the press quoted Savimbi
as denouncing the peace talks as a plot by Crocker to get rid of UNITA. Where
did that come from, we wondered. Had South Africa planted that thought? Had
Savimbi gone off the deep end? Had he misunderstood Chet? Was this a red
herring?

We were creeping toward agreement on a communiqué announcing a cease-
fire and the beginning of withdrawal, but each side needed assurance that it
would not look like the loser. The Angolans wanted to make sure they did not
appear to be forsaking SWAPO, their fighting and political organization. The
Cubans felt the same way. We went through a lot to get to that agreement and
we groveled a little.

In September, we talked about protectional borders, the dismantling of the
armed forces, and timelines for the Cuban troop withdrawal. The Angolans
wanted thirty-six months; the South Africans wanted twelve months—two
years apart, but it was a beginning. We also had a breakthrough when the South
Africans agreed that a UN technical team and peacekeeping force could go to
Namibia, but we had a little setback when the South Africans added that no
military from Australia or the United States would be acceptable on the United
Nations Transition Activity because those two countries were opposed to the
apartheid government. The Australian ambassador called on me to express his
displeasure with this demand.

About this time, we had a visit from a "senior officer," a confidential visitor
who was trusted by Savimbi. He told us that Savimbi was depressed and had no
faith in Chet, whom, he felt, was not forthcoming. I emphasized again to Chet
the importance of keeping open the lines of communication to Savimbi
because he was suspicious. "He hasn't lasted this long as a bush fighter without
being suspicious," I said. "It is what has kept him alive."

I also ran into a Russian I had first seen in Washington when I was head of West African Affairs.

"Remember me, Ambassador?" he asked.

"Yes, what are you doing here?"

"Watching you," he said. He wanted to know how the talks were going.

"Maybe you can tell me," I answered. Since the Soviets were funding both the Cubans and the Angolans, he had access to both, as well as information I did not have.

We scheduled a meeting for early October in New York to work out remaining problems and then headed to a final, three-way signing of the Namibia Accords in Brazzaville at the end of November and the final protocol in New York in December.

November 29 arrived with last-minute confusion about who would attend the signing ceremony in New York. Chet was to be there, Secretary Shultz would arrive bearing letters from President Reagan, and Pik also would be there to sign. We did not know the other members of the South African delegation at Brazzaville. Alarcón from Cuba was coming, as well as Cuba's Foreign Minister Malmierca, but neither Carlos Aldana, a powerful figure in Cuba's Communist party, nor any Cuban military. With Larry Napper, one of the world's great drafters of diplomatic documents, we worked through the night ironing out the rest of the reference to the verification process, Brazzaville Protocol, and set a date for the trilateral signing in New York. We were now down to tweaking sentences to incorporate everyone's ideas.

The next evening in Brazzaville, Chet and I met the Soviet deputy foreign minister Anatoly Adamishin at the Soviet ambassador's home. We left that meeting, which included an unreasonable amount of vodka, caviar, dumplings, and nuts, for more conferences. The next morning we caucused, then held bilaterals for almost three hours with the Angolans and Cubans in a poorly ventilated room. The Cubans smoked cigars until the air was green. I was sweating profusely and getting drunk from the cigar smoke, and I thought my interpreter would die.

At the signing of the Brazzaville Protocol in December 1988, Chet spoke with some emotion. The long process had taken a physical toll on him. That day he said that the ceremony signified "the end of a sad chapter in Africa's modern history and the beginning of a new chapter." He paid tribute to both the United

States and our Soviet counterparts for working together despite "some differences in perspective and roles in the negotiating process." He continued, "It has
been a case study of superpower effort to support the resolution, of reaching a
resolution on regional conflicts. The United States does not have the blueprints
for the solution of every problem around the world, but we are prepared to
involve ourselves in the search for constructive solutions, when such a role is
welcomed and appropriate." We were realists and that was what made this protracted but successful negotiation possible; we recognized that massive solutions
could be based on the concrete historical realities of a given situation. "Just as
man cannot eat slogans, neither can statesmen solve problems with rhetorical
clichés and abstract formula. We have tried to chart a clear course and stick with
it. This is an approach that may sometimes fall short of shifting fashions and popular hopes of instant results, but over time, this is the approach that gives confidence and predictability to success. It is the approach that works."

Ten years after the UN Security Council adopted resolution 435 and nine
months after Chet initiated negotiations, the final signing ceremony was held at
the UN in New York, December 22, 1988. I was so hyped up I could barely walk.
South Africa, Angola, and Cuba signed the Tripartite Agreement, paving the way
for Cuban troop withdrawal and independence of Namibia. I joined others on
the secretary's plane for New York, where we motorcaded to the UN. The ceremony was held in the Security Council chambers with Secretary Schultz offici-
ating on behalf of the United States. Angola's Van Dunem signed and then made
a speech; Cuba's Isidoro Octavio Malmierca did the same. Both speeches were
political and sharply critical of the United States, which was most unusual at
such an historical event. They said the United States supported South Africa in
its invasion of other countries, interfered in other nations' affairs (meaning
Angola), and mistreated Cuba by imposing an embargo after the Cuban missile
crisis.

   In my opinion, both men were dopes and should have acknowledged that the
United States had wrought a miracle. Schultz would not let it pass. He made a
point of noting his displeasure and his disagreement with their remarks. Speaking for South Africa, Pik followed with a surprisingly restrained speech, and I
commended him on his talk. South Africans are not known for pulling their
punches.

Secretary Shultz delivered a graceful speech, saying that a new era of peace and prosperity had begun. "As the guns fall silent across the borders of southwestern Africa," he said, "the world will look to the nations of that vast region, turning to resolution of their pressing internal problems through peaceful means." Shultz also praised Chet for taking the lead in seeking a resolution to this problem.

When we all went down to Namibia to witness the changing of flags, UN Secretary General Perez de Cuellar officiated, giving a great speech, yet never once mentioned the U.S. role. Without the United States, Perez de Cuellar never would have been able to deliver that speech.

What we had accomplished was remarkable. As summarized in a U.S. government publication, "The peace plan included the withdrawal of Cuban troops from Angola, the withdrawal of South African troops from Namibia, the demobilization of Namibian military units, the return of refugees, the release of political prisoners, the repeal of discriminatory and restrictive laws, registration of voters, and election of an assembly to draft a constitution." That constitution included the environmental protection of the desert nation, making Namibia the first country in the world to promise constitutionally to protect the Earth.

Could all of this have been done by someone other than Chet as leader of the delegation? Perhaps, but Chet not only was resourceful, he was relentless. He never gave up, and he had around him a group of close and exceptional personal aides working in concert.

When we finally achieved success on Namibia, I was invited to dinner at the British ambassador's house, down the street from mine in Cape Town. The British had not been involved at all in the Namibian process. I walked into the house, and he said, "By God, we showed them, didn't we?"

"Yes, Robin," I said. "We did."

What occurred at Brazzaville will go down in history as one of the world's greatest negotiating successes. It is clearly one of the more fundamental ones in Africa.

The civil war in Angola appeared to have ended peacefully. The United States and the Soviet Union ceased support of their constituencies in Angola. We ended U.S. financial aid to UNITA, and the Soviets stopped supporting the MPLA. Namibia gained its independence in March 1990, and elections were finally held, although they took two years to arrange. The MPLA party's Jose

Eduardo dos Santos claimed victory over Savimbi. When I told Savimbi that I was instructed by President George H.W. Bush to tell him the United States would no longer support him and UNITA, Savimbi seemed resigned to hearing a message that he did not like. Nevertheless he said to me, "Mr. Ambassador, you have the reputation of never mincing words. Please tell the president that I will abide by the election." I carried the message, but Savimbi did not keep his word. The civil war in Angola went on. I had been Savimbi's pawn.

POSTSCRIPT
SOUTH AFRICA

In the middle of the Namibian peace talks, I was offered a new assignment. It would be my penultimate job—the director general of the Foreign Service. I had dreamed of sitting in the director general's chair for most of my Foreign Service career. From the day I took the oath of office as a newly minted officer, I was well aware of the obstacles, both real and imagined, that stood in my way, but I studied the Foreign Service with the intent of being an officer of substance. I was determined that no gaps would exist in my qualifications. I steadily advanced to increasingly responsible jobs with timely promotions.

In about nine months, my tour of duty in South Africa would be up, and I expected to be rotated to another post, but not even in fantasy did I expect to be offered the director generalship. And yet, as much as I wanted the job, we were at a critical stage in the Namibian negotiations. Some people believed that the U.S. involvement in Namibia was disingenuous and a stalling tactic to prolong advancement in South Africa. Our hard work in South Africa seemed perilous and capable of collapse. I still had so many tasks yet to perform there. I was committed to a peaceful transition and to replacing the present government, but I did not want to replace a white despotic government with a black despotic government. With all of this in the balance, could I walk away from Namibia and South Africa? It was a wrenching decision. I was surprised, elated, and overwhelmed at the offer before me, but I hesitated. I could have paraphrased the familiar adage and made it my own by saying, "When the gods want to break your heart, they grant you your deepest wish."

I told outgoing Director General George Vest that I thought I should stay in South Africa another year, being uniquely placed and qualified to finish the job. Then, to round out my qualifications, I should serve a tour in Indonesia and take the director generalship later.

"Ed," he said, "do you want to be director general of the Foreign Service?"

"Yes," I replied. "I have dreamed of having this job."

"Then take it now. You will only get the offer once in your career. You have done what no one else could have done, and that is to craft the demise of the apartheid system. You must know when it is time to move on to the next challenge. That time is now, and the challenge is being director general. The Service needs you at the top."

Vest thought the time had come to appoint a black director general, and I was the black he wanted for the job. He told me that I would shortly receive a cable from the secretary of state proposing that President George H. W. Bush nominate me to the Senate. Vest's straight-shooting remarks put me back on the sensible path and made me realize something I knew—nobody is irreplaceable. I told Vest to send the cable. He had given me a lecture I could well have delivered myself, because I lived by the creed of holding an assignment for just so long, then moving on to the next venture.

I talked about my impending departure when I had dinner in Cape Town with South African authors Danielle and Wilbur Smith. "What in God's name is wrong with your government?" Danielle said, furious at the news that I was leaving. "We've got an ambassador here who is our best bet for avoiding a civil war, and they pull you out!" I told her that a three-year tour of duty was customary, that the director general was the top Foreign Service job in the State Department, and that the administration had sent me word that I was the person for the job at this time in history.

When I was assigned to South Africa, I never thought that I was hand-picked or had special qualifications for the job. I was selected, appointed, and told to try making a change without violence. I lived the assignment and its challenges day and night, but when the next assignment was identified, it was time to go. I know the policy of reassignment established by Kissinger is healthy for the Foreign Service. New assignments keep the Service vibrant and alive. George Vest was right. I had already done the things that needed to be done in South Africa. We had crossed the Rubicon, and there was no question that South Africa was going to change. Apartheid was finished. I would watch from afar how the new South Africa moved into the future with the heart of a lion but on the trembling legs of a fawn. It was hard, but I went.

I was saddened to leave South Africa. That assignment affected me as no other before or since. Wherever I am, the memory of golden South Africa sunlight colors my days, and the people I met there slip into my dreams at night. South Africa is an indelible part of my life.

In January 1989, George Herbert Walker Bush was sworn in as America's forty-first president. Having been Reagan's vice president, he knew why the president had sent me to South Africa. He thought the objective had been obtained. President Bush had been a congressman, the head of the CIA, an ambassador to China, and ambassador to the UN, so he came into office with a rock-solid background. He was professional in his approach to South Africa, and he let the Afrikaners know that the Bush administration was different. This administration would traffic no nonsense about such issues as access to sea-lanes, minerals, the price of coal, or sanctions. This new administration had more important objectives than South Africa. The message President Bush sent South Africa, one reporter wrote, was "Don't get cute."

The Aftermath

The Leaders

P. W. Botha had a stroke in February 1989, and that was the beginning of his downfall. Shortly thereafter, he was deposed as leader of the National Party, and the end of his presidency was in sight. F. W. de Klerk led the fight to oust Botha as party head and then became acting president. In my last meeting with de Klerk before leaving South Africa, I asked him about his plans. "We've been talking about change in Africa since I got here," I said. "What are you going to do?" De Klerk smiled, smoking as usual, and said, "Well, Ambassador, you and everybody else will just have to wait and see."

In 1990, de Klerk released Mandela from jail and rescinded the orders banning the ANC, the PAC, the South African Communist Party, and other illegal organizations. Restrictions were lifted on the UDF and the media. He announced that henceforth South Africa would cease to manage political activity. With those actions, de Klerk ended apartheid, shrugging off the heavy Afrikaner yoke that South Africa carried for so long and taking a giant step into a new South Africa. De Klerk was not a revolutionary, but he was a moderate and a realist. It could be argued that the country would have changed anyway, naturally, but without de Klerk and his colleagues it also could have taken four or five more turbulent years.

Following the election of President Mandela, Foreign Affairs Minister Pik Botha was appointed minister of Mineral and Energy Affairs. He retired from politics in 1996. A few years after that, Pik reportedly said that Afrikaners should work more closely with the majority government, and he expressed

interest in joining the ANC. He did join and is now an accredited, card-carrying
member. Pik was always a realist and something of an opportunist. His membership reflects at least two realities: the ANC will likely be the majority party
well into the future, and if Pik intends to remain in South Africa, his personal
future is enhanced through active membership in the ANC.

The Country

The South African whites were right when they forecast an economic and societal breakdown if the national government changed. The year 1994 had changes
that hit the nation like an earthquake. In late April, South Africa held its first
one-person, one-vote election, and Mandela was elected president. Everything
shifted. The social needs of the majority black population were so great and the
expectations so large that they swamped the new, unprepared government.

Five years later, only 27 percent of blacks, contrasted to 96 percent of
whites, had running water in their homes. Unemployment was 40 percent for
blacks and 4 percent for whites.[1] To further imperil the country's economic
stability, young, white South Africans began moving abroad to work. White
professionals left the country en masse. Since 1948, when the Nationalist Party
won power, South Africa's economy had been state-controlled and -managed.
That system was a carefully designed economic model—a partnership
between the titans of business and the Nationalist Party, based in part on policies put in place by the National Socialist Party in Germany in the 1930s. When
political change came in South Africa in 1994, it was a shocking thunderclap. It
was now time to equalize at the least the amounts of money that targeted
blacks; affirmative action was becoming a newly imposed norm. Whites were
uncertain where they would fit and what would happen to them. Two things
had to happen if the economy was not to come apart: the white exodus had to
be minimized, and all citizens, especially the affluent, had to embrace the new
economic system of blacks and whites for South Africa. This is still emerging.
Sanlam, Anglo-American, De Beers, the petrol industry, and the ancillary mining interests all must play a part.

Creating a new economic system takes time, but the impoverished black citizens were not inclined to be patient. They had waited too long. Frustration
ignited fury in the black townships. Fighting broke out in KwaZulu between
the Inkhata Freedom Party and the ANC, and the rate of violent crime soared.
Some sixty-four thousand women and children were raped every year. As the
government struggled to provide water, electricity, education, and medical

This was a historic day. Nelson Mandela was making his first visit to the United States. I greeted him in the Jefferson Room at the State Department. Winnie Mandela is center.

care for the population, funding was unavailable for the arts that had catered to the tastes of the white minority, and performing arts organizations such as the National Symphony Orchestra fell silent.

In 1996 Ann Paton, Alan's widow, wrote me a grim eyewitness account of the country:

> A state of anarchy seems to prevail almost everywhere—certainly in the universities. And corruption is rife. Money is "disappearing" as a result—millions of rands—as many of those in high places are not too scrupulous about lining their own pockets, and voting themselves huge salaries and perks. I suppose it is inevitable in a "developing" country, but South Africa does not exactly fall into the category of "developing country." Education is going straight down to a very low level, and the brain drain is now exacerbated because of this. People are now leaving to make sure of giving their children a good education. People walk in fear—I personally know of five people who have been murdered in this area in the last two years. And yet we stay in this beautiful country, hoping against hope that it will all come right. But I fear for the future of Alan's beloved country.

Some things did not change. Soweto is still a sprawling, poverty-pocked townsite with meandering dirt roads, dusty sidewalks, and inadequate running water, toilets, and electricity. Ironically, after apartheid, Soweto became one of the most popular tourist sites in South Africa. Tour guides take European and American visitors through the townsite and point out the house where Mandela lived. Many of the tourists photograph the shabby homes, stop to hear choirs practicing in the churches, and give coins to the local street children. Some of the visitors weep.[2]

South Africa's Truth and Reconciliation Commission, chaired by Archbishop Tutu, began in 1995 as a national effort to heal the wounds of apartheid atrocities. The hearings, founded on the religious tenets of confession and forgiveness, were an alternative to the Nuremberg Trials after World War II. The intent of the commission's investigations—testimonies of twenty thousand victims and admission of guilt by hundreds of the perpetrators—was to expose the crimes of apartheid, salve the pain, and thus move the country forward. It was a heroic but flawed effort. Some, including the family of Steve Biko, rejected outright the idea of granting amnesty to murderers and torturers. Former State President P. W. Botha would not testify. Chief Buthelezi refused to cooperate. Winnie Mandela was charged with eighteen offenses, ranging from torture to murder. F. W. de Klerk was harangued for hours, then he sued the commission for an apology and to excise his examination from the records. The impartiality of the commission was called into question when ANC crimes were not equally enumerated, and a number of ANC leaders did not testify but were granted amnesty anyway.[3]

In 1999, on the one hundredth anniversary of the Anglo-Boer War, Britain's Queen Elizabeth made a state visit to South Africa, publicly remembered the "tragic chapter in the history of both our countries," and expressed sadness at the loss of lives. Some Afrikaners wanted a full-fledged apology and demonstrated in protest. They cited the number—27,927 Boer women and children and 20,000 blacks who died as prisoners of war in the British concentration camps.[4]

South Africa is a country dealing with an emergency evolution of its economic, political, and social structures. When Mandela came out of prison, he was welcomed with *toi toi* (drum beat) dancing. The euphoria is gone now. People are counting how many new houses have been built and how many electric lines have been extended into the townships where there was no light. First the national government and then the provincial and municipal governments underwent a crisis and massive restructuring of the delivery of public utilities. A Coloured woman working with thousands of people in temporary housing told me that they do not talk about affirmative action. "They don't give a damn who's sitting in the office, black or white. They just want the water service to work. They want water."

The central government has been wrestling with capacity building and transforming itself from a revolutionary government into a party that learns to compromise with other parties, to allocate resources, to deliver goods and services, and to bring about a better life for the people. It is learning to deal with a majority population with a history of deprivation who now feels a sense of entitlement and angry impatience. For the first time, token university fees were instituted, and students walked out or marched in protest, saying they were entitled to a free education.

The government is struggling towards a workable policy for combating the HIV-AIDS virus, which continues to escalate.

So many want so much, and they all want it now, but this is not a transformation that can happen magically and instantly. It is a process. This change is like a great ocean turning over. It takes time.

The Afrikaners

The South Africa government ministers were wrong about AIDS. They had not heeded my warning, but instead insisted that AIDS was little more than a problem for some blacks. That error was monumental. The infection exploded into a national cataclysm. More people have contracted the disease in South Africa than in any other country in the world. By 2003, more than five million South Africans had been infected with HIV-AIDS, and some six hundred were dying daily. Equally wrong were the black ministers who followed the white South Africans into office and refused to believe that AIDS was sexually transmitted. Notable among those was President Thabo Mbeki, who questioned both the cause and nature of the disease and the available medical treatment.[5]

The Black Revolutionaries

Mandela left prison February 11, 1990. Thousands of people awaited him. He raised his fist in the air, he wrote in his autobiography, and a roar rose from the crowds. "I had not been able to do that for twenty-seven years," he said, "and it gave me a surge of strength and joy."[6] The following year he was elected president of the ANC. In 1993 he, along with de Klerk, was awarded the Nobel Peace Prize. In 1994, in South Africa's first multi-race elections, Mandela was elected president of the country. His inaugural address called for reconciliation and affirmed his determination to build a peaceful society of all races. He appointed

ministers from the National Party, ANC, and Inkhata. His vision as elected leader
of the nation mirrored his statement as a prisoner in the dock at the Rivonia
Trial: "I have fought against white domination, and I have fought against black
domination. I have cherished the ideal of a democratic and free society in which
all persons live together in harmony and with equal opportunities. It is an ideal
which I hope to live for and to achieve. But if needs be, it is an ideal for which I
am prepared to die." In 1999, at age eighty-one, he did not stand for reelection,
saying the robust country needed a younger man, and he was succeeded as president by Thabo Mbeki.

Winnie Mandela continued to fall from grace. The murder of fourteen-year-
old Stompie Moeketsi Seipei and her infamous necklace speech ("If they betray
us, we will necklace them.") toppled her star into a steady descent. Rumors of
her multiple lovers were an affront to the people's icon, Nelson Mandela, and
reports of her working with Robert Brown in an attempt to license the Mandela name on products further damaged her credibility. When she built a lavish
home in the midst of Soweto's matchbox houses, it was derisively called "Winnie's Palace." From 1986 to 1989, her football team of young thugs ran rampant, terrorizing the community, and were accused of a rash of beatings, rapes,
torture, and killings. Posing as bodyguards dressed in soccer uniforms, they
accompanied her everywhere, from meetings to funerals. More and more, the
top black leadership began to consider her as an irritant and damaging to the
cause. I once saw Joe Marks become almost uncontrollable with rage when he
heard about one of her outrageous public statements. "That woman is doing
her husband irreparable harm. She has to go," Joe said. Winnie and Mandela
were divorced in 1996.[7]

Walter Sisulu died in May 2003 at age ninety and was given a state funeral in
Orlando Stadium that was attended by tens of thousands of mourners. The government dipped its banners and accorded him the honors due a hero. With wisdom and courage, this modest self-made man, the son of a black mother and a
white father who did not acknowledge him, had become a guiding force of a
nation. Like the biblical figure he admired, Sisulu was a David who slew the
giant of apartheid. Mandela mourned him eloquently and publicly. "Sisulu
stands head and shoulders above all of us in South Africa," Mandela said. "You
will ask what is the reason for his elevated status among us. Very simple, it is
humility. It is simplicity. Because he pushed all of us forward and remained quietly in the background."

Albertina, Sisulu's widow, still lives in Soweto. I stay in contact with her and call on her whenever I am in South Africa. She continues to work to help the people of her country and currently is making plans to build an after-school shelter for children. The black children of working parents disappear off the streets, either kidnapped or murdered, at a horrifying rate, she told me; she wants to provide them a safe shelter.

Chief Buthelezi became Home Affairs minister in the new government, an appointment made in 1994 by Mandela. The chief survived scurrilous charges of collaboration with the South African government's security forces and the Truth and Reconciliation Commission's accusation that Inkhata massacred hundreds of people during the fierce clashes in 1990 with the ANC. Some South Africans maintain that Inkhata and Buthelezi murdered more people in that violent period than the South African government did in all of apartheid.

On one of my visits back to South Africa, Buthelezi hosted a dinner at his Johannesburg hotel suite for my companions and me. I saw the Buthelezi I remembered of old—clever, charming, and verbose. Over drinks he read aloud a three-page statement he had prepared and then presented us with printed copies. The meal began with a long blessing by the chief's kinsman in their tribal language, and then our host said with a chuckle, "We assume that God speaks Zulu."

Father Mkhatshwa was named executive mayor of Pretoria (officially, Executive Mayor of Tshwane, which is the name of the area) in 2000. In making the appointment, President Mbeki told him, "We believe you are one of the very few who can build and transform local government." When the priest and I had breakfast in Johannesburg a few years ago, Father Mkhatshwa told me about taking a helicopter tour of Pretoria, Mamelodi, Alexandra, and environs just weeks after assuming the mayoral post. The poverty was glaring and visible. "I could see the suffering of the people from the air," he said. "It is a huge beast that must be tamed."

The White and Coloured Revolutionaries

Ann Paton left South Africa. Alan was such an important part of that country that her leaving was reported in the *New York Times*. They had lived in a middle-class neighborhood in Durban, and she wrote to me how she regretted her decision: "But I can't stand it any longer. Several of my friends have had their houses broken into and I've had mine broken into. I can't live in a society where you have five locks on the door." She moved to Chelsea in London.

Johan Heyns and I spoke for the last time, as we had done so many times before, in the study of his home in Johannesburg. We talked about soliciting the support of small-town dominees and encouraging them to preach about cooperation with the new South Africa. In 1994 as he sat in that same study, he was assassinated by an Afrikaner for betraying the white cause. It was Guy Fawkes Day, and Renee, his widow, said the family could hear fireworks popping outside. They were absorbed in a game of gin rummy, with grandchildren playing on the floor at their feet. She turned to Johan to say how close the firecrackers sounded and saw that he had been shot in the back of the head. What she had heard was not a loud firecracker, but the gunshot of the killer firing through the window.

The last time I saw Allen Boesak, in March 2003, he had not changed a bit. He talked to me in English while making deals in Afrikaans on the telephone. As always, he was living like a prince and dressed to the nines. After Mandela's election, Boesak was slated to be ambassador to the European Union in Brussels, one of the more important ambassadorships in the world. While waiting for confirmation, charges were brought against him, alleging corruption in the management of the Kagiso Trust that he chaired. Mandela did not desert him, though. Remembering the role that Boesak had played in the struggle, Mandela appeared in court on his behalf. Still, he was found guilty. If it were possible for a Coloured to have been elected president after apartheid, Allen would have been the first candidate. Instead, he became a disgraced leader, but a man who still manifests a deep devotion to a new, democratic South Africa.

Archbishop Tutu continued in his inimitable style, speaking his mind, falling out with President Mandela, growing in international stature. His Grace retired as archbishop of Cape Town in 1996 and was named archbishop emeritus. He continues sermonizing, writing, and speaking around the world. One of the last times we interacted, I was welcoming him to Norman, Oklahoma, to receive an honorary degree from the University of Oklahoma.

The U.S. Embassy Staff

Most of my own staff at the U.S. Embassy in South Africa continued to build distinguished careers. While I was still in South Africa, Tim Bork, my USAID counselor for developmental affairs, was replaced by Dennis Barrett, the highest-ranking American Indian in the Foreign Service. Dennis is a fine Foreign Service officer who did an outstanding job in South Africa and later became ambassador to Botswana. Tim's career took a bumpier ride. He was always intensely passionate about his work for social justice and, like all of us, Tim had drunk of the rare wine that is South Africa. He had a hard time adjusting to a routine work life after he was transferred to Washington. Eventually he retired from the Agency for International Development and went to work first for the Ford Foundation and then for the Carnegie Foundation. At Carnegie, he initiated a large grant for a national debate on the United States and Africa. He longed for an ambassadorial appointment, and I supported him, but it was not in the cards. He took it hard. Sometimes politics and political appointments take precedence over qualifications.

Karl Beck, my black political officer, served in Germany, and upon falling ill for a while, returned home to Fort Myers, Florida. For some time, he had some difficulty receiving clearance to rejoin the Peace Corps. He prevailed and continues to serve with distinction as Peace Corps director in Central Asia.[8]

Liz Pryor and Bob Frasure, two of my most valuable staff members, had the roughest time at the hands of the South African government. From the autumn of 1987, the Afrikaners harassed them with growing hostility. Liz was followed and knocked down, and her car was run off the road on two occasions. Her house was bugged and then burglarized twice with no signs of forced entry. Her jewelry, passports, and diplomatic papers were stolen. Bob and his wife, Katharina, received threatening phone calls and letters. A rock was thrown through the window of their home with a message attached, and they were sent photographs and audiotapes to prove the government's surveillance. Also, one time that Bob and I accompanied Pik Botha to his hunting lodge in the Northern Transvaal, after an opulent *brai* and lots of drinks, Pik pointed to Bob and said, "You are being watched. Take it from a friend. Watch yourself." Indicating Bob, Pik said, "He knows where the bodies are buried." To the Afrikaners, Bob was the most effective person in the embassy and Liz was masterful with the press. Pik's words were a clear and chilling warning—the Afrikaners intended to get rid of them. In the summer of 1988, we reported by cable to Washington that the U.S. Mission was on a tightrope with increasingly acrimonious attitudes toward personnel, and that the confidence within the embassy was eroding. That summer, I had both Liz and Bob transferred out of South Africa to other appointments.

Liz was transferred back to USIA in Washington, where she served in various assignments, excelled in her assignment to the U.S. NATO mission, and then returned to the State Department.

Bob went to the embassy in Addis Ababa, Ethiopia, as the deputy chief of mission. After that, he and his family returned to Washington, where he served in the European Bureau. In 1992, he was named the first U.S. ambassador in

Estonia, and he then returned to Washington to become deputy assistant secretary in the Bureau of European Affairs. In August 1995, Bob was on an official
peace mission to Bosnia as chief negotiator, traveling in the party of Assistant
Secretary of State Richard Holbrooke. Bob and other negotiators were riding
in an armored car that swerved to avoid an oncoming vehicle, hit a pile of rub-
ble, and plunged two hundred meters off a steep mountain road. Bosnian soldiers pulled three people out of the burning vehicle, but Bob and two other
U.S. diplomats died in the accident. I was one of the first people Katharina, his
widow, asked to be notified. I called her immediately. The loss I felt at his death
was a chasm beyond measure and beyond words.

It is hard for me to assess my own effectiveness in South Africa. I do not collect
accolades to hold up and admire any more than I collect butterflies; it smacks
of vanity and is too ephemeral in the great churning tides of history. I can cite
what others have written about me, but with the disclaimer that, for good or
ill, the accounts are merely personal perspectives. I was the right person at the
right time, Norma M. Riccucci writes in *Unsung Heroes*, because I had good
communication skills, an aptitude for relationship-building, and an ability to
pull together disparate people with my "dignity, self-discipline, control, and a
low-key, non-threatening style."[9] Negotiation is not possible without communication among all parties, so it was important for me to reach out to South
Africa's black communities and almost unfathomable to me that my predecessors in the U.S. Embassy had not done so.

One of my successors in South Africa, Ambassador Princeton N. Lyman,
praised my "imposing physical presence, commanding demeanor, and outspoken views on the evils of apartheid" both in the press and in my confrontations
with President Botha. He is correct that I attended "all too frequent funerals of
activists slain during the state of emergency in the late 1980s." Ambassador
Lyman also quoted Karl Beck with accuracy in saying that I went from being
accused by black leaders of being a "house nigger" to becoming something of a
celebrity. "It went from this kind of racist ugly contempt," Karl said, "to the
point where he was mobbed everywhere he went. On planes from Cape Town
people would just want to come up and touch him."

It was not Edward Perkins the person who attracted this adulation; it was
Ambassador Edward Perkins, a delegate of the people and of the government
of the United States, and personal representative of the president. I had been

well trained, I believed in my oath of office, and I took my duty seriously. Armed with that, I moved forward with action as boldly as possible, remembering the quote from Goethe: "Whatever you would do, begin it. Boldness has courage, genius, and magic in it."

I have returned to South Africa many times, most often in my role as a trustee of the Woodrow Wilson National Fellowship Foundation and its project to develop well-trained and university-educated public-service administrative personnel who will help build the infrastructure of the new South Africa. I have been impressed and heartened by some of the young leaders I have met—young blacks and Afrikaners, civil servants, and political appointees—who are carrying out the work of the government. Some of them work in substandard conditions, in offices that resemble ramshackle townships, but they are working. They have much to learn and a long way to go in capacity building, but I have been surprised at how much confidence and optimism they exhibit. They are the new order, working together to build a new South Africa. One civil servant told me, "We pride ourselves in South Africa that we work across the color line in solving problems." They are doing pretty well in this unusual—and historical—social transformation that is taking place in South Africa. As Pliny the Elder wrote, "Out of Africa always something new."

In late January 1989, I returned to attend the groundbreaking for the U.S. Embassy in Pretoria. I turned the first shovel of dirt. Later I unveiled the bust of Martin Luther King Jr. that we hoped would stand in that embassy in perpetuity. KaNgwane chief minister Enos Mabuza joined me for the dedication ceremony. When I spoke, I quoted from King's *Letter from Birmingham Jail*, expressing the hope that "the dark clouds of racial prejudice will soon pass away and the deep fog of misunderstanding will be lifted from our tear-drenched communities. And in some not-too-distant tomorrow, the radiant stars of love and brotherhood will shine over our great nation, with all their scintillating beauty."

Terror Lekota, the prisoner I first saw in the dock at the Delmas Treason Trial, became minister of defense. Ours was a teary reunion in 2003 when I saw him in the office that Afrikaner Magnus Malan had once occupied.

"Do you have any idea what it means to me to see you sitting in this office?" I asked him. "After all of the cruelty that this country went through and what you personally went through. They put you on trial for your life and the first thing you say to me now is, 'We are learning how to live with each other, the Afrikaners and the blacks, just what you hoped, Ambassador.'" He and I returned to the waiting room, still holding hands. The people were mesmerized at the drama being enacted between the two of us. Terror said to everybody in the room, "Here is the man who made it possible for me to be alive today."

He and I talked a lot about what happened just as the change was coming about. He told me something I suspected but had not known for sure—the special branch of the Afrikaner intelligence went on a killing spree, eliminating lots of people, some of whom were in jail, and others they ferreted out and classified as enemies of the state. "One of those people was my brother," Terror told me, "and another was my father." Like so many of his countrymen, Terror is still willing to forgive in the greater interest of the unity of South Africa. That willingness to forgive is one of the most remarkable characteristics of black South Africans.

My last hunting trip as ambassador to South Africa was the outing with Pik. They were culling the herds. One morning we were deep in the wild looking for wildebeest. The tracker spotted one, and the foreign minister made the shot. Then both men went to the dead animal, opened a new bottle of wine, poured some into the blood flowing out of the animal, and drank lustily from the bottle. In Africa, whenever the life of an animal is taken, its spirit is honored. I saw an acknowledgement of that spirit constantly in West Africa and in South Africa. At every important event, some reference was made to the spirit. Sometimes it was in song or dance, but it was always a reminder that the spirit is never far from us. That is what I saw on the hunt. Those two people, one white and one black, were totally of the soil at that moment.

It is my hope that South Africans think of me as a person who got involved in their strains and stresses and fights. I could be a change-agent because Americans are revolutionaries at heart. That is what makes our country continue to advance and what made America's intervention in South Africa so different from the European intervention. The United States was intervening because we are a revolutionary society. When the South Africans remember me, I hope they say, "This is the guy who came down here and represented his government at a time when we did not trust Americans. He helped turn South Africa around. And he helped turn America around."

For me South Africa was a journey long and deep. I went as an ambassador, and I came back a changed person. I took that experience with me back to America and into the Office of Director General of the Foreign Service.

DIRECTOR GENERAL
CHANGING THE FOREIGN SERVICE

Lawrence Eagleburger, who became deputy secretary of state about the time I became director general, called me into his office and said, "Ed, this goddamned Foreign Service has got to change. Otherwise, we won't be relevant in government any more." I agreed that we needed to change and that more minorities and women must be brought into the Service if we were to accurately represent the face of America.

"You're the big chief for a while," he said. "You have to change it." That was a tall order. Organizations are hard to change. As director general, I was dealing with a workforce of approximately twenty-five thousand people worldwide: Foreign Service, Civil Service, U.S. citizens, and nationals of their respective countries who worked for an embassy or consulate. Bureaucracy is a slow-moving ship that is exceedingly difficult to steer. The Foreign Service, like other bureaucracies, is not inanimate. It is a mass of humans, with all their personal and professional frailties, prejudices, and strengths. The job of the director general is to make sense out of all of this in the greater interest of running the United States diplomatic service. I was always asking myself two questions: What would make me a better Foreign Service officer? How can I make this enormous workforce better? People are the greatest tool we have. Dealing with people's lives is a grave responsibility. They depend on their job to make money, but once they get past the basic needs, 95 percent of the workforce looks for something beyond that in job satisfaction. If people are not satisfied with their job, no amount of money will make them happy. My diaries from my years as director general tell a more complete story of humans than almost anything I have experienced in my career. I got an education during this assignment that I could not have received at any university, corporation, or other institution.

My office in the State Department overlooked the Washington Monument and provided a spectacular view of the Fourth of July fireworks display. As Lucy, Sarah, and I sat there watching the gigantic fireworks in 1989, I mulled over what I wanted to accomplish. Suddenly I envisioned a new paradigm for the Foreign Service. I saw that we needed to redefine the culture of the Service and develop a new prototype of Foreign Service officer. I needed to make it possible for all Foreign Service activities across the United States government to relate to each other and to U.S. foreign-policy initiatives, regardless of agency, for the greater consideration of foreign policy. I learned quickly that the governance procedures for Civil Service employees in the Department of State needed major surgery to ensure an equal status with Foreign Service employees and to eliminate the second-class-citizen stigma attached to them. And I needed to define a way to keep in touch with the Congress and its appendages.

My job as director general was yet another assignment of managing change and resolving conflict. All conflict is about people. Resolution requires knowing who they are and what they think. In South Africa, my job was to effect political change without violence, and that work was public and risky. Trying to change the Foreign Service would be deep, quiet work against steady resistance. The status quo was entrenched, and opposition to change was deep seated and strong. The conflict-resolution skills required of me again included a clear vision of the goal, strategy based on research, persistent effort, and good communication skills.

We were not seeking change within the Foreign Service merely for the sake of change. Since the 1970s, our society had begun to bulge at the seams. We were looking for a new way of existing in a world that was quickly changing. In the 1960s I had come into a rigid Foreign Service where the majority of the senior officers dressed conservatively in gray, brown, or black suits. Stripes were the norm, as were oxfords, no radical ties, and short hair. I was shocked in the 1970s when I saw a senior Foreign Service officer wearing long sideburns and flower-power stickers on his car. I was not the only one startled by his appearance. My boss lamented, "Did you see Peter? My God, what's the Service coming to?" Now we had to reform ourselves to meet the demands of the times or run the risk of being frozen out of policy.

The Rogers Act of 1925 had created a Foreign Service that consisted principally of a corps of political reporting officers from which most career ambassa-

On the steps of the U.S. Capitol with Rep. Constance Morella of
Maryland as director general of the Foreign Service, 1989. This assignment was yet another task of managing change and conflict resolution.

dors were selected. Now we needed a different kind of officer—an officer who
could be multifunctional. New officers needed to understand they would have
to possess a wide range of knowledge by the time they reached the senior Foreign Service. This included understanding the essential elements of the Foreign
Service: intelligence, defense, development, administration, consular affairs,
and the Service's interaction with the FBI, Drug Enforcement Administration,

and Treasury activities. New officers would need to understand economics, be proficient in several foreign languages, and perceive the environment as a foreign-policy tool. They needed skills in management, conflict resolution, and development administration.

It was not, however, merely a matter of saying that an officer had to be multifunctional. We had to make sure that the culture of the Service also changed so the promotion system valued that multifunctionality. These changes were threatening to people who were already in the Service. It is hard to get people to be creative when they are accustomed to working by standard operating procedures. Every change I proposed became a little battlefield.

I could see the issues stretching before me like so many mileposts:

* We needed to bring order to the administration of senior officers in the Service's up-or-out system. Too many senior officers were walking the halls and collecting their salary but not holding responsible assignments.

* We needed a system to recruit minorities and women more effectively. America was stepping into the era of women's rights, civil rights, and equal employment, and the Service had to be an active participant. This was a fight. Senior officers came to see me and said, "You're ruining the Service." They stopped me in the hall and told me, "You're diluting the Service if you let these people in." Those remarks reflected the elitism of the old Foreign Service and the officers who sought to recreate the Service in their own image. They considered minorities and women to be "those people." Behavioral science is a legitimate part of public administration and political science. In a complex organization, we must overcome the natural tendency to not interact with a person who is different from the norm. Along with many other institutions and corporations, the Foreign Service needed sensitivity training, and a course was subsequently enacted.

* We needed to take a new look at secretaries, their career paths, and their training for the new world we were entering, specifically the use of electronics and computers.

In summary, I saw that we needed a holistic model of recruiting, training, promotion, and management of officers' careers. My assignment, in short, was to create a new Foreign Service.

It was an interesting challenge and I had only four years to do it—the amount of time I had promised the secretary of state that I would serve as director general. In theory, I had the authority to direct these changes. The Foreign Service Act of 1980 vests broad personnel authorities in the secretary of state, and these authorities largely have been delegated to the director general. It is a short, straight line of command.[1] I had a particularly good relationship with President Bush and Secretary Baker. Both were clear about their expectations. The president told me that he wanted me to deal with both career and non-career ambassadors who were political appointees. This is unusual, but the president kept his word. When a politically appointed ambassador was discovered using narcotics, I went to Baker and asked him his pleasure. "It is the pleasure of the president," he said, "that you handle it like any other employee." Secretary Baker had told me up front, "I rely on you to run the Foreign Service and to manage the Civil Service in the State Department. When you need me, I'll be here, but I do not intend to get into your business." I consider Baker one of the great secretaries of state. He was cold, calculating, and decisive. He wasted no tears. He told me that if I ever needed to see him urgently to call his special assistant, Margaret Tutwiler, and she would arrange it. One time I did exercise that channel of communication involving an issue that could have become an explosive subject—the political appointee involved with narcotics. The unstated rule is that nothing is to embarrass the president of the United States. I defused it by persuading the ambassador to resign.

Each president and each secretary of state I have worked with has had a different relationship with the Foreign Service. I came into the Service on the watch of President Nixon, who did not particularly like the Foreign Service. When Nixon was out of government, during the Kennedy and Johnson administrations, he traveled abroad extensively as a private citizen at the expense of Pepsi Cola. All too often, Foreign Service officers who met him at the airports treated him with disdain, and Nixon never forgot it. He appointed Kissinger to be national security advisor with the thought that the two of them would run foreign policy from the White House and cut out the State Department. Nixon was not inclined to give any credence to the ability of the Foreign Service, so the Service did not fare well under his administration. When he was reelected, all presidential appointees sent him a customary and perfunctory letter of resignation. This included career officers and political appointees serving as ambassador. Traditionally, career ambassadors remain in place until the end of their tour of duty. President Nixon took the unusual step of asking his chief of staff if he could ask for the resignations of Foreign Service officers as well, since they are appointed by the president with the advice and consent of the Senate. Clearly he was looking for a way to emasculate the Foreign Service. He soon backed off when he recognized it would cause too much of a stink.

Dwight Eisenhower and Lyndon Johnson got along pretty well with the Foreign Service. I got to know Johnson during one of my assignments in Washington. He was a man bigger than life, but also a person with flaws. With too much energy, he lived high and recklessly and did not take care of his health. Johnson did everything with the force and power of a Texan. On a trip to Southeast Asia, he liked the way a tailor shop made shirts and ordered thirty or forty of them on the spot. In the Philippines, he danced with the beautiful Imelda Marcos so long that she signaled her husband to cut in and rescue her. I never met Lady Bird Johnson, but I understand that she was a formidable woman. She demonstrated a view toward minorities that was surprising, since her husband took up the mantle of promoting civil rights unabashedly and unashamedly. When a White House staffer sought to help Mrs. Johnson into a car, she reportedly turned to him and said, "Get your black hands off me." I was disappointed when I learned about that.

Jimmy Carter's relationship with the Foreign Service was good but not exceptional. I believe that Carter saw it as too elitist. He set up an ambassadorial selection committee consisting of prominent people from outside the government. President Carter wanted to bring in the best and the brightest to be ambassadors, and he was not convinced that he could find the best and the brightest inside the career Service. To his credit, he backed Secretary of State Cyrus Vance's efforts to increase the numbers of minorities and women in the Foreign Service.

Gerald Ford, one of the nicest people I have ever met, got along well with the Service, but he had his own views about who should be appointed ambassador, and some of his choices were political hacks. President Reagan appointed more than an average number of political appointees, but he had a good relationship with the Foreign Service. He met a number of Service officers when he traveled, and he never forgot them. George Bush got along very well with the Foreign Service—better, in my judgment, than any other president I have known. I do not give high marks to Bill Clinton, who did not seem to care all that much about the Foreign Service. When President Clinton went to Australia, our ambassador there could not persuade him to make the cus-tomary stop by the embassy to greet the employees. Every other president since Eisenhower has dropped by the embassy in Australia, planted a tree, or met the employees.

The director general has the power to appoint people and manage the Service, which includes hiring, training, and assigning on a worldwide basis; discipline, initiating separation; and setting policy for all the agencies permitted by law to use the provisions of the Foreign Service Act. Having the authority is one thing; being able to wield it to institutionalize bureaucratic change was quite another.

The Foreign Service is not a culture in which when an order is given, some-thing changes. It is an unusually closed system, difficult to penetrate by non-career officers and almost impossible to understand by people outside of the system. Even now, after serving as director general and spending a career of appointments all over the world, I find it very difficult to explain this extraor-dinary organization known as the Foreign Service. It is a country with its own mores, customs, and language.

No issue was more pressing or more difficult than increasing the number of minorities in the Foreign Service. When I became director general, I felt the irony of coming full circle. In the 1970s, when I was a junior officer, some of my black colleagues and I drafted a proposal—a hopeful plan of idealistic young men and women—to encourage the hiring and promotion of minorities in the Foreign Service. Now I was the head of the Foreign Service, and that same subject was on my desk. In 1989, I saw the issue of minority hiring with older and wiser eyes. Beneath my suit and tie, I wore the scars of bureaucratic and political battles. I knew that not all could be won and that even just causes sometimes fail.

What's more, I knew that I was not infallible. I remember well being part of the three-person interviewing team when a candidate came before us who was not the stereotypical Foreign Service officer candidate. He was a black man in a green suit, aggressive in nature, and bedecked with jewelry. We questioned him at length as my colleagues sought a reason for turning him down, and I designed questions to justify our bringing him into the Service. My two colleagues voted against him, but I voted for him and argued that the Foreign Service needs all kinds of people. All too soon, I said, their rough edges will be knocked off and they will fit like a sardine in a can, but before they do, perhaps their different contributions can be helpful to us. I argued so persuasively that my colleagues reversed their stance and we voted him in. It was the wrong decision. The young candidate did not succeed. I must have shared my two colleagues' conviction that the candidate was not suited to the Service, but I subordinated that instinct to my desire to bring more blacks, more minorities, and more women into the Service. That particular candidate was doomed to fail in the Service. It was a dreadful error, and I was responsible for it. I had been wrong on that occasion, and I reminded myself that in all the change I planned to initiate in the Foreign Service, people's lives and careers were at stake. I could be wrong again.

One of my first activities in June 1989, the first month on the job and even before the Senate had confirmed my nomination, was to lob a volley announcing my position on change. I appeared before the Open Forum, a State Department dissent channel that is the only place in the U.S. government where anybody can express a view—open, unfettered, and without repercussions—about a policy being exercised at post. This sends a message directly to the secretary of state. The person who uses the dissent channel is not considered a pariah but rather someone who feels very strongly about something. I have never known anyone to be hurt for expressing an opinion at the Open Forum. Sometimes things are changed as a result of the dissent; sometimes they are not. My address to the Open Forum was about South Africa, the fight between the administration and the Congress, and the evolution of my own philosophy in South Africa as a change-agent.

If I were to reform the Foreign Service, I needed more than authority and vision. I needed to marshal resources. Early on I formed a close working relationship with Jill Kent, the extraordinary chief financial officer of the State Department. She had come from Treasury with Baker about a year earlier. Jill saw the goal immediately and joined in the vision. We were on the same wavelength. Together we sought a philosophy of public administration that would meld together the allocation of financial resources (her responsibility) and the people resources (my responsibility) for the greater consideration of foreign policy.

I began my director generalship determined to beef up every officer's knowledge of economics. Until then, we had considered economics an esoteric subject to be learned by a few select officers. I wanted to change that. I wanted all officers to have knowledge of economics in their knapsacks, to be able to understand economic analysis, to offer input to an economic plan of action, and to converse intelligently with their economics officers. To advance in the Foreign Service, an officer needs many skills: oral and written communication, an understanding of the legal basis of our country, of history, and of what makes a society move. This includes economic activities—beef, rice, shoes, coal, oil, pecans. Many officers had a weak education in economics. The Foreign Service had to come of age and learn how to push American business abroad.

I brought in a senior officer to rewrite the precepts for promotion. That is how you get people's attention. When I spoke with the director of the economics faculty, I told her that I wanted her to offer new classes, an economics familiarization course, and another at an advanced level. She was horrified. She said that it could not be done, that we could not teach economics in a six-week course. We can teach them some of it, I told her, and the alternative was to send the officers to universities, in which case people would begin to wonder what her job was. I was insistent, and she designed an abbreviated course. The policy was to send everybody through it. It was a sweeping change and, like all change, resisted by some. I learned of a young officer in the basic training classes who said, "I did not come into the Foreign Service to sell cars." I asked the instructor to send the young man to me. I knew that directive alone would be a sobering experience for the officer—when I was a young Foreign Service officer, I tiptoed past the office of the director general. The young man appeared before me, and I suggested to him that if he thought he could not sell cars, then he should look for another career—a nice, clean profession where he would not have to get his hands dirty with business. Commerce is part of the Foreign Service, I told him. Selling American cars—or beef or wheat or dairy products—is part of diplomacy. Foreign Service officers have to be able to talk about chickens, eggs, cattle, and rice, which are all important in the lifeline of a nation. One of the realities of the global economy is that the United States produces more than we can consume and thus we must look for overseas markets. Today's Foreign Service officers must be facilitators for the private sector in seeking those markets and in convincing foreign governments to accept enlightened investment policies. The economy is a primary factor in making a

country strong, and officers have a hand in keeping it strong. Now, the economics course that I initiated is institutionalized and a regular part of an officer's training.

I also wanted to require more language training in the Foreign Service. Senator Paul Simon (Democrat–Illinois), who had written the book *The Tongue-
Tied American: Confronting the Foreign Language Crisis*, wanted every embassy to
be staffed by Americans who spoke the language of the country. Just before I
became director general, the State Department agreed. Then we discovered
that we could not accomplish it as quickly as the senator wanted, so I was asked
to negotiate a new timeline with him. Instead of a four-year deadline, he
agreed to give us six years. A year later, the new under secretary of management said it could not be done in six years either and wanted me to go back to
Senator Simon. I said I would not do it, because we had made the agreement in
good faith. "Why don't *you* call him?" I asked the under secretary. I was finally
convinced to revisit Senator Simon, and I laid the cards on the table. "Mr.
Ambassador," he said to me, "you and I talked about this last year and you personally said six years is all you needed. Here you are again asking for an indef-
inite delay. I won't do it. I realize it is not totally your fault, but you're the
director general. Goodbye, sir." I went back and told the controller and the
under secretary to find the money for the training because we were going to do
it in six years.

Management skills were something else I wanted to improve among the senior officers. The ambassador is the senior officer in a country, and although
intelligence officers have a different reporting system, by regulation the
ambassador is privy to every intelligence report sent. The intelligence officers,
in effect, work for the ambassadors, but ambassadors and intelligence officers
do not always get along. I have seen intelligence officers, sometimes the entire
intelligence mechanism, pulled out of a country because the ambassador insists
on his or her way of doing things. It is essential, therefore, that an officer who
becomes an ambassador understand how to use the country team effectively.
Everything must fit within some concept of a strategic plan. Deputy Secretary
Eagleburger supported me in insisting that officers coming up through the Service learn to be managers, rather than administrators, which are different.

The proclivity of Foreign Service officers is not to be combative or confrontational because they have not been so in their world. Until they reach a
position such as deputy chief of mission, theirs has been silent work with little

or no experience in management. Consular officers have better experience because they manage resources. Administrative officers get much better experience because they must relate resources to policy needs. Political officers get the least amount of training as managers, yet 50 percent of those who reach ambassadorial rank come from the political area. I wanted to change that and give them the skills they would need. I introduced the concept of management, allocating resources toward an acceptable set of goals.

A couple of senior officers were so upset about it that they went to Congress, and I was called to testify before the House Committee on Foreign Affairs. Congressman Steve Solarz (Democrat–New York) made a guest appearance at the committee hearing to question me. "I want to ask you about this management concept you are putting forth," he said. "I thought our officers were supposed to report events and evaluate them." I told him about an embassy's being made up of people not just from the Foreign Service, but also from Treasury, Agriculture, Justice, Labor, Defense, USAID, and USIA. They are all part of an ambassador's staff with resources that must be managed if the objectives of the country plan are to be achieved. "An ambassador cannot do that, Congressman," I said, "if he or she spends all of the time reporting on events and evaluating them." Solarz did not agree, and we got into a shouting match. Finally, the committee chairman said, "Okay, that's enough of that. Congressman, thank you very much for your appearance. Mr. Ambassador, fine. Thank you." My plans for management training moved forward.

MINORITIES AND WOMEN

Some people were uneasy that I had been assigned as director general. I was the first black officer to have the job, and they did not know what I would try to do with my newfound power. Would I go overboard in pushing minority hiring and promotion? I recognized this concern and spent considerable time and effort in meeting personally with Foreign Service employees in the United States and in posts around the world to explain face-to-face the new direction. I told them what I was trying to accomplish, and I let them ask questions. I gave them the opportunity to size me up and to answer their silent question: Who is Perkins?

Sensing that they had a sympathetic voice in me, a number of minority people came to see me about their experiences with unfairness. This led me to the

subject of grievances filed by employees of the Foreign Service. I became concerned about the sizeable number that were on their way to court action, not
just from minorities, but also from employees across the board of the State
Department and Foreign Service. I wanted to reduce that high number. As I
sought a way to settle them amicably, I applied two rules: (1) if the grievance is
perceived to be legitimate, we will find a remedy satisfactory to the grievant,
and (2) if it is found not to have merit, our review of it will be quick and to the
point, and our remedy will not preclude the employee from pursuing other
channels, including the court system. I did not want a grievance to be considered an affront to the institution. Sometimes employees have legitimate com-
plaints, and as agents of the institution we have a right to try to reach a
satisfactory remedy. I did not want employees who filed a grievance to be
tainted. When it appeared that an employee really had been wronged, I wanted
an agreement from the lawyers that I could exercise my legislative rights and
make a settlement. Generally, the lawyers were cautious, because they did not
want to set a precedent that could be followed. I found this reasoning to be
rampant.

When I came aboard as director general, one of my priorities was implementing legislation that authorized the State Department to launch a Foreign Affairs
Fellows Program. This program provided undergraduate scholarships to ten or
twelve selected students from minority populations who agreed to enter the
Foreign Service upon graduation. The Congressional Black Caucus had helped
develop this program to provide a steady intake of minorities into the Foreign
Service at entry level. Many of us had worked hard to get the intern program
into action, but implementation of the legislation was stalled in the Congress.
    The legislation authorizing the program was in place, but the funding was
not, so the State Department had not acted. With no money, the program was
not going anywhere. Once again, Jill Kent came to the rescue. I asked her to
carve out enough money from the State Department budget to fund the first
cohort of students and the program's management by an outside contractor.
Much to my surprise and joy, she assented immediately. "I can see that something like this is needed," she said, "so we'll find the money for it." And she
found it. A Jewish woman from Detroit, Jill had no reason to be particularly
favorable to such a program except that logic told her it was needed. I asked

policy personnel and then an outside consultant to write the paradigm for the program—and in a hurry—but I heard a chorus of opposing voices. Finally I had to take a position rare to me, and I said baldly, "This is going to happen, period. If you can't do it, I'll bring in somebody else who can."

I know some Foreign Service people did not actively oppose the fellowship program but stood back passively and said, "Let Ambassador Perkins try it. It's going to fail anyway." I was bound and determined that it would not fail. I worked to sell the program inside the personnel bureau, including lobbying a white woman recruiter. She became a great advocate. When Ivan Selin, under secretary of state for management, and I interviewed her, we both thought she would do the job. Some of my black colleagues were skeptical. "Do you expect a white woman to do what you want done?" We do not live in a totally white society, I told them; nor do we live in a totally black society. I was convinced that she was a solid citizen, and I was right. She turned out to be the most vocal champion of the program in the personnel bureau.

I was addressing governors about this time, telling them what we were doing in the Foreign Service and about the intern program in particular, when a propitious suggestion came from Virginia governor Douglas Wilder. He urged us to have the legislation amended to include disadvantaged whites in the population we were soliciting. To prove his point, the governor invited me to take a trip through Appalachia, a place I had never been. This trip through the mining country of Kentucky, West Virginia, and lower Pennsylvania taught me two things. I learned how important it is for Foreign Service officers to understand all of America, and I learned how a large percentage of the Appalachian population is locked in a cycle of poverty. Hampered by a substandard education and low self-expectation, many are blocked by a sense of hopelessness. As I drove through the countryside, I saw people, old and young alike, sitting on the porch from morning to night. "If you get some people from Appalachia into the Foreign Service through a superior education," Governor Wilder said, "think what it will do for the people attached to them—mothers, fathers, sisters, brothers." So we amended the legislation. It took a while to get Appalachian university students for the Foreign Service, but we did.

David Schwartz at the Foreign Service Institute wrote the paradigm for the fellowship program, accomplishing what others could not or would not do. He included several of the historically black and Hispanic, as well as Appalachian, colleges and universities. The Woodrow Wilson National Fellowship Foundation was contracted to manage the program, and we chose the first cohort in 1990. We were up and running. It was and still is a terrific program.

The Foreign Service is not a friendly place for people who enter by any way other than through the normal examination process, so we had to institute safeguards to ensure that no member of the cohorts was unjustly railroaded out. Continuing the program was another problem. Each cohort has to be reauthorized by the director general, who has to get the money from the chief financial officer. It was not difficult since we had established the precedent, but officers rotate out and presidential administrations change. After Jill left, the next chief financial officer was not sympathetic to anything that took away from the main funding programs. Selin was gone, and his replacement was not as supportive. And I was in my next post when I got the call alerting me to the funding crisis. I knew it was an attempt to kill the program. I called my successor as director general and asked him, "Do you want me to go to Congress?" They found the money. This has happened almost every year since 1992. I get a call saying the intern program is not being funded, then I call the director general and offer, or threaten, to go to Congress and argue for funding for the program. If I were director general today, I would work to get a line item in the budget to fund the internship program and avoid this precarious year-to-year fighting.[2]

Congress and the Civil Rights Commission were beating on the State Department to manifest our commitment to equal employment opportunity. In June 1990, the deputy secretary of state convened a meeting of assistant secretaries in the Department of State on the subject of equal employment opportunity. It was clear that we had a long way to go. "We are shameful," he said. "We're not moving fast enough. I'm telling all of you to get busy. Find women. Find minorities. Put them in top jobs, and come back to me in a month. I'll ask the same questions."

The director of Equal Employment Opportunity and Civil Rights (EEOCR) did not move fast enough to satisfy the commission. This office reported to the secretary of state, who had neither the time nor the interest in supervising that work, so I met with the head official periodically to find out what was happening and how we could fend off the criticism. It was a Sisyphean experience—and I was trying to push the rock uphill. A mode of no-communication and no-action caught me between the EEOCR Commission and the congressional members. Both looked at the director general as having the ultimate responsibility for meeting report deadlines. When a report on the status of women in the State Department was six months late, I was called to the Hill to testify. Senator Olympia Snow (Republican–Maine) dismissed out of hand my explanation that the report was the responsibility of another office in State. "Ambassador Perkins," the no-nonsense senator said, "you are a senior official in the State Department, and you are the head of personnel. This is a personnel matter. I don't care who is internally responsible. I want you to get that report up here."

My answer was succinct: "Yes, Senator." I started working with EEOCR to help that office get the various reports completed on time.

Minority hiring problems continued to crop up. One affirmative-action program that was particularly unpopular among Foreign Service officers was that of midlevel entrants. This is the program a handful of junior black officers conceived when Kissinger was secretary of state. It was designed as a temporary solution to filling midlevel ranks with women and minorities. The rationale was that these entrants would have sufficient professional experience outside the Service to hit the ground running and would quickly advance to become senior officers. Bringing in people at midlevel was quite a bold step, but it was based on fairness, efficiency, and the needs of the Service. Meanwhile, we also accelerated the program in bringing in minority officers at the bottom who would work themselves up through the ranks. After about ten years, we reasoned, the Service would better represent women and minorities. Otherwise, it would have been thirty years before the Service had minority midlevel and senior officers in sufficient numbers. The midlevel-entry program was especially disliked by white male officers and a few black officers because in an up-or-out system, it seemed to slow the promotion rate. I empathized with those who believed the promotion rate was being affected. A career service does not work unless people are constantly on the move up or on the move out. Behind each person is someone waiting to be promoted into the space being occupied. Later we tested the back-door program, and we discovered that it did not disrupt the normal promotion rate of those who came in at the bottom. For now, however, the midlevel entry program was hounded by a built-in bias. One senior officer told me, "You can't bring people like that into the Foreign Service. They don't know how to do it."

There had been some failures in the midlevel entry program for minorities, and we recognized that, regardless of previous accomplishments, it is quite difficult for a person from the outside to come into the Foreign Service, pick up the culture, and succeed without some assistance. I rejected the idea that it could not be done, so I asked the head of the division of Foreign Service counseling and assignments and others to find a way to make this a more successful program. We launched a "grafting" system designed to integrate new, midlevel people into this culture quickly, inculcating in them all the things we professional officers learned on the way up. This grafting program had several features: (1) The posts were chosen carefully. I did not want the appointees going to a hostile post where the ambassador could not care less about the new officer's success. (2) A formal mentor was assigned to each new officer and instructed to stay in touch. (3) I phoned the head of each post and said, "You're going to get a minority midlevel officer. We do not want this officer failing because nobody paid attention to him or her. Your responsibility will be to make a success out of this person." (4) I urged the ambassadors to spend time with them, and I asked that the deputy chiefs of mission be given the role of monitoring their progress.

The success of the grafting program depended on the people involved and especially on the ambassador. A few ambassadors would neither give it their attention nor delegate the work. In some instances, non-career ambassadors were at a disadvantage because they had come in at the top and did not understand the Foreign Service culture themselves. They did not know what to teach. Some politically appointed ambassadors were particularly sympathetic and well disposed to the minority officers. Sometimes, non-minority ambassadors felt threatened by the minority officer's desire to achieve—minority achievers could be threatening. I quickly learned that you could not bat a thousand when you were bringing people into the Service from the outside. Even superstars in their jobs on the outside may not be superstars in the Foreign Service.

Women and minorities were not always given a good shot at assignments, and black women had a tougher time than black men in the Foreign Service. That was especially true in European posts, which were considered the prime jobs. Even to place minority officers there I fought what I called the "European anti-minority Mafia." Even if they managed to be assigned to European missions, some black female officers found lack of support and obstacles in their way. Sometimes I sat in on the meetings of the assignments panel, which surprised the panel members at first. I made it clear that they were there because as director general I had delegated that authority to them, and that I was reviewing that authority. I wanted to make sure that due process did indeed obtain.

An ambassador in France complained that too many women were being assigned to principal-officer jobs there. "What if they were all men?" I asked him, "What would you say?"

"It's not the same thing," he replied.

"It is the same thing," I told him. "You've just gotten used to having male officers."

Another ambassador said, "If you're looking for representation, I've done my bit. I have three women."

"I'm looking for two things," I replied. "I'm looking for competence and representation. If all the best officers happen to be women, so be it. Put them there." He was smart enough not to fight it.

Some ambassadors did not want any women officers at all. A politically appointed ambassador in Ireland, a venerable gentleman of another era, was adamantly opposed to receiving women officers. He refused to accept them.

As with any affirmative-action initiative, questions were raised by the lawyers as to whether the internship program or the midlevel-entry program could be challenged in court. I suggested that people stop concentrating on the impediments to these essential programs and focus instead on how to make them work. I was prepared for the legal challenges. I even went directly to the assistant attorney general for civil rights at the Department of Justice to defend these programs, because I believed in their power to effect the kind of changes that would make for better foreign-policy administration. Although the midlevel program eventually was discontinued, the internship program was modified in light of Supreme Court precedent and remains a powerful recruiting tool to this day.

The hope for the Foreign Service is the Foreign Affairs Fellows Program (now called the Pickering Fellows), which is the most successful intake program for minorities that we have ever tried. This is the one that will make the difference. It is the best method yet devised for insuring that the Foreign Service, a tool of the United States, does in fact look like the United States, with a healthy representation of minorities and women. If we could get enough money, this would be the best way to select not just minorities, but all people who want to come

into the Foreign Service. We could eliminate the existing examination process
and be assured of a steady cadre of people who are highly likely to succeed.

SACRED COWS—THE FOREIGN SERVICE EXAMINATION AND THE FOREIGN SERVICE INSTITUTE

There is no way that a modern personnel system can operate without due
process of law. Before 1972, few built-in guarantees existed in the Foreign Service to prohibit capricious actions or to offer an officer selected out the opportunity of review. It took a tragedy, the suicide of an officer who had been
selected out, to introduce the concept of due process. His widow and the
American Foreign Service Association became advocates in fighting for due
process. As a result, a different method of assignment was introduced. A review
of the results of the Promotion Board now triggers another review under the
Standards Review Panel. I sat on both of these boards in my midlevel career. A
question still lingers about the need for further reform of due process and of
the entrance standards. This would entail examining the sacred cow of the Foreign Service—the examination procedures that bring new officers into the
Service. The existing examination concept has been criticized for not including
a representative number of women and minorities of all stripes.

The examination is a rigorous exercise, but not impossible to pass. The exam
has been reduced from the two-day ordeal that it was when I entered the Service to one-half day. The entrance examination seeks to determine the candidate's knowledge of United States history and basic laws, economics,
quantitative analysis (arithmetic, algebra, and perhaps a couple of problems in
geometry), world history, English language, art, and some current events. I
remember a question from my examination that stumped me: What was the
Chautauqua Experience? I had never heard of the Chautauqua Experience.

The examination was made up by the Educational Testing Service at Princeton when I was director general, and it cost us about $600,000 a year. When I
asked the question "Are we getting our money's worth out of this expensive
examination?" it hit like a bombshell. Officers were dumbfounded.

"You want to get rid of the Foreign Service examination?" they exclaimed.

"No," I said, "I'm just asking if there isn't another way to bring people into
the Foreign Service without sacrificing excellence." I proposed—radically, it
seemed to some—that the examination process might best be moved from the

Office of Recruiting and Examination and that the Board of Examiners be placed directly under the director general. When I met with the Board of Examiners, they had got the word that I was in the mood for changing things. Everybody seemed genuinely interested in doing the best thing to create a different kind of Foreign Service. Then, best intentions began to deteriorate. I suggested we use a simplified version of the test, as the Civil Service does. Dinah Lynn Chang, representing the Office of Personnel Management headed by Connie Newman, brought test experts to talk to the board. In my diary I noted, "Boy, were they good. They spoke in English!" The test they had devised was direct and to the point; it asked questions in plain English that covered a wide range of skills—economic, administrative, listening, and a modicum of political skills. I was most impressed with the test and its clarity.

The board rebelled. Half of the Board of Examiners were academics, and it was they who were especially appalled. Tradition, they cried, you are threatening tradition. "In this case, tradition means something we don't need," I said. "I think we've outgrown it." Without the examination, they argued, the Service might be tainted. People might get in who would not have made it in under the old system. I had discussed this with Secretary Baker and Deputy Secretary Eagleburger, both of whom agreed that it was a ridiculous situation. Despite their support, I did not prevail. I did not get rid of the traditional Foreign Service examination. Perhaps I was faint of heart. Recently I was asked again what I thought of the examination, and I said that it has outlived its time. "Yes," said the director general at the time, "but there is a constituency out there that still wants it." And they still have it.

Baker and Ivan Selin had decided that the Foreign Service Institute (FSI) should not continue to stand alone as a separate activity, but should be a part of the Office of the Director General. We adopted the philosophy that like activities should be together. I was directed to make it happen. Such changes never happen smoothly because nobody wants to lose the perceived prestige of a stand-alone agency. Nonetheless, I explained my mandate to the director of the FSI and to the deputy director, and they seemed to accept the decision. All was going well, and we made an official suggestion to the Congress to incorporate FSI into the director general's office. Then the bottom fell out. What I did not know at the time was that a rear-guard action had been launched. It was a most effective campaign. The Congressional Oversight Committee refused to endorse the change, and it became clear to me that the resistance movement had succeeded. The FSI continues to stand alone. In retrospect, I do not know if incorporating the FSI into the director general's office would have been beneficial. The under secretary was trying to reduce the number of agencies that reported directly to him and streamline the huge conglomerate known as the management family (Consular Affairs, Security Affairs, Personnel, Administration, FSI, and numerous ad hoc arrangements such as the Office Overseeing the Construction of the Embassy in Moscow). The debate is moot, though, because the merger did not happen. I understand that my name is still blighted in some parts of the FSI as the rascal who tried to bring FSI under the Office of the Director General.

SECRETARIES

One of the issues I dealt with early on as director general was the changing role of secretaries in the Foreign Service and Civil Services. Subjects ranged from salary to the new world of secretarial work, including the advent of the Internet and the growing use of computers. During my tenure, we quit requiring secretaries to have shorthand skills, which used to be a key component. Now secretaries manage offices, make appointments, and exercise judgment, weighing priorities and options about the demands on an ambassador's time. The clerical corps was looking for its role in the new Foreign Service, so for institution-building, I had lots of lunches with secretaries, asking for their views and their recommendations. We formed a Secretarial Task Force, developed an assignment policy for them, restructured the grading system for their ranks, and created a ladder diagram so that secretaries could see how they could progress up the ladder.

We changed the way secretaries are counseled vis-à-vis their career, and we also recommended that a certain number of secretaries be put in a special category by function rather than by name. These are the secretaries who rise to the top of the ladder and work for an ambassador or an assistant secretary. Secretaries who work for a career ambassador can go with that ambassador on reassignment. Some secretaries spend twelve or fifteen years with one person, going from assignment to assignment. My last secretary had three assignments with me: director general, the United Nations, and Australia.

We also looked at intangible perks that could enhance secretarial jobs. Too often embassy secretaries can get lost in the shuffle. I encouraged chiefs of mission to put secretaries on invitation lists for social functions, which are actually official events, and I encouraged ambassadors to set aside funds so the secretaries could entertain their counterparts in government. This would go a long way in helping the secretaries build their own networks. Intangibles can be psychological income and are often just as important as tangible benefits.

Another issue was the new people being recruited into the secretarial corps who were ill prepared to meet the public. Most were women, and many were from minority populations. I could see that few had the advantage of a useful education. Our job, as I saw it, was to teach these new employees how to use the English language and how to dress. Our teaching leaned heavily on spelling, sentence structure, speaking correctly, and the organization of the Department of State. Appropriate dress for work was another issue altogether. "You'll get into trouble trying to tell a woman how to dress," said the head of training new secretaries. "I agree," I said, "so you will have to figure out a way to influence that." She did. We embellished the training course with fashion designers who gave lectures on makeup and dress. We took photographs of the groups when they first arrived and when they graduated. There was no comparison; they were completely but subtly transformed. I spent a lot of time with the secretaries and attended their graduation ceremony, sharing with them my appreciation for how secretaries had helped me on my way through the Foreign Service.

Embassy communicators, much like secretaries, are all too often unseen and underappreciated people working behind closed doors. Their role was also changing. Years ago communicators had to be able to climb a telephone pole and string cable, making sure it was classified. They had to clear buildings, using devices that warned if clandestine listening instruments were planted. Now they are different. They are highly technical people who run the code rooms and telecommunication activities, moving thousands of words across space. The old-line communicators talked about meeting incoming planes and retrieving the heavy diplomatic pouches. The new communicators emphasized their technical skills and not their physical ability. It was a hell of a problem. How would we classify these diverse skills as to grade? How much do they get paid? One old-timer suggested it ought to be determined by a contest as to who could climb a pole and string wire the fastest. I would have lost my mind if I had not had some training in public administration and behavioral science. That stood me in good standing because I could see the organization as a living instrument, not some pristine organic activity where people are put in boxes. Organizations do not work like that.

COMMUNICATION

I spent considerable time trying to foster openness in the governance system of the Foreign Service. Until about 1972, the administration of the Service had been done behind closed doors. I wanted to let in more air and light and tell people what was going on, especially with the new evolution of the Foreign Service. I embarked on this communication campaign in several ways.

When I had a brown-bag lunch with the new Foreign Service Class of 1990, I told them about the tremendous opportunities for young officers, the unfolding events in Eastern Europe, China, the unification of Germany, and the new burdens placed on Moscow and Africa. "In Eastern Europe, almost for the first time, we are being asked to give assistance in public administration, business management, journalism, and law," I told them. "Africa has so much potential that we need to have the best and brightest officers involved in all elements of our policy there. We can influence the making of institutions, and there is no more effective way to sway the course of events than doing things like this." My intent was to show these young officers the glittering possibilities that lay before them. I wanted them to be hungry for opportunity; I wanted to see them eager to reach out and grasp the future.

I traveled a great deal, talking to officers at posts around the world, telling them what was happening in Washington with the new Bush administration and how the Foreign Service was changing. I visited posts in Australia, Ethiopia, New Zealand, Hawaii, Papua New Guinea, throughout Asia, Europe, South America, and Canada. I tried to meet with every employee in every agency in the United States government, and I took note of their concerns. Along the way I met both competent and incompetent officers and a few caricatures of the old Foreign Service. One consul general was so inept at dealing with people that I made sure he was not selected for promotion to deputy chief of mission, a job that requires people skills. He is out of the Service now, which is where he should be. I made it a habit to pick out some employees who made an impression on me. For example, in Sydney I met a political officer who was a new employee, a midlevel entrant, and exceptional in her work. I advised her on the concept of tenure in the Foreign Service. She was subsequently tenured.

I am sure that one thing that helped her was accepting the fact that she was the main element in the process—that she was in control of the direction in which her career went.

Although it is generally unusual for the director general to visit the small posts at the ends of the earth, it is important for the members of those missions to have people visit them. It was a good learning experience for me as well. I learned from the Peace Corps volunteers in Papua New Guinea, for example, how the country had gone directly from the Stone Age to the Technological Age during World War II and still clung to ancient customs. They talked to me at some length about the concept of payback, which is a way of avenging a real or perceived wrong. This ingrained custom had tragic ramifications at the Papua New Guinea mission. When one of our female officers at the post discharged a servant, the incident was perceived as being unjust. Men of the servant's clan destroyed the officer's fence, broke into her home, and assaulted her. We got her out of there as fast as we could. It was a personal calamity with international reverberations. In that culture, it was she and not the assailants who violated societal norms. The current Peace Corps officers were still disturbed by the incident, and I talked with them about their understandable reactions of fear, anxiety, and uncertainty.

I also traveled across America, visiting universities, especially predominantly black and Hispanic universities, where I spoke about the Foreign Service in the hope of recruiting young officers. I spoke with governors and state government officials in an effort to place Foreign Service officers in domestic assignments. Legislation permits assigning officers to governors, mayors, and governmental organizations. The intent is to allow the officer to learn more about the country that he or she serves and for the community to learn more about the Foreign Service.

Unlike a book, a life does not fall neatly into chapters. People and situations from my previous posts bled into my tenure as director general. I was often pulled back toward the fire of Liberia, asked repeatedly to intervene and to urge Doe to leave the country. I had to decline, explaining that United States policy had moved on, and our political interest in Liberia had waned. I was director general in February 1990 when de Klerk announced the unbanning of the ANC and other organizations, releasing all political prisoners, including Nelson Mandela. As director general I visited Namibia for the final episode of that country's independence, and it was on that trip that I finally met Mandela. I was in Secretary Baker's party, which called at Mandela's temporary residence in Windhoek. Joe Slovo, the secretary general of the South African Communist Party, was also there. Mandela and I embraced. "I did not realize you were such a big man," he said to me. "He is a big man in many ways," Secretary Baker said. Winnie embraced me as well.

In the mixed bag that is the director general's job, I was assigned the job of monitoring the progress toward getting a holiday set aside honoring Martin Luther King Jr. While I was director general Terror Lekota and his colleagues were released because the South African Supreme Court dismissed their case. As director general I swore in Bob Frasure to an ambassadorship and then received news of his death in Bosnia.

The flesh and sinew of the Foreign Service was never far from my attention. It was not a job of dry paper and policy; it was a job of people. I presided at retirement ceremonies for ambassadors where I initiated the custom of presenting the flags of office to retirees, and at the funeral of an ambassador killed while fulfilling his work at post. I dealt with political appointees suffering withdrawal pangs and trying to wrangle another appointment; with senior officers' anguish at retirement or of being selected out of the Service; with officers, including an ambassador who was charged with sexual harassment; and with the benefits of officers' spouses, including wives bereft by death, wives bitter at devoting themselves to helping an officer succeed in his career and then being abandoned by divorce, with spouses of both sexes trying to find fulfilling work on post in a dual-career marriage; and with a senior officer suspected of espionage. That incident was a celebrated case—Felix Bloch, one of the brightest Foreign Service officers and a former chargé d'affaires to the U.S. Embassy in Vienna. In 1989, he was the highest-ranking State Department official suspected of espionage. In the face of separation proceedings commenced by the department, Bloch opted to resign from the Service. Once the officer resigned, his life unraveled. His wife left him, and I last heard he was working in a grocery store.

The career concerns of the senior officers were as sensitive and legitimate as those of young or minority officers. Senior officers were concerned about the new rules, especially the length of time people have in grade before they must be promoted to the next grade. Or, if they reach the highest grade, how long do they have there? When I became a career minister, I had ten years to serve in that grade before having to retire or being promoted to the honorary grade of career ambassador. The number of officers in each grade is limited, and the higher up the promotion ladder one is, the fewer position opportunities are available. There are never more than two or three on active duty as career ambassadors or twenty-five or thirty career ministers. I well understood from my own experience the pressure senior officers felt as they worried about time in grade.

I wrestled, sometimes unsatisfactorily, with the thorny problem of trying to transfer incompetent Civil Service officers who did not want to move. In the Foreign Service, the rank is in the person, so a person can be transferred any place. In the Civil Service, however, the rank is in the job and unless they are assured of a comparable job elsewhere, they won't budge. If they have satisfactory job ratings, which is usually the case, that is not reason enough to initiate separation procedures for incompetence. I attempted to arrange for the removal of a USUN employee who was unacceptable to the permanent representative. Because of her evaluations, we were unsuccessful.

I saw a number of firsts as director general: the first blind officer hired by the Service, the first Native American named ambassador, and the first woman named head of the medical division. In retrospect, my two most effective accomplishments were establishing a paradigm to bring a representational group of minorities and women into the Service and establishing the multi-functionality of officers. Without multi-functionality, which has been given short shrift, the Foreign Service may not survive.

"In view of the way the world is shaping up now," a Foreign Service officer asked me recently, "would you say the continuance of the Foreign Service is assured?"

"I would not," I replied.

My stay in personnel ended like a lightning bolt. I had planned on serving as director general for four years, but after I had been on the job for about three years, Secretary Baker called me and said, "The president wonders if you would like to go to the UN as ambassador." I was stunned. Career officers are seldom appointed to the United Nations post. There was no way I would turn down this opportunity. I was headed for a cabinet position, tall cotton for a farm boy from Louisiana.

At my swearing in as the United States ambassador to the United Nations, with Secretary of State James Baker.

THE UNITED NATIONS

My family and I had gathered at our Washington, D.C., home January 1 to observe the New Year of 1992 with traditional Southern fare for good luck and prosperity: hoppin' john, pigs' feet, ham hocks and black-eyed peas, cornbread, greens, and pecan pie. It was the beginning of the year of the monkey in the Chinese zodiac. To honor our family's mixed heritage, we augmented the Southern food with tofu and other dishes prepared Chinese style, with Asian herbs and sauces. My mother was present for the holiday, as were both daughters and Kathy's future husband, Jeffrey Kovar.

It is Lucy's New Year tradition to clear the house of unnecessary clutter. It is my personal tradition to review the past year's work and see how I can improve myself professionally for the upcoming year. The year 1992 would prove to be a time of exciting change for our family. Kathy and Jeff would marry in September, Sarah would graduate from the University of Pennsylvania and go to China for graduate study at the university in Nanking, and Lucy and I would move to New York for a new appointment that was coming my way.

Secretary of State James A. Baker phoned on January 13 and asked me to come see him. "You'd better sit down," he said when I entered his office. He told me that President George H. W. Bush wanted to nominate me for the United Nations appointment and he wanted my reaction. This was completely unexpected. Although I was bowled over by the news, I told Baker that I would like to go. "Don't you think you should talk with Lucy about this first?" he asked me.

The job at the UN is the highest-ranking job that a Foreign Service officer can aspire to as ambassador. I had never even considered the possibility that one day I would hold it. "You'll be a whiz," the secretary assured me. "Don't worry about it. Just bone up on all of the issues worldwide." When I told Lucy and our daughters about the offer, they were ecstatic, so I called Baker and said that if the president wanted me to go to the UN, I would be honored to do so.

The official title of the U.S. ambassador to the United Nations is a mouthful—Permanent Representative of the United States to the United Nations (USUN) and Representative of the United States in the Security Council with the rank of Ambassador Extraordinary and Plenipotentiary. The "extraordinary and plenipotentiary" tag is an international title and means that the ambassador speaks for the head of state on matters of state. The shorter name for the job is either ambassador or perm rep.

I was starry eyed at the prospect of working in the UN. A new world order was being shaped there, and the United States was a power in this creation. The hot issues at the UN were the Middle East—the area in general, as well as Iraq and the Persian Gulf, specifically—Central America, Cambodia, South Africa, Somalia, and Yugoslavia. My job, I was told, would be to advance United States foreign-policy objectives through the UN and to work to strengthen that august body in peacekeeping, countering terrorism, preserving Israel's rights, and building coalitions.

President Bush echoed my enthusiasm in his letter of appointment to me. "We are entering a new, exciting time of change in international relations," he wrote. "The postwar era is drawing to a close. As leader of the democracies, our Nation faces an historic opportunity to help shape a freer, more secure, and more prosperous world, in which our ideals and our way of life can truly flourish. . . . I look to you, as my personal representative to the United Nations, as my partner in this task."

Secretary of State Baker signed in with his own directions to me, pointing out the possibility of new relations with the new states of the former Soviet Union and "an invigorated Security Council," which had created seven new peacekeeping operations in the last twelve months. "This important UN body now works more as its founders intended," Baker wrote, and directed me to "play a major part in ensuring no changes proceed which jeopardize Council effectiveness." As invaluable as the UN is in its primary role of international peacekeeper, Baker's letter of instruction reiterated a note of well-known caution. "It must be clear the UN cannot serve as the option of first resort for all internal struggles, civil wars, or ethnic conflicts. Where UN peacekeeping operations are appropriate, you should insist they be effective and credible, and logistically and financially realistic."

Even more than its international peacekeeping and security missions, the UN is known for its work in human rights. I foresaw that my work at the UN offered possibilities to improve the global environment, food policy, agricultural development, trade, and health delivery. It is easy to support this worldwide work from a national perspective. The United States must look at a preferred state of affairs in the world. Quite simply, it is in the national interest of the United States to have a world where people have enough to eat, a roof over their heads, and access to at least rudimentary medicine.

The UN's myriad activities include the United Nations Development Program to enhance the growth of small-scale business activities, and the World Health Organization, which leads the fight to eradicate diseases such as cholera and AIDS. The International Labor Organization pushes for enlightened labor laws around the world, and the UN advocates improvement of the plight of women around the world.

Yet for all of its high-minded works, the UN had fallen victim to American derision from 1970 to the time of the Reagan administration. The nonaligned movement had come into its own, involving countries that considered themselves aligned neither with the West nor the East. Out of this group of nations came a growing chorus of anti-American invective. When Reagan became president, part of the Republican Party platform was to address the U.S. role in the UN. Jeane Kirkpatrick, then an unknown professor at Georgetown University, wrote an article saying that we deserved more credit for our support of UN causes, especially considering the money we paid into the UN. This was the beginning of serious anti-UN rhetoric.

As the office director of West African Affairs in the State Department during the first years of the Reagan administration, I helped develop a mathematical model to track how nations voted in the UN. We could see from that model what percentages of the votes were against the United States. Encouraged by Reagan, Kirkpatrick spoke out more and with a gusto that had never before been experienced at the UN. The United States began to withhold its dues to encourage the UN to reform itself. The huge cadre of people working under the title of International Civil Servant continued to grow into a bloated, inefficient staff that ate away at the budget. Congress refused to allocate the money to pay the dues because it was convinced both that the UN had too many people working for it and that the United States should not help perpetuate this situation. That continues to be the principal concern today. I would learn that the secretariat, the administrative department of the UN, is full of nonfunctioning people whose job is to create paper, put it into stacks, then create more paper to stack.

The UN found itself with more issues on its plate than it could manage with its budget and the large number of ineffectual employees. As the U.S. pushed for reform, constructive discussions between the United States and Secretary General Perez de Cuellar plummeted to zero. I believe that Ceullar's pique is the reason he failed to mention the United States when the flag of independence was raised over Namibia. At the ceremony, he completely ignored the U.S. role in negotiating that independence.

After the end of the cold war, the dissolution of the Soviet Union, and the Gulf War, the United States found itself leading a coalition, and the United Nations was back in business in a proactive way. About the time I became the U.S. perm rep, the UN was rejuvenated. The Security Council, which is the real power, was more vigorous than it had been and had passed some resolutions with teeth in them. I asked myself if the UN could be an effective tool of the United States in carrying out foreign policy. My answer was yes, but the United States has to play a leadership role. I was ready to roll up my sleeves and try.

Professionally, the perm rep post was a risky appointment to accept at the time, because 1992 was a presidential election year. The UN ambassadorship is often a highly political appointment and thus subject to the flutter of a political whim. I had never before hesitated to take risks professionally, and I did not do so now. I considered the appointment to the UN to be the most demanding test of my career. It was a pinnacle to be scaled. I moved post haste to familiarize myself with all issues before the UN. First, I went through a series of briefings, and then I had all the briefing material put into books. I was overwhelmed at the enormity of those books, shelves of them, and the magnitude of the issues they contained. One of the best calls I made in preparation for the post was a visit with Kirkpatrick, who had served as perm rep in 1981–85. She told me to think of the USUN as a challenge and the Security Council as a state legislature.

Approval of my appointment dragged on for months, and while I waited for Senate confirmation, I got caught in a thicket of personnel problems as venomous as sea urchins. By the time my appointment was confirmed in April, some of the stars in my eyes had dimmed.

The personnel problems in the USUN were multiple. My predecessor, Ambassador Thomas Pickering, had gotten crosswise with the State Department. The

UN job gave him the world stage. He was often in the news and on national TV talk shows. Somewhere along the way, he made a mistake. He let it be inferred that the successful conclusion to the Gulf War was due in no small measure to his diplomacy, which slighted the president and the secretary of state. Pickering's ego seemed out of hand. I never heard either Bush or Baker say a word about it, but I did hear Margaret Tutwiler, Baker's right hand, express her disdain for Pickering. The UN ambassador is considered a cabinet-level officer, and as such, is one of three State Department officials who have a dedicated car and driver. The other two are the secretary of state and the deputy secretary. Margaret felt that Pickering's car should be taken away and that he be required to use the department car pool like everyone else. Pickering also had some falling out with the Bureau of International Organizations Affairs (IO) headed by John Bolton, and thus lost more political friends in the State Department. I told myself right then, "I can't make a success at the UN if I am at odds with the State Department." I made an appointment to talk with Margaret about the USUN mission and ask her opinion. I was launching a disarming campaign and making a blatant effort to gain an ally. She and I never became bosom buddies, but she was supportive. Whenever I was scheduled to appear on a news program such as "Meet the Press," I made sure the public affairs officer notified her and asked if Secretary Baker had any talking points for me.

The tension within the USUN mission was intense. Pickering did not want to leave his post at the UN, but the president had decided he was going, and there was no way he could stay after that. Mrs. Pickering was equally adamant about staying. A chef and housekeeper told me that for some time she refused to pack. The Pickerings had poisoned the air against me, I was told. "They have shucked and buried you," said Irvin Hicks, who was going to join me at USUN as one of the ambassadors.

I was also catching hell with the press. An article appeared in the *Wall Street Journal* saying that President Bush was replacing Pickering, a superior senior Foreign Service officer, with a second-rate officer—me. The writer implied that I was inadequate, that I had no experience in multilateral affairs, and that the only substantial job I ever had was a kind of special appointment as ambassador to South Africa. It was a terrible article. The black community in Washington came up in arms and wanted to picket the State Department in protest. I advised against it, saying that the reporter was muckraking and that none of us should get down in the dirt with him. We took the high ground and made no public response. When I learned that the USUN's public affairs officer was the person responsible for this negative media slant and that he was suspected of orchestrating two newspaper articles assailing me as not being capable of the job, I took drastic and definitive action. I sent word to the mission that I wanted him transferred and out of there before I arrived.

By now I knew that I would have a rough time—jealousy among some of my colleagues, personnel problems within the mission, and a tug-of-war over leadership of the USUN mission. The IO's executive office wanted more involvement in casting policy, and that had to be sorted out. Did Bolton and IO run the mission, or did I? Congress would have a role, too. On top of this, I anticipated obstacles within the UN community itself. I began to feel that I was back in South Africa, fighting on two or three fronts.

I was genuinely concerned. I wondered if I would have the loyalty of all the people. Irv Hicks and I developed a war strategy of how I should take command of the troubled mission without causing more anxiety among the staff, yet making sure it was understood that it was a new day with a new leadership.

Despite all of this brouhaha, as soon as news of my appointment appeared in the press, people began drifting by my office asking for an appointment and hoping to go with me to the UN. We have UN missions in Kenya, Austria, Geneva, Montreal, and Rome—all connected in one way or another to the permanent representative of the USUN—but the mission in New York is the granddaddy of them all, and the posts there are highly coveted. The USUN has a huge staff (more than one hundred when I assumed control), a sizeable number of whom are Civil Service people.

My hearing before the Senate Foreign Relations Committee took place April 1, and I wore jade cufflinks for good luck. Ironically, the other ambassador on the docket was Pickering, who was being sent to the embassy in India. I invited Ambassador Pickering to go first at the hearing, and he moved through it relatively smoothly. When I was up, Committee Chairman Clayborne Pell asked me about one of the hottest issues at the UN: "Can Israel get a fair deal at the UN?" Other senators asked me about the civil war in El Salvador: "What do we do when the Farabundo Marti National Liberation breaks the cease-fire agreement?" Senator Jesse Helms wanted to know. Senators Paul Simon, Nancy Kassebaum, and Daniel Moynihan asked my definition of self-determination, UN reform, and my position on peacekeeping—specifically, if I would support the peacekeeping budget's being in the Defense Department and not in the State Department?

Compared to my examination for the South African ambassadorship, this hearing was remarkably affable. George Shultz called to congratulate me, and I asked for his suggestions for the UN. "You don't need any," he said graciously.

I was sworn in as perm rep May 7, and Lucy and I moved to New York to take up residence in the USUN Ambassador's apartment at the Waldorf-Astoria Hotel, where all the American perm reps have lived. Across the hall from us lived Motown record producer Phil Spector. General MacArthur's widow lived on the thirty-fifth floor.

The U.S. Embassy, a twelve-story building constructed in the late 1940s especially for the mission, is on First Avenue directly across the street from the

My family meets the president that had just appointed me to be the U.S. ambassador to the United Nations. (*left to right*) President George H. W. Bush, me, Lucy, Katherine, and Sarah.

UN building. It is not a good place to work because long ago the staff outgrew the space. The office is crowded, and people are jammed together. Past the security checkpoints, the entrance is tastefully decorated with fresh flowers and a waiting room. One of the first things I saw as I entered were the names of all the previous perm reps, with their years of service and their home state. It is a distinguished list, including George H. W. Bush, Warren Austin, Henry Cabot Lodge, Arthur Goldberg, Jeane Kirkpatrick, Andrew Young, Donald McHenry, Vernon Walters, Adlai Stevenson, and Daniel Moynihan.

On my first day at work, May 15, Alexander Watson, the deputy perm rep, met me at the entrance and welcomed me to the mission, setting a cordial tone. Alex was a fantastic officer who demonstrated an amazing skill at holding together the agitated staff during the difficult time of the changeover from Pickering to me.

Then we got down to business. At 8 A.M. I had an intelligence briefing in my office. This report covered the entire world. It was a composite report of all the intelligence agencies. The intelligence officer handed me the file, sat there while I read it, then took it away. Every day would begin this way.

At 9 A.M. I had an executive meeting with the counselors and ambassadors—political counselor, economic counselor, administrative counselor, and the three ambassadors. At this meeting we covered all of the active problems spread before us and decided which ones we had to deal with that day, either in the Security Council or bilaterally with another of the perm reps. Bob Gray, the political counselor, usually took the lead. He is a senior officer with impeccable qualifications, and he had been there long enough to know exactly what was going on. He had a good ear for the vulnerability of the perm reps. He could advise me how to talk most effectively to this one, what not to say to that one, or when to go to a second-in-command to enlist support in persuading the perm rep to vote our way.

There is absolutely no way I can quantify the totality of the issues we dealt with every day. Bob and his colleagues were with me step for step, preparing direct and straightforward memoranda for me that kept me well briefed and thoroughly prepared. They guided me through the intricate maze of the UN as if it were child's play. Prepped by them, I appeared at the Security Council, presented my credentials to the secretary general, Boutros Boutros-Ghali, and made my premiere addresses. They did their homework, I did mine, and miraculously I made no mistakes.

The names of the U.S. perm reps to the United Nations are listed at the U.S. Mission to the United Nations, along with their home state and years of service. I proudly listed Oregon beside my name.

Boutros-Ghali is an Egyptian who dresses impeccably, in dark suits and a white or blue shirt with a tastefully chosen tie. He speaks with a European-Arab accent and seemed French both in his training and his thinking. He holds a Ph.D. in international law from Paris University. He struck me as a person who genuinely wanted to make a difference at the UN. He also had an eye on history, specifically how history would view him, and he revealed a bit of egotism. Boutros-Ghali was particularly interested in effecting positive change in Cyprus and Libya, but he could not do this without cultivating the Permanent Five. The Perm Five members are Britain, China, France, Russia, and the United States. He was aware of the power of the United States, but not totally appreciative of it. I think he felt the United States was exercising more power than diplomacy in dealing with some issues, especially Libya and Yugoslavia.

The first official call I received was from Dr. Haris Silajdzic, the foreign minister of Bosnia-Herzegovina. He made a plea for both the United Nations' and the United States' intervention in the former Yugoslavia. "Our people are being slaughtered," he told me. When I first spoke at the General Assembly in late May, Yugoslavia was the subject. I welcomed three new members of the United Nations—Bosnia-Herzegovina, Slovenia, and Croatia. I said that what was left of Yugoslavia was not necessarily a successor to the old Yugoslavia, that the fighting must stop, and that Montenegro and Serbia must apply for membership in the United Nations if they wished to be treated as nations. I called for Serbia and Montenegro to step down from their harassment and end their violent campaign to reestablish the status quo with Serbia as the seat of power. "That's history," I said. The representatives of Serbia, Croatia, Slovenia, and Bosnia-Herzegovina rose to their feet in the back of the chamber and applauded.

The General Assembly is essentially a debating society, and every member of the UN has an opportunity to talk. It can pass resolutions, but they are not binding on the members. Occasionally, the resolutions from the General Assembly lead to Security Council resolutions, which are binding. In the 1950s, the Soviet Union was boycotting the Security Council the day the vote came up about the Korean War. The Chinese had crossed the Yalu River and the American delegate in the Security Council, under Chapter VII of the UN Charter, proposed a police action to halt the aggression of the Chinese and North Korea. If the Soviet member had been present, he would have cast a veto, but he was absent and the resolution passed. A United Nations peacekeeping force has been stationed in Korea ever since. No Soviet/Russian delegate has been absent since then.

Sometimes Robert Muller, the counselor for host-country affairs, joined us for the daily executive meeting. He had the job of working with the City of New York and the mayor's office and of making sure the foreign missions were happy and accommodated. If some ambassador was abusing his wife, Robert knew about it and advised me how to handle it. If someone did not pay the rent or failed to pay traffic tickets—a notorious UN diplomatic problem in New York since parking is scarce—he knew about it. Robert had good credentials for the job; he was a former detective with the New York City Police Department.

The executive session was my first meeting with the ambassadors, Irv Hicks, Alex Watson, George Moose, and Shirin Tahir-Kheli, a naturalized citi-

zen from Pakistan. I went directly from that to a meeting with the senior staff
in a large conference room. At 12:15, UN Chief of Protocol Joseph Verner Reed
briefed me about my presentation of credentials to the secretary general at
12:30. Then I chaired a coordinating committee of the Perm Five members of
the Security Council to review a proposed draft of a Security Council resolution on Yugoslavia. After that I attended my first Security Council Consultation
Committee meeting, followed by a Security Council meeting on the subjects of
Slovenia and Croatia.

That meeting ended at 6:30. I barely made it home for the last half of a
reception I hosted at the residence for the USUN staff. Thus ended the first day.
It set the pace for all of the days I spent at the UN. After the final meeting of the
day, I usually got home about 8:30. The daily routine was extended when the
General Assembly was in session from September through December, a hectic
time, with lots of visitors in town trying to arrange meetings and gathering for
business lunches. Security Council meetings often stretched far into the night.
Also, at the UN work does not stop on the weekend. It is a frantic pace, twenty-
four hours a day, seven days a week.

The second day on the job, I met with all of the mission staff in a big audito-
rium on the twelfth floor. I made these points: (1) I wanted team action; (2) I
wanted everyone to work together; and (3) I wanted to make sure there were
no surprises for me, ever. I told them that I believed the United Nations was a
great idea whose time had come and that I was proud and privileged to be a
part of this team. "I'm not the only player here," I told them. "All of you are
players, too." Then I walked through the mission, through all of the floors, visiting every employee at his or her desk. One day on my way to the Security
Council, the political counselor who usually attended with me was not around,
and I asked a senior Civil Service employee to go with me.

"I've never been there," he said.

"Well, you're going today," I replied.

"What do I do?"

"Sit behind me and make sure that I don't make any mistakes." As we headed
to the Security Council building he said, "You know, Ambassador, this is the
first time in my twenty years here that I've ever walked across the street with
the perm rep of the United States." I had no answer. I found that the mission
needed to be far more open with every employee, especially since working

conditions were not optimal. I started a new policy at Wednesday morning
general staff meetings. After the reports, I went around the room and asked if
anyone had comments. Once I stopped at a secretary and asked her name and
where she worked. "What do you think about our policy on this?" I asked her.

"No one ever asked me before," she said.

"You should get used to it," I said. "Everybody at this mission is a part of the
mission, not just me, the counselors, and the ambassadors." That set the tone I
wanted.

When I first spoke to the Security Council, the subject of my address was Cuba.
Ricardo Alarcón, Cuba's perm rep, had asked to appear before the Security
Council to make a complaint against the United States. "Fifteen years ago," he
said, "one of our airliners was shot out of the sky. We have reason to believe the
United States did it. We don't want it to be forgotten, so we want to make a
presentation of it." The United States was adamant in our reply that we had not
shot down the plane, and my address was a rebuttal to Alarcón's accusations.

I first met Alarcón during the negotiations for the removal of the Cuban
troops from Angola. Later he became president of the Legislative Assembly of
Cuba. Now, in 1992, we were both perm reps at the UN. I greeted him with a
handshake when we entered the chamber as the newspaper cameras flashed.
That threw them somewhat off balance. He spoke on Cuba's behalf, airing the
grievance that the United States harbors, aids, and abets criminals against the
best interests of Cuba and, by implication, Venezuela. His speech was the most
unbelievable trash I have ever heard. I rebutted with several denunciations about
its being a waste of time, the absurdity of the charges, and the restatement of the
United States' position. According to our mutually accepted prearranged plan,
the Security Council president thanked us politely and gaveled down the discussion. Alarcón went wild. "Wait, wait," he shouted, "I have to make my rebuttal. I've got to answer these charges." The president reminded him of our
agreement of procedure, but Alarcón protested. "Let him talk," I said, and he
did, alleging that in my address I had implied that the United States considered
this subject a waste of time because of the color of the skin of the people who
died in the airline crash. They were black people. "Absolutely ridiculous," I said,
and that was the end of my initial address before the Security Council.

YUGOSLAVIA

My first week as perm rep, I tackled one of the hottest issues at the UN: Yugoslavia.

Yugoslavia had been in turmoil since Marshall Tito died in 1980. After World War II, I witnessed six republics of the Balkans merge into the socialist nation of Yugoslavia, then separate again. In only four decades, modern Yugoslavia rose like a violent eruption from the ocean floor, then sank again, the waters of history closing over it. In 1992, the federation was in its death throes and in constant demand for UN attention.

In May, I got a call from the State Department saying that the Yugoslavs had allowed big guns to be implanted around the airport in Sarajevo so they could control the movements of the Bosnians and shoot their planes out of the sky if necessary. Secretary of State Baker had sent word to the Yugoslav foreign minister that they had forty-eight hours to change this. Furthermore, Yugoslavia was to provide security for the UN relief columns going into Bosnia-Herzegovina. "Until this happens," Baker said, "there will be no Yugoslavian airplanes flying to the United States. None will be allowed to land anywhere in the U.S." That evening at ten o'clock I finally reached Boutros-Ghali and relayed to him what the U.S. had said to Yugoslavia.

Meanwhile, Yuri Petrovsky, the political counselor at the Russian mission, proposed a new approach to handling Bosnia-Herzegovina. We had been working on soft ground, and it was coming apart. A number of people were reminding me that it was Serbia, not Croatia, that was the United States' friend during World War II. Croatia had been a German ally, but here we were beating up on the Serbs. "You might lose more than you gained," someone warned me. Petrovsky suggested a new approach to handling Bosnia-Herzegovina, which was that the United States and the Soviet Union jointly set the pace to insure that one was not played off against the other. Boutros-Ghali told me that he thought it was a possibility the United States should consider, although it was at variance with a position he espoused earlier that day. When we met that morning, the secretary general had cautioned me against either the U.S. or the UN interfering in the Yugoslavian breakdown. The ethnic divides were particularly sensitive. Intervention, he said, might produce more problems than we were prepared to deal with.

The Russians, Yugoslavia's closest ally of old and ethnically a kin nation, were troubled by the United States' pushing for sanctions against Yugoslavia.

Consequently, the Russians tried to do everything they could to push Serbia into an action that would cause the U.S. to pull back. The French were beside themselves with contentiousness when I reported that Secretary Baker wanted to go all the way and impose sanctions in response to the hard lines being taken by Yugoslavia.

Meetings about Yugoslavia went on and on. To clarify the United States' position, I convened the full U.S. delegation along with my staff. Colin Powell, chairman of the Joint Chiefs of Staff, was represented by his deputy. Ralph Johnson came from the National Security Council, and a representative also attended from the State Department's Bureau of International Organizations Affairs. There is always jockeying in the federal government, especially among the national security agencies (the State Department, the Defense Department, and the National Security Council) about who takes the lead. I called this meeting to make it clearly understood that as the perm rep of the United States, I was calling the shots on establishing this policy on Yugoslavia. I had no problems after that.

United Nations Security Council permanent members met in groups—the Perm Five, the Perm Three, or the Perm Two, for example—and in informal consultations (the entire Security Council in session but behind closed doors) to draft a resolution of sanctions against Yugoslavia. The ambassador from Kyrgyzstan petitioned me for aid for a disaster that had just occurred there, and the United States granted it.

When I met with the non-aligned group of nations, they were skeptical about the United States' intentions regarding the proposed resolution about sanctions against Yugoslavia. The Chinese representative told me that his government had instructed him to abstain, which was a way of saying that China favored the resolution but could not vote for it. The British and the Belgians agreed with the resolution. The French wanted to drop the banning of sports activities. We stood fast, saying the Yugoslavs would be hurt more by a ban on sports activities than almost anything else because it would affect more people. France agreed to vote yes but would issue a statement deploring the sports ban. India wanted to change the preambular paragraph referring to successive governments, but, as I expected, Washington said no. About this time, in late May, the secretary general's report on Yugoslavia revealed that Serbians were killing Bosnians, raping Bosnian women, and killing their children. Later India and Zimbabwe, among others, complained that the timing of this report had undue influence on the vote.

At last the text was agreed upon and the resolution came to a vote in the Security Council in late May. After eight speakers—Cape Verde, China, India, Morocco, Zimbabwe, Hungary, Japan, and Venezuela—the vote was taken: thirteen for, none against, and China abstaining. After the vote, five speakers came forward—Belgium, the United States, the Russian Federation, France, and the U.K. The resolution passed.[1] It was printed in French and English and released to the press. This process is representative of the give-and-take in developing a resolution in the Security Council. During my time at the UN, I witnessed only one other such resolution of such complexity.

Months later, the Organization of Islamic Conferences (OIC), a rather unfriendly organization headed at the time by the Turkish ambassador, addressed the General Assembly on the Yugoslav issue, specifically with concern for Bosnia-Herzegovina, the Muslim part of Yugoslavia. The OIC wondered aloud if the United States, the United Kingdom, and France had considered Islam as we developed our foreign policy. It seemed to them, the organization said, that Christianity was the only consideration. The Turkish ambassador came to see me because I was the P-5 coordinator, and said the conference had come to the conclusion that Western policy was value-laden along Christian lines rather than being even-handed. He wanted the U.S., U.K., and French perm reps to so inform our respective governments.

I called Edward Djeridjian, assistant secretary of Near East and South Asia Affairs, and told him of my experience with the Turkish ambassador, saying that I wanted to recommend that we make a statement on Islam and how our foreign policy relates to it. He relayed this to Secretary Baker, who did not authorize the statement. He thought it would be too risky. I persisted and Edward went back to the secretary and said, "Edward Perkins urges us to do it." "Okay," Baker said, "you write a speech, and let's go over it and try to define how our foreign policy relates to Islam and other monotheistic religions." Djeridjian did that, and it was an immediate hit. I happened to be giving a speech about that time, and someone in the audience asked the very question, what did the U.S. foreign policy say about Islam. I could answer with the new policy just prepared. Everyone in the audience wanted a copy of it.

We also had trouble with Greece on the subject of Yugoslavia. The problems reached far back in history. Macedonia, also a part of the old Yugoslav Federation, had been part of Greece in Biblical times and Greece still claimed it in perpetuity. When we began to deal with the new republics, Greece would not agree that Macedonia could someday become the Republic of Macedonia. We settled on calling it "the former Yugoslavian territory known as Macedonia."

It was August before the UN finished the Security Council resolution acknowledging the dissolution of Yugoslavia and recognizing the independence of Bosnia-Herzegovina, Croatia, and Slovenia and the issue of prisoners of war in Croatia. This had taken time because we had to overcome the objections of China, India, and Zimbabwe. The extensive work on this resolution is an indication of the difficulty in dealing with the complex issues and balancing the diverse desires of UN members. Roping rainbows would be easy by comparison.

The crisis dragged on. In December, I asked the senior staff to prepare a think cable on Bosnia. It was time that we did something about that situation. I was in favor of enforcing the no-fly zone, destroying Serbia's army and air force and therefore the ability of the Bosnian Serbs to play war. We would have to move fast if we were to get a resolution before the end of the year, so I decided that we should visit the capitals and resolve differences between the U.S., U.K., France, Russia, and Belgium. At issue was the definition of targets, the length of time that can elapse before the no-fly zone is effected, and the degree of control by the secretary general. By the end of the month, Slobodan Milošević, a Serbian nationalist, apparently had won the presidential election, and I was convinced that Yugoslavia would panic. Since May, the UN had imposed economic sanctions on Serbia and Montenegro, called for a cease-fire in Bosnia-Herzegovina, and imposed a naval blockade on Yugoslavia and a no-fly zone over Bosnia. How to enforce this was the problem.

As we wrestled with these issues, none of us in 1992 guessed just how long Yugoslavia's problems would lumber on, leaving in its wake human suffering of colossal proportions. As history has shown, the breakup of the Yugoslav Federation was accompanied by violence and genocide of the worst sort. As the decade of 1990 ended, the Kosovo Liberation Army rebelled against Serbian rule and multitudes of Kosovo Albanians fled the killing and the atrocities visited upon them. Ethnic cleansing took root; thousands of innocent people were placed in Serbian detention camps and lost their lives. Hundreds of thousands of Muslims were driven from their Bosnian homes. In 2001, Milošević was arrested and put on trial for war crimes. The final destiny of Yugoslavia, from breakup to independent nations, and to the trial of Milošević as an international human rights criminal illustrates, in no small way, the inability of the people of the region to be heroic together.

THE MIDDLE EAST

The more I studied the Middle East, the more fascinating I found it. I knew the history of the area, that the mighty Muslim Ottoman Empire was felled by Russian expansion and European wars, then divided as spoils by Britain and France after the two world wars. I knew that Britain created modern Iraq, Kuwait, Jordan, Palestine, and Israel, and the Saudis had tribes before the Roman Empire extended itself into what are now Saudi Arabia and the Middle East. I also knew that the United States' close relationship with Israel is unlike any other U.S. relationship. No U.S. president would dare to make a radical change in U.S.-Israeli relations' policy without consulting, within his country, as well as other nations.

What I did not know when I became perm rep, but what I was learning fast, is that Islam is the key to understanding the Middle East and the Arab nations. In the United States we do not know enough about Islam. Our substantive understanding of this complicated subject is essential to solving world problems. I should have read the Koran long before I did. I cannot see how I completed my doctoral studies without looking at the effect of Islam on public administration, because the two subjects are intertwined in the institutions of government and community. Public administration exists to embrace the things that make a difference in individual lives, work, community, travel, food, safety—governance at all levels. The public administration I studied had a decidedly Western orientation. On the Islamic side of the fence, public administration is connected almost irrevocably with the Koran.

Before going to New York and the UN, I plunged into the study of Islam, trying to make up for my lack of knowledge. My operating bible was UN Security Council Resolution 242, the Oslo Accords, and the decision taken by the Americans at a Madrid conference shortly thereafter to be the continuing broker in the peace process between Israel and the Arab states, urging each side to be reasonable.[2] James Bill, a professor from William and Mary College, briefed me thoroughly on Islam and the Middle East. He spent a couple of days with me and left me with this reminder: "To learn about the Arabs, don't just have a

surface understanding, especially with the fundamentalists. These are the people who are manifesting a set of grievances that have built up over the years.
They are convinced they are right. If we are going to have peace, we have to
understand them so we know where they are coming from when we talk." I
noted in my journal, "This is what the United States' government has failed to
do so far." We see fundamentalism as a threat. We need to look at them not as
an enemy, but as another element to understand thoroughly. I believe that our
destiny as a nation is caught up in it. We do ourselves a dishonor by not having
an in-depth understanding of this religion and of the expansion of Islam that is
marching through Africa, Central Asia, and China.

While Boutros-Ghali was secretary general, the United Nations played a key
part in the effort to get Iraq back into its bottle. In 1990, before Iraq invaded
Kuwait, the UN had imposed heavy trade sanctions and prohibited air traffic to
and from Iraq. After the Gulf War cease-fire in 1991, President Bush and Secretary Baker got on the telephone and personally invited a number of Arab
nations to join the United States in creating the status quo ante. Despite his
defeat in the Gulf War, Saddam Hussein intended to be the driving force in the
Middle East. He wanted to be more powerful than Iran, Saudi Arabia, and
Kuwait, and he wanted nuclear weapons in order to achieve arms superiority.
Not only did Hussein consider Kuwait historically the nineteenth province of
Iraq, he had been humiliated by the war. I believed that he would do whatever
necessary to regain face. He considered the United States the chief villain and
the primary obstacle in his march to glory.

Iraq had not complied with UN resolutions or the demands to eliminate all
weapons of mass destruction, so international sanctions remained in place.[3]
Now, in 1992, the country's infrastructure was in shambles. Breakdowns in
food supply and health care had resulted in an enormous civilian mortality
rate, including 800,000 children. Hussein's dictatorship was iron-fisted and
brutal as thousands of Kurds and political dissidents were murdered or simply
disappeared. In the language of UN resolutions, the repression of the Iraqi civilian population, especially the Kurdish-populated areas, and the massive flow of
refugees across the borders reflected the "magnitude of the human suffering."
The UN declared the situation to be grave and Iraq deserving of condemnation
for the violations of human rights.

The Perm Three (the United States, France, and the United Kingdom) sought sanction language to reply to Iraq's Ambassador Al-am-Bari. I was the conduit through which the U.S. talked to Iraq. Washington spoke to me, I spoke to Ambassador Al-am-Bari, and he spoke to his government. In this way, we delivered points back and forth. I found myself feeling sorry for Al-am-Bari and his successor, Ambassador Ham Doun. They were caught in the crossfire but stayed true to their mission of carrying out the national interests of their country. Never once did either of them deplore the situation.

In July, Rolf Ekeus, the head of the UN Commission on Inspection regarding Iraq, reported that he was still in discussion about an inspection of an agricultural warehouse. He was convinced that the Iraqis intended to cooperate, but the Iraqis were stonewalling. As of July 24, we were considering bombing Baghdad. This action, to get Iraq back to its reestablished borders, would be under the auspices of the UN Security Council resolution that created a Gulf coordinating committee with the U.S. as leader.

I testified on the Hill later that month, and the questions from Lee Hamilton's Subcommittee on UN Affairs and Human Rights were all about Iraq. The subcommittee wanted to know about the ongoing Iraqi inspection. Two congressmen, Tom Lantos and Robert Torricelli, were the most obtrusive. Saying Hussein had regained the upper hand, they wanted war. My exchange with them became quite heated.

The Iraqis subsequently agreed to the warehouse inspection, and Ekeus reported to the Security Council that he had found nothing in the building. Still, the Iraqis were not behaving, and by August we said that we intended to declare a no-fly zone in Iraq. In response to the UN action of 1991, Iraq complied inch by inch. The Iraqis had moved back inside their own borders to establish the status quo ante. Kuwaitis lobbied hard and heavy for a resolution, and the United States was beginning to back the Kuwaitis' request. As the Perm Five met on Kuwait, the secretary general told me that his under secretary was working to get a memorandum of understanding that would permit humanitarian aid workers access to Iraq, especially to work among the Kurds. The Iraqis, however, wanted all humanitarian workers out of Iraq, especially out of the south. They linked this with the no-fly zone, which they knew was coming.

The Security Council sent a rapporteur, a Dane named Max Vanderstoel, to Iraq and chronicle the human-rights violations there. He reported that the

Iraqis were going for broke in all directions. The plight of the civilians and the flood of refugees rendered the situation critical and threatened international peace and security in the region.

In September, I went to the Middle East, making calls on the governments of Egypt, Israel, and Syria to make sure that I understood from them what I was to say in the upcoming resolution and to carry instructions to them from the United States government. I was accompanied by Brad Hanson, originally from Georgia, who had studied at the American University in Cairo. He spoke Arabic, had traveled a great deal around the Middle East, and was now a Foreign Service officer and Arab specialist at the USUN mission.

We landed in esoteric Damascus, Syria. The biblical account of Paul's Damascus road experience was much in my mind. This was the closest I had been to the Middle East peace process. I knew that I needed a clear understanding of the history of Syria, the Golan Heights, Israel, and Iraq. They are all kindred, just as the Yugoslavs are related to each other. The people of the Middle East are separated by the evil sides of religion and nationality; because of that, they have murdered many people to establish superiority. I needed to know more about this ancient, arcane world.

In Syria, I raised myriad issues with the minister of State for Foreign Affairs, but he responded substantially to only one—the Middle East peace process. He said that Syria had made a big step in agreeing to the condition on which to base talks, and he hoped that Israel would respond favorably. He said that he was happy that the United States did not intend to push for the dismemberment of Iraq. The issue of the Golan Heights—that Israel return the conquered area—he said, was nonnegotiable. It remains that way today.

In Cairo, I tried to meet with the Arab League's secretary general, but he was ill and could not receive me. I suspect that he was diplomatically ill, because he thought I would say something that he did not want to hear, namely that we wanted the League to be more supportive of the peace-process efforts. I did meet with the intelligent and well-informed foreign minister of Egypt and a gaggle of his assistants. After that stimulating meeting and a lunch hosted by the U.S. ambassador, I had time for sightseeing. I visited the pyramids, the slowly eroding Sphinx, and the age-old Citadel, as well as the *souk*, one of the world's grand central markets.

From Cairo, we traveled to Jerusalem for a series of instructive meetings with the Israelis, who wanted to present their side of the peace process. It was

a seminal meeting with Prime Minister Yitzhak Rabin, who was not only cordial but, for him, downright friendly. I asked if he would agree that non-
governmental organizations could work in the refugee settlements, which
until then the Israel government had refused. In a turnaround, Rabin agreed.
"We're kidding ourselves if we think the settlers are going anywhere," he said.
"They are with us forever. So, yes, the humanitarian organizations can come
in." That afternoon, when I toured a refugee camp, my prevailing thought was:
People are being created here who will be either a friend to stability or an
enemy to the existence of Israel. It has turned out to be the latter. The young
people in those settlements have known no other life. They have grown up
being told that the Israeli military forces are their enemy. What I saw in 1992
came to bear fruit a decade later in spontaneous eruptions in the Palestine territory and in Israel. I believe that what Rabin was thinking when he told me he
would allow these humanitarian organizations into the settlements was that
maybe, just maybe, it would help create a different atmosphere. Perhaps it
would be a promising step toward making the people in the refugee settlements into citizens who have a stake in peace. Rabin was assassinated in 1995
while attending a peace rally in Tel Aviv. Middle East peace talks sputter on,
but the escalating violence continues to this day.

After I returned to the UN, an open formal session was held in the Security
Council on November 23 about the Kuwait-Iraq issue. Twenty-one nations
spoke. The U.S. and U.K. made the toughest statements, calling on Iraq to
comply with UN Security Council Resolution 687. Iraq's Deputy Prime Minister Tariq Aziz must have either wanted to deliberately enrage the Security
Council or to make points with Hussein with his soliloquy. His accusations
were so wild that I insisted the council president's exit statement be amended
to reference them. In the course of the debate, Aziz sunk to name-calling and
referred to the Kuwaitis as "that person," a deplorable action that lowered
Iraq's status even further. Iraq now appeared to be some kind of outlaw nation.

In December, we received word that the Iraqi government apparently had
decided not to allow the United Nations' humanitarian-relief trucks to proceed through Iraq territory to take care of the Kurds. Then our monitoring
forces intercepted two Iraqi fighters in the Iraqi no-fly zone, destroying one
and possibly the other. The State Department wanted a menu of violations
delivered to the Iraqi ambassador. I delivered a copy to Ambassador Ham
Doun myself so he could send it to Baghdad. Later that day, a call came saying

At the General Assembly of the UN. When the secretary of state attends a session, he or she is given the perm rep's chair. Here, Secretary Lawrence S. Eagleburger, seated to my left, takes his rightful place.

the government of Iraq had now apparently reversed its decision and would allow the convoy to proceed.

As contemporary history has shown, the end of the year 1992 was not the end of conflict in Iraq. The UN remained, in Security Council resolution language, "seized of this matter." For a decade the UN sought Iraqi compliance, attempted to conduct inspections, passed more resolutions, and threatened attack. In 2003, a U.S.-British force invaded Iraq and overthrew Hussein. This brought to an end Hussein's reign, but the struggle begun so long ago seems destined to continue.

SOMALIA

Somalia had been battered into the ground by civil war, then decimated by famine. The year before I became perm rep, some 300,000 Somalians had died of starvation. During the spring and summer of 1992, the UN sent in unarmed military observers to monitor the cease-fire and begin humanitarian relief efforts. Nevertheless, I believed that the country was ripe for a revolution.

By August I felt the country was beyond redemption as a modern nation unless a proconsul action was installed. The question was, who would take on the task? I suspected that no country would want to shoulder that job. Much of the world looked to the United States to take on the responsibility, in part because the U.S. had contributed considerable financial aid to Somalia over the years. By November we knew that the UN peacekeeping force was not working very well. It was inadequate to secure the humanitarian efforts. Food sent into the country was corralled by warlords and profiteers, who often took control of the Red Cross boats and the other aid conveyances of humanitarian gifts, warehoused the goods, and sold them to the highest bidder. Some two thousand people were dying daily of starvation, and the Somalian warlords continued to wage war among themselves.

We decided within the USUN Mission that I propose to President Bush that the United States intervene on a humanitarian basis and provide the armed force necessary to protect the distributors of food and to ensure that it was distributed to the people who needed it. The president, now nearing his last month in office, agreed and asked us to communicate to the secretary general that the U.S. would be willing to lead a coalition of nations in making Somalia safe insofar as distributing food—but not a step further. The United States' offer was that the United States would lead, command, and control, with participation by other nations and under the UN flag.

The secretary general favored using the U.S. plan, but some of his advisors objected. Perhaps they thought that a U.S.-led mission would imply that the UN had failed and that the United States stepped in to save the situation, as we had in Korea, Desert Storm, and other incidents. The secretary general was reluctant to take this to the Security Council for another reason. The UN members would see this as a most unwelcome precedent, moving into a country without the invitation of a government. The normal eye would see this as a greater danger—aggression and the violation of the concept of sovereignty. I knew that China, India, and other nations would be wary about such a resolution. It would raise memories of Tibet for China and Kashmir for India. They would think, suppose Tibet pushes the self-determination rule under the charter. Suppose the Kashmiris push the self-determination rule under the charter.

Then, a nation such as the United States, compelled by human-rights interests, might push for a resolution to go in and help.

December 3, 1992: I was present at the making of history. United Nations Security Council Resolution 794 was passed, accepting the U.S. offer to field a force in Somalia of about twenty-five thousand combat troops to ensure that humanitarian aid got to the Somalian people. The U.S.-led United Task Force authorized the United States as commander of the coalition to ask others to help, similar to Desert Storm, and it placed the operation under the auspices of the United Nations. For the first time, the UN approved entry into another country without an invitation and a military force for humanitarian purposes. The action was called "Operation Rescue Hope," and it was expected to be over in one month.

The resolution was a radical move toward peacekeeping, using military force based on humanitarian issues and needs. In my judgment, it was a giant stride towards meeting the challenges of modern society. It was a historic

As perm rep to the United Nations, I worked with Colin Powell,
who was then chairman of the Joint Chiefs of Staff.

effort to move beyond the niceties of observing borders when necessary to break the rule of sovereignty. When I talked with U.S. Information Agency officer Karen Aquilar about how to explain this in an innovative public-relations campaign, I told her that we had to present it in a way that was not threatening to less-powerful nations. Smaller nations who could not defend themselves could easily see this as a precedent for the United States or another powerful nation to ride roughshod over them in the future.

By December 9 the landing was going well, and by the end of December, we had secured Somalia. The secretary general, however, still wanted a northern operation and disarmament of warlords as a basic objective. He hoped we would stay longer. Two things happened.

First, Boutros-Ghali had a long-standing animus with the foremost Somalian warlord, whom he wanted caught and prosecuted. The secretary general suggested that the U.S. fold that task into our humanitarian protection. He wanted us to push north, clear land mines, and disarm the warlords. We said no. We would distribute food and clear and confiscate weapons of war in accordance with carrying out our mission, but the United States would not attempt to make Somalia safe. He tried to exercise pressure on the United States through the media. I was sent to the secretary general to tell him personally that the president was not amused.

"I must have made a mistake," Boutros-Ghali said.

"Perhaps your note taker took down the wrong notes," I said.

"Yes, that might have happened."

Second, Colin Powell, his deputy, and I worked on establishing the mission and refined it until we felt it was exactly the way it ought to be. The mission was agreed upon by the Defense Department, the State Department, the White House, and the United Nations. The United States planned on pulling out of Somalia before the new Clinton administration came into office.

However . . .

Somewhere along the way that plan was changed. The United States decided to stay longer. Later, the Clinton administration increased the safekeeping action, and a series of mishaps occurred. The worst of these was the death of two soldiers. They were killed, and their bodies were dragged through the streets of Mogadishu. Television news cameras captured the event and broadcast it widely. Almost immediately, the United States ended activities in Somalia and left the country in the hands of a UN commander. What began as a noble idea in the USUN mission turned out to be disastrous. The mission changed, but the strategy did not. One lesson to be learned from that experience is that when using military force, the purpose has to be very clearly stated and the operation must stay within the paradigm already established. Go in with clearly defined objectives that have been agreed upon by all involved, complete the mission, then leave. If necessary, go back to the drawing table and redefine the mission. Do not change courses in the middle, and do not add something at the end. We should never forget that lesson.

Another lesson I learned from this experience is the importance of preparing soldiers for the customs they will encounter in the country. We are not a nation that can sit by and watch between 2,000 and 5,000 people starve to death each day without doing something about it, but our efforts may not always be appreciated. Some of the Somali peasant women sitting on the stoops in Mogadishu made contemptuous gestures at the black U.S. troops passing by. This was not specifically an anti–black American gesture. Somalis trace their tribe to the Queen of Sheba and consider themselves better than darker-skinned Africans.

Early in my career I was shocked to learn that the United States did not assign nonwhite officers to Iceland because the Icelandic government, fearful of miscegenation, did not want them. Later, as director general, I reinforced a policy of simply saying that we send our men and women everywhere in the world, and that included women to Arab countries. If a country will not accept them, then we will not send anybody. Accept all U.S. soldiers or none at all. I think that is the right policy, because that is what we are as a nation. We cannot tailor our external expression based on the receiving countries' prejudices.

United Nations operations in Somalia were ended in 1995. Currently, Somalia is unreconstructed and continues to be in need of economic development, health delivery services, nutritional aid, education, and a government based on the stable state.

TRAVEL

Since I was a virtual member of the cabinet, my presence was often requested in Washington. On one such occasion, I was invited to be present at an appearance of Boris Yeltsin before Congress. In 1991, the Soviet Union broke apart into separate independent states and Yeltsin was elected president of the Russian Republic, defeating USSR president Mikhail Gorbachev. Yet, when Yeltsin visited Washington in June 1992, Gorbachev still held the real political power and was still recognized as premier of the Soviet Union. This was a matter of great sensitivity to Yeltsin, an outspoken and often abrasive man. As a boy he had lost a thumb and finger while tinkering with a live grenade. As a young man he had mastered construction skills, then trained as an engineer. As a politician, he was brash and impatient for reform. Now he was in Washington to pay a courtesy call on President Bush. He was met at the White House by a woman who was a Security Council Russian expert—Condoleezza Rice.

"Is this the door Gorbachev went through to see the president?" Yeltsin asked her.

"No," she said, "Gorbachev was head of state. He went to the front entrance."

"That is the way I want to go."

"You can't," Rice said.

Yeltsin sat down, Condoleezza told me, and refused to move. She sat down, too, and also refused to budge. After about five or six minutes, Yeltsin gave up and followed her directions. They had communicated nonverbally but clearly. He knew that he had met an immovable force, and she recognized how far she could go.

The communication process at the UN is intricate. It was difficult for me, as the American ambassador, to pick up the phone and call another ambassador without his wondering if there was a message behind my message. Even casual conversations in the UN corridors or outside the Security Council chambers can be misconstrued by the press or passersby and spun into stories as fanciful as they are erroneous. Therefore, an enormous amount of time is expended on courtesy—attending functions, hosting receptions and luncheons, seating people appropriately, and using the occasions to exchange messages. It is time consuming, but it is valuable because it puts people in touch with each other in ways they could not otherwise meet without going through an enormously complicated protocol. Social events offer an informal conduit of communication. I rarely met formally or exchanged a démarche with either the North Korean delegate or the Chinese ambassador, but we could chat while walking around a buffet table. In five minutes of seemingly innocent conversation, we could pass one another a message and get a response.

The USUN ambassador is an ambassador-at-large, so my duties included touching base with various capitals in Europe and Asia. On one such a trip to Paris, President François Mitterand's military advisors briefed me in impeccable English on the military issues facing the French government. In London on the same trip, my escort officer was the first blind Foreign Service officer whom I had sworn in when I was director general. I had insisted that the London Embassy take him, and to this day I believe the mission returned the favor by assigning him to me as my control officer. He assisted me ably, but he remained as disagreeable as ever.

In Geneva on the same trip, I had another round of political jousting for authority. I was at a conference of the United Nations United States missions. John Bolton, assistant secretary for the Bureau of International Organizations Affairs, was a brilliant person, but he had trouble accepting the fact that the UN ambassador outranked him. He would turn up unannounced in New York and meet with UN officials without notifying the USUN. He did that when I was perm rep, and I called his aide and said, "I want to be courteous to John by conveying this through you. Tell him that I do not want him having meetings with anybody unless he gets permission from this mission. Tell him like that."

Bolton told me that he thought I had been notified. "Not so," I said, and I went on to clarify my position. "This is a mission. This is not a city. It is the United States' mission and you are an official of the U.S. government. Not even the president would come to New York without letting me know he was coming. I want to be notified. I may want to sit in on some of the meetings, which is my right. If you are discussing things which will affect my mission and the way I carry out my duties for the president and the secretary, you are honor-bound to tell me what you talked about." In Geneva, he and I had round two. Among other things, I addressed the IO group on the importance of honest communication and cooperation between the USUN mission and IO. It would appear that, like the biblical poor, inner-departmental jockeying for position is with us always.

Some people were still smarting about my replacing Pickering at the UN. When I attended the United Nations Conference on Environmental Development in Rio de Janeiro that June, an official from one of the nongovernment organizations said, "Mr. Ambassador, you have big shoes to fill at the UN." My patience with this subject was wearing thin. "I am accustomed to filling big shoes," I replied.

President Bush arrived at the Rio conference and said, "Ed, they tell me I don't have to make a speech while I am here." I was surprised. "The president of the United States cannot come here and not make a speech," I told him. He called a speech-writing meeting early the next morning. He wrote the speech himself, with all of us standing around contributing to it. I noted that he had to say something about a Commission on Sustainable Development, which would be an important conference follow-up at the UN in New York. "How do you think this ought to go?" he asked me. "Mr. President, if you will just say that you look to your ambassador at the UN to take the lead in helping to establish a Commission on Sustainable Development, that is all I need." That is what he said, and that was the basis on which the commission was established.

While in Rio I met with Boutros-Ghali and said it was time the UN did something to stop the fighting in Haiti. He had just met with Mrs. Sadako Ogata, the director general of refugees for the UN High Commission for Refugees, and she proposed using Santo Domingo for the refugees pouring out of Haiti. I raised the possibility of a UN peacekeeping force in Haiti. Boutros-Ghali was sympathetic but said that he wanted the Organization of American States, not the UN, to take care of Haiti. Consequently, the UN did not become involved until later.

My travels as perm rep took me to the Far East—China, Japan, Thailand, Cambodia, and Korea.

In August 1992, I was in Seoul to inspect the United Nations Command. Korea is by far the largest United Nations force ever assembled since the inception of the UN in 1945. I had been in Korea thirty years earlier, as a rifle-carrying marine, after the UN's intervention in Korea under Chapter 7 of the UN Charter, which meant utilizing armed activity to stop the aggression and to move the aggressors back to the status quo ante. When I returned on this trip, it was the first time in history that someone stationed there as a trooper had come back as an ambassador representing the UN.

The question in 1992 was if North Korea and South Korea, members of the United Nations, could begin talks about a possible rapprochement. In my discussions with the South Korean foreign minister, I raised the question of possible negotiations, but when a North Korean ambassador approached me about our engaging in informal talks, the State Department did not give me permission to talk with him. That decision was shortsighted but not unusual. During the Carter administration, Andrew Young talked without official permission to the Palestine Liberation Organization representative at the UN. Their meeting raised such a furor, led in no small part by the U.S. Jewish community, that he had to resign. The Libyan ambassador also approached me and said, "You and I need to be talking with each other." I agreed, but again no such permission was granted. The same thing had happened when Cuba's Ricardo Alarcón asked me during the Namibia-Angola negotiations if he and I could not "start talking on this level and try to resolve some of the differences between us." Assistant Secretary Elliott Abrams had a fit and absolutely prohibited it. When I saw Abrams in Washington years later, I asked him if he had changed his mind about the Cubans. "No," he said, "I am even more determined." I was disappointed. It is my judgment that as diplomats we should engage in open and informal communications where possible. Often my experience in doing so has been a successful movement toward a new page in the negotiation.

While in Korea, I met with the U.S. Mission and Ambassador Don Gregg's country team. I wanted to know about South Korea in this new era; about the elections in North and South Korea; about the nuclear nonproliferation treaty, which had reciprocal implications for both North and South Korea; about the Northern Pacific peninsula bordering Japan, China, North Korea, and South Korea; and about relations between Japan and South Korea, which were not good but moving on an improved path. Japan was paranoid about taking the blame on the issue of "comfort girls," South Korean women who had been put into sexual slavery for Japanese soldiers in the Pacific War. The surviving women were pariahs both in their own society and in Japan.

From Korea, my accompanying aide, T. J. Rose, and I went to Cambodia so that I could have a look at what was happening under the auspices of the Paris Peace Accords. Brokered by the United States, France, Indonesia, and Japan in part, the Peace Accords called for a cessation of hostilities inside Cambodia between the Khmer Rouge on one side, other Cambodian factions on the other side, and His Royal Highness Prince Norodom Sihanouk somewhere in the middle.

To my amazement, a passenger on the plane to Phnom Penh happened to be Khieu Samphan, one of the original authors of a plan titled *Some Thoughts on Restructuring Cambodia's Social and Economic Activity*. This document, written during the 1950s while Samphan and other Cambodians were students at the University of Paris, became the operative bible for the Khmer Rouge's bloody excesses in trying to restore Cambodia to what they considered cultural purity. The Cambodian killing fields of 1975–79 witnessed one of the worst acts of genocide of the century. An estimated two million Cambodians were killed, tortured, or starved to death. Schools, stores, banks, hospitals, religions, and the family unit were all banned. Now here on the same aircraft was one of the instigators of that ethnic purge. When the plane landed, Samphan slipped off the plane with his entourage and melted into the crowd. I did not see him again until later in the trip.

In 1992, Cambodia was a landmass, not a nation. It had no real government or head of state. Under the terms of the Paris Peace Accords, Japan, Australia, and America operated huge aid programs there. Australia undertook to reestablish public safety in Cambodia, using troops from other nations under the auspices of the United Nations. T. J. and I flew on to Siam Riap to meet with HRH Prince Norodom Sihanouk of Cambodia, but before the meeting we took a day's side trip to Angkor Wat. According to legend, this lost city in the creeping jungle was built by gods. Spread over some forty miles, the vast array of stone temples, statues, and carvings is an engineering marvel. At the center of this twelfth-century masterpiece is a pyramid temple, carved with exquisite bas-relief carvings and art and surrounded by a great moat. It was a daunting adventure to witness the grandeur of this lost era of Khmer history. At the end of our day's tour, poor T. J., sorely affected by the heat, humidity, and expanse of the place, was feeling more daunted than adventurous. He had not expected life in the Foreign Service to be so rigorous.

En route to Angkor Wat, which had been desecrated by the Khmer Rouge, I saw that the trees had been cut down waist-high by gunfire. We could not get off the main road because of the land mines. I was jarred by the juxtaposition— the artistry of an ancient civilization, the triumphant vegetation, and the destruction of humanity and art as a result of ethnic violence. To use the term "ethnic cleansing" in reference to such violence and death seems to me to be a cruel distortion of the English language.

That evening, we called on His Royal Highness Prince Sihanouk at his summer palace. T. J. and I sat in chairs below him. We were joined by the prince's chief of protocol, a woman who had been in his family for decades. I was taken by the obeisance she paid him. As soon as she entered the room, she dropped to her knees and crawled to him in a sign of respect. All evening the prince sent her coming and going to fetch things, and each time she came into the room, the process was repeated.

I told Prince Sihanouk that I was instructed to say to him that the United States hoped he would agree to be king of Cambodia once more, with the completion of the stacking of arms of the combatants in compounds as required by the UN. I also told him that the United States saw him as the only unifying element in Cambodia and that all of the factions would rally around him and not feel threatened.

I found him to be peripatetic, petulant, short-tempered, somewhat child-like, and not unaware of the importance of his royal person. He was about seventy years old, an accomplished film producer and director and composer. An excellent musician, he played the clarinet in the style of the bygone Paris jazz era. But he had led an excessive life and had been in poor health for some time. More germane to my official visit and our conversation, Sihanouk has a low respect for Americans. His 1973 memoir was titled *My War with the* CIA: *Cambodia's Fight for Survival*.

I told him that the United States was genuine in its desire to see peace reign in Cambodia, but he was very suspicious of the United States and recited for me what he considered our perfidy. He hinted that the United States was an enemy of the world's nonwhite population. I sought to introduce a little pleasure into the conversation when I told him that I was aware of his having helped to solve a problem created when a U.S. vessel was captured in North Korean waters a few years earlier. The surviving sailors, one of whom was a black American, were taken prisoner and placed in Cambodia's custody. Sihanouk treated them very well, even having white civilian suits made for them to wear when they met the press. "Oh you remember the incident?" the prince asked, beaming. "Yes," I said, "we were all very pleased that you did that. It manifested the humane side of Your Royal Highness." From then on, things got easier, and he began to halfway trust me, but he never once forgot that I was an agent of the United States. We talked into the night, eating fruit, nuts, dates, and tea. About midnight he finally thanked me for coming and thus signaled that the meeting was over. Still, one never takes leave abruptly of the king. "Your Royal Highness," I said, "if I may, I'd like to ask your permission to leave, as the French express it, to *demandez le route*." "*Avec plaisir*," he replied.

When I met with Cambodia's foreign minister, Hun Sin, what he most wanted was assurance that the United States would not back out of the peace process and that we would continue to insist that it continue until elections were held. I assured him that we would stay the course and that the UN Security Council would do the same. Later that morning, I attended a meeting of the Supreme National Council of Reconciliation of Cambodia in which Sihanouk presided as head of state, UN Special Representative Akashi presided as co-chairman, and the Perm Five representatives were all in attendance. Khieu Samphan attended for the Khmer Rouge and spoke arrogantly, calling for provisions that were above and beyond those already agreed upon. The meeting was a formal passing of power, grasped out of the air, to the newly designated but not yet accepted king of Cambodia. It was followed by a constitutional convention and then lunch. Sihanouk did most of the talking. Among other things, he said that the UN transition authority for Cambodia would be needed for a long time, and he urged us not to leave until the process was well underway. He called for numerous bottles of champagne to be opened and drunk, making many toasts. So ended the initial effort to reestablish Cambodia as a nation state.

Sihanouk did accept the role of king and maintained palatial residences at Phnom Penh, the capital of Cambodia, and in Pyongyang, North Korea. The Cambodian government remained divided; the different factions alternated representatives to the UN one month at a time. When the going gets tough, Sihanouk disappears, sheltered either by the Chinese or the North Koreans, until it is safe to return. His wife, Her Royal Highness Princess Monique, has spent a large part of her time in Paris, where she had become something of a grande dame.

Much in the manner of a Greek tragedy, Cambodia progresses slowly. In the UN, we worked on the Cambodia issue continuously. The French, once the colonial power in Cambodia, had a dinner specifically to talk about Cambodia and to make sure we were all singing the same tune, especially about the Khmer Rouge and our support of King Sihanouk. However, Cambodia became less and less important in the worldwide scheme of things. In the national characteristics of that area of Southeast Asia, the Cambodians are the most peaceful-minded, endowed with a Khmer gentleness. The Vietnamese are harder, resilient, tough, and more industrious and warlike. Consequently, the Chinese, the Laotians, the Thais, and the Cambodians all fear the Vietnamese. My prediction is that the greatest threat to peace in that area will come from Vietnam.

Continuing the official tour, my next stop was Beijing, where, to T. J.'s chagrin, we began the day with a good Chinese breakfast—*kung di soup*, spring
rolls, pickles, steamed dumplings, and Chinese tea. Vice Foreign Minister Tiam
Zengpei hosted us at a great dinner. In that informal setting, I managed to
deliver a majority of my talking points: UN reform, budgets, and adherence to
human rights; Security Council work on disarmament; North and South
Korean relations; and the bilaterals on Yugoslavia and the need for Serbia and
Montenegro to seek UN membership. I made these points because China had
abstained from the resolution inviting Croatia, Bosnia-Herzegovina, and Slovenia into the UN as separate countries. I also brought up women's issues, a subject not always accepted by the Chinese as anyone's business except their own.
I noted in my diary that the Chinese reacted harshly to my mention of the
"Spratlys," a group of islands in the North Pacific claimed by China, Japan, and
the Philippines.

In 1992, the feeling in China was that the United States was not being totally
fair in its criticism of China's human-rights practices. I was there, in part, to
see how these two large nations with some influence on the rest of the world
can live together and work together peacefully. The issues that would affect the
relationship between China and the United States for some time to come were
human rights, trade, women's issues, equal pay for equal work, not using
prison labor in factories, and removing enslaved conditions. The note-taker at
one session whispered to me that the minister had not answered one of my
questions. "He is not going to do so," I replied. I have known Chinese people
for a long time, and when they feel a subject is none of our business, they do
not comment. They just don't say anything.

One of my duties in Beijing was to attend the opening of one of the world's
largest McDonald restaurants near Tiananmen Square. Sarah came down from
Nanking, where she was studying, to visit me. I saw a young woman wearing a
Chinese student's uniform and a pigtail down her back, and for a second I did
not recognize her as my daughter. Her Chinese was so fluent that she was able
to argue her way past the hotel desk and register to stay with me in my suite,
despite the fact that her student I.D. had expired and she had not received governmental permission to stay at the hotel.

In November, Bill Clinton was elected president, which ended the administration of George H. W. Bush. As Lucy and I watched the election results on television, I felt pride in the American people as we peacefully went about the job of changing presidents and passing the torch to a new administration. I have dealt with different countries for so long and have seen so much turmoil over the wrestling for power that I rejoice in our system, which permits the transfer of power peacefully. That peaceful transition is absent from so many countries in the world that one could easily lose hope. Our system gives me sustenance each day that I live and work as a servant of the people and wage war for peace.

The two-fold speculation was that (1) the new president would not give much attention to foreign affairs, which indeed was true early in his administration, and (2) Clinton probably would want me to stay on at the UN, a guess that was completely wrong. One day in mid December, I heard on the TV news that President Clinton had announced that Madeleine Albright would be his new ambassador to the UN.

"We tried to get them to get word to you and to us before they made the announcement," Eagleburger told me. "They were completely oblivious." To hear of the appointment this way was an extreme discourtesy and annoyed me mightily. New Secretary of State Warren Christopher apologized to me later. So did Tim Wirth, a personal friend of the president, who called it an unacceptable breach of courtesy. A young staffer on the campaign trail with the president had advised him differently: "We don't have to say anything [to Perkins]," she said. "He's the enemy." Because I had been appointed to the USUN post by a Republican president. "This is a political act," an outraged friend protested to me. "It's a political post," I replied.

On Christmas Eve, my family and I walked through the cold winter night to attend midnight Mass at St. Patrick's Cathedral, a couple of blocks from the Waldorf-Astoria. We were given reserved seats on the front rows, joining Ambassador Irv Hicks, New York mayor David Dinkins and his wife, and former New York mayor Edward Koch. John Cardinal O'Connor officiated and gave special recognition to Lucy and me, and to my work at the USUN. I was grateful for his prayers.

As 1992 ended, several of the same issues that I had dealt with since my arrival as perm rep were still active and not totally resolved—Yugoslavia, Somalia, the Middle East, Cambodia, and South Africa, to name some. On the last day of the year, the final two issues compelling my attention in the Security

Council were Iraq and Israel. Israel had expelled eighty-two Palestinians into Lebanon, claiming they were aiding and abetting unrest. The Non-Aligned Movement (NAM), organization of over one hundred countries who are not formally aligned with or against any major power bloc, was intent on a resolution in the Security Council condemning Israel for its action. The United States took the lead in developing a resolution that we considered to be rather balanced. It did not satisfy either side, but the Palestinians were the unhappiest. Operating through the NAM, they considered it far too soft. After meeting with the NAM caucus, I reported back to Washington. Following consultation with Washington, I again met with the NAM caucus and told them that the U.S. position on the peace process had not changed and that we would continue to be an honest broker. The caucus then met, redesigned some sentences, and was prepared to delete offending language.

I contacted Washington to sell it. There I learned that we had not exactly been negotiating in good faith. Washington really did not want a resolution, Under Secretary of State Arnold Kantor told me. Evidently we had been playing for time, but I was not told. The NAM caucus then came back saying the statement was so watered down, negotiations were being postponed. I called Kantor and told him that he had his wish—the statement was not going to happen.

I scrambled to tie up as many issues as I could before the January 21 presidential inauguration. Madeleine Albright and I had settled on a transition date at the end of January. I would leave one day and she would arrive the next. My tenure as perm rep had ended as abruptly as it began. Lucy and I shipped our things, packed up the car, and drove to Washington, where I was given an office, a secretary, and temporary assignments.

At age sixty-five, I had two choices. I could retire from the Foreign Service, or I could be assigned to another ambassadorial post.

AUSTRALIA
DOWN UNDER AND BEYOND

I wanted another overseas assignment. The much-coveted Australia ambassadorship was available, and I asked for it. More than that, I lobbied for it. Australia is the only post I ever sought.

I was offered the mission in Switzerland, but I turned it down because I felt I would have little to do there. Switzerland is a nice place to be, but I could not envision spending three years on an assignment that seemed to me to be much like an extended vacation.

I had always wanted to go to Australia, a country at the end of the world and a staunch political ally. The United States has maintained relations with Australia in six shooting wars (World War I, World War II, Korea, Vietnam, the Persian Gulf War, and the Iraq War). Australia is the anchor of the ANZUS Treaty—a defense security pact among Australia, New Zealand, and the United States for the Pacific region. John Foster Dulles was secretary of state when this pact was signed in 1951. The treaty established an alliance for Australia and the United States to share defense technologies and intelligence, notably at the Joint Defense Facilities at Pine Gap, Australia.

My getting the appointment was a long shot. The Australia ambassadorship ordinarily is given as a reward for large monetary contributions to political parties. I was a career ambassador, not a campaign contributor, and I had never even met President Clinton. I fully expected someone on Clinton's staff to say, "Who does this guy think he is?" Two secretaries of state—Warren Christopher and Eagleburger—argued persuasively on my behalf, a couple of other people joined in, and lo and behold, the president appointed me.

The press repeatedly wondered why in print. Since the Aboriginals are a subject of embarrassment to most white Australians, some questioned why Clinton was sending a black American as ambassador. Some supposed that the appointment was my payoff for the difficult assignments I had had throughout my career. I accepted the answer President Clinton gave. When I met the president, it was in the company of Australia's prime minister, Paul Keating, who was in Washington on an official visit. President Clinton introduced us at a luncheon and said, "Prime Minister, this is one of our best Foreign Service officers I'm sending you. It is an indication of what we think of the relationship between our two countries." The Australians were delighted that they were getting a career officer. They had only one before, Marshall Green in 1965. Gough Whitlam, who was prime minister at the time, believed then and forever after that President Nixon had sent Ambassador Green to watch him and to prevent him and his government from straying too far to the left politically.

The appointment papers were more complicated than ever before, and it was October 1993 before I completed clearance and arrived in Australia. The U.S. Embassy is always located in a nation's capital city, so in Australia the embassy is in Canberra. This is where Lucy and I settled into the ambassador's residence. In 1942, during World War II, Eleanor Roosevelt visited Canberra to check on the construction of the American Embassy. President Roosevelt wanted the embassy to represent a specific period in American history, and he chose the Williamsburg period. Consequently, the American Embassy in Canberra is reminiscent of Virginia, and the building is a magnificent structure. Mrs. Roosevelt planted the first tree on the lawn, and it has grown into a magnificent oak. When she declared that the fireplaces in the official residence would not draw and asked the Australian architect to change them, he refused. When Lucy and I built a fire in the winter, we noted that the fireplaces worked fine. The tree Mrs. Roosevelt planted is now a magnificent oak. A great luxury of this residence is its heated swimming pool, which was especially important to me because it provided my primary exercise. Both of my knees were deteriorating, and other forms of exercise were difficult.

The official residence in Canberra is surrounded by a great expanse of land, so I asked the gardeners to plant a vegetable garden and showed them how to do it. I have loved mustard greens from the time they were a staple on my grandfather's farm, so we grew mustard greens in my Australian garden. The cooks learned to prepare them just as my grandmother had, simmered slowly with chunks of pork. My grandmother used salt pork and cooked the greens in a big, iron pot suspended over the fireplace. We grew so many greens on the farm that she would keep the fire going for four or five hours.

At a luncheon for the prime minister of Australia, one of the first things President Clinton asked me was "What size shoe do you wear?" Secretary of State Warren Christopher joined us.

Occasionally the American Embassy does what it can to support community fundraising, and we did so in Canberra by opening the ambassador's residence to the public in an event for the Red Cross. The morning of the residential tour, Lucy examined the gardens and discovered that the gardeners had not finished weeding. Before the public arrived, I found myself out in the garden pulling weeds. The gardeners never made that mistake again.

The United States also has consuls general in Melbourne, Perth, and Sydney and a one-person consulate in Brisbane, since closed. Australia is a large country, comprising six states and with jurisdiction over seven islands and territories, including the Australian section of Antarctica. I crossed the Australian continent many times, visiting the consuls and meeting as many Australian citizens as possible. I came to champion the cause of the Norfolk Islanders, and I was particularly involved with the issues of the Aboriginal people. I concentrated on health-delivery services for the Aboriginals, as well as governance, law and order, education, and culture—the glue that links communities. I also supported Aboriginal art, music, and architecture.

Australia is an island-continent, renowned as the smallest, flattest, and, with the exception of Antarctica, driest continent in the world. It is also one of the most urbanized countries on the globe, with about 70 percent of the population living in the country's ten largest cities. Despite the fact that its land mass is almost comparable to that of the United States, its population is considerably smaller. Australia's population is 20 million, compared to the United States' roughly 296 million. The continent's isolation for millions of years resulted in a zoological delight of rare flora, fauna, animals, and birds—kangaroo, koala, platypus, flightless emu, waratah (the floral emblem of New South Wales), and banksia trees.

Whenever I called on Prime Minister Keating, either in Canberra or in Sydney, we discussed United States–Australia relations. The prime minister said they could not be better. "Obviously a country with only one-fifteenth of the population of the United States can't compete with the United States, but we can do some things out here that you as a big power can't do. Indonesia is one country where we can do that. You must not ignore 190 million people." He meant that Indonesia is a big country in Australia's neighborhood, and the United States must have a positive relationship with that country, with which Australia could help. He was true to his word.

Many Americans, I discovered, think Australians are all like Crocodile Dundee, a rugged Outback character much like our own Davy Crockett, or they imagine the national character of Australia to be much like our own in the United States. Not at all. There is a big difference between the two countries, although it may not be immediately apparent. When we step off the plane in Sydney or Melbourne or Perth, at first glance it looks much like America: Kentucky Fried Chicken, McDonald's, Toys R Us, IBM, Citibank, the Bank of America—it's all there. The root of the differences in national character lies in the political histories of the two countries.

I have often said in speeches that America is a revolutionary society, with a certain fiber of civil disobedience. It is this revolutionary spirit that has allowed our imperfect society to continue to grow as a nation. Australia is a British Commonwealth nation. My credentials were addressed to "Her Majesty, Queen Elizabeth II, Queen of Australia." For a moment, I thought a mistake had been made, and then I remembered that her representative is not the prime minister, but the governor general of Australia, to whom I presented my credentials in 1993. Australia is a nation with a reverence for its attachment to the United Kingdom and the queen. At tea with a monarchist, I learned that he and his wife did not want a president like the American president, with the powers of the American president. "Australia needs to grow into that situation," he said. "We are evolving toward independence." I reminded him that Americans did not grow into independence; we took it. "That's the difference between Australia and America," he said. "We've never had a revolution in Australia, so there is a distinct difference between your having taken your independence and our evolving as we have."

An Australian woman asked me if the president of the United States could appoint someone to the cabinet who is not a member of Congress. The president cannot appoint a member of Congress to the cabinet unless that member resigns from Congress, I told her; that is the separation of powers defined by the Constitution. She was flabbergasted. "Then how does he control the party?" she asked. "He doesn't control the party," I said. "The party recognizes that if it is unified, everybody benefits. The party has to be unified to gain the White House." I told her that the makers of the Constitution, especially Jefferson, Washington, Monroe, and Hamilton, were steeped in the teachings of John Locke, who postulated that the law of God did not intend for men to exercise tyranny over one another. They based the Constitution on this theory, the most important part of which is the separation of powers to keep it in balance. The judiciary is separate from both the legislature and from the executive. She listened to all of this and said, "I am learning from you something that I have never heard of." It was not the first time I had heard such incredulity from a non-American. The system of the United States is based so much on faith that a foreigner finds it difficult to understand how it can function effectively. Not effectively, I reply, but rather, democratically.

Australians are similar to Americans, I found, in their openness, love of life, strong work ethic, and equally strong dislike of being constrained. A difference in our national characters is that Americans place more value on individual achievement. We tend to be competitive and goal driven. Australians, by contrast, seem to feel that one should not get too far ahead of one's contemporaries. In Australia

I came to be good friends with writer Colleen McCullough, who told me that she left her native Australia because she felt a bias against achievement in general and a particular bias against women achievers. Jim Wolfensohn, president of the World Bank, left Australia for essentially the same reason; he needed to feel a sense of societal value on individual accomplishment. I empathize with them. I think it an absolute must that each of us achieve to the best of our abilities. This is the opposite of what communism generally advocates, which is that individual achievement creates imbalances and injustices. That is untrue. The greatest protection I can have is for every individual to be all he or she can be. I have always had a strong will to achieve. I have to achieve to stay alive mentally and physically. I believe it is natural to strive to achieve, that to deny this impulse is like denying water to a growing plant.

Australia is an enormous country. Western Australia, the most vocally independent of the six states, is as far from Canberra as California is from Washington, D.C. It takes as much time to travel from Perth to Canberra as it does from San Francisco to Washington, D.C. The independent nature of Western Australia reminded me of the American West, with its independent attitude regarding issues such as water rights and cattle grazing. When I visited the exhibition hall in Western Australia, I saw prominently displayed a book titled *Secession: the Case of Western Australia*. I asked my host, Western Australia's premier, Richard Court, if it had been put there for my benefit. He just smiled and did not answer. Some, but by no means all, of the recent debate in Australia about Aboriginal rights is in Western Australia.

THE ABORIGINALS

When my mother visited us in Australia, she asked, "Where are the people?" She meant black people. There were few to be seen. As a white nation, Australia was similar to South Africa, except that blacks are the minority in Australia. Aboriginal and Torres Strait Island people total less than 2 percent of the Australian population. Only about 400,000 of the Australia population are black. Blacks in Australia, however, are much worse off in terms of preparation to participate in government or the economy than the blacks of South Africa. Australian whites are superior in technology, education, and numbers. They will be forced to make changes, which will give the Aboriginals a step up the ladder, but I predict that the white population of Australia will be in control for a long time to come.

In my first staff meeting at the embassy, I announced a new policy. There was only one black employee at the time, so I told the personnel officer, "I want to see a multiethnic embassy, and I want you to hire some Aboriginals. I want to get to know as many Aboriginals as I can, and I want to go and see them where they are."

One of our jobs at the American Embassy was to create more awareness in Australia of this minority, the first Australians, to make sure their plight received attention, and to include them in our cultural events. If American musicians, writers, or painters were visiting, we made sure they met their Aboriginal counterparts in a cultural exchange. I urged visiting American representatives to learn about the black Australians.

European Australians refer to nonwhite Australians as Aboriginals, not as Australians. Soon after I arrived in Australia, I received a briefing on the Mabo Land Title Decision from the High Court, the resolution of a suit against the government by a Torres Strait Islandsr, Eddie Mabo. This decision confirmed the Australian Aborigines' title to land if they could show consistent residency since the beginning of their existence in Australia. Since the Aboriginals can prove conclusively that they have been on the land for more than sixty thousand years, the High Court nullified the claim of *tera nullus*, or empty land, which is what European Australians had maintained. The Mabo decision would cause increasing frustration among the white Australians.

Some months later, I went to Palm Island, an Aboriginal settlement just off the coast of Queensland, to participate in a tribal ceremony that closed a colorful tale. About 115 years earlier, Barnum and Bailey circus arranged to have six Aboriginal men come to the United States. Some say the men were kidnapped from Palm Island and exhibited as savages. One of them by the name of Tambo Tambo contracted pneumonia and died in Cleveland, Ohio. The circus left town, but the body remained behind in a Cleveland funeral home. Barnum and Bailey would not allow the other five to bury the man with honor in the Aboriginal tradition, which would have exorcised evil spirits according to their belief. Over the century, the body mummified, forgotten in a basement. When it was discovered, the Australian Embassy in Washington was notified, and arrangements were made to return the remains to Palm Island. There a shaman would exorcise the demons from the body, and Tambo Tambo's spirit would be at peace. It was my job to represent the U.S. government in officially handing over the body to the Australians.

Lucy and I arrived on the day of the funeral, February 23, 1994, and were met by representatives of the island's thirty-five Aboriginal tribes. The body had been put in a miniature boat, taken out into the harbor, and then allowed to float back to shore. I received the remains from this little boat and physically handed them to the tribal representative. My official role was over, but I stayed on and joined the procession that marched from the pier toward the mountain that had been designated as a sacred place for the remains of Tambo Tambo.

We reached a fork in the road. Here, I had been instructed earlier, I would be expected to go with the women, children, and the uninitiated to the hotel, where a feast would be held once the burial was over. Instead, the tribal representative asked me and my associate to join them, so we continued the march to the top of the hill. Three clergymen were among the procession. Two of them represented Christianity, and one was a fetish priest representing Paganism. Each had a role in the burial ceremony. The day was still, but suddenly I distinctly felt a rustle in the air, like a wind passing among us. As the body was lowered into the ground, everything grew quiet; there was no sound at all, and no leaves moved, but the breeze swept by. We completed the burial with each of us throwing a shovelful of dirt onto the coffin and then began our walk back down the hill. I asked the tribal senior elder if he had noticed anything unusual taking place while we were there. "Yes," he said, "the wind. That was the spirit of Tambo Tambo finally coming to rest at last."

After the resplendent feast, I was given a tour of the island. I had just experienced the mystical side of the Aboriginals. Now I was about to witness the physical degradation of the tribes.

"I want to see your problems," I told my tribal guide.

"The biggest problem we have is welfare," he said. People did not have to work to subsist. I learned about the extensive drug abuse and alcoholism among the young people, especially among the young Aboriginal men; the high suicide rate; unbridled sex and rampant teenage pregnancies; and what they called "Saturday night massacres," which was violence resulting from drunkenness. Education was not valued. In the last ten years, I was told, only one teenager had left the island to go to the university.

"What is the answer?" I asked him.

"I don't know," he said. "We seem to be getting deeper and deeper into

despair. When the government controlled this place, they promoted agriculture. We had rice, beans, corn, and other things the government harvested and
sold on the mainland. The government gave it up, and we have not been able to
replace it. Nobody wants to work that hard. And, we have not been able to agree
on how the island is to be managed. Tambo's funeral is the first time we've been
able to get together on a single purpose. Maybe this is a good thing. Maybe it will
bring us together."

What I saw in Palm Island was a lack of hope. Palm Island was a mirror of the
larger Aboriginal community, which has been harmed by welfare, which the
government intended as a benevolent policy. I saw similarly bleak conditions in
the Aboriginal district of Sydney. This area is much like Crossroads in South
Africa. Both areas seemed to me to lack a work ethic, a can-do attitude, and a
sense of self-governance and self-reliance. How do you instill this in people?

In Australia, I think the roots of this plight can be traced to the Europeans
who, when they arrived in the 1880s, treated the Aboriginals as non-people and
did not bring them into the mainstream. It also reflects a difference in cultural
thinking. Much like Native Americans, Aboriginals prize community, whereas
the majority white culture values individualism more highly. This raises the
issue of minorities' acceptance of mainstream values. In the United States, especially in disadvantaged areas, the person who tries to succeed is often labeled a
copycat of the majority culture. It suggests that the person is trying to be something he or she is not. This mentality encourages some young black males and
young Hispanics to shy away from excelling, lest they be singled out as not fitting into their group culture.

Is this true in Australia? I do not know. I saw so many Aboriginal teenagers
destined for a life of hopelessness. Yet I saw other Aboriginal communities
whose people were determined to take matters into their own hands and fight
the tendency to sink. In Alice Springs, I met a family with two sons. The mother
was half Aboriginal, and the family had sent the boys to Canberra so they could
go to school with Europeans and, in that culture, aim at individual excellence.

One of my most extraordinary interlocutors was Lois O'Donahue, chairman
of the Aboriginal and Torres Strait Island Commission, a national civil rights
commission.[1] Lois is half Aboriginal. Because she was half white, she had been
taken away from her mother when she was young to live with a white family.
Until 1975, the national policy was to assimilate and integrate Aboriginals and
thereby destroy their culture. Thousands of Torres Strait Islander children and

Aboriginal children with European features were removed from their parents and placed with white families. Often the indigenous mothers never knew what happened to the children. In the late 1990s, a report entitled *Bringing Them Home* examined the impact of this cruel—and failed—assimilation effort. Then the national policy was changed, the Aboriginals were given the right to vote, and the government adopted a policy referred to as "taking care of the Aboriginals." This meant a welfare program in totality, from cradle to grave, in a mistaken effort to make up for past wrongs. The result was the elimination of the will to achieve, so decried by Aboriginal leaders today.

The most accomplished Aboriginal I met was Noel Pearson, a barrister in the Cook Island area who was a spokesman for Aboriginal conditions, legal needs, and relationships with the central government. I brought up his name at a dinner party with white Australian political leaders, and they dismissed him as "that radical guy." The tone was much the same white Americans might use to diminish radical minority leaders such as Russell Means or Stokely Carmichael. One day I spent six hours with Noel talking about the Aborigines. "What are your greatest problems?" I asked him. "The dole," he said. It had depleted the people's will to achieve. "We can't get rid of the dole," he said, "and we can't live with it."

When I went to Arnhem Land, the large northern area in Australia recognized as belonging to the Aboriginals, I toured the famous recreational area. Parks and rivers are government-operated, with a large part of the proceeds going to the Aboriginals who live there as heirs to the land. A white government ranger had been assigned to squire me around by plane and Land Rover. I wanted to see everything. "Mr. Ambassador," he said, "you may see some things you don't like." "Don't hide anything from me," I replied. "I've seen too much already."

I particularly wanted to meet a top Aboriginal leader in Arnhem Land, but I was stalled by a series of excuses. Then, while leaving a community center, which was much like a general store stocked with everything from essentials to liquor, my guide said, "Here is the leader now." Clearly he had been drinking for several days.

Back in the car I asked my guide, "When do the welfare checks arrive?"

"Thursday," he said.

"That's why I couldn't get an appointment with him, isn't it?" I said.

"Yes," the guide said, "when the welfare checks come in, they drink until the money is gone, usually Sunday." I saw this repeated in several Aboriginal communities. Unwittingly, the government had created a policy that was destroying a large part of the Aboriginal community. Now Australia is at a crossroads and neither the white nor the Aboriginal societies know what to do to solve the problem.

Aboriginals are almost nonexistent in Tasmania, an island south of Melbourne where the white citizens made a conscious decision to eliminate all Aboriginals. The last native-born Tasmanian Aboriginal died about ten years before I became ambassador.

In 1998, Australia made a national move toward atonement and reconciliation with activities across the country. It was a public acknowledgment of the forced removal of indigenous children from their families. The event was proclaimed National Sorry Day.

THE PACIFIC WAR

I learned immediately how reverently the Australians kindle the memory of the U.S.-Australia alliance in the Pacific War. The Battle of the Coral Sea, fought May 7 and 8, 1942, was the first major defeat of the Japanese. The Japanese Imperial Navy had set its sights on capturing Port Moresby, New Guinea, in hope of breaking the Allied line from the continental United States to Australia and thereby expanding into the South Pacific, controlling the Coral Sea, and closing off Australia. The great fleets of Japan and the United States met in those waters. Two days of heavy battle were fought solely by aircraft launched from their mighty aircraft carriers. Both sides suffered serious losses, many planes and a carrier each, but the Japanese Navy was soundly defeated and withdrew. The Battle of the Coral Sea and the Battle of Midway a month later marked the turning point in the Pacific War. They saved Australia from being invaded by the Japanese, and the Australians continue to be thankful to the Americans who came to their aid.

In Australia, the annual commemoration of the Battle of the Coral Sea is an important, almost sacred, celebration. The Australian government, the local communities, and the Australian-American Association solemnly commemorate the Australians and Americans who gave their lives during World War II to defend Australia. All in the same week, in late April or early May, simultaneous celebrations are held in Canberra, Sydney, Brisbane, Perth, Melbourne, and

Adelaide. The celebration is culminated by the Coral Sea Ball, the posh event of the season.

Every year, the White House appoints someone to represent the U.S. president at the Coral Sea Celebration. The president's representative goes one direction, the ambassador another, so there is an official representative of the president of the United States at all of the events. It happens this way year in, year out, straightforward and simple, but for some reason the White House seems always to delay in naming the president's representative. Craig Smith from the White House personnel office came for a visit, and since he was from Little Rock and a close friend of President Clinton, I asked him to use his influence with the president to get us a high-level representative for the Coral Sea ceremonies. I seemed to ask everyone I met to help with this cause. I called Vernon Jordan in Washington, another of the president's friends, and asked him to weigh in and see if he could persuade Hillary Clinton to come and represent the president. I asked for Colin Powell and U.S. Supreme Court Justice Ruth Bader Ginsburg. I suggested Jimmy Carter. I even asked for Mel Gibson, Tom Cruise, and Nicole Kidman.

In 1994, President Clinton's representative was Jack H. Watson Jr., White House chief of staff during the Carter administration, and the Australians felt slighted. He was a fine person, but not the luminary they wanted. The following year, I began early trying to get a representative of stature, someone with a title that would please the Australians. For months I devoted considerable effort to securing an appropriate representative from the United States to attend the celebration. The Australians put such stock in the ceremony that they consider it an affront to have to have a presidential representative whom they consider a minor governmental figure. Every time I met with the foreign minister or representatives of the Australian-American Association, their refrain was the same: "We want someone of substance."

Every year, we repeated this exercise, chasing around the stump for a suitable representative. Month after month, I sent repeated requests to Washington. When it became hard to accomplish, my requests grew more frequent, more urgent, and my patience grew thin. Finally, in mid-April 1995, as the ceremony was almost upon us, I made a personal call to the State Department's Bureau of East Asian and Pacific Affairs Washington. I presented a crisis scenario, and at last secured the name of the man to be the president's representative—Admiral Ronald J. Zlatoper, commander in chief of the Pacific Fleet, the world's largest navy command. I reported the selection to the Australians, and they were quite pleased. The admiral and his wife, Barry, arrived in early May 1995 for the Coral Sea celebration, and they were splendid representatives.

In 1996, Secretary of Navy John H. Dalton and his wife, Margaret, represented the president admirably. Dalton obviously had done his homework. He was up to date on issues the two countries were addressing, even touchy subjects such as agriculture subsidies for American wheat farmers. He exhibited exceptional knowledge of the history of the armed forces of Australia, especially the Royal Australian Navy.

The first event of the extended commemoration was the Coral Sea Remembrance at a monument outside the Australian defense ministry to honor the men and women of the United States armed forces who gave their lives in helping to defend Australia against a Japanese invasion. It was a moving affair. I felt humbled when I saw how the Australians conduct such ceremonies with much more seriousness than Americans.

To Australians, having "someone of substance" to represent the United States president at the Coral Sea celebration is of utmost importance. In May 1996, Secretary of the Navy John H. Dalton spoke about the "Legacy of Friendship" and read a message from President Bill Clinton at the Coral Sea Memorial Service at Canberra, Australia.

Australia's preparations for the celebration were extensive and detailed. During World War II, the largest concentration of American men and women in uniform outside of the United States were stationed at Townsville in Queensland state, the area in upper Australia nearest the battle site. In the Townsville Town Hall, the American Stars and Stripes flies alongside the Australian flag every day as a gesture of gratitude. When I visited the city of Townsville, I found several houses where Yanks had made friends and were still remembered fondly. Following the tradition of careful planning for the event, the mayor of Townsville called on me well in advance of the Coral Sea celebration to lay plans. He asked for a U.S. Air Force plane for display purposes, and I was able to accommodate him.

Later during my tour of duty in Australia, the fiftieth anniversary of the cessation of war in the Pacific was celebrated there, and the country pulled out the stops for a glorious celebration. One festivity was a big dance in Brisbane, Queensland, for which the Fifth Air Force Band was imported to play the kind of music that was popular during World War II. It was an absolute blowout. Scores of women who had been teenagers when the Yanks were stationed there came to dance with me, the American ambassador representing the United States, as a symbolic act of thanks for the dance, for the American music, and for America.

Yet the American presence in Australia during World War II was not without strife. Some Aussie soldiers resented the attention paid to American soldiers by Australian women. As in Europe, the Americans were criticized for being "overpaid, oversexed, and over here." In Brisbane in November 1942, a fight broke out among three Australian soldiers and two U.S. military police. One factor was race—local girls were dating black American soldiers. The fight escalated into a near riot that eventually included some four thousand soldiers, resulting in one death and several injuries. It is referred to as the Battle of Brisbane.

Also in Brisbane I visited the former headquarters of General Douglas MacArthur. The Australian-American Association, active since 1938, presented a plaque commemorating MacArthur. Some of the older people in the group remembered the general. He worked almost around the clock, they told me, from 7 A.M. until late at night. The huge oaken table that MacArthur used as a desk was still there. When I sat in the chair he had sat in, at the desk he had used, I felt I was on hallowed ground. The Australians harbor immense respect for MacArthur. He was passionate about his mission in the Pacific, and he could not understand why military forces were diverted to Europe when he needed them in the Pacific War.

MacArthur had no telephone in his office. Whenever he deigned to speak with someone on the telephone, he got up from his desk and walked into the next room to use it. By and large, he dispatched his subordinates to do all the telephoning. The two people MacArthur did favor with a telephone conversation were the president of the United States and the emperor of Japan.

I was invited to Albany, in Western Australia, the site of one of the United States' largest submarine bases during World War II. When Lucy and I stepped onto the train platform, we were greeted by the town crier, a retired American submariner named Homer White who had married his Aussie sweetheart after World War II and made his home in Australia. He was dressed in a costume of yore, and officially cried out, "Hear ye, hear ye. Arriving on platform number [whatever it was]—the American ambassador."

In Albany I participated in the tolling of the bell for the submarines still out to sea, all those vessels not yet returned from patrol duty. In the hushed April dawn, the bell's toll—once for each lost submarine—seemed to be searching the wide sea for the men who met their fate at the hands of the Japanese in submarine warfare. The Dawn Service began after World War I, in remembrance of the Australian and New Zealand Army Corps (ANZAC) soldiers who fought at Gallipoli during World War I. Now ANZAC Day is held every April 25 to pay honor to all Australian servicemen and women. The commemoration held at Albany is especially poignant because Albany was the last Australian land to be seen by the World War I ANZACs as they sailed off to battle. Many did not return. At the first Dawn Service at Albany in 1923, a small group gathered to watch as a man in a small dinghy cast a wreath into the waters. The wreath floated out to sea while a priest and WWI veteran spoke these words: "As the sun rises and goeth down, we will remember them." Some seventy years later, the forlorn bell of that ceremony reverberated through me.

One of the great events in Australia every year, usually in the spring, is the Air Show Down Under, a spectacular air show with planes and pilots from the American, the Russian, the Australian, the French, the British, and the German air forces. The great air show in March 1995 included a breathtaking Russian plane that took off, turned its nose vertical, and headed straight up as if it were a torpedo in the sky. I had never seen a plane go straight up in the air. In just seconds it accelerated to the speed of sound. My military representative turned to me and said, "I think we've got our work cut out for us."

In Australia, I continued the tradition of celebrating July 4, the American national holiday, with an enormous party at the official residence in Canberra. Lucy and I hosted three Fourth of July parties while in Australia, just like the ones I remembered from growing up in America—hot dogs, hamburgers, and a band. I had a distinct memory of the iced tea my grandmother made on the farm for two annual holidays—June 19 and July 4. June 19, now often known as June-teenth, is the official black holiday commemorating the emancipation of slaves by Abraham Lincoln. On those holidays the extended family gathered to clean family cemeteries and then celebrated with a picnic. For both occasions, my grandmother made a special tea with tea leaves she had cured, brewed, and sweetened, then chilled with chunks of ice purchased from the icehouse. I tried to combine both of those holidays and replicate my grandmother's ice tea for the embassy's annual party. One year, my mother attended the Fourth of July celebration in Australia, and she was in high heaven. She said she never dreamed that she would see her son living in a huge mansion with hundreds of people floating in and out.

All American ambassadors around the world celebrate the Fourth of July in some fashion, but I speculate that few get into the spirit of it as I did. I pulled out all the stops. For the 1995 party, tents were erected on the grounds; red, white, and blue colors festooned everywhere. Since July is mid-winter in Australia, blow heaters were installed in the tents for warmth. Cakes and flowers arrived from the Hyatt hotel. All sections of the embassy submitted names, and we worked on the invitation list for a month or more. We sent out more than 800 invitations and received 664 acceptances, but more people streamed in after the party began. What a grand day. A Dixieland jazz band from San Francisco was touring Australia and agreed to play pro bono in exchange for the American hol-iday fare and drinks. A female staff member gave me a pair of red, white, and blue suspenders and a Stars and Stripes tie, and I wore them for the party, stand-ing in the receiving line and greeting people with my suspenders showing. The Australian singer Colin Slater sang a cappella the Australian national anthem and then "The Star-Spangled Banner." His voice was like a thousand bells fused into an electrifying sound. The white Australian blues and jazz singer Lee Gunness, with a soul-lifting voice like Mahalia Jackson, sang "Home on the Range" and "Waltzing Matilda." If I closed my eyes I would have thought I was hearing a black woman from the American South. She told me that she had lived in New Orleans and learned to sing in Southern black churches. Almost all of the guests were Australians, but we learned of a group of nearly forty young Americans who were in the country on a tour, and we invited them to the party. They were so grateful that they stayed afterward to help clean up. I had been impressed by the dignity and solemnity of the Australians' patriotic celebrations, but when I saw the July Fourth party splayed out across the lawn, I noted how the majesty of our nation blends with the ordinary character of the United States, and I was deeply thankful to be a citizen of our country.

In the embassy we once talked about why the United States was represented in Australia, and I said, "Our reason for being here goes back to the Constitution. On my car are two flags. One is the national ensign, the Stars and Stripes, and the other is the president's flag, which has on it the Great Seal. Suppose you become an ambassador," I said to one of the officers. "Do you know what this seal means? Can you explain it to me?" She could not, but I would be surprised if more than half a dozen ambassadors can explain the flag that they fly on their car. The presidential flag looks very magisterial, and many Australian students asked me about it. By Constitutional decree, I told them, the president's representative displays the same flag as the president because the ambassador is an extension of the president. The flag is a symbol of the sovereign. The American bald eagle on the Great Seal represents the nation and signals both war and peace. In one claw the eagle holds thirteen arrows. The arrows signal "Don't tread on me." In the other claw, the eagle holds olive branches, to signify peace. The thirteen arrows, the thirteen leaves of the olive branches, and the thirteen stripes all represent the original thirteen states and the beginning of the republic. The red and blue banner in the eagle's beak reads *E Pluribus Unum*, meaning "out of many, one." The Great Seal is always in the custody of the secretary of state and in a glass case on display and available to the public in the State Department's display hall. I was a young junior officer in the Foreign Service when I first saw the Great Seal and heard the curator explain it. She was very patriotic and almost in tears by the time she finished talking. That visit and her talk have stuck with me ever since. The flag's background is blue, symbolizing the spirit of the American people. It is sky blue, reflecting America's sky's-the-limit attitude.

TRADE RELATIONS

Further solidifying the relationship between the United States and Australia was central to my duties. I spent time in Melbourne attending the National Investment and Trade Conference. In Canberra I called on representatives of the Australian Wheat Board to talk about an export-enhancement program. While I was in Australia, there was a set-to between our two countries involving the importation of wheat from the United States. The Australians were concerned that we did not exercise enough caution to ensure that we did not also export a pest indigenous to Texas. A similar issue arose regarding fruit flies coming into the United States from Australia (New South Wales and Victoria).

In Western Australia I talked with dynamic Premier Richard Court about getting more U.S. businesspeople to set up and operate businesses in Perth and Western Australia. He was convinced that they would make a profit, pay taxes, and provide employment opportunities for Australians. He is succeeding in this dream.

I worked to correct the negative impression conveyed by the Australian governmental press releases and statements from the trade minister about agricultural-export subsidies. These press releases conveyed the impression that the United States was the biggest subsidizer of agricultural exports. The United States was being pilloried in the Australian press, but the European Union countries that were even larger subsidizers escaped unscathed. "The United States' subsidized agricultural exports are a minor part of subsidized agricultural exports in the world and in this region," I told Secretary for Foreign Affairs Michael Costello. "The disproportionate attention we get in your media creates the impression among the Australian public that the United States is a main source of agricultural export subsidies. Feeding this impression does not help our relationship." Mike smiled and said, "Ed, you are right in everything you say. But you are a big country, and you can take it." We left it at that, but the Department of Foreign Affairs and Trade did try to ameliorate the situation.

I went to Hobart, Tasmania, headquarters of the Commission on the Preservation of Antarctic Marine Life (CMARL), to deliver a talk about the environment. Earlier I had learned about krill, which are small, shrimplike creatures about as big as half a human thumb and live by the millions in Antarctic waters. They are a primary food source for whales. An environment issue of CMARL is to ensure that all fifteen nations that signed the Antarctic Treaty are dedicated to preserving the food chain in Antarctic waters. I discovered that delegates from the U.S. State Department and the National Science Foundation were headed to Hobart for a CMARL conference. They were accustomed to flying into Australia for the meeting with perfunctory notification for country clearance, but without inviting the embassy. "Where does the American ambassador fit in?" I asked. After some stammering, the reply was: "I gather that you want to be involved." I said that as the senior American official in the country, I was entitled not only to be a member of the delegation but to head the delegation, and I notified Washington of that desire, which was effected. During the CMARL meeting, I met with all the nongovernmental organizations represented on Tasmania that were involved in any way with the environment—woodchips, fisheries, and forest areas. They did not know one another, but from that meeting they began to exchange information.

I spent considerable time working on the Asia Pacific Economic Cooperation (APEC) forum, which had been formed in 1989 to enhance Pacific economic growth, cooperation, and trade. The idea for APEC was developed by the faculty of the School of Economics and Political Science at the Australian National University. My sources told me that Premier Bob Hawk had adopted the idea and pushed it to what resulted as APEC, but that the faculty never received any credit. In 1994, I traveled to Djakarta to participate in the APEC forum meeting in Indonesia. While there, I spoke with U.S. Commerce Secretary Ron Brown and discussed preliminary plans for him to visit Australia. He never made it. Flying to Croatia through one of the worst storms in the area's history, he and thirty-four others were killed in a U.S. Air Force plane crash in 1996.

At a dinner in Djakarta hosted by the Indonesian minister for investment, I had just sat down when I was approached by former vice president Walter Mondale, then ambassador to Japan, who said, "Am I glad that you're here. They have to have a keynote speaker tonight, and what about you?" He was the ranking appointee of President Clinton, I argued, but he replied that he had spoken the night before, and "they want another American tonight." The subject, he said, was to be "Investment as a Foreign Policy Tool." President Clinton was also attending the APEC forum, so I suspected that Mondale had cleared this impromptu assignment with the president before approaching me. I recognized that I had lost the battle. "You owe me one," I told him. Instead of eating dinner, I jotted notes for the speech, interrupted by everybody who passed by to clap me on the shoulder and say hello. Afterward I received word that the president was pleased. It was a great experience in being prepared.

At a luncheon the next day for the prime minister of Australia, I had a good conversation with President Clinton. He always appeared comfortable and full of fun, but when I looked into his eyes I saw that he was not missing a damn thing going on around us. As we chatted, he asked what size shoe I wore. I told him 13D and he replied, "It sure is good to find someone whose feet are bigger than mine." "What size do you wear?" I asked him. He laughed and said, "13C."

I had been in Australia about two months when one of the first issues on my plate was a thorny commercial issue—landing rights for American airlines. I joined the campaign to try to persuade Australia's Department of Transport to exempt U.S. civilian official aircraft, particularly scientific research flights, from landing charges. This issue had been brought to a head by the National Science Foundation's desire to bring a C-130 to Canberra in 1995 for experiments by American, Australian, and European scientists. I told the Australian government that the U.S. policy worldwide was not to land U.S. government-owned aircraft in places where landing charges were collected. Australia was one of the few such places. If the landing charges were not lifted, the National Science Foundation might be forced to make other plans with a different location. We were given a favorable decision, and the experiments went on as scheduled.

Two U.S. airlines, United and Northwest, flew to Australia and they wanted the right to pick up passengers at intermediate points en route. Northwest petitioned for Fifth Freedom rights, a part of the International Aviation Law that entitles an aircraft to pick up passengers at intermediate points for the final destination. Northwest flew from Detroit to Osaka, Japan, and from there to Australia, but could not pick up passengers in Osaka because Australia's Quantas airline opposed it. United had a similar problem and was standing by to see the outcome of Northwest's campaign. Part of my job was to negotiate a change in this policy. My staff in the embassy's commercial section worked hard with me on this, and just before Christmas 1993, Australia's chief negotiator called to tell me that the government was prepared to grant American air carriers Fifth Freedom Rights. It was a triumph, and my staff and I met with the Australians to toast the decision and praise the civility of their decision. Then we all went back to work.

I kept waiting to hear a word of appreciation from Northwest, the airline that had initiated the request and which had pushed us to lean heavily on the Australians, but none came. I called the State Department and asked, "Have you heard from Northwest? Are they happy or what?" In March, I learned second-hand that Northwest had decided the Australia route was too expensive and was closing it. Surely they had known this all along. My officers were crushed. I sent a hot rocket back to the State Department saying, "This is absolutely unacceptable. Just unacceptable. Northwest needs to say something to the officers at State, Treasury, and Commerce in Washington and in the embassy here who worked all this time to get them what they wanted, and as of now, they have not had the courtesy to say a word." I never heard from them.

Some time after that I ran into Ambassador Mondale and reminded him that he owed me a favor. Not only was Northwest Airline's hub in Minneapolis, Mondale's city, but he sat on the board of Northwest. I told him the story and he was incredulous.

"You haven't heard from them?" he asked.

"Not a word."

"Leave it to me," he said. Two months later I saw him in Hawaii and told him that I had still had not heard either from Northwest or from him. "Leave it to me," he said. I have yet to hear from Northwest or from Mondale on the subject, and to my knowledge, the State Department and the embassy are still waiting. We could change Australia's commercial policy, but we could not wrangle a courteous communication from this American corporation. From that day, I have never flown on Northwest.

VISITORS

Part of an ambassador's job is receiving official visitors from the United States, and we welcomed a number of congressional representatives and other distinguished visitors in Australia. Secretary General Boutros-Ghali of the United Nations and a group traveling with him stopped en route elsewhere to hear a report from the Australian government about the propriety of further nuclear testing. The French had decided to have these tests in the South Pacific, which created boycotts against the French Embassy in Canberra. Robert McNamara, as intense personally as he is professionally, served on the commission, and he was among the party who heard the results of the report. One morning about five o'clock while I was walking around Lake Burley Griffin, I met McNamara out power-walking and dripping with sweat. Here before me, I thought, is a man possessed.

Edwin Moses, an Olympic gold medallist who was recognized as one of the greatest track-and-field athletes in history, was then working for the Olympic Committee, and he came by to meet on Olympic business. Sydney would host the Olympic Games in 2000.

The nongovernmental activist Ralph Nader came to Australia to deliver a series of lectures. He spoke well, but I had the impression that he had run out of issues. He spoke in opposition to the new World Trade Organization, but not for any real quantifiable reason that I could ascertain.

I hosted a reception in honor of Dr. Ray Marshall, secretary of labor in Carter's administration, a consultant, and a University of Texas professor. It was a distinct joy getting to know this man, whom I consider one of the best secretaries of labor, whose sole peer is Frances Perkins, who served under President Franklin D. Roosevelt. At my invitation, General John Shalikashvili, chairman of the Joint Chiefs of Staff, visited Australia. He was committed to maintaining good relations between the United States and Australia, and his visit was of immense value.

Supreme Court Justice Antonin Scalia held forth in brilliant conversation at a small luncheon to which I had invited my deputy chief of mission, Karen Weaver, and two young Australian legal practitioners who tried to challenge Justice Scalia. It became clear immediately that they were outmatched—Karen said she was made speechless by his wisdom—and lunch proceeded in conversation that was both fascinating and eclectic. He was a refreshing delight. I had invited the justice to stay at the residence during his three-day trip. He breakfasted with me each morning. Our talks were a rare experience, similar to a seminar on ethics, history, legal matters, and the challenges facing modern society.

Edward Teller, father of the hydrogen bomb and a founder of nuclear physics, arrived to open a conference on breast-cancer awareness for his friend, Gina Rinehart. I also invited Dr. Teller to stay at the residence. A Hungarian refugee, Dr. Teller was a massive man who walked with a shepherd's staff. He was taller than I, craggy, with pronounced eyebrows and lots of white hair. He was about eighty-six years old, and I thought he might like to retire early that evening. "Not at all," he said. "I want to talk." This was slightly daunting to me. What could I talk about with a famous scientist? I looked up his biography in *Who's Who,* and it was about three pages long. He was a man of lively curiosity, and he wanted to know about me and the Foreign Service. When I confessed that I did not know what to say to him, he said, "The same thing you say to anybody else."

"Do you have any second thoughts about inventing the H-bomb?" I asked.

"No," he said. "Someone had to invent it. It was out there to be invented. I think it is better for a nation that is as responsible as the United States to have invented the H-bomb. It is good that we have it because we are not going to use it. As long as we've got it, other nations will be very careful about how they develop it and subsequently use it."

He was opening the breast cancer awareness conference, he told me, because he was a close friend with Gina's father, Lane Rinehart, another Hungarian refugee. "I am not an expert on breast cancer," he said, "but when I developed the H-bomb, I developed a special camera to be used in the detection process. This camera can isolate minute portions of anything. I wondered if we could use this camera to isolate portions of a breast that is heir to breast cancer, to avoid those terribly invasive procedures that are in practice so a woman need not lose all of her breast but only one small portion. I tried it and it works." He described this as a biopsy system for detecting cancer in the breast in the hopes of obviating the need for mastectomies. There was an interest in having noted physicist Edward Teller come to Canberra to speak about breast cancer awareness. "It is important for people to know that I am not interested in killing people," he said. "I am interested in preserving people."

We talked for about an hour and a half that evening, and the next morning he was up as early as I, about five o'clock, ready to continue our conversation about the H-bomb from the night before.

At a Melbourne charity event jointly hosted by Boston and Melbourne, the speaker representing the city of Boston was Michael Kennedy, second son of the late Robert Kennedy. Michael was full of life, exuding confidence and a little cockiness, and he was full of praise for Melbourne. He gave a great speech. His ebullient presence transformed the dinner into the kind of activity that adds to the zest of the relationship between the United States and Australia. When we were introduced, he said, "I have wanted to meet you ever since I heard you were going to South Africa. That fit my idea of courage." Personal courage was one attribute the Kennedy family has manifested in many ways. The next morning I happened to see Michael in the hotel's executive dining room. He had just showered after jogging, and came into the dining room dressed in a bathrobe and slippers. "Ambassador," he said, "I was hoping I would see you here. I have something which I am sure my father would want you to have." He pulled out of his bathrobe pocket a little paperweight with an excerpt from a speech Robert

Kennedy had given in Soweto, South Africa, in 1966. The paperweight was inscribed with this quotation from Archimedes: "Each time a man stands up for an ideal, or acts to improve the lot of others, or strikes out against injustice, he sends forth a tiny ripple of hope, and crossing each other from a million different centers of energy and daring, those ripples build a current which can sweep down the mightiest walls of oppression and resistance."[2] Michael paid me a great compliment when he said that his father would have been proud that I had represented the United States as ambassador to South Africa. Three years later, Michael was killed in a skiing accident. It was almost unfathomable to think that his unbridled energy was stilled.

In November 1994, former President George H. W. Bush and former First Lady Barbara arrived for a speaking tour sponsored by Citibank. Lucy and I escorted them around Melbourne and Sydney. His speech at the luncheon I attended was superb. He spoke about leadership, a moral stance, and the value of family and friends. I could see that he was reconciled to passing the baton to his sons, Jeb and George W., and he spoke of them glowingly and respectfully. The Bush visit was invaluable in further cementing relationships between the United States and Australia. Before they left, I thanked President Bush for the honor of his appointments, as director general of the Foreign Service and as ambassador of the United States to the United Nations. And I thanked him and Barbara Bush for the service they have given to our country and for what they continue to do to advance the cause and fortunes of the United States.

Travel

As in my other assignments, as ambassador to Australia I traveled widely across the country. Since many people think of Australia as a whites-only country, some saw my presence as a lesson in diversity. I went everywhere. I believed that it was important for the people of Australia to see the American ambassador all over the country, without pretentiousness, pomp, or ceremony. I often reduced the number of people traveling with me so that it would not be seen as an entourage. In this way I saw more than I would have had I been surrounded by people. Sometimes Lucy and I would hop on a small plane and drop down to visit Aboriginal villages. When Sarah visited from Thailand, where she was teaching school, she joined us. We visited Broome, a village near Papua, New Guinea, where the Aboriginals live in degradation. We went to Turkey's Creek, arriving at 10 A.M., which is just about teatime. Water in a big cast-iron tub was being boiled over an open fire. It was the same kind of tub my grandmother washed clothes in on the farm. A huge cake, a large crock of butter, and a pot of jam were nearby. Lucy and Sarah looked at me as if to ask, "Are we really going to do this?" I stepped forward and made a cup of billy tea—a dipper of boiling water poured over leaves of bush tea—cut a slab of cake, slathered it with butter and jam and handed it to Lucy. Then I made one for Sarah and for myself. Whenever I think of teatime, I remember the billy tea in Turkey's Creek. I have been told repeatedly that the Aboriginals still talk about me. I was the only American ambassador they had ever seen.

We saw the famous tourist sights—the Great Barrier Reef and the stunning Ayers Rock, known now by its Aboriginal name Uluru. In New South Wales we rode in open-sided vehicles to visit the beautiful Snowy Mountains by way of Coomba Park and Thredbo, traveling through a snowstorm though it was December and in the middle of summer. In Kangaroo Valley we stayed overnight in a bed and breakfast located in a valley near a small creek, which Lucy commented was not a good feng shui location. In Hunter Valley, I toured coal mines, including the Peabody Mine, operated by an American company, and met with the United Mine Workers union. There I saw an excellent mining activity, highly productive, but heard concerns from the miners about personnel issues. I am not quite sure why they brought it to my attention, but I spoke to the mine operators about it, who were somewhat surprised at my knowledge and involvement.

I took the C-12 turboprop, our embassy airplane, to Alice Springs in the Northern Territory, which is an enormous expanse of desert. The place is as flat as a griddle with a clear sky for about 350 days of the year. We flew over miles and miles of red, dry land, stopping en route at Leigh Creek, pronounced "crick" by the local citizens. Leigh Creek looked like a storybook post—a little station with fuel and amenities such as cigarettes, toothpaste, and candy. It was an oasis in the desert, run by a woman whose job it is to refuel planes. It was 40 degrees Centigrade (about 101 degrees Fahrenheit) when I arrived, with a totally cloudless sky and no humidity. Incredibly, the woman had rigged a little watering system for a small garden of flowers at the station. The Northern Territory of Australia was like another world. I was seeing it much as it must have been a million years ago, and yet this woman had managed to bridge today and yesterday through her garden spot in the middle of the desert.

The United States' interest in the northwest cape is the potential for offshore drilling for gas. One U.S. company that has an activity in this lonely but lovely area is Phillips Petroleum. In Western Australia, I visited Exmouth to tour the naval base Her Majesty's Australian Ship *Holt* (H.M.A.S. *Holt*), named for an Australian prime minister, Harold E. Holt, who lost his life while swimming in rough seas off the coast of Melbourne. Originally the base was formerly occupied by the U.S. Navy, but in 1993 it was transferred to the Australian government. All of the American troops were gone when I visited. The commanding officer, Captain Crispin George, carved a piece of scrimshaw for me to commemorate the visit, which I keep on my desk at home.

The Solar Observatory Station is located in Exmouth. Its primary purpose, of course, is to observe solar activity primarily, but it also observes satellites, planes, and unmanned flying objects. The observation station, operated jointly by the U.S. and Australian governments, is the best cooperation I have ever seen between two governments. The personnel live in trailers specially built to withstand the extreme heat of the area. I was so interested in the work of the observatory that Major Cecilia "Celia" Askue of the U.S. Air Force spent about two hours talking with me about the solar system and the sun's effect on weather. That evening, at a party on the Indian Ocean beach, Lucy and I witnessed the spectacular view of a simultaneous moonrise and sunset. This occurs only once a year, and we happened to be there at exactly the right time. The next day, we continued our trip along the pristine coastline in the sparsely populated northwest cape. In Perth, I was pleased to see the environmentally conscious efforts of Alcoa at its bauxite-mining facilities, one of the largest in the world. Bauxite is mined close to the surface, much like strip mining, but this U.S. aluminum corporation is restoring environmental areas, trying to keep the ecosystem exactly as it was found. I came away convinced that Alcoa's concern for the environment and ecosystem represents a role of corporate America for the future.

In the rugged western area, I met with the two associations of pastoralists and graziers, which is how they describe sheepherders and cattlemen. One big farm that I visited included twenty-five thousand acres, thirty-thousand sheep, and several thousand cattle. It was worked by a man, his wife, and a handyman with a helicopter and several trucks. I found Western Australia to be a macho, can-do state, proud of its ability to get along without the help of "those people back east." I called on as many ministers of state government as I could find and, to a person, they were all independent-minded. Gas and oil are the industries up in the northwest, and fishing is in abundance in the south. Western Australia also has the Margaret River and some of the finest wineries in the world. A great concert is held annually in the Margaret River area, and when I was there I heard the complaint that when singer Gladys Knight was the guest artist, she accepted the fee, demanded a pink dressing room with a pink toilet, but got in a car and left for the airport as soon as the concert was over. Margaret River people were still smarting over the fact that she had not stayed to mix and mingle.

We rode a small prospector train to Kalgoorlie, a former gold rush town, where the custom of dressing for dinner was like stepping back in time. Women there might wear overalls and boots during the day, but in the evening they put on frocks for dinner. Men donned ties, opened a bottle of whiskey for a drink, then joined the ladies at the table. I learned that President Herbert Hoover had worked in Coolgardie and Kalgoorlie gold mines as a young engineer in the 1890s. It is said that he lived on sardines and cocoa and traveled by camels and horses.

In Kalgoorlie, he resided at the Palace Hotel; Kalgoorlians still talk about his crush on a young barmaid. He wrote her a poem extolling his love for her, and it is now framed and proudly displayed in the bar. Some years later, Hoover bought a floor-to-ceiling mirror in San Francisco and sent it back to Kalgoorlie in gratitude for the hospitality he had enjoyed there. It is installed in the foyer of the Palace Hotel.

From Kalgoorlie, Lucy and I traveled on the Indian Pacific train across Australia. From Perth, Western Australia, to Adelaide, South Australia, the train trip was thirty-two hours. There was nothing to see but endless flat, dry, treeless plains with a raw beauty of its own—and millions of rabbits. Rabbits had been imported early from England and because they have no natural predator in Australia, they have multiplied. And multiplied. Nothing has controlled them—not poison, not fences, not even the introduction of rabbit stew from Ireland. The only civilization we saw on that sparse land were occasional camps of railroad engineers living in trailers and stationed there to service the train.

In Adelaide, the City of Churches, the governor of South Australia was Her Excellency Dame Roma Mitchell, a tall, stately woman about eighty years old. Dame Mitchell was Australia's first woman Queen's Council, first woman supreme court judge, and the first woman governor of South Australia. At a social function, nobody knew how I was to behave around her since she did, after all, represent the queen. One certainly does not go ask the queen to dance, but saying, "I didn't get as far as I have by observing protocol all the time," I went to

Dame Mitchell and said, "Governor, would you like to dance?" She was delighted. Thank God it was a slow dance—I don't know if I could have mustered the nerve for a boogie-woogie. The Australian protocol officer tried to smile through it all, but his face was set in ice as he said, "Only the Americans."

Not far from Canberra, in a place called Tidbinbilla, is a Deep Space Network station that was the first to receive the statement from the first man on the moon. When Neil Armstrong said, "One small step for man, one giant leap for mankind," it was first heard here. When I saw this isolated station, I thought it looked like the moon itself. Because of that space station, one of the people on my staff in Canberra was a representative from the National Aeronautics and Space Administration.

Not all of my travel was limited to Australia. I was in Washington for the Australia–United States ministerial talks of 1994 and in New York the following year to address the Asia Society. Before leaving New York, the Australians wanted to pay a call on Vice President Al Gore to thank him for his help, especially on the Korean Energy Development Organization. I went with them. The party included Australia's Foreign Minister Gareth Evans, Defense Minister Robert Ray, Secretary of Foreign Affairs Costello, and the Australian Ambassador in Washington, Don Russell. We also talked Earth Day and about ANZUS. To my eye, the vice president seemed slightly artificial. He was too quick to know everything and he asked few questions. Since he fancied himself a computer whiz, he wanted to demonstrate his mastery of the Internet, but he could not boot up his computer. I think his secretary usually turned it on for him every morning, and that day she had not done so. He finally gave up and said, "Well, obviously I am not as good as I thought I was."

ANTARCTICA

One of the most exciting trips I undertook was a trek to Antarctica in 1995. I was highly excited about my first and only visit to the ice continent, which ranks as one of my most memorable experiences. Six months earlier, I had had both knees replaced with titanium joints. I worked arduously every day in physical therapy in order to be in shape to make the trip—seeing Antarctica was an opportunity I did not want to miss. Furthermore, I wanted to be the first Foreign Service officer in history to serve on all seven continents.

The first stop was Christchurch, New Zealand, headquarters of the backup station for all of our stations in Antarctica—one at McMurdo Sound, a second at the South Pole, and a third on the western side of the continent. I was briefed by the representative of the National Science Foundation and by the Navy commander about the Navy's Deep Freeze program. Before leaving New Zealand, we were given an enormous supply of Arctic clothing. When I reached Antarctica, I found that every single piece had a special use and was necessary. It was the summer season in Antarctica, which meant about 27 degrees below zero Fahrenheit at McMurdo Sound and 45–50 degrees below zero Fahrenheit at the South Pole.

The next day we flew to McMurdo Sound, the main station for U.S. activities in Antarctica and the site of Robert Scott's first headquarters in 1912. We took off from New Zealand in a C-130 on wheels and landed about seven hours later on skis that had been retrofitted to enable the C-130 to land on the ice. The passengers on the flight included my colleague, the U.S. ambassador to New Zealand, Josiah Horton Beeman. "As soon as the plane touches down," the pilot told us, "put on your sunglasses." It was evening, but the light was blinding. The sun never sets during the summer season, and two more months of daylight stretched ahead. The day lasts from October 1 until March 1, and then the long night sets in. We checked into our quarters and then attended a dinner hosted by the station agent. At about 10 P.M., he urged us to go to bed, although it was still complete daylight. Draw the blackout curtains to simulate night, he advised us. I had problems getting used to around-the-clock sunshine and sleep was difficult for me the first several days because a sliver of daylight crept through the blackout drapes.

The next day I had an opportunity to observe the results of a giant clean-up program that had been in process for several years. The United States and one or two other signatories to the Antarctica Treaty had decided to clean the refuse left by explorers since 1917. Antarctica is the driest climate in the world, and on that continent nothing decays. Almost ninety years of refuse had accumulated. The United States engaged a contractor from the Northwest to clear it away, and when I arrived, the refuse was all boxed—hundreds of boxes—stacked, and ready to be loaded onto a ship and taken back to North America for destruction.

I visited a small cabin reportedly built during the historic expedition of British explorer Sir Ernest Shackleton and his crew as they attempted to be the first to cross Antarctica in 1917. The shack, which included an apothecary, was remarkably intact. The explorers might have just stepped out the door. Beside the door I saw a stack of seal meat butchered for fuel, a half-dressed penguin on the kitchen table and, saddest of all, the skeleton of a chained pet dog left behind. The dog probably had been devoured by the predatory seagull skewer bird with its long, needle-shaped beak. Nearby was a penguin rookery with a huge penguin population. Adult penguins formed a collective battle shield against the skewer birds, which feed on penguin eggs and baby penguins. The stench of that rookery is still with me.

I have enormous respect for Steve Emslie, a U.S. scientist who spends every summer alone in a small tent studying the penguins and their habits. He is touted as the most knowledgeable person in the world about penguin behavior. Antarctica is one of the few places on the planet where humans and animals share space in mutual consideration of each other. In Antarctica, humanity is but a tiny speck. It was a humbling experience that I felt more keenly every day I was there.

Ambassador Beeman and I visited a number of two-person observation stations in small tents observing the environment. Our trip to Dry Valley in the southern mountain range in Antarctica was a highlight of our trip. Some of the scientists have ascertained that several thousand years have passed since rain fell there; sand indicates that the area was once underwater. The plain is littered with huge black boulders, some the size of large living rooms and some the size of large houses. Some of the boulders resemble houses with rooms carved out by the corrosive sand and wind over several thousand years. After the helicopters landed, we saw a towering glacier that was advancing about one-half inch a year.

It was a thrill for me to visit the South Pole and the U.S. station there. The headquarters is situated in a giant igloo, large enough to house sleeping quarters, a common kitchen and dining area, and an enormous storage area to accommodate the supplies of the station's 25–50 scientists and support personnel who live there. We made the trip in a plane piloted by a U.S. Navy Reserve pilot who is part of the Navy Reserve Unit's employment base and the National Science Foundation. She was also a noted archaeologist, and as we flew over several crevices, she gave us a scientific explanation of what we were seeing. She pointed out a crevice into which a man had fallen while skiing en route to the South Pole. His body will lie there intact for thousands of years.

Just before I landed, a Norwegian scientific explorer had arrived at the pole on skis, pulling a small sled. She worked for her keep at the station, as visitors are required to do. The day I arrived, she was baking chocolate chip cookies for afternoon tea.

I found the American population at the pole to be fairly diverse, much more so than I had expected. I was happy to see this, because it seems only right that on Antarctica America put forth its best face. One evening as I sat in the dining hall at McMurdo Sound, I noticed a tall, dignified black man in a coat and tie whom I had not seen before. I wondered what role he played at this distant station. When I met him at a small cocktail party, he told me that he was in charge of the food-service program for the entire continent. He was originally from Louisiana, I learned, about twenty miles from where I was born. "I now know why there was catfish on the menu this evening," I replied. I had traveled to the far reaches of an unknown continent and was eating fried catfish with another man from Louisiana. "Welcome," he laughed. "Enjoy yourself."

The ice at the pole is reportedly three miles deep. The air is thin and dry. I noticed as I walked outside that small particles floated in the air, glittering like diamonds. I asked one of the scientists about this phenomenon, and he replied that it was my breath freezing as soon as it hit the air. I took off my mittens to take a photograph, and my fingers immediately ached as they began to freeze. My admiration for the men and women working in Antarctica knows no bounds. The scientists there are delving far into space, looking for secrets that will affect the way we live in other times. Those who provide support for U.S. efforts provide extraordinary service that makes it possible for the Antarctic polar program to endure such hardship and make our lives better.

In June 1996, Lucy and I began to make farewell trips to the consulates in Melbourne, Perth, Brisbane, and Sydney. On July 31 we packed our personal things and flew back to the United States. After almost forty years, I was retiring from the Foreign Service. I was not, however, retiring from an active professional life.

A wise friend once told me never to try to create the past, for it is always a disappointment. I had my sights on a new adventure. I had decided that I wanted to be involved in higher education, and after considerable deliberation I chose to accept the offer to join the University of Oklahoma. This decision was made in no small part because of my admiration for David Boren, who had retired from a political career to become the president of OU in Norman, Oklahoma. When I was weighing offers from several universities, I consulted Larry Eagleburger, Colin Powell, Henry Kissinger, and others; they all said the same thing: "Go to the University of Oklahoma." One friend was aghast at the decision, but that is

Graduation Day, May 1997, at the University of Oklahoma. Former U.S.
president George H. W. Bush gave the commencement address and was
awarded an honorary doctorate degree by OU President David Boren (*right*).

because he envisioned Oklahoma as dry beds of sand and cows dying in the
desert. He could not be more wrong about the geography.

At this university smack in the heartland of America, my title is: William J.
Crowe Chair Professor and Executive Director of the International Programs
Center. In this role, I teach graduate courses in the various elements of generic
making of American foreign policy. The experience of interacting with some
incredibly bright students continues to serve as an elixir to me. Teaching is both
a reward and a learning process.

As executive director, I probably enjoy one of the most exciting engagements
in the country—that of helping the president of the university to international-
ize the University of Oklahoma across all disciplines and increase the university's outreach throughout the state and nation. I have the privilege of carrying
the flag of this public university throughout the United States and much of the
world. Presiding over this process with President Boren, I have participated in

Our daughters, Kathy (*left*) and Sarah, tell us they have benefited
from their multi-cultural heritage and a life of world travel.

secondary diplomacy efforts. I believe that public universities are uniquely prepared to perform this role and, what is more, that they are obligated to make a
difference in this milieu.

I also serve on the board of the Woodrow Wilson National Fellowship Foundation, out of Princeton, New Jersey. This work takes me back to South Africa
almost every year, as we seek to help build the infrastructure with well-educated
and -trained administrators to work in governmental and nongovernmental
activities at national, regional, and local levels.

Lucy and I make our home in Norman and maintain a residence in Washington, D.C.

And what became of the two little girls who shared our adventures around
the world, who lived in foreign countries spinning with revolutions and political
upheaval, took tea in the Outback, embraced their family culture in China, met
U.S. presidents and foreign leaders, and stood politely through ceremonies in
the White House and State Department? Our daughters, Katherine and Sarah,

both received first-class educations and matured into responsible young women. We wanted them to become independent thinkers and highly qualified professionals, and they have become just that. Both went to graduate school; both learned several languages; both have married fine men; and their marriages appear to be good examples of mutually beneficial partnerships. Katherine is an official in the U.S. Department of State, as is her husband, Jeffrey Kovar. Their young sons are Nathan Noble Liu and Robert Hale. Sarah became a China specialist. She learned to read, speak, and write Chinese, and she studied in China at the University of Beijing and the University of Nanjing. She works in the nongovernment sector, and her husband, Kwabena Koro Nuri, works for the U.S. government in the field of banking. Their daughter is named Sofia Yasmeen, and their son is Kadin Perkins.

When people ask me, "How do you like retirement?" I reply, "I think you need to ask a different question. That question is, 'How has the movement been from your previous incarnation to the new incarnation?'" I subscribe to a belief in Maslow's theory of hierarchical needs. After the basic needs of food, water, shelter, and safety are met, we move through education and self-esteem toward the highest level—self-actualization, or the need to be all that one can be. Self-actualization is what keeps a person vibrant and young in spirit and mind. The same thing is true of a nation. The United States is among the youngest and most successful nations in the world. We would not have achieved this success if we had been a lackadaisical nation. China, South Africa, the Soviet Union, and other communist countries have found that holding people down does not work. History has proven repeatedly that nations do not prosper indefinitely when they try to keep the lid on individual economic development and the desire for individual political development, which is the right of people to determine how they want to be governed.

In my rich and challenging career I have learned that circles are never closed, either personally or professionally. I am grateful to the philosophers—the Reverend Martin Luther King Jr., Sun Tzu, Miyamoto Musashi, and the practical diplomacy of Dr. Ralph Bunche—who teach that humans have unlimited potential toward a greater justice for all. I believe that what we have achieved to date as nations, communities, and as humans is just the beginning, and that there is, and always will be, much more to accomplish. I believe that a warrior for peace

must have an inner core that can meet the demands for principle over expediency. I believe in diplomacy that allows people to grow. A continuing miracle is that people have the capacity and the desire to grow and to improve themselves. This is hope born anew through the centuries. From my study of the Greek philosophers, I remember the words of Sophocles: "Wonders there are many, but none more wonderful than man."

As a representative of government, I have learned that lessons one thinks are personal are lessons for citizenry as it charges its representative government to pursue a conduct-of-relations strategy insuring that the compact among citizens is (1) a living one and (2) will contribute to the greater good of all members. I believe that a nation's foreign policy is not the purview of an exclusive few, but rather the responsibility of all citizens. When I meet with community organizations, I urge them as citizens to become involved in foreign relations and foreign policy. Alan Paton told me that our Constitution made us better as a people than we would have been without it. What must follow is a personal commitment to the enhancement of the individual citizen and community support systems.

I believe in the unity of the citizenry and the individualism of the citizen. As a diplomat, and certainly as a citizen, I have come to know that power writ large is within the scope of this belief. It has been a lifelong learning exercise. The diplomatic world in which I have been privileged to operate has been the focus of efforts to increase power, prestige, and a sense of relativism in the world order of nations. In her brilliant examination of the successes and failures of the Roman Empire, writer and historian Colleen McCullough has inspired me to look anew at the conduct of relations activities on behalf of the United States. The definition of a great nation is under revision, and citizens are at pains to master the lessons that come with the changes. I ask myself continually if a great nation among the world order of nations will adhere to my notion of nationhood and to my sense of community.

The role of the United States is enormous in affecting the course of the world. I know the source of that power comes from many rivers. I have benefited much from remembering and enhancing power through diversity. Most especially I have advocated embracing the diversity of ethnicity. The United States has an abundant supply of this resource, and I am a part of it. As a participating citizen and professional I have sought to make this diversity work for me. I vowed never to let my racial heritage inhibit my achievements or my growth toward excellence and never to permit others to make this a problem for me.

I spent one long afternoon with the late author James Michener at his home in Austin, Texas. His book *The Covenant* had been invaluable to me in forming U.S. policy toward South Africa in the last years of apartheid government.

I am wedded to the philosophy that a society in continuous revolution is moving toward being better today than it was yesterday. As a citizen and diplomat, I have returned to the inherent meaning of Manifest Destiny, and this was especially poignant and acute during my assignment as ambassador to the Republic of South Africa. Inevitably it led me back to citizenship and community.

I spent one long afternoon with the late author James Michener at his home in Austin, Texas. Our discussion brought me face-to-face with citizenship and community and with my participation in them. His book *The Covenant*, in the main about South Africa, and his exceptional understanding of America was invaluable to me in forming U.S. policy towards South Africa in the last years of apartheid government. He and I talked that afternoon about the political, historical, social, and economic glue that holds us together. We talked about what makes a country great, and we agreed that tolerance for individualism and unity must always obtain.

Circles are never closed. We must never let them close. I hold near to my heart the lesson I learned as a boy in that segregated black high school in Arkansas: *finis est non tamen*—the task is not yet complete.

Notes and Sources

The primary sources for this book were the voluminous official government documents of my files and my own papers and diaries. I also consulted colleagues who had been with me on this journey for their first-person recollections. I reread secondary sources, especially books that I had used in preparing for my postings, and pertinent magazine and newspaper articles of the time—not that I always agreed with their reports. An informational source unavailable to me during much of my career was the Internet with official websites, which I consulted later.

"Fire with Fire"

For information about the Delmas Treason Trial and the people involved, see Mosiuoa Patrick (Terror) Lekota, *Prison Letters to a Daughter* (Johannesburg: Taurus, 1991); Rose Moss, "A Matter of State," *Boston Review: A Political and Literary Forum* (Boston Critic, Inc.: February 1989); "Champion of Justice," *The Natal Witness Opinion* (Pietersmaritzburg, South Africa, February 18, 2003); "Pride vs. Arrogance: The New Patriotism," plenary address by Prof. Kader Asmal, MP, Minister of Education at the Values, Education and Democracy Conference, Kirstenbosch, Cape Town, South Africa, February 23, 2001; and Delmas Treason Trial, Department of Historical Papers, University of Witwatersrand Library (www.wits.ac.za).

"Jesus Christ and Huey Long"

A portrait of the Louisiana of my youth can be found in: Federal Writers Project, *Louisiana: A Guide to the State*, American Guide Series (New York: Hastings House, 1941); and T. Harry Williams, *Huey Long* (New York: Alfred A. Knopf, 1969).

"High School in the Big City"

For more detail of the state at the time I lived there, see Federal Writers Project, *Arkansas: A Guide to the State* (New York: Hastings House, 1941).

"Portland—Portal to the World"

Lancaster Pollard, *Oregon and the Pacific Northwest* (Portland: Binford and Mort, 1946).
Federal Writers Project, *Oregon: The End of the Trail* (Portland: Binford & Mort, 1940).
From *The* [Portland, Ore.] *Oregonian*: Michelle Cole, "Diversity Comes Late to Newspaper's Pages," December 4, 2000; R. Gregory Nokes, "Ambassador from Portland," September 10, 1987; Michelle Cole, "Diversity Comes Late to Newspaper's Pages," December 4, 2000; "Ex-Portlander Shuns Spotlight of New Post," November 6, 1986; B. Meechan, "At War in the 1940s," December 24, 1999; and also numerous other issues of the newspaper.

533

I am grateful to Madeleine Owens, Miss Arbuckle's niece, for biographical information about her aunt, and conversations with Glenn Pattee, Carmen Walker, Joy Brock, Clarence Pruitt and Jackie Swint were also helpful.

"Young Warrior"

For further reading I recommend: Morris J. MacGregor Jr., *Integration of the Armed Forces, 1940–1965* (Washington, D.C.: Center of Military History United States Army, 1981); and Bruce Cumings, *Korea's Place in the Sun: A Modern History* (New York: W.W. Norton & Company, 1997).

"Japan: Land of the Rising Sun"

1. Keiko Matsui, "Night Waltz," Tarzana, Calif.: Sin-Drone Records, 1992.

Kenneth G. Henshall, *A History of Japan, From Stone Age to Superpower* (New York: St. Martin's Press, 1999).

John W. Dower, *Embracing Defeat: Japan in the Wake of World War II* (New York: W.W. Norton & Company, 1999).

"Taiwan"

Jonathan D. Spence, *The Search for Modern China* (New York and London: W.W. Norton, 1999).

"Education and Eisenhower's Little War"

John Lewis Gaddis, *Now We Know: Rethinking Cold War History*, A Council on Foreign Relations Book (Oxford: Oxford University Press, 1998).

Neil Sheehan, *A Bright Shining Lie: John Paul Vann and America in Vietnam* (New York: Random House, 1988).

Bernard B. Fall, *Street Without Joy* (Mechanicsburg, Penn.: Stackpole Books, 1972).

Kenneth J. Conboy and Andrade Dale, *Spies and Commandos: How America Lost the Secret War in North Vietnam* (Lawrence: University Press of Kansas, 2000).

James E. Parker Jr., *Covert Ops: The CIA's Secret War in Laos* (New York: St. Martin's Press, 1997).

William J. Duiker, *Ho Chi Mihn: A Life* (New York: Hyperion Books, 2000).

"The Foreign Service of the United States"

The Foreign Service of the United States is the official nomenclature of the Foreign Service, also known variously as "the diplomatic service" or "the diplomatic service of the United States." The Stein case study of February 1949 provides a useful historical development of the Foreign Service. The report is a case study of the development of the Foreign Service Act of 1946 or Public Law 724 (PL 724). See sections 211 and 212 of the PL 79-724, otherwise known as the Foreign Service Act of 1946.

The Foreign Service intake process is through entry examination, which is specified in law. The examination process is managed by the Board of Examiners of the Foreign Service as specified in the appropriate public law (that is the Foreign Service Act of 1946) and as superceded by the Foreign Service Act of 1980. The examination is a two-part process. The written examination, given about once a year, is largely academic and is administered by an outside professional testing service. Those who successfully pass the written examination are invited to take an oral examination.

An example of the eastern character of the leaders of the Foreign Service in 1946 is demonstrated by looking at the educational history of several people in the higher echelon: Selden Chapin, former director general of the Foreign Service, was from Pennsylvania, went to St. Paul's private school, had a U.S. Navy career of about six years, and was appointed Foreign Service officer in 1925. He had a distinguished career and retired at the class of career minister, which is the highest operational rank in the Foreign Service. Andrew Brisbin Foster, also from Pennsylvania, attended the Episcopal Academy, Dartmouth, and St. John's College at Cambridge University and studied in Switzerland. He also represented the kind of officer who was likely to succeed in the Foreign Service. Edmund Asbury Gullion, from Kentucky, attended Western High School in Washington, D.C., went to the Emerson Institute, and graduated from Princeton University. Julian Fiske Harrington from Framingham, Massachusetts, graduated from Columbia University. Edward Tudor Lampson, from Connecticut, a graduate of Kingswood School preparatory school, received a B.A. from Amherst and a Ph.D. from Harvard.

For further information about the Foreign Service, I recommend:

Andrew L. Steigman, *The Foreign Service of the United States: First Line of Defense* (Boulder, Colo.: Westview Press, 1985).

Martin Weil, *A Pretty Good Club: The Founding Fathers of the U.S. Foreign Service* (New York: W.W. Norton, 1978).

Chris Argyis, *Some Causes of Organizational Ineffectiveness Within the Department of State* (Washington: Department of State, 1967).

William Barnes and John Heath Morgan, *The Foreign Service of the United States: Origins, Development and Functions* (Washington, D.C.: Historical Office, Bureau of Public Affairs, Department of State, 1961).

Henry A. Kissinger's speech at the swearing in of the 119th Foreign Service Officer Class on June 17, 1975: "The Department lacks an effective system for addressing or deciding priorities among areas or specialties. What is needed, therefore, is a new approach—a mechanism for coordinating resources and goals and reprogramming existing resources from less important functions to areas that demand priority attention. I have, therefore, recently established a Priorities Policy Group (PPG) to provide the mechanism for linking decisions for resource allocations to the broader consideration of foreign policy."

Juan Williams, "Man in a Trap," *The Washington Post Magazine*, March 1, 1987.

"GHANA IN A TIME OF TURBULENCE"

Thomas L. Friedman, "Here Comes the Sun," *The New York Times*, May 4, 2002.

Prof. A. Adu-Boahen, *The Ghanaian Sphinx: Reflections on the Contemporary History of Ghana, 1972–1987 (The J.B. Danquah Memorial Lectures, 1988)*, under the auspices of the Ghana Academy of Arts and Sciences.

For further reading, I recommend:

Apter, David E. *Ghana in Transition.* 2nd ed. Princeton, NJ: Princeton University Press, 1972.

Bing, Geoffrey. *Reap the Whirlwind: An Account of Kwame Nkrumah's Ghana from 1950 to 1966.* London: MacGibbon and Kee, 1968.

Nkrumah, Kwame. *I Speak of Freedom: A Statement of African Ideology.* New York: Praeger, 1961

Osei, Akwasi P. *Ghana: Recurrence and Change in a Post-Independence African State.* New York: P. Lang, 1999.

"Liberia in Revolution"

Colonization:African-American Mosaic Exhibition (Library of Congress), (lcweb@loc.gov).

James Smith, "Liberia's Ugly Past (Part III): The True Whig Party in Unusual Waters" (www.theperspective.org).

Life magazine, June 1980.

For further reading, I recommend:

Beyan, Amos Jones. *The American Colonization Society and the Creation of the Liberian State:A Historical Perspective, 1822–1900.* Lanham, Md.: University Press of America, 1991.

Dendel, Esther Warner. *New Song in a Strange Land.* Boston: Houghton Mifflin, 1948.

Ellis, Stephen. *The Mask of Anarchy: The Destruction of Liberia and the Religious Dimension of an African Civil War.* London: Hurst, 1999.

"Director of West African Affairs"

For further reading, I recommend:

Beckett, Paul, and Crawford Young. *Dilemmas of Democracy in Nigeria.* Rochester, NY: University of Rochester Press, 1997.

Magyar, K. P. *United States Interests and Policies in Africa: Transition to a New Era.* New York: St. Martin's Press, 2000.

Morrison, J. Stephen, and Jennifer G. Cooke. *Africa Policy in the Clinton Years: Critical Choices for the Bush Administration.* Washington, D.C.: CSIS Press, 2001.

"Mr. Ambassador"

1. In 1997, Johnson-Sirleaf was a presidential candidate in Liberia. She came in second. In 2005, she ran again and was elected. According to the Associated Press, her campaign buttons read "Ellen—She's Our Man."

"A Black Ambassador to South Africa?"

1. One important contact was Maurice Tempelsman, Jackie Kennedy's companion. He had numerous business interests in Africa and knew many of the key actors, black and white, within both the Afrikaners and the English business communities.

I spoke with Patricia de Lille, a Coloured revolutionary from South Africa who was in the United States on a visitor's grant and F. Allen (Tex) Harris, deputy director of the Office of Southern African Affairs.

In New York and in Washington I met the South African ambassador to the United Nations, Chris von Schoending, and the South African ambassador to Washington, Herbert Beukes. At the AFL-CIO I saw Lane Kirkland and learned that the AFL-CIO had lost contact with the black unions in South Africa. When I met Vernon Jordan, a member of the South Africa Group, he asked me where was I born. I told him Louisiana, and he said, "Mr. Ambassador, you'll do great."

I tried to see Randall Robinson of TransAfrica, but he refused to come to the State Department. He wanted me to come to him. A key person I did meet was Gay MacDougal, a black lawyer of the Lawyers' Group for Human Rights. The Group of 100, started by one hundred black men, asked me to speak at lunch one day.

In Washington, I had lunch at a restaurant near 14th and K streets with Coretta Scott

King, widow of Martin Luther King Jr. She exuded warmth and understanding for the mission I was attempting. She told me that she hoped that I could bring news of her proposal for the Martin Luther King Center for Non-Violent Social Change in South Africa.

En route to South Africa, I stopped in London and had dinner with Denis Worrall, the South African ambassador to the Court of St. James, and with Tiny Rowland, a successful entrepreneur in Africa without many claims to morality. I met Afrikaner Fleur de Villiers, and I visited with the U.S. ambassador to the Court of St. James, Charles Price. Robin Raphael, the political officer in our London embassy who was responsible for watching African affairs, briefed me on South Africa. Later Robin became my political counselor in South Africa.

John Samuel, an Indian, was head of the Education Trust, an organization set up to handle scholarships for black South Africans. We would later look to him for setting up controls to keep track of the people who were sent abroad to study.

2. Jon Qwelane, "Dear Mr. Perkins, you are just not welcome." *Sowetan Sunday Star*, November 24, 1986.

3. Juan Williams, " Man in a Trap," *The Washington Post Magazine*, March 1, 1987.

For further reading, I recommend:

de Klerk, F. W. *The Last Trek—A New Beginning: The Autobiography*. New York: St. Martin's Press, 1999.

Mandela, Nelson, *Long Walk to Freedom: The Autobiography of Nelson Mandela*. London: Little, Brown and Company, 1994.

Mead, Gary, *South Africa*. Lincolnwood, Ill.: Passport Books, 1997.

Meredith, Martin, *Nelson Mandela: A Biography*. New York: St. Martin's Press, 1997.

Michener, James A. *The Covenant*. New York: Random House, 1980.

Pakenham, Thomas. *The Boer War*. London: Futura Publications, 1988.

Reader, John, *Africa A Biography of the Continent*. New York: Vintage, 1997.

Sampson, Anthony. *Mandela: The Authorized Biography*. New York: Alfred A. Knopf, 1999.

Sparks, Allister. *The Mind of South Africa*. New York: Alfred A. Knopf, 1990.

Thompson, Leonard. *A History of South Africa,* revised edition. New Haven, Conn., and London: Yale University Press, 1995.

Waldmeir, Patti. *Anatomy of a Miracle: The End of Apartheid and the Birth of the New South Africa*. New York: W. W. Norton, 1997.

Wheatcroft, Geoffrey. *The Randlords: The Men who Made South Africa*. Johannesburg: Jonathan Ball, 1986.

"Let Them Know I Am Here"

Books I found particularly informational were: David Harrison, *The White Tribe of Africa* (London: British Broadcasting Company, 1981); and Graham Leach, *South Africa: No Easy Path to Peace* (Methuen: London Ltd., 1987).

"Making Policy in South Africa"

Michael J. Garrison and Thomas T. Huang, "Black Sash Leader Attacks Apartheid," *The Tech*, 105, no. 38 (October 1, 1985).

Helen Suzman, *In No Uncertain Terms: A South African Memoir* (New York: Alfred A. Knopf, 1993).

For more information about Steve Biko, I recommend Mamphela Ramphele, *Mamphela Ram-phele—A Life* (Claremont, South Africa: David Philip Publishers, 1995).

Rodney Davenport and Christopher Saunders, *South Africa: A Modern History* (London: MacMillanPress, Ltd., 2000) .

Walter and Albertina Sisulu, *Walter and Albertina Sisulu: In Our Lifetime* (Claremont, South Africa: David Phillip Publishers, 2002)

Govan Mbeki, *The Struggle for Liberation in South Africa: A Short History* (Claremont, South Africa: David Phillips, 1991).

"Fission and Frustration," *The Financial Mail* (October 16, 1987), p. 29. This South African publication listed some of the rash of "extra-parliamentary" organizations, both left and right, that had sprung up: "Idasa, UDF, Azapo, the Five Freedoms Forum, Detainees' Parents' Support Committee, End Conscription Campaign, Black Sash, AWB, Blanke Bevrydingsbeweging, Inkatha, Inyandza, Unity Movement, TIC, NIC, the Anti-PC Committee, ANC, PAC, SACP, Jews for Social Justice, Jodac, Lawyers for Human Rights, Actstop, Soyco, Labour Monitoring Group, Trac, Tag, Lurk. . . ." The list appeared endless. "On the surface," according to the article, "such heterogeneity and fission should make government laugh. It isn't—it fears the Right in the next election and cracks down stronger by the day on the Left and its media—indeed, the media as a whole. This may simply be a holding operation of a party about to rupture further and make a messy exit from history's stage."

Reiner Leist, "Interview from Blue Portraits," September 1991 (www.anc.org.za/people/sisulu).

Newsweek, September 29, 1997.

Bruce W. Nelan, "New Man in the Townships," *Time*, February 23, 1987.

For information about the Zulus, Buthelezi recommended Donald R. Morris with intro. by Mangosuthu Chief Buthelezi, *The Washing of the Spears: A History of the Rise of the Zulu Nation Under Shaka and Its Fall in the Zulu War of 1879* (London: Da Capo Press edition, 1998).

For information on Martin Luther King, I recommend:

Branch, Taylor. *Parting the Waters: America in the King Years, 1954–64.* New York, London, Toronto, Sydney, Tokyo: A Touchstone Book Published by Simon & Schuster, 1989.

Oates, Stephen B. *Let the Trumpet Sound: A Life of Martin Luther King Jr.* New York: HarperPerennial, 1994.

"The White Tribe"

1. Harald Pakendorf, "Another Voice," *Sunday Times*, December 28, 1986.

See also Geoff Cronje, *'n Tuiste vir die nageslag* (A Home for Posterity) (Johannesburg: Publicite, 1945), which discusses the plan for repatriation of all Indians back to India. The book was dedicated to Afrikaner mothers as protectors of the purity of blood of the Boer nation.

"Tightening the Screws"

1. The Comprehensive Anti-Apartheid Act of 1986 (CAAA), Public Law 99-440, was enacted into law on October 2, 1986. The reference is the Congressional Record of September 12, 1986, pp. 6768–6777. Also on that same date, a statement was issued by the president of the United States that the administration "will implement the law." The CAAA was a signal move representing a near-unanimous feeling throughout America that we as a people stood for something akin to "doing the right thing." Readers who want to know more about that tur-

bulent struggle over a significant foreign policy move are urged to consult the act and the sense of the Congress notes accompanying it.

2. Ken Owens, *The Citizen*, May 1987.

3. Simon Barber, *The Cape Times*, May 12, 1987.

4. Ned Temko, *Christian Science Monitor*, June 25, 1987.

5. *The South African Advisory Committee Report*, dated February 10, 1987, is massive and covers just about every single element in a conflict resolution sense. One of the members of the committee was Frank Thomas, a black American from Queens and president of the Ford Foundation at that time, who had caused to be written an extensive report titled *Time Running Out*.

6. Foreign representatives in the Republic of South Africa at the time included Ambassadors (unless otherwise noted) C. E. McDonald, Australia; Alexander Christiani, Austria; E. A. J. D. Kobia, Belgium; R. S. MacLean, Canada; Major-General L. Prussing, Chile; H. K. Yang, Republic of China; Consul-General N. Horn, Denmark; Chargé d'Affaires H. K. I. Mantyvaara, Finland; J. P. Dupont, France; Immo Stabreit, Germany; L. E. M. Tsilas, Greece; D. Ariel, Israel; M. Piersigilli, Italy; Consul-General S. Horiuchi, Japan; P. A. van Buuren, The Netherlands; Consul-General B. Lindstom, Norway; J. M. P. de Villa, Portugal; A. de Castilla, Spain; Envoy Extraordinary J. Lundvik, Sweden; J. O. Quin, Switzerland; R. W. Renwick, United Kingdom of Great Britain and Northern Ireland.

7. Two Coca-Cola executives involved in the divestment were Don McHenry, former U.S. ambassador to the United Nations and a Coca-Cola board member, and Carl Ware, who was in charge of the South Africa Coca-Cola program. Both are black Americans. When they called on me, they suggested some useful stances that I should take in public debate in South Africa. They also had recommendations on bursaries and getting young black South Africans back into schools.

8. In 1986, the Commerce Department in Washington released the 1985 figures on U.S. direct investment in South Africa. The dollar value of U.S. direct investment in South Africa had been declining since the end of 1981. At the end of 1985, it was $1.3 billion, which was about half the level that it was at the end of 1981. In interpreting this change, the Commerce Department noted that sanctions were working.

9. Key black businessmen included Peter M. Mashego from Mashalltown, a black suburb of Johannesburg; Lionel Grewan, executive director of the Signatory Association; Dusi Tshabalala, the dynamic managing director of the Tshabalala Group of companies; H. H. Diamlenze, a successful entrepreneur; Mandela David Msomi, from the African Travel Services, Ltd., and also a member of Micor, which was the group of Johannesburg companies trying to establish a black bank. P. W. Modise, who had helped develop the Freedman's Bank in New York, came to South Africa to advise the fledgling bankers. Richard Maponya, president of Maponya's Discount Stores, was one of the first blacks to buy a house in an upscale suburb of Johannesburg when the Group Areas Act was discarded. His wife, Christi Khaboza, was equally adept at business and operated her own businesses. Peter Rabali was the national chairman of the National African Federated Transport Organization, whose membership was all the black taxi and truck drivers.

10. For more about Percy Qoboza, read "In Memoriam: Percy Qoboza," *Neiman Reports* 53, no. 4 (Winter 1999), and 54, no. 1 (Spring 2000); and "Hundreds Attend Qoboza Funeral," *Pretoria News*, January 25, 1988.

"Angola-Namibia: The Long Struggle for Peace"

1. Joint Press Statement, Department of State, Nov. 8, 2000: Other Angolan members of the delegation were General Franca Ndalu, deputy minister of Defense and chief of staff of the armed forces; Vanancio da Moura, deputy foreign minister; Colonel José Maria, security advisor to the president; Ambassador Elisio de Figueiredo, Angolan ambassador to Great Britain; Antonio Pitra, legal advisor.

2. The Cuban members of the delegation also included: Jorge Risquet Valdez, politbureau of the Communist Party (ccp); General Ulises Rosales del Toro, chief of staff, ministry of the Revolutionary Armed Forces; Carolos Aldana Escalante, secretariat, Central Committee (ccp); Raul Roa Kouri, deputy foreign minister; Rudolfo Puente Ferro, Central Committee (ccp) and deputy head of the general department of foreign relations (ccp).

3. Other members of the South African delegation were Piet Koornhof, ambassador to Washington; R. Killen, ambassador to London; J. H. Beukes, deputy director general; Neil Barnard, director general, National Intelligence Service; Derek Auret, Foreign Affairs; Brig. G. Sonnekus, South Africa Defense Force; J. Boshoff, nis, Andre Jaquet, Foreign Affairs, J. Sunde, Foreign Affairs, Robert Desmarais, Foreign Affairs. Neil van Heerden's assistants were Derek Auret and Robert Demarais.

4. In addition to me, the U.S. delegation included Larry Napper, a Foreign Service officer from the State Department, Washington; Larry Silverman, from my embassy in Cape Town; Robert Frasure, my political counselor at the South Africa Embassy; James Woods, deputy assistant secretary of Defense; Colonel Charles Snyder, from the Pentagon and assigned to the State Department; Michael McKinley, State Department; John Ordway, Earl Irving, desk officer for Congo Brazzaville; John Byerly from our legal staff in State; Alex Schiabo; Robert Cabelly, Chet Crocker's chief of staff; Ambassador Herman Cohen, National Security Council; William Bellamy, Department of State; and Jimmy Kolker, U.S. Embassy in London.

"Post Script: South Africa"

1. "In Apartheid's Wake, A Word Still Divides," *The New York Times*, October 3, 1999.
2. "Where Apartheid Ruled, Tourists are Swarming," *The New York Times*, September 24, 1999.
3. R. W. Johnson, Editorials/Opinion, "An Earnest Exercise Hasn't Healed South Africa," *The New York Times*, November 4, 1998.
4. "No Apology But 'Sadness' Over Anglo-Boer War," *Agence France Press*, November 11, 1999; "Anglo-Boer War Shaped S. African History for Generations," *Agence France Press*, October 7, 1999; "Britain Acknowledges 'Shameful' Neglect of Women, Children in Boer War," *Agence France Press*, October 10, 1999.
5. John Murphy, "South Africa Struggles to Build aids Program," *Baltimore Sun*, October 14, 2003; Mark Schoofs, "South Africa Won't Provide aids Drugs in Hospitals," *The Wall Street Journal*, June 28, 2001.
6. "Mandela Reminisces on His Release from Prison Ten Years Ago," *Agency France Presse*, February 8, 2000. For details, read Mandela's biography, *Long Walk to Freedom*.
7. Andrew Selssky, "Convicted Murderer Implicated Winnie Madikizela-Mandela in a Killing," Nando Media and Associated Press, November 29, 1999; "Winnie's Fall Makes Big News Abroad," *The New York Times*, February 18, 1989.

8. Karl Beck's work is acknowledged with admiration in Princeton N. Lyman, *Partner to History: The U.S. Role in South Africa's Transition to Democracy* (Washington, D.C.: United States Institute of Peace Press, 2002).

9. Norma M. Riccucci, *Unsung Heroes: Federal Execucrats Making a Difference* (Washington D.C.: Georgetown University Press, 1995).

"DIRECTOR GENERAL: CHANGING THE FOREIGN SERVICE"

1. In reforming the Foreign Service, I utilized the *Thomas Report* and the *Bremer Report*, which dictated that every agency operating under the Foreign Service Act of 1980 be administered the same way. These new studies concentrated on a rational way of allocating resources for the greater good of foreign policy, somewhat a replay of Kissinger's State Department work in the 1970s. The reports focused on training for the modernity of the times.

2. An unofficial watchdog activity helps look after the Foreign Affairs Fellows Program. Ambassador Ruth Davis, the highest-ranking black female in the Foreign Service, Richard Hope, and two or three others are vigilant and valiant. I, too, keep an eye on the program. With these efforts we should be able to keep the program going for the next ten years. By that time, a critical mass should have emerged—officers who came up through the cohorts and who have constituted themselves into a network around the world.

"THE UNITED NATIONS"

1. Resolution 757, adopted May 30, 1992, called for, among other things, the immediate cessation to fighting in Bosnia and Herzegovina, cessation of forcible expulsions and "attempts to change the ethnic composition of the population," the establishment of conditions for humanitarian assistance to and from Sarajevo, the declaration of economic sanctions, and the prohibition of air traffic to and from the Federal Republic of Yugoslavia (Serbia and Montenegro).

2. UN Security Council Resolution 242 was adopted November 22, 1967, after the Six-Day War earlier that year. The goal was "the establishment of a just and lasting peace in the Middle East" and called for "withdrawal of Israeli armed forces from territories occupied in the recent conflict."

3. UN Security Council Resolution 688, adopted on April 5, 1991. Also see UN Security Council Resolutions 706 (1991), 712 (1991), and 778 (1992).

For an inside look at the UN, I recommend:

William F. Buckley's witty and well-written book, *United Nations Journal: A Delegate's Odyssey,* and Daniel Moynihan's book, *A Dangerous Place.* Senator Moynihan gave me much insight on such things as the United Nations Development Program (UNDP) and the UN's Economic and Social Organization (ECOSOC).

Also informative are:

Brill, James A. *Eagle and the Lion: The Tragedy of American Iranian Relations.* New Haven, Conn., and London: Yale University Press, 1989.

Lesch, David. *The Middle East and the United States: Historical and Political Reassessment.* Boulder, Colo.: Westview Press, 2003.

"Australia: Down Under and Beyond"

1. *USA Today*, April 21, 2004, reported that when Australian prime minister John Howard decided to abolish the Aboriginal and Torres Strait Islander Commission and appoint a panel in its place, an Aboriginal woman "pointed the bone" at him, meaning that she put a curse on him.

2. Robert F. Kennedy's speech, originally titled "Day of Affirmation Address," came to be known as the "Ripple of Hope" speech. He delivered it at the University of Capetown in Capetown, South Africa, on June 6, 1966.

ACKNOWLEDGMENTS

Just as no career is built alone, in isolation from others, no book is produced singlehandedly. It is, of course, impossible to mention all who have had something positive to add to the making of this memoir, but I do wish to give special thanks to those in Oklahoma who helped my dream of producing this work become reality. The staff of the University of Oklahoma Center for International Programs—in particular, Kathy Shahan, Julie Horn, Donna Cline, and Loretta Selvey—deserve special mention for the extraordinary support they gave me throughout the life of this research. Graduate assistants John Van Doorn and Mitchell Fuller, both professors now, have my thanks for helping me review official archives at the Department of State in Washington and at the U.S. Mission to the United Nations in New York. They also aided in the selection of material for use not only in this memoir but also in the Diplomatic Archives of the University of Oklahoma Libraries system. They quickly mastered bureaucratic rules, made friends with several archivists, and made an impossible objective achievable. John Van Doorn helped design the first plan of action for the research and the follow-on University of Oklahoma Diplomatic Archives, which will contain my official and personal papers, plus those of Oklahomans who have served as United States ambassadors. Other graduate assistants, Angela Rogers, Chris Grossman, Charlotte Carter, and Ann Jones, also provided enormous help in researching materials and recording relevant information crucial to the project.

Special thanks go to Barbara McClurkin, selected to be the first archivist for the diplomatic archives. She gave invaluable assistance in locating materials among the many volumes of papers, checking names, dates, events, and accuracy of statements made by me and my numerous contacts.

I developed special affection for the legion of typists—especially Teresa Finders, Annette Harker, and Michele Moore, who transcribed my dictation as I annotated my mountain of diaries and official papers into 6,000-plus pages for the archives. This mountain of resource material became the basis for this memoir.

I owe unlimited thanks to the Department of State, especially to Margaret Grafeld and her associates in the Department of State, who went beyond expectations to accommodate my numerous requests for declassification and shipment of documents to me, and to Mary Ann Alt and her colleagues at the United States Mission to the United Nations. All gave unstinting help, made files available for my review, and hurried along requests for declassification in a timely and efficient manner.

As this project progressed over the past five years, I have been assisted greatly by the University of Oklahoma Press, especially Director John Drayton and the skillful copy editing of Robert A. Clark and Ariane C. Smith. Mr. Drayton offered continuous encouragement, guidance, and sympathy. I am indebted to him for gently easing me into the realities of the publishing world.

There are no bounds to my gratitude to Edith Kinney Gaylord for her very generous financial and psychological support, which made this project possible. An unswervingly honorable and highly concerned citizen, Ms. Gaylord made it possible for me to pursue this project of which I had dreamed for some time. When the project started and the grant was given, Ms. Gaylord was already in poor health. I remain saddened that I did not have the opportunity to meet this remarkable citizen. The world will probably never know just how much Edith Kinney Gaylord contributed to societal changes for the betterment of humanity. I am especially enriched because she cared about the unusual and excellence. Her lawyer, longtime confidante, and friend, Bill Ross, was not only my channel of communication to Ms. Gaylord, he also became a good friend to me. It was through Bill Ross that I learned of Ms. Gaylord's tremendous appetite for helping to ensure the triumph of justice in key elements of society. I owe Bill a great debt of gratitude for his wisdom and advice during the research of this project.

University of Oklahoma President David L. Boren introduced my proposed project to Ms. Gaylord. He convinced her of the worthiness of the research and subsequent publication. I am indebted to him for this extraordinary expression of confidence in the project and in me. I am also grateful to President Boren for conceiving of the idea of a diplomatic archive at the University of Oklahoma to house official and personal papers of Oklahomans who have represented the United States as ambassadors to various countries. I am very pleased that the archives will also contain my official and personal papers as well. I first came to know then Senator Boren during my turbulent assignment to South Africa as U.S. ambassador. He gave his personal backing to my efforts to help bring about change in South

Africa, adding to efforts to displace the apartheid government and political/social system that constituted the power base in South Africa. Senator Boren's support of my diplomatic efforts continued through my assignments as Director General of the Foreign Service and as United States Permanent Representative to the United Nations and Representative in the Security Council. Inviting me to compete for a vacant academic chair at the university upon completion of my diplomatic career, President Boren has continued to support and encourage me. That support has contributed enormously to this project.

The women who served as my special assistants during my presidential appointee assignments, Norma Jaegar and Nancy Buss Garnett, deserve special mention. Norma served with me in Liberia and South Africa, enduring continued racist remarks and taunting in South Africa because she dared to serve as my special assistant and openly defended the policy of pushing for political and social change in South Africa. She kept every scrap of information that related to the workings of the U.S. mission policy in South Africa during my stewardship, much of which served as a point of reference for my comments about South Africa. She was as steady as a rock in her determination to support my efforts and me. Ms. Garnett served with me during my assignments as director general of the Foreign Service, ambassador to the United Nations, and finally as ambassador to the Commonwealth of Australia. Her support represented the highest ideals of the Foreign Service. She, too, kept enormous files representing the many profiles I assumed as a representative of the president. Most, or all, of these have served as reference points in this research. Both women represented the highest ideals and standards of the U.S. Foreign Service, professionalism, personal integrity, and citizenship. I am fortunate that my path crossed theirs.

The Reverend John W. Gravely, a colleague and fraternity brother throughout my Foreign Service career, served as a valuable sounding board for much of this project. His advice and counsel have been invaluable as, moving through the many lives portrayed in this memoir, I sought to maintain a balance. I am grateful and owe much to John. Herbert Harrington, Nicholas G. W. Thorne, Abe S. Ashcanase, and Mary Pearl Dougherty have been valuable career counselors and in that role have helped keep this project in focus and on level ground. I owe a special debt of gratitude to Herbert because of shared experiences pre-Foreign Service, especially the inculcation of the study of Asian philosophy, which has served me so well during my professional and personal life experiences. Nick and Abe have both been mentors and Foreign Service colleagues. Mary, as for so many others during her Foreign Service career and during her lifetime, was a personal mentor and valuable listener.

I want to thank my cousin, Marie Maxey, for her encouragement in pursuing this project and for her support throughout my diplomatic career. She was like a sister to me.

Readers of the manuscript, Dr. Richard O. Hope and J. Brooks Spector, provided comments that were invaluable, and I am indebted to them for their careful scrutiny.

John Smelcer, Adriaan Crew, and Ida Cooper were important for my additional research in South Africa, and I thank them for their assistance and their knowledge.

Anya Van Ditmarsch provided insight and information on Liberia, United States–Liberia relations, and the cultural divide amongst Liberians during the fall and slow rise of Liberia as a nation.

I want to express gratitude to William Lacy Swing, ambassador to Liberia during my first assignment as deputy chief of mission. Under his tutelage I learned many vaulable things, including the lesson of eating humble pie once in a while.

Connie Cronley, my collaborator, has been with me from the day I began to seriously considered writing a memoir. Her writing skills have served me beyond description as we ventured through the many avenues of this project. She internalized the project to an extent that permitted us to discuss ideas, language, and construction without inhibition. Moreover, we have developed enormous respect for each other. I have come to appreciate Connie not only as a writing collaborator but also as a great citizen with respect for nation and community.

My final acknowledgment is a salute of gratitude to my family for their support and great friendship in all things we are about. Daughters Katherine Karla and Sarah Elizabeth and their families have been consistently supportive of this research project. I am grateful for their unstinting support. No words can convey my thanks for the love and support of my wife and mate, Lucy. She has remained by my side as we made repeated treks across the burning sands in various climes on difficult and interesting assignments around the world—always with great cheer. Lucy is an unrelenting and ardent supporter of the democratic ideal, and an extraordinary representative of her adopted homeland. As such, she has added her support to me in uncounted ways. My success, such as it has been, would not have been possible without Lucy.

Whatever faults or mistakes discovered in this work must be attributed to me, for I am solely responsible.

INDEX

Abidjan, Côte d'Ivoire: 221, 227

Aboriginal and Torres Strait Island Commission: 505

Aboriginals (Australian): 497, 500, 503, 504, 506, 507; rights of, 502

Abrams, Elliott: 490

Abrams, Ken: 414

Accra, Ghana: 170, 181, 188; described, 171–172

Acheampong, Ignatius Kutu: 173

Adamishin, Anatoly: 417

Adams, John: 151

Adams, John Quincy: 151

Addis Ababa, Ethiopia: 431

Adelaide: 508, 523

AFL-CIO: 182, 316, 317

African American Labor Center (AALC): 317

African Defense Force: 334

African Development Bank: 221

African Frontline States: 406

African National Congress (ANC): 7, 10, 247, 248, 254, 290, 296, 301, 302, 305, 306–309, 318, 334, 345, 354, 367, 368, 390, 391, 393, 394, 423, 424, 426, 428, 429, 458

Afrikaans Dutch Reformed Church: 339. See also Dutch Reformed Church

Afrikaans Gereformeerde Kerk (AGK). See Afrikaans Dutch Reformed Church

Afrikaner National Party: 414

Afrikaners: 254, 279, 281–284, 287, 291, 295, 298, 318, 319, 322, 325, 335–337, 341, 350, 355, 356, 359, 363, 366, 367, 373, 375, 379, 380, 384, 385, 387, 395, 396, 423; after aparthied, 427; and Namibia, 405, 406, 408, 410, 413; as described by Boesak, 345; fears of, 370; government of, 361; idealogy of, 348–349; national identity of, 280, 281; populism and, 368; reaction of to Perkins article, 374; religion of, 338–339, 342; treatment of dissidents, 339, 340; treatment of other races, 296; women, 349

Agency for International Development (USAID): See U.S. Agency for International Development

Agriculture Department: 218, 232

Ahtisaari, Martti: 411

AIDS: 332, 376, 427, 463

Akuffo, Frederick W. K.: 173, 187–189

Al-am-Bari: 479

Alarcón, Ricardo: 411, 417, 472, 490

Albany, Australia: 511

Albright, Madeleine: 495, 496

Alcoholism: 160

Aldana, Carlos: 417

Alexander, Beverly: 233

Alexandria: 327

Algeria: 222

Ali, Muhammad: 183

Alice Springs: 521

Allende, Salvadore: 232

American Brands Incorporated: 386

American Chamber of Commerce: 387

American Colonization Society: 195

American Cyanamid Corporation: 386

American Federation of Government Employees: 162

American Foreign Policy, Three Essays (book): 163

American Foreign Service Association: 162

ANC: *See* African National Congress

Anderson, Marian: 63

Angel, Bob: 387

Angkor Wat: 491

Anglican Church: 299, 309, 320

Angola: 253, 301, 332, 334, 364, 405, 409–412, 418, 472; and Namibian negotiations, 415–416; civil war in, 406, 407; U.S. relations with, 408

Anna and the King of Siam (movie): 138

Antarctica: 499, 500, 514, 524–527

ANZUS Treaty: 497

apartheid: 275, 287, 296, 299, 300, 306, 331, 332, 336, 350, 352, 356, 373, 383; and churches, 339–340, 338–339, 342–346; ended by de Klerk, 423; ideology of defined, 337; inception of, 284–285, 385; opposition to, 247, 248, 254; status of races under, 297

Aquilar, Karen: 485
Arbuckle, Ruth: 53, 55, 58, 60, 270
Arkansas Agricultural, Mechanical, and Normal
    College: 43
Armacost, Michael: 242, 352
Armed Forces Revolutionary Council (AFRC): 187,
    190, 191
Armstrong, Neil: 524
Arnhem Land: 506
Art of War, The (book): 10, 98, 255
Arten, John: 106
Ashanti: 180
Asia Pacific Economic Cooperation (APEC): 515
Askue, Cecilia "Celia": 522
Association of American Foreign Service Wives: 162
ASTAB bookstore: 184
Atomic Energy Commission: 232
Aubert, Alvin: 81
Austin, Warren: 468
Australia: 441, 454, 456, 491, 500; U.S. relations
    with, 497, 500, 514
Australian and New Zealand Army Corps (ANZAC):
    511, 524
Australian-American Association: 510
Austria: 466
Ayers Rock: 521
Azanian People's Organization (AZAPO): 305, 315
Aziz, Tariq: 481

Baghdad: 479
Baker, Herbert: 285
Baker, James A.: 391, 439, 442, 453, 458, 459, 461,
    462, 465, 473, 475, 478; photo with Perkins, 460
Baker Initiative for Economic Reform: 391
Baker International: 386
Bamako, Mali: 223
Bangkok: 138, 141, 144, 147; description of, 143
Bantu Laws Amendment Bill: 339
Baoulé tribe: 227
Barclay's Bank: 383
Barkley, Richard: 291, 303, 321
Barnard, Neil: 333
Barrett, Dennis: 430
Barry, Marion: 226
Basilica of Our Lady of Peace: 227
Bassett, Ralph: 56, 58, 72
Battle of Blood River: 279, 280, 283
Battle of Midway: 507
Battle of the Coral Sea: 507
Beck, Karl: 5, 289, 290, 310, 319, 370, 374, 375,
    431, 432
Beeman, Josiah Horton: 525, 526
Beijing: 494
Belgium: 475, 476

Bell and Howell: 386
Benin: 171, 220, 225, 226
Benjamin Franklin Room of State Department: 152,
    153, 269–270
Bernstein, Rusty: 308
Beukes, Herbert: 270
Biko, Steve: 306, 307, 341, 374, 426
Bilbo, Theodore: 42
Bill, James: 477
Bizos, George: 6, 7, 311
Black, Shirley Temple: 230
Black Chamber of Commerce (South Africa): 393
Black Consciousness Group (South Africa):
    305–306
Black Sash: 298, 299, 340
Black Women's Political Caucus: 264
blacks (South African): 249, 254, 256, 265, 274, 275,
    277, 280, 284, 288, 290, 292, 294, 307, 312, 337,
    345, 350, 367, 376, 384; after aparthied, 424;
    and AIDS, 332; and labor movement, 316–318; as
    employees of embassy, 293; assassination of,
    295; at war with Boers, 279; disappearance of
    children of, 295, 299, 319; divisions among,
    300–301, 303, 315, 319; economy of, 392–395;
    education issues for, 304, 305; employment of,
    386, 387, 388; exclusion of from politics, 296;
    goodwill of toward whites, 375; hopes of (1987),
    368; place in Afrikaner religion, 282; possibility
    of government by, 371; relegated to migrant-
    worker status, 281; townships of, 323–329
Bloch, Felix: 458
Bloemfontein: 275, 279
Boer War: 281, 298, 385, 426
Boers: 278–280; exiled following Boer War, 281
Boesak, Allan: 297, 300, 344, 345, 401, 430
Bogle, Dick: 64
Bok, Derek: 359
Bolton, John: 465, 466, 488
Bong Mining Company: 207
Book of Five Rings, The (book): 10, 98, 100, 255
Bophuthatswana: 324, 332, 388, 393
Boraine, Alex: 356
Boren, David: 8, 379, 381, 528; confronts P. W.
    Botha, 380
Bork, Tim: 289, 290, 315, 317, 340, 376, 430
Bosnia-Herzegovina: 458, 470, 473, 475, 476
Botha, Elise: 330
Botha, Pieter W. (P. W.): 254, 260, 285, 287, 288,
    301, 303, 330, 333, 335, 361, 366, 383, 384, 386,
    423, 426; conflict with Reagan, 302; confronta-
    tion with Nunn and Boren, 379–380; photo of
    with Perkins, 286
Botha, Roelof "Pik": 302, 335, 395, 401, 412, 413,
    415, 417, 418, 423, 431, 434; joins ANC, 424

Botha, Stoffel: 333
Botswana: 290, 334, 364, 430
Boutros-Ghali, Boutros: 468, 469, 473, 478, 485, 489, 517
Brazeal, Aurelia: 347
Brazzaville: 414, 415, 417
Brazzaville Protocol: 417
Brisbane: 499, 507, 510
Britain and British: *See* United Kingdom
Broederbond: 283, 298, 316, 332, 337–339, 350
Broederbond: The Super Afrikaners (book): 336–337
Brown, Ben: 401
Brown, John: 191, 192
Brown, Matthew: 97
Brown, Robert: 250, 428
Brown, Ron: 515
Brown, Samuel S.: 75
Brown v. Board of Education: 14, 109, 155
Bruce, Bob: 229
Buchanan, Pat: 249
Bunche, Ralph: 530
Bureau of African Affairs: 217
Bureau of International Organizations Affairs: 465, 466, 488
Bureau of Narcotics: 218, 219
Bureau of Near East and South Asian Affairs: 162, 163
Burger, Warren: 397
Burkina Faso: 171, 229
Burroughs, John: 153, 345, 375
Burton, Mary: 299
Bush, George H. W.: 380, 420, 422, 423, 439, 440, 461, 462, 465, 468, 478, 483, 487, 489, 495, 520
Bush, George W.: 520
Bush, Jeb: 520
Bushido: A Modern Adaptation of the Ancient Code of the Samurai (book): 98, 99, 102
Busia, Kofi: 182
Buthelezi, Mangosuthu Gatsha: 325, 326, 351, 377, 426, 429

Cabelly, Robert: 252
Cadbury Chocolates: 383
Cairo: 480
Cal-Tex Oil: 386
Cambodia: 138, 139, 462, 489–493, 495
Camp Pendleton, Calif.: 113
Camp Stoneman, Calif.: 76, 77
Campbell, Joseph: 415
Canada: 406, 410
Canberra: 498, 499, 500, 502, 505, 507, 512, 514
Cape Town: 275, 277, 278, 283, 289, 302, 304, 315, 320, 321, 329, 330, 346, 350, 370, 379, 399, 422
Cape Verde: 220, 225, 226, 475

Caprivi Strip: 301
Carlucci, Frank: 252, 321, 351, 353–355
Carmichael, Stokely: 506
Carnegie Foundation: 431
Carter, James E.: 171, 184, 216, 413, 440, 508
Carter administration: 210, 218, 236, 357, 372, 490, 518
Casey, Bill: 333, 372
Casey, William: 249
Castro, Fidel: 409
Center for Strategic and International Studies: 265
Central America: 462
Central Bank of France: 222
Central Intelligence Agency (CIA): 185, 218, 249, 333, 347, 372, 423; and Angola-Namibia, 407
Central Pretoria Prison: 343
Cesaire, Aime: 306
Chad: 220, 221
Chang, Dinah Lynn: 453
Chase Manhattan Bank: 207
Chaveas, Peter: 400
Chiang, Mai-Ling Soong: 124, 128
Chiang Kai-shek: 123–125, 128
Chicago Council: 359
Chikane, Frank: 401
Chikane, Moss M.: 5
China: 474–476, 483, 489, 494
Chinese Nationalists: 125, 127
Chisholm, Shirley: 264
Christchurch, New Zealand: 524
Christiani, Alexander: 382
Christopher, Warren: 495, 497
Chu, Calix: 130, 132
CIA. *See* Central Intelligence Agency
Cilliers, Piet: 348
Cincinnati, Ohio: 75
Ciskei: 324
Citibank: 207, 240
Civil Rights Commission: 448
Clinton, Bill: 440, 441, 495, 497, 498, 508, 515–516
Clinton administration: 485
Clinton, Leo: 43
CNN: 214, 251
Coca-Cola: 386, 391
Coetsee, Kobie: 311–312
Cohen, Hank: 353, 355
Colgate Palmolive: 386
Coloured Dutch Reformed Church: 344, 345. *See also* Dutch Reformed Church
Coloureds (South African): 254, 278, 284, 295, 297, 304, 319, 327, 337, 345, 346, 371, 376, 393, 414, 426, 429; parliament for, 296; townships of, 329
Commerce Department: 218

Commission on the Preservation of Antarctic
    Marine Life (CMARL): 514, 515
Committee of One Million: 125
Communist Party of South Africa: 354
community capitalism: 391
Comprehensive Anti-Apartheid Act (CAAA): 267,
    292, 358, 365, 385
Congregationalist Church: 345
Congress of South African Trade Unions (COSATU):
    306, 316, 318
Congressional Black Caucus: 261, 446
Conservative Party (South Africa): 342
constructive-engagement policy: 248, 252, 266,
    355, 361, 366, 372, 383, 412
Contact Group of United Nations: 406, 407
Coolgardie: 523
Coomba Park: 521
Cooper, Al: 387
Coral Sea Celebration: 508, 510
Cordon Sanitaire: 405, 412
Costello, Michael: 514, 524
Côte d'Ivoire: 171, 195, 220, 221, 226–227, 231,
    237, 245
Cotton, Ola Mae: 44
Council of 100: 262
Council on Foreign Relations: 357
Court, Richard: 502, 514
Covenant, The (book): 255
Crawford, Roger D.: 387
Croatia: 470, 471, 473, 476
Crocker, Chester "Chet": 236–237, 247–250,
    252–254, 261, 266, 290, 300, 319, 330, 347,
    352–355, 360, 372–374, 399, 402, 415; and con-
    structive–engagement policy, 236; and Namibia,
    407, 408, 410–413, 416, 417, 419
Crossroads: 305, 328, 375, 382, 505
Crown Cork and Seal Company: 386
Cruise, Tom: 508
Cry the Beloved Country (book): 284
Cuba: 405, 472, 490; and Angola, 406, 407, 410,
    418; and Namibian negotiations, 415; U.S. rela-
    tions with, 408–409, 411–412
Cullen, Countee: 41

Dai Ichi Insurance Building: 83, 89
Dalton, John H.: 509
Damascus, Syria: 480
Davidow, Jeff: 415
Davis, Benjamin O.: 75
de Gaulle, Charles : 221, 222
de Klerk, F. W.: 335–336, 423, 426–427, 457
de Klerk, Wimpie: 336
de Lange, Pieter: 338, 348
de Villiers, Fleur: 361, 362

Dean, John Gunther: 139
DeBeers, Mona: 369
Defense Department: 218
Delmas Treason Trial: 5, 6, 11, 311, 319, 350, 433;
    moved to Pretoria, 8
Dellums, Ron: 365
Dennis, Cecil: 198, 202
Dennis, Charles C.: 198
Diem, Ngo Dinh: 139, 140
Diepkloof: 284
Diepkloof Prison: 400
Dijkhorst, Kees van: 6
Dilio, Kay: 69
Dingane: 278
Dinkins, David: 495
Diouf, Abdou: 227, 231, 232
District Six: 328
Djakarta: 515
Djeridjian, Edward: 475
Doe, Jackson: 239
Doe, Samuel K.: 197–199, 204, 205, 207, 210, 212,
    213, 216, 235–236, 253, 260, 262, 457; and Jean-
    Claude Duvalier, 241, 242; appetites of, 211;
    dark side of, 213–214; inauguration of, 238;
    meets Perkins, 199–200; overthrow and death,
    245; photo of, 201; survives coup attempt, 237;
    visits U.S., 215
domino theory: 125
Dorman, Leslie: 162
dos Santos, Jose Eduardo: 419–420
Doun, Ham: 479, 481
Dressler Industries: 386
Drug Enforcement Administration: 437
Dubach, U. G.: 105
DuBois, W. E. B.: 41, 172, 194; search for grave of,
    185–186
Duke, Doris: 118
Dulles, John Foster: 125, 497
Duncan, Sheena: 299, 340
Durban: 304, 329, 333, 346, 377, 429
Durban Umshlangu: 305
Dutch East India Company: 277
Dutch Reformed Church: 294, 298, 300, 320, 338,
    340–344, 395; members reconsider apartheid,
    338. See also South African Dutch Reformed
    Church, Afrikaans Dutch Reformed Church,
    Coloured Dutch Reformed Church
Duvalier, Jean-Claude "Baby Doc": 241, 242

Eagleburger, Lawrence S. "Larry": 157–159,
    163–168, 230, 231, 355, 435, 444, 453, 482, 495,
    497, 527
Eagleton, Thomas: 266
Eastland, James: 42

Eastman, Ernest: 235
Egypt: 480
Eichelberger, Robert: 83, 86
Eighth Army: 83, 86, 88, 94
Eisenhower, Dwight: 123, 440
Ekeus, Rolf: 479
Eli Lilly: 387
Emslie, Steve: 526
Energy Department: 218, 232
English-speakers (South African): 298, 350, 356,
    363, 369, 385, 395
Equal Employment Opportunity and Civil Rights
    (EEOCR): 448, 449
Estonia: 432
Ethiopia: 456
Evans, Gareth: 524
Ewe tribe: 180, 188, 192
Executive Women's Club (Johannesburg): 369
Exmouth: 522
Eyadéma, Gnassingbé: 226, 231

Fanon, Frantz: 306
Fantis: 179
Fauntroy, Walter: 248
Federal Bureau of Investigation (FBI): 232, 437
Fick, P.: 6
Fifth Marines: 113
Firestone Rubber: 207
519th Military Police Battalion: 85
Fleet Marine Training: 113
Flegel, Dorothy: 62
Ford, Gerald: 216, 440
Ford Foundation: 431
Ford Motor Company: 386, 391
Foreign Affairs Fellows Program: 446, 447, 451
Foreign Service: 147; description of, 150–151, 435;
    examination for, 452–453; minorities in, 441,
    450; needed changes in, 438; reforms of,
    442–446, 454–456
Foreign Service Act of 1946: 147, 160
Foreign Service Act of 1980: 439, 441
Foreign Service Institute: 169, 447, 453, 454
Fort Beaufort: 328
Fort Knox, Kentucky: 73–76
Fort Lewis, Washington: 73
Fraga, José Arbescu: 411
France: 406, 410, 474–477, 479
Franklin, John Hope: 227
Frasure, Robert "Bob": 5, 289, 290, 302, 303, 315,
    322, 330, 333, 336, 338, 346, 348, 362, 364, 370,
    371, 373, 377, 394, 412, 431, 432, 458; and
    Namibia, 410
Fredericks, Wayne: 387
Free Mandela movement: 248, 306, 309, 403

Free South Africa movement: 248
Freedom Charter: 10
Freeman, Chaz: 347
Freeman, Inez: 65, 67
French Financial Union: 222
French Foreign Legion: 106
Friedmann, Gene: 291

Ga tribe: 180
Gambia: 220, 225, 228
Gandhi, Mahatma: 297, 319, 343
Garvey, Marcus: 172
Gazankulu: 324
Geldenhuys, Jannie: 412
General Accounting Office: 160
General Motors: 358
Geneva: 413, 466
George, Crispin: 522
George Washington University: 256
Georgetown University: 265, 333
Germany: 405, 406, 410, 431
Get Ahead Foundation: 328
Ghana: 199, 220, 226; Catholic Church in, 180; con-
    ditions in '70s, 174–175, 176; history of,
    172–173; Soviet Union influence in, 184; U.S.
    relationship with, 171, 183
Gibson, Abner: 34
Gibson, Mel: 508
Gilstrap, Carly: 56, 58, 68
Ginsburg, Ruth Bader: 508
Godley, MacMurtrie: 138, 139
Golan Heights: 480
Goldberg, Arthur: 468
Goldberg, Dennis: 308
Goodyear Tire & Rubber: 386, 387
Gorbachev, Mikhail: 486
Gore, Al: 524
Gorée Island: 227
Goulding, Merrick I.: 411
Graham, Katharine: 261
Grahamstown: 375
Grant, Henry Titus: 21, 22, 33, 39, 46, 47, 49, 53,
    64, 65
Grant, Tiny Estelle Noble Perkins: 15, 20, 22, 34,
    39, 49, 53, 65; photo of, 66
Gravely, John: 153, 155, 156, 255
Gray, Robert "Bob": 63, 468
Gray, William (Bill) III: 261, 355
Great Trek (1938): 283
Greece: 475
Green, Marshall: 498
Greenburg, Jack: 262
Gregg, Don: 490
Griffin, Monte: 56, 57, 58

Grootfontein: 414
Group Areas Act: 339, 370
Guevara, Che: 308
Gugulethu: 328, 393
Guinea: 195, 220, 221, 222
Guinea-Bissau: 220, 225, 226
Gulf War: 464, 483
Gunness, Lee: 512

H. H. Robertson Company: 386
Haig, Alexander: 216, 248
Haiti: 241, 489
Hakone Recreational Club: 88
Hamilton, Lee: 479
Hanson, Brad: 480
Harrington, Herbert: 255
Harris, F. Allen "Tex": 356, 357, 360, 377
Harrop, Bill: 238
Harvey, Allen: 285
Hatch, Orin: 266
Hatfield, Mark O.: 64
Haute Volta. See Burkina Faso
Hawaii: 116–119, 456; racism in, 118
Hawk, Bob: 515
Haynesville, Louisiana: 38
Heath, Edward: 394
Heere XVII: 277
Helms, Jesse: 266, 466
Hero With a Thousand Faces (book): 415
Heunis, Chris: 333
Heyns, Johan: 294, 338–339, 341–342, 348–349,
     429–430
Hibbard, George: 58
Hicks, Irvin: 465, 466, 470, 495
Higginbotham, Leon: 357
Hill, Charlie: 250, 352
Hill, George: 67, 70
Hines, John: 167
Ho Chi Minh: 139, 140
Hobart, Tasmania: 514
Hofmeyr, Jan: 341
Holbrooke, Richard: 432
Holt, Harold E.: 522
Homelands: 296
Honolulu: 359
Hoover, Herbert: 523
Hope, Bob: 114
Hotel Portland: 62, 63
Houphouet-Boigny, Félix: 227, 231
Hughes, Langston: 41
human rights: 221
Hungary: 475
Hunt, Leamon Ray: 163
Hurley, Patrick: 124

Hussein, Saddam: 478, 482

IBM: 386, 391
Imjin River: 93
Immorality Act: 339
"In Your Hands" (article): 373
Inbusana, Walter: 307
India: 474–476, 483
Indian National Congress: 318
Indians (South African): 254, 295, 304, 319; parlia-
     ment for, 296; stand on apartheid, 297
Inkhata Freedom Party: 326, 424, 428–429
Inouye, Daniel: 165, 166
Institute for a Democratic Alternative South Africa:
     356
Institute for Strategic Studies: 362
International Cooperation Administration: 243
International Labor Organization: 463
International Monetary Fund (IMF): 181, 211, 221
International Postal Union: 211
International Relations Club: 69
International Visitors Program: 378–379
Iran: 478
Iraq: 462, 477–482, 496
Islam: 240, 241, 475, 477, 478
Israel: 477, 480, 481, 496

Jackson, Cornelius: 43–44
Jackson, Jesse: 261, 356, 402; meets with Perkins,
     263–264
Jacobs, P. B.: 6
Jaegar, Norma: 291
Japan: 475, 489–491; occupation after World War II,
     84–85, 87–90; racism in, 88
Jefferson, Thomas: 151
Jefferson County Courthouse: 38
Jefferson High School: 55, 58, 59, 62
Jerusalem: 480
Jewish community: 346
Johannesburg: 275, 310, 313, 328, 340, 346, 347,
     368, 370, 394, 400
Johannesburg Three: 402, 415
Johnson, Lady Bird: 440
Johnson, Lyndon: 440
Johnson, Ralph: 474
Johnson, Yeloue Yormie: 245
Johnson & Johnson: 386, 387, 388
Johnson administration: 359
Johnson-Sirleaf, Ellen: 237, 239–241, 262
Jordan: 477
Jordan, Vernon: 262; photo with Perkins, 263
Joy Manufacturing Company: 386
Justice Department: 218

Kalgoorlie: 523
Kamakura, Japan: 96
KaNgwane: 324, 325, 433
Kantor, Arnold: 496
Kashmir: 483
Kassebaum, Nancy: 265, 266, 268, 272, 379, 466; photo with Perkins family, 267
Katrada, Ahmed: 308
Keating, Paul: 498, 500
Keetmanshoop: 414
Kennedy, John F.: 139, 217, 243
Kennedy, Michael: 519, 520
Kennedy, Ted: 381, 402
Kent, Jill: 442, 446, 448
Kenya: 171, 315, 466
Kérékou, Mathieu: 226
Kerry, John: 240, 266
Keyes, Alan: 352–354
Khayelitsha: 328
Khmer Rouge: 490–491, 493
Khotso House: 340
Kidman, Nicole: 508
Killen, P. R.: 286
King, Coretta Scott: 262
King, Martin Luther Jr.: 10, 143, 291, 297, 306, 308, 321, 340, 341, 343, 346, 363, 404, 433, 458, 530
King Williamstown: 375
Kinshasa: 414, 415
Kirkpatrick, Jeane: 353, 463–464, 468
Kissinger, Henry: 141, 155–156, 163–164, 167–168, 405, 422, 439, 449, 527; direction of Foreign Service by, 157–160; Sub-Saharan Africa policy, 406
Kitchen, Helen: 265
Kitt, Eartha: 388
Klopper, Henning: 283, 367
Knight, Gladys: 523
Koch, Edward: 495
Kodak: 386
Koli Koli Pass: 116
Kopel, Molly: 386
Kopp, Frank: 103
Korea: 76–81, 83, 88, 113–114, 470, 483, 489, 490
Korean War: 93, 106
Kosovo Liberation Army: 476
Kovar, Jeffrey: 461, 530
Kovar, Nathan Noble Liu: 530
Kovar, Robert Hale: 530
Krahn tribe: 200
Ku Klux Klan: 14
Kurds: 478, 481
Kuwait: 477–479
KwaMashu: 328
KwaNdebele: 324, 393

KwaZulu: 324, 325, 424
Kyoya, Tomiko: 89; photo of, 90

Labor Department: 218
Ladysmith: 319
Lagos Murtala Mohammed International Airport: 221
Lamco: 207
Langa: 328
Lantos, Tom: 479
Laos: 138–139
Lattigan, Esther: 339
Lautenberg, Frank R.: 355, 379
League of Nations: 405
Lebowa: 324
Lee, John: 376
Leigh Creek: 521
Lekota, Patrick (Terror): 5, 7, 8–9, 433, 434, 458
Lesotho: 364
Letter from Birmingham Jail (book): 10, 25, 308, 321, 343, 363, 433
Levy, Arnold: 379
Lewis and Clark College: 105
Lewis and Clark Expedition: 63
Liberia: 149, 220, 235, 242, 247, 253, 291, 457; coup attempt in, 237; debts of, 212; economy in, 206–207; elections in, 238; history of, 195–197; home of Voice of America, 244; Perkins arrives in, 236; racial conflict in, 198–199; revolution in, 202; United States relationship with, 209, 212
Libya: 201, 212–213, 216, 245, 469, 490
Life, Wally: 387
Limann, Hilla: 180–181, 192
Liu, Lucy Cheng-mei. *See* Perkins, Lucy Cheng-mei Liu
Lodge, Henry Cabot Jr.: 153, 468
London: 361–362
Long, Huey: 32, 33, 368, 390
Lonrho Africa: 394
Lopius, Markus: 63
Louw, Saki: 375
Lugar, Richard: 250, 265
Lusaka: 334
Lutheran Church: 414
Luthuli, Albert: 7, 307
Lyman, Princeton N.: 432
Lyons, Stephen T.: 189

M. Hart Corporation: 386
Mabo, Eddie: 503
Mabo Land Title Decision: 503
Mabuza, Enos: 325, 393, 433
MacArthur, Douglas: 83–86, 89, 93–94, 510–511
MacArthur, Jean Marie Faircloth: 84, 89

Macedonia: 476
Magoba, Mmutlanyane Stanley: 344
Malan, Magnus: 333–335, 412, 433
Malawi: 332, 364
Malaysia-Singapore Federation: 169
Mali: 220–222
Malmierca, Isidoro Octavio: 417, 418
Mamelodi: 301, 323, 327, 328, 393
Mandela, Nelson: 7, 9, 140, 232, 248, 299,
    307–309, 311, 312, 354, 360, 381, 383, 384, 425,
    426, 430, 458; elected president, 424, 428;
    released from jail, 423, 427; urges black leader-
    ship to meet with Perkins, 310
Mandela, Winnie: 306, 309, 311, 382, 403, 425,
    426, 428; meets with Perkins, 312–314
Mann, Betty: 67
Mao Tse-tung: 123, 125, 145, 177, 308
Maponya, Richard: 393
Maputo: 335
Marcos, Imelda: 440
Margaret River: 523
Marine Corps: 107, 147, 153, 377; attributes of,
    111, 112; segregation in, 112–113
Marks, Joe: 335, 393, 428
Marshall, Ray: 518
Masonic Order (Liberia): 207, 208
Matsumoto, Hideiko "Sleepy": 91
Matthews, Baccus: 202
Mauritania: 220, 222, 228
Mbeki, Govan: 7, 308, 390, 391
Mbeki, Thabo: 254, 318, 427, 428, 429
McCain, John: 379
McCarthy, Joseph: 125
McCullough, Colleen: 502, 531
McElroy, William "Mac": 156, 162
McGann, Steve: 291
McGee, Pat: 319
McHenry, Donald: 468
McMann, Ned: 302
McMurdo Sound: 525, 527
McNamara, Robert: 321, 517
McRoberts, Don: 328
Mcunu, Ernest J.: 386
Mdantsane: 328
Meacham, Marian: 56, 58, 67, 70
Meadowlands: 328
Means, Russell: 506
Meer, Fatima and Ismail: 318–319
Meike, Futaba: 91, 92, 93, 104
Melbourne: 499, 507, 520
Merrill High School (Pine Bluff, Ark.): 40, 41
Mesurado: 207
Methodist Church: 344
Mhlavi, Raymond: 308

Michaels, Lucky: 393
Michener, James: 255, 532
Middle East: 462, 477–478, 495
Milošević, Slobodan: 476, 477
Milwaukee High School: 55
Mind of South Africa, The (book): 336
Minnesota Mining and Manufacturing: 386
Mitchell, Roma: 523, 524
Mitchell's Plain: 297, 329, 376
Mitterand, François: 488
Mkhatshwa, Smangaliso: 343, 344, 379, 380, 429
Mlangeni, Andrew: 308
Mmusa, Edison: 273, 274, 313
Moberly, Patrick: 384
Mobil Oil Company: 386, 387
Mogadishu: 485–486
Mokoena, Aubrey: 309, 403, 404
Molefe, Popo Simon: 5
Mondale, Walter: 247, 515, 517
Moniba, Harry F.: 238
Monroe, James: 151, 196
Monroe, Louisiana: 13
Monrovia, Liberia: 195, 237–238, 244–245, 251,
    260; description of, 199
Montenegro: 470
Montgomery, Jim: 347
Montreal: 466
Moose, George: 470
Morella, Constance: 437
Morgan, Nancy: 222
Morocco: 222, 475
Moses, Edwin: 518
Motlana, Ntatho and Sally: 309
Motsualedi, Elias: 308
Motsuenyane, Sam: 393, 394
Mount Holyoke College: 235
Movement for Justice in Africa (MOJA): 201, 210
Moynihan, Daniel: 466, 468
Mozambique: 253, 301, 332, 334, 364, 405, 406
Mugabe, Robert: 253
Muller, Robert: 470
Multnomah Public Library: 54
Murphy, Edward: 132
Murray, Hugh: 373
Musashi, Miyamoto: 98, 101, 102, 368, 530
Mydans, Carl: 272
Myrick, Bismarck: 210

Nader, Ralph: 518
Naidoo, Jay: 317, 318, 326
Naigow, Peter: 240–241
Namibia: 253, 301, 355, 404, 405, 411, 421, 458,
    464; governed by South Africa, 406, 408, 410;
    negotiations for independence of, 413–420

Nanking: 494
Napper, Larry: 417
Natal: 278
Natal Indian Congress: 297, 319
National Association for the Advancement of Colored People (NAACP): 74, 155, 185, 262
National Party (South Africa): 284, 324, 332, 335, 336, 337, 339, 342, 346, 361, 374, 423, 424, 428
National Security Council: 159
National Union of Mineworkers: 313, 316
Native Land Act (1913): 324
Naudé, Christian Frederick Beyers: 294, 339, 340, 341
Ncome River: 279
Nelan, Bruce: 323
New Guinea: 520
New South Wales: 500
New York: 466
New Zealand: 456, 497
Ngue, Chris: 401
Nguesso, Denis Sassou: 414
Nickel, Herman: 265, 303
Niebhur, Reinhold: 343
Nieuwe Gereformede Kerch (NGK). See Dutch Reformed Church
Niger: 220, 221; American diplomacy in, 223–225
Nigeria: 171, 218–219, 250; conditions in, 220–221
Nixon, Richard: 141, 176, 216, 439–440, 498
Nkrumah, Kwame: 172, 173, 180, 185, 192
Nobel Peace Prize: 427
Noble, Anna: 17
Noble, Ellis: 19
Noble, Elmer (Bud): 18, 30
Noble, Jo Willie: 18, 34
Noble, Katye Bell: 19
Noble, Mattie Oney: 18
Noble, Minnie Pearl: 18, 34
Noble, Nathan: 15, 16, 24, 25; death of, 29
Noble, Sarah Elizabeth Stovall: 16, 23, 47
Noble, Savannah: 15, 18, 22, 23, 30, 33, 34
Noble, Virgil: 19
Non-Aligned Movement (NAM): 496
Norfolk Islanders: 499
Norman, Oklahoma: 527, 529
Northwest Airlines: 516–517
Nuclear Non-Proliferation Treaty: 382
Nujoma, Sam: 411
Nunn, Sam: 8, 379
Nuri, Kadin Perkins: 530
Nuri, Kwabena Koro: 530
Nuri, Sofia Yasmeen: 530
Nyanga: 328

O'Connor, John Cardinal: 495

O'Donahue, Lois: 505
O'Farrell, Patrick: 182, 317
Obasanjo, Olusegun: 220
Obayed, Hisham: 411
Octagon Theatre: 86
Office of Equal Employment Opportunity (EEO): 154–156, 162
Office of Management Operations: 164, 169
Office of West African Affairs: countries covered by, 220; photo of staff, 219; review of Perkins tenure at, 232
Ofuna, Japan: 97
Ogata, Sadako: 489
Ohene, Elizabeth: 192
Okinawa: 104, 137
Oliver, C. S. (Cecile): 53, 54, 55, 58, 270
one-person, one-vote: 247, 336, 354, 373, 424
Open Forum: 442
Operation Rescue Hope: 484
Operation Rolling Thunder: 141
Orange Free State: 374
Organization of American States: 489
Organization of Islamic Conferences (OIC): 475
Oslo Accords: 477
Ottoman Empire: 477
Ouachita River: 13
Ovambo tribe: 414
Owens, Jesse: 63
Owusu-Afriye, George: 180, 182

Pace College (Soweto): 387
Pacivera, Manuela: 411
Palestine: 477
Palestine Liberation Organization: 490
Palestinians: 496
Palm Island: 503, 505
Palmer, Allison: 160
Palmer, Joan and Don: 106, 107
Pan-Africanist Congress (PAC): 305–307, 423
Papua New Guinea: 456–457
Parker, Frank: 370
Parsons, Howard: 138, 145, 149
Pasqual, Carlos: 376
pass law: 278
Passman, Otto: 141
Patina, Lester: 393
Paton, Alan: 283–284, 341, 425, 531
Paton, Ann: 425, 429
Pattee, Glenn: 67
Peabody Mine: 521
Peace Corps: 180–181, 223, 290, 431, 457; work in Liberia, 203–204
Pearlman, Ina: 374
Pearson, Noel: 506

Pearson Amendment: 233

Pell, Clayborne: 466

Pennue, Harrison: 197

Peoli, Isidoro Malmierca: 411

People's Liberation Army of Namibia (PLAN): 405

PepsiCo: 386, 391

Perez de Cuellar, Javier: 407, 419, 464

Perkins, Edward J.: 217; activities in Ghana,
178–183; and Eastern philosophy, 95, 98, 99,
100–102, 143, 255, 368; and farm life, 24–25,
26–28; and Liberian Embassy affairs, 242–243;
and non-violent philosophy, 289–290, 297; and
problems in South African embassy, 347;
appointed deputy chief of mission (DCM), 170;
arrival in Liberia, 199; as Director General of
the Foreign Service, 421–422, 436, 439, 456,
459; assessment of work in South Africa,
432–434; assigned to Ghana, 169, 171; attends
Afrikaner church, 294; awarded Order of
Liberia, 260; celebrates the Fourth of July in
Australia, 512, 513; confronts Ghanaian mob,
189–190; considers appointment to South
Africa, 251; danger to in South Africa, 255; doctoral studies at USC, 144–145, 158–159; encourages dialogue in South Africa, 370, 373;
enlistment in army, 73; enters Foreign Service,
152–154; enters Lewis and Clark College, 105;
formulates embassy policymaking in South
Africa, 289–293; given carte blanche authority
in South Africa, 259; impressions of Japan,
88–90, 92–93; in Ghanaian revolution, 187–189;
in Korea, 77–81; intern in USAID program, 137;
interviews with Senate committees, 265–269,
466; introduced to South Africa, 42; Marine
Corps and, 107–113, 119–121; joins PPG staff,
164; joins University of Oklahoma, 527; language proficiency, 144; as Director of West
African Affairs, 217, 232; meets Lucy Cheng-
mei Liu, 127–128; meets Samuel Doe, 199–200;
meets with blacks in South Africa, 309–319;
meets with Jesse Jackson, 263–264; meets with
Winnie Mandela, 312–314; moves to Arkansas,
37; mustered out of the army, 94; named ambassador to Liberia, 235; nominated for ambassador
to United Nations, 461; Portland speech of,
360–361, 369; presents credentials in South
Africa, 285–287; promoted to career minister,
402; reform efforts in Foreign Service,
442–445, 450; relationship with South African
Press, 321–323; religious philosophy of, 343,
345; relocates to Portland, 49, 51; replaced at
United Nations, 495; reports to White House,
351–354; revolutionary philosophy of, 177;
seeks Australia ambassadorship, 497; service in

Hawaii, 116–119; service in investigation unit,
114; South African reaction to, 260; Soviet contact with, 184; speaks across U.S., 357–362; stationed in Japan, 83; sworn in as ambassador to
South Africa, 270–272; takes oral examination
for Foreign Service, 148–149; travels as United
Nations ambassador, 489–494; travels to West
Africa, 220–229; visits fellow ambassadors in
South Africa, 381–383; visits Nigeria, 220;
White House interviews of, 255–260; work
ethic of, 45; work in Liberia, 205–207

Perkins, Frances: 518

Perkins, Katherine Karla "Kathy": 8, 134, 187, 199,
235, 256, 329, 397, 403, 404, 461, 529, 530

Perkins, Lucy Cheng-mei Liu: 161, 187, 202, 216,
235, 251, 285, 288, 319, 329, 349, 375, 380, 436,
461, 498, 504, 520–522, 527, 529; courtship and
marriage of, 127–135

Perkins, Sarah Elizabeth: 8, 135, 161, 187, 199, 202,
216, 235, 319, 359, 397, 436, 461, 494, 520–521,
529

Persian Gulf: 462

Perth: 499, 502, 507, 523

Peterson, Sharon: 356

Petrovsky, Yuri: 473

Peurifoy, Mrs. John J.: 144

Phillips Academy (Andover, Mass.): 235, 359

Phillips Petroleum: 522

Phnom Penh: 493

Pickering, Thomas: 464–466, 468, 488

Pickering Fellows. See Foreign Affairs Fellows Program

Pienaar, Louis: 410

Pietermaritzburg: 370

Pine Bluff, Ark.: 22, 34, 37–38, 40, 43, 47–48

Pine Bluff Commercial (newspaper): 46

Pine Gap, Australia: 497

Player, Gary: 392

Pleasant Grove, Louisiana: 15, 30, 31

Po, Fernando: 196

Poindexter, John: 256, 257

Popular Movement for the Liberation of Angola
(MPLA): 406, 407, 411, 413, 419

Population Registration Act: 295

Port Elizabeth: 305, 374, 375, 390

Port Moresby, New Guinea: 507

Portland: 51–53, 60, 65, 70, 360; racism in, 53, 59, 63

Pottsdam Declaration: 83–84

Powell, Charles: 384

Powell, Colin: 354, 474, 485, 508, 527; photo with
Perkins: 484

Pretoria: 5, 8, 274–275, 283, 288, 293, 303, 304,
323, 328, 332, 338, 346, 350, 384, 386, 393, 399,
429, 433; U.S. Embassy in, 274–275

Pretorius, Andries: 274, 279
Price, Charles: 362, 384
Priorities Policy Group (PPG): 157–159, 164, 169, 198
Progressive Freedom Party (PFP): 299, 369, 374
Pruitt, Clarence: 64
Pruitt, Joy Brock: 60, 61, 70
Pryor, Elizabeth (Liz): 290, 291, 321–322, 333, 370, 373, 375, 431; and Namibia, 410
Public Order Law: 299
Pyongyang: 493

Qaddafi, Muammar: 245
Qoboza, Percy: 403, 404
Queen Elizabeth II: 426
Queensland: 503
Queenstown: 375
Quiwonkpa, Thomas: 237, 239, 240
Qwaqwa: 324

Rabin, Yitzhak: 481
Race Classification Act: 339
Racine, Georges P.: 387
Racism: 53, 58, 61, 73, 118
Ramaphosa, Cyril: 313, 316
Ramphele, Mamphela: 318
Rand Afrikaans University: 338
Raphel, Robin: 410
Rawlings, Jerry John (J. J.): 186–188, 191–194
Ray, Robert: 524
Reagan, Ronald: 4, 214–215, 233, 239, 250, 251, 256, 290, 309, 321, 331, 351, 366, 369, 385, 417, 423, 440; conflict with Botha, 302; imposes sanctions on South Africa, 248; interviews Perkins, 256–259; photo with Perkins family, 269; questions Perkins, 351–352
Reagan administration: 223, 236, 247, 254, 261, 300, 336, 357, 360–362, 372, 463; and constructive-engagement policy, 248
Red Cross: 483, 499
Reed, Joseph Verner: 471
Reed College: 56–57, 65
Regan, Donald: 256–257
Renwick, Robin: 384
Replacement Depot, Seoul, South Korea: 77
Rhodes, Cecil: 278
Ribeiro, Fabian Defu: 301
Riccucci, Norma M.: 432
Rice, Condoleezza: 487
Rinehart, Lane: 519
Rio de Janeiro: 488–489
Rittenhouse, Thomas J.: 120
Rivonia Treason Trial: 7, 308, 390, 428
RJR Nabisco: 386

Robb, Charles: 379
Robben Island: 9, 310
Roberts Field (Liberia): 212
Robeson, Paul: 63
Robinson, Randall: 248, 261
Rogers, Steve: 370
Rogers Act of 1925: 436
Roland, James Howell: 91
Roman Catholic Church: 343–344
Rome: 466
Roosevelt, Eleanor: 498
Roosevelt, Franklin D.: 124, 498, 518
Rose, Jerry: 291
Rose, T. J.: 490, 491, 494
Rosenberg, Allison: 356
Roux, Jannie: 285–287
Rowland, Tiny: 394
rubber industry: 206
Rupert, Anton: 348
Russell, Don: 524
Russia: 476

Sachs, Albie: 301, 318, 335
Salter, Thomas: 18
Samphan, Khieu: 490, 491, 493
San Francisco Peace Treaty: 87
San people: 254, 277, 278
sanctions: 248, 250, 256, 257, 265, 317, 355; British view of, 383; policy papers concerning, 388; urged in U.S. Congress, 365
Sanlaam: 284
Sarajevo: 473
Saudi Arabia: 477, 478
Savimbi, Jonas: 407, 411, 416, 420
Scalia, Antonin: 518
Schwartz, David: 447
Scott, Robert: 525
segregation: 14–15, 38, 39, 46, 55, 60, 61, 63, 73, 74, 87, 112, 337; difference of in South Africa and U.S., 336–337
Seipei, Stompie Moeketsi: 314, 428
Sékou Touré, Ahmed: 221, 222
Selin, Ivan: 447, 453
Senate Foreign Relations Committee: 466
Senegal: 220–221, 226–228, 231
Senghor, Leopold: 226
Serbia: 470, 473–474
sexism: 161
Shabazz, Betty: 264
Shackleton, Ernest: 525
Shaka: 278
Shalikashvili, John: 518
Sharpeville Massacre (1960): 307–308
Shaw, Johnny: 48

Shultz, George: 4, 68, 248, 250, 256, 270, 290, 321,
    351–354, 356, 369, 417–419, 467; calls Perkins
    re South African Ambassadorship, 251, 253; New
    York address by (1987), 372; photo with
    Perkins, 249; qualities of, 258–259
Siam Riap: 491
Sibiya, Gordon: 392
Sierra Leone: 171, 195, 220, 228, 237
Sihanouk, Norodom: 490–493
Silajdzic, Haris: 470
Silverman, Larry: 410
Simmons, Jake: 379
Simon, Paul: 444, 466
Sin, Hun: 492
Sinatra, Frank: 388
Sinclair, Jean: 299
Singapore: 141
Singapore model of governance: 367
Sisulu, Albertina: 309–312, 380, 401, 428; visits
    Washington: 380–381
Sisulu, Walter: 7, 9, 308, 310–311, 428
Sisulu, Zwelakhe: 379
Siverson, Sandy: 276
Slabbert, Frederick Van Zyl: 356
slavery: 14, 222, 278
Slovenia: 470–471, 476
Slovo, Joe: 308, 318, 458
Smith, Danielle and Wilbur: 422
Smith, Nico: 294, 339, 348
Smith, Ray: 252
Smith, Robert: 179, 181
Smuts, Harry: 414
Smuts, Jan Christian: 42, 414
Snider, Ray: 291
Snow, Olympia: 449
Sobukwe, Robert: 307, 341
Solarz, Steve: 445
Somalia: 315, 462, 482–486, 495
South Africa: 42, 364, 405, 436, 442, 462, 466, 495;
    1987 elections in, 365; American business inter-
    ests in, 385–388; and AIDS, 332; and Namibia,
    406–408, 412, 414, 416; Carter administration
    relations with, 247; Chinese in, 297; dangerous
    to Perkins, 9, 10; economic and societal changes
    in, 424, 426–427; government of, 333–336; his-
    torical background of, 277–285; integration in,
    293; international relations with, 381–385; labor
    movement in, 316–318; military in, 377; news-
    papers in, 322; partitioning considered for, 366;
    Perkins's arrival in, 273–277, 285–287; prob-
    lems and people in (1986-1987), 253, 294–297;
    sanctions against, 248, 250, 256, 258, 265, 317;
    townships in, 323–329; U.S. approach to (1987),
    354; U.S. investment in, 389

South African Communist Party: 318, 390, 423, 458
South African Council of Churches: 339–340
South African Defense Force: 301, 414
South African Dutch Reformed Church: 281, 282
South African Miner's Union: 306
South African Students Organization: 306
South African Winery Consortium: 393
South West Africa: See Namibia
South West Africa People's Organization (SWAPO):
    253, 405–408, 411, 414, 416
Southeast Asia: 137–138
Soviet Union: 201, 204, 210, 212, 213, 216, 231,
    405, 406, 470, 473; and Anglola-Namibia,
    407–408, 411, 417, 419; dissolution of, 464
Soweto: 247, 304–305, 309–310, 312, 314, 323,
    327–329, 332, 377, 382, 387, 425–426
Soweto Citizens League: 309
Soweto Committee of Ten: 309
Soweto Women's League: 377
Soweto-by-the-Sea: 327
Sparks, Allister: 280, 336
Spector, Phil: 467
St. George's Cathedral (Cape Town): 309, 320–322,
    350
Stabreit, Immo: 382
Stanley Corporation: 207
Stellenbosch: 348
Stellenbosch University: 296, 339
Sterlington, Louisiana: 13
Stevens, William: 199
Stevenson, Adlai: 468
Stovall, Benjamin Franklin: 16
Stovall, Emerline: 16; photo of, 17
Strydom, Hans: 336
Sugamo prison: 83
Sullivan, Leon: 262, 357–359
Sullivan Principles: 357–358, 385, 387
Sullivan Signatories' Association: 388
Sun Tzu: 98, 102, 183, 530
Suzman, Helen: 299–300, 346
Swakopmund: 413
Swaziland: 364
Swing, William: 195, 199, 202, 205, 215, 216, 235, 236
Swint, Jacqueline: 60
Switzerland: 497
Sydney: 499, 500, 507, 520
Sye, Harold: 255
Syria: 480

Tahir-Kheli, Shirin: 470
Taipei: 123, 126
Tambo Tambo: 503–505
Tambo, Oliver: 254, 307–308, 318
Tanzania: 315, 364, 406

Taylor, Charles: 245
Teichner, Martha: 321
Teiko, Miura: 97
Tel Aviv: 481
Teller, Edward: 518–519
Terreblanche, Sampie: 298
Thailand: 138–141, 143–144, 147, 489
Thatcher, Margaret: 383–384
Thokoza: 328
Thomas, Helen: 226
Thomas, Moses: 17
Thorne, Nicholas G. W.: 147–149, 151, 167
Thredbo: 521
Tiananmen Square: 494
Tibet: 483
Timbuktu, Mali: 223
Tito, Marshall: 473
Todman, Terrance: 250–251
Togo: 171, 220, 225–226, 231, 240, 290
Tojo, Hideki: 83
Tolbert, William R.: 197, 202, 211
Tomoyuki, Yamashita: 84–85
Toot, Gloria: 264
Torres Strait Island: 502–503
Torricelli, Robert: 479
Townsville: 510
TransAfrica: 248
Transkei: 324
Transvaal: 278
Transvaal British Indian Association: 297
Treasury Department: 218, 232, 438
Treurnicht, Andries: 342
True Whig party (Liberia): 207–208
Truman, Harry S: 75, 79, 93, 94, 233
Truth and Reconciliation Commission: 426, 429
Tuareg people: 223
Tubman, William V. S.: 197, 208
Turnhalle Constitutional Conference: 406
Tuthill, John W.: 354
Tuttle, Robert: 255
Tutu, Desmond: 309, 322, 344, 359, 365, 401, 402, 426, 430
Tutu, Trevor: 328
Tutwiler, Margaret: 439, 465
Tuzon, Liberia: 206
212th Military Police Company: 85, 90, 93

Ulundi: 318
Umkhonto we Sizwe (MK): 308
Umlanga: 328
Unger, Leonard: 139
Union Carbide: 386
Union for Total Independence of Angola (UNITA): 406–407, 411, 416, 419, 420

Unisys Corporation: 386
United Airlines: 516
United Democratic Front (UDF): 5, 7, 8, 290, 308–310, 345, 423
United Gold Coast Convention Party (UGCC): 172
United Kingdom: 477, 479, 501; relations with South Africa: 383–385
United Nations: 388, 411, 418, 461–462, 464; and Middle East, 477–478; and Namibia, 405; and Somalia, 483–486; General Assembly of, 470; Resolution #242, 477; Resolution #342, 253; Resolution #385, 406–407; Resolution #435, 355, 407, 410, 418; Resolution #687, 481; Resolution #794, 484; Security Council of, 470–472, 474, 476, 479, 481, 495–496; U.S. attitude toward, 463
United Nations Development Program: 463
United Party (South Africa): 42, 298
United Technologies Corporation: 386
Universal Military Training (UMT): 76
University of Ghana: 189, 191
University of Maryland in Taipei: 137
University of Oklahoma: 430, 527, 528
University of Pennsylvania (Philadelphia): 359
University of South Africa: 394
University of Southern California: 144
Unsung Heroes (book): 432
Urban League: 63, 106
U.S. Agency for International Development (USAID): 137, 147, 155, 170, 211, 243, 264, 290, 340, 376–377, 392, 430–431
U.S. Information Agency: 485
U.S.-Japan Security Treaty: 87
U.S. Military Assistance Advisory group: 126
U.S. Operations Mission (USOM): 138
USG Corporation: 386

van der Merwe, Elizabeth: 349–350
van der Westhuizen, Pieter: 335
Van Dunem, Alfonso: 411, 418
Van Heerden, Neil: 401, 412
van Niekerk, Willie: 332
Van Tonder, Neels: 412
Vance, Cyrus: 164, 413, 440
Vanderstoel, Max: 479
Vanport: 52, 56, 67, 70
Vanport Recreational Center: 67, 69
Venda: 324
Venezuela: 472, 475
Verwoerd, Hendrik Frensch: 284, 285, 296, 303, 337
Vest, George: 421, 422
Vietnam: 138, 139, 140, 141, 145, 493
Vlok, Adriaan: 333
Voice of America: 244

Voortrekkers: 278, 279, 283
Vorster, John: 307

Waldorf-Astoria Hotel: 467, 495
Walker, Carmen Parrish: 67, 68, 70, 270
Walker, John: 153
Walker, Walton H.: 87, 88
Wallace, Henry: 70
Walters, Vernon: 468
Ward, Robert: 118
Washington, Booker T.: 41
Washington, D.C.: 137, 148, 152
Washington, James: 185–186
Waterkloof: 341
Watson, Alexander: 468, 470
Watson, Jack H. Jr.: 508
Weaver, Karen: 518
Weh-Syen, Thomas: 200, 205
West African Affairs: 235
Western Sahara: 220, 222
White, Homer: 511
White, Robert: 18
White, Stanford: 63
White, Walter: 74
White House Public Information Office: 232
Whitehead, John: 239, 250, 254, 300, 352
Whitlam, Gough: 498
Wilder, Douglas: 447
Wiley, John: 395, 396
Wilkins, Ivor: 336
William and Mary College: 477
Williams, Juan: 262
Windhoek: 414
Winterveld: 393
Wirth, Tim: 495

Wolfensohn, Jim: 502
Wolpe, Howard: 236, 237, 240, 355
Woodrow Wilson National Fellowship Foundation:
    433, 447, 529
Woodson, Robert: 390
World Health Organization: 463
World Trade Organization: 518
World War II: 26, 38, 52, 83, 118, 405, 507, 510–511
Worrall, Denis: 383
Wright, Richard: 41

Xerox: 386
Xhosa tribe: 278

Yalu River: 93, 470
Yeltsin, Boris: 486–487
Yew, Lee Kwan: 169
Yokohama: 85–87, 89, 90–91, 94
Yokohama Golf Country Club: 88
Yokosuka Naval Base: 121
York (slave): 63
Young, Andrew: 173–174, 468, 490
Yu, Lee Kwan: 367
Yugoslavia: 462, 469–471, 473–477, 495

Zaire: 364, 407, 414
Zambia: 301, 332, 364, 406
Zengpei, Tiam: 494
Zimbabwe: 253, 332, 364, 405, 475–476
Zion Baptist Church (Philadelphia): 357
Zlatoper, Ronald J.: 508
Zululand: 318, 325
Zulus: 278–279
Zushi, Japan: 97
Zwelithini, Goodwill: 318